Labor's Giant Step

Twenty years of the CIO

Labor's Giant Step

by Art Preis

PATHFINDER PRESS, NEW YORK

Library of Congress Catalog Card Number 72-79771
ISBN 0-87348-263-8 paper, 0-87348-024-4 cloth
Manufactured in the United States of America

First Edition 1964
Second Edition 1972
Second Printing 1974
Third Printing 1978

Pathfinder Press
410 West Street
New York, N.Y. 10014

Permission to use quotations are acknowledged as follows:
From *CIO—Industrial Unionism in Action* by J. Raymond Walsh; copyright 1937
by the author; published by W. W. Norton and Company, Inc. and reprinted
by their permission. From *Tailor's Progress* by Benjamin Stolberg; copyright
1944 by Doubleday & Company, Inc. and reprinted by their permission. From
The Automobile Industry and Organized Labor by A. J. Muste; published 1935 by
the Fellowship of Reconciliation and reprinted by their permission. From
John L. Lewis—An Unauthorized Biography by Saul Alinsky; copyright 1949 by the
author; published by G. P. Putnam's Sons and reprinted by their permission.
From *Labor on the March* by Edward Levinson; copyright 1938 by the author,
copyright 1956 by Louise Levinson; published by University Books, Inc. and
reprinted by their permission. From *The Roosevelt I Knew* by Frances Perkins; copyright 1946 by the author; published by Viking Press and reprinted
by their permission. From *American City* by Charles Rumford Walker; copyright 1937 by the author; published by Farrar and Rinehart and reprinted by
their permission. From *Sidney Hillman: Statesman of American Labor* by Matthew Josephson; copyright 1952 by the author; published by Doubleday & Company, Inc.; reprinted by permission of Harold Ober Associates Incorporated.

TO ETHEL MARY
whose love, devotion and care
made everything possible
who was my invaluable assistant
throughout the preparation and writing
of this book and who
gave it its title —
ON OUR 30th ANNIVERSARY
January 16, 1964

Contents

Foreword

When Art Preis put the finishing touches on this book shortly before his death in 1964, he had completed a history of what was, in his words, "the most significant event in modern American history." The history of the CIO, from its turbulent beginnings in 1935 as a split in the conservative AFL until its merger twenty years later with that same parent organization, provides a panorama of one of the stormiest periods of labor radicalism in American history.

Since the merger of the AFL and CIO in 1955, the bureaucratization of the unions has continued. The stifling of union democracy; the growing remoteness and independence of the union bureaucrats from the rank and file; their increasing subservience to the interests of the employing class and its government; the consequent alienation of the workers from the unions, and the failure of the unions to act as media for the political sentiments of the rank and file: these are still the main features of the unions today.

Although the unions appear to have changed little in the intervening years, there has been significant change in American life. The post-World War II prosperity and world economic domination of American capitalism have yielded to growing economic difficulties at home and increasingly severe competition abroad. The years of cold-war witch-hunt, with which this book closes, have given way to successive political crises and a period of intense radicalization. The youth—particularly the students on high-school and college campuses—have been the shock troops of this radicalization, and their influence in the antiwar, women's liberation, and Black and Chicano liberation movements has changed the entire atmosphere of American life. This change is having and will continue to have an effect on the organized labor movement.

The labor movement today presents the most striking contrasts. On the one hand, the union officials continue to behave as they did in the past, with some nearly perfect historic parallels. Thus, despite initial rumblings of dissatisfaction, they greeted Nixon's 1971 wage freeze just as their forebears greeted Roosevelt's wartime wage freeze: rather than blame the profit-gouging of big business for the inflation, they assisted the government in squeezing the cost of the war out of the workers' paychecks.

The labor bureaucrats try to use the union machinery to suppress militancy or independence among the workers. On the other hand, the impact of the radicalization on the long-silent working class has produced serious stirrings of discontent that the organized union movement has to reckon with. With the demographic changes in the country as a whole, the composition of the unions has shifted. An increasing number of workers are women, they are Black or Brown, and they are young. Frequently they bring their experience in the high-school and college radicalization into their unions. In many of the mass-production industrial unions, Black caucuses have been formed to combat the super-oppression of Black workers; many local unions have passed resolutions against the war in Southeast Asia; women's caucuses have developed to fight for the special needs of women workers. Rank-and-file caucuses for union democracy or for a militant stand against the employers have appeared. Employers complain that their young workers have no respect for authority or pride in their work. As the radicalization continues, it will undoubtedly precipitate confrontations within the unions, like those recounted in this book, over how to deal with the complicated political and economic issues that must inevitably arise.

How will the bureaucratic leaders of the unions respond to this new awakening in the union ranks? We learn from Preis how in the past they have tried to derail, defuse, and crush the militancy of the workers. What programs will the various radical organizations propose for this new chapter in the class struggle? *Labor's Giant Step* explains how revolutionaries can avoid the pitfalls of the past and lead this new upsurge to a successful conclusion.

Because it arms this generation of militants with the lessons drawn from the experiences of the last generation, this history is more than a dramatic story. It focuses a spotlight on the treachery of all the misleaders, and explains what drove them to subordinate the needs of the workers to the interests of the masters of capital.

*   *   *

Present-day union officials and some historians of the labor movement have deliberately underplayed the importance of the role of radicals in organizing the union movement. From the earliest days of American labor, the best and hardest-working organizers were the men and women who were radicals and who saw in the organized ranks of the working class the crucial forces of social change. The CIO unions in particular were built in large part by the selfless work of the best militants in the working class, many of them members of radical organizations, who seized the opportunity to organize the industrial workers at a time when the conservative leaders of the AFL craft unions refused to do so. Many of them, like Art Preis, came directly off the campuses in the early thirties and threw in their lot with the workers' movement.

The new CIO in the action-packed years of 1935-39 had the potential to organize labor not only for economic struggles but for a broad political struggle, through an independent labor party, that could challenge the capitalist system itself. All the elements were present except the most important of all: the leadership. None of the political currents or bureaucratic cliques that achieved control of the union movement wanted it to make a break with capitalism.

Thus, *Labor's Giant Step* is not simply a history of the CIO; it is a history of radicalism in the CIO, and a mercilessly honest account of how the various political tendencies stood up to the test of leading the American working class at the time of its greatest upsurge.

Neither the Social Democrats, who represented a privileged layer of the union bureaucracy, nor the Stalinists, who reflected the interests of the ruling bureaucrats of the Soviet Union, were capable of pursuing a revolutionary strategy in the labor movement.

But there were also the rank-and-file militants themselves, many of them leaders of the heroic battles waged under the CIO banner, who were radicals and rose to positions of local leadership. To a large extent, they were dispersed and demoralized by the lack of a serious class-struggle program as an alternative to the conservatism of the union bureaucrats. The revolutionary party that had such a program was not influential enough to popularize it widely.

The chapter "Three Strikes That Paved the Way" is partly auto-biographical, because Preis was one of the young organizers and leaders of the famous 1934 Toledo Auto-Lite strike. He had attended Ohio State University, and during the height of the depression began organizing among the unemployed. Shortly after the Toledo victory, Preis joined the Trotskyist movement and later became labor editor of *The Militant.* Along with the other Trotskyists who led the Minneapolis teamsters to victory in 1934, he was a living representative of those fighters who, despite their small numbers and meager resources, set the example for the entire working class in the crucial days preceding the 1937 sit-down strike wave; they give us a glimpse of what the CIO could have been.

Preis learned in the course of the struggle that the dynamic mass organizations of the workers needed class-conscious political leaders in order to meet the needs of the millions who were joining the new movement. That is why this is a frankly partisan book, partisan to the workers' cause and to the fight for socialism. It tells not only what happened, but what could have happened, and what can still be done. It is the story of untiring efforts within the labor movement to develop a class-struggle program and to create a class-conscious leadership.

A class-struggle program is essential to victory. A new historical opportunity for the working class is in the making. It still remains for a class-struggle left wing in the unions to be organized. And that is why a new edition of *Labor's Giant Step* is being brought out at this time. It will help today's militant workers develop a program; show them how to fight; give them a chance to know their past, to learn where they came from, who they are, and what they can do. They can change the world.

NAOMI ALLEN

March 1972

Preface

This is not a history of "collective bargaining" or "labor-management relations." It is not a recital of institutional activities and personages. This book deals with the titanic clash of great contending classes as reflected in the twenty years of the CIO. It is the history of the class struggle in the United States, the most proletarian nation of all, from 1929 through 1955.

Strikes, next to social revolutions, are the most overt expression of the class struggle. From 1936 through 1955, during the 20 years of the CIO's independent existence, there was a staggering total of 78,798 strikes in the United States, involving 42,366,000 strikers.

Even allowing for workers who have struck more than once, this figure puts in the pale the corresponding strike figures for all other countries. If we break down the above strike figures by decades and compare them with the decade just before 1933, we will observe a tremendous intensification and expansion of the class struggle, reaching its peak in the second decade of the CIO. Below are the U. S. Bureau of Labor Statistics (BLS) strike totals for 1923 through 1932; 1936 through 1945; and 1946 through 1955:

Number of Strikes and Strikers
(By Decades)

Years	Number of Strikes	Number of Strikers
1923–32	9 658	3 952 000
1936–45	35 519	15 856 000
1946–55	43 279	26 510 000

These figures scarcely support the widely circulated fiction of an America without a proletariat or a class struggle. The greatest single strike in our history — the 116-day national steel strike — occurred as recently as the fall and winter of 1959.

On June 16, 1959, during the prolonged steel negotiations, United Automobile Workers President Walter Reuther charged that the steel industry was spearheading a "class struggle...precisely as Karl Marx wrote that it would be waged." And he added fearfully: "If the labor movement begins to respond in kind, we will prove together that Karl Marx was right." Well, Karl Marx *was* proved right — again.

But figures, however accurate, always seem cold. The living evidence of the class struggle in America is summoned up most vividly in the history of the CIO. That is the subject of my book.

*   *   *

The first nine chapters of this book were published serially, May 9 through July 4, 1955, in *The Militant,* the weekly that reflects the viewpoint of the Socialist Workers Party. The series bore the general title, "Twenty Years of the CIO." It had been planned as a full history of the CIO in connection with the projected merger of the AFL and CIO in December 1955. Circumstances prevented my continuing the history as scheduled and I did not resume the task until 1958. The nine original chapters, however, are retained with but slight modifications.

At this writing I know of no other full history of the CIO either published or in preparation. There are several valuable books covering the first two years, including Edward Levinson's *Labor on the March* and J. Raymond Walsh's *C. I. O. — Industrial Unionism in Action.* There are a few books which deal with limited periods or special aspects of the CIO. There are several histories of individual unions affiliated at one time or another, and biographical works on labor leaders like John L. Lewis, Sidney Hillman and Philip Murray who played important roles. I cite some of the works in the context of my book.

I have been struck, however, by the lack of any rounded historical studies of the CIO. The labor leaders most directly involved do not appear interested. Political tendencies like the Communist (Stalinist) Party and the Socialist Party-Social Democratic Federation, which exercised considerable influence in the CIO at certain stages, have not seen fit, as yet, to sponsor a full-scale history. There are several and related reasons for this reluctance.

None of these labor leaders and tendencies has a scientific and consistent historical viewpoint. They see little or no connection between the conditions and events which brought the CIO into being and the present status and problems of organized labor. They have no desire to rekindle the memory of the great struggles of the CIO, or to inspire and enlighten the new generation of workers. These union officials want to stifle the class struggle, not lead it. They see no practical value in furnishing the workers with a textbook, however watered down, about how the industrial workers built and maintained their unions in twenty years of class battle.

Moreover, a careful, honest review of labor history since 1929 reveals such inconsistencies and contradictions, such absurd and conflicting views and judgments by all tendencies among the top labor leaders, that a history such as I have undertaken can prove only an embarrassment to them. The Stalinists, whose shifts and turns I trace in some detail, provide one well-known example. But they are not alone. A comparison of statements and actions over the years by surviving CIO leaders, from John L. Lewis and David Dubinsky among the founders, to Walter Reuther, David McDonald and James Carey who inherited the CIO in its last stages, cannot help their prestige.

We do not lack samples of the approach to labor history of such union leaders as Lewis and Reuther. Take Lewis's description of Reuther as "an earnest Marxist chronically inebriated, I should think, by the exuberance of his own verbosity." This is nonsense, because Reuther was anti-Marxist even when he was a mild Norman Thomas-type Socialist for a few years in the depression Thirties.

Reuther himself ventured to publish a history of the United Automobile Workers in the June 1956 issue of the *United Automobile Worker*. He expunged from that history the UAW's founding convention, convened August 26, 1935, at the Fort Shelby Hotel in Detroit. Reuther did not attend; he was not yet a member. It was at this convention that AFL President William Green conferred an international union charter on the newly formed United Automobile Workers in accordance with the May 9, 1935 decision of the AFL Executive Council. The second convention, which Reuther's account lists as the first, was held in May 1936, at South Bend, Indiana. The UAW did not formally affiliate with the CIO until the following July.

The effect of this rewriting of history has been to erase the true role of Reuther's factional opponents, such as George Addes of Toledo who was the union's first secretary-treasurer, in the founding of the UAW. By postdating the UAW's founding to 1936, Reuther can pose as a charter member and founder.

Except for the Marxist tendency, no group in the labor movement envisages an independent historic role for American labor. The differences between a Reuther, a James Hoffa, a David Dubinsky, a George Meany, a Stalinist or a Social Democrat are minor compared to one major characteristic they all share in common: their utter lack of faith in the independent power of the working class. They all see the problems of modern capitalist society—its inherent economic crises, political reaction and wars—as the product of mere "misunderstanding" and "error." It requires, in their opinion, only the efforts of "men of good will" and the intervention of "liberal" government to bring about an epoch of "peaceful coexistence" between hostile classes and nations alike. All these tendencies seek an agency or power outside the working class itself on which to lean and from which to solicit favors and benefits. This attitude and its source were brilliantly analyzed by the late Leon Trotsky, exiled leader of the Russian Revolution. Trotsky said:

"Monopoly capitalism does not rest on competition and free private initiative but on centralized command. The capitalist cliques at the head of mighty trusts, syndicates, banking consortiums, etc., view economic life from the very same heights as does state power; and they require at every step the collaboration of the latter. In their turn the trade unions in the most important branches of industry find themselves deprived of the possibility of profiting by the competition between the different enterprises. They have to confront a centralized capitalist adversary, intimately tied up with state power. Hence flows the need of the trade unions—insofar as they remain on reformist positions; that is, on positions of adapting themselves to private property—to adapt themselves to the capitalist state and to contend for its cooperation. In the eyes of the bureaucracy of the trade union movement the chief task lies in 'freeing' the state from the embrace of capitalism, in weakening its dependence on trusts, in pulling it over to their side. This position is in complete harmony with the social position of the labor aristocracy and the labor bureaucracy, who fight for a crumb in the share of super profits of imperialist capitalism. The labor bureaucrats do their level best in words and deeds to demonstrate to the 'democratic' state how reliable and indispensable they are in peacetime and especially in time of war..." (Leon Trotsky, *Trade Unions in the Epoch of Imperialist Decay.*)

The truth of this analysis is confirmed by the entire history of the CIO. It is the main thread running through the activities of the CIO leadership. At every step of the way they sought to subordinate the interests of the workers to the dictates of the capitalist state or to entrust the workers' interests to the decisions of the capitalist government. If they did not fully succeed, it is because of the very nature of the unions, their class base, their inherent function.

That function was defined at the dawn of the modern trade union movement by Friedrich Engels, Karl Marx's colleague and co-thinker. In a letter he wrote in March 1875, Engels spoke forcefully of the need for "the organization of the working class as a class by means of the trade unions. And that is a very essential point, for this is the real class organization of the proletariat, in which it carries on its daily struggle with capital..." Elsewhere Engels wrote: "The very existence of Trades Unions is proof sufficient of the fact: if they are not made to fight against the encroachments of capital, what are they made for?..."

Today, as in Engels' time, the unions are the *combat* organizations of the working class. Despite all efforts of the pro-capitalist labor leaders to deny or subordinate that function of the unions, to convert the unions into non-class "community service" organizations devoted to everything but the defense of labor, the unions retain their basic class character and function. We see this vividly demonstrated in the history of the CIO.

I regard the class struggle as the most dynamic element of modern society, and therefore view the rise of the CIO as the most significant event in modern American history. It foreshadows the even more momentous developments of the class struggle to come.

These developments, I firmly believe, will unfold on the political field. If "present society is mainly divided into two great antagonistic classes," as Engels said in his statement on the need for unions "to fight against the encroachments of capital," then we must conclude with him: "A struggle between great classes of society necessarily becomes a political struggle." He added:

"In every struggle of class against class, the next end fought for is political power."

Before the industrial workers were organized, AFL leaders like William Green and Daniel J. Tobin disdainfully dismissed the factory workers as "unorganizable" and not even "fit" for unionism. Even John L. Lewis and other founders of the CIO were astonished to find themselves caught up in the surging sweep of a movement from below that fought with new weapons like the sit-down strike and rose in great mass actions that could not be contained.

Today's labor leaders dismiss the possibility of workers' rule because the workers lack "class consciousness" just as the old craft union leaders claimed the industrial workers had no "union consciousness." But a lack of class consciousness does not mean the absence of classes. Classes exist independently of the lack of social awareness or of illusions. Sooner or later, objective reality punctures the illusion. The worker then sees himself as a worker. Class consciousness asserts itself and brings in its wake conscious class struggle. The first stage of awakening class consciousness was achieved, in fact, with the rise and consolidation of the CIO. The second stage will be marked by a further giant step—the formation of a new class party of labor based on the unions.

An awakening of *political* class consciousness will place the American workers in the center of the arena of world history. For the decisive question before the entire world today is: Who shall rule in the United States, this greatest bastion of capitalist imperialism, the workers or the super-rich? A workers and farmers government in this country will become a new starting point for the forward march of all humanity.

On the eve of World War II, James P. Cannon wrote in the June 15, 1939 *Socialist Appeal* what I believe remains the great prophetic truth for our generation. He said:

"The proletariat of the United States is the source of unlimited power, it can lift the whole world on its shoulders—that is the unshakable premise of all our calculations and all our work...the workers of America have power enough to topple over the structure of capitalism at home and to lift the whole world with them when they rise!"

Art Preis

New York
May 1, 1961

"...making history is what really counts...."

A reception for Art Preis, celebrating the publication of his book Labor's Giant Step — Twenty Years of the CIO *was held in New York on November 21, 1964. It brought together a number of leading participants in the early struggles for industrial unions which preceded and paved the way for the CIO.*

Among those honoring Preis were Farrell Dobbs, national secretary of the Socialist Workers Party; A. J. Muste, a leading figure in the U. S. antiwar movement; Sam Pollock, president of the Butcher Workmen's Union in Cleveland, Ohio; and Tom Kerry, editor of the International Socialist Review.

Farrell Dobbs was a leader of the historic Minneapolis teamsters strike of 1934. A. J. Muste was head of the Conference for Progressive Labor Action, the militant union trailblazing movement of the 1930s. Sam Pollack was one of the trio, along with Ted Selander and Art Preis, known in the 1930s as "the Three Muste Steers" because of their close collaboration with "A. J." in the heroic battles of the unemployed and the industrial workers of Ohio. Tom Kerry was a participant in the West Coast maritime strike of 1936.

It was fitting that, in addition to the veterans, many young people, representing the new generation of socialists, attended the reception.

The high point of the evening was Art Preis's speech. Indeed, his appearance at the reception — like the completion of his monumental work on the CIO — was further proof of his strength. For a series of severe illnesses in the past few years had necessitated a number of operations, and had deprived him of his hearing. A little more than a month after the reception, on December 26, he died.

Preis addressed his remarks particularly to the young people in the audience. He confided to them: "I don't want to knock the writing of history, but making history is what really counts."

This is a rare and wonderful occasion.

Just think, we have as participants and guests with us this evening men and women who fought on the picket lines 30 and more years ago in strikes that made labor history.

Here is Farrell Dobbs, who, with Marvel Dobbs, stood shoulder to shoulder with the Dunne brothers, Carl Skoglund and Kelly Postal, writing that imperishable chapter of the American class struggle, the 1934 Minneapolis truckdrivers strikes.

We are honored to have as one of our speakers Sam Pollock, who, with Ted Selander, challenged and smashed an injunction and mobilized the Toledo Auto-Lite workers in a six-day battle with the National Guard in May 1934. That battle won the first union contract in the automobile industry.

And there is that grand old fighter for the rights of labor, A. J. Muste, who was the adviser and strategist in the Toledo Chevrolet strike of 1935. It was the first successful strike in a General Motors plant or any plant of the automotive "Big Three." I can still see and hear William Green's representative Francis Dillon screaming "Muste's men! Muste's men!" at the Chevrolet strikers in Toledo's Civic Auditorium after they booed down Dillon's sell-out agreement.

And there are others here tonight who do us honor.

You know that Anne Chester, with Bob Chester and Mary Henderson, did a monumental job in putting out *Labor's Giant Step.* But did you know that Anne Chester fought on the picket lines in that terribly fierce Paterson silk strike of 1931 and again in 1934?

Karolyn Kerry went out in 1935 to help the horribly exploited agricultural strikers in California's Imperial Valley and Tom Kerry fought in the bitter 99-day West Coast maritime strike of 1936.

I don't want to knock the writing of history — but making history is what really counts.

You are not paying tribute tonight to a book, but to the men and women who wrote, in life, the greatest chapters of that book.

When I went as a young man of 22 into Toledo, Ohio, on Jan. 2, 1933, I got the shock of my life. That industrial city was a ghost town — hardly any autos on the streets, half the stores vacant, most of the banks failed.

The workers and their wives and children walked around in rags. They looked starved and they were starved.

Then and there, all on our own, without one drop of experience, strangers in town, Ted Selander and I determined to organize the unemployed. We had phenomenal luck and success. By August 1933 we were ready to launch our first big-scale "mass action"— although I don't remember that we even knew that phrase.

We called a strike of the unemployed on relief. Sound fantastic? Well, it was. It was a strike of the workers in the relief warehouse.

You see, "relief" was a handout of old potatoes, sour prunes and moldy beans — and damn little of those. Those on relief worked at sacking this food in burlap bags. Then they got this food — called "commissary relief" — as payment.

Well, we called a strike against commissary relief for cash relief. The strike was to begin on a Tuesday morning, at 9 a.m., at an open-air meeting in front of the Lucas County Courthouse.

But the previous Saturday night Ted and I went to a nearby township where we had called a meeting of the rural unemployed. We were to meet in an open field.

When we got there another organization was out in force in a field across the road. It was the Ku Klux Klan burning a cross. This was not down in Alabama or Mississippi. This was in northern Ohio, 31 years ago.

We had barely arrived when several county deputies' cars came blasting up the road. Ted was picked up and shoved into a patrol car. Then a big deputy came right up to me and bellowed, "Where's Preis?"

I said, "I think he went down that way." As soon as the deputy moved away, I sauntered across the road in the dark. There was a young worker in overalls at the wheel of an old beat-up Model T Ford.

I whispered, "The cops are after me. Can you give me a lift away from here?" He had never seen me before. But he took me in his car over a terrible backcountry road to Toledo.

When I got to Toledo, my troubles only began. I had no place to stay — no home, no money.

I had met Ethel at a YWCA forum, so I decided to go to her house and see if she would let me use the phone so I could try to find out what was happening to Ted. Ethel asked me no questions. I was able to phone a civil-liberties lawyer.

He called back and told me Ted was in the county jail and so were all the other members of our strike committee. I was the only one still at large to call the strike on Tuesday morning.

Unfortunately, there was a warrant out for my arrest on 21 counts, including plotting to blow up the relief warehouse. When I told Ethel what the situation was, she didn't hesitate.

Now, Ethel was a very proper young lady, but she hid me out. She put me in a tiny alcove in back of the third floor stairwell. I was there three nights and two days.

On Tuesday morning came the moment of truth. I had to go to the county courthouse, stand on the monument, and call the strike. At any second I expected the heavy hand of the law to fall on my shoulder.

I began to speak although there wasn't a single person there. Then, out of nowhere, the unemployed started to gather: from doorways, alley ways, around the corners. In five minutes there were 5,000 demonstrating unemployed.

And at the peak of the demonstration, the arrested strike leaders were released. They filed right onto the monument and we had a grand reunion.

Our strike lasted a month, and we won cash relief — $1.65 per week per person, whether we needed it or whether we didn't. That was the first successful strike of any kind in Toledo since 1919.

Yes, only 31 years ago there was not a single recognized union in any plant of basic industry in the United States. The Ku Klux Klan and the Black Legion, another secret terrorist society, were lynching union organizers.

I don't think anyone dreamed that within a year we would have the Minneapolis drivers strikes, the Toledo Auto-Lite strike, and the San Francisco general strike. As I look back at that time, never did organized labor's prospects look so bleak.

And yet we were at the very threshold of a mighty upsurge that was to swiftly transform the relationship of class forces in the United States.

That is a lesson for the youth of today.

The class struggle goes on.

We will see a new upsurge.

We cannot fix the day or the hour, just as we could not foresee the rise of the CIO. But this generation's socialist youth will get its chance.

You must study, work, prepare, organize.

Your chance will come.

And you will finish the job that my generation and the generations before me began.

PART I

THE RISE
OF THE CIO

1929-1940

The "Golden Twenties" Collapse

On December 5, 1955, the largest labor organization ever known in any capitalist land was formed by the merger of the Congress of Industrial Organizations (CIO) and the American Federation of Labor (AFL). This merger marked the twentieth anniversary of the CIO, whose industrial unions and name are preserved under the combined name, the AFL-CIO.

A new generation has grown up since the CIO's birth on November 9, 1935, out of a split from the old AFL. Young workers now in their twenties, who join a union as a matter of course, cannot even remember when there was no CIO. Yet, the rise of the CIO was, without doubt, the greatest event in modern American history.

The heroic past of the CIO, the titanic events that brought it forth, are dimmed not only by time. The capitalist propagandists and the union leaders themselves have deliberately tried to bury and hide the true nature and significance of the CIO's history. It has been surrounded with falsifications, distortions and myths.

It is necessary to recall for the new generation the record of the CIO, its achievements and shortcomings, its victories and defeats. Young workers must be armed with the lessons and traditions of the CIO as a powerful weapon for the further advance of the American labor movement.

The CIO did not suddenly emerge full-blown from the heads of a few of the more aggressive AFL leaders like John L. Lewis, the CIO's founding president. Its origin went back to the earliest struggles of modern American labor. The vision of industrial unionism—combining all workers of an industry regardless of craft, skill, race, color, national origin, religion or politics — was one of the great inspirations of the pioneer American unionists and, especially, of the socialists.

Eugene V. Debs, the great socialist leader, had led the famous 1894 railroad strike in an attempt to organize the American Railway Union as an industrial organization. The Industrial Workers of the World (IWW), popularly known as the Wobblies, in the decade before and during World War I had fought for industrial unionism and led battles which wrote imperishable pages in American labor history. The Communist Party of the Twenties, before its degeneration under Stalinism, advanced the program of industrial unionism within the AFL and in several great post-World War I strikes.

But the immediate origin of the CIO dates to the fateful year 1929—to the beginning of the great depression-and-war era that continues to this very day.

There are some big differences between the America of 1929 and 1960—and the CIO played a major part in producing them.

In 1929, there were fewer than three million members in the AFL. By 1955 the CIO alone had almost twice as many; the AFL itself boasted 10-1/2 millions. When these two labor bodies merged, they formed a massive organization almost six times as large as the AFL 30 years ago.

In the "golden Twenties," workers in the mass production industries — steel, auto, rubber, textiles, oil, chemicals, etc. — were unorganized and atomized. They had no rights—no means of self-defense from even the most brutal aggressions of the employers. They were fired at will, speeded up to a killing pace, worked for 10 and 12 hours a day straight time at wages dictated by the bosses.

Today, a majority of mass production workers are unionized. Even where they suffer poor leadership, the unions in industry put some restraints upon the unrestricted brutalization of labor that was practiced by the monopoly corporations back in 1929.

The difference between the two periods is shown markedly in the scope and character of strikes. A few thousand strikers in the Twenties evoked screaming headlines in the capitalist press. Almost all picket lines were crushed with bloody violence by police, deputies, troops and armed professional strikebreakers.

Today, strikes are so commonplace that only the most gigantic industry-wide walkouts are treated as front-page news in the national press.

In 1929 there were 921 strikes, involving 289,000 workers for a loss of 5,352,000 man-days. In 1953 there were 5,091 strikes involving 2,400,000 workers and a man-day loss of 28,300,000. The bosses themselves called 1953 a "quiet" year on the labor front. In 1959 strike figures zoomed with the record-breaking 116-day national steel strike.

A change has also taken place in the attitude of the American people toward capitalist "free enterprise," a phrase now generally held in derision. It is widely recognized that capitalism cannot stand on its own legs. It must be propped by vast government aid, especially war spending, to stand even temporarily. Moreover, few will now dispute the responsibility of government for social welfare. Even die-hard Republicans vote in Congress for social security improvements. Yet, as late as 1932, the third year of the great depression, the AFL officially opposed federal unemployment insurance.

Twelve years of depression, followed by 18 years of wars, war preparations and war scares, have undermined the sense of security that prevailed back in 1929. The American people are no longer blind believers in a natural and inevitable progress under capitalism. Their minds are plowed deep with doubts and fears.

But there were no doubts and fears in the mind of AFL President William Green on September 1, 1929, when he issued his annual Labor Day message. "The organization of the unorganized has gone ahead with startling success," he boasted. Even "the wage earners of the South have awakened to the necessity of organization." He found that "collective bargaining is coming to be accepted more and more as a preventive of labor disputes" and bragged that strikes had been reduced from 3,789 in 1916 to 629 in 1928.

"To give labor's victories in detail would fill pages," he opined. "It is sufficient to say that labor is progressing at a greater speed than for any year in the past, that it knows what it wants and is aware of the way to secure it, and that it will grow in numbers and in strength every year in the future."

Green was wrong in every particular. Within a few months the onset of the great depression, which continued to the very year of America's entry into World War II, blasted every one of his claims, although he never admitted it to his dying day.

On September 1, 1929, Green did not so much as mention unemployment or even hint at the possibility of depression. The sole reference to unemployment that day came from Secretary of Labor James J. Davis, who conceded that "we do have a bit of unemployment in America" but that it existed "even in the best of times" and that much of it was "seasonal."

It is unlikely that Green or Davis had read *The Militant* of February 15, 1929, containing the platform of the Left Opposition which was expelled from the Communist Party in 1928 for fighting bureaucratic Stalinism. This forerunner of the Socialist Workers Party, analyzing the economic situation, reported that already there was "a standing army of unemployed workers numbering several millions" and a "growing series of wage cuts." It stated:

"American capitalism has been unable to overcome the serious depressions in agriculture and in the coal, textile, lumber, oil, shipping and other industries, nor will it be able to prevent the coming decline in iron and steel and automobile industries... the internal contradictions of American imperialism, bound up with its world economic interdependence, are maturing a severe crisis..."

The declaration in *The Militant* emphasized: "The main reservoir of labor militancy is in the masses of unskilled and semi-skilled workers in the unorganized, basic industries. The full horror of the capitalist rationalization falls directly on them, and the attacks of the capitalists in the present depression and coming crises strike them first and hardest." The task of class-conscious militants, the paper pointed out, was to turn to these unorganized masses and "lead in the work of organizing them into new industrial unions."

The full fury of the economic storm forecast in *The Militant* was signaled by the collapse of the stock market in October 1929. Blue-chip stocks, which had boomed to hundreds of points on the index, fell almost overnight to five, four, three and even zero.

But this catastrophic decline in stock values was merely the reflection of a profound dislocation of the entire American economy. Between 1929 and 1933 industrial production dropped 48.7%. The national income fell from $81 billion in 1929 to $39 billion in 1932. The index of total payrolls sank in one year—November 1929 to November 1930—from 95.1 points to 68.5, or almost a third. In the same period the employment index fell from 94.8 points to 76.5.

Unemployment rose almost continuously to its peak in March 1933, with estimates of the jobless ranging from 13,300,000 (National Industrial Conference Board) to 17,920,000 (National Research League).

Republican President Herbert Hoover simply denied the severity of the situation. His own committee, headed by Col. Arthur Wood, had reported in December 1930 that there were "probably" between 4,500,000 and 5,000,000 unemployed and had recommended a $2 billion federal construction program to provide jobs. Hoover claimed, however, there were only 2,500,000 jobless. He asked for an emergency "employment" fund of from $100,000,000 to $150,000,000. But his failure to grasp the situation was not unique. The Democratic governor of New York, Franklin Delano Roosevelt, in September 1931 when there were more than a million unemployed in that state, asked only $20,000,000 for relief.

The symbol of the depression became the "Hoovervilles" — the tarpaper-and-tinsheet shack communities that grew up in the dumps of America's cities and towns where evicted families were forced to live. An estimated 1,500,000 homeless, including thousands of women and young girls, wandered the roads of the country. Mass hunger amidst plenty — want despite an unparalleled capacity to produce — was the sign of American capitalism.

After the first shock of the economic crisis the unemployed began to organize. The leadership of this movement was first in the hands of the Communist Party. It pursued at that time an adventuristic, sectarian policy that in the end disorganized its own movement. But the demonstrations initially led by the Communist Party first aroused the American workers from their shock and pressured the earliest relief measures. The demonstrations of the unemployed were met with brutal suppression; many were killed, wounded and jailed.

On March 7, 1932, a demonstration of unemployed seeking jobs at the Ford River Rouge plant was dispersed by machine guns, with four dead and many wounded. Then, in July, came the savage attack on the unemployed World War I veterans who had come to Washington to seek payment on their bonuses. On Hoover's orders Gen. Douglas MacArthur, riding a white charger at the head of his troops, drove out the 25,000 veterans and their families with tear gas, fire and bayonets.

What did the labor leaders, headed by Green, do on the matter of unemployment? J. B. S. Hardman, editor of *Advance,* organ of the Amalgamated Clothing Workers, in a 1934 symposium in a book called *Challenge to the New Deal,* summarized the AFL leadership's attitude:

"The Communists staged hunger demonstrations and marches. The liberals organized unemployment insurance conferences. The socialists advocated remedial legislation and relief measures. The men of the Conference for Progressive Labor Action promoted Unemployment Leagues. The AFL alone carefully guarded its record of safety and sanity and did about nothing."

Not absolutely nothing. One day in February 1932, about 100 AFL bureaucrats led by William Green marched a mile from the AFL headquarters to the White House and asked Hoover to spend some money for relief. Then they marched a mile back. This ended their "uprising" for the duration of the depression.

Seeking to preserve their profits and to foist the whole weight of the depression on the workers, the corporations instituted wave after wave of wage cuts. By 1931 total wages and salaries were halved over 1925.

A few months after the stock market crash Green had attended a conference of employers summoned by Hoover. There the AFL leader pledged a no-strike policy (this had always been his policy anyway) if the employers would pledge not to cut wages. A "gentlemen's agreement" was made. The only "gentlemen" turned out to be the AFL leaders. In June and July, 1930, 60 corporations and industries announced wage cuts. The AFL did nothing.

Between March 1930 and March 1931 the Bureau of Labor Statistics reported 2,937,925 workers in manufacturing industries suffered average wage cuts of 9.4%. In mining, wages of 110,669 anthracite workers were slashed 9.2%, while 213,028 bituminous miners received wage cuts of 16.2%. At that time United Mine Workers President John L. Lewis toured the mining areas putting down strikes and counseling acceptance of the cuts. That was the role of all the AFL leaders.

By 1931, Lewis's union had shriveled to 60,000 members from a 400,000 peak in 1920. Green's 1929 prophecy of the AFL's uninterrupted growth was swept away in the depression. The AFL membership, which stood at 4,029,000 in 1920, was declining at the rate of 7,000 a week by 1931. It fell by 1933 to a low of 2,127,000.

Those figures are history's commentary on the policy of narrow craft unionism in a mass production country.

2

"New Deal"—
Myth and Fact

Hoover's administration was washed away in the November 1932 elections by a flood of popular hatred that was to submerge the Republican Party in Washington for the next 20 years. It was said of this defeat that "even Mickey Mouse could have beaten the 'Great Engineer.'" Franklin D. Roosevelt, Hoover's Democratic successor, did not win because of personal popularity or program. He was not even well known to the national public.

Roosevelt's big election campaign pitch was "government saving." He said in his nomination acceptance speech of July 2, 1932: "For three long years I have been going up and down this country preaching that Government—federal, state and local—costs are too much ... I propose to you, my friends, and through you, that Government of all kinds, big and little, be made solvent and that the example be set by the President of the United States and his cabinet."

As for unemployment relief, he explained that "primary responsibility for relief rests with localities, now, as ever" — that is, with bankrupt local communities. He wound up with the oft-quoted declaration: "I pledge you, I pledge myself, to a new deal for the American people."

After Roosevelt's death in 1945, his Secretary of Labor Frances Perkins, in her naively revealing *The Roosevelt I Knew,* spilled the beans about the "New Deal." She wrote that when Roosevelt took office in March 1933, "the New Deal was not a plan with form or content. It was a happy phrase he had coined during the campaign, and its value was psychological. It made people feel better ... "

This "happy phrase" concealed the real purpose of the medicine in Roosevelt's prescription. He was intent on saving dying American capitalism and he was ready to use all means to that end.

His first major official act after he took office on March 4, 1933, was to save the big banks and big depositors at the expense of the small banks and small depositors. His bank moratorium on withdrawal of deposits and other emergency bank measures consolidated the big banks while thousands of the small ones never opened again or paid back only a fraction of deposits.

Dr. Broadus Mitchell, in *Depression Decade,* an able study of the depression era from 1929 to 1941, makes a telling point in connection with the bank moratorium. "Some felt at the time, and have continued to believe since, that this was a moment when the country, and Congress, would have followed the President in making the banks national property ... Such an action would have meant that the New Deal, instead of reforming glaring defects in order to preserve the capitalist system, would have set about superseding it." Raymond Moley, one of Roosevelt's closest associates of the early "New Deal," wrote in his book, *After Seven Years:* "It cannot be emphasized too strongly that the policies which vanquished the bank crisis were thoroughly conservative policies. If ever there was a moment when things hung in a balance, it was on March 5, 1933 — when unorthodoxy would have drained the last remaining strength of the capitalist system. Capitalism was saved in eight days." The man who promised to drive the "money changers from the Temple" actually gave them a new lease on it.

The picture of Roosevelt as a "friend of labor" giving the people concessions out of the tenderness of his heart—this portrait painted by both the conservative trade union officialdom and the Stalinists —is completely false. Roosevelt was a clever, adroit politician who carefully gauged popular sentiment. His slightest concession to the workers was given grudgingly out of fear of the masses and to prevent their moving left. He voiced this in his 1932 acceptance speech, saying that "a resentment against the failure of Republican leadership ... the failure of Republican leaders to solve our troubles may degenerate into unreasoning radicalism ... To meet by reaction that danger of radicalism is to invite disaster."

Ferdinand Lundberg, in *America's 60 Families,* a classic study of the big capitalists who run this country, concluded that the "New Deal" was neither "revolutionary nor radical"; in reality it was "conservative." He wrote that "its mild tentative reformist coloration" was a "concession in the face of widespread unrest."

The labor leaders and liberals who have built up the popular myth about Roosevelt's "humanitarianism" and "love for the little man," rest their case mainly on two claims: (1) that he "gave relief and jobs to the unemployed"; (2) that he "gave labor the right to organize."

Let us examine his aid to the unemployed. Speaking of the annual average of more than 12 million unemployed during Roosevelt's first term, his relief administrator and intimate colleague Harry L. Hopkins boasted in his book, *Spending to Save,* published in 1936, that "in the last three and a half years we have spent almost six billion dollars in helping these families maintain themselves." The average annual expenditure for the unemployed ran about $1-1/2 billion, while the total yearly cost of government was a little more than $7 billion. When it came to war, however, Roosevelt was to spend $79 billion in 1943, $95 billion in 1944 and more than $100 billion in 1945.

The Emergency Relief Act of 1933 granted only $500 million to the states to continue the starvation doles previously given some of the unemployed. By 1935, Roosevelt was to declare his intention to "get out of this business of relief" and to abandon three-quarters of the unemployed to the tender mercies of local relief agencies without funds.

Roosevelt's works program never provided jobs for more than 25% of the jobless. His first such program, the Civil Works Administration started in November 1933, lasted only three months. It paid $15 a week, with minimum wages of 40 cents an hour in the South, 45 cents in the Midwest and 60 cents in the Northeast. The Federal Emergency Relief Administration program, which got under way in the summer of 1934, began to fold up in the spring of 1935. It employed an average of fewer than 2,000,000 workers, at a wage of $12 a week.

The peak of the work relief program was reached under the Works Progress Administration (WPA). This paid the "prevailing wage rates" of the local communities — as low as $19 a month in the South and $40 a month in the North for common labor. At its peak, WPA wages, including skilled, professional and administrative, averaged only $45.91 a month.

Relief jobs were systematically increased before national elections and hundreds of thousands were fired shortly after the votes were counted. In 1936, for instance, mass WPA layoffs were discontinued in the fall before Roosevelt's second-term election. Immediately afterwards, 400,000 WPA workers were fired en masse, most of them still displaying their Roosevelt campaign buttons.

Throughout the entire first two terms of the Roosevelt administration, there were continuous unemployed demonstrations, relief works strikes and riots. The highest relief, the most relief jobs and the biggest wages were in direct proportion to the number of unemployed struggles.

Miss Perkins tells how she met an elderly lawyer, a Harvard graduate who got a WPA job in a park, "and he would always ask me to take a message to the President — a message of gratitude for a job which paid him $15 a week and kept him from starving to death."

How pitiable seems such gratitude in the light of America's tremendous productive capacity and the liberality Roosevelt was to display in providing hundreds of billions in "relief" for war profiteers in World War II. Roosevelt's program for the unemployed seemed generous only by comparison with Hoover's. But in terms of even minimum subsistence standards it was, as the Unemployed League put it, "not enough to live on and just too much to die on."

The main prop of the Roosevelt myth is that he gave American labor "the right to organize." This claim is based on Section 7(a) inserted into Roosevelt's chief piece of early "stabilization" legislation, the National Industrial Recovery Act, known as NRA, enacted in June 1933. Actually, the right to organize had been fully sanctioned in the Norris-LaGuardia Anti-Injunction Act of 1932, adopted in Hoover's administration.

To be sure, labor already had that right to organize — whenever it exercised the right and fought to maintain it. If there were no such right, how could the AFL have existed at all? In fact, 14 years earlier the AFL had organized more than four million workers. Had the workers not been ready and eager for organization, Section 7(a), affirming their right to organize and bargain collectively and to pick their own union representatives free from employer interference, would have had no effect in any sense.

The facts are that the workers were already on the move when Roosevelt took office and Section 7(a) was a reluctant response to labor pressure. The same upsurge of protest against conditions that had swept Roosevelt into office was also expressed at the start of 1933 in the biggest strike wave since the early twenties. These strikes were especially significant because many occurred in unorganized, company-dominated basic industries, particularly auto. Between January 1, 1933 and the signing of the NRA in mid-June, there had been strikes at four Briggs plants, Motor Products, Hayes Body, Murray Body, Hudson Body and Hudson Production, Willys Overland, Chevrolet (Oakland, Calif.) and White Motor.

A. J. Muste, in his 1935 pamphlet, *The Automobile Industry and Organized Labor,* published by the Fellowship of Reconciliation, reported: "As one observer expressed it, 'Early in 1933 hell began to pop. Strike followed strike with bewildering rapidity. The long-exploited, too-patient auto slaves were getting tired of the game.'"

The original draft of NRA said nothing about collective bargaining rights. Long afterwards, in her book, Miss Perkins admitted that Section 7(a) was written into the bill only after protests by William Green. She comments: "Written in general terms, 7(a) was a problem in semantics. It was a set of words to suit labor leaders, William Green in particular."

Other labor leaders also are credited with responsibility for 7(a); namely, the late Sidney Hillman, president of the Amalgamated Clothing Workers, and John L. Lewis, United Mine Workers president. Pre-1940 accounts, including Edward Levinson's *Labor on the March,* agree on Lewis as the actual author.

Saul Alinsky, author of a soberly written and fully documented biography of John L. Lewis, has described the campaign of flattery, intrigue and pressure used to squeeze from Roosevelt his grudging consent to Section 7(a), "a set of words" written so vaguely that it could be interpreted to assure the "rights" of company unions as well as of genuine labor organizations.

Many workers undoubtedly were misled into thinking that 7(a) meant that the government really would protect them in their right to join a union. Even before NRA became law on June 16, 1933, Lewis sent an army of union organizers into the coal fields, shouting "The President wants you to join the union." In her book, Miss Perkins complains that this organizing slogan was raised "with more drama than truth" and that "Section 7(a) was subject to excited interpretations by organizers who gave working people an exaggerated notion of their rights." Lewis himself, many years later, admitted to Alinsky: "Roosevelt was not too friendly to Section 7(a); and, if there was any time when I began to question and wonder and have reservations about the President, it was at that time."

Section 7(a) did at least have the effect of getting some of the union leaders out of their office chairs and doing a little organizing. In some instances, the immediate results were phenomenal. The mine union signed up 300,000 new members in two months; the International Ladies Garment Workers Union, 150,000; the Amalgamated Clothing Workers, 50,000. There was a spurt of unionization in steel and a few other industries where organizations of a sort existed.

But even if Section 7(a) played a certain part in helping to organize some workers, it could not keep them organized or protect them against boss reprisals. Immediate events were to prove that to the hilt.

3

War on Labor
under the NRA

Section 7(a) was an incidental afterthought and not the main aim of the NRA. As Secretary of Labor Perkins subsequently admitted, the NRA "rested on the idea of suspending the effect of the anti-trust laws in return for voluntary agreements by industries for fair competition, minimum wage levels and maximum hours." NRA was surrounded with a gigantic propaganda campaign, including parades, Blue Eagle symbols everywhere, radio speeches, and thousands of business men swarming into Washington for industry conferences to set up codes of "fair competition."

Lundberg summed it up in his *America's 60 Families,* observing that the NRA sought to guarantee the status quo of worker and employer, "one in possession of little, the other in control of much," in order to "restore industrial stability." The government exempted from the requirements of the anti-trust laws those industries which agreed to the codes. In most cases, the codes were the very agreements already maintained by the trade associations, with the government now enforcing them. In some cases the codes were the exact copies of those agreements. Thus, the government served to underwrite monopoly more openly and broadly than ever before. "In almost every instance," notes Lundberg, "the authorities responsible for enforcing each code were simply the leading executives of the trade associations."

Matthew Josephson, author of the semi-official biography, *Sidney Hillman: Statesman of American Labor,* concedes: "Perhaps the Blue Eagle was part fraud, and under its frowsy wings too many business chiselers raised wages 10 per cent while marking up wholesale prices as much as 50 or 100 per cent and scheming to curb production."

The Blue Eagle, or the "Blue Buzzard" as it came to be called by the workers, was a total fraud. Edward Levinson, in *Labor on the March*, observed that "the code authorities, completely dominated by employers, assumed the function of fixing hours and wages, frequently — with the acquiescence of the federal government — without even consulting the employees."

The textile industry adopted the first code, which General Hugh S. Johnson, head of the National Recovery Administration and chum of Wall Street financier Bernard Baruch, called a "model." It fixed minimum wages of $13 a week in the North and $11 in the South. The average weekly wage in the industry by June 1934 was $10.86.

In coal the minimum wage was fixed at $14 a week. The steel industry, which had been working a 10 to 12-hour day, provided in its code for an "eight-hour" day — that is, an "average" of eight hours a day over a six-month period. So long as the "average" was maintained, a particular workday could be any number of hours at straight-time wages.

The auto code fixed minimum wages of 40 to 43 cents an hour — as low as $16 a week for a 40-hour week. The per capita weekly earnings of all auto workers in 1934 averaged about $25. "However, employment is notoriously seasonal even in good times," reported Muste in his previously cited pamphlet. "Thus, for example, the automobile plants under the code in 1934 lost 36.3 per cent of possible man hours. A sample study by the Henderson staff revealed that 45 per cent of all workers in the group received less than $1,000 a year. In one factory studied, one-third received less than $400 for the year 1934 and three-fifths less than $800."

The auto code, moreover, contained the notorious "merit clause," approved by Roosevelt personally. This declared that auto employers "may exercise their right to select, retain, or advance employes on the basis of individual merit, without regard to their membership or non-membership in any organization." This was a formula for enforcement of the open shop and for discrimination against real unionists on the basis of "individual merit." Subsequently, Roosevelt inserted a further qualification, the "proportional representation" clause. This permitted company union spokesmen to receive positions on bargaining committees on a proportional membership basis along with bona fide unions and "the government makes it clear that it favors no particular union or particular form of employes organization or representation."

The final score of NRA and Section 7(a), before the Supreme Court in May, 1935, voided the entire Act as contravening the anti-trust laws, is contained in a comparison of the growth of the AFL and of

company unions during the NRA's two-year history. The AFL recruited—and retained—500,000 new members, bringing its total
membership to 3,600,000. Company union membership, however,
increased more than twice as much in the same period—rising from
1,263,000 to about 2,500,000 in 1935, according to a Bureau of Labor Statistics survey.

Roosevelt himself, in a radio appeal for the NRA, on July 24,
1933, had stated: "The workers of this country have rights under
this law which cannot be taken from them, and nobody will be permitted to whittle them away but, on the other hand, no aggression
is necessary now to attain these rights ... The principle that applies
to the employer applies to the workers as well and I ask you workers to cooperate in the same spirit."

By "aggression," of course, Roosevelt meant strikes. But the
workers were not for cooperation with the employers and government in maintaining wages of $12 to $15 a week, "merit clauses"
and recognition of company unions. The workers resorted to the
only weapon which had ever enforced their rights and improved their
conditions—strike action. In the six months following enactment of
NRA, the workers were forced to commit a host of "aggressions"
in an attempt to get the most elementary rights; first of all, union
recognition. The number of strikes totaled 1,695 in 1933 compared
to 841 in 1932 and the number of strikers almost quadrupled in the
same period, from 324,000 to 1,168,000.

Some 35,000 members of Hillman's Amalgamated Clothing Workers were forced to strike in New York City against the code minimums proposed. The 60,000 dressmakers of David Dubinsky's International Ladies Garment Workers Union followed suit. A dozen
or more strikes flared in auto. Fifty thousand silk workers in Paterson and elsewhere went out against NRA-proposed minimums of
$12 to $13 a week. More than 70,000 miners stayed out of the pits
in August and September.

If the workers had "rights under this law which cannot be taken
from them," as Roosevelt claimed, the coal miners couldn't find
what these rights were. The murderous opposition of the employers
to unions is typified in the following account of one event in the strike
of coal miners in steel company captive mines of Western Pennsylvania. The August 5, 1933 *Militant* reported:

"The miners' wives from the outset joined directly in the battle
taking the blows with their husbands and giving blows as the powerful picket line extended over a far-flung territory. One miner is reported killed in typical Pennsylvania steel trust fashion: shot down
in cold blood by company plug-uglies while carrying the American

flag at the head of a picket line. Several other miners are expected to die from wounds received and many are suffering from lighter injuries."

The treacherous role of both Roosevelt and his labor lieutenants was also shown in this mine strike. Roosevelt ordered an investigation of "communism" in the strike. He also ordered the mine union leaders to end the strike. Philip Murray, then a United Mine Workers (UMW) vice president, told the *New York Times* of his interview with the President.

"The President then said to me, 'Philip, I want you to get these men back to work.' I replied, 'If there is anything in God's world that I can do for you, I will be glad to try.'" Concerning Roosevelt's command Murray further told the *Times:* "Any union or union officials who refuse to obey their command will not live long."

Murray accepted an agreement promising "union conditions" but not union recognition in the U. S. Steel mines. It took seven years and another big strike to get a union contract in the captive mines.

What followed the signing of the NRA was not the recognition of labor's rights but the most ferocious assault on American labor in its history. Labor was forced into what was a virtual civil war fought on three thousand miles of picket lines for five years. Hundreds of workers were killed, thousands wounded, tens of thousands arrested or otherwise victimized from 1933 to 1938.

Summarizing six months of "New Deal" atrocities against labor, from July 1, 1933 to January 1, 1934, the American Civil Liberties Union charged that "too many employers confuse Roosevelt's New Deal with Coolidge's New Capitalism.

"The methods of that era are used flagrantly to smash labor's efforts to organize despite the NRA. At no time has there been such widespread violations of workers' rights by injunctions, troops, private police, deputy sheriffs, labor spies and vigilantes.

"More than 15 strikers have been killed, 200 injured and hundreds arrested since July 1. More than 40 injunctions of sweeping character have been issued ... Troops have been called out in half a dozen strike districts. Criminal syndicalist charges are being used against active strike leaders. The National Labor Board and its regional boards (set up under NRA) have lacked the will or the power to overcome the defiance of employers. Labor's rights to meet, organize and strike have been widely violated by employers who fear neither General Johnson nor Attorney General Cummings. Only where labor has been well organized and has struck with determination have its rights been respected." (*New York Times,* February 11, 1934.)

In 1934 there were to be 52 strikers murdered and the toll was to mount until the climactic Memorial Day massacre in the 1937 Little Steel strike.

During this period of the NRA the AFL did little officially to organize the unorganized. Hostile to industrial union forms of organization, fearful of militant action by the workers, conciliatory to the bosses and government, the craft union officials who dominated the AFL made only timid gestures in the direction of organizing the unorganized.

In August 1933, the AFL Executive Council was prevailed upon to issue charters for so-called federal locals. These were local unions directly attached to the AFL rather than to an affiliate and ruled by the AFL top officers. In announcing this policy, William Green made it amply clear that such federal unions would be of a temporary nature and ultimately would be divided among the numerous craft unions claiming jurisdiction over the various types of work done by members in the same shop. "In following such a plan of organization (federal locals)," said Green, "the American Federation of Labor is not in any way departing from the form of organization and traditional policy which it has pursued from the beginning."

Many radicalized workers, particularly those under Communist Party (Stalinist) influence, at that time rejected participation in the AFL unions. The Stalinists were then following the line of building separate "revolutionary" unions and called all other labor organizations "social fascist." The August 25, 1933 *Daily Worker* reported how the CP's trade union secretary Jack Stachel answered an appeal urging workers to join the AFL: "Stachel said we are against this, except in certain cases like the Railroad Brotherhoods, as the AFL is organizing the workers for betrayal and not for struggle."

James P. Cannon answered this ultra-leftist line in the September 2, 1933 *Militant*. He said: "We do not expect Green & Co. to organize the masses of unskilled workers in the basic industries for effective struggle. The resurgent struggles of the masses ... will probably break out of the formal bounds of the AFL and seek expression in a new union movement." He added to this forecast of the coming of the CIO, however, that "the center of gravity at the present moment is unquestionably in the conservative mass organizations. That is where we must be."

It was precisely radical workers active in "conservative mass organizations" of the AFL who gave the impetus to the next great stage of labor struggle. They sparked the upsurge that led to the CIO through three strike battles such as this country had never seen before—the Toledo Electric Auto-Lite, the Minneapolis truck drivers and San Francisco general strikes.

4

Three Strikes
That Paved the Way

The National Industrial Conference Board, in a survey of collective bargaining under the NRA, could boast in March 1934 of "the relatively small proportion of employes found to be dealing with employers through an organized labor union." At the same time, said the board, "Employe representation [company unions] appears to have made considerable progress" and "it is clear that individual bargaining has not in any way been eliminated by Section 7(a) of the Recovery Act."

In that same month, the *American Federationist,* organ of the top AFL leadership, complained: "In general there has been no increase in real wages...The codes will not safeguard real wages...The government monetary policy points toward diminishing real wages."

Worst of all, the wave of strikes following the enactment of NRA in June 1933 was ending in a series of defeats. Where the union leaders themselves did not rush the workers back on the job without gains—not even union recognition, the strikes were smashed by court injunctions and armed violence. Behind the legal restraining orders and the shotguns, rifles and machine guns of police, deputies and National Guardsmen, the scabs and strikebreakers were being herded into struck plants almost at will.

It was at this stage, when strike after strike was being crushed, that the Toledo Electric Auto-Lite Company struggle blazed forth to illuminate the whole horizon of the American class struggle. The American workers were to be given an unforgettable lesson in how to confront all the agencies of the capitalist government — courts, labor boards and armed troops—and win.

Toledo, Ohio, an industrial city of about 275,000 population in 1934, is a glass and auto parts center. In June 1931, four Toledo

banks had closed their doors. Some of the big local companies, including several suppliers to the auto industry, had secretly transferred their bank accounts to one big bank. These companies did
not get caught in the crash.

But thousands of workers and small business men did. They lost
their lives' savings. One out of every three persons in Toledo was
thrown on relief, standing in lines for food handouts at a central commissary. In 1933, the Unemployed League, led by followers of A. J.
Muste, head of the Conference for Progressive Labor Action (later
the American Workers Party), had organized militant mass actions
of the unemployed and won cash relief. The League made it a policy
to call for unity of the unemployed and employed workers; it mobilized the unemployed not to scab, but to aid all strikes.

On February 23, 1934, the Toledo Auto-Lite workers, newly organized in AFL Federal Local 18384, went on strike. This was
quickly ended by the AFL leaders with a truce agreement for negotiations through the Regional Labor Board of the National Labor
Board, which had been set up under the NRA.

Refusing to be stalled further by the labor board or to submit to
the special Auto Labor Board, which Roosevelt had set up in March
to sidetrack pending auto strikes and which had upheld company unionism, the Auto-Lite workers went on the picket lines again on
April 13.

The company followed the usual first gambit in such a contest. It
went to a friendly judge and got him to issue an injunction limiting
picketing. The strike had begun to die on its feet when a committee
of Auto-Lite workers came to the Unemployed League and asked for
aid. What happened then was described shortly thereafter by Louis
F. Budenz, in the previously cited collection of articles, *Challenge
to the New Deal,* edited by Alfred Bingham and Selden Rodman. This
is the same Budenz who about a year later deserted to the Stalinists,
served them for ten years and finally wound up as an informer for
the FBI against radicals.

However, at the time of the Auto-Lite strike, Budenz was still
an outstanding fighter for labor's rights and civil liberties. He had
edited *Labor Age* during the Twenties and had led great battles against
strikebreaking injunctions at Kenosha, Wisconsin, and Nazareth,
Pennsylvania. It was he who suggested the tactic for breaking the
injunction and he had addressed the thousands massed on the picket
line after the injunction was smashed. While he was still uncor-
rupted, Budenz wrote about the Auto-Lite battle:

"The dynamic intervention of a revolutionary workers organization, the American Workers Party, seemed to have been required

before that outcome [a union victory] could be achieved. The officials in the Federal Automobile Workers Union would have lost the
strike if left to their own resources.

"The merit of this particular AFL union was that it did strike.
The Electric Auto-Lite and its two affiliated companies, the Logan
Gear and Bingham Stamping Co., were involved. But when the company resorted to the injunction, the union officers observed its terms.
In less than three weeks, under protection of the court decree, the
company had employed or otherwise secured 1800 strikebreakers
in the Auto-Lite alone.

"That would have been the end, and another walkout of the workers
would have gone into the wastebasket of labor history. The Lucas
County Unemployed League, also enjoined, refused however to let
the fight go in that way. Two of its officers, Ted Selander and Sam
Pollock, [and several auto local members] wrote [May 5, 1934] Judge
R. R. Stuart, advising him that they would violate the injunction by
encouraging mass picketing. They went out and did so. They were
arrested, tried and released—the court warning them to picket no
more. They answered by going directly from court, with all the
strikers and unemployed league members who had been present, to
the picket line. Through the mass trials, Selander and Pollock got
out a message as to the nature of the capitalist courts. The picket
line grew."

The unexampled letter sent by the local Unemployed League to
Judge Stuart deserves to be preserved for posterity. It is an historic
document that ranks in its way with the great declarations of human
freedom more widely known and acclaimed. The letter read:

May 5, 1934

His Honor Judge Stuart
County Court House
Toledo, Ohio

Honorable Judge Stuart:

On Monday morning May 7, at the Auto-Lite plant, the Lucas
County Unemployed League, in protest of the injunction issued
by your court, will deliberately and specifically violate the injunction enjoining us from sympathetically picketing peacefully
in support of the striking Auto Workers Federal Union.

We sincerely believe that this court intervention, preventing
us from picketing, is an abrogation of our democratic rights,
contrary to our constitutional liberties and contravenes the
spirit and the letter of Section 7a of the NRA.

Further, we believe that the spirit and intent of this arbitrary injunction is another specific example of an organized movement to curtail the rights of all workers to organize, strike and picket effectively.

Therefore, with full knowledge of the principles involved and the possible consequences, we openly and publicly violate an injunction which, in our opinion, is a suppressive and oppressive act against all workers.

Sincerely yours,

Lucas County Unemployed League
Anti-Injunction Committee

Sam Pollock, Sec'y

By May 23, there were more than 10,000 on the picket lines. County deputies with tear gas guns were lined up on the plant roof. A strike picket, Miss Alma Hahn, had been struck on the head by a bolt hurled from a plant window and had been taken to the hospital. By the time 100 more cops arrived, the workers were tremendously incensed. Police began roughing up individual pickets pulled from the line. What happened when the cops tried to escort the scabs through the picket line at the shift-change was described by the Associated Press.

"Piles of bricks and stones were assembled at strategic places and a wagon load of bricks was trundled to a point near the factory to provide further ammunition for the strikers... Suddenly a barrage of tear gas bombs was hurled from upper factory windows. At the same time, company employes armed with iron bars and clubs dragged a fire hose into the street and played water on the crowd. The strike sympathizers replied with bricks, as they choked from gas fumes and fell back."

But they retreated only to reform their ranks. The police charged and swung their clubs trying to clear a path for the scabs. The workers held their ground and fought back. Choked by the tear gas fired from inside the plant, it was the police who finally gave up the battle. Then the thousands of pickets laid siege to the plant, determined to maintain their picket line.

The workers improvised giant slingshots from inner tubes. They hurled whole bricks through the plant windows. The plant soon was without lights. The scabs cowered in the dark. The frightened deputies set up machine guns inside every entranceway. It was not until the arrival of 900 National Guardsmen, 15 hours later, that the scabs were finally released, looking a "sorry sight," as the press reported it.

Then followed one of the most amazing battles in U. S. labor history. "The Marines had landed" in the form of the National Guard but the situation was not "well in hand." With their bare fists and rocks, the workers fought a six-day pitched battle with the National Guard. They fought from rooftops, from behind billboards and came through alleys to flank the guardsmen. "The men in the mob shouted vile epithets at the troopers," complained the Associated Press, "and the women jeered them with suggestions that they 'go home to mama and their paper dolls.'"

But the strikers and their thousands of sympathizers did more than shame the young National Guardsmen. They educated them and tried to win them over. Speakers stood on boxes in front of the troops and explained what the strike was about and the role the troops were playing as strikebreakers. World War I veterans put on their medals and spoke to the boys in uniform like "Dutch uncles." The women explained what the strike meant to their families. The press reported that some of the guardsmen just quit and went home. Others voiced sympathy with the workers. (A year later, when Toledo unionists went to Defiance, Ohio, to aid the Pressed Steel Company strike, they found that eight per cent of the strikers had been National Guardsmen serving in uniform in the Auto-Lite strike. That was where they learned the lesson of unionism.)

On May 24, the guardsmen fired point-blank into the Auto-Lite strikers ranks, killing two and wounding 25. But 6,000 workers returned at dusk to renew the battle. In the dark, they closed in on groups of guardsmen in the six-block martial law zone. The fury of the onslaught twice drove the troops back into the plant. At one stage, a group of troops threw their last tear gas and vomit gas bombs, then quickly picked up rocks to hurl at the strikers; the strikers recovered the last gas bombs thrown before they exploded, flinging them back at the troops.

On Friday, May 31, the troops were speedily ordered withdrawn from the strike area when the company agreed to keep the plant closed. This had not been the usual one-way battle with the workers getting shot down and unable to defend themselves. Scores of guardsmen had been sent to the hospitals. They had become demoralized. By June 1, 98 out of 99 AFL local unions had voted for a general strike.

A monster rally on the evening of June 1 mobilized some 40,000 workers in the Lucas County Courthouse Square. There, however, the AFL leaders, frightened by this tremendous popular uprising, were silent about the general strike and instead assured the workers that Roosevelt would aid them.

By June 4, with the whole community seething with anger, the com-

pany capitulated and signed a six-month contract, including a 5% wage
increase with a 5% minimum above the auto industry code, naming
Local 18384 as the exclusive bargaining agent in the struck plants.
This was the first contract under the code that did not include "proportional representation" for company unions. The path was opened
for organization of the entire automobile industry. With the Auto-Lite
victory under their belts, the Toledo auto workers were to organize
19 plants before the year was out and, before another 12 months,
were to lead the first successful strike in a GM plant, the real beginning of the conquest of General Motors.

While the Auto-Lite strike was reaching its climax, the truck
drivers of Minneapolis were waging the second of a series of three
strikes which stand to this day as models for organization, strategy
and incorruptible, militant leadership.

Minneapolis, with its twin city St. Paul, is the hub of Minnesota's
wheat, lumber and iron ore areas. Transport — rail and truck — en-
gages a relatively large number of workers. In early 1934, Minneapolis was a notoriously open-shop town. The Citizens Alliance, an
organization of anti-union employers, ruled the city.

On February 7, 8 and 9, 1934, the Citizens Alliance got the first
stunning blow that was to shatter its dominance. Within three days
the union of coal yard workers, organized within General Drivers
Local Union 574, AFL International Brotherhood of Teamsters, had
paralyzed all the coal yards and won union recognition. The *Minneapolis Labor Review,* February 16, 1934, hailed "the masterly manner
in which the struggle was conducted... there has never been a better example of enthusiastic efficiency than displayed by the coal
driver pickets."

The February 24, 1934 *Militant* reported that Local 574 "displayed
a well organized, mobile, fighting picket line that stormed over all
opposition, closed 65 truck yards, 150 coal offices and swept the
streets clear of scabs in the first three hours of the strike."

The most painstaking and detailed preparation had gone into this
strike. The organizers were a group of class-conscious socialists,
Trotskyists who had been expelled from the Stalinized Communist
Party in 1928, and workers sympathetic to the Trotskyist point of
view. Soon their names were to ring throughout the whole northwest
labor movement and make national headlines. They included the
three Dunne brothers — Vincent, Grant and Miles— and Carl Skoglund, later to head 574.

"One of the outstanding features of the strike," the original *Militant*
report stated, "was the Cruising Picket Squad. This idea came
from the ranks and played a great role in the strike." This "cruis-

ing picket squad" was the original of the "flying squadrons" that were to become part of the standard picketing techniques of the great CIO strikes.

The late Bill Brown, then president of 574, revealed another important aspect of the coal yards battle. "I wrote Daniel Tobin, international president of the union for an OK [to strike]. Two days after the strike was over, he wrote back that we couldn't strike. By that time we'd won and had a signed contract with increased pay."

The Dunne brothers, Skoglund and their associates proved to be a different and altogether superior breed of union leaders compared to the type represented by the craft-minded bureaucrats of the AFL who were content to build a little job-holding trust and settle down for life to collecting dues. After the first victory they set out to organize every truck driver and every inside warehouse worker in Minneapolis. A whirlwind organizing campaign had recruited 3,000 new members into Local 574 by May.

On Tuesday, May 15, 1934, after the employers had refused even to deal with the union, the second truck drivers strike began. Now 5,000 strong, the organized drivers and warehousemen promptly massed at a large garage which served as strike headquarters. From there, fleets of pickets went rolling by trucks and cars to strategic points.

All trucking in the city was halted except for milk, ice and beer drivers who were organized and who operated with special union permits. The city was isolated from all truck traffic in or out by mass picketing. For the first time anywhere in connection with a labor struggle, the term "flying squads" was used—the May 26, 1934 *Militant* reported: "Flying squads of pickets toured the city."

The Local 574 leaders warned the membership over and over to place no reliance or hope in any government agents or agencies, including Floyd B. Olsen, the Farmer-Labor Party governor, and the National Labor Board. They preached reliance only on the mass picket lines and militant struggle against the employers.

From the start, the strike leaders summoned the whole working-class populace to their support. The very active unemployed organization responded at once. A 574 Women's Auxiliary, with a large membership, plunged into the strike, doing everything from secretarial work and mimeographing, to running the huge strike kitchen and manning picket trucks.

Some 700 of them marched in a mass demonstration to the Mayor's office to demand the withdrawal of the "special" police. The march was led by Mrs. Grant Dunne, auxiliary president, and Mrs. Farrell Dobbs, auxiliary secretary and wife of a young coal

driver who was a strike picket dispatcher. A decade later Farrell
Dobbs became editor of *The Militant* and then national secretary of
the Socialist Workers Party.

The Citizens Alliance had called a mass meeting of small business men, junior executives and similar elements and steamed them
up for an armed attack on the strikers. They were urged to become
"special deputies" and strikebreakers.

They selected the City Market, where farm produce was brought,
as the center of the struggle. The sheriff moved in deputies to convoy farm trucks in and out of the market square. The pickets were
able to halt all but three trucks. Brutal terror was then the answer
to the strikers.

"The Mayor doubled the police force, then tripled it," reported
the May 26, 1934 *Militant*. "Gunmen were imported to get after the
leaders of the strike. Determined attempts were made to break
through the picket lines on Friday night and Saturday. Two hundred
arrests were made... Saturday night the 'regulars' and 'special' police rushed a truck load of women on the 'newspaper row' and beat
them unmercifully, sending five to the hospital."

The next day some 35,000 building trades workers declared a
strike in sympathy with the truck drivers. The Central Labor Union
voted its support. Workers, many from plants which weren't even
organized, stayed off their jobs and flocked to join the pickets.

On May 21 and 22 there was waged a two-day battle in the City
Market that ended with the flight of the entire police force and spe-
cial deputies in what was called by the strikers "The Battle of
Deputies Run."

Word had come to the strike headquarters that the police and
bosses were planning a "big offensive" to open the City Market to
scab trucks on Monday and Tuesday. The strike leaders pulled in
their forces from outlying areas and began concentrating them in the
neighborhood of the market.

On Monday, a strong detachment of pickets was sent to the market. These pickets managed to wedge between the deputized business men and the police, isolating the "special deputies." One of
the strikers, quoted in Charles Walker's *American City,* a stirring
and generally reliable study of the Minneapolis struggle, described
the ensuing battle:

"Then we called on the pickets from strike headquarters [re-
serve] who marched into the center of the market and encircled the
police. They [the police] were put right in the center with no way
out. At intervals we made sallies on them to separate a few. This
kept up for a couple of hours, till finally they drew their guns. We

had anticipated this would happen, and that then the pickets would be unable to fight them. You can't lick a gun with a club. The correlation of forces becomes a little unbalanced. So we picked out a striker, a big man and utterly fearless, and sent him in a truck with twenty-five pickets. He was instructed to drive right into the formation of cops and stop for nothing. We knew he'd do it. Down the street he came like a bat out of hell, with his horn honking and into the market arena. The cops held up their hands for him to stop, but he kept on; they gave way and he was in the middle of them. The pickets jumped out on the cops. We figured by intermixing with the cops in hand-to-hand fighting, they would not use their guns because they would have to shoot cops as well as strikers. Cops don't like that.

"Casualties for the day included for the strikers a broken collar bone, the cut-open skull of a picket who swung on a cop and hit a striker by mistake as the cop dodged, and a couple of broken ribs. On the other side, roughly thirty cops were taken to the hospital."

The strikers were victorious in another sense: no trucks moved.

The next day, the showdown came. The bosses' private army of 2,200 "special deputies," plus virtually the entire police force, were mobilized in the market place to break the strike at its central point. A striker gave the following account in the June 2, 1934 *Militant:*

"A skeleton patrol was sent to patrol the market streets and to report any move to start delivery. Word quickly comes back; hundreds of special deputies, special police and harness bulls armed with clubs and guns, squad cars of police with sawed-off shot guns and vomiting gas... A truck starts to move, but pickets jump to the running boards and demand that the scab driver stop. A hired slugger raises his club and slashes at a picket. Down the picket drops as if dead. The fight is on.

"Phone rings at the concentration hall [Central Labor Union headquarters]: 'Send the reserves!' Orderly, but almost as if by magic, the hall is emptied. The pickets are deployed by their leaders to surround the police and sluggers. The police raise their riot guns but the workers ignore and rush through them. 'Chase out the hired sluggers,' is their battle cry. The cowardly sluggers take to their heels and run. The police and strikers use their clubs freely. Many casualties on both sides. The workers have captured the market!"

Two of the "special deputies" who had volunteered to club strikers to death were killed themselves in the wild melee. One was Arthur Lyman, Citizens Alliance attorney and vice-president of the American Ball Company. The market was strewn with deputies' clubs and badges. The police disappeared.

The employers then agreed to move no trucks. On May 25 the

strike was settled, with union recognition, no discrimination in re-hiring of strikers and arbitration of wages, which the employers had increased previously to forestall a strike and avoid dealing with the union.

An interesting sidelight of the second strike was a leaflet issued by the Communist Party denouncing the Dunne brothers and Skoglund as "traitors" and "agents of the bosses" and calling for "rank and file leaders," although the strike committee was composed entirely of 75 workers on the trucks.

A significant observation was made by Walker in *American City:* "Throughout, the nub and core of dispute was a matter of fundamental principle and strategy—for both sides—known as 'recognition of the inside workers.'... To the employers, the 'banana men, the chicken pickers, and the pork picklers' who worked inside their warehouses were outside the jurisdiction of a truck union. But why did they care so much? They cared because their inclusion meant that a kind of industrial union would be set up in the trucking industry of Minneapolis. Without the inside workers, they would be dealing with a pure and simple craft union of truck drivers, weaker in bargaining power, easier to maneuver and smash. To the union, the issue of the 'inside workers' meant the same thing, a step toward industrial organization, a strong union..."

Not only the Minneapolis employers were disturbed by the industrial union implications of Local 574's campaign. AFL Teamsters President Daniel Tobin was no less upset by the Minneapolis truck drivers' victories. For he, too, was a bitter opponent of industrial unionism. He was to play a key part in the AFL in blocking an industrial union policy. Meanwhile, he openly joined with the Minneapolis employers in the next stage of the struggle.

The leaders of 574 put no trust in the employers to live up to the agreement in the second strike. They promptly began preparing the union for another battle in the event the bosses reneged. They gave the employers a month or so to comply with the pact. When the employers stalled, chiseled and ignored the union, the firm answer was a strike, called July 16, 1934.

One of the reasons the employers were emboldened to force the union's hand was a declaration by Tobin in the Teamsters magazine denouncing the Local 574 leaders as "radicals and Communists." This red baiting had no effect on the Minneapolis workers. On July 6 a parade of some 10,000 AFL members had proclaimed in advance their support of the coming strike. The meeting of business agents of the Building Trades Council denounced Tobin's red baiting and affirmed their support of 574. Only the bosses and their newspapers took the cue from Tobin and began screaming "Reds" and "Bloody Revolution."

The blood, however, was drawn by the other side. Police and employers deliberately planned to lure isolated picket trucks into an ambush and shoot down the unarmed workers without warning. This was to be a pretext for sending in the National Guard to break the strike.

The trap was sprung on the fifth day of the strike—"Bloody Friday," July 20. *American City* quotes a strike picket on what happened that day in the wholesale grocery district:

"For two hours we stood around wondering what was up for there was no truck in sight. Then as two P.M. drew near a tensing of bodies and nervous shifting of feet and heads among the police indicated that something was up. We were right, for a few minutes later about one hundred more cops hove into view escorting a large yellow truck. The truck, without license plates and with the cab heavily wired, pulled up to the loading platform of the Slocum-Bergren Company. Here a few boxes were loaded on... At five past two the truck slowly pulled out... It turned down Sixth Avenue and then turned on Third Street toward Seventh Avenue. As it did a picket truck containing about ten pickets followed. As the picket truck drew near the convoy, the police without warning let loose a barrage of fire. Pickets fell from the trucks, others rushed up to pick up their wounded comrades; as they bent to pick up the injured, the police fired at them... One young worker received a full charge of buckshot in the back as he bent to pick up a wounded picket.

"The rain of bullets then became a little heavier so I and three other pickets hopped a fence and walked to headquarters... Pickets by the dozens lying all over the floor with blood flowing from their wounds, more coming in and no place to put them. The doctor would treat one after another who urged him to treat others first.

"The Minneapolis papers printed hundreds of lies about what had happened but none was brazen enough to claim that the strikers had any weapons at all."

This was substantially confirmed by the Governor's own investigating committee which, after the strike, found that the police had planned the attack in advance and fired to kill on unarmed pickets.

One worker, Harry Ness, died shortly after the shooting. Another, John Belor, died a few days later in the hospital. Some 55 workers were wounded. Within 20 minutes of the massacre, the National Guard rolled into the area. It was their signal.

But if this terrorism was expected to smash the strike, the bosses got an unpleasant surprise.

All union-driven taxicabs, ice, beer and gasoline trucks, which had continued to operate by union permit, immediately went on strike. The police were cleared from all areas near the strike headquarters. Then, when Harry Ness was buried, the whole working class of Minneapolis turned out in an historic demonstration for his funeral. Some 40,000 marched in the funeral cortege. They took over the streets. Not a cop was in sight. The workers themselves directed traffic.

Governor Olsen declared martial law. The military commanders began handing out "permits" for trucks to operate under the protection of the troops. Soon thousands of trucks were being manned by scabs and strikebreakers. The union did not take it lying down. The leaders gave an ultimatum to Olsen to withdraw the permits and to issue others only with the union's approval.

Then followed a war of attrition for several weeks. The strikers defied the troops and renewed their mobile picketing, keeping the military officials and cops on a merry-go-round. The guardsmen launched an attack in force on the Local 574 strike headquarters, arresting 100 members, including Bill Brown and the Dunne brothers, and throwing them into specially constructed military stockades. But the union rank and file, trained in democratic self-reliance, held firm and ran the strike as usual. So great was the outcry and protest—including another mass demonstration of 40,000—that the union members and leaders were released in a few days.

Two of the tribe of Roosevelt's labor board mediators—"meditators" as the workers called them—were shipped into Minneapolis early in the strike. They were Father Haas, a Catholic priest, and E. H. Dunnigan. They had at once proposed a settlement based on some concessions to the workers which the bosses had flatly rejected. In the end, with the troops out in force—almost one soldier for every striker—Father Haas and Dunnigan tried to put over a watered-down version of their original proposals. When they went to sell the proposition to the rank-and-file Strike Committee of 100, they were subjected to such a devastating cross-examination that they were utterly routed. A new mediator was sent in and Father Haas had to retire to a sanitarium.

On August 22, after five weeks of the toughest battling against all the forces of the employers and government, the strikers won. The bosses capitulated and signed an agreement granting the union its main demands. This included the right to represent "inside workers," which the employers had threatened to fight to the bitter end as industrial unionism.

While the Minneapolis truck drivers were battling their way to victory, the San Francisco general strike—involving 125,000 workers at its peak—carried the American class struggle to new heights.

On May 9, 1934, from 10,000 to 15,000 West Coast members of the AFL International Longshoremen's Association went on an "unauthorized" strike. Soon the strike included 25,000 workers, many of them members of seamen's organizations who joined in sympathy.

The original demands had been for a coast-wide agreement, union control of hiring halls and a closed shop. The strikers added demands for $1 an hour instead of 85 cents and the 30-hour week instead of 48.

From the start, the strike was waged with great militancy. Frederick J. Lang, in his book *Maritime, A History and Program,* wrote: "It was a real rank-and-file strike, with the 'leaders' swept along in the flood. It encountered every weapon then in the arsenal of the employers. The shipowners hired their own thugs who tried to work the docks and man the ships. The city police of every port on the Coast were mobilized on the waterfronts to hunt down the strikers. The newspapers, launching a slander campaign against the strikers, called on the citizenry to form vigilante committees to raid strike headquarters, the actual organization of this dirty work being entrusted to the American Legion and other 'patriotic' societies."

ILA President Joseph Ryan hastily flew into San Francisco from New York in an effort to squelch the strike. Over the heads of the strikers and their local leaders, he signed an agreement giving up the main demand—the union-controlled hiring hall. He was repudiated by the strikers in a coast-wide poll.

The chief strike leader was the then unknown Harry Bridges. He was under Stalinist influence but fortunately, at that time, did not adhere so closely to Communist Party policies as to carry out its line of not working inside the "social fascist" AFL unions. Under the radicalizing effect of the depression, maritime workers were influenced by various political tendencies—Stalinist, IWW (Industrial Workers of the World) and others—with the Stalinists playing the dominant role.

Ryan—a consort of shipowners, stevedore bosses, gangsters and Tammany politicians, who 20 years later was to be dumped by these elements when he was no longer useful to them—tried to split the strike by making separate settlements in each port. He succeeded only in Tacoma. AFL President William Green joined in denouncing the strike and yelling "reds" and "communists."

On July 5 the bosses tried to smash the strike by attacking its strategic center, San Francisco's waterfront, with calculated force and violence. At the "Battle of Rincon Hill" the police blasted away with tear gas, pistols and shotguns at the waterfront pickets. They killed Howard Sperry and Nick Bordoise and wounded 109 others. As in the third Minneapolis strike and the Toledo Auto-Lite battle, the deliberate massacres perpetrated by the police were the signal for sending in the National Guard.

The murder and wounding of strikers did not crush the workers. Instead, San Francisco labor answered with a tremendous counter-attack—a general strike. For two days, the working class paralyzed the city. The workers took over many city functions, directing traffic and assuming other municipal tasks. On the third and fourth days, the general strike petered out when the AFL leaders, who were swept along in the first spontaneous protest against the killings, ordered an end to the stoppage.

The bosses and police, with the aid of organized vigilantes, vented their fear and hatred of the workers on the small radical organizations, not daring to hit directly at the unions. Thirty-five gangs of vigilantes, heavily armed, raided headquarters of Communist, I W W and Socialist groups. They smashed furniture, hurled typewriters and literature out the windows, beat up many defenseless workers. In some instances, the police who arrived after the vigilantes left completed the work of destruction. They jailed more than 300 persons.

After 11 weeks, the longshore strike was ended on July 31 with an agreement to arbitrate. It was a poor settlement, but the workers returned to the job in an organized body. Within a year, in job action after job action, they won the union hiring hall up and down the Coast. Their struggle gave impetus to maritime organization on the East Coast, leading in 1937 to establishment of the CIO National Maritime Union, and opened the way for organization of West Coast industrial labor.

Too little credit has been given to the Toledo, Minneapolis and San Francisco strikes for their effect on the subsequent industrial union movement, the CIO. But had these magnificent examples of labor struggle not occurred, in all likelihood the CIO would have been delayed or taken a different and less militant course.

It was these gigantic battles—all led by radicals—that convinced John L. Lewis that the American workers were determined to be organized and would follow the leadership that showed it meant business.

"Lewis watched the unrest and flareups of violence through the summer of 1934. He saw the Dunne brothers of Minneapolis lead a general strike of truck drivers into a virtual civil war. Blood ran in Minneapolis," wrote Alinsky in his *John L. Lewis — An Unauthorized Biography*.

"In San Francisco a general strike spearheaded by Harry Bridges' Longshoremen's Union paralyzed the great western city for four days.

"Before that year was out, seven hundred thousand workers had struck. Lewis could read the revolutionary handwriting on the walls of American industry. He knew that the workers were seething and aching to be organized so they could strike back. Everyone wanted to hit out, employer against worker and worker against employer and anyone else who they felt was not in their class. America was becoming more class conscious than at any time in its history..."

Of course, "civil war" was going on in towns and cities from coast to coast and blood was being spilled in scores of other places besides Minneapolis, Toledo and San Francisco. These latter cities were unique, however, in this: *they showed how the workers could fight and win. They gave heart and hope to labor everywhere for the climactic struggle that was to build the CIO.*

5

Industrial vs. Craft Unionism

A great part of the strength of the Minneapolis, Toledo and San Francisco strikes of 1934 flowed from success in spreading the strikes and involving large sectors of the working class. They broke the bonds of craft and grasped the weapon of class struggle. These unifying struggles showed the need for a broader, all-embracing organizational structure to organize the unorganized and defend labor against the united assaults of the employing class.

During this same period, however, the need for industrial organization was being proved in a negative way. The workers in great mass production industries like auto, steel, rubber and textiles suffered terrible debacles because of the policies of the craft-minded AFL leaders.

In March 1934, some 200,000 auto workers were waiting for a strike call against the infamous NRA auto code with its "merit" and open-shop clauses. A call actually did go to 44,000 GM workers to strike on March 21, but Roosevelt personally intervened and got the AFL leaders to agree to a postponement. On March 25, AFL President Green and his personal representative in auto, William Collins, accepted Roosevelt's establishment of an Auto Labor Board, headed by Dr. Leo Wolman, and the "proportional representation" proposition. This latter denied exclusive collective bargaining rights to the majority union and permitted recognition of company unions on the basis of their proportional strength in Auto Labor Board elections. The strike was called off indefinitely.

By July, Collins was complaining in the *American Federationist* that the "President's agreement" was not working out. "This settlement was by no means satisfactory to the unions," Collins wrote. "Nevertheless, union representatives looked upon it as their patriotic duty to accept the settlement, since it was the direct request of President Roosevelt that they should do so..." It was their "patriotic duty," in short, to accept a program for strangling the auto unions. After the March, 1934 agreement, Roosevelt extended the auto code four times despite official AFL protest.

By February 1935, the membership of the AFL federal auto locals had dwindled from 100,000 to 20,000. When the Wolman board took a poll in April 1935 to determine "proportional representation" in a number of plants in Michigan, of the 163,150 votes cast, 88.7% were for unaffiliated representatives; 8.6% for leaders of AFL federal locals. This was not a vote against unionism. It was a vote of no-confidence in the AFL. "The AFL campaign had been a complete failure, except in the Toledo sector, where the rank and file ignored both the Wolman Board and the AFL, struck against the Electric Auto-Lite Company," noted Levinson in *Labor on the March.*

The auto fiasco was duplicated in steel. Organized in the old Amalgamated Association of Iron, Steel and Tin Workers, headed by the crusty bureaucrat Mike Tighe, the new members had brushed aside Tighe's objections, drafted demands and set up a committee to present them to the steel barons. A month later, in mid-June 1934, Green submitted a plan for a settlement without a strike to a special union convention. It was the same "plan" as in auto — an "impartial" board appointed by Roosevelt. The scheduled steel strike was called off indefinitely.

The first fruit of the steel plan was a series of wage cuts in August and September. In December, Roosevelt proclaimed a three-point "truce" plan which agreed in every major particular with the program of Myron C. Taylor, then head of U. S. Steel. Point 1 in effect recognized company unions. By this time Tighe was able to report to the AFL Executive Council that of the 100,000 members who had poured into his union, only 5,300 remained as dues-paying members.

The rubber workers, centered mainly in Akron, Ohio, went through an almost identical betrayal. A tremendous strike sentiment spread through the rubber plants in early 1935 and reached a high pitch in April. Some 30,000 rubber workers in Akron were poised for strike. At the last moment, Green's representative Coleman Claherty put over a deal calling off the strike in return for another Roosevelt settlement withholding a union contract and recognizing company unions along with real ones.

A special feature of this betrayal was the role of the Stalinists. The Communist Party, which had considerable influence at that time among the rubber workers, celebrated its recent turn to the

"People's Front" — collaboration of "progressive" capitalists and workers — by going along with the rubber sellout. An official AFL representative spoke from the same platform as Earl Browder, then CP national secretary, at a CP meeting where Browder remained demonstratively silent on the pending deal between the AFL leaders and Roosevelt. The CP was to perform hundreds of similar services for the pro-capitalist labor officialdom in the next 20 years.

The most tragic and despicable betrayal of the period came in the great national textile strike which began on September 1, 1934. This strike climaxed a tremendous upsurge of unionization during which the AFL United Textile Workers climbed from 50,000 members in June 1933 to more than 300,000 in June 1934. The heart of this upsurge was in the deep South, where the most abused and exploited industrial wage slaves in America thronged to the union as to a mighty crusade.

No more heroic record of labor struggle has been written than in the battle put up by the more than 400,000 textile strikers. Sixteen strikers were killed, hundreds wounded. They confronted, in addition to scores of thousands of police, deputies and armed strikebreakers, the largest military display of troops in this country since World War I. More than 40,000 National Guardsmen in 16 states were sent against the strikers. Roosevelt at one point alerted federal troops and was preparing to order them into Rhode Island when the Democratic-controlled Rhode Island legislature hastily voted a resolution urging Roosevelt to withhold his order for fear of the political consequences.

In the South, the strikers organized flying squadrons, modeled on the Minneapolis pattern, and went from town to town and mill to mill calling out the workers. The response was overwhelming. This was to remain the high tide of Southern labor struggle for more than two decades. To this day, the Southern workers have not recovered from the crushing blow delivered by their own leaders, headed by Thomas F. McMahon, an old-time labor skate.

At Roosevelt's request the textile union leaders called off the strike for nothing more than his promise to make another government "survey" of conditions in the industry, where wages as low as $3 to $4 a week prevailed in some Southern plants. The mill owners never assented to this settlement even verbally. "For the strikers it was the peace of defeat," Edward Levinson correctly wrote in *Labor on the March*. He reveals: "There were indications that the Federation leaders had asked the President to provide a plausible pretext for ending the walkout which had developed into a battle far more serious than the old Federation leaders had bargained for."

More than 15,000 of the best union militants were barred from the plants after the strike ended.

Even Northern manufacturers are still profiting from the 1934 sellout of the Southern textile workers. The South still provides the most inviting haven for runaway plants seeking cheap, non-union labor.

But the drive of the industrial workers toward organization was irrepressible in spite of all treachery and defeats. American labor absorbed terrible blows and then came back swinging. In May 1935, it again scored a solid punch—once more in Toledo.

The workers at the Toledo Chevrolet transmission plant, reversing the Detroit pattern, voted in favor of the AFL union in April 1935. They gave mighty General Motors three weeks to recognize and deal with their union and then struck. The same leadership who had saved the Auto-Lite strike aided and guided these newly unionized workers. Members of the Workers Party, just formed from a merger of the Communist League of America (Trotskyists) and the American Workers Party (Musteites), advised the rank and file.

Such precision, organization and power were displayed by the strikers that the plant was shut down tight in a few minutes. All the workers marched from the plant onto a mass picket line. A March of Labor, combining the workers of five other strikes, was set up to give aid wherever required on any picket line. After the Auto-Lite strike, there was no attempt to operate with scabs. Even the top GM officials from Detroit had to have written permits from the strike committee to enter the plant.

The strike was a bottleneck, halting production of transmissions for the whole Chevrolet system. Within a week, some 35,000 Chevrolet workers were out all over the country, with strikes in Cleveland, Norwood and Cincinnati, Ohio, and Atlanta, Georgia. The Toledo strike committee, made up entirely of rank and filers from the plant, moved to spread the strike to all GM plants, starting with the Buick plant in Flint, Michigan. Delegations were sent to Flint and Detroit, but Green intervened to block further walkouts.

Green had sent his personal representative Francis J. Dillon into the strike area to try to halt it. The Toledo workers knew what his game was — the main source of their information being their own strike paper, *Strike Truth,* edited by the author. This was the first strike paper in the industry and was modeled after *The Organizer* of Minneapolis Drivers Local 574. After three weeks, Dillon was able to ram a compromise settlement down the strikers' throats at a dramatic mass meeting, where the strikers at first refused him the floor. They weakened when he left the hall screaming, "Muste's

men!" and issued a statement threatening to withdraw the Local
18384 charter, covering 19 plants.

Submitting under the pressure of this threat, the newly organized
workers nevertheless were able to squeeze from General Motors a
small wage increase and a published stipulation that management
would meet with the union committee, although there was no signed
contract. This was the first time GM had failed to smash a strike.
The workers marched back into the plant as an organized body,
more solidly unionized than before. From that time on, every GM
worker was able to say: "If the Toledo workers could do it, we can
do it." Two years later they were to prove it.

In March 1935, pressure from the federal auto locals had forced
the AFL Executive Council to agree to establishment of an auto
workers international union. The Toledo local, aroused by Dillon's
treachery in the Chevrolet strike, demanded his removal and the
immediate convening of a constitutional convention for the auto workers. Fearful that they would move without his approval, Green finally called a convention for August 26, 1935.

The auto militants, with veterans of the Toledo Auto-Lite and
Chevrolet strikes in the lead, lost no time in launching a campaign
for a genuinely democratic international union and a fighting program. A group of prominent participants in the great Toledo battles
organized the first caucus in the auto union's history. Calling themselves the Progressives of United Automobile Workers Union Local
18384, these pioneer UAW builders published and circulated a program for the projected new auto workers international union that can
still serve as a model for any union in its general spirit and conception. Among the framers and signers of this program were James
Roland, chairman of the Toledo Chevrolet Strike Committee, Louis
Didisse, Kenneth Cole, who later became the first secretary of the
Toledo CIO Council, Richard Meyers, Henry Tanner, Dallas Patton,
Eugene Cole, C. C. Smith, Carl Cannon, Joe Ditzel, Wilber King,
Dean Gaston, William Prior, Kenneth Munson, Willard Warren,
J. Martin, William Weston, Fred Marks, George Huston, Harry
Nofen, E. K. Nation, Frank Walentowski, Mrs. S. Buder, Erwin
Wiley and Roy Slee. None of these workers is prominent in the UAW
today; some drifted from the industry long ago. But the establish-
ment of an international automobile workers union and the unique
character of that union in its heyday owe more to these almost unknown and forgotten rank-and-file leaders who initiated the struggle
against the AFL bureaucracy than to others better known, like Walter
Reuther, who arrived a little later on the scene and reaped where
these earlier militants had planted.

Among the policies advocated by the Toledo militants in their published program was "militant action" and an active national organizational campaign to "organize all unorganized automobile workers this fall." They called for "confidence in the organized power of labor"; no compulsory arbitration; "against 'NO STRIKE' agreements"; and "no trust in governmental boards and agencies... which without exception, aid only the employers." They emphasized "no discrimination against members or prospective members because of color, creed, nationality, political belief or affiliation." They called "for a democratically controlled convention" with "free elections from the floor of a chairman and all committees by majority vote" and "all decisions to be reached by the same means."

They also proposed an "International Union organized on industrial lines with full jurisdiction over all who work in or around automobile or automobile-parts plants." They urged the auto workers, further, to insist on an "International Union controlled by the membership with all officers, organizers, executive boards democratically elected by the membership and subject to their recall." But what must have seemed to William Green the most revolutionary and Bolshevik proposals of the Toledo militants were their last two:

"For dues to be kept at an absolute minimum commensurate with the needs of the International Union.

"For all officers to receive wages comparable to those received by the workers in the plants; in no case are wages to exceed the sum of $2,500 per year."

When the first United Automobile Workers convention finally convened in Detroit on August 26, Green used every device at his command to keep the new international union strictly under the thumb of the AFL Executive Council. The constitution proposed by Green for the UAW called for appointment of the new union's president by Green himself. Led by the Toledo delegation, which was the largest single contingent in the convention and the most influential, the delegates passed a motion, by a vote of 164.2 to 112.8 to elect their own president. After a three-day floor fight, Green personally took over. He declared either he would appoint the top officers or there would be no charter. He then appointed Dillon president, and Homer Martin, of Kansas City, a one-time preacher, as vice-president.

Green simply turned the gavel over to Dillon after proclaiming that owing to the "deep division" in the convention it was necessary for him to appoint "probationary" officers. All motions or objections contrary to this procedure were ruled out of order. Dillon, speaking "as the president of your union," intoned that they were members of the AFL "and you all understand it, and it is done in a perfectly legal, orderly way."

As for limiting union officers to a skilled worker's pay, this had Green and Dillon almost apoplectic. They saw to it that the new UAW officials got a top salary of $6,500 (about $16,000 at this writing) a year for president and scaled down proportionately for lesser posts. If the UAW leaders were able over the next couple of decades to boost the highest going salary in their union to only $22,000 a year for president, compared to $50,000 in the steel and miners unions, their grievance must be directed first of all at those now obscure delegates to that first UAW convention who had the notion that the best union leaders are those who do not live too high above the scale of the workers they are supposed to serve.

Learning from the auto workers' experiences, the rubber workers held a convention the next month and refused to back down before Green's threats. They voted 44 to 9 against appointment of officers and then proceeded to elect their own officers, selecting Sherman Dalrymple as their first president.

The example of the auto and rubber workers, who had pushed through all obstacles to win their own industrial unions, gave a tremendous impulsion to the whole movement for industrial unionism. It hardened the minority of AFL leaders, particularly John L. Lewis, who had been pushing for industrial union organization since 1933.

At the October 1933 AFL convention, Elizabeth Christman of the Women's Trade Union League had offered an industrial union resolution. But it was not voted on after a test vote was taken on a resolution to ratify the AFL council decision which ordered the Brewery Workers, an industrial organization, to turn over its truck driver members to the AFL Teamsters. The vote was 13,877 to 5,859.

Lewis did not press the Christman resolution but agreed to submit the matter to a special conference of 75 unions in Washington on January 24, 1934. This conference adopted a resolution which declared organization of the unorganized to be "imperative" but "bearing in mind that in the pursuit of organization the present structure, rights and interests of affiliated national and international unions must be followed, observed, and safeguarded." Craft "jurisdictional rights" could not be touched.

But the issue would not down. At the AFL convention in San Francisco in October 1934, the Executive Council itself proposed an organizing "campaign" to accept the membership applications of workers seeking unionism. The council reported: "There was a virtual uprising of workers for union membership. Workers held mass meetings and sent word they wanted to be organized." But a compromise resolution that appeared to grant the principle of industrial organization contained a rider limiting the scope of such industrial unions—commanding them "to protect the rights of existing craft unions."

The real test, once more, was on the brewers-teamsters issue, which the convention decided, by a vote of 15,558 to 9,306, in favor of the teamsters.

It was Teamsters President Tobin who voiced the contemptuous attitude of the craft union leaders — the "aristocrats of labor" — to the mass production workers. Describing how he ran his own union, Tobin said: "We have to use force in our organizations. If we didn't use force and enforce decisions, we would not have an international union of 135,000 members — and they are not the rubbish that have lately come into other organizations."

Tobin had previously written: "The scramble for admittance to the union is on... we do not want to charter the riffraff or good-for-nothings, or those from whom we cannot make wages or conditions, unless we are compelled to do so by other organizations offering to charter them under any conditions... We do not want the men today if they are going on strike tomorrow." Riffraff, rubbish and — strikers, that was the AFL craft moguls' opinion of the industrial workers.

It is hard to believe, in view of the above-cited facts of history, that AFL President George Meany, addressing the CIO auto workers convention March 29, 1955, on the AFL-CIO merger plans, could still claim: "There never was a trade union reason for disunity."

But there was a group within the AFL leadership—no less pro-capitalist, no less bureaucratic, no less conservative in their political outlook than the opponents of industrial unionism—who nevertheless could see "the revolutionary handwriting on the wall" and understood that the moment must be grasped if the old union leadership was to retain its dominant position over organized labor.

Thus, at the October 1935 AFL convention in Atlantic City, International Typographical Union President Charles P. Howard, although himself head of a craft union, tried to make Green, Tobin, John Frey, Matthew Woll, "Big Bill" Hutcheson and the others opposed to industrial unionism see the light. He argued their own self-interest.

"Now, let us say to you that the workers of this country are going to organize, and if they are not permitted to organize under the banner of the American Federation of Labor they are going to organize under some other leadership... I submit to you that it would be a far more serious problem for our government, for the people

of this country and for the American Federation of Labor itself than
if our organization policies should be so molded that we can organize
them and bring them under the leadership of this organization."

John L. Lewis's role at this convention is most vividly remembered for his "punch heard round the world," when he symbolized
the coming split with a solid haymaker to the jaw of Carpenters'
President Hutcheson, who had called Lewis a rude name. But Lewis's
speech at the convention was a masterly, eloquent, fighting sum-
mation of the arguments for industrial unionism.

"At San Francisco they seduced me with fair words," Lewis apolo-
gized for his compromise of 1934. "Now, of course, having learned
that I was seduced, I am enraged and I am ready to rend my seducers
limb from limb..."

He pointed out how the organization of the coal miners had reached
an impasse because of the failure to organize the steel corporations
which owned the captive mines.

"... Great combinations of capital have assembled great industrial
plants, and they are strung across the borders of our several states
from the north to the south and from the west in such a manner that
they have assembled to themselves tremendous power and influence,
and they are almost 100 per cent effective in opposing organization
of the workers under the policies of the American Federation of
Labor...

"If you go in there with your craft union they will mow you down
like the Italian machine guns mow down the Ethiopians in the war
now going on in that country...

"... The strength of a strong man is a prideful thing, but the unfortunate thing in life is that strong men do not remain strong. And
that is just as true of unions and labor organizations as it is true of
men and individuals.

"And, whereas today the craft unions of this country may be able
to stand upon their own feet and like mighty oaks stand before the
gale, defying the lightning, yet the day may come when this changed
scheme of things — and things are changing rapidly now — the day
may come when those organizations will not be able to withstand the
lightning and the gale. Now, prepare yourselves by making a contribution to your less fortunate brethren. Heed this cry from Macedonia
that comes from the hearts of men. Organize the unorganized..."

But they did not heed. The convention voted down the minority's
industrial union resolution by 18,024 votes to 10,993. On October 19,
1935, came the symbolic blow that sent Hutcheson toppling.

The next morning, after the convention adjourned, Lewis sat at
a breakfast table of the President Hotel with Philip Murray, Thomas

Kennedy and John Brophy of his own union, and ITU President Howard, David Dubinsky of the International Ladies Garment Workers, Max Zaritsky, head of the Hat, Cap and Millinery Workers, McMahon of the Textile Workers, and Sidney Hillman of the Amalgamated Clothing Workers. They had all supported the industrial union resolution. Lewis outlined to them his bold plan for industrial organization.

Three weeks later, on November 9, the same union officials, with the addition of Harvey Fremming of the Oil Field, Gas Well and Refinery Workers, and Thomas Brown of the Mine, Mill and Smelter Workers, met in Washington. That day they issued their historic announcement. They had constituted themselves as a committee within the AFL "to encourage and promote organization of the workers in the mass production and unorganized industries." They called themselves the Committee for Industrial Organization and their main activity would be "educational and advisory." Lewis was elected chairman; Howard, secretary; and Brophy, executive director.

It is true that in his oratory Lewis spoke of organizing 25 million workers. The CIO was never to surpass six million. But it is doubtful if the men who launched the CIO envisaged the powerful impact it would make or the road it would travel. They were not imbued with far-reaching social ideas. They took their step as a practical proposition, primarily for what they considered the interests of their own international unions.

In later years they were to picture themselves as the creators of a mighty movement, who built the CIO solely out of their own powers. This is the way it may have seemed. They were, however, merely like surfboard riders on the crest of a wave; the power and motion were in the wave and they had learned to ride it. Vast social forces and intense class struggle had been set loose by the crisis of capitalism. They adapted themselves to the circumstances.

It is doubtful if the CIO would have been formed, or if the industrial union movement would have arrived as quickly as it did, if not for the exceptional qualities of Lewis. There has been a vile campaign to denigrate and discredit Lewis, to low-rate his real role. Lewis has many weaknesses —political conservatism, blind belief in capitalism, contempt for union democracy —which he shares with virtually all other top union officials. But it was Lewis, with his boldness, his self-reliance, his aggressiveness and courage, stamping him as a man of superior character and moral fibre, who pushed through the CIO's formation. When his detractors are long dead and forgotten, the American working class will remember and honor Lewis as the founder of the CIO.

6

CIO's Political Coalition with Roosevelt

The Committee for Industrial Organization remained formally within the structure of the AFL until 1938. In November 1936, the AFL convention confirmed the Executive Council's suspension of all international unions which had associated themselves with the CIO. Formal expulsions began in January 1938 when the Executive Council revoked the charters of the United Mine Workers, the Federation of Flat Glass Workers and the Mine, Mill and Smelter Workers unions. In March 1938, it ordered expulsion of all CIO unions from city and state federations. The next month, the AFL Executive Council expelled the Amalgamated Clothing Workers, the Amalgamated Association of Iron, Steel and Tin Workers (then within the CIO Steel Workers Organizing Committee), the United Textile Workers (within the CIO Textile Workers Organizing Committee), the United Automobile Workers, the United Rubber Workers and the Oil Field Workers.

Dubinsky's International Ladies Garment Workers Union escaped the expulsions. He played the part of "honest broker" in seeking a reunification agreement on terms which would have subjected 20 of the 32 CIO unions to possible redivision among numerous craft unions. Dubinsky publicly attacked the establishment of the Congress of Industrial Organizations and did not attend its first constitutional convention. The ILGWU remained in a position of suspension until restored to full status in the AFL in 1940.

A CIO constitutional convention was not held until October 1938, when its permanent name, the Congress of Industrial Organizations, was adopted. But the split was definitive, in fact, from the start. The CIO proceeded at once, in November 1935, to its own independent activity and organization. For the most part it ignored the warnings, threats, summonses, suspensions and curses of the AFL leaders.

In the November 16, 1935 *Militant* — the same issue which told of the "deep split" within the AFL and the formation of the CIO — another great and related event was described. A story from Akron, dated November 11, reported that all workers in the truck tire department of the Goodyear plant had protested a wage cut by a two-hour "strike" — "the third department in Goodyear that sat down at work while a delegation went to management" to demand restoration of wage rates. Management gave in. This is the earliest reported CIO-inspired "sit-down" strike — the tactic that was to become inseparably associated with the heroic rise of the CIO.

The Firestone workers on January 28, 1936 decided to use the same tactic. Some 2,500 of them "sat down" to force the rehiring of a fired unionist. This time they stayed overnight—several nights, in fact. After first refusing to meet with a union committee, the company finally capitulated. The union won virtually all its demands. Spontaneous sit-downs began to sweep through all the rubber plants.

A full-scale strike of 15,000 Goodyear workers developed, with mass picketing. On February 25 the company officials and city authorities determined on a show of violence to smash the strike. The local unionists mobilized their forces for a defensive battle. The CIO had sent them financial aid and voiced its support. This was a tremendous inspiration to the strikers in this first great battle under the CIO banner. The February 29, 1936 *Militant* reports the climax of the strike:

"As the zero-hour neared, hundreds of pickets packed into the strike headquarters across from the struck plant. Thousands more took the streets in front of the picket posts. Each picket was well provided with 'firewood.' Up the hill marched the forces of law and order. Grimly the strikers waited. The cops in the lead, the strike-breakers marched closer and closer to the massed rubber workers. The line refused to budge. Finally, Police Chief Boss halted his men a few feet from the taut strikers. Nervously he looked the situation over. He was outnumbered.

"Breaking down, he cried out, 'I've never led anyone into a goddam slaughterhouse, and I'm not going to now.' The cops broke ranks, the deputies marched down the hill again, to the accompaniment of tremendous jeers and boos from the massed pickets. One of the deputies suddenly clutched his stomach and became violently ill. The strikers, with their magnificent demonstration of militancy and determination, had carried the day."

The settlement of the five-week Goodyear strike also revealed the weak side and limitations of the CIO leaders. They persuaded

the strikers to accept a vaguely-phrased compromise settlement
put forward by a Roosevelt administration mediator.

Contrary to the popular belief, the CIO leaders did not differ
essentially from the AFL craft leaders in considering strikes only
as a "last resort." They were not "strike-minded." Indeed, the first
year of the CIO saw a sharp decline in the number of strikers. From
a high of 1,467,000 in 1934, the number of strikers fell to 789,000
in 1936.

What preoccupied the minds of the CIO leaders was politics. They
didn't rush out to organize strikes. Their first big moves were to
mobilize the workers for political action. Where the AFL leaders
had traditionally opposed political organization of the workers and
had merely made personal pronouncements in favor of candidates
for public office, the CIO right from the start sought to organize
the workers politically.

The CIO leaders were not motivated by belief in class politics.
On the contrary, they hoped to use the workers' voting strength as
a means of winning the "good will" of the Roosevelt administration
and bargaining for small concessions through government intervention on behalf of labor. Their politics was a device not to advance
the independent class power of the workers but to "get in good" with
the reigning capitalist political machine and solicit favors from it.

In Roosevelt's fourth year of office, at the May 1936 Amalgamated
Clothing Workers convention, Sidney Hillman complained that less
than 15% of the workers were organized, that "the mass-production
industries have gone back to long hours and wage-cutting, while we
still have ten or twelve million people unemployed." Nevertheless, to
the CIO leaders "everything now turned on the re-election of Roosevelt in 1936." (*Sidney Hillman: Statesman of American Labor,* by Matthew
Josephson)

In February 1936, to the great consternation of the CIO leaders,
AFL Teamsters chief Daniel J. Tobin, one of the most powerful
opponents of the CIO faction, was appointed to head the National
Labor Committee of the Democratic Party.

Lewis, Hillman, Dubinsky and their colleagues feared that the
AFL was getting the "in" with Roosevelt. The President, of course,
did play the AFL against the CIO, a policy he was to pursue throughout his entire administration. But this hastened Lewis and Hillman
to "cook up," as Hillman later expressed it, Labor's Non-Partisan
League to mobilize labor votes for Roosevelt.

Lewis, who many years later admitted that he had had doubts and
suspicions of Roosevelt as far back as the beginning of NRA in 1933,
nevertheless proclaimed in 1936 that "labor has gained more under

President Roosevelt than under any president in memory. Obviously it is the duty of labor to support Roosevelt 100 per cent." He did not say that more company unions had been organized, more workers killed, wounded and jailed, more troops called out against strikers under Roosevelt than under any president in memory. He did not tell how Roosevelt had strengthened the big banks and industrial corporations and helped to tighten the stranglehold of the monopolies on the American economy.

Labor's Non-Partisan League was represented, at the time of its formation, as a broad step in the direction of independent labor political action. Its main purpose, however, was just the opposite. It was created to be a bridge back from independent political action for hundreds of thousands of unionists who then customarily voted Socialist or Communist or were clamoring at the time for a labor party. This was particularly true in the key state of New York, where the great majority of workers in the garment industry had traditionally opposed the capitalist parties.

Dubinsky and Hillman especially needed the LNPL and even a separate American Labor Party as a means for channelizing the votes of their union members into the Roosevelt stream. Hillman's biographer Josephson has described the game:

"For Hillman the first and most important task was to 'sell' the idea to his own union people... Many of the union members, especially in New York and Chicago, had grown up in the tradition of supporting the Socialist Party, at least locally, and shunning our Tammany Halls. What Hillman advocated now was a distinctly *opportunistic* approach. The new League, unlike La Follette's Progressive Party of 1924, was to function mainly through one of the two major parties, and particularly the Democratic Party, in order to ensure Roosevelt's re-election. Some left-wing unionists had their doubts about Roosevelt... As an 'honest broker' in politics he often gave the effect of facing both ways, especially on the company-union issue. Moreover, in the Democratic Party's Southern stronghold CIO organizers were still welcomed by armed mobs of vigilantes or Klansmen..." (Original emphasis.)

Hillman, of course, did not tell his membership that he was proposing to completely abandon their traditional policy of independent political action. "We have had a policy, which was not to endorse either of the two political parties, and that if we took a position it should be along Socialist lines," he admitted to his General Executive Board in late April 1936. "The position of our organization is known: that we are for a labor party. We are today bound... to help bring about a labor or farmer-labor party — what is commonly known as independent political action. But in the last two years things have happened... since the coming of the Roosevelt Administration. We have participated in making the labor policy of the Administration."

The labor leaders had participated merely as backdoor beggars at the White House whining for crumbs. Their simplest requests had been rejected, as in the case of the company-union clauses in the NRA codes.

Announcement on April 2, 1936 of the formation of the LNPL was followed on July 16, 1936 by the formation of the American Labor Party as a New York State affiliate of LNPL.

"The thought was to channel the 'regular' Socialists into the Roosevelt camp," writes Josephson. In addition to Dubinsky, Hillman and Alex Rose of the millinery workers, the founders of the ALP included such conservative unionists as Joseph P. Ryan, who was to have himself voted lifetime president of the AFL International Longshoremen's Association, George Meany, then head of the New York State Federation of Labor, as well as the right wing of the Socialist Party. The new party "also enjoyed the support of Governor Herbert Lehman, A. A. Berle, and Mayor La Guardia — all in all a remarkable amalgam of AFL and CIO unionists, as well as Republican Fusionists, New Deal Democrats and Socialists," comments Josephson. He leaves out one other ally — the Stalinists. They, too, joined the unholy alliance and played a decisive part in this "People's Front" for the betrayal of labor's independent political action program.

It should be noted that AFL leaders who could not stomach the CIO as an organizer of the unorganized industrial workers could join with it in a "non-partisan" body to harness the workers to capitalist politics for the re-election of the "New Deal" President.

Dubinsky, one of the key sponsors of the ALP, had actually been a member of the Socialist Party in 1936. He resigned and joined the Roosevelt camp. Benjamin Stolberg, in *Tailor's Progress,* a history of the ILGWU and its president Dubinsky, relates that the garment workers would not register "en masse" in the Democratic Party and that this led Dubinsky to conceive of the device of "fusion" to corral the garment workers' votes. Stolberg writes:

"In New York, where the great majority of them [garment workers] live, they were used to the device of fusion, which cuts across all parties. Mayor La Guardia had shown what could be done by mixing all sorts of political factions in the name of roaring progress. Dubinsky and other New Deal labor leaders decided to combine those trade union and 'good government' forces which had been the backbone of the fusion movement in New York into a labor party. They felt that the socialist traditions of the workers could thus be canalized into support of the New Deal, which could give them a good deal of political power. The American Labor Party was to be that strangest of all animals — a non-partisan political party."

Dubinsky's biographer further relates that when the Stalinists had gained considerable power in the ALP, "one of the reasons the right-wingers continued to stay in the ALP was that the New Deal wanted them there. Without them there could have been no ALP and the politicians in the New Deal needed such a party in New York State."

The history of the CIO was to constantly appear as an admixture of two elements. On the one hand, mass organization of the industrial workers was to lead to titanic strike battles, most often initiated by the militant ranks despite the leadership. On the other, the workers were to be cheated of many gains they might have won because of the intervention of the government which had the backing of the CIO leaders themselves. Unwilling to "embarrass" the Democratic administrations, forced by the very fact of their political alliance to cover up the anti-labor acts of the New Deal and Fair Deal regimes, the CIO leaders kept one arm of the CIO — its political arm — tied behind its back. Reliance on the capitalist government and on one of its major political wings crippled the CIO. That is what really caused its early, and not unrealizable, dream of 25 million members to be shattered.

7

Flint '37 —
"Gettysburg" of the CIO

Class collaboration and class struggle — two irreconcilably opposed theories and methods which have always contested with each other in the labor movement—strove for supremacy within the CIO from its start. This clash of theories and methods was especially bitter during the CIO's crucial first two years.

The top CIO leaders were class collaborationist to the bone. They sought "peaceful coexistence" between predatory capital and exploited labor — between robber and robbed. They believed they could persuade the employers that unions are a "benefit" to the capitalists themselves and thereby secure gains for the workers by the simple means of "reasonable discussion" across the conference table.

In addition, they denied the capitalist class nature of the government and the major political machines, Republican and Democratic, particularly the latter party. Lewis appears to have had an almost touching faith in the honesty of capitalist politicians and to have placed an inordinate dependence on Roosevelt to give the CIO strong backing in its developing steel and auto campaigns. Lewis held this view all the more strongly because the Democratic Party graciously accepted more than a million dollars from the United Mine Workers and Labor's Non-Partisan League to help finance Roosevelt's 1936 election campaign. There is no evidence that Roosevelt and the Democratic leaders had agreed to any quid pro quo—any return for value received. Lewis just assumed it. Didn't the capitalists always get substantial returns for their political contributions? Wasn't labor's money just as good?

Fortunately for the success of the CIO, the concepts of the top CIO leaders did not always prevail. The strident notes of the class struggle broke through the "class harmony" chorus and set the dominant tone during the decisive days of the rise of the CIO. The bridge to victory proved to be not the conference board, nor the inside track to Roosevelt in the White House, but the picket line — above all, that "inside picket line," the sit-down.

Following formation of the LNPL to help re-elect Roosevelt, the CIO launched its big organizing drives in mass production industry. Lewis and his lieutenants had determined that the spearhead of the CIO offensive would be in steel. Lewis was particularly concerned with steel because of its importance for the miners union. He used the most eloquent of arguments — the offer of a $700,000 campaign fund ($500,000 from the miners and $100,000 each from the Ladies Garment Workers and Amalgamated Clothing Workers unions) to swing the old Amalgamated Association of Iron, Steel and Tin Workers leaders into the CIO. On June 13, 1936, ten days after the Amalgamated Association had been absorbed, the CIO leaders officially announced the opening of the steel drive.

The drive was placed in the hands of a Steel Workers Organizing Committee composed completely of top officials of unions outside the steel industry, with the exception of Tighe and Joseph K. Gaither of the Amalgamated Association. Most of the steel committee were selected from Lewis's own officialdom in the United Mine Workers. Philip Murray, Lewis's first lieutenant in the UMW, was named SWOC director. There was not a real worker in the lot. The steel workers had a handpicked leadership imposed on them from the top. From the start, the voice of the ranks was stifled and their initiative choked off.

The steel organizing campaign, however, was conducted in style. Murray sent 433 full-time and part-time organizers into the steel areas. Thirty-five regional offices were opened and a paper, *Steel Labor,* was issued. As a special inducement, the SWOC asked no dues. It was not until April 1937, after the United States Steel Corporation contract was signed, that the SWOC began to collect $1 a month dues; in June 1937, a $3 initiation fee was added.

In December 1936, Lewis and Myron C. Taylor, then board chairman of U. S. Steel, engaged in secret "exploratory" discussions on the possibility of a union contract. Just what would have come of these discussions if they had proceeded without any outside intervening factor is hard to say. The CIO front suddenly and dramatically shifted from swank hotel suites and skyscraper offices to the grimmer battlefield of the massive industrial plants of General Motors. Without a by-your-leave to Lewis or anyone else, the GM workers challenged the auto industry's giant in an immediate showdown battle. The GM sit-down strike of the winter of 1936-1937 became the major point of CIO combat. Flint, Michigan, became the "Gettysburg" of the CIO.

The United Automobile Workers, which joined the CIO formally in July 1936, was the closest to a rank-and-file controlled organization in the new CIO. By their own efforts in battle against the AFL Executive Council, the auto workers had established their own international union in 1935. At the UAW's second convention, the last week of April and beginning of May 1936, they completed the job by ousting William Green's handpicked President Dillon, and electing their own officers under their own constitution. The first fight at the convention occurred over Dillon's attempt to prevent the seating of the militant Toledo delegation, comprising 17 per cent of all delegates. It was these veterans of the Toledo Auto-Lite and Chevrolet strikes who set the pace.

This convention unanimously adopted a resolution calling for formation of a national labor party. Only a personal plea from Lewis to the convention, with an impassioned appeal by the newly elected UAW President Homer Martin, secured passage of a last-minute rider to the political resolution to support Roosevelt in the forthcoming national elections. Principles of union democracy were built into the constitution and practice of the UAW so firmly then, that more than two decades of bureaucratization have not eradicated them entirely. The convention rejected a resolution to bar "communists" and opened the union to all auto workers regardless of race, creed, religion, national origin or politics. It must be added that young militants of all radical tendencies, especially the Socialist Party (whose left wing then included the Trotskyists) and the Communist Party, played a most active and influential role in the convention.

There were several flashes of lightning before the GM storm. On November 13, 1936, a spontaneous sit-down strike halted operations of the Fisher Body No. 1 plant in Flint. The union won its point and the UAW started to sign up new members by the hundreds. Robert Travis, a member of the 1935 strike committee in Toledo Chevrolet, and Wyndham Mortimer, a Cleveland auto worker on the UAW board, were sent into Flint to aid the drive. Both of them were already under Stalinist influence, but they were still fresh from strike struggles and retained a good bit of their native militancy.

In the next several weeks there were successful sit-down occupations at the Bendix plant in South Bend, Midland Steel Products in Detroit, and a five-day sit-down at Kelsey-Hayes wheel plant in Detroit. Meanwhile, a strike flared at Fisher Body in Atlanta over the discharge of four men wearing union buttons. When the Atlanta workers appealed for an extension of the walkout, the CIO strategists termed such a move "premature." Four weeks later, a strike erupted at the Kansas City Fisher plant. On December 21, Lewis and the UAW leaders wired Knudsen of General Motors for a collective bargaining conference. They were told to take it up with local plant managers.

Disgusted with stalling around, some 7,000 workers at Cleveland Fisher Body, organized by Mortimer, struck December 28, 1936. They announced they would not work until a national GM contract was signed. More than a thousand strikers occupied the plant. Two days later, on the morning after they had presented management with a contract demand, workers in Fisher Body Plant No. 2 in Flint saw inspectors who supported the union being transferred. They sat down. At Plant No. 1 that evening the night shift saw important dies being loaded onto trucks and boxcars for Grand Rapids and Pontiac. They, too, sat down. The production of bodies for all GM cars came to a halt.

Within three weeks 15 other GM units were closed by strikes, including the Fleetwood and Cadillac plants in Detroit and plants in Jamesville, Wisconsin; Norwood, Ohio; Atlanta; St. Louis; Kansas City and Toledo. At the most crucial stage of the struggle the Flint Chevrolet No. 4 plant, where motor assembly was centered, was seized and occupied by the strikers. By the end of the strike, some 140,000 of GM's 150,000 production workers either sat down or "hit the bricks," as traditional picketing in a strike was described.

Victory or defeat for the GM workers depended on a simple strategy: keeping their buttocks firmly planked on $50 million worth of GM property until they got a signed contract. GM's strategy was to get the workers out of the plants by hook or crook so that the police, deputies and National Guard could disperse them by force and violence. All the maneuvers between Lewis and the UAW leaders on the one hand and Roosevelt, Frances Perkins, Michigan's Governor Frank Murphy and General Motors on the other, involved the sit-down issue essentially.

In his book *C.I.O.—Industrial Unionism in Action,* published late in 1937, the former Harvard economist, J. Raymond Walsh, who became CIO research and educational director, stated flatly that the CIO leaders had not called the GM strike. "The CIO high command, preoccupied with the drive in steel, tried in vain to prevent the strike; it was fed by deep springs of resentment among thousands of men against a corporation grossly derelict in its obligations," wrote Walsh. There was certainly no strike call and no broad strike strategy.

It was not until January 3, 1937, when the strike was already spreading like a brush fire through the GM plants, that 200 UAW delegates convened in Flint, created a board of strategy headed by Kermit Johnson of Flint, and authorized it to call a formal corporation-wide strike. The next day GM was served with a set of eight demands, including union recognition and a signed contract; abolition of piecework; the 30-hour week and six-hour day; time and a half for overtime; minimum pay rates; reinstatement of discharged unionists; a seniority system; sole collective bargaining rights for the UAW; and union participation in regulating the pace of the belt lines.

Once the GM strike was under way, Lewis publicly voiced the CIO's approval. On December 31, 1936, he declared: "The CIO stands squarely behind these sit-downs." When GM's Knudsen demanded evacuation of the plants before considering collective bargaining, Lewis repeated the demand for a national contract embodying sole collective bargaining rights.

On January 2, GM secured the first of its injunctions. A Judge Black issued an order to vacate the plants and to desist from picketing company property. When the sheriff attempted to read the order, the sit-downers laughed him out of the plants. Thousands of other workers continued their mass picket lines on the outside. But the injunction was never enforced; it was disclosed that Judge Black was a GM stockholder, with 3,365 shares then valued at $219,000.

On January 8 came the announcement of the formation of the Flint Alliance as "a voluntary movement of employes who wish to return to their work and are against the strike." This back-to-work movement, open to all citizens at large and not only GM workers, was headed by George E. Boysen, ex-mayor and former Buick paymaster.

A direct physical clash came on January 12. The company had shut off the heat that afternoon in an attempt to freeze out the sit-downers in Fisher Body Plant No. 2. Several hours later the Flint police announced there would be no more food allowed to enter the plant for the strikers. The cops blocked off the entrance and then knocked down a ladder to a window through which supplies were being shipped. A union sound truck with Walter Reuther's brother Victor at the microphone called on the police to end their blockade. The plea was ignored.

A body of pickets finally stormed the entrance, forcing the police aside and carrying coffee and bread in to the sit-downers. Around 9 P.M., half of Flint's police force suddenly fell with clubs on the pickets at the entrance. Some were scattered, others were driven into the plant. Tear gas was fired into the plant. Police sent volleys of buckshot through the windows. The strikers fought back with everything from hurled nuts and bolts to soda pop bottles. A three-hour battle ensued. During the course of the struggle the strikers captured the sheriff's car and three police cruisers. When the police reformed ranks at midnight to make a new attack, the strikers brought into play their "secret weapon"—a plant fire hose that soaked the police with freezing water and finally drove them back to the other side of a bridge leading to the plant gates. Twenty-four strikers had been injured; 14 had gunshot wounds. The "Battle of the Running Bulls" was the last attempt to recapture any GM plant by force. GM announced it would not try to use strikebreakers, a move it could scarcely employ anyway so long as the plants were occupied by strikers.

What force failed to do, GM sought to achieve through guile. The newly elected Democratic Governor Frank Murphy invited GM's Knudsen and UAW President Martin to Lansing on January 15. After a meeting, Murphy announced that a truce agreement had been reached for the sit-downers to leave five of the major struck plants on the weekend and then GM would start to negotiate on Monday. The Cadillac and Fleetwood workers in Detroit marched out of the plants with banners and brass bands. The next day, Sunday, January 17, the Flint workers were to leave their forts. Then the union learned that GM had wired Boysen of the Flint Alliance that "we stand ready always to discuss with your group" as well as with the legitimate union.

The truce blew up. Workers who were half way out of some plants rushed back in and took defensive posts. Others, preparing to leave, remained and locked the doors. Now the siege was on in earnest. Lewis announced: "G. M. was caught in a barefaced violation of the armistice and so the evacuation of the plants was stopped. The men are not going to leave them."

Lewis believed his ace-in-the-hole was Roosevelt. The union leader sought to get the President to come out firmly in support of the GM workers. On January 21, Lewis told a press conference: "The administration asked labor for help to repel this attack [on Roosevelt in the 1936 elections] and labor gave its help. The same economic royalists now have their fangs in labor. The workers of this country expect the administration to help the workers in every legal way and to support the workers in General Motors plants."

Roosevelt's reply the next day was a cold rebuke to Lewis: "Of course I think in the interests of peace that there come moments when statements, conversations, and headlines are not in order." A few days later Roosevelt sought to balance this off with criticism of GM Board Chairman Alfred P. Sloan, when the latter refused to confer with Lewis in Secretary of Labor Perkins' office. Roosevelt said this was a "very unfortunate decision" and left it at that.

GM was not averse to intervention by Roosevelt, if no other course was open. The *Detroit News* had come out in the third week of the strike with a front-page editorial, "Let Roosevelt Do It." GM understood Roosevelt's role very well. His task was not aid to the workers, as Lewis assumed, but to get the company off the hook with the smallest possible concessions. These GM concessions would be represented as a "patriotic" response to the President's request, not as a surrender to union pressure.

On January 31, Madame Perkins threw the administration's weight on the side of GM by telling the press that she had proposed to Sloan the day before that the strikers were to quit the plants "as an expression by the union of good faith in General Motors" before any negotiations were to begin.

Subsequently, at the most critical point of the strike, Roosevelt phoned from the White House to Lewis in Detroit to try to persuade Lewis to agree to a one-month contract in return for getting the workers to leave the occupied plants. He raised the offer to two and then three months, but Lewis stood firm for a minimum of a six-month pact.

While the shadow play was being enacted by Lewis, Knudsen, Murphy, Perkins and Roosevelt between Washington, Detroit and Lansing, the live drama was unfolding in Flint. There 1,500 members of the National Guard, sent by Governor Murphy, set up an encampment in preparation for driving the strikers out of the plant if so ordered. The company next sought another injunction as the legal basis for compelling Murphy to use the troops to invade the plants and force the strikers out.

On Tuesday, February 2, GM found another compliant judge, Paul V. Gadola, who issued an injunction ordering the strikers to evacuate the two Fisher plants by 3 P.M., Wednesday. A critical challenge faced the Fisher Body sit-downers.

Anticipating the Fisher injunction, however, the strikers moved on February 1 to occupy a still more strategic plant, Chevrolet No. 4 where the Chevrolet motors were assembled — a real bottleneck. The leader of the Chevrolet unionists was Kermit Johnson, a militant left-wing Socialist. Chevrolet No. 4 had not been shut down, as it was not certain whether the union had sufficient strength in the plant. A bold stratagem was devised to capture the plant by reinforcements from the outside.

A diversion was created. Several thousand strikers marched to Chevrolet Plant No. 9 from the union headquarters. They were led by Roy Reuther and Powers Hapgood. GM informers, as had been expected, had tipped off management about the march on No. 9. Armed Flint detectives and company guards had been installed in the plant. The workers inside began yelling "sit-down!" and a forty-minute battle was waged inside the plant. The Women's Emergency Brigade, organized and led by Genora Johnson (now Dollinger), fought heroically on the outside, smashing the windows to permit the tear gas to escape from the plant.

During this diversion, a group of Chevrolet No. 4 men, with some squads from Chevrolet No. 6, marched boldly into the No. 4 plant, shut down operations, barricaded doors and gates and set up patrols. Steel gondolas, weighing hundreds of pounds apiece, were piled against doors and windows from floor to ceiling. That night, troops with bayonets marched ominously outside — but Murphy did not dare give an order to attack.

The seizure and holding of Chevrolet Plant 4, which proved to be the key to victory, was an imaginative and bold stratagem carried out by workers with iron nerves. Kermit Johnson, chief author and organizer of this stratagem, worked in Plant 4 and had the inside knowledge necessary to conceive of the plan. In the February 11, 1959, issue of *The Searchlight,* official publication of UAW Chevrolet Local 659 in Flint, Johnson has given the most authentic account on record of this amazing struggle, which he and a few others of the strike strategy committee had worked out in a week of almost continuous meetings. Johnson writes:

"Plant 4 was huge and sprawling, a most difficult target, but extremely important to us because the corporation was running the plant, even though they had to stockpile motors, in anticipation of favorable court action. G. M. had already recovered from the first shock of being forced to surrender four of their largest body plants to sit-down strikers. They already had the legal machinery in motion that would, within a short time, expel by force if necessary the strikers from the plants. If that happened, we knew the strike would be broken, and the fight for a union in General Motors would be lost. Even the top leadership in the CIO, including John L. Lewis, were seriously worried about the G. M. situation. When Lewis' right-hand man, John Brophy, approved our plan of action, he did it with great reluctance and complete lack of confidence. He couldn't conceive of a successful strike in a plant that was less than one-fourth organized.

"I was remembering all these things and many others as I walked through the plant gate that afternoon, February 1, 1937. I was doing a lot of thinking... I thought about last night's final secret meeting, held deep inside the South Fisher plant. What a farce that had been! I laughed to myself and felt like a conspirator when I recalled all the pretense we'd gone through to arrange a meeting for one despicable man, a stool pigeon. Thirty men had been secretly picked for that meeting by Bob Travis, Organizational Director, and his aide, Roy Reuther, including Ed Cronk and myself from Chevrolet. The four of us who alone knew the actual plans put on a real show that night selling the right guy the wrong bill of goods. It seemed like a dirty trick to dupe so many good men, but to make the big fish swallow the bait we had to have a lot of little fish nibbling. I was sure we had convinced the stool pigeon that today at 3:30 P.M. the men in plant 9 would stage a sit-down strike. I was sure because he asked so many pointed questions about strategy, and because others, taking a natural part in the discussion, helped to allay any suspicions he might have had.

"Now, at exactly 3:10 P.M. I was upstairs in the toilet at the west end of Plant 4. I had nothing to do but wait and hope that everything was moving according to schedule. At this very minute someone was rushing into the mass meeting downtown, yelling 'Trouble at Plant 9!' Bob Travis would be chairing the meeting and Roy Reuther would be clamoring for the floor to make a motion and an impassioned plea that the meeting be adjourned so that they could all go to Plant 9 and help their brothers in the fight against their common enemy. I could see them now, cheering wildly and singing 'Solidarity' as they thundered down the rickety stairs of the union hall. There wouldn't have to be a vote taken; they wouldn't even wait for it, because this was action and that's what they wanted. Who could blame them for having bitterness in their hearts after witnessing the police brutality that had taken place in the past few weeks...

"3:25 P.M. I was down on the main floor, and the minutes were going fast. I was walking slowly in the aisle trying to be as inconspicuous as possible, but I couldn't understand why Ed and his men weren't here; they were long overdue. The next few minutes seemed like hours, and as I ambled toward the door, my previous confidence was rapidly giving way to fear — fear that we'd lost our one big gamble. My thoughts were moving a mile a minute, and I was rehashing the same plan over and over, but this time all its weaknesses stood out like red lights. I had never realized before how many if's there were and how every if was so utterly dependent upon every other if. No wonder John Brophy had been skeptical. Why this was like a mathematical problem without a single known quantity, or like trying to — and then the door burst inward and there was Ed! Great big Ed, his hairy chest bare to his belly, carrying a little American flag, and leading the most ferocious band of twenty men I have ever seen. He looked so funny with that tiny flag in comparison with his men who were armed to the teeth with lead hammers, pipes, and chunks of sheet metal three feet long. I felt like crying and laughing at the same time.

"When I asked where in hell the three hundred men were that he had guaranteed to bring with him, he seemed dumbfounded. I don't think he'd ever looked back from the time he had dropped his tools, picked up the flag, and started his line plunge to Plant 4. It didn't take a master mind to know that trying to strike a roaring plant of more than three thousand men and almost as many machines with just twenty men was absolutely impossible. We huddled together and made a quick decision to go back to plant 6 for reinforcements, and if that failed to get out of Chevrolet in a hurry. Luckily we encountered little opposition in Ed's plant, and in a short time we were back in Plant 4 with hundreds of determined men.

"Although we didn't know it then, a real war was going on in and around Plant 9, the decoy. Every city cop and plant police were clubbing the strikers and using tear gas to evacuate the plant. In retaliation the men and women from the hall were smashing windows and yelling encouragement from the outside.

"Back in Plant 4 a relatively peaceful operation was proceeding according to plan; a little late, but definitely moving now. Up and down the long aisles we marched, asking, pleading, and finally threatening the men who wouldn't get in line. For the first hour the men in Plant 4 were being bullied not only by us, but by management as well. Almost as fast as we could turn the machines off, the bosses following our wake would turn them on, and threaten the men with being fired. As the lines of marchers grew longer, the plant grew quieter, and finally after two hours every machine was silent.

"The men were standing around in small groups, sullenly eyeing members of supervision. No one knew who belonged to the union because no one had any visible identification. We had successfully taken the plant, but we knew that our gains had to be immediately consolidated or we'd face counteraction. We had a few men go through the plant and give a general order that all who didn't belong to the union should go upstairs to the dining room and sign up. While the vast majority were thus taken care of, a few hundred of us were left unhampered to round up the supervisors. It didn't take long to persuade them that leaving the plant under their own power was more dignified than being thrown out. Herding the foremen out of the plant, we sent them on their way with the same advice that most of us had been given year after year during layoffs. 'We'll let you know when to come back.'"

The next day, when Judge Gadola issued his injunction setting a deadline for the following day, the strikers held meetings and voted to hold the plants at all costs. The Fisher No. 1 workers wired Governor Murphy: "Unarmed as we are, the introduction of the militia, sheriffs, or police with murderous weapons will mean a blood bath of unarmed workers. . . We have decided to stay in the plant. We have no illusions about the sacrifices which this decision will entail. We fully expect that if a violent effort is made to oust us many of us will be killed, and we take this means of making it known to our wives, to our children, to the people of the state of Michigan and the country that if this result follows from an attempt to eject us, you [Governor Murphy] are the one who must be held responsible for our deaths."

Early the next day, all the roads into Flint were jammed with cars loaded with unionists from Detroit, Lansing, Pontiac and Toledo. More than a thousand veterans of the Toledo Auto-Lite and Chevrolet strikes were on hand. Walter Reuther, then head of the Detroit West Side UAW local, brought in a contingent of 500. Rubber workers from Akron and coal miners from the Pittsburgh area joined the forces rallying to back the Flint strikers. No police were in sight. The workers directed traffic. Barred from Fisher No. 2 and Chevrolet No. 4 by troops with machine guns and 37-millimeter howitzers, the workers from other areas formed a huge cordon around Fisher No. 1.

But when the showdown came, the sheriff refused to try to enforce the injunction. He passed the buck to Governor Murphy. New Dealer Murphy stalled, fearful of committing political suicide if he used the troops against the workers. On February 8, the company tried to freeze the strikers out once more by turning off the heat. The strikers opened all windows and threatened to freeze the firefighting equipment in the plants, thus causing a violation of GM's fire insurance contracts and leaving its property unprotected by insurance. GM howled at Murphy to enforce the injunction and he, in turn, went literally screaming in rage to Lewis: ". . . you've got to do something about this, Mr. Lewis. I demand that you do something."

Lewis replied: "I did not ask these men to sit-down. I did not ask General Motors to turn off the heat. I did not have any part of either the sit-down strike or the attempt to freeze the men. Let General Motors talk to them."

This was the literal truth. The GM strike was an uprising of the rank and file. Its leadership was mainly local young workers with radical social and political views. A short while later most of them, like those under Stalinist leadership who became the most servile supporters of Roosevelt, and the Reuther brothers who broke their Socialist Party connections, became more and more adapted to capitalist politics and class collaboration. But for that one brief period of the historic GM sit-down, they were still close enough to the militant ranks, still sufficiently imbued with socialist ideas and the traditions of the old IWW and socialist fighters, to rise with the masses. The men they were then would have spit upon the men they were to become.

Once more, after he had pleaded with Lewis to betray the strikers, Governor Murphy tried the threat of troops to frighten them. On the night of February 9 the National Guard in Flint, with 1,300 reinforcements, was alerted to seal off all highways and prevent reinforcements for the strikers. The sit-downers refused to budge; they made weapons of defense in assembly-line fashion and awaited the attack. Late that night, Murphy again went to Lewis and showed him an order he had signed for the troops to empty the plants by force the next day. Lewis told him: "Tomorrow morning, I shall personally enter General Motors plant Chevrolet No. 4. I shall order the men to disregard your order, to stand fast. I shall then walk up to the largest window in the plant, open it, divest myself of my outer raiment, remove my shirt, and bare my bosom. Then when you order your troops to fire, mine will be the first breast that those bullets will strike."

Murphy, his nerve broken, fled from the room. General Motors, fearful that any attack on the strikers in their determined mood would mean devastation of its plants and machinery, cracked. The muscular rumps of the GM workers pressed down on the chests of GM's corporate owners until they cried "Uncle!" On February 11, 1937, GM signed a six-month agreement. It provided that the company would not recognize or deal with any other organization in the 17 plants closed by the UAW, that all unionists and strikers would be rehired, that unionism could be discussed on company property during lunch and rest periods, and that negotiations would proceed at once on wages, hours, production speedup, and other issues.

It wasn't much of a deal by present standards. But it was an inspiring victory to all American labor in 1937. The floodgates of class struggle were opened. The cry "sit-down!" echoed from one corner of the land to the other. One month after the end of the GM strike, some 193,000 workers engaged in 247 sit-downs; nearly a half million took up this weapon before 1937 ended. The number of all strikes rose from 2,172 in 1936 to 4,740 in 1937, with 1,861,000 workers involved. That is the way the CIO was built and consolidated.

8

The Sit-Down Wave
and Little Steel Defeat

Under proper conditions, the sit-down is the most effective strike tactic ever devised. Although used in this country as far back as 1892 and employed by the IWW before World War I, the sit-down became a veritable tidal wave during the first two years of the CIO. It swept all before it in the period following the conquest of GM.

The sit-down was, in fact, an international phenomenon of the mid-Thirties. It appeared simultaneously in a number of capitalist countries. In 1934, coal miners at Terbovlye, Yugoslavia, in Pecs, Hungary, and in Katowice, Poland, stayed down in the pits in desperate actions that won victories. Greek tobacco workers took over a factory that same year. Some 3,000 Spanish copper miners in 1935 remained in the Huelva pits for ten days. Coal miners in Wales, Scotland and France adopted the tactic successfully. In Pondicherry, India, textile workers applied it with complete effect. And in France during 1936, a million workers sat down at one time in the key industries.

Within a month of the GM settlement the sit-downs spread to every kind of industry and trade, from Chrysler auto workers in nine plants to 5-and-10¢ store saleswomen, Western Union messengers, restaurant and hotel employes, milliners, bindery workers, garbage collectors, glass blowers, and tire builders. They sat down in movie theatre projection booths, WPA projects, shirt factories, and on shipboard.

The workers showed marvelous ingenuity and expended great labor in conducting long sit-downs or "stay-ins," as they were also called. Their chief problems were food, bedding, sanitation, recreation, discipline, and defense. Elaborate organization and committees were required to keep everything running smoothly. Outside committees and women's auxiliaries kept food supplies pouring in to the sit-downers. Bands, entertainers, radios, phonographs, checkers, and cards were obtained. Rigid rules against smoking and drinking were enforced. Cleanliness even went a nose ahead of godliness — the strikers kept the premises spotless always, while they sometimes missed Sabbath services. There is not a single reported case of dirt or damage as the result of a sit-down except in the tiny fraction of cases of police attack and invasion.

The very non-violence of the sit-downs infuriated the employers and their government agents. It was impossible for police or troops to provoke violence without clearly initiating it themselves. They had to attack and break into plants where there was obviously no disorder, because strikers were on the inside, strikebreakers on the outside. Thus, only 25 sit-down strikes were broken by police of the more than 1,000 sit-downs reported by the press in 1936 and 1937.

Sit-downs maintained high morale among strikers. Prolonged picketing outdoors in rain, cold, or snow can become a real ordeal. The sight of strikebreakers, escorted by armies of police, marching into a struck plant does no good to the spirit of strikers. As J. Raymond Walsh noted in his 1937 book on the CIO: "Nothing pleases a striker like the sight of smokeless chimneys. The sit-down does the job most easily and surely."

The sit-downs heightened the sense of comradeship and solidarity among the strikers. The strength of all became the strength of each. One GM striker expressed it to Lewis's biographer Alinsky: "It was like we was soldiers holding the fort. It was like war. The guys with me became my buddies. I remember as a kid in school readin' about Davey Crockett and the last stand at the Alamo. You know, mister, that's just how I felt. Yes sir, Chevy No. 4 was my Alamo."

But, unlike the Alamo, the sit-downs seldom ended in defeat. Almost all won partial or complete victories. It must be added that despite the Wagner Labor Relations Act of 1935, which supplanted the defunct section 7(a) of the NRA, more than 50 per cent of the sit-downs were for simple union recognition. (It should be noted in passing that former Secretary of Labor Perkins recalled in her book on Roosevelt that he had taken no part in formulating or pushing the Wagner Act through Congress, that he "was hardly consulted about it," and that "it did not particularly appeal to him when it was described to him.") The Wagner Act proved no more effective than section 7(a) in protecting the workers' right to organize and bargain collectively. It took a couple of million workers in the 1936-37 sit-down wave to actually seize that right by the seizure of hundreds upon hundreds of factories and other places of work.

The sit-down tide gradually ebbed after 1937. In some states, employer-dominated legislatures enacted laws with severe penalties for "trespass" on company property during strikes. A number of local and state courts found them "illegal." But they had almost ceased to occur by the time the United States Supreme Court issued unfavorable ruling on them in 1940.

Even before the courts had effectively intervened, however, the union leaders themselves had put the lid on sit-downs. The very success and effectiveness of this form of labor combat frightened the union officialdom. The sit-down gave tremendous power to the rank and file. In a few hours or days they were able to win from the bosses more than the union leaders could gain by years of "labor statesmanship" in "across the table" conferences.

AFL President William Green, of course, openly attacked the sit-downs. Directly after the CIO's GM victory, Green solemnly warned that the sit-down had "grave implications detrimental to labor's interests" and "must be disavowed by the thinking men and women of labor." He further claimed that "temporary advantages gained through sit-down strikes will inevitably lead to permanent injury." He added: "Both personally and officially, I disavow the sit-down strike as a part of the economic and organization policy of the AFL."

Of course, scores of AFL unions participated in the sit-down wave and, although primarily a CIO weapon, the sit-down won not a few victories for the AFL.

Lewis had commented on Green's remark: "He again sells his own breed down the river." "He 'bends the pregnant hinges of the knee that thrift may follow fawning,'" added the CIO chairman, in an effective if rather obscure quotation from Shakespeare's *Hamlet*. But the CIO leaders were by no means enthusiasts about this method of struggle. They were merely swept along for a while in the spontaneous flood.

"Some CIO leaders confess to a private anxiety, and hope that the sit-down will give way to more familiar tactics," reported Walsh, an intimate of the CIO top leaders, in his *C.I.O.— Industrial Unionism in Action.*

It is important to note that the sit-down technique was confined almost exclusively to the new unions and to newly organized workers, especially those organizations where more democratic policies prevailed. Of the 484,711 sit-downers between September 1936 and June 1937, some 278,000 belonged to new unions and 182,000 to unions formed since the start of NRA in 1933. There were 247,095 auto sitters; 42,167 in rubber; 22,270 in textiles; and 12,996 in iron and steel. But in old unionized industries there were hardly any — 300 in mining and none in the garment trades. In the old unions the bureaucracies had the workers more "harnessed" and "disciplined."

What most disturbed the CIO as well as the AFL leaders about the sit-downs was the revolutionary implication of the workers' seizure, even temporarily, of the means of production. The union officialdom, abject servants of the capitalist system, saw in the sit-downs a defiance of the dogma of the sacredness of private property and free enterprise. If workers could seize the plants to enforce their union economic demands, why could they not seize them as part of a more far-reaching social program? Why could they not eliminate the private owners altogether and organize production on the basis of social ownership?

Such revolutionary ideas are inherent in the very nature of the sit-down. The workers of America, by the enthusiasm they displayed in grasping this weapon, showed themselves far less inclined than their leaders to hold private property in the means of production as sacred. They quickly understood where the heart of the owners' power lay, and they put their hand on that heart when they took over his property. It is a lesson they will recall in future struggles where the issues appear to them as great and the stakes as high as in 1937.

By the end of 1937 the list of industrial corporations which had bowed to the CIO and signed union contracts read like a substantial list of "Who's Who in Big Business." The downfall of GM had a decisive effect on the negotiations secretly under way with U. S. Steel, which controlled about 40 per cent of the basic steel industry.

On March 2, 1937, Carnegie-Illinois, largest U. S. Steel subsidiary, received a SWOC delegation and signed a contract negotiated by Lewis. It granted recognition to the SWOC as the bargaining agency for its members, a ten per cent wage increase, the eight-hour day, 40-hour week, time and a half for overtime, vacations with pay, and seniority rights.

Reporters and commentators at the time credited Lewis with a "single-handed" victory. Lewis did take full advantage of favorable circumstances and skillfully "wrapped up" the deal with a corporation which at its founding in 1901 had adopted a special resolution never to recognize a union. But Lewis did not do the job "single-handed."

He had had the able aid of a "negotiating committee" of 140,000 GM sit-downers, particularly the brave auto workers of Flint who held the GM plants for 44 days. The defeat of mighty GM gave pause to Thomas Lamont of the House of Morgan, that controlled U. S. Steel, and to Myron Taylor, the steel company's head.

They were particularly anxious to avoid the GM experience because they had promise of a big pickup in profits from what was
becoming the fastest developing market—war orders. British armor plate contracts were in the offing, if U. S. Steel could assure
prompt deliveries. The House of Morgan also had reason to believe
that Roosevelt was preparing to swing the country more and more
in the direction of war preparations. Why risk the loss of British
orders and the chance to bid on U. S. contracts by forcing a strike
that might well end with the workers squeezing out even bigger concessions than Lewis was willing to accept?

The U. S. Steel contract inspired a rush of new members into the
SWOC. Within a week, some 20,000 more workers got their union
cards and 30 steel companies agreed to collective bargaining conferences. Within three months 140 companies representing 75 per
cent of the industry, including 14 U. S. Steel subsidiaries, were under union contract.

There was a negative side to this development. The gains of the
steelworkers appeared to come from the top. The steelworkers
themselves did not have to go through a great struggle to get them
and the CIO leadership, the SWOC leaders in particular, never
made any attempt to impress on the steelworkers their immense
debt to the GM sit-downers. Although the SWOC had more than
400,000 members by July 1937, they had no say whatsoever. Only
in 1942, when SWOC Chairman Philip Murray felt he had all the
union's machinery firmly in his own grip, was the United Steelworkers of America established with elected officers. This absolute control of the steel union from the top was to have repeated
unfortunate consequences for the steelworkers. The first example
of this came swiftly in Little Steel.

Five of U. S. Steel's leading competitors comprised the group
known as Little Steel. They were Bethlehem Steel, Republic Steel,
Youngstown Sheet and Tube, Inland Steel, and Weirton Steel. This
group determined to fight to the death against recognition of the
SWOC. The union's appeals to the law — the Wagner Act — only
brought sneers from the hard-bitten owners of these corporations.
Tom Girdler, head of Republic Steel, declared there was nothing in
the law requiring an employer to sign a written contract. The companies, as was later revealed by the Senate Civil Liberties Committee headed by the younger Robert La Follette, had stocked millions of dollars worth of arms and ammunition for a war on unionism.

Every effort of Philip Murray and his assistants to secure union
recognition was brushed aside. It was either accept a total and
humiliating defeat without a struggle or strike. On May 26, 1937, a

strike call was issued to 75,500 workers of Bethlehem, Youngstown Sheet and Tube, Republic, and Inland, with Weirton reserved for a later attempt.

The initial walkouts were virtually 100 per cent effective. "Next day the steel towns breathed clean air for the first time in years. The mills were as empty as a Monday-morning church," wrote Walsh in his book.

The subsequent terrible defeat the CIO suffered in Little Steel can not in any wise be blamed on the workers. Their response to the strike call was magnificent. Their heroism and courage in the face of the murderous assaults of the company thugs, deputies, police, and National Guards have never been surpassed in the annals of American labor. There were 18 strikers slaughtered, scores wounded, hundreds arrested — some 200 union members and local leaders were jailed in the Youngstown, Ohio, area alone. Memorial Day 1937, when ten were massacred outside the Republic plant in South Chicago, stands as one of the darkest days the American workers have ever known.

The responsibility for the Little Steel defeat rests squarely on the top SWOC leaders. They did nothing to prepare the workers for effective defense against the strikebreaking forces of the local and state governments. These union leaders told the workers that all the "New Deal" public officials were "labor's friends" and that the strikers should "welcome" the National Guards, state troopers and police sent to keep "law and order" by Democratic governors and mayors who were among Roosevelt's key henchmen. Nothing proved more demoralizing and disorienting to the strikers than to be greeted with hot lead and cold steel by the armed strikebreaking forces who the union leaders said were being used to "protect" the strikers and "keep the mills closed."

In Pennsylvania, Governor Earle, who had been elected in 1934 as the first Democratic head of the state in 44 years, declared martial law at Johnstown when local police and vigilante terror failed to break the strike at Bethlehem's Cambria plant. The plant, which had been closed for a week, was reopened by the state troopers. The head of the troopers issued his own "injunction," limiting the number of pickets to six at the lower Franklin gate, the main entrance for the scabs. The commander of the troopers claimed that the road running directly past this gate must be kept open as a highway. The angry and frustrated strikers could watch from a distance as Earle's troopers herded an ever greater number of scabs into the plant. Eventually, the strike was broken and the union crushed.

In Ohio, Roosevelt's political colleague, Democratic Governor

Davey, sent the National Guard — the same Guard that had been fought to a standstill in the 1934 Toledo Auto-Lite strike—into the steel areas. The National Guard officers held a secret conference with the Republic Steel executives and then moved systematically from Youngstown to Warren, Niles, Dayton, Massillon, and Cleveland, smashing picket lines, arresting strikers, escorting scabs into struck mills.

In Youngstown, two strikers were killed by deputies who claimed that the strikers' wives had called them names. The National Guard finished the job. Every organizer was arrested. Hundreds of union men were held in "technical custody," jailed without charges or bail. Union headquarters were raided repeatedly. After the strikers — at the behest of the pro-Roosevelt Stalinists, in this instance — had welcomed the guardsmen as heroes, Governor Davey had announced that the "right to work is no less sacred than the right to strike." This meant keeping the plants open and protecting the scabs. Morale was gradually broken and the strike caved in.

A similar process took place in Canton. Governor Davey's guardsmen occupied an area several miles square around the plants and permitted no one to enter or leave without a military pass. All highways to the city were blocked off to prevent sympathizers from other towns coming to the aid of the Canton strikers. Hundreds of workers were arrested and held incommunicado. One worker was beaten to death—but two doctors were procured to testify that death was due to "heart-failure." Troopers driving children from a Canton playground nervously jabbed with bayonets three youngsters who jeered them. The cut children had to be treated at the medical corps room of the Canton armory.

At Massillon, Ohio, a group of special deputies, armed with tear gas shotguns supplied by Republic Steel, opened fire at night into pickets changing details at SWOC headquarters. Two strikers fell fatally wounded, 13 were treated for wounds at the hospital. The deputies invaded the union hall, confiscated the records and broke up the furniture. A midnight man hunt began, with 150 dragged from their homes to jail. All picketing and meetings were then banned. The strike was broken.

The most evil day of the strike was May 30. A Memorial Day meeting had been called by the union in South Chicago. The meeting decided to hold a protest parade past the struck Republic plant. About 1,500, including women and children, were in the line of march. Union leaders, including Stalinists, told them that Roosevelt, the Wagner Act and Chicago's own "New Deal" Democratic Mayor Kelly had "guaranteed" the right to peaceful picketing.

As the marchers, in holiday mood, crossed a large trash-strewn field in the direction of the Republic plant, they saw a solid line of 200 police drawn across their path. A group of about 300 advanced to the police line and a leader began to talk to the police. Suddenly, the police opened fire with tear gas shells. Then, as the marchers broke and began to run in retreat, the police opened fire with their revolvers, sending hundreds of bullets into the panic-stricken crowd. The police then charged with swinging clubs and blazing guns, beating down or shooting every laggard. In a couple of minutes, ten lay dead or fatally wounded — every one shot in the back. Another 40 bore gunshot wounds — in the back. One hundred and one others were injured by clubs, including an eight-year-old child.

A Paramount News cameraman recorded the event. It was such a ghastly sight that the film company refused to exhibit the newsreel for fear of "inciting riots." It was subsequently shown in secret to the La Follette Civil Liberties Committee in the Senate and this showing was described in a contemporary press account. After telling how dazed individuals were shown caught in the midst of the charging police, the *St. Louis Post-Dispatch* of June 16, 1937, said:

"In a manner which is appallingly businesslike, groups of policemen close in on these isolated individuals, and go to work on them with their clubs. In several instances, from two to four policemen are seen beating one man. One strikes him horizontally across the face, using his club as he would a baseball bat. Another crashes it down on top of his head and still another is whipping him across the back...

"A man shot through the back is paralyzed from the waist. Two policemen try to make him stand up, to get him into a patrol wagon, but when they let go of him his legs crumple, and he falls with his face in the dirt, almost under the rear step of the wagon. He moves his head and arms, but his legs are limp. He raises his head like a turtle, and claws the ground...

"There is continuous talking, but it is difficult to distinguish anything, with one exception — out of the babble there rises this clear and distinct ejaculation:

"'God Almighty!'

"A policeman, somewhat disheveled, his coat wide open, a scowl on his face, approaches another who is standing in front of the camera. He is sweaty and tired. He says something indistinguishable. Then his face breaks into a sudden grin, he makes a motion of dusting off his hands, and strides away. The film ends."

Lewis and Murray looked to Roosevelt to save the Little Steel strike. On June 30, with the blood of many scores of steel strikers still fresh on the streets of a half dozen towns and cities, Roosevelt spurned the plea of the union leaders, grandiloquently quoting Shakespeare's *Romeo and Juliet:* "A plague on both your houses!"

Lewis, who had remained silent at the President's treacherous actions during the GM strike, could no longer contain himself. In a September 3 (Labor Day) coast-to-coast radio broadcast, Lewis scored the Roosevelt administration:

"Shortly after Kelly's police force in Chicago had indulged their bloody orgy, Kelly came to Washington looking for political patronage. That patronage was forthcoming, and Kelly must believe that the killing of the strikers is no liability in partisan politics... Labor next year cannot avoid the necessity of a political assay of the work and deeds of its so-called...beneficiaries. It must determine who are its friends in the arena of politics and elsewhere...

"Those who chant their praises of democracy but who lost no chance to drive their knives into labor's defenseless back must feel the weight of labor's woes even as its open adversaries must ever feel the thrust of labor's power.

"Labor, like Israel, has many sorrows. Its women weep for their fallen and they lament for the future of the children of the race. It ill behooves one who has supped at labor's table and who has been sheltered in labor's house to curse with equal fervor and fine impartiality both labor and its adversaries when they become locked in deadly embrace."

This scathing indictment of Roosevelt was not followed by a political break. Lewis was still to continue, for a time, his support of the Democratic machine and the "New Deal" administration. The other CIO leaders—Murray, Dubinsky, Hillman, etc.—did not even give support to Lewis's verbal attack on Roosevelt. Murray, whose strike "strategy" had been merely dependence on Roosevelt and "New Dealers" like Davey, Earle and Kelly, said not a word.

Later the story was to be circulated that the Little Steel strike had been a "mistake," that Murray had been induced to call the strike because of "misleading" and "over-enthusiastic" reports from local organizers and leaders in the Little Steel areas. The strike was lost only because of "misleading" and "over-enthusiastic" belief in Roosevelt and the other Democratic capitalist "friends of labor." Had the SWOC leaders prepared the workers for a real battle, with dependence only on their own organized strength, there would have been a different story to tell, as the Toledo, Minneapolis, San Francisco, and Flint strikes had already proved.

The Little Steel defeat was the first serious setback for the CIO. It slowed up but did not halt the CIO's drive. The eight unions with

900,000 members that had formed the CIO in November 1935, grew to 32 international unions with a membership of 3,718,000 in September 1937. The AFL Executive Council in September announced a total AFL membership of 3,600,000 — less than that of the CIO. However, the AFL leaders claimed 1,000,000 new members, demonstrating that the impetus given to organized labor by the CIO's campaign had benefited the AFL as well.

9

The Roosevelt Depression and CIO Retreat

By September 1937, the heroic days of the CIO were over. In the following two years, the CIO added only 400,000 to the 3,700,000 membership reached in its first 22 months. The strike statistics clearly indicate a period of retreat. The monthly average of strikes fell more than half between 1937 and 1939, as follows:

Year	Monthly Av. No. of Strikes
1937	395
1938	231
1939	192

Economic conditions were the principal basis for this retreat. The CIO's rise had coincided with a favorable economic upturn from June 1935 to August 1937. Physical volume of industrial production had fallen from 110 points on the index in 1929 to 58 in 1932. By increasing government spending from $4.6 billion in 1932 to $9.7 billion in 1935 and by inflating the government debt from $36 billion to $50 billion in the same period, Roosevelt had managed to jack up production to 87 points in 1935; 103 in 1936; and 113 in August 1937 — higher than in 1929. Roosevelt publicly boasted: "We planned it that way."

In late August, Roosevelt's "prosperity" bubble burst. Within three months the industrial production index dropped 27 per cent. In fact, the Roosevelt "recession" was the most precipitate the country had ever known—the decline in four months was three times as great as the drop during the first five months after the October 1929 stock market crash. Not until after the outbreak of World War II in September 1939 and after Roosevelt had launched the greatest arms budget in U. S. peacetime history was the depression to be liquidated in 1941 and 1942.

The pro-Roosevelt labor leaders and the Stalinists have gone to extravagant lengths to bury the fact that Roosevelt failed utterly to solve the problem of capitalist crisis and depression within a peacetime economy. Yet the figures of mass unemployment during Roosevelt's first two terms, according to the official estimates of both the CIO and AFL, are the single most damning refutation of the Roosevelt myth. Unemployment never fell below eight million during the entire "New Deal"—the government's own special census reported a flexible "8-1/2 million to 11 million" jobless at the August 1937 "prosperity" peak. In 1940, a year after the war had started in Europe, the CIO reported more than ten million unemployed. Here are the unemployment statistics from 1933 through 1940:

Year	CIO Estimate	AFL Estimate
1933	12 643 000	13 271 000
1934	10 845 000	11 424 000
1935	10 050 000	10 652 000
1936	8 756 000	9 395 000
1937	8 109 000	8 282 000
1938	11 030 000	9 979 000
1940	10 276 000	9 104 000

The "New Deal" proved to be a brief, ephemeral period of mild reforms granted under pressure of militant mass action by the organized workers, both unemployed and employed. By late 1937, Roosevelt had adopted the policy of propping up basic industry with government war orders, while cutting relief expenditures even though unemployment rose. The "New Deal" became the "War Deal."

The shift of policy was publicly proclaimed in Roosevelt's "Quarantine the Aggressors" radio speech of October 5, 1937. This belligerent speech urged a policy of building big military forces. In this very speech, Roosevelt also announced that "the Federal Government with the return of prosperity must more and more narrow the circle of its relief activities and reduce the amount of Federal revenue to be expended in the amelioration of human want and distress..."

This "return to prosperity" was a lie. Roosevelt's Secretary of the Interior Harold Ickes noted in his diary on January 1, 1938: "It is clear that the budget will not be balanced for the next fiscal year and this does not surprise me. Unemployment is increasing rapidly. Only a few days ago, President Knudsen, of General Motors, announced that 30,000 more men would be laid off January 1, this in spite of very large earnings by GM last year." (*The Secret Diary of Harold L. Ickes — The Inner Struggle, Vol. II.*)

In 1938, however, Roosevelt cut relief and work-relief expenditures to $2,176,000,000 from the peak $2,944,000,000 for 1937 and the 1935 sum of $2,321,000,000. At the same time, war spending rose steadily as follows:

Year	Federal War Spending
1935	$ 689 000 000
1936	900 000 000
1937	929 000 000
1938	1 029 000 000
1939	1 206 000 000
1940	1 657 000 000
1941	6 301 000 000

In the spring of 1939, Roosevelt called for the firing of 1,500,000 unemployed from WPA work-relief rolls. By 1940, some 2,000,000 had been fired. WPA strikes and unemployment demonstrations had led to mass arrests throughout the country. FBI agents were used to spy on the jobless and as *agents provocateurs*. In Minneapolis, 25 unemployed were sent to jail on FBI testimony, after Roosevelt had proclaimed: "You can't strike against the government."

The legend now fostered depicts the Roosevelt of that period as a shining humanitarian. Actually, the records of the time reveal deep disquiet among Roosevelt's liberal and labor admirers. Only the Stalinists appear to have covered up completely for Roosevelt, as they were the first to push for a Roosevelt third term.

Even Sidney Hillman, an obsequious supporter of Roosevelt, had to complain about the President's relief-budget slashes before the Amalgamated Clothing Workers convention on May 9, 1938: "As far as labor is concerned, as far as the progressive forces of the country are concerned, we will not permit budget balancing at the expense of hungry, starving men and women and children."

The link between war spending and relief cuts was pointed out by none other than Vice-President Philip Murray of the United Mine Workers. Murray, who was to succeed Lewis as head of the CIO the following November, told the UMW convention in January 1940 he preferred to see the government spend ten billion dollars "to put the idle to work rather than to spend one dollar for American-made bullets to be used to kill someone."

Long before this, the "New Deal" had been laid to rest. On March 1, 1938, the *New York World–Telegram,* chief newspaper of the Scripps-Howard chain, had reported that "President Roosevelt had declared a quiet armistice on new reforms." This "armistice" was to last a long time. Five years after Roosevelt's death, Murray complained in his article in the March 27, 1950 *New Republic:* "Since 1938, Congress has taken a leave of absence from social welfare legislation." Not only were social reforms at an end, but Roosevelt sought more and more openly after August 1937 to appease Big Business. Arthur Krock, the authoritative Washington commentator of the *New York Times,* observed on November 21, 1937 that "for the first time since 1933, the President [has] accepted the idea of aiding industry on its own terms..."

The impact of war on the depression is described in Price Administrator Leon Henderson's *First Quarterly Report,* U. S. Office of Price Administration, April 30, 1942. Henderson, Roosevelt's chief economic advisor, testified:

"The impact [of war in Europe] upon American markets was immediate. Memories of the first World War—memories of insatiable demand, of shortages, of inflation—were rekindled and there was an immediate and sharp increase in buying. The businessman who customarily bought one carload put in an order for three. Prices rose precipitately, basic commodities and basic raw materials both jumping about 25 per cent in the single month of September [1939]. The rise of prices itself evoked widespread accumulation of inventories that further fed the streams of buying. A speculative boom was on.

"Employment in manufacturing increased almost 10 per cent by the end of the year. Pay rolls rose 16 per cent. The Federal Reserve index of industrial production, which stood at 106 per cent of the 1935–39 average in August, rose to 125 in December. This was an all-time high..."

But war in Europe did not, of itself, turn the trick. Economic conditions in the United States returned to their former condition of slump during the so-called *Sitzkrieg* or "phony war." The invasion of the Low Countries and France in April and May 1940 was the signal for Roosevelt to call for all-out U. S. war preparations. In July 1940, Congress appropriated $12 billion for military spending and by March 1941 the total appropriation surpassed the $35 billion expenditure for all of World War I.

The CIO's retreat under unfavorable economic conditions and Roosevelt's pro-war campaign is reflected in the events within the most democratic and dynamic CIO union, the United Automobile Workers. At the third annual UAW convention, held in Milwaukee late in August 1937, there began the intense factional struggle between top leadership cliques for control of the union. Heading one faction was Homer Martin, whose specialty was redbaiting. The other faction — self-styled the "Unity" caucus — included the Stalinists and Walter Reuther. The Stalinists at this stage proposed to ban all caucuses in the UAW. This convention ended up with a compromise division of posts.

In September 1937, the UAW National Executive Board, including the Stalinists and Reuther, voted unanimously to ban all union-local newspapers, and to subject all union-local printed matter to NEB censorship. At the same time, they voted to inform General Motors it could fire any workers engaged in "unauthorized" strikes. Reuther and the Stalinists joined in signing a letter to this effect and the October 1937 *Communist* magazine declared that the Communist Party was "against unauthorized strikes."

The power fight between the Martin and the Unity factions came to a head in early 1939, after Martin suspended the majority of the Executive Board. He then tried to drag the UAW back into the AFL. Split conventions were held, but the pro-CIO convention in Cleveland won the overwhelming support of the auto workers. Reuther worked with the Stalinists until 1939, although his first break with them came in 1938 in a squabble over a post for his brother Victor in the Michigan CIO.

In June 1940, the UAW signed the worst General Motors contract ever, without providing for proper grievance machinery, and with weakened seniority. At this time the Stalinists took the lead in getting GM locals to rescind previous resolutions for the 30-hour week at 40-hours pay. Reuther, in charge of the union's GM division, helped ram the contract, giving only a one and a half cent hourly pay increase, down the GM workers' throats. He used the "national emergency" as a ramrod. He said that "now we must accept even a bad agreement for the good of the country."

At the July 1941 UAW convention, Reuther, heading the then most conservative wing of the UAW, shoved through the first antidemocratic amendment to the UAW constitution — a discriminatory amendment barring "communists" from elective or appointive offices in the international.

The CIO retreat was reflected in virtually every one of its affiliates. At a national SWOC conference in December 1937, the question of setting up a steel international with elected officers was shunted aside. No analysis was made of the reasons for the Little Steel defeat. Philip Murray assumed absolute and unlimited powers. By February 1938, both the steel and textile organizing drives were brought to a halt, with their organizing staffs reduced to a quarter of their original size. Two years later, at the May 1940 SWOC conference, Murray's eagerness to aid Roosevelt's third-term campaign led him to invite Mayor Kelly, whose cops had killed ten steel workers in the 1937 Memorial Day Massacre, to address the gathering. The Republic Steel delegates walked out in a body when Murray introduced Chicago's New Deal mayor.

Almost forgotten today is the alliance of the Stalinists with the CIO leadership in that period and the treacherous class-collaborationist role the followers of the Communist Party line followed. Those who recall the strikebreaking, speed-up, incentive pay policies of the Stalinists during World War II, may forget that this was the continuation of the line the Stalinists pushed before the war, interrupted briefly only during the period of the Stalin-Hitler pact. Every section of the top CIO leadership played ball consciously, at one time or another, with the Stalinists. Indeed, the Stalinists, by virtue of their false label of "communists," were able to deceive and disorient union militants who would not trust the old-line union leaders. They were invaluable to the CIO leadership in helping to bureaucratize the CIO and harness its native militancy. Recognition of this fact does not detract from the tribute due to thousands of hard-working, self-sacrificing workers under Communist —and Socialist Party — influence to whom much credit is due for organizing work in many local unions and areas. Most of them were disoriented and disgusted eventually by the Stalinist twists and turns.

With the consent of Lewis, Hillman, Murray, etc., the Stalinists moved in to take over leading city and state CIO councils. Joseph Curran of the CIO National Maritime Union, Michael Quill of the Transport Workers, and Harry Bridges of the West Coast Longshoremen faithfully followed every twist and turn of the Stalinist line. The Stalinists were a powerful force in the steel, rubber, auto, and electrical unions. Lewis appointed Bridges the West Coast CIO director in October 1937.

The Stalinists were then calling for "collective security" by a military alliance of the Soviet Union and the "Western democracies"; that is, those capitalist imperialist countries which were lined up against the Axis imperialist powers: Germany, Italy and Japan. The inducement the Stalinists offered Wall Street for a war pact was the use of the American Communist Party to help stifle the class struggle in this country.

In April 1938, during a jurisdictional fight with the then independent Sailors Union of the Pacific, which was defying the National Labor Relations Board ruling, Harry Bridges proclaimed the slogan, "You can't strike against the government." Later, Roosevelt and Truman used this same slogan when they seized railroads and plants to break strikes. Bridges introduced in February 1940 a "five-year peace plan" offering a no-strike guarantee for five years in the maritime industry in return for a compulsory arbitration setup.

The Stalinists initiated the CIO campaign for a third term for Roosevelt. They introduced a resolution to this effect at the November 1938 CIO convention. Lewis, as chairman, ruled the resolution out of order. However, the new CIO National Executive Board of 42 contained 15 Stalinists or Stalinist sympathizers.

Even after the Stalin-Hitler pact in August 1939, the Stalinists continued to give "qualified" support to the Roosevelt third term. In November 1939, all Stalinist delegates voted for third-term resolutions at the New York and New Jersey state CIO conventions. Quill said at the New York CIO convention: "We believe that endorsing a third term at this time is correct." But he warned the labor movement to "see that President Roosevelt and any official of the American government should never attempt to drive the American people into war."

The Stalinists withdrew their support from Roosevelt in 1940 and gave undercover backing to the Republican Willkie. But after the Nazi attack on the Soviet Union on June 22, 1941, Quill, Curran, Bridges, and the rest of the Stalinist followers in the CIO again became rabid supporters of Roosevelt and the capitalist war.

Politics dominated the developments in the CIO during this period and led to the first serious open internal conflict among the top CIO leaders. This struggle revolved around the growing enmity between Lewis and Roosevelt.

During the General Motors strike, and even more sharply during the Little Steel strike, Lewis had clashed with Roosevelt over the latter's anti-union acts. In fact, as early as February 1, 1937, Lewis spoke in favor of a third party based on a combination of labor and the farmers, at a dinner meeting sponsored by *Common Sense* magazine. By 1939, according to Alinsky, Lewis's biographer, the CIO leader "was becoming increasingly interested in the establishment of a third political party."

But, unfortunately, Lewis never seriously pressed the idea of a labor party. Instead, he kept his resentment against Roosevelt to himself and his intimates and did not take the CIO membership into his confidence. He continued after the Little Steel rebuff from Roosevelt to try to patch up their political alliance. During the 1938 elections, at Roosevelt's personal request, Lewis again contributed large sums of United Mine Workers money to the Democrats. A big share of this money was spent to aid the Roosevelt-Democratic faction in Maryland. A leader of this faction was Congressman Allen E. Goldsborough, later awarded a federal judgeship by Roosevelt. Nine years later Federal Judge Goldsborough was to repay Lewis for his political help by fining him and the UMW three and a half million dollars for violating an injunction. Roosevelt likewise personally solicited and obtained funds from Lewis for Senator Alben Barkley's campaign in Kentucky. Barkley, too, repaid his political debt by snarling attacks on the later mine strikes.

As late as the November 1939 CIO convention, Lewis took no open stand against a third term for Roosevelt. Lewis held the position of a "neutral," voicing the hope for a "progressive" candidate for president. At this time Lewis spoke sharply against any drive toward war, but also backed Roosevelt's "neutrality" measures, which were a smokescreen for the war drive. Hillman, however, was the author of the neutrality resolution and was working hand-in-glove with Roosevelt against Lewis and seeking to undermine Lewis in the CIO.

When Roosevelt, without consulting Lewis, appointed Hillman to the National Defense Advisory Committee, the CIO president felt that Roosevelt was deliberately trying to win over the CIO leaders with favors and appointments and to build a faction inside the CIO to destroy Lewis. It was this that brought Lewis to an open break with Roosevelt.

That Lewis was correct in his assumption has only recently been affirmed by Matthew Josephson in his laudatory biography of Hillman. Josephson tells how Roosevelt entertained the highly flattered Hillman at the President's Hyde Park estate in the summer of 1939. "Roosevelt feared greatly that the CIO, which had given him such mighty aid in the campaign of 1936, might be turned against him through the enormous influence of Lewis," reveals Josephson. "In his dilemma, Franklin Roosevelt, with keen intuition, turned to Sidney Hillman for help. In Hillman the President sensed a rival force within the CIO, one that might be used to divide the growing opposition in the labor movement or wean it away from Lewis. Hence the marked personal attentions shown to Hillman at Hyde Park and elsewhere."

On January 24, 1940, at the 50th Anniversary convention of the United Mine Workers, Lewis proclaimed his political break with the Democrats and Roosevelt. He declared that "the Democratic Party is in default to the American people" on every major domestic and international issue. He charged that Roosevelt had "broken faith" with the American workers. "In the Congress, the unrestrained baiting and defaming of labor by the Democratic majority has become a pastime, never subject to rebuke by the titular or actual leaders of the party." He added that Roosevelt's candidacy "would result in ignominious defeat."

Immediately, other CIO leaders, including Hillman and Rieve of the United Textile Workers, repudiated Lewis's statement and declared themselves in support of a third term for Roosevelt. On February 11, 1940, Lewis issued another blast at Roosevelt, when the latter hit a youth convention which had passed an anti-war resolution protesting loans to Finland in the Soviet-Finnish war. Lewis reminded Roosevelt that the 2,400 delegates at the UMW convention had also voted against loans to Finland and "after all, who has a bigger, greater right to protest against war, or any part of war, or the diplomatic intrigues of war, or the subtle politics preceding war, than the young men who, in the event of war, would become cannon fodder?"

Roosevelt had already made plain that "national defense" was designed to put handcuffs on labor, to prevent strikes and freeze wages. On May 21, 1940, he told a press conference: "Labor will not attempt to take advantage of its collective power to foment strikes and interfere with the national defense program to squeeze higher wages from employers in the so-called war industries." At an early conference of his newly appointed National Defense Advisory Committee, Roosevelt made plain to Hillman, his labor captive, what was expected of him: "Sidney, I expect you to keep labor in step."

In August 1940, Lewis told a cheering convention of the United Auto Workers in St. Louis: "Some day in this country the people are going to lose confidence in the existing political parties to a degree that they will form their own party." With Lewis beginning to voice such independent sentiments, it was no wonder that an estimated 25,000,000 to 30,000,000 people tuned in on the evening of October 25, 1940, to hear a political statement by America's most popular labor leader.

For most of Lewis's speech, his audience, including virtually every member of organized labor, heard a devastating attack on the Roosevelt war program and Roosevelt's assumption of executive powers. "... Those who hear these words, and who have studied the public addresses of the President, from his Chicago 'Quarantine speech' to his Charlottesville 'stab in the back' address, and thence to Dayton and Philadelphia, will understand his... objective. It is war. His every act leads one to this inescapable conclusion. The President has said that he hates war and will work for peace, but his acts do not match his words..."

Millions of workers were hanging on Lewis's every word. Millions of them were waiting for him to announce a new bold independent political course — a call for the labor party about which he had spoken only a few weeks before. Then came the anti-climax. "... If not Roosevelt, whom do I recommend to do the job of making secure our nation and its people? Why, of course, I recommend the election of Wendell L. Willkie..."

To the workers, there was obviously no more sense in voting for Willkie, the Republican tool of the utilities, who spoke for both "peace" and military aid to Britain, than in voting for Roosevelt who introduced the draft and also promised that "our boys are not going to be sent into any foreign wars."

There was a further point Lewis made in his radio speech. He said that a victory for Roosevelt would be "the equivalent of a vote of no confidence" in Lewis by the members of the CIO. If Roosevelt were re-elected, Lewis said he would "retire as president of the CIO, at its convention in November."

At the CIO convention, on November 18, 1940, two weeks after Roosevelt's election, Lewis ended his term of office as CIO president and refused a renomination. His choice as his successor was Philip Murray.

Alinsky has bewailed Lewis's break with Roosevelt as "the great American Tragedy of the labor movement." He is dead wrong. Lewis's tragedy is great indeed but it is not his break with Roosevelt. His tragedy has been his inability to break with the kind of politics represented by his coalition with Roosevelt.

It was not with Roosevelt the individual but with Roosevelt the capitalist reform politician that Lewis formed his political ties. In turning from Roosevelt to Willkie, Lewis had hoped to form the same kind of tie with another political agent of the same ruling class that Roosevelt represented. Had Lewis used his tremendous influence and prestige to summon American labor to build its own party at that crucial juncture, the American working class would be at least 20 years further ahead today. Lewis's failure in this regard is the real tragedy.

PART II

PRELUDE
TO WAR

1940-1942

10

Internal Conflicts and Factions

On December 9, 1955, fifteen years after the momentous CIO convention of 1940 discussed in the previous chapter, the head of the newly merged American Federation of Labor and Congress of Industrial Organizations addressed the National Association of Manufacturers. George Meany, a bitter AFL foe of the CIO in its rise, celebrated his recent accession to the AFL-CIO presidency by discoursing on his union philosophy before an assembly of labor's industrial enemies. He climaxed his remarks to the NAM with the boast:

"I never went on strike in my life, never ran a strike in my life, never ordered anyone else to run a strike in my life, never had anything to do with a picket line."

In that boast we have a certain measure of the difference between the CIO and AFL during their period of rivalry. We can hardly conceive of any CIO leader, however timid and conservative, daring to boast publicly that he had never had anything to do with strikes.

Not that the top CIO leaders differed from a George Meany in their basic social and political outlook. They too advocated peaceful coexistence between exploited labor and exploiting capital. They yearned for a passive, quiescent, strikeless labor movement. But the composition, structure and dynamism of the industrial unions, confronting the unyielding arrogance of the giant monopoly corporations, repeatedly thrust the CIO leaders, however unwilling, into at least nominal leadership of bitter strikes. The year 1941 was to supply a number of examples.

The CIO's turbulent external struggle was matched by almost continuous internal conflict and change. The origin and industrial composition of the CIO, the historical conditions that provided the soil for its growth, also nurtured opposing tendencies, political groupings, shifts and splits, both within the national CIO and its component unions.

When John L. Lewis, principal founder and first president of the CIO, withdrew in 1940 from its presidency and in 1942 from the CIO itself, it was a measure of the intensity of the internal conflict within the CIO and of the exceptional pressure on it by outside hostile elements.

Within seven years of the first meeting of the Committee for Industrial Organization, forerunner of the completely independent Congress of Industrial Organizations, four of the CIO's eight founding unions had broken away from it. The International Ladies Garment Workers Union, the Hatters, Cap and Millinery Workers Union, and the International Typographical Union, whose presidents had been members of the CIO founding committee in 1935, did not attend the 1938 constitutional convention establishing the CIO as a separate association of unions. The ILGWU and the milliners rejoined the AFL in 1940. The ITU re-entered in 1944 only after the AFL rescinded its compulsory assessment for a "war chest" to fight the CIO. In October 1942, the United Mine Workers, which had provided most of the money and organizing staff for the early CIO drive, was also to leave the CIO, although the UMW did not rejoin the AFL until January 1946. In a following chapter, I shall deal at more length with the UMW split from the CIO.

It is especially instructive to consider the role of the ILGWU and its president, David Dubinsky. The ladies garment workers, concentrated mainly in the New York area, had a rich socialist tradition. Dubinsky himself had belonged to the Socialist Party, but was a right-winger whose "socialism" was of the holiday variety. Members of his school of Social Democratic politics covered their class-collaboration policies and their conservative bureaucratism in the unions with a veneer of social demagogy and appeals for social reforms. By 1936, Dubinsky deserted the socialist movement openly and jumped on the Roosevelt band wagon.

Dubinsky had been swept along in the great labor upsurge from 1934 to 1937. His own membership, brought up on the socialist tradition of industrial unionism, was afire with the new vision evoked by the struggle led by John L. Lewis inside the AFL for industrial organization. But Dubinsky never really made a clean break from the old AFL machine and his old AFL cronies.

First of all, he was frightened by the atmosphere of militancy, the pressure for union democracy that prevailed inside the new unions like the auto and rubber workers. He feared the growth of a rank-and-file faction that might contest his bureaucratic grip on the ILGWU. (This union, under his domination, continues to this day to embrace some of the lowest-paid workers in all industry, and did not have a major strike from 1933 to 1958.) In June 1940, the ILGWU convention, hammered by Dubinsky's arguments that the purposes of the CIO had already been fulfilled and that the "Communists" controlled the CIO, voted to rejoin the AFL. Max Zaritsky's milliners union followed the same course.

There was another and perhaps weightier reason for Dubinsky's abandonment of the CIO. This was the pressure of Roosevelt. The latter was determined to mobilize labor for the war for which he was consciously preparing. He needed the help of the labor leaders to force the workers to submit to the inevitable wartime regulations and deprivations. His personal hatred of Lewis, attested by a number of the late President's intimates, was almost beyond reason. He was out to destroy Lewis or at least reduce his influence to a minimum. Roosevelt considered the elimination of Lewis as indispensable to his scheme for absolute control of the workers in the war for which he was planning. And he wasn't altogether wrong, as the wartime events were to prove.

Toward this end, Roosevelt had manipulated and maneuvered in 1940 and 1941 to effect a "shotgun" merger of the AFL and CIO on terms which would have been most disadvantageous to the development and preservation of industrial unionism. It would also, in Roosevelt's opinion, have left Lewis in a weakened position, since Roosevelt figured that the less independent elements of both the AFL and CIO leaderships would combine against Lewis.

Both Saul Alinsky in his excellent biography of Lewis, and Matthew Josephson in his semi-official book on the late Sidney Hillman, confirm the fact of Roosevelt's attempted intervention in the labor movement to force a merger with the aim of submerging Lewis.

At the November 1940 convention of the CIO, Hillman and his associates of the Amalgamated Clothing Workers had tried to press the issue of "unity." This meant unity under the terms laid down by the AFL Executive Council, that would have left the new industrial unions wide open for dissection by numerous craft unions. There is little question that Hillman was acting under instructions from Roosevelt. Hillman was not only fully committed to Roosevelt's war program; he was completely submissive to the President and appeared to regard him as the actual leader of the labor movement.

Lewis took up the challenge in one of his most scathing speeches. He told the CIO convention delegates:

"Five years ago a little group of men representing some eight organizations in the American Federation of Labor... highly resolved that come high or come low they would go forward... And one of those men was Mr. Dubinsky... who swore by every God that ever sat on high that he, Dubinsky, would never waver in the cause, and he signed the scroll and by book, bell and candle vowed to affiliate with this movement. And where is Dubinsky today?... He has crept back into the American Federation of Labor. He abandoned his fellows, and he abandoned what he claimed was his principle. He has gone into that organization on his adversary's terms. He is crying out now, and his voice laments like that of Rachel in the wilderness, against the racketeers and the panderers and the crooks in that organization.

"And Zaritsky, he was the man representing the Millinery and Cap Workers. He said, 'Me too.' And now above all the clamor come the piercing wail and the laments of the Amalgamated Clothing Workers. And they say, 'Peace, it is wonderful.' And there is no peace.

"There is no peace because you are not yet strong enough to command peace upon honorable terms. And there will be no peace with a mighty adversary until you possess that strength of bone and sinew that will make it possible for you to bargain on equal terms..."

Lewis concluded with a direct defiance of the Hillmanite threat of a possible split: "Dubinsky took the easy way. Zaritsky took the easy way. If there is anybody else in the CIO who wants to take the easy way, let them go..."

In a radio address on the evening of the day he was elected CIO president to replace Lewis, Philip Murray echoed Lewis's sentiments with a warning to Roosevelt "not to force a shotgun unity between the AFL and CIO." Roosevelt had not yet succeeded in effectuating the full breach between Lewis and his lieutenant Murray.

Roosevelt did not cease his interference with the labor movement. During 1941 he addressed himself openly to the conventions of both the CIO and AFL, trying to force them into a merger, stating:

"In this hour when civilization itself is in the balance, organizational rivalries and jurisdictional conflicts should be discarded... The establishment of peace between labor organizations would be a patriotic step forward of incalculable value in the creation of true national unity."

But within a few months — after Lewis, in January 1942, had issued his own unexpected proposal for "accouplement" of the CIO and AFL —Roosevelt frantically summoned CIO President Murray and charged him on no account to agree to any merger proposal.

The President complained that Lewis's move was nothing but a plot to create division between organized labor and the White House. By this time—a few weeks after Pearl Harbor—Murray was completely the creature of Roosevelt. Murray hastened to remind the world that he was president of the CIO and "all arrangements in behalf of the Congress of Industrial Organizations will necessarily have to be initiated through the office of the President of the Congress of Industrial Organizations."

A few days thereafter, Roosevelt instructed Murray and AFL President Green each to designate three representatives to "consult with him [Roosevelt] frequently on matters relating to labor problems." Murray quickly complied, selecting himself, President R. J. Thomas of the United Automobile Workers, and Secretary-Treasurer Julius Emspak of the United Electrical Workers, then a notorious Stalinist associate. The entire press noted the absence of Lewis's name.

The conflict between the Lewis forces and the Murray-Hillman-Stalinist bloc, which I will discuss in more detail later, was only one indication of the lack of homogeneity in the CIO. There were other elements which contributed toward divergencies.

It is noteworthy that, with the exception of the Amalgamated Clothing Workers, led by Sidney Hillman, all those old-line well-established unions with hardened leaderships which had entered the early CIO, left it within a few years. The Amalgamated had had only a short association with the AFL's United Garment Workers and had entered the AFL only in 1933. Therefore it felt no great pull back to the "parent" organization. Thus, the unions which finally comprised the CIO were mostly new organizations which arose in mass production industries in the Thirties.

These new unions, however, were not all led by new leaders or leaders who came out of the industries involved. The steel, textile and packinghouse unions, for instance, were originally dictatorially run by organizing committees hand-picked by Lewis and the top CIO leadership. For years these unions were denied status as international unions with their own constitutions and elected leaderships.

Murray and his office aide David J. McDonald got control of the steelworkers through appointment by Lewis. Murray was one of Lewis's vice-presidents in the United Mine Workers. Lewis looked on Murray as a faithful lieutenant who could be trusted to follow orders in directing the steel organizing drive which was initiated in 1936.

The UMW was particularly concerned about the captive coal mines owned by the steel companies. Lewis considered the organization of the steelworkers a means of bolstering the UMW's bargaining power with the captive-mine owners.

Every attempt of the steelworkers to secure their own international union and elect their own officers had been rebuffed by Murray. In 1942, however, when Murray was approaching his open break with Lewis, he summoned a constitutional convention and established the United Steelworkers of America, with himself as president and McDonald as secretary-treasurer, plus large salaries for both.

Sidney Hillman and the Amalgamated Clothing Workers "fathered" the Textile Workers Organizing Committee and supplied most of its funds and organizers. Hillman hoped to strengthen the Amalgamated by organizing the starvation-wage textile plants, in many of which men's clothing manufacturers had interests.

Hillman had decided to convert the Textile Workers Organizing Committee into an international union in early 1939. Among the groups loosely combined under the TWOC was the old United Textile Workers Union headed by Francis J. Gorman. In a factional war, Gorman split a small group from the TWOC and returned to the AFL. Hillman declared Gorman expelled from the TWOC.

Hillman then called a convention of the TWOC which in May 1939 established the Textile Workers Union of America, with its own constitution and elected officers. While Emil Rieve, head of the hosiery workers union and Hillman's trusted lieutenant, was named TWUA president, Hillman continued as chairman of the Executive Board until April 1941. Establishment of the TWUA fitted well into Hillman's larger aims. He was already trying to bolster his own hand in the developing conflict between Lewis and Roosevelt, a conflict in which Hillman was committed to Roosevelt from the start.

It is interesting to note that the CIO packinghouse workers were kept in an Organizing Committee status under Stalinist domination until October 1943, when the United Packinghouse Workers of America was founded.

A whole group of new CIO unions or unions which achieved a real growth only within the CIO framework, early fell into the bureaucratic grip of the Stalinists. These included the National Maritime Union led by Joseph Curran, the International Longshoremen's and Warehousemen's Union headed by Harry Bridges, and the United Electrical Workers (UE).

The UE, largest of the CIO unions which the Stalinists were to succeed in dominating, had been led originally by a coalition of Stalinists and non-Stalinists. Among the latter was James B. Carey, who was named president of the UE when it was formed in 1937.

Carey came into conflict with the Stalinists during the brief period of the Stalin-Hitler Pact — from September 1939 to June 22, 1941 — when the American Communist Party's slogan was "The Yanks Are Not Coming."

Under the tutelage of Hillman, who was pressing with every means at his command to wipe out all opposition in the CIO to Roosevelt's war program, Carey tried to suppress the Stalinists. He opened a campaign in the UE locals for passage of a resolution to bar communists from office. The UE General Executive Board, with a Stalinist-influenced majority, ruled such resolutions unconstitutional. In this same period, Carey accepted a post on Roosevelt's National Defense Mediation Board against Stalinist disapproval.

By the time of the UE's August 1941 convention, Hitler's invasion of the Soviet Union had turned the Stalinists into super-patriots and howling warmongers in the CIO and everywhere else. They no longer had any principled differences with Carey, nor he with them. But the factional war between them had continued on its own momentum and Carey continued to press his anti-democratic proposal to bar communists from holding UE office.

Carey was unseated as UE president and replaced by Albert J. Fitzgerald. The latter actually was a Hillmanite but had agreed to a compromise on the anti-communist resolution, since by this time Hillman and the Stalinists were joined in unholy alliance to destroy Lewis and advance the pro-war policy of Roosevelt. Carey later was compensated for his loss of the UE presidency by his retention in the post of CIO secretary-treasurer.

But when people think of the CIO, even to this day, they are apt to think first of the United Automobile Workers. If you were to ask almost any group of workers to name a "typical" CIO union, the chances are they will cite the UAW. The UAW, however, was far from typical. In fact, it was unique.

"Dynamic" was the word used most often to describe the UAW through most of its years. Other unions also waged great strikes and their members had no less fighting qualities than the auto workers. But the struggles of the auto workers always had an extra flair.

They raised the sit-down strike to the level of a national institution in the General Motors strike of 1936-37. They organized colorful mass picketing. They maintained the "flying squadrons," those shock troops of the picket line with their overseas-type caps and uniformed blouses, as permanent groups in many of the key locals. They most clearly exemplified the militancy, the ingenuity, the will to fight that imbued the ranks of industrial labor in the Thirties and powered the mighty upsurge that built the CIO.

Behind the traditional dynamism and militancy of the UAW was a special element: the relatively high level of union democracy that prevailed, particularly in its first ten to twelve years. The power of the rank and file to make its voice heard and its will felt reached a high point for the modern American labor movement in the UAW-CIO. Until Walter Reuther finally succeeded in establishing one-man rule in the late Forties, the internal life of the UAW for years was a succession of factional struggles, revolts and opposition movements against all attempts to strengthen the top bureaucratic leaders against the ranks.

Within a period of eleven years, from 1935 when the UAW was chartered as an international union by the AFL Executive Council until Walter Reuther gained the presidency in 1946, the UAW ranks gave the boot to three international presidents. In 1936 the UAW convention ousted Francis Dillon, a president appointed by William Green in 1935. They elected a member of their union, Homer Martin, in his place. Martin, after attempting to use the iron hand, ended up in 1939 with a small split-off which he took back into the AFL, where it eventually degenerated into a racket run by outright gangsters. In Martin's place, the 1939 UAW-CIO convention elected R. J. Thomas, one of the leaders who had come up from the ranks. At that time, Thomas was considered a compromise "neutral" choice between competing factions, including the Reutherites and Stalinists. Thomas fell in 1946, when Reuther defeated him for the presidency.

The stormy conventions of the UAW became famous—or notorious, according to the point of view. The members jealously guarded their right to maintain organized caucuses, to press for policies and leaders they preferred. Those open factional struggles of tendencies were a source of dismay, indeed of horror, to the old-line union officials who dealt ruthlessly with even the mildest opposition and never let a member "talk out of turn."

The relative difference in union democracy between the UAW and other major CIO unions can be indicated by two incidents at conventions of the steel and auto workers in the early Forties.

On the opening day of the founding convention of the United Steelworkers, May 19, 1942, CIO and SWOC Chairman Philip Murray, in his keynote address, served due warning on any and all who would try to promote policies or leadership other than his own:

"I shall fight any attempt that is made to have little backroom caucuses while this convention is going on. So if any of the boys are thinking right now of midnight sessions in strange places in the city of Cleveland, just begin to forget about it right now."

If dissenters were meeting in "midnight sessions in strange

places," it was because had they met in daylight in known places they feared they might be visited by squads of burly elements with weighty arguments in their hands. Caucus meetings at UAW conventions, however, were usually wide-open affairs.

Compare the atmosphere at the 1942 steelworkers convention, as indicated by the above-quoted statement of Murray's, to that of the 1943 UAW convention.

In debate on the wartime no-strike pledge, Emil Mazey, a delegate of Briggs Local 212, spoke from the floor against the pledge, in opposition to the entire top officialdom from Thomas to Reuther and including a powerful wing of Stalinists. Mazey's argument, under the circumstances, is of especial interest. He said:

"Despite the war, the interests of the employers and the workers remain diametrically opposed. We have given up our struggle against the employers but the employers have not ceased their class struggle against us during the war."

He then turned to John Anderson, the Stalinist floor whip from Local 155 (not to be confused with the well-known militant John W. Anderson of Fleetwood Local 15), and repeated: "Yes, Brother Anderson, the class struggle does go on in spite of the war."

This was not strange language to the auto delegates. Mazey wasn't shouted down or ruled out of order. He was heavily applauded. He remained a prominent, indeed a leading member of the UAW. At this writing, although his views are considerably altered, he holds the post of UAW secretary-treasurer.

What was significant in this event was that, at the height of war jingoism, a worker well-known for his militant and radical views could speak so freely and openly on a union convention floor. In the UAW, it must be stressed, all political views found some avenue of expression in the continuous struggle for correct program and leadership. New ideas found a favorable climate and the membership was educated in progressive social and political ideas. Far from weakening the auto workers union, this internal democracy was the wellspring of its power and tremendous growth. Instead of "falling apart with dissension," as top CIO and some UAW officers so fearfully foretold, the UAW became the first million-member union in the history of American labor.

When poll-tax Senators from one-party-ruled Southern states and political agents of boss-ruled Northern machines today seek laws to enable the corporation-dominated government to intervene in unions and to impose "democracy" from the outside, they are not thinking of the real union democracy manifested in the early years of the UAW. These political elements or their like had "viewed with alarm" the uprisings of the UAW rank and file and the relatively free play of ideas in the best days of the UAW. In those years, they berated the UAW and the CIO leaders for not "disciplining" and "controlling" the auto workers.

In this chapter I have given a panoramic view of the CIO, of the type of unions which composed it, the conflicts within it and the splits that occurred at the very time the CIO industrial workers were to enter their second great wave of strike battles. The year 1941, on the very eve of U. S. military participation in World War II, was to become another period of gigantic clashes, of major victories for the CIO — and a few defeats. The defeats we recall for the lessons they teach. But 1941 shines for American labor as the year when some of the seemingly most impregnable fortresses of the open-shop system fell under the renewed onslaught of organized industrial labor. 1941 — when the Ford empire was battered into submission, Bethlehem Steel fell before the power of marching thousands, and the captive coal mines became union-shop territory.

11

Triumphs at River Rouge and Bethlehem

Since Franklin D. Roosevelt's death in April 1945, a voluminous literature has grown up around his memory. Despite the material continuously pouring forth, there are two major areas of Roosevelt's policies and activities as President that remain murky: on labor and on the war.

The confusion derives both from the deliberate designs of Roosevelt himself and the myths fostered and elaborated by certain of his followers, particularly among the Democratic liberals, the labor bureaucrats and the adherents of the Communist Party. These groups seek a prop for their present policies in the still potent name of Roosevelt.

Labor's role in the war preparations and in war itself was Roosevelt's decisive concern. From the first, Roosevelt had moved to muzzle all militant sectors of labor and all union leaders or tendencies that might insist on the preservation of labor's rights and conditions during the war. Above all, he sought to suppress the right to strike. This became the biggest and most hotly disputed issue between the workers and the government, between the union ranks and the leaders, in the years immediately preceding and during World War II.

It is false to claim, however, as so many of the present-day labor leaders do, that Roosevelt's opposition to strikes was simply a wartime policy, an "emergency" measure. Not the least of the fictions circulated about Roosevelt is that he supported labor in its struggles against the employers. There is no real evidence of this.

Virtually all claims for Roosevelt's alleged friendliness toward organized labor and its struggles can be traced back finally to the claim that he "gave" labor "the right to organize." In an earlier chapter, I have shown that even the famous Section 7(a) of the National Recovery Act of 1933 was an afterthought and was incorporated into the act only under the direct demands of Lewis and Green. The subsequent Wagner National Labor Relations Act, which was upheld by the Supreme Court in 1937, reaffirmed the right of union collective bargaining. But this was a right won in fact by direct mass struggles — strikes.

A union denied the right to strike is like an automobile without fuel: it has no ability to move; it can't go anywhere on its own power. True enough, the Wagner Act had an ambiguous reference to the right to strike; that is, it contained a clause which said that nothing in the Act should be construed as a denial of the right to strike. But it did not directly uphold the right to strike.

From 1933 to 1939 there had been 17,862 strikes involving 8,261,000 workers, most of them seeking union recognition. During Roosevelt's first two terms, the National Guard, financed and equipped by federal funds and trained by Regular Army officers, played its most active strikebreaking role. From 1933 to 1935 alone, out of 42,737 National Guards who were called to active duty, 32,645 or 77 per cent were used to break strikes. In the one year, 1935, the National Guard was employed in 73 strikes in 20 states, a majority of them under Democratic "New Deal" administrations. As late as the November 1938 convention of the CIO, its officers' report complained that "the use of the National Guard to break strikes has been subsidized by Federal government... The use of the National Guard to break strikes has increased in recent times."

It is not on record that Roosevelt ever attempted to use his immense presidential influence and powers to halt or even to protest against governmental armed violence employed against the American workers during the prewar period. There is nothing to show that he ever wanted to halt it except through surrender by the workers to the employers.

The acceleration of war preparations and the heightening of "national defense" propaganda, after the start of the European phase of World War II in September 1939, sparked Roosevelt's more and more open campaign to destroy the right to strike and to establish government control over wages and conditions of employment in private industry.

When WPA relief workers had struck against $15 a week wages in July 1939, Roosevelt had declared that "you cannot strike against the government." During 1940, the Roosevelt administration, acting largely through the National Defense Mediation Board, moved to curb virtually every strike in private industry as a "strike against the government," since there was scarcely a major corporation that did not deal directly or indirectly with the government.

Roosevelt had delivered his dictum that "labor will not attempt to take advantage of its collective power to foment strikes" in May 1940. In April 1941, the month of the big Bethlehem Steel and Ford strikes, the CIO published a pamphlet entitled *The Right to Strike—Keystone of Liberty*. Its conclusions stand in marked contrast not only to Roosevelt's attitude, as indicated even before the war began, but to the CIO leaders' own position a few months later, after the Pearl Harbor events. This pamphlet said in part:

"The right to strike is basic to all workers' rights and to all liberty in the United States. Without this right, labor has no real protection against low wages and living standards. Labor must keep this right in order to remain free, in order to keep and improve standards won over past years of struggle.

"The right to organize and bargain collectively implies the right to strike, since strike action is the only way organized workers have of enforcing collective bargaining. Though collective bargaining is guaranteed by the National Labor Relations Act, employers often refuse to obey the law of the U. S. Strike action is then the only way by which they can be forced to recognize unions and bargain collectively.

"The right to strike... is inherent in all free nations. Yet today this American right is under sharp attack, in Congress, in the press, on the radio. Every day sees new proposals to take away the right to strike or to curb it so severely that its value to workers would be destroyed."

This gives us some idea of the anti-labor drive being whipped up as the Bethlehem and Ford struggles came to a head in the spring of 1941.

As early as January 18, 1939, CIO President Lewis had written to Roosevelt to protest the issuance of government contracts to violators of the Wagner Act and other federal labor laws. He named among others the Bethlehem Steel and Douglas Aircraft corporations. Roosevelt had replied coldly that the government could not require government contractors "to adhere to the letter of the Labor Law." In two subsequent letters to Roosevelt, Lewis pointed out that Bethlehem Steel, Ford Motors and other corporations which had been ruled in violation of the federal labor laws by both federal courts and the National Labor Relations Board, had received more than $13 billion in war contracts. He accused Roosevelt of "business appeasement," of deliberately scheming to aid the anti-union corporations to evade the labor laws in return for their cooperation in accepting war contracts. It must be noted that the corporations were refusing to accept war orders except under conditions which would not interfere with their peacetime business and which would provide guaranteed profits and new plants built by the government.

On August 11, 1940, a Steel Workers Organizing Committee conference in Bethlehem, Pennsylvania, had launched a new campaign to organize ten of the biggest mills and shipyards of the Bethlehem Steel Corporation, largest and key firm among the Little Steel group that had so murderously smashed the 1937 strike. Bethlehem Steel had consistently refused to pay the legal $5 a day minimum wage on government contracts. The SWOC conference declared that failure of the company to bargain collectively with the SWOC "will compel the workers to enforce their rights by economic action" — that is, by strike.

Sidney Hillman, it was suspected at the time, played an important role in delaying and stalling action by the CIO against Bethlehem Steel, Ford Motor and other offending corporations. He had approved a directive of the National Defense Council to enforce the 40-hour week on government contracts — "except in emergencies." Later he agreed to an order requiring union mechanics in army arsenals to work a 48-hour week at straight-time wages, instead of the legal 40 hours.

Several months before the November 1940 presidential elections, SWOC Chairman Philip Murray had told Hillman the union was definitely preparing strike action at Bethlehem Steel. We now know from the testimony of Matthew Josephson, Hillman's semi-official biographer, that Hillman was acting under a direct order from the White House to "soft-pedal" the issue of labor-law compliance by corporations with government contracts. Hillman himself feared any developments, such as strikes against labor law violators, that might embarrass Roosevelt before the elections. He therefore put pressure on Murray, then the CIO vice-president, and Van A. Bittner, then western regional director for SWOC, to hold off the Bethlehem strike at least until after the elections. They did not offer much resistance to Hillman's persuasion.

Eugene Grace, Bethlehem Steel chairman, had announced on October 31, 1940, that his company would not negotiate with the CIO. He declared that Bethlehem Steel did not consider a signed contract a necessary part of collective bargaining.

At about the same time as the SWOC renewed its campaign to organize Bethlehem Steel and secure a contract, the United Automobile Workers convention in St. Louis voted to intensify its Ford drive, which had been launched two and a half years before, at the Milwaukee convention, with a special $1 per capita assessment.

The drive had bogged down badly because of the do-nothing policies of the UAW top leaders. The new UAW President R. J. Thomas was a wishy-washy type, flopping back and forth between the pro-Lewis and the pro-Hillman tendencies. Reuther had definitely joined forces with Hillman and was obstructing militant policies in Ford's, although Reuther and Richard Frankensteen, another UAW vice-president, had suffered fearful beatings at the hands of Ford Service men when the two union officials back in May 1937 had courageously attempted to hand out union leaflets on the Ford overpass into the River Rouge plant.

The Roosevelt administration on November 7, 1940, one day after the elections, announced that Ford had been awarded a War Department contract for more than $123 million worth of aircraft engines. This juicy award to Ford came as 25 UAW members were in jail awaiting hearings on charges arising out of their distribution of union leaflets a week before at the River Rouge plant.

The workers in the open-shop plants were seething with unrest and pressing for action. They were well aware that the corporations were being granted immense war contracts handing them profit increases amounting to hundreds of per cent. At the same time, living costs were steadily climbing as capitalists hoarded necessary supplies, scarcities developed, and prices were pegged higher and higher.

A spark was needed to set the inflammable labor situation alight. This was the 12-day strike of 3,700 UAW members at the Vultee Aircraft plant in Los Angeles. When the Vultee workers went on strike November 15, 1940, for increases above the 50 cents an hour minimum wage and for other benefits, they became the target of a furious redbaiting onslaught. Auto unionists then following the line of the Stalinists were playing an influential role in the UAW on the West Coast. This fact was seized upon for a tremendous campaign by the Stalinophobes and just plain labor-haters to smear the strikers as "communists" and to attempt to smash the strike.

Government agents swooped down on the strikers. The FBI issued a statement charging the strike was "fomented" by "reds" and "subversive elements." The Dies Committee, so called for the Texas Democrat who then headed the House Un-American Activities Committee, began a "probe." Attorney General William Jackson called the strike "communist." Hillman denounced the strike through the Labor Commission of the National Defense Council. The November 23 *New Leader,* organ of the Social Democratic Federation, which voiced the views of right-wing socialists and former socialists from whom the Dubinsky-Reuther types had sprung, headlined its story of the strike: "Reds Cripple Vital Plane Production at Vultee."

But the Vultee strikers had one "small" factor in their favor — the support of the West Coast workers. AFL construction workers employed in building new government-financed Vultee plants laid down their tools. AFL truck drivers refused to go through the CIO picket lines with materials and equipment. AFL waitresses took charge of the strikers' commissary. Local tradesmen and neighboring farmers contributed many tons of food to feed the strikers and their families. After twelve days, the company had to yield and grant, among other concessions, a 12-1/2-cent hourly raise and two weeks' vacation with pay. Immediately, there was a noticeable spurt in organization throughout the aircraft industry and in Ford, Bethlehem and other industrial corporations.

The UAW International Executive Board, which met in the last week of December 1940 in Cleveland, ignored the signs of the time as revealed in part by the Vultee events and shunted aside the big issue of the Ford campaign. The board voted to turn all questions relating to the Ford drive over to a Ford director appointed by the CIO rather than the UAW. In effect, the entire top leadership of the UAW, from Thomas to Reuther, "washed its hands" of the Ford situation, just as they had stood apart from the Vultee struggle.

Despite the inaction of the UAW top leadership and the fact that the CIO Ford director did little more than issue leaflets and urge dependence upon a forthcoming National Labor Relations Board collective bargaining election, the River Rouge and Lincoln plants of Ford Motors were "aflame with unionism" in January 1941, according to the eyewitness report in the January 25 *Socialist Appeal*, predecessor of *The Militant*.

"Thousands upon thousands of men in Ford are now union. Union men under union instructions have entered the hellish gates of the Ford empire wearing union caps and union buttons!...Ford is jittery. He has dished out thousands of dollars for newspaper advertisements and he has tried his best to get public sympathy by blaring about his support of 'National Defense.'

"How different things are now than six months ago. Now the wave of unionism has so engulfed River Rouge that Service men [Ford's private army of thugs] are offering themselves for sale to go to work for the union. They feel the ship will soon change hands.

"There are about 8,000 Service men in Ford. Most of them have criminal records. As befits the petty-larceny criminals they are, they hold no loyalty to Ford...

"Union men now give out leaflets without fear. The plant gates of the Rouge empire are no longer the portals to an impenetrable anti-union hell. When a Service man does dare to attack a union man, many union brothers are ready and able to protect their union brother — and to exact a little revenge for past brutalities. There is enough steam up in the Ford empire among the men to blow the anti-union lid off for all time."

The news that workers dared to openly display union caps and buttons inside the feudal-like Ford empire brought joy to organized and unorganized workers everywhere. For Ford was the very epitome of industrial exploitation and wage slavery. Henry Ford, the founder, had established such a system of speed-up and harassment, enforced by a vast private army who operated much like Nazi storm troopers, that it was said that Ford's made an old man out of a young worker in five years. Men who were even suspected of union sentiments were lucky if they were merely thrown out of the plants and evicted from their homes.

Such were the zeal, militancy and numbers with which the Ford workers flocked to the CIO banner within a few weeks that the attention of the whole labor movement became riveted on the Ford battle. AFL President William Green suddenly revealed an intense interest in the Ford workers. He announced on February 3 that a "majority" of the Ford production workers in the Detroit area "have taken the necessary preliminary steps to become organized into American Federation of Labor unions." The steps were so "preliminary" in fact that the Ford workers hadn't even been aware of them. Brazenly ogling for a sweetheart contract behind the backs of the Ford workers, Green praised the Ford management's labor relations: "None of these [Ford] employees was ever discriminated against by the management of the Ford Motor Company because of membership in the American Federation of Labor."

That same week, however, the War Department, fearful of touching off an explosion by any provocative move, announced that it would not award a $10 million contract to Ford because he had refused to accept the inclusion of a labor clause binding him to respect the labor laws. Of course, a previous $123 million army contract, which had been awarded without such a labor clause, was not withdrawn.

By February 7, 1941, the top UAW leaders had decided to get into the act once more. That day UAW President Thomas, together with CIO Ford Director Michael F. Widman, demanded an immediate conference with Ford Company officials for bargaining purposes. The union leaders' letter asked for the conference "in order to avoid any necessity for a strike." A Ford spokesman informed the public press that "the company will not take the trouble to reply to the union."

Thereafter, the union leadership took no real steps toward mobilizing and preparing the workers for strike action. No mass meetings were called, no broad strike committee established, no strike kitchen set up. Most important of all, they made no effective move to counter the special final weapon Ford planned to use to break a strike — race hatred.

Ford had deliberately and shrewdly established the policy of employing Negro workers at a time when most industries denied them jobs. He set up a special division of personnel for hiring of colored people. In the spring of 1941 some 10,000 Negro workers were employed by Ford, about ten per cent of his labor force. He built the idea with careful publicity that he was a special friend and benefactor of the Negro people. He contributed to Negro church groups and influential individuals. And he sought their support in his war against unionism.

As the union movement swept his plants, Ford even staged a banquet in Detroit for 300 people, invited by Donald J. Marshall, Ford's director of colored personnel. In attendance was "nearly every colored minister in the city who came at special invitation to get the free meal and listen to Marshall's harangue against the CIO," according to the account in the *Pittsburgh Courier,* a Negro publication. "Those Negro ministers in Detroit who have expressed sympathy for the CIO were not invited..."

In his banquet speech Marshall threatened: "The Negro will regret the day if he helps to turn the Ford shop over to the CIO." He meant that if the CIO won, the usefulness of the Negro workers to Ford would be over and he would get rid of them. To emphasize the point one pastor at the banquet moaned: "It will be a sad day for us [the Negro people] if the Ford company changes its policy."

At that time, Horace E. Cayton, co-author of *Black Workers in the New Unions,* wrote two articles in the *Pittsburgh Courier* explaining Ford's game. He told how Ford had tried to buy and tie to himself certain Negro leaders and then described Ford's real attitude toward the Negro workers:

"Ford's policy toward the Negroes, however, is one that had been born of self-interest and has not offered the Negro much except employment. That Ford has hired more Negroes than other companies is a matter of fact. He has done this, however, to provide himself with 'strike insurance.'

"It is the testimony of most persons familiar with the Ford plant that Negroes are definitely limited in their ability to be promoted within the Ford plants and are pretty largely confined to the lower wage income brackets. Likewise, all workers in the Ford plant, including Negro workers, suffered from the speed-up, the possibility of brutal treatment from Ford's service men, and enjoy a wage which is about ten cents an hour below that of workers in other automobile plants."

Cayton concluded that the "CIO has made a desperate effort to break down color barriers and it presents the greatest hope for Negro laborers since the Knights of Labor."

The Ford struggle brought to the fore the issue of anti-Negro discrimination and the need for unity of Negro and white workers in common action against the exploiters of all labor. Out of the Ford, Bethlehem Steel, and other great union battles came a new awareness of the vital contribution that Negro labor can make to the labor movement, and of the necessity for the labor movement to take the lead in the struggle for full equality and civil rights for the Negro people.

But it must be admitted that in the Ford campaign the union leadership did not make a very convincing appeal to the Negro workers. It was mainly the latter's own good sense and feeling of solidarity with the rest of the workers that brought the bulk of the Negro workers into the union fold.

By the first week in March, the struggle inside the Ford plants had become so intense and bitter that the UAW finally filed notice with the Michigan Labor Board of intent to strike the Ford Motor Company. The March 8, 1941 *Militant* reported from Detroit: "The tension is becoming unbearable inside the River Rouge plant. For the past two weeks, union men wearing their union buttons are being physically attacked and slugged by the Service men and quite a few have been sent to the hospital.

"It is not, however, a one-sided battle. In the past week, more and more of the Service men are getting a dose of their own medicine. Today Service men do not dare enter certain departments that are 100% organized."

Daily skirmishes over periods of weeks developed into full-blown departmental sit-down strikes. On March 13, some 3,000 men in one division of River Rouge sat down in protest against the firing of eight union men. Within one hour the formerly cocky and self-confident Harry Bennett, Ford personnel director and head of the Service men, caved in and agreed to rehire the fired men. He said, "It was all a mistake." This was the first strike victory in the history of Ford. But, as for bargaining in good faith in event of a union victory in the impending NLRB poll, Bennett said: "The CIO

will win it [the poll], of course, because it always wins these farcical elections and we will bargain with it because the law says so.
We will bargain till hell freezes over but they won't get anything."

What Bennett was thinking about, in part, was the new government agency that Roosevelt was planning to set up to take over the
power of decision in labor disputes. That very week a joint announcement by Roosevelt, Knudsen, Secretary of Labor Frances
Perkins, and Hillman proclaimed that steps were being taken to set
up a new War Labor Board, such as existed in World War I, to intervene in all labor conflicts and through which the unions would be
required to mediate their demands. The new agency was to be called
the National Defense Mediation Board.

But the Ford workers, with unerring instinct, had begun to rely
only on their own organized power. On March 18, another 6,000
workers sat down in the Axle Building. Their union committee was
invited into management's office and before they left they had secured the reinstatement of 12 fired union men. The next day, the
B Building struck and the company immediately brought back several
fired men to their jobs in a company bus. On March 21, Ford's
representative called in the union committee and agreed to return
more than 1,000 fired unionists to their jobs.

But all Ford's wiles, his millions of dollars of publicity, his
hundreds of millions of dollars of government financing, his thousands of armed goons, the government's no-strike campaign, the
timidity and even treachery of the union leaders could not prevail.
On April 2, 1941, the miracle that many said could never happen,
did happen. The Ford workers took matters into their own hands.
They shut down the Ford empire.

When the real showdown came, Ford's elaborate defenses crum-
bled away. His attempts over the years to form an anti-union bulwark of the doubly exploited Negro workers proved useless. Out of
10,000 Negro workers in Ford, less than 1,500 remained in the
plant. The April 12 *Militant* reported that "thousands" of Negro
workers joined the union right after the start of the strike and "many
are out every day on the picket lines side by side with the white
workers."

The strike was precipitated by Ford himself. He decided he did
not dare to wait any longer because of the union's ever growing
strength and because a CIO victory in the forthcoming NLRB poll
might prove of great moral and propaganda value to the union. Eight
union committeemen were fired. It was apparently the intention to
force either a strike that Ford's Service men would drown in blood
or a union retreat that would cripple the CIO's prestige.

The company refused to meet with a committee of the rolling mill men on the eight fired workers. The rolling mill men began to roll. While federal and state mediators moved into the situation and Ford stubbornly said the eight would never work in his plants again, the workers in the rolling mill and other key River Rouge departments were banding their forces together and marching through the plant to confront the Service men. And they went prepared to defend themselves physically from Ford's storm troopers. They gathered support as they went, closing down department after department. Finally, even the most poorly organized departments joined in. At last, the killing pace of the Ford production line had been slowed to a dead stop. Harry Bennett, his bully boys routed, could only let out a bleat for "state troopers to clear the illegally seized plants." He had found out, when River Rouge was stopped cold, that hell could indeed freeze over.

At 12:15 A.M. Wednesday, April 3, some nine hours after the strike had actually begun, the UAW officers declared the strike was officially on and ordered the workers to evacuate the plants. By the tens of thousands the workers who had been sitting tight marched out in mass, singing "Solidarity Forever."

But the problem remained: Could the strikers prevent the thousands of heavily armed Ford Service men, plus city and state armed forces and possibly federal troops, from herding scabs and strikebreakers into the plant? The entire River Rouge works lay within Dearborn, Ford-ruled municipality. The plant resembled a fortress-island. For a mile along one side of Miller Road was the plant; on the other side, Ford's private parking lots. The situation was similar at the side entrances. Half the workers came to work in their own cars, customarily parked in the Ford lots; the other half came by trolley cars and buses which stopped directly beside overpasses into the Ford plants. The problem was to prevent scabherding and yet avoid direct combat with the Service men and government armed forces, which might result in many dead and wounded. The rank-and-file strike leaders, advised by experienced militants of the General Motors and Toledo strikes, put into effect a previously worked-out strategy.

Vast, impenetrable and immovable barricades of automobiles were set up, blocking off all the main arteries into the Ford fortress. The pickets in their cars even took control of the county-owned drawbridge, thus barring shipment of supplies by water on the River Rouge. Parked bumper to bumper for great distances and surrounded by massed determined pickets at every vital point, the barricades of cars formed an impassable barrier into or out of the plants.

At 6 A.M. Wednesday, Ford's Service men gathered at the gates in full force. They bristled with arms and waited for action. They waited and waited. But no one showed up. Not a single scab. Not even a rat could get through the barricades of cars and strikers.

Only one serious battle took place. About 1,500 of the 10,000 Negro workers, who had been pumped full of anti-union poison for months, had remained in the plants. They attempted three forays out of the plants against the mass picket lines, but were beaten back each time. Thirty-six pickets were injured, but the strikers considered it a small price to pay for the satisfaction they felt when the whistle blew. River Rouge, biggest plant in the world and hell-hole of the auto industry, lay silent and dead.

From union locals scores and even hundreds of miles away members rushed to the Ford barricades. All the equipment of other auto locals was thrown into the battle — loudspeakers and sound-cars, mimeograph machines, cooking utensils for the strike kitchens. The misled men in the plants could get no food or fresh bedding. The blare of the loudspeakers, the singing of the pickets kept them from sleep.

The UAW-CIO took complete control and was the sole policing force of a ten-square-mile area surrounding the River Rouge plant in Dearborn. UAW pickets, wearing their overseas-type caps, directed traffic. It was probably the most orderly and disciplined area in the whole history of Michigan.

On April 7, sixth day of the strike, the Ford Motor Company meekly agreed to a "truce" providing that the company would not operate the plant during negotiations, and the union would open the road barriers to allow the resumption of traffic.

In the meantime, Philip Murray and other CIO officials, anxious to end the strike on almost any terms, had been holding feverish conferences with Governor Van Wagoner, federal and state "mediators" and Ford officials. The top UAW officials agreed right at the start to give away half the original demands of the Ford workers. The NLRB in Washington scheduled an election in 45 days instead of the original 60 days. At a huge mass meeting on April 14, with the top CIO and UAW leadership hammering away at the ranks, a narrow majority was secured to end the strike without a formal signed contract, but with negotiations to proceed between the union and company and no discrimination against strikers.

On May 22, the UAW-CIO swept to victory in an NLRB election with a more than 70 per cent majority. Within a month, the Ford Motor Company signed the first *union shop* agreement in the automotive industry. Not only did Ford recognize the union — he recognized that every worker employed in his plants would have to join the union.

The battle of Bethlehem Steel coincided with that of Ford. As more than a billion dollars in government contracts poured into Bethlehem's vaults, the workers in its plants all over the country became increasingly incensed. Corporation executives everywhere were voting themselves bigger and bigger salaries, bonuses, and stock awards. Eugene Grace, head of Bethlehem Steel, stood right at the top of the heap.

Then, in a 38-hour strike at the large Lackawanna, New York plant, some 13,000 steelworkers in the last week of February won the first real union victory in the fifty-odd years' history of the Bethlehem corporation. When more than a thousand unionists were fired in a company attempt to intimidate the rest of the men, a walkout was called, beginning at 9 P.M., February 26.

The company began sending cars through the picket line with "superintendents" and "assistant superintendents." When the ninth "assistant superintendent" started to drive through, the massed pickets got tough and said enough "superintendents" were already in to run an empty plant. Members of 65 CIO local unions as well as many AFL members joined the picket lines.

At the Buffalo gate of the plant, a total mobilization of Buffalo city police appeared in the morning. An all-day battle took place with police and scabs trying to smash through the massed pickets and the steel strikers blocking them with hundreds of bodies. By the end of the day, despite all possible reinforcements, the police were exhausted. It was demonstrated that a lot more endurance is gained handling steel ten hours a day than by walking a beat and twirling a club.

By the second morning, Grace gave in and agreed to reinstate the thousand men who had been given "indefinite suspensions." He also agreed that management would meet with the union committee to negotiate and settle grievances — something which the company had sworn it would never do. Not only was this the first time Bethlehem Steel yielded to a strike; it was the first strike victory in any major plant of the steel industry. The U. S. Steel contract in 1937 had been negotiated without a strike and the Little Steel strike of the same year had been smashed. It was this first victory that gave heart to the rest of the 80,000 Bethlehem Steel workers for the more decisive struggle soon to come.

Particularly noteworthy was the role of the Negro workers in the Lackawanna strike. "No group played a more commendable role than the Negro workers," reported the March 8, 1941 *Militant*

from Buffalo. "The lowest paid and the most oppressed of the Bethlehem workers, the Negro workers gave an unexampled demonstration of union courage and fighting qualities. Negro workers were
in the forefront of every battle on the picket lines." Undoubtedly,
their example helped to influence the Negro workers at River Rouge
in the Ford strike a few weeks later.

On March 25, 1941, the parent plant of Bethlehem Steel at Bethlehem, Pa., was shut down, with 19,000 of the 21,000 employees
responding to the official strike call. This strike was forced on the
union when the company sought to hold a company union election on
its property. The company had announced a move to bolster its
"Employes' Representation Plan" in order to roll back the CIO tide
that was sweeping over its vast domain. This move was particularly
provocative because the National Labor Relations Board nine months
previously had ordered Bethlehem Steel to dissolve its company
union. A week before the strike flag-draped ballot boxes had been
placed in all departments of the many mills of the company-dominated nine miles of the Bethlehem Valley.

At the Lackawanna plant, after their two-day strike, the workers
had disposed of the company union election quite simply. The local
SWOC leaders asked management who owned the ballot boxes. Not
wishing to admit openly that this was a company-sponsored election,
the company spokesman said the ballot boxes "belong to the men."
"OK," replied the committee, "If they belong to the men, the men
don't want them and wish to do away with them." In a short time,
the workers in every department reduced the booths and ballot
boxes to kindling wood.

But the key to a definitive victory over Bethlehem Steel lay in
the parent plant. A sizable section of the workers in this plant were
on the fence, sympathetic to the union but waiting to see if it would
act decisively before they "stuck their necks out."

When the company forced the issue by preparing to hold a company-union election, the SWOC leadership had no choice but to prevent the election through strike or to retreat into certain defeat.
The strike, when it was finally called, was so strongly and enthusi-
astically supported that it swept into the union fold most of the on-
the-fence elements.

The first night of the strike there was no disorder. Massed in
the thousands, the workers, with their wives and children out to
support them, discouraged the few scabs who attempted to enter
the plant. Nobody was hurt. A few hundred scabs had remained in
the plant to give a semblance of activity inside the plant in order to
discourage the strikers. The scabs were working 16 hours a day.

Within three to four days, the ambulances were clanging into the plant frequently to remove strikebreakers who had collapsed from physical exhaustion and lack of proper food and sleep.

Meanwhile the forces of "law and order" had been mobilizing. These included not only the plant guards, city, county, and state police, but a force dressed in the uniforms of the dreaded Pennsylvania "Cossacks," the infamous coal and iron police, a special body that had been recruited for strikebreaking purposes from professional thugs and criminals of the Pittsburgh, Philadelphia, and other large city underworlds. For decades this force had spread terror and murder in the Pennsylvania coal and steel towns during strikes.

Since the company held options on all available meeting halls in the vicinity of the mills, the strikers were forced to meet at a hall several miles away. On the second night of the strike, while most of the workers were away at a special union meeting, the State Mounted Police and the coal and iron police launched a full-scale attack on the thinned picket lines. There were about a thousand people, many of them children and women with babies in their arms, standing in front of the main gate, with the floodlights on them.

A squad of mounted police rode out of the gates and without warning charged into the unsuspecting crowd. A large force of police on foot, armed with 30-inch riot sticks, rushed behind the mounted police into the crowd. Women and children were knocked down and clubbed. The crowd broke and ran. The police chased them up side streets.

On one side street mounted police encountered a group of women on the porches of a row of frame houses. When the women jeered the police, they rode their horses onto the sidewalks along the porches, clubbing the women and driving them into their homes.

News of the assault finally reached the strike meeting. The sentiment of the workers was overwhelmingly for rushing to the picket line in a body and taking on the coal and iron cops. But top SWOC leaders argued for caution and persuaded the strikers to discontinue the picket lines, at least temporarily. Until the next afternoon there were no picket lines. Had the company been able to mobilize an army of scabs quickly enough, the strike might have been smashed right then and there.

John Riffe, SWOC representative, had told the strikers that certain unnamed government officials asked him to withdraw the pickets and had assured him the government would make the company come to terms. On the very day of the assault, however, the government had awarded another $75,000,000 war order to Bethlehem and subsequently didn't lift a finger to enforce the NLRB order to disband the company union.

The strikers did not stay inactive long. They issued an ultimatum to the police that if they were not permitted to picket they would fight for the right. Confronted by this ultimatum, backed by thousands of tough steelworkers just aching to teach the uniformed thugs a lesson, the police backed down and agreed to "limited" picketing. Riffe once more advised "caution" and told the workers to set up "token" picket lines of ten or a dozen men before each gate. The workers complied for a few hours but gradually the lines began building up to mass strength again. Meanwhile, directly across the street from the main gate, an "unofficial" picket line of hundreds and at times thousands of workers formed and kept a 24-hour vigil. (I walked that picket line accompanied by Ruth Querio, a veteran of the Unemployed Leagues who had helped organize unemployed workers in the Allentown-Bethlehem area during the Thirties. Hundreds of Bethlehem steelworkers had first learned about mass labor action through the Unemployed Leagues.) That night the company agreed to meet the union committee.

Next morning, at a huge overflow mass meeting, with thousands of workers unable to jam into the hall, the company's terms were announced. Bethlehem Steel agreed not to recognize the company union as the sole bargaining agent, and to recognize the SWOC as the sole bargaining agent for its members, with the right to post union bulletins in the plant and to establish union grievance machinery.

After a heated debate, the strikers accepted these terms, although they had originally asked for increases above the 42-1/2-cent hourly minimum wage, sole collective bargaining rights and an end to the man-killing speed-up. When they reached their decision, the strikers poured out of the meeting hall and formed a victory parade, marching 12 miles through the city of Bethlehem that had just ceased to be a company town.

The author marched in that parade that day, reporting it in the April 5, 1941 *Militant*. I described the jubilation, the feeling of real liberation that building a union and winning a strike meant in an open-shop town like Bethlehem in those days.

"'It's bigger than the day they signed the Armistice,' an exultant steel striker behind me exclaims...

"Not until this moment have these Bethlehem Steel workers fully understood what the union is, what it represents, its size, its solidity, its power...

"Now, when the parade swings forward, they see the UNION as

it really is. They see it whole, its numbers, its dynamic power in action, stretched forward and behind as far as the eye can see.

"'God Almighty!' the worker beside me breathes one final exclamation to the world in general. 'Bethlehem ain't never seen a crowd this big before.'...

"We are marching uphill. The head of the line appears six blocks in the distance, rising over the crest of the company's toll bridge, with its sign, 'One Cent for Pedestrians. Three Cents for Motor Vehicles.'

"Day in and day out the workers who have entered the realm of Bethlehem Steel over this little bridge have given their offerings to the power and greed of the corporation. Millions of pennies have paid for the bridge ten times over.

"No pennies today! Over the bridge the parade rolls in a solid stream. Ten thousand marchers and not one penny. 'Let 'em try and collect their goddam penny today!' A symbol of industrial servitude is ground into dust under 20,000 feet crossing a small bridge...

"A head in front of me jerks sideways and upwards. A huge fist waves high in the air. 'Hide, you rats, you dirty scabs! Go on, hide! We can smell you from here.'

"I look where the fist is pointed. I see three pairs of eyes, wide open, scared, staring over a third floor window ledge of a plant building. 'It'll be a miserable thing for those scabs when this bunch gets back in the plant,' a short, middle-aged Hungarian worker says, almost in half-pity. Another marcher answers with a loud burbling lip-sound, scornful and merciless."

It was a beautiful spring for labor, that spring of 1941.

That same April which saw the Ford and Bethlehem Steel citadels fall before the CIO onslaught, also witnessed a strike of 400,000 Appalachian soft-coal miners for a dollar a day wage increase and paid vacations. John L. Lewis bluntly refused to accept the "mediation" of Roosevelt's new National Defense Mediation Board and to approve work without a contract. The mine owners, unable to use the government machinery for stalling strikes and wage demands, were forced to give in. The miners, always a model of union solidarity and discipline in a struggle, won wage increases of from 16 to 22 per cent, paid vacations for the first time and equal wage boosts for Southern and Northern miners.

In the course of this fight, Lewis issued a blistering attack on Roosevelt's new Mediation Board, stating: "We are not going to follow this new formula that seems to have been discovered by the Mediation Board in Washington when they wire strikers to go back to work and bust their strike, and then come back to Washington to

mediate for remnants of it. The United Mine Workers of America
do not mediate that way, and this present stoppage will not be settled that way."

By the end of April, both the Big Steel and Little Steel corporations had announced ten-cent hourly wage increases for 603,000 steel
workers. The coal miners mopped up all remnants of resistance,
except in the South, to their wage demands and got signed contracts.
By the end of May, an "unauthorized" strike of 40,000 General
Motors workers in Flint, Detroit and Saginaw had won a general
wage boost of ten cents an hour, previously approved by the Mediation Board but which the company had refused to grant. More than
1,500,000 CIO workers, aided by the powerful strike thrusts of the
Ford, Bethlehem Steel, and mine workers, won wage increases.

In good part, these gains were won despite the union leaders,
who were already enmeshed in the war machinery and strikebreaking
apparatus of the government. These victories once again revealed
the potency of industrial unionism and the power of the workers in
independent organized mass action that relied neither on maneuvers
of the top union leaders nor on "friends of labor" in the government.

12

Roosevelt—
Open Strikebreaker

Throughout most of the "New Deal" Thirties, the Roosevelt administration had been careful to avoid open and direct intervention against strikes. To be sure, the federally financed National Guard, then at the disposal of the various state governors, was used many times against strikers, but Roosevelt himself managed to stay clear and play the part of a "mediator" and a "neutral."

After the 1940 election, Roosevelt no longer kept up the pretense of neutrality. His administration and agencies directly intervened in most strikes. At first this intervention took the form of appeals to the strikers to end their walkouts, without satisfaction of their demands and grievances. Concentrated government pressure was put on strike leaders. Statements by public officials and agencies were used in an effort to arouse public hostility to strikes and to encourage harsh newspaper attacks on strikers.

The administration was cautious at first not to express too open hostility to strikes that had the formal backing of the top union officials, such as the Ford and Bethlehem Steel battles. But as early as the Vultee strike in November 1940, the Roosevelt administration dared to take open direct action. The formula in the Vultee strike was a "red" scare with FBI and congressional "probes," plus denunciation of the strike by the administration as a "blow to National Defense." Stage by stage, Roosevelt's strikebreaking went from redbaiting and intimidation, to direct orders to strikers to go back to work, to the use of federal armed forces to smash picket lines.

Two strikes about which little is heard in labor circles today, but which evoked screaming national headlines in 1941, provided the occasions for the Roosevelt administration to open its direct strikebreaking program. In both cases, it must be noted, the strikes were alleged to be led by Communists and were opposed or un-supported by top union officials. The first was the 75-day Allis-Chalmers strike early in 1941. The second was the North American Aviation strike in June.

The strike of UAW-CIO Local 248 at the Allis-Chalmers Manu-facturing Company plant in West Allis, Wisconsin, began on Janu-ary 22 as a protest against systematic company moves to weaken and break the union. Although the UAW had a contract, the manage-ment was infiltrating the workers' ranks with pro-company elements and encouraging attempts to organize an AFL local in competition with the CIO. Anti-UAW elements were interfering with the recog-nized union's activity, picking fights with UAW members and gen-erally taking the company's part on issues arising in the plant. When the UAW local asked that these pro-company elements be disciplined or removed, the company refused and intensified its anti-union activity. The strike resulted.

The response to the strike call was overwhelming. In a plant of 7,500 workers, as many as 5,000 marched on the mass picket lines. After four weeks of an effective strike, with no hint of a break in the union ranks, the Office of Production Management, a new Roose-velt-appointed agency with Knudsen and Hillman as co-directors, intervened. On March 1, the OPM co-directors called union and company representatives to Washington. There Knudsen and Hillman proposed arbitration, with agreement by the company to carry out the union's demand if it was found that the union's charge of com-pany anti-union activity was correct. The union promptly accepted the arbitration offer. The company rejected it.

This fact, however, did not incline the government toward a sympathetic attitude to the workers. Instead, having some inti-mation that the Allis-Chalmers workers could expect little or no support from the UAW leaders and apprised that some of the Local 248 leaders were under attack as Communists, the government launched an offensive against the strikers.

First came threats. On March 21, the press reported that the War and Navy departments were "seriously considering" taking over the struck plant. While the company would receive "full re-muneration" for the use of its plants, a government spokesman said that work "would be carried forward with workers taken from civil service lists." *(New York Times, March 22.)* This meant that strikers would lose their jobs.

When the threat failed to intimidate the strikers, the Roosevelt administration decided on the then unprecedented step of ordering the privately-employed strikers back to work. Roosevelt first hid himself on his yacht and Hillman took a convenient vacation, in case the move should backfire. OPM Director Knudsen and Navy Secretary Frank Knox on March 26 wired the company: "We must ask you to notify your entire force to return to work." A copy was sent to the union with the addition: "We expect your full cooperation in carrying out the above program."

The anti-labor atmosphere at this time can be sensed from a couple of samples of press and Congressional comments. In an editorial entitled "Breaking a Strike," the March 27 *Washington Post* wrote: "Summoning courage which has heretofore been lacking, Secretary Knox and OPM Director Knudsen yesterday ordered the company to reopen its plant and proceed with work. This is the most favorable piece of news that has come out of the strike situation in recent months. In effect, Messrs. Knox and Knudsen have undertaken to break a strike."

Chairman Sumners of the important House Judiciary Committee said in a committee session that he would not hesitate "a split second" to pass a law to send strikers "to the electric chair." Secretary of War Stimson and Undersecretary Patterson called a special press conference to announce their endorsement of the Knox-Knudsen telegrams. The company sent a notice to every worker individually that it was starting "full resumption" of operation on March 28 "in compliance with the United States government's wires to us and to the union." City and county police agencies announced full mobilizations "to protect workers entering the plant."

Local 248 responded with a huge mass meeting that made plain no worker would re-enter the plant until a satisfactory union settlement was made. By this time, realizing that the very life of the union was at stake, officials of the UAW regional office in Milwaukee issued a statement backing the strikers. CIO President Murray felt impelled to demand in a wire to Knudsen: "By what power are you and Secretary Knox authorized to issue ultimatum... Why do you not insist upon compliance [by the company] with your original proposal?"

The various Washington officials were reported astounded by Murray's statement. "Defense officials were taken aback by the vehemence of Mr. Murray's challenge," said Louis Stark in the March 28 *New York Times*. Knudsen and Knox replied to Murray: "You were familiar with our proposal to issue an appeal to the workers to return to work and negotiate while the plant was in operation."

Now faced with opposition from the top CIO and UAW leaders as well as the strikers, the administration officials beat a retreat and denied they had issued any ultimatum to the strikers. They then

asserted that "the original strike vote had been obtained by fraudulent means." The March 30 *New York Times* reported, however, that
"more than 5,000 UAW workers... voted today at a mass meeting
to persist with their strike at the Allis-Chalmers Company plant,
hooting down appeals of government officials..." There evidently
was no fraud about the workers' desire to continue the strike.

Inspired by the Roosevelt administration's strikebreaking intervention, the local police on March 31 made a violent assault on the
Allis-Chalmers picket line. For the first time in American labor
history, an armored car manned by police firing tear gas bombs
through slits in the steel plates smashed through a picket line of
3,000 workers. Many were sickened and injured, but the line closed
up and picketing went on.

In the meantime state militia had been sent to the scene. The
workers, however, could not be driven back to work at bayonet
point. After three days Governor Heil withdrew his troops and ordered the plant shut.

On April 7, after 75 days, the union voted to end the strike when
the company agreed to accept the terms the union would have settled for at the beginning. The agreement provided a "maintenance
of membership" clause—a watered-down version of the union shop
—which guaranteed the membership status as of the time of signing
the contract.

Just two months later Roosevelt moved into the most open and
violent phase of his anti-strike program. This was his use of federal troops to smash the picket lines of peaceful strikers at the
North American Aviation plant in Inglewood, California.

Looking back, it seems incredible that the workers had not struck
long before. The UAW-CIO had gone through a prolonged NLRB
election procedure, first winning a plurality and then, in a run-off
against the AFL on March 13, 1941, gaining an outright majority.

North American's minimum wage was 40 cents an hour, ten cents
less than an unskilled laborer's relief wage on WPA. It was far below
the subsistence standard of living computed by government agencies
and lower than the average of all Southern California aircraft plants.

When the company finally agreed to open negotiations on April 16,
the workers asked for a 75-cent hourly minimum and ten cents an
hour more for all workers. In 1940, even before receiving huge
government war orders, the company had made a net profit of $855
for every worker in its employ. But when the union made its wage
demand, North American's President J. H. Kindleberger scoffed:
"I don't have to pay any more to my workers because most of them
are young kids who spend their money on a flivver and a gal."

After being stalled for five weeks with this kind of talk, the union membership on May 23 voted for strike. The issue then went to the National Defense Mediation Board. The workers stayed on the job 13 days past their strike deadline. When it became clear that the NDMB intended to stall indefinitely, the 12,000 North American workers struck on June 5.

The NDMB turned the case over to the White House. Roosevelt acted with dispatch. He ordered the workers to end their strike and announced he was sending U. S. troops to be on hand Monday morning, June 9, to open the plant in the interests of the "national emergency." Why he did not order the company to pay decent wages as a means of ending this "threat" to the "national emergency" the President did not say.

Roosevelt acted with confidence because he felt he had the backing of high CIO and UAW officials. In speaking of those who were at the President's side when he signed the order for the troops to smash the strike, Roosevelt's secretary, Stephen Early, spoke of "Mr. Hillman and the others." Hillman—that was a name to conjure with. It was a "Labor" seal of approval.

After the strike was broken, at a meeting of 250 CIO executives in Washington on July 7, Lewis denounced Hillman as a "traitor" who was "standing at Roosevelt's elbow when he signed the order to send troops to stab labor in the back..."

On the very day the strike was called, the UAW international union officials dispatched Richard Frankensteen to the strike scene. That same night, without consulting the strike committee, he broadcast a denunciation of the strike over a national radio hookup.

On Sunday night, June 8, a meeting of 10,000 workers massed outside the plant. The local strike leaders revealed that Frankensteen himself had conferred with the local union committee when the strike date had been originally set, had urged them to fight for the 75-cent minimum wage demand, and had actually suggested the strike date, pledging the full support of the international union. When he spoke to the mass meeting, ordering the workers back to work and waving a telegram from Philip Murray condemning the strike, he was hooted down and forced to retire.

The next morning the embittered workers massed at the plant. There to meet them was the first large contingent of what was to grow by nightfall into an army of 3,500 federal troops. Thus, the United States government waged its first military engagement of World War II on American soil against American workers resisting hunger wages.

Roosevelt did not send inexperienced draftees to Inglewood. He sent professional soldiers of the 15th Infantry, described by the June 10 *New York Daily News* as "composed of bronzed veterans recently returned from long service in the Orient. To even get into the 15th, a soldier has to have seen previous Army service..."

The events of that "day of infamy," June 9, 1941, are preserved in the graphic eyewitness report by Bill Morgan in the June 14, 1941 *Militant*. Here is how he described "Operation North American":

"When the troops marched in yesterday morning, the strikers were lined up 6,000 strong around the plant. As army trucks filled with armed soldiers, their steel bayonets glistening in the hot sun, first rolled up the road, some of the younger and less experienced workers cheered. The older workers smiled grimly. The soldiers didn't return any greetings. They looked straight ahead.

"Then the troops formed ranks, bayonets thrust forward, and began to deploy toward the line of pickets. Machine guns were quickly placed at strategic spots, their deadly nozzles bearing directly on the mass of workers.

"'Move on!' came the grunted command. No worker cheered now. They began a reluctant retreat, giving ground slowly, a step at a time.

"Suddenly a bayonet flashed and there came a sharp cry. Carl Clemment, one of the pickets, had been stabbed in the thigh for not moving fast enough.

"The troops moved ruthlessly. They drove the workers back with blows from their rifle butts. Cries broke out from the workers' ranks. 'Heil Roosevelt!'"

By nightfall, the troops, armed with trench mortars, anti-tank guns, machine guns, automatic rifles, and two anti-aircraft guns, had cleared a mile-wide area around the plant and established martial law.

The next day, on advice of the local strike leaders, the workers yielded to overwhelming armed force and agreed to return to work. As acts of reprisal, the troops at the gates excluded some leading militants. The UAW international officials struck the final blow: they suspended the local union officers.

Although the breaking of the North American Aviation strike was formally labeled a plant "seizure," the leading voices of American capitalism jubilantly hailed Roosevelt's action. There was no fear for "property rights" or profits. Secretary of War Stimson himself allayed concern, telling the press:

"J. H. Kindleberger [North American's president] has a good reputation with the government... There are not enough like him. We do not want to do injury to such a man. You may draw your own inference from this."

The June 10 *New York Times* reported that "the strong action of Mr. Roosevelt had the wholehearted support of Wall Street." The *Wall Street Journal* of the same day said: "The Government's firm stand in the North American Aviation strike... produced a strong final hour on the New York Stock Exchange. The War Department's statement that the strike had been 'broken open'... had decidedly favorable implications."

A question about which press and President alike maintained near-total silence was the legality of Roosevelt's action. On this, the June 11 *New York Herald Tribune* lifted one corner of the veil: "A guffaw swept the press conference as a reporter asked the Chief Executive: 'Mr. President, do you have any comment on specific legislation empowering you to do what you did yesterday in the North American case?'"

But not everyone thought the illegal use of American troops against American workers exercising their right to strike was amusing. Indeed, the American workers were appalled and the instantaneous outcry that swelled from local union ranks all over the nation came as a sharp rebuke to the President and to the CIO and UAW officials who had countenanced and, in the case of elements like Hillman and Frankensteen, even approved the use of troops.

Murray sensed the feeling of popular outrage. Although he had urged the North American workers to comply with Roosevelt's order to end their strike, he had to issue a statement denouncing use of the troops to break the strike:

"The injection of armed forces of the nation into a private industrial dispute must also be condemned. Such action can only serve to create a status of enforced labor in this nation, and enforced labor can only create bitterness on the part of the working people."

At the same time, Murray defended the demands of the workers and the right to strike and attacked the usurpation of compulsory powers by the NDMB. He said:

"At the present time the rising corporate profits and the increasing cost of living of the working people amply justify the demands of the workers... the workers must continue to enjoy their fundamental right to strike. This right cannot and must not be impaired by government officials or legislative action. No mediation board... should usurp or be given authority to impose compulsory arbitration or to interfere in any way with the basic rights of labor."

But Murray carefully refrained from mentioning the author of the actions and policies he condemned. He did not refer to Roosevelt either by name or office. He deplored sin and shielded the sinner.

No such schism existed where John L. Lewis was concerned—

and his voice was still potent in the CIO. He was still chairman of Labor's Non-Partisan League, which had served since 1936 as a political vehicle for the CIO. The LNPL statement on the North American events — on the administration's simultaneous threat to draft strikers into the army and its moves to inspire anti-strike legislation — did not defer to Roosevelt.

Calling the series of events of the week of June 9 "the blackest in American labor history" (it surely seemed so at the time to many unionists), the LNPL on June 16 stated: "Responsibility for the wholesale sacrifice of fundamental principles of government labor policy must be pinned squarely on the Roosevelt administration.

"In a virtual tidal wave of reaction the administration sponsored legislation advances far along the totalitarian path of forced labor. It embraced compulsory arbitration, perverted the conscription act into a strikebreaking weapon, deserted the unemployed, accepted a blanket condemnation of strikes and, finally, ordered federal troops with drawn bayonets on strikebreaking duty."

But Lewis offered no remedy for what the LNPL statement called "the most severe crisis in the history of the modern American labor movement." He had no independent class position and could only flounder around in the field of political action.

The issues involved in the Allis-Chalmers and North American strikes dominated the stormy 1941 convention of the United Automobile Workers which opened on August 4 in Buffalo.

The right wing, pro-war Hillman tendency, led by Reuther, had a clear-cut position. It was out to execute a factional power-play to undercut the Stalinist elements and also, by raising the "communist" issue, to smear the genuine rank-and-file militants who dared to strike amidst the war preparations and without "authorization" of the UAW tops.

The great majority of the UAW delegates were imbued with its tradition of militancy and union democracy, but they lacked a clear program and firm leadership. The chief spokesman for the opposition to the right wing was George Addes. He had risen from the ranks in the 1934 Toledo Auto-Lite strike and wielded considerable influence as UAW secretary-treasurer of long standing. He was associated with the Lewis tendency which opposed government intervention in the unions. But he was very weak in his anti-war position—the war question underlay the whole struggle in the UAW and was decisive in determining its outcome.

Those most directly under attack by the UAW right wing as a result of the Allis-Chalmers and North American strikes were the followers of the Communist Party line. Far from wanting to defend these or any other strikes, or to associate themselves with Lewis's opposition to government interference, the Stalinists were now trying to crawl into the Hillman camp. They were already voicing the most extreme pro-war and anti-strike propaganda.

The Communist Party had long before abandoned any struggle for socialism. Since 1935 it had advanced the concept of class collaboration in the form of the Peoples Front of working class and "progressive" capitalist organizations. Then, in August 1939, Stalin and Hitler had signed their "non-aggression" pact, which Stalin boasted "has all grounds to be prolonged and stable." This "prolonged and stable" friendship lasted 22 months, until June 22, 1941, the day Hitler's armies invaded the Soviet Union. That was just 11 days after the termination of the North American strike.

During the 22 months of the Stalin-Hitler pact, the American Communist Party adopted a type of pseudo-militancy. After five years of open and ardent support of the Roosevelt administration, the Stalinists temporarily assumed the posture of opposition. This opposition was principally a verbal one. Contrary to the propaganda put out by the reactionary press, radio, government spokesmen, and union right-wingers, the Stalinists in the unions during this period played an essentially conservative role.

In the year 1941, there were 4,288 strikes, involving 2,363,000 workers, compared to the 4,740 strikes and 1,861,000 workers who struck during the explosive year of 1937. These 1941 strikes involved huge war corporations and industries, including Ford, Bethlehem Steel, General Motors, and the whole coal industry. Far from having to "foment" strikes, the heads of Stalinist-led unions could no more prevent the workers from striking against 40-cent wage scales than the old-line conservative union bureaucrats could hold back the more than 2-1/4 million workers who hit the picket lines in "authorized" strikes. More workers went on strike in 1941 than in any previous year in American history except 1919, and the relatively small strikes the Stalinists are given credit for leading were just a few trickles feeding the flood.

The Communist Party took a stand before June 22 in favor of the Lewis tendency as against Hillman's. A CP document, published in the May 9, 1941 *Daily Worker,* had stated: "The issue is the Lewis program of winning increases versus the Hillman program of sacrifices." It must be noted that the Stalinists in pushing "the Lewis program" went all-out in uncritical praise of the UMW leader and never advanced an independent class position.

On June 17, less than a week after Roosevelt smashed the North American strike but five days before Hitler's invasion of the Soviet

Union, William Z. Foster, the National Chairman of the American Communist Party, charged in the *Daily Worker:*

"...When President Roosevelt sent federal troops against the aviation workers and broke their strike, it was a taste of the Hitleristic terrorism that Wall Street capitalists have in mind for the working class. These war-mongering imperialists, who dominate the Roosevelt administration, are determined to compel the workers to accept lowered standards of living and restricted civil liberties, as part of their bigger plans to force the unwilling American people into a 'shooting' war...Organized labor...should realize that an Administration which commits such a monstrous act is an enemy of the workers and cannot be supported by them..."

Six weeks after the statement by Foster, UAW President R. J. Thomas, a strong-voiced man of weakly held views, was able to taunt the Stalinist elements at the UAW convention on their own rabid warmongering:

"I was called a war-monger by certain people [the Stalinists] a few months ago when I advocated material aid to Britain. Today, we can hear these same people wanting to go much further than I want to go today. I predict that these same people will be advocating we go to war. I still say we should keep ourselves on record as against any foreign adventures."

Although Thomas himself advocated going to war at the same time the Stalinists did—when Roosevelt said so—he did put his finger on the factor that determined the outcome of the 1941 UAW convention battles over the Allis-Chalmers and North American strikes: the complete capitulation of the Stalinists to the war program of American imperialism.

No sooner had the convention opened than a minority on the Credentials Committee reported that an attempt was being made to refuse to seat the delegates from the Allis-Chalmers local. The technical grounds were that the Local 248 members had nominated and elected delegates at the same meeting, contrary to the constitutional provisions. A motion to seat the Allis-Chalmers delegates immediately was sidetracked by a motion to refer the matter to the Credentials Committee which, it was claimed, had not yet made a final recommendation on the matter.

The next day, the confused delegates voted about 1,700 to 1,200 for a recommendation to refuse seating the ten Allis-Chalmers delegates. Reuther led the attack with a tirade against communists. Other top leaders followed. Addes alone opposed the move. But, most significantly, the leaders of the Stalinist faction made only the most feeble gestures on behalf of the Allis-Chalmers workers.

The debate over the North American Aviation strike revolved around three reports from the convention Grievance Committee: a majority report backed by Reuther; a minority report backed by extreme right-wing supporters of Frankensteen; and a "super-minority" report (so called because it was reported out of committee by a single individual) supported by Addes. All three reports proposed degrees of punishment for Lew Michener, California regional director and International Executive Board member, who was being made the scapegoat for the alleged crime of the North American strike.

Reuther's majority report called for barring Michener from holding any office, elective or appointive, for one year. The minority right-wing report proposed expulsion of Michener and the barring of all union representatives who opposed Frankensteen's strikebreaking from all elective or appointive posts for five years.

The "super-minority" report, which made no criticism of Frankensteen's strikebreaking and his support of the use of troops, was a product of an unprincipled deal between Addes and Frankensteen for practical electioneering purposes. (Hasty deals and factional shuffles were constant within the UAW leadership; principles and program were subordinated to power politics.)

It was left for rank-and-file delegates to bring out the real issue. One Fisher Body delegate from Flint said: "I am not so sure the California boys were wrong or made a mistake. They went out on a justified strike. You talk about unauthorized strikes. Why wasn't it authorized? In Flint in 1937 we built this union with unauthorized strikes. The Ford workers went out on an unauthorized strike... that's how they built their union."

Among the Stalinist—minded delegates there was considerable confusion. Those closest to the ranks and particularly to the locals under attack, felt the necessity of making some kind of defense of the denounced strikes. But the recognized national floor leaders of the Stalinist faction remained silent when the North American workers were under fire. They accepted Addes's deal with Frankensteen whereby Michener, who was closely associated with the Stalinist policy, was barred from the International Executive Board for one year and the North American strike branded a "mistake."

Indeed, one North American delegate, Jack Montgomery, who was known to hold the Stalinist line, actually pleaded with tears in his voice: "All right, we made a mistake. But by God, boys, give us a break."

The final vote on the three resolutions found the "super-minority" report, which laid down the least severe penalty, winning by a slim majority of 97 votes. The Reutherite majority report and the extreme right-wing "minority" report split the remaining votes.

The convention wound up by adopting a Reuther-sponsored constitutional amendment barring from elective or appointive office anyone "who is a member of or subservient to any political organization, such as Communist, Nazi or Fascist which owes its allegiance to any foreign government." The reference to "Nazi or Fascist" was intended as a smear, to link the American Stalinists, who were pro-union, to the most extreme capitalist reaction, fascism, whose aim is to smash all unions. This amendment was significant as the first infringement on the basic democratic principles originally written into the UAW constitution, which provided equal rights of membership for all workers covered by the UAW charter regardless of race, creed, nationality, religion, or political views.

Instead of fighting the Reuther amendment on principled grounds, the Addes group proposed to add "Socialist" to the list of proscribed political views. This was thought to be a clever flank attack on Reuther who, in any event, had resigned from the Socialist Party three years before. Despite the confusion compounded by Addes, a sizable vote of 1,062 was registered against the anti-democratic amendment with 1,968 in favor.

The triumph of the Hillman-Reuther forces testified to the tremendous outside pressure of super-patriotic pro-war propaganda and to the treachery of the Communist Party whose flip-flop helped disorient many militants.

13

The Fight against
the National Defense
Mediation Board

In order to enforce a no-strike policy, the Roosevelt administration had to proffer the unions some substitute means which could be represented as a court of appeals for workers' grievances. The National Defense Mediation Board was rigged up as that agency.

The plan for this tri-partite board, composed of four labor, four employer and three "public" representatives, has been attributed to Hillman, who wanted to have labor disputes handled separately from the agency of war production mobilization. This plan was a virtual duplicate of the War Labor Board which had served the corporations so well during World War I. Hillman projected his plan in anticipation of the Ford and Bethlehem Steel strikes which he had hoped — vainly, as it proved — to head off into the swamps of government mediation.

Having obtained Roosevelt's more than willing support for the plan, Hillman personally announced it to the press on March 14, 1941. On March 17, the press reported that Murray had agreed to support the proposition and would name two CIO representatives to the new NDMB. The AFL would have a similar number of seats.

Murray named himself and UMW Secretary-Treasurer Thomas Kennedy to the board. The AFL representatives were George Meany and George M. Harrison. Industry was represented by W. C. Teagle, Cyrus Ching, Roger Lapham and Eugene Meyer, all hard-boiled, unyielding corporation heads. President Clarence Dykstra of Wisconsin University, President Frank P. Graham of the University of North Carolina, and William H. Davis, a patent lawyer, were designated the "public" representatives. The latter, in actuality, were simply three additional votes for the employers.

Murray's support of the NDMB came as a shock to a large part of the CIO members. Just a week before, the March 10 *CIO News* had published a report of Murray's memorandum to the Labor Policy Commission of the National Defense Commission which raised five strong points of objection to any new war labor board:

"1. Such a board 'will necessarily find its attention directed against labor in order to maintain the status quo as much as possible,' and will strive to stop 'wage increases or improvement of working conditions for labor.'

"2. Compulsory arbitration will result from board activities, since it would enter situations where collective bargaining was in process to 'bring terrific pressure to bear on labor to agree to arbitration in practically all situations.'

"3. Policy-making powers assigned to the board could easily bring about interference with the workings of the Wagner Act, the wages and hours act, and the Walsh-Healey Act, since the agencies administering these acts would be unable to resist the board's pressure.

"4. This in turn would make the Labor Relations board merely a formalized agency 'confined entirely to avoiding labor disputes,' stripping it of the power to require employers to bargain collectively under the Wagner Act.

"5. The setup of the proposed board carries strong anti-labor possibilities in the three members supposed to represent the public. These members 'are to settle controversies, make special investigations, hold hearings and issue reports, and arbitrate disputes,' making them real powers in the board, since the other members representing labor and industry would simply have advisory powers.

"'It has been the experience of labor that representatives from the public are usually taken from the ranks of retired businessmen,' Murray wrote."

On the last point Murray proved wrong in detail, but not in principle. Two of the "public" members were heads of universities. The third depended on corporations for his legal clients.

Of course, the board got its authority with the workers from the presence of the union leaders on it. Without them the board would have appeared for what it was: a body of seven pro-corporation members who were given an "impartial" coloration by the minority of four labor members. The latter had merely to withdraw and the board would collapse.

Events quickly confirmed Murray's initial warning. The role of the NDMB as a pro-employer body designed to impede strikes and impose unfavorable settlements on the unions was clearly illustrated during the autumn series of strikes in the "captive" coal mines.

These mines belonged to seven basic steel corporations and supplied them exclusively with coal. The seven companies controlled 70 per cent of American steel output. They employed about 53,000 coal miners, 95 per cent of whom were United Mine Workers members, and five per cent, non-union. Although the UMW had contracts covering the captive mines, these contracts did not include a union-shop clause such as the rest of the coal industry had signed.

On July 6, 1941, the UMW had scored one of the greatest triumphs in its history, compelling the Southern soft coal operators, after threat of a renewed strike, to sign a new contract which eliminated for the first time the 40-cent daily wage differential between Northern and Southern miners. This gain, after decades of struggle, would set the example for Southern workers in steel, textile and other industries that maintained a Southern wage differential.

The UMW's Southern contract also included two clauses, secured despite the contrary recommendation of the NDMB. One clause gave the UMW the right to strike "throughout the entire area covered by this agreement when necessary to preserve and maintain the integrity and competitive parity of this agreement." The other extended the union shop into the mines of the "Bloody" Harlan County, Kentucky, Coal Operators Association, sole operators, except for the owners of the captive mines, to refuse to sign a union shop agreement in 1939. Over the years, scores of Harlan County miners had paid with their lives to win this union security; four had been shot to death in the spring strike of 1941.

After patiently negotiating with the captive-mine owners for months after the other coal operators had accepted the union shop terms, some 53,000 workers struck on September 14. Amid a crescendo of threats and abuse from administration spokesmen, congressmen and the press, the miners returned to work on September 19 under a 30-day truce, pending the outcome of mediation by the NDMB.

The NDMB stalled past the 30-day deadline and then, on October 24, announced that it had "no recommendation" to make on the disputed issue. It proposed binding arbitration if both parties agreed in advance to accept any decision.

At midnight, Saturday, October 25, the captive-mine workers went out again. The next day, Sunday, Roosevelt himself intervened. He sent a letter to Lewis saying that "in this crisis of our national life there must be uninterrupted production of coal..."

Subsequently, it was claimed that Roosevelt had called on U. S. Steel's Myron C. Taylor to confer with Lewis and cooperate in preventing a shutdown. This move was devious and something of a cover-up for Roosevelt. It was his own NDMB which had stalled to the advantage of the steel companies.

The miners did not respond to Roosevelt's veiled threat, even though rumors were broadcast that he was preparing to send troops into the areas as he had done in the North American Aviation strike. Lewis replied to Roosevelt within 24 hours. On October 27 he wrote the President:

"For four months the steel companies have been whetting their knives and preparing for this struggle...If you would use the power of the state to restrain me, as an agent of labor, then, sir, I submit that you should use that same power to restrain my adversary in this issue, who is an agent of capital. My adversary is a rich man named J. P. Morgan..."

Roosevelt issued, in all, three rapid-fire demands that the miners return to work. These were accompanied by threats of drastic governmental action against them if they did not comply.

In addition, Roosevelt threatened to give the green light to the open-shop, no-strike legislative drive which the Democrats were pushing in Congress. The latter were denouncing Lewis as everything from a "dictator" (Senator Connally) to a "traitor" (Senator Ellender). A certain Senator Harry S. Truman of Missouri expressed "outrage" at Lewis's defiance. Truman advised Roosevelt that he could easily end the strike by appealing to the miners over the heads of their leaders.

Roosevelt's threat of anti-labor laws was intended to frighten the rest of the CIO into putting pressure on Lewis to capitulate, before Congress enacted restrictions on all unions. But this received no open support within the labor movement except from the Stalinist elements, who followed the line of the *Daily Worker,* which said editorially on October 30:

"Labor has a responsibility, for its own protection and that of the nation, summarily to reject the policy of John L. Lewis...The governmental agencies have correctly asked the workers to restrain their use of the right to strike."

However, CIO President and SWOC Chairman Philip Murray on October 29 issued a public statement attacking the use of the argument of "national defense" to conceal the open-shop aims of the steel barons. He said:

"The cloak of national defense used by the large [steel] corporations to escape responsibility is no justification for their refusal to accept the provisions of the Appalachian agreement [commercial mines contract]."

On October 29, the third day of the captive mines' closure,

Myron C. Taylor and Lewis conferred privately in Washington and then went to the White House to see Roosevelt. The press then announced that Lewis and Taylor had agreed to resubmit the issue to the NDMB for a definitive opinion, which, however, would not be binding on either side. Lewis was led to believe that he had a tacit understanding with Taylor that U. S. Steel would accept a pro-union shop decision if the board voted it.

The UMW called off the strike on October 30 but fixed another strike deadline for November 15, by which date the NDMB was expected to render an opinion.

The opinion was delivered five days before the deadline. On November 10 the NDMB voted nine to two against the union shop in the captive mines — the two AFL representatives voting with the employers and "public" members of the board. This decision was comprehensible only as a political reprisal by the Roosevelt administration against Lewis. For the NDMB itself, only a few weeks previously in the joint AFL and CIO machinists strike in San Francisco, had ruled in favor of a "uniform pattern" of the union shop.

Murray and Thomas Kennedy, both UMW officials and members of the NDMB, promptly resigned from the board. They declared that it held the position that "labor unions must be denied the right of normal growth and legitimate aspirations, such as the union shop, and that the traditional open shop policy of the anti-labor employers must prevail." As for the anti-union-shop vote of the AFL members on the board, Murray correctly branded it "arch-treachery and treason."

With the resignation of the CIO members, the NDMB simply faded away.

In the midst of the captive-mine struggle, Roosevelt showed he was strictly impartial when it came to strikebreaking. He publicly ordered AFL Teamsters President Daniel J. Tobin, head of the Democratic Party's National Labor Committee since 1932 and one of the President's most willing lackeys, to call off immediately a strike of Railway Express drivers in Detroit. Tobin agreed but pleaded with Roosevelt to give him two days to get his executive board together. Roosevelt peremptorily commanded Tobin to call off the strike at once regardless of circumstances — and Tobin did.

But Lewis and the coal miners did not jump when Roosevelt or anyone else snapped his fingers. The UMW went quietly ahead preparing for battle by the November 15 deadline. Inspired rumors were circulated that Roosevelt was preparing to order 50,000 federal troops into the mine areas. Army Intelligence agents were reported circulating through the mine fields and army headquarters were hastily set up in Pittsburgh.

On Saturday, November 15, following the decision of the UMW wage-policy committee, the captive mines were again shut down tight. The following Monday, November 17, the CIO opened its fourth national convention in Detroit. Despite the predominately pro-war sentiment of the CIO leaders, they did not dare ignore or repudiate the coal strike. The convention unanimously adopted a resolution in support of the mine strike and in condemnation of the NDMB ruling.

Murray revealed the conflict and cross-purposes in his mind even as he spoke for the resolution. "I support national defense— but be that as it may, in the Mine Workers case the Union's demands must be supported on their merits... The decision of the Mediation Board is the rankest kind of governmental discrimination... I whole-heartedly support the President's foreign policy. But I will fight for the retention of the economic liberties and economic gains of the workers."

Of course, support of U. S. involvement in the war and also of "the economic liberties and economic gains of the workers" were mutually exclusive aims. But even Lewis tried to straddle these two issues. His foreign policy was expressed at the CIO convention in an amendment backed by Murray's group, the Hillmanites and the Stalinists. Where the latter proposed not merely aid to Britain, Russia and China, but naval convoys to accompany U. S. shipping, Lewis's group opposed the convoys but supported the war aid.

Michael Quill, Transport Workers Union president, attempted to amend the resolution of support to the miners. He proposed to instruct all CIO vice-presidents to hurry to Washington and "place themselves at Roosevelt's command to settle the mine strike."

Although Roosevelt could not count on Murray as the chief spokes-man of the CIO to aid him against the miners, he was assisted by the Hillmanites and Stalinists who tried to sabotage any active CIO aid to the mine workers. But the captive-mine strikers could count on the help of hundreds of thousands of miners in the commercial pits. The latter struck in sympathy and almost 200,000 were out by the time of the settlement. As for Roosevelt's threat of troops, Lewis said: "If the soldiers come, the mine workers will remain peace-fully in their homes, conscious of the fact that bayonets in coal mines will not produce coal."

On November 22, Roosevelt capitulated. He agreed to name a three-man arbitration board which would be guaranteed in advance to approve the union shop demand. This board would be composed of Lewis, Benjamin Fairless of U. S. Steel, and John Steelman of the U. S. Conciliation Service. Lewis agreed to this "arbitration" and called off the strike.

Only much later was it revealed that Roosevelt may have given in to the miners on November 22 because that day he had received an intercepted and decoded Japanese message which indicated that the Japanese government considered war with the United States might begin almost at any moment. Certainly he must have feared the reaction among the five million CIO members whose pressure had forced the CIO convention to voice unanimous backing for the miners. He could not afford to enter a shooting war abroad with millions of resentful and hostile industrial workers at home.

After a decent interval of 16 days, the "arbitration" board made public its "decision." It granted the union shop to the captive-mine workers by a vote of two to one, Fairless dissenting.

But the tremendous victory of the coal miners was scarcely noticed. For the decision was announced on December 7, 1941. Everything was drowned out that day by the reverberations of exploding bombs at Pearl Harbor.

Almost every top union leader, including Lewis, promptly lined up with the war machine. Murray had declared in advance, at the CIO convention two weeks before: "I say to the government of the United States of America, the National CIO is here with its heart, its mind, its body, its everything, its life, its blood, and its limbs, prepared to make whatever sacrifices may be necessary..."

Lewis issued a statement: "With all other citizens I join in the support of our government to the day of its ultimate triumph over Japan and all other enemies."

The top union officials, with one honorable exception, did more than voice their support of U. S. participation in the war. They publicly proclaimed a no-strike pledge "for the duration." Only the late Matthew Smith, founder and president of the then independent Mechanics Educational Society of America, a small national union of tool and die makers, refused to make a no-strike pledge. As for Murray, he was later to boast before the September 1944 convention of the United Automobile Workers, that "on the 17th day of December, 1941, ten days after our country had become involved in the war... *Without formal request upon the part of the President of the United States,* we all voluntarily agreed to give our Commander-in-Chief, and through him to the people of our country our No Strike commitment." (My emphasis.)

Thus, according to Murray's testimony, the workers were deprived at one blow of their right to strike by the voluntary surrender of the union leaders. This action was taken without consultation of the union membership. The events of the war years were to reveal, however, that the union ranks and the union leaders were continents apart on the question of the no-strike policy.

MESA President Matthew Smith said of the no-strike policy: "The AFL and CIO did not sell out their membership. They gave them away."

This was not an unfair charge. Although none of the CIO and AFL top leaders would have admitted it openly, they were quite prepared to sacrifice labor's basic rights and just demands — indeed, they well knew that support of the war meant the tearing down of labor's rights and living standards.

At the CIO convention two weeks before Pearl Harbor, several of the Hillmanite delegates had let slip the underlying attitude of the pro-war labor leaders.

Leo Krzycki, of the Amalgamated Clothing Workers, urged the convention: "Let us say that in these extraordinary times we are willing for the time being to shelve the things we are entitled to."

Jacob Potofsky, who was to become ACW president following Hillman's death in 1946, told the convention: "The CIO is strong. Its strength gives us the assurance we can win our just demands without resort to our ultimate right to strike."

Murray did not echo this cynical lie. Instead, he appealed to Roosevelt and the corporation heads not to put the squeeze too strongly on labor:

"And to you, Mr. President, I ask you in the spirit of justice, in the spirit of righteousness, to sit down and ponder just a little more than you have, the need of giving labor in America a chance...I ask you, Mr. American Businessman, to mete out to labor more than you have — more of the things to which they are entitled."

This was a plea designed not so much to tame the tiger's ferocity as to fool the workers into believing that an appeal to the tiger's sense of "justice" and "righteousness" might get it to curb its appetite for fresh, raw meat.

14

The Minneapolis
Labor Case

A major struggle involved the CIO in 1941 when it received into membership a local of some 5,000 Minneapolis truck drivers who were defending their union democracy against the gangster-ridden Tobin machine of the AFL Teamsters. This developed into an historic civil liberties case with national and international repercussions.

On December 8, 1941, the day after Pearl Harbor and at the very moment Congress was formally declaring war, a group of 17 men and one woman faced a federal district judge in a Minneapolis court room. They were members and leaders of the Minneapolis General Drivers Local 544-CIO (formerly AFL) and of the Socialist Workers Party. They heard the judge pronounce sentence of federal imprisonment upon them for their outspoken socialist opposition to imperialist war. They had been tried, convicted and sentenced under the Smith "Gag" Act of 1940, which Roosevelt had signed into law over the protest of both AFL and CIO leaders as well as every civil liberties organization in the country.

The leaders of Minneapolis General Drivers Local 544-AFL had conducted a series of victorious strikes in 1934 which opened the way to unionization of the entire Northwest. When the war in Europe first began, the *Northwest Organizer,* official weekly of the Minneapolis Teamsters Joint Council to which General Drivers Local 544 belonged, had attacked Roosevelt's war plans in its September 7, 1939 issue.

"The workers have no interests abroad to defend. No member of the Minneapolis Milk Drivers Union — or the General Drivers Union, or the City and Sanitary Drivers, or the Federal Workers Section, or the Electrical Workers Union or any other union — has any 'interests' abroad to defend.

"The Standard Oil Company, General Motors, General Electric, Ford, J. P. Morgan have interests abroad to defend. We haven't. If the big boys want to go abroad to defend their investments, let them go.

"J. P. Morgan has a gun. He just returned from a sojourn in Scotland where he was shooting grouse. If he wants to defend his investments, let him take his gun and fight for them. But don't let him try to force us to fight for him. And don't let him try to lie about any fake 'war for democracy.' We can all see how much democracy came out of the first World War."

How true these words proved to be!

For those who still believe the propaganda that this country was precipitated into World War II by the Japanese "sneak attack" at Pearl Harbor, I refer them to the most complete and documented study of the U. S.—Japanese negotiations prior to Pearl Harbor: *President Roosevelt and the Coming of the War; A Study in Appearances and Reality,* by the great American historian, the late Professor Charles A. Beard.

The Roosevelt administration's deliberate step-by-step drive toward war from 1937 onward is now a matter of public record. We know from the postwar testimony of General George Marshall before a congressional committee that late in November 1941, at a secret meeting of Roosevelt's so-called War Cabinet, the main topic of discussion was how to maneuver Japan into firing the first shot.

An entry in Secretary of War Stimson's *Diary,* dated November 25, 1941, reads: "The question [at a White House conference] was how we should maneuver them [the Japanese] into the position of firing the first shot without allowing danger to ourselves."

World War II was in a very real sense a continuation and extension of World War I. It was a renewed explosion of the imperialist rivalries and competition for international markets, cheap raw materials and new fields for profitable capital investment that had touched off the first world war.

While continuously building up his war preparations, from passage of the conscription act to the abandonment of the neutrality act and the initiation of secret submarine warfare, Roosevelt had to maintain the pretense that he would not take this country into war. On the eve of his crucial third-term election, in his campaign radio speech of October 30, 1940, Roosevelt had promised:

"And while I am talking to you, fathers and mothers, I give you once more assurance. I have said this before, but I shall say it again, and again, and again: Your boys are not going to be sent into any foreign wars."

This promise was intended to lull the growing suspicions and even hostility of the workers, whose patience with the Roosevelt administration had worn thin. For one thing, the depression had continued to grind on. The National Industrial Conference Board had estimated unemployment in January 1940 at 10,000,000. In his message to Congress on January 3, 1940, Roosevelt had conceded that "we have not yet found a way to employ the surplus of our labor."

The CIO resolutions and literature of the period give a reflection of the mood of the American workers. For instance, commenting on Roosevelt's 1940 congressional message, the January 8 issue of the *CIO News* bitterly attacked his proposal "to put through deep slashes in relief, public works and social services and agencies, while adding huge sums to arms expenditures ... The cheers which rang from the tory benches of Congress when President Roosevelt promised to slash appropriations for unemployment relief and all other than war purposes, will have a bitter echo in millions of Americans' homes in the coming year."

This mass mood well indicates why Roosevelt had to seek re-election by promising not to take this country into any "foreign wars" and why he and his colleagues secretly connived to maneuver the Japanese imperialists to "fire the first shot." He also had to silence every conscious expression of opposition to imperialist war inside the labor movement. First and foremost was the leadership of Minneapolis General Drivers Local 544-AFL.

The militant leadership and policies of Local 544 had worked a transformation of the Northwest labor movement. Average weekly wages for truck drivers in Minneapolis rose from $11 in 1933 for a 60-hour week to over $33 a week for 44 hours in 1940. They had won conditions that were the envy of workers everywhere at that time, including paid annual vacations, seniority, and many other benefits. Minneapolis had been transformed from a notorious open shop city to a union town. And it was done entirely by the independent action of the workers themselves.

But from the start of their struggles, the Minneapolis drivers found their most bitter enemy inside their own international union—Daniel J. Tobin, International Brotherhood of Teamsters' president.

Tobin was a simon-pure representative of business unionism, the labor philosophy of most of the AFL leadership. The organization of workers was to him primarily a business designed to serve his personal interests and the personal interests of the bureaucrats on his payroll. The idea of leading the working class in battle against the capitalist class for broad economic, social and political aims appalled him no less than it did the employers. Thus, from the start, he joined with the Minneapolis employers in fighting Local 544 and its leadership.

The Minneapolis union lent funds and seasoned organizers to new unions throughout the Northwest. It spearheaded a tremendous expansion of unionism throughout a great open-shop area. In August 1938, this organizing drive was climaxed by the winning of the first over-the-road drivers contract, with union wages and conditions, including the closed shop, in an 11-state area ranging from Montana to Ohio and Minnesota to Oklahoma.

The initiators and leaders of this AFL Teamsters triumph were the men who had organized and led Local 544. Farrell Dobbs, former secretary-treasurer, was the first secretary of the North Central Area Negotiating Committee. Tobin fought this organizing drive bitterly and had demanded its discontinuance. The over-the-road drivers were real proletarian types in contrast to the city driver-salesmen who had previously predominated in the Teamsters. Tobin didn't want this huge influx of new, militant workers into his union.

But he couldn't resist the vision of all that per capita rolling in after the Central States over-the-road contract brought 200,000 new members — more than the entire 135,000 members of the IBT in 1935. Tobin thrust his fears of streamlined, aggressive, industrial unionism momentarily into the background. He even appointed Dobbs organizer for the IBT in charge of the over-the-road field.

The employers and their political agents kept up their unrelenting war against the union and its leaders. In November 1937, Pat Corcoran, chairman of the North Central District Drivers Council and a close co-worker of Local 544, was shot to death by an unknown assassin. It is generally accepted in the labor movement that he died at the hands of gangsters hired by the bosses.

These same bosses then initiated a campaign of slander against the leaders of Local 544, claiming they were "gangsters" and "racketeers" who were "misusing union funds." The employers association smuggled a couple of agents into the local. These agents, backed by unlimited funds, then brought suit against the union for monies allegedly due them.

After a three-year fight, in which the union's financial records were made public and scrutinized down to the last penny of receipts and expenditures, a hostile judge in October 1940 was forced to give the union and its leaders a clean bill of health. The "Fink Suit" was finally thrown out of court.

But the leaders had to reckon with an even more powerful combination of foes — Tobin, Roosevelt and the FBI. In the spring of 1941, Tobin determined to smash the leadership of Local 544 at any cost and by any method. He haled its officers to his Washington headquarters in early June. He ordered them to recommend to the local union's Executive Board that they ask Tobin to send in a "receiver" with dictatorial powers to run the union and to remove any officer or member. The local's delegation replied they had no power to give away the democratic right of the membership to control the affairs of their own union and to elect their own officers.

On arrival home, the delegation learned that Tobin had been scheming with Minnesota Governor Harold E. Stassen and State Labor Board Chairman Blair to sign sweetheart contracts with the employers under contract with Local 544.

In the face of such outright treachery, the Local 544 leaders and members determined to break from Tobin's grip and seek a charter from the CIO. On June 9, 1941, at a general membership meeting with more than 4,000 drivers present, the local voted overwhelmingly to accept a charter from the CIO as Motor Transport and Allied Workers Industrial Union, Local 544-CIO.

At this meeting, Farrell Dobbs, who two years earlier had quit his IBT post to become national labor secretary of the Socialist Workers Party and, later, editor of *The Militant,* was a guest speaker. He summarized Tobin's motives in seeking to destroy Local 544 and its leadership:

"In Daniel J. Tobin's eyes, this union is guilty of four great crimes.

"Our first crime is that we believe in fighting the bosses all the way. Tobin doesn't believe in this. I hope you all read the little editorial on the inside front cover of the June issue of Tobin's personal organ [*Teamsters Journal*], wherein he states:

"'Business agents and salaried officers of unions are going to be held mainly responsible by the state and federal governments for the actions of their members as time goes on. In most instances paid representatives of local unions are in a position to stop trouble. In some few instances they are not strong enough to stop the rank and file, but in those instances where they fail or where they are unable to protect the rank and file from themselves, they should notify the International Office of such failure.'

"Translated out of Tobin's language into English, that paragraph is a warning and a threat to every official of every IBT local that Tobin doesn't want the drivers asking for higher wages, he doesn't want any trouble, he doesn't want any strikes, he doesn't want to pay out any money for strike benefits. And God help any business agent or officer who can't hold down the drivers and get them to lie down. If they can't do it, Tobin will have their scalps...

"Local 544's second crime in Tobin's eyes is that the delegates from this union to the last convention of the IBT—Tobin permits a convention once every five years—voted against his proposal that he be given dictatorial powers to force arbitration upon any affiliated local. One of the delegates to take the floor against this reactionary program was Miles Dunne [then Local 544 president] who made such an effective speech it took Tobin half an hour to get the convention to order... By agreement with other progressive delegates, Miles Dunne made his talk; together, the convention was able to deal Tobin a stiff defeat, something unheard of at IBT conventions.

"Local 544's third crime, according to Tobin, is that representatives of this union took the lead in organizing the over-the-road drivers and achieving the 11-state area contract. In this drive about two hundred thousand new members were brought into the IBT. Tobin fought against this successful campaign from the start. He tried to disrupt our drivers' council that launched the over-the-road campaign. Once the successful fight was over, Tobin immediately clamped down and began to expel or push aside all those whom he couldn't absolutely control and integrate into his machine.

"Our fourth crime is that the Local 544 delegates voted against Tobin's request to raise his annual salary from $10,000 to $30,000 a year...

"There stands Tobin with his $30,000 sack of dough over his shoulder, almost tipping him over backward, holding up his hand to the drivers, and howling, 'Don't strike, boys, I got mine.'"

This was the background of the internal union situation into which Roosevelt was to intervene — as an ally of Tobin. It was for Tobin that the President of the United States was to summon the might of the federal government.

On June 13, four days after the Local 544 membership voted for affiliation with the CIO, the President's secretary, Stephen Early, issued the following special White House press statement on the internal union struggle in Minneapolis:

"Mr. Tobin telegraphed from Indianapolis that it is apparent to him and to the other executives of his organization that because they have been and will continue to stand behind the government, that all subversive organizations and all enemies of our government, including Bundists, Trotskyists and Stalinists, are opposed to them and seeking to destroy loyal trade unions which are supporting democracy.

"Mr. Tobin goes into considerable detail and states he is going to issue a statement from the Indianapolis office of the teamster's union. When I advised the President of Tobin's representations this morning he asked me immediately to have the government departments and agencies interested in this matter notified and to point out to you that this is no time, in his opinion, for labor unions, local or national, to begin raiding one another for the purpose of getting membership or for similar reasons." (*New York Times,* June 14, 1941.)

Far from rushing to "raid" Local 544 or claim its jurisdiction, the CIO representatives had scrutinized the local and its leaders most carefully. Frank Barnhart, regional director of the United Construction Workers Organizing Committee, CIO, on June 28 revealed in a press statement:

"Before granting a charter to Local 544 the CIO made a careful investigation of the union and its leadership. As a part of its investigation, representatives of the CIO consulted the Minneapolis Police Department [!] and were informed by them that the leaders of Local 544 had no criminal record and were in no sense classed as labor racketeers. A further irrefutable evidence of the honorable record of the leadership of Local 544 is contained in the finding of Judge Carroll during the court hearing which involved an examination of all the books, records, minutes, contracts, financial transactions, etc., of Local 544."

This intervention by Roosevelt was unprecedented. It was all the more brazen because it was well known that Tobin was chairman of the Democratic Party's National Labor Committee and Roosevelt's response to Tobin's appeal could be regarded only as payment for political favors received.

On June 30, Roosevelt acted. Under the President's direct orders, as Early's statement proved, squads of U. S. marshals and FBI agents invaded the St. Paul and Minneapolis headquarters of the Socialist Workers Party. They confiscated quantities of *The Militant* and other publications, and numerous books, including Marxist classics by Marx, Engels, Lenin and Trotsky, available in many university and public libraries. The warrant said the raid was made because these classics were "reportedly" on sale at the SWP halls— as they had been for more than a decade.

The next day, July 1, a federal grand jury composed entirely of rural residents from outside Minneapolis moved to indict 29 persons, all but three of them members or former members of Minneapolis unions, for "seditious conspiracy." The American Civil Liberties Union promptly protested to Acting Attorney General Francis J. Biddle that the indictments were "obviously dangerous to the preservation of democracy."

The CIO had issued a statement on June 28, declaring the attack on Local 544 and the SWP "nothing but a smear campaign against the CIO." It added:

"Unable to bend the workers to his will by the other vicious tactics which he has employed, Dan Tobin has persuaded Roosevelt to carry out this action in payment of his political debt to Tobin... It is deplorable that the functions of the U. S. Department of Justice have been perverted in this reprehensible manner."

On July 1, the very day the Department of Justice took its demand for indictments to the grand jury, a mass meeting was held in the Lyceum Theatre in Minneapolis to welcome Local 544 into the CIO. More than 200 telegraphed greetings from CIO bodies all over the United States were read to the meeting. CIO President Philip Murray and John L. Lewis sent warm messages.

One CIO spokesman, Cecil Owens from Washington, told the meeting: "Your coming over to the CIO created a sensation in Washington. For a few days it appeared that the national administration had dropped its campaign of 'Aid to England' for a campaign of 'Aid to Dan Tobin.'"

Lee Pressman, national legal counsel for the CIO and personal representative of Murray, was the main speaker. His remarks are particularly significant because he was a Stalinist and a bitter political foe of the Local 544 leaders and the Socialist Workers Party. But Pressman felt impelled on this occasion to repress his extreme political partisanship. He pointed out:

"When a single local union like 544 joins the CIO, why is there all this excitement? Why have you become a national issue?... The tradition behind your local union leads right to the origin of the CIO... Your 1934 strikes gave meaning to the needs of the workers for strong unions. The CIO has carried out concretely on a national scale what you started in 1934."

General Drivers Local 544 of Minneapolis was, in this author's opinion, the greatest local union the American labor movement has ever known. It was the prototype of the model union — militant, democratic, aggressive, independent of the employers, of the capitalist government and of capitalist politicians and parties. Its leaders, like the Dunne brothers (Vincent, Miles and Grant), Carl Skoglund, Farrell Dobbs, and Kelly Postal, were absolutely selfless and wholly dedicated to the cause of labor.

These men, and others who fought at their side, were students of the labor movement and its history, informed in economic, social and political theory. In every respect they stood above the Lewises, Murrays and Reuthers, let alone the exclusively business-unionism, narrow craft types like Tobin, William Green or George Meany.

Above all, they were firm socialists in the Eugene V. Debs tradition, unyielding opponents of company unionism in politics and implacable foes of the private monopoly—private profit system. That is why Roosevelt determined to eliminate them in advance of his entry into the war.

Acting on the demands of the Roosevelt administration, the handpicked grand jury indicted 29 persons, including, with the above mentioned Local 544 leaders, James P. Cannon, founder and national secretary of the Socialist Workers Party; Albert Goldman, attorney for the SWP; and Felix Morrow, editor of *The Militant*. Grant Dunne died before the trial; the other 28 stood trial.

Kelly Postal, secretary-treasurer of Local 544, was at the same time indicted by a county grand jury for allegedly embezzling AFL funds when, at the motion of the Local 544 membership, he transferred their money to the new CIO local. Acquitted in the federal "sedition" trial and in one trial involving the transferred funds, Postal was tried again on a similar count. He was railroaded to prison for larceny, although it was conceded by the prosecution that he had acted at the order of the members; not one penny was taken for himself. He died in July 1958, an honest, sterling fighter for labor who had been framed and branded as a "thief."

After the indictment of the 29, the American Civil Liberties Union, in an August 20 letter signed by the noted liberals John Haynes Holmes, Arthur Garfield Hays and Roger Baldwin, exposed the government's charges. They declared that "it seems...reasonable to conclude that the government injected itself into an interunion controversy in order to promote the interests of the one side which supported the administration's foreign and domestic policies."

Besides the Roosevelt administration, Tobin and the Minneapolis employers, there was only one other element who joined in the hounding and persecution of Local 544 and the SWP leaders. The August 16, 1941 *Daily Worker* boasted:

"The Communist Party has always exposed, fought against and today joins in the fight to exterminate the Trotskyite Fifth Column from the life of our nation."

The CP daily complained, however, that the Justice Department planned to try the 29 as socialist revolutionists (which they were) and not as "agents of fascism" (as Stalin did in his Moscow Frameup Trials).

The Minneapolis Labor Trial, as it became known, began on October 27 in Minneapolis before Federal District Judge M. M. Joyce. The 28 defendants were tried under two laws. Count one of the indictment was based on an 1861 statute passed during the Civil War against the Southern slaveholders, then in an actual armed rebellion. This count charged a "conspiracy to overthrow the government by force and violence."

Count two of the indictment charged the publication and circulation of literature, the establishment of an organization and membership therein "to teach, advocate and encourage" the "overthrow of the government by force and violence." This count was based wholly on the Smith Act of 1940 which had never before been used. It was, in fact, the first federal law since the infamous and quickly-repealed Alien and Sedition Act of 1798 to make mere advocacy of views a "crime."

The details of the trial were reported in *The Militant* for the year 1941. Two pamphlets — *Socialism on Trial,* containing the verbatim testimony of the chief defendant, James P. Cannon; and *In Defense of Socialism,* the closing defense argument of Albert Goldman—are remarkable textbooks on socialism and its principles, presented in the heat of an historic labor trial. They completely disprove the government's attempt to equate socialism and Marxism with "force and violence."

The government's case was based first of all upon quotations torn out of context from the publications of the SWP and its predecessor groups going back to 1928, and from the Marxist classics going back to 1848 — all publicly sold and available in most public libraries.

The prosecution also put 37 witnesses on the stand. They testified that various defendants allegedly had told them privately about their political views. According to these witnesses, the defendants were particularly voluble about the use of "force and violence." Of the 37 government witnesses, 22 were on Tobin's payroll or known supporters of his machine in the Teamsters; two were FBI agents who had been planted in Local 544; one was an agent of the Associated Industries, Minnesota employers' organization. The other 12 were of only minor significance and gave no important testimony.

On December 1, 1941, the jury brought in its decision. On the "seditious conspiracy" count under the old Civil War law, all defendants were acquitted. Under the new Smith Act, which many at the time thought would unquestionably be thrown out when the case was appealed to the higher courts, 18 defendants were convicted, ten acquitted.

During a two-year appeals fight directed by the Civil Rights Defense Committee, an organization of prominent liberals and labor figures, more than six hundred labor, Negro and civil liberties organizations backed the 18 Minneapolis Case victims. These organizations included the national CIO, the United Automobile Workers, the United Rubber Workers, the AFL International Ladies Garment Workers and others, representing in all more than five million members.

The case involved the most basic constitutional rights — free speech, free press, freedom of assembly. But the United States Supreme Court, a majority of its members appointed by Roosevelt, three times refused even to review the case. On the evening of December 31, 1943, the convicted people went to federal prisons for terms ranging from one year to 16 months, with time off for good behavior.

Today, even in the purely legalistic sense, the 18 have been vindicated. Rulings of the highest federal courts in the cases of the Communist Party leaders convicted in the recent series of Smith Act trials would bring acquittal for the first 18 Smith Act victims if they were brought to trial today. The latest ruling, at this writing, is the reversal of the conviction of six CP members tried under the Smith Act. The United States Court of Appeals on August 5, 1958, held that mere teaching or advocacy of overthrow of the government, by force or otherwise, does not constitute "a call to action" and is not felonious.

Further verification is presented by Roosevelt's wartime Attorney General Francis Biddle, who indicted and prosecuted the Minneapolis defendants, in his autobiographical book, *In Brief Authority*. Biddle comments 21 years after the trial: "History showed that sedition statutes — laws addressed to what men said — invariably had been used to prevent and punish criticism of the government, particularly in time of war. I believed them to be unnecessary and harmful.

"I authorized a prosecution so that the law would be tested at the threshold..." claims Biddle, sidestepping the fact that Roosevelt ordered intervention at Tobin's request. However, when the Supreme Court three times refused to review the case, Biddle kept silent, even though he now admits "I should not have tried to test the criminal provisions of the statute in this particular case. The two Dunne brothers and their twenty-seven associates were the leaders of the Trotskyist Socialist Workers Party, a little splinter group [which] by no conceivable stretch of a liberal imagination could have been said to constitute any 'clear and present' danger to the government..."

In the course of the war, with its leaders imprisoned and with Tobin's goons and the government bringing every threat and pressure to bear on the Minneapolis drivers, Local 544-CIO was finally crushed. But its record and tradition remain as an example for the new generation of unionists, who will certainly face a new crisis of American capitalism in this epoch of economic instability and wars.

PART III

THE CIO
IN THE WAR

1942-1943

15

Roosevelt's
War Labor Curbs

For America's monopoly capitalists Pearl Harbor meant golden opportunities. The barons of steel, auto, oil, aircraft, chemicals, and other requisites of the war machine strove to dredge unlimited profits out of the bloody mash. They not only dictated the terms of war contracts; they staffed all the agencies of government with their own trusted agents.

Gone were the dismal years of depressed profits and unsalable inventories. The government offered an assured and insatiable market for their wares—at top prices. As quickly as they delivered the "hardware" of war, it was consumed—blown up, shot down, or sunk at sea. New orders would then come in, faster than could be filled. Everything was sold—even defective copper wire cables that broke like pieces of string, armor plate that cracked, shells that dropped short on our own troops, ships that split apart at sea.

The voracious war demand meant enormously increased pressure for output—longer hours of work, speed-up, the diversion of labor power from production of the "nonessentials" of living to the "essentials" of killing and dying.

The corporations and their government agents unleashed a savage drive on labor's standards of living and job conditions. Wages were to be frozen. Jobs also were to be frozen so that workers might not be lured by competing firms with offers of higher pay. "Excess" purchasing power was to be drained into the war coffers by a new withholding tax on wages and by "voluntary" purchases of government bonds, to be repaid ten years later in debased currency.

Above all, the workers' power of organized resistance — their right to strike — was to be smashed. In attempting this, the war profiteers had plenty of encouragement and advice from top union officials. A few days before Pearl Harbor, Hillman, as a co-director of the OPM, had sent Roosevelt a lengthy proposal for the complete control of labor after the anticipated entry into the war. "A way must be found to stop defense strikes," Hillman urged. "We are all agreed that 'strikes as usual' can no more be tolerated than 'business as usual.' "

Industry unhesitatingly grasped Hillman's formula of "no strikes as usual and no business as usual." In the name of patriotism, they demanded that the workers accept the arrangement ironically labeled "Equality of Sacrifice."

This called upon the workers to sacrifice their peacetime union conditions and wage standards; the industrialists and financiers to "sacrifice" peacetime business for war business. Labor was to accept wartime restrictions on its right to fight for higher wages. Capital was to agree to restrictions on its right to produce civilian goods while expanding war production at guaranteed profits.

For propaganda purposes, the labor leaders gave another interpretation to the "Equality of Sacrifice" slogan. They sought to represent it as a sharing of the hardships and losses of war. Roosevelt too, on several occasions early in the war, made gestures intended to reinforce this fraudulent interpretation. These included his never-enforced proposition to limit individual wartime income to $25,000 a year after taxes. But the corporation executives and owners knew what "Equality of Sacrifice" really meant. It was a smart gimmick to defraud labor.

The initial step was to disarm the labor movement by formal acceptance of the unconditional surrender of the labor leaders. The Roosevelt administration organized a week-long industry-labor conference in Washington, starting December 16, 1941. From this conference, attended by nine top labor leaders which included Murray, Lewis and Julius Emspak for the CIO, the employers emerged with a threefold commitment from the union officialdom: (1) the surrender of the right to strike—or the "no-strike pledge"; (2) settlement of all labor demands through negotiations, mediation and arbitration; (3) establishment of a government War Labor Board empowered to handle all labor disputes.

The last point of the program was imposed by Roosevelt. He issued the executive order initiating the establishment of a War Labor Board even before any conference agreement had been reached.

As the war progressed, the union leaders complained that the no-strike, compulsory-arbitration agreement was merely part of a "contract" or "understanding" whereby labor was assured of its rights and standards in return for sacrificing its most effective weapons. They referred to "breach" of a "contract" that had never been signed. This was how Lewis, during the 1943 mine strikes, explained his acceptance of the three-point surrender.

It is a fact, however, that the union leaders emerged from the industry-labor conference without inclusion in the final agreement of the chief point of the original AFL-CIO declaration of aims. This had said that "all workers have a right to a living wage, as a minimum, sufficient to maintain full efficiency, good health and well-being for themselves and their families." The employers flatly refused to accept such statement of intent.

While the employers and their government gave not a single guarantee to labor, the corporations were exacting maximum guarantees regarding war contracts and profits. At a conference in January between the auto industry and the OPM, the industrialists demanded and secured so-called escalator clauses permitting the contractor to add to the final price materials and labor costs not estimated in the original contract. They also secured provisions for tax amortizations which enabled them to obtain ownership of new, government-built plants for next to nothing.

Justice for labor and the protection of its rights were to reside in the new 12-man War Labor Board which Roosevelt named on January 12, 1942. Although the CIO had resigned from and smashed the National Defense Mediation Board only two months before, the CIO leaders again agreed to serve as labor window-dressing for a board modeled on the NDMB, but with even greater powers and pro-corporation bias.

William H. Davis, who had been roundly condemned by the CIO when head of the defunct NDMB, was named by Roosevelt to head the new board. Dr. Frank Graham, another "public" member of the NDMB who had voted, like Davis, for the steel corporations, also was appointed to the WLB.

The old NDMB had engaged only in voluntary mediation and could make no binding decisions. The new WLB was given power, by executive decree, to invoke compulsory arbitration. It had binding authority. Moreover, the union leaders entered the WLB in a hopelessly weak position, having surrendered in advance the right to strike.

As the union leaders gave ground completely before the employers and as the workers bowed before reactionary pressure following the first stunning impact of Pearl Harbor, some spokesmen of the corporation-dominated war machine dared to express publicly their inmost hatred of labor and their real aims for the future of unionism.

Admiral Ben Moreell, chief of the U. S. Bureau of Yards and

Docks, speaking in October 1942 to a Toronto meeting of the AFL Building and Construction Trades Department, openly threatened:

"I will admit that no one can live without labor, but they certainly can live without labor unions. They are living without them in Germany, and in Italy, and in Japan and they seem to be doing right well—at least for the moment—and, in my opinion, they will damn well live without them here if all of us don't get in there and pitch."

Admiral Emory S. Land, of the U. S. Maritime Commission, on October 19, 1942, told an approving convention of the Investment Bankers Association that, in his opinion, union "organizers ought to be shot at sunrise."

Thus, the American ruling class and its martial agents conceived their "war against fascism" as a simultaneous war against American labor.

* * *

As Roosevelt summoned the nation after Pearl Harbor for his military crusade to attain the "Four Freedoms"—especially "freedom from want" — all over the globe, the U. S. Bureau of Labor Statistics, in a mid-April 1942 report, revealed truly shocking facts about "freedom from want" here at home.

Over 25 per cent of all employed workers in December 1941 earned less than $20 a week. Over 50 per cent earned less than $30 a week. Only 13 per cent of income earners in industry, including supervisory and executive employees, earned as much as $50 a week, a sum below the minimum decency and comfort standard of living fixed by the government itself.

Pearl Harbor accelerated the speed of rising living costs. By the end of January 1942, the CIO leaders felt impelled by rank-and-file discontent to initiate a drive for industry-wide wage increases. Meeting in New York City on January 26, the CIO National Executive Board issued a call to all affiliated unions to demand "substantial wage increases." President Murray said that by March 1942 living costs including taxes would be 20 per cent above the January 1941 level. This would wipe out all 1941 wage gains and impose an actual ten per cent general wage cut.

To quiet the growing demands for wage increases, Congress passed and Roosevelt signed the War-Time Price Control Bill. This bill, giving the Office of Price Administration power to fix prices of consumer goods, was designed actually to give a legal cover to price gouging. Roosevelt himself had to admit, as he signed the bill, that he had "doubts as to the wisdom and adequacy of certain sections of the Act." On January 30, OPA, headed by Leon Henderson, issued a statement saying it expected "nothing sweeping or radical" from the measure but hoped it might have at least a "psychological" effect on manufacturers and merchants. The January 28 *New York Times* quite candidly denounced the bill as "a thoroughly bungled and discreditable job, a mere mockery of its own declared purposes."

The "declared purposes" of this price control law were to prevent a general rise in prices; fix maximum prices that might legally be charged for certain goods; and to set up agencies for policing prices. The real purpose was to provide a basis for the claim that prices were being controlled and, therefore, wages must be controlled. The prices of war goods sold to the government were fixed by the corporations themselves, acting through their "representatives" in the war procurement divisions. As for retail prices of civilian goods, it would have taken a vast army even to begin to police the millions of daily transactions. Price control was a fraud.

This was pretty much the belief of the industrial workers. For instance, United Automobile Workers delegates from 90 General Motors plants met in Detroit on February 7, 1942, and adopted demands for a dollar-a-day pay increase and the union shop.

Motivating the wage demand, Walter Reuther, then GM director for the UAW, pointed out that the auto workers were "worse off than they were a year ago" despite the 10-cent hourly boost in the previous spring.

The GM workers' major demands followed those the United Steelworkers had made on four of the Little Steel corporations: Bethlehem, Republic, Inland, and Youngstown Sheet and Tube. Murray had immediately shunted the Little Steel demands into the hands of the War Labor Board. The UAW leaders followed suit with the GM proposals. Murray's move indicated what he really had in mind when he had promised at the CIO National Executive Board meeting to "fight" for "substantial wage increases" and union security.

On February 23, in a radio address, Roosevelt explained his program. He stressed "the one thought for us here at home to keep uppermost... uninterrupted production. I stress that word *uninterrupted*." He urged "three high purposes for every American": (1) "We shall not stop work for a single day. If any dispute arises we shall keep on working while the dispute is solved by mediation, conciliation or arbitration — until the war is won"; (2) "We shall not demand special gains or special privileges or special advantages for any group or occupation"; (3) "We shall give up conveniences and modify the routine of our lives if our country asks us to."

One "high purpose" Roosevelt did not mention, as virtually every newspaper noted at the time, was the limitation or elimination of war profits. The CIO leaders seemed not to notice the clear anti-labor implications of Roosevelt's "three high purposes." Murray had complained that "certain government and industry officials" were conducting a "premeditated publicity campaign" seeking to "prejudice the public mind, and, if possible, the War Labor Board" against the steel union's demands. The chief culprit whom Murray carefully refrained from naming was Roosevelt. The pro-Big Business press was not so shy. The old *New York Sun,* a traditional Republican fixture on the tables of the Wall Streeters, had to admit on February 24:

"In his speech last night, the President placed the emphasis definitely upon labor... [this] did more probably to brighten the atmosphere in Washington today than anything else he said in his speech last night."

Roosevelt followed his February 23 radio speech with a series of more specific demands and commands, designed not only to freeze wages but to force the unions to surrender contractual conditions already won and enjoyed.

His first move was against premium pay for work on Saturdays, Sundays and holidays. Union contracts customarily provided for time and a half on Saturdays and double time wage rates for working Sundays or holidays. General Motors initiated the attack on contractual standards when it refused to continue paying double time for Sunday work. This was the first issue submitted to the War Labor Board by the UAW.

Donald Nelson, newly-named head of the War Production Board which had supplanted the Office of Production Management, appearing on March 24 before the House Naval Affairs Committee, stated the Roosevelt administration's position on premium pay. Nelson said that if the unions did not agree within 30 days to give up premium pay for week ends and holidays which did not fall on the sixth and seventh consecutive days of work, the administration would press for a law to compel such surrender. As one New York daily put it, this was a "velvet-gloved ultimatum" to labor.

The top union officials of the CIO and AFL yielded immediately, and without consultation with the ranks. They agreed to abrogate premium-pay clauses in hundreds of newly signed contracts.

This giveaway of their hard-won rights did not go down easily with the workers. Resentment was so rife among the auto workers that the UAW leaders had to call a special national delegated convention in Detroit to cram the decision down the workers' throats.

The most significant aspect of this convention was the united front of the top leaders — Thomas, Addes, Frankensteen, Reuther, and the Stalinists — against the ranks. The fight lasted for two days. Every trick was employed to break down or confuse the opposition. The resolution to give up premium pay contained a section on "Equality of Sacrifice" so worded as to give the false impression that sacrifice of premium pay would be conditional on measures by the government to eliminate war profits.

One of these measures was described in a letter to the convention from Roosevelt. He promised: "It is the intention of the government to renegotiate contracts with the employers wherever necessary to insure that the savings from relinquishment of double or premium time go not to the employer but the nation."

In this same letter, he said that premium pay "in wartime... puts a brake upon production. It causes factories to close on Sundays and holidays." This implied that the employers could not afford to pay overtime and premium rates. But when he spoke of the need to "renegotiate contracts," he made it plain that the corporations were being reimbursed by the government for every cent of overtime and premium wages.

In the end, with 150 courageous delegates standing on their feet to vote opposition openly, the UAW resolution to give up premium pay was adopted. Just before the vote was taken, Roosevelt's letter was reread to the convention and Frankensteen bellowed into the microphone: "Are you going to tell the President of the United States to go to hell?"

At the subsequent steelworkers convention in May, Philip Murray cited the UAW's surrender on premium pay to press the steel delegates into adopting a similar resolution.

Late in April, Roosevelt convened his "war labor cabinet" of CIO and AFL officials and demanded that they accept "voluntary" wage "stabilization" in the form of a wage freeze. In return for this he said he would try to persuade Congress to withhold pending legislation for a compulsory wage freeze. Then on April 27 in his message to Congress, Roosevelt called for wage stabilization by action of the War Labor Board. He also urged pressure for mass purchase of war bonds by personal pledges of not less than ten per cent of weekly wages and limitation of credit and installment buying. He spoke vaguely of limiting profits to a "reasonably low level." A week later he acted by executive fiat in the shipyards wage negotiations.

A general wage increase had been automatically provided by a cost-of-living escalator clause in the industry-wide shipyards "stabilization" agreements, signed in 1941 by both CIO and AFL unions at the insistence of the government itself. Roosevelt issued a virtual ultimatum against any such increase in a strongly-worded telegram on May 2 to the Chicago wage conference of government officials, shipyard owners and CIO and AFL leaders representing 800,000 shipbuilding workers. He said:

"The situation that now confronts you is that the full percentage wage increase for which your contracts call, and to which, by the letter of the law, you are entitled, is irreconcilable with the national policy to control the cost of living."

But the escalator clause was designed to meet an already increased cost of living. Moreover, further wage increases under this clause were dependent on further price rises — and Roosevelt had given assurances that prices would be controlled. What need to fear extension of this escalator clause if his promises on price control meant anything?

Most of the union leaders greeted Roosevelt's wage proposals and mandates with sullen silence, or went along with complaints and misgivings. Of the major tendencies in the CIO only the Stalinists and the Hillmanites gave quick and wholehearted endorsement to Roosevelt's "3-point" and "7-point" programs. The April 26 *Daily Worker* demanded that organized labor accept the latter program "as a whole," particularly compulsory wage stabilization through the War Labor Board. On May 3 the *Sunday Worker* claimed "the primary duty of labor — to make plain its determination to back the President's plan."

Acceptance of a wage freeze, as even the dullest and most conservative union leaders could see, might have disastrous consequences for union organization. Few unorganized workers would want to join and pay dues to unions they felt would have little prospect of winning improvements for them, especially in wages. These union leaders were not concerned so much with the effect of wage stabilization on living standards as with its effect on the stability of dues payments. Catering to this, the WLB devised an inducement for union officials to help enforce the wage freeze. This was the so-called maintenance of membership clause.

The WLB, with its employer members dissenting, on April 25 reaffirmed a nine-month-old ruling of the old National Defense Mediation Board granting a "maintenance of membership" clause in the case of the CIO Industrial Union of Marine and Shipbuilding Workers at U. S. Steel's Federal Shipbuilding and Dry Dock Company in Kearny, New Jersey. The company had refused to abide by the original ruling and in 1941 had provoked a strike and "seizure" by the navy. The navy had not, however, enforced the NDMB ruling.

"Maintenance of membership" was not the union shop or the closed shop. The union shop requires, as a condition of continued employment, that all workers hired must join the union after a stipulated time. The closed shop requires that only union members be hired to begin with. But, as the WLB ruling pointed out, the "maintenance of membership" clause in the Federal Shipbuilding case "does not require any old employe, any new employe or any employe whatever to join the union at any time."

It meant that a worker who is a member of the union at the time of the signing of the contract, or who voluntarily joins the union after the contract has been signed, must pay his dues for the life of the contract. Provided he pays his dues, he can actually engage in anti-union activities and still not be fired.

The reason for offering the "maintenance of membership" clause was to ensure that the union ranks were kept under the thumb of "responsible leaders." Pointing out how smart it was for employers to play ball with such "responsible labor leaders," the WLB said:

"Too often members of unions do not maintain their membership because they resent the discipline of a responsible leadership. A rival but less responsible leadership feels the pull of temptation to obtain and maintain leadership by relaxing discipline, by refusing to cooperate with the company, and sometimes with unfair and demagogic attacks on the company. It is in the interests of management, these companies have found, to cooperate with the unions for the maintenance of a more stable, responsible leadership."

WLB Chairman Davis, in an April 29 news interview, directly connected the question of "union security" with the enforcement of a general wage freeze.

"We're going to have to call on the leaders of labor to put this [wage stabilization] over," said Davis. "That being so, that is another reason for upholding the hands of leaders of organized labor."

Thus, "maintenance of membership" was to be the union leadership's reward for policing the unions for the employers and enforcing the no-strike pledge, wage freeze, speed-up and other onerous conditions.

But the Roosevelt administration did not entrust this job solely to the union leaders. Roosevelt personally led the attack on wage standards. On May 22, 1942, for instance, he told his press conference that he would do all in his power to prevent what he called "unwarranted" wage increases voluntarily granted by corporations. The matter had been put to him in connection with a report that three West Coast aircraft firms were preparing to offer wage boosts. Even where corporations expressed willingness and ability to pay, Roosevelt declared, no plant would be permitted to grant raises "which would make workers in other plants unhappy." (*New York Times,* May 23.)

Roosevelt, however, was not loath to make the American workers unhappy on other scores. On May 7 his Secretary of the Treasury Henry Morgenthau, Jr., had placed the administration's plan for drastic tax increases on lower incomes before the House Ways and Means Committee.

Prior to 1941 most American workers had been free of direct income taxes. Annual incomes under $2,500—equivalent to more than $6,000 in 1959 — were exempt. In 1941 Roosevelt signed a war tax bill which taxed single persons with incomes as low as $750 a year and married couples with incomes as little as $1,500. Although the tax was originally designed to place the burden on those most able to pay — the rich — the 1941 law imposed income taxes on 17 million persons in the lower brackets who previously had been exempt.

Morgenthau's plan placed income taxes on single persons getting only $600 a year and couples with but $1,200. Those in the previously taxable brackets, with incomes from $750 to $2,500 a year, would suffer tax increases of from 200 to 1,000 per cent. Only two months before, on March 3, Morgenthau himself had said that these lower-income groups should not be taxed because "our studies at the Treasury show that the very lowest income groups have all they can do to feed and clothe themselves and their families." The Roosevelt-Morgenthau tax program was substantially adopted and by the end of the war income taxes were levied on incomes as low as $500 a year. About 30 million wage earners, who would have been exempt in 1939, were having income taxes up to 20 per cent deducted in advance from their wages.

The administration, by a series of decrees, began to impose rationing of many necessities on the premise of providing a fair division of scarce commodities. Auto tires and gasoline were put on the ration list in January; meats, butter, cheese, canned fish and edible oils in March. Rationing limited the supplies available to workers, but the well-to-do could get what they wanted through expensive black market sources or by eating in restaurants. A year after Pearl Harbor most necessities, from safety pins to clothing and housing, had become extremely scarce. With scarcity, prices soared. Price-gouging was legalized by the OPA, whose function turned out to be —not controlling prices but sanctioning prices already illegally advanced. In the one month of August 1941, for instance, the OPA raised legal prices on more than 500 food items.

As the squeeze tightened, the greed and voracity of the industrialists and financiers became so extreme that some sections of the administration and Congress felt it necessary to put some restraining pressure on the war-contracts corporations.

Late in January 1942, the Special Senate Committee for Investigating the National Defense Program, with Senator Truman of Missouri as chairman, had issued a report of its nine-month survey of war contracts. This report, which lifted the veil from only a portion of the war profiteering and frauds, dripped with the sordid facts of corruption, graft and profiteering that saturated every war industry and government war agency.

The OPM, the report disclosed, was controlled "by persons holding important positions with large companies who were willing and anxious to serve on a dollar per year or without compensation basis." On January 5, the report said, no less than 255 "without compensation" men were in the OPM "dealing with matters involving the welfare of the class of clients by whom they were formerly employed and by whom they naturally expect to be employed in the future." These corporation agents, the report further complained, were in position to inform their companies of impending shortages so they could grab up scarce materials and supplies.

Among the corporations named as benefiting from the government war contracts were the Big Three of auto: General Motors, Ford and Chrysler; "nineteen favored manufacturers of military aircraft": Bethlehem Steel, Aluminum Corporation of America and several of the large shipbuilding corporations.

James E. Barnes, representative of the Todd Shipbuilding Corporation, boasted to the Senate hearing: "If it wasn't for taxes, we couldn't have handled our profits with a steamshovel."

Nine of thirteen shipbuilding companies investigated by the Special Senate Committee got guaranteed net profits — above taxes — from government contracts in 1941, which were greater than the worth of their entire properties in 1939.

Almost immediately following the Truman report, the House Naval Affairs Committee issued a report disclosing further facts about the "excessive and unconscionable profits" of the shipbuilding corporations, some of them subsidiaries of the giant steel corporations. The committee assumed seven per cent to be a fair profit. However, profits made by 15 large companies that held 60 per cent of all shipbuilding contracts averaged between 20 and 40 per cent. On some individual contracts profits ranged as high as 246 per cent.

This same committee interjected into its report an attack on the union movement having no connection with naval affairs. It complained of the fact that 117 separate AFL, CIO, and Railway Brotherhood unions, organized for non-profit purposes and representing more than 6,000,000 members, had combined assets of $82,594,959. The congressmen called this an "astounding concentration of wealth," although it was less than one-twentieth of the assets of General Motors Corporation alone and one-fifteenth of the amount of the war contracts handed in one year to Bethlehem Steel.

The war gave a tremendous impulsion to the further concentration of wealth in the hands of a few big corporations and financial cliques. The Senate Committee on Small Business reported on February 5 that the War Production Board was "utterly ruthless to small business." Out of 184,230 manufacturing establishments, a mere 56 had received more than 75 per cent of all army and navy contracts, including aircraft. "The remaining fragments of the defense program is distributed among about 9,000 prime contractors" and over "174,000 manufacturing establishments have received no contracts at all, even through sub-contracts."

James E. Barnes, spokesman for the Todd Shipbuilding Corporation, holder of more than a billion dollars in naval contracts, told the Senate Naval Affairs Committee on February 5 that Todd's 1942 government business totaled $200,000,000, of which $20,000,000 was net profit—equaling ten per cent of the face value of the contracts, but 50 per cent of the company's invested capital of $40,000,000!

The official hullabaloo about war profits quickly subsided. It was intended simply to impress the people that the government was "doing something" about war profiteering and that the workers should, therefore, willingly give up even their bare necessities.

Replacing the OPM in January 1942, the new War Production Board took up where the OPM left off. Donald Nelson, named by Roosevelt to head the WPB, was a "loan" from Sears, Roebuck & Co., giant mail-order firm, where he was executive vice-president. He spoke of a reorganization of the war procurement setup but hastily added that "any revolutionary changes would only bring delay." He announced he was setting up six major divisions under the WPB. "Each of the six major divisions and most of the secondary groups are headed by executives who handled similar work in the OPM," reported the January 22 *New York Times*.

Sidney Hillman, however, was "overlooked" in this reorganization. He had been associate director-general of the OPM. He was "reorganized" out of the new WPB. The administration didn't bother to notify him of the change. He read about it in the papers. Subsequently, Hillman was elbowed completely out of the government when Roosevelt named Paul V. McNutt, former governor of Indiana, known as the "Hoosier Hitler" in labor circles because of his brutal strikebreaking of the 1938 Terre Haute general strike, to head the new War Manpower Commission. Hillman had been shamelessly pleading for the post. Roosevelt's action was a heavy blow to

Hillman, who suffered the first of the heart attacks that were to lead to his death four years later.

Following the issuance of the Truman report, Nelson appeared before the Senate Investigating Committee. He was asked if the kind of "good men" he wanted for his WPB setup did not have "an unconscious bias toward maintaining the present industrial setup." Nelson shot back: "Isn't that a criticism of all business men?"

Two days later Nelson told a private gathering of representatives of some 250 principal holders of war contracts:

"To hell with stopping to count the cost. Start turning the stuff out and we can argue the terms at our leisure. Turn it out by inefficient methods if necessary... but get the stuff moving."

The monopoly corporation agents lapped this up. The war contractors used not only "inefficient methods"; they turned over to the war agencies—for hard cash—material and equipment so defective that it cost the lives of many soldiers and seamen.

Throughout the war, defective Liberty ships cracked apart and sank at sea with heavy loss of lives. Soviet representatives here in 1944 refused to accept delivery of a score or more Liberty ships unless they were rebuilt. No steel or shipbuilding executives were ever tried or penalized for these crimes.

The Wright Aeronautical Corporation was accused by the Truman committee in July 1943 of falsifying tests on airplane engines, destroying records and forging others, etc. "I have no doubt a lot of kids in training planes have been killed as a result," said Truman. More than 25 per cent of their engines failed in army inspection.

Attorney General Biddle admitted on August 23, 1943, that war-contract frauds in World War II were "much bigger than they were in 1917 and 1918." He revealed that 123 federal indictments had already been filed, with 1,279 investigations pending, and only 71 cases had been disposed of. He complained that most of those convicted had received very light penalties. Only in the cases of a few small companies were company officials given short prison sentences.

Anaconda Wire and Cable Company was indicted on December 21, 1942, for conspiring to sell the government defective communications and other combat wire. The company was shown to have devised all sorts of ingenious methods for side-stepping government test requirements. The trial judge called its practices "revolting" and the prosecuting attorney described its actions as "the most obnoxious fraud ever presented to a court of the United States." However, the defendants were let off with money fines totaling $31,000 and no prison sentences. The frauds had profited the company many times the amount of the fines.

A valuable study of the war profiteering corporations is *Wartime Crimes of Big Business*, by George Breitman. Breitman points out that these wartime crimes were committed by such firms as U. S. Steel and Curtiss-Wright, which "are not two-bit businesses unrelated to the rest of industry. On the contrary, they are among the most powerful groups in American Big Business, being two of the 25 companies which hold 50% of the war contracts."

But these cases were played down and most of them eventually buried. The press generally paid small attention to them. The capitalist government had bigger fish to fry. It was preparing to "cook the fat" out of labor's living standards.

16

The Wartime Wage Freeze

A general offensive against wage increases, despite steeply rising living costs, was launched with the announcement on July 15, 1942 of the War Labor Board decision in the Little Steel case. This was the decision that came to be known as the "Little Steel Formula."

As was to be expected, the industry and "public" members of the WLB lined up solidly against the union representatives in the Little Steel decision. The board majority denied the United Steelworkers' demand for a dollar-a-day wage increase, despite a report of the board's own special panel that the industry could easily afford the wage boost without raising prices. The steelworkers were awarded just 44 cents per day more. The award was based on the following formula, as stated by the board:

"For the period from January 1, 1941 to May 1942...the cost of living increased about 15%. If any group of workers averaged less than a 15% increase in hourly wage rates during or immediately preceding or following this period, their established peacetime standards have been broken. If any group averaged a 15% increase or more, their established peacetime standards have been preserved."

To begin with, the preservation of the "established peacetime standards" meant continuation of the low-level depression wages which had continued right up to Pearl Harbor, as the Bureau of Labor Statistics figures showed.

By using the cost-of-living figure of January 1, 1941 as the yardstick, the WLB deliberately chose a period prior to the great strike wave of 1941. Most CIO workers had won increases that year and under the Little Steel Formula would therefore receive little or no further increases. Actually, the WLB fact-finding panel had found that living costs had gone up 13 per cent since April 1941. Thus, the 5.5 per cent granted the steelworkers left at least an eight per cent disparity between their "peacetime standards" as of April 1941 and the time of the WLB ruling.

On July 20, the *CIO News* complained that the WLB decision in the Little Steel case was "predicated" on the policies of the Office of Price Administration, which "instead of concentrating its attention on price fixing and democratic rationing of consumer goods, has maintained its attack against legitimate and equitable wage adjustments for the workers." The OPA policies, of course, were determined or at least approved by Roosevelt and enforced by his appointees. The *CIO News* omitted this fact.

Just prior to the ruling Murray had hinted to the press that the United Steelworkers might reject anything less than the union's demand. Asked whether the CIO could do this, he had answered: "I understand that this is still a democracy. Labor understands it has the right to go after wage increases and nobody has said that the workers must accept wage rates that somebody negotiates for them."

On the eve of the decision, Murray had even threatened to hold a referendum vote of the steelworkers on the issue. But he quickly wilted after Roosevelt summoned him for a private conference. He then agreed to the WLB decision.

Although the four WLB labor members had said that "the wage ruling struck a heavy blow at the foundations of collective bargaining," Murray pushed through a unanimous vote at the United Steelworkers Policy Committee meeting to accept the WLB decisions. The steel union leaders were consoled somewhat by the board's award of a "maintenance of membership" clause.

The steel union's Policy Committee sought to condition its surrender with the statement: "We now look toward the President to carry through the remaining portions of the National Economic Program, such as an effective tax program, a real effective freezing of prices of goods, rents and other items of cost to the people."

They were to keep looking vainly for fulfillment of the rainbow promises of "equality of sacrifice" right to the war's close.

Two weeks after its Little Steel decision, the WLB used the same formula to deny a ten-cent hourly increase in the Tonawanda, New York, Remington Rand case. This time the WLB majority made plain that the formula was intended to apply to all the workers in every industry. A section of the ruling said: "The National Association of Manufacturers has called attention to the fact that over two-thirds of the manufacturing industries of the country have already made increases to or in excess of the level fixed by the War Labor Board's formula... contrary to some reports it [Little Steel

Formula] does not guarantee to labor that existing standards of living will be maintained throughout the war."

If the CIO leaders appeared ready to give away the workers' rights and conditions at a mere nod from Roosevelt, the CIO ranks were not so yielding. The first flare-up occurred at the United Automobile Workers convention in August.

A rank-and-file revolt swept the convention on its second day, August 4, against the fraudulent "equality of sacrifice" program and the surrender of premium pay. Stamping, shouting delegates forced the War Policy Committee, headed by Reuther, Frankensteen and Addes, to withdraw a resolution endorsing sacrifice of overtime pay. This resolution contained the complaint that the AFL and certain employers were not complying with the equality of sacrifice program and it threatened to end the UAW agreement to comply unless the government enforced sacrifices universally "within thirty days."

Stalinist speakers, who had come forward as the most avid defenders of the resolution, were roundly booed by the delegates. Frankensteen, the board member who had approved Roosevelt's use of troops in the North American aircraft strike, was prevented from speaking for 20 minutes as the delegates clamored for a vote after an already prolonged debate.

The UAW leaders confused the issue the next day with a "revised" version of the resolution which contained instructions to the UAW secretary-treasurer to notify all employers of the 30-day limitation on the universal enforcement of the premium-pay ban. This was, in reality, a call on the government to ban premium pay by law within 30 days. But before another full-blown debate could develop, CIO President Murray was introduced to give a long patriotic harangue and the vote was then taken. A majority of the delegates accepted the revised resolution.

Thomas, Addes, Reuther and Frankensteen went to Washington on August 28. They asked Roosevelt to halt all premium pay for weekends and holidays — that is, they asked for the imposition of a wage cut on all organized labor.

Roosevelt happily complied with this demand. On September 9, he decreed abolition of all premium pay for weekends and holidays, abrogating all union contracts providing for such overtime pay. In effect, this established a precedent for government cancellation of any aspect of union contracts deemed by Roosevelt "against the interests of the war program."

At this time, Roosevelt also initiated his program to freeze workers to their jobs. He issued two decrees on September 14. One decree empowered War Manpower Commissioner McNutt to transfer 2,300,000 federal employees to any jobs, including private factories, without their consent. The other ordered workers in the lumber and nonferrous metals industries in 12 states not to leave their jobs without permits on penalty of being reclassified and drafted for military service.

CIO President Murray had already given Roosevelt a signed blank check. He had said on Labor Day: "I am going to support you and the CIO is going to stand by you, come what may."

What came were the succession of decrees against labor.

The Little Steel Formula was quickly expanded into a universal wage freeze. WLB Chairman Davis told the Senate Banking Committee on September 15 that the Little Steel Formula would automatically disqualify 75 per cent of wage earners from any further increases. "If workers want more pay," he said, "they must work overtime to get it." Indeed, with soaring prices, mounting taxes, and bond deductions, most workers exhausted themselves with long hours to make ends meet.

On September 17, the WLB rejected the dollar-a-day demand of the General Motors workers. Using the Little Steel Formula, the board granted the GM workers a raise of just four cents an hour. Two days later the board ruled to penalize an AFL union at the General Electric Company in Buffalo by denying it a union security clause because it had gone on strike for just a few hours in June. Thus, the WLB was assuming not only compulsory arbitration powers, but enforcement and punitive powers over the unions.

Under his claimed wartime powers as Commander in Chief and decree powers granted him just the week before by Congress, Roosevelt on October 5 issued a far-reaching decree affecting wages. He set up the Office of Economic Stabilization and named James Byrnes as director or "economic czar." Byrnes was a notoriously antilabor and anti-Negro Democrat from poll-tax South Carolina who had served in the Senate and had been appointed a Supreme Court Justice by Roosevelt.

The same order directly froze wages at the September 15, 1942 level. It stated: "The National War Labor Board shall not approve any increases in wage rates prevailing on September 15, 1942, unless such increases are necessary to correct maladjustments or inequalities to eliminate substandards of living, to correct gross inequities."

It was left to Byrnes to decide what would be "gross inequities." In any event, the decree ruled out raises for most of the workers.

Moreover, the decree forbade increases by "voluntary agreement, collective bargaining, arbitration or otherwise" unless filed with the WLB and approved by it. The unions were thus deprived of the right to bargain with the employers independently of the government.

To soften the anti-labor effect of his order, Roosevelt appended a section purporting to limit salaries to $25,000 a year. It did not touch on the main sources of capitalist income — dividends, interests and rents. The wording of this phase of the decree is a model for all shyster lawyers:

"*Insofar as practicable,* no salary shall be authorized to the extent that it exceeds $25,000 *after the payment of taxes* provided however that *such regulations shall make due allowance for the payment of life insurance premiums, required payments on fixed obligations...and shall make provision to prevent* undue hardship." (My emphasis. A. P.)

As it worked out under Byrnes, everyone accustomed to more than $25,000 a year net salary was indeed considered to suffer "undue hardship" if cut to that level. This salary limitation was never seriously enforced.

A week after his appointment, Byrnes issued his first order on wages. He officially enjoined the War Labor Board to freeze all wages on the basis of the Little Steel Formula and ordered the WLB to disapprove all negotiated wage increases that exceeded the limits allowed by this formula.

The WLB then turned down the demand of the Ford workers for a dollar daily raise and denied so much as a cent increase. At the same time, the WLB adopted a program providing for direct investigation of all local unions involved in any strike and the securing of "full information as to the relations of the local officers to the strike and their efforts locally and in cooperation with the international officers to prevent its occurrence."

This was designed to put local union officers on the spot by compelling them to state publicly their attitude toward each strike.

In the last week of October, Roosevelt signed the new tax law which imposed income taxes on 29 million more workers and low-income farmers who had been previously exempt. It provided for a "victory tax" for all persons, married or single, earning $12 a week or more.

When the CIO convened its five-day national convention in Boston, November 9 to 14, its officers and delegates painted a dismal picture of the treatment of labor. Frankensteen of the UAW bewailed the difficulties of organizing the aircraft industry: "We no longer have the approach we once had of telling these workers that if they join with us we have a very tangible something to put in their hands, that we can get them a wage increase... No longer can we step in and organize a plant, and if we are unsuccessful in bargaining we can no longer strike..."

Lewis Merrill, head of the United Office and Professional Workers of America, confessed that while the labor force in the country had increased by 12 million since 1935, the CIO had not grown substantially since the peak of its offensive in 1937. It now had about five million members and was surpassed by the AFL, which the CIO had outnumbered in 1937. "The ratio of organized labor to the new working class that has been brought forth in this country has been obviously in the direction of representing a smaller proportion of that total working force..."

Lee Pressman, national CIO counsel, conceded that "as of a week ago there was in Washington, in the offices of the National War Labor Board, about three or four thousand wage agreements. The entire administrative machinery of the Board has completely broken down... with agreements piled up in some room over in some warehouse somewhere." But Pressman also voiced the "danger" of "criticizing the Board to such a degree that it will be interpreted to mean that we want the Board terminated."

Murray complained that the new income tax law "passed this year has meant a nation-wide wage cut which creates serious dangers to food budgets."

After five days of complaining, the CIO leaders wound up pledging their all to Roosevelt. Murray's closing address prophesied that "the record will show that this convention will undoubtedly go down in history as perhaps the greatest parliament of labor ever conducted anywhere, any place, any time in the history of this country."

Murray's evaluation of the historic role of the 1942 CIO convention was wholly exaggerated. None of the rank and file was heard. Every tendency within the top bureaucracy had united against the ranks. There was not one dissenting voice. Lewis and the United Mine Workers had pulled out of the CIO the month before and their powerful influence could no longer serve as a restraint upon the rest of the CIO leaders. In effect, every speaker recited: Roosevelt's in his White House, all's right with the world. About the only positive action of this "greatest parliament of labor" was its renewal of the no-strike surrender.

Yet, even as the CIO leaders were boasting of their effectiveness in preventing and halting strikes, the strike statistics for 1942, the first full year of America's entry into the war, belied the impression they sought to give that the class struggle had been completely smothered.

There were no fewer than 2,968 strikes that year, involving 840,000 workers. The number of strikes surpassed that of any year back to 1919, except the record-breaking years of 1937 and 1941. The number of strikers was greater than in 1936, 1938 and 1940, and every year between 1919 and 1933. But the labor leaders had done their work well in one respect. With the aid of the government and employers, they had quickly broken most strikes. The man-days idle in 1942 due to strikes was the lowest since 1930.

The year 1942 proved to be only a brief calm between storms. The period of the war was one of continuous and mounting class struggle. The American working class did not submit meekly to the war patrioteers and jingoes. The record proves they fought back magnificently to defend their standards and rights despite the treachery and strikebreaking of most of their own leaders.

17

The Break
between Lewis
and Murray

At the November 1941 CIO convention, the CIO's total membership had been reported as exactly five million, including those who had merely signed application blanks. There were 41 national and international unions; 33 state councils; and 204 city, county and district councils. The three largest CIO unions were the United Mine Workers with 600,000 members; the Steel Workers Organizing Committee, 500,000; and the United Automobile Workers, 400,000.

The CIO as a whole never grew significantly beyond this point. By the end of World War II, the union leaders were to claim around 6,000,000 members, but the increase over the pre-Pearl Harbor period was mainly a result of the wartime expansion of employment in already organized sectors of industry. There was little CIO extension into unorganized areas and industries. The organization of the South, which Murray at the 1941 convention had proclaimed as "Task Number One," was scarcely mentioned at the 1942 convention.

An indication of the brake placed on its dynamic drive was the shift in the relative strengths of the CIO and AFL. Recouping from the AFL's all-time low of 2,060,933 members in 1937, when the CIO had spurted past the parent body, the latter reported at its 1941 convention an all-time membership peak of 4,669,036 paid-up card holders. Allowing for dues exemptions for illness, retirement and unemployment, the AFL was once more about equal in membership to the CIO.

The very success of the CIO benefited the AFL, which also capitalized on the general upsurge of union sentiment inspired by the CIO victories. Some employers were persuaded to sign AFL contracts rather than deal with the "radical" CIO. In 1941 the OPM had agreed to make the AFL Building and Construction Trades Department the sole bargaining agency for all war construction, in return for a union commitment to forego premium pay for Sundays, holidays and night work when these fell during a regular shift. This same sacrifice was then foisted on the CIO industrial workers in the spring of 1942 by government edict. The AFL had also gained at the expense of the CIO with the re-entry of Dubinsky's ILGWU in 1940.

A far more serious loss for the CIO was the breakaway of the United Mine Workers in October 1942. The miners were not only the largest union in the CIO, but had provided from 80 to 90 per cent of the financing of its organizing drive and a big percentage of its organizing manpower. Virtually the entire top leadership of the steelworkers came from the mine workers. The militancy and solidarity of the miners were a source of inspiration to the rest of the CIO workers.

Lewis, after he had stepped out of the CIO presidency in November 1940, tried not to interfere with Murray's conduct of that post. Nevertheless, he had continued to play a dominant role in the labor movement and outshone Murray by leading a struggle against government intervention in labor conflicts, particularly in the captive mine strikes. Murray had appointed Lewis, along with himself and Emspak of the UE, as one of the three CIO representatives at the industry-labor conference called by Roosevelt shortly after Pearl Harbor.

The underlying conflict between Murray and Lewis, based on their opposite attitudes toward Roosevelt and toward reliance on the government labor machinery, broke through soon after the conference. On January 17, 1942, Lewis told the press he had proposed, via a letter to Philip Murray and William Green, a meeting of the CIO and AFL with a view to "accouplement" — merger — of the two largest labor bodies in America. Lewis had written:

"It is obvious that if accouplement could be achieved with unified and competent leadership, the results would be advantageous and in the public interest...I address this letter to each of you in my capacity as a member of the standing negotiating committee of the Congress of Industrial Organizations, acting under the authority of its third constitutional convention."

Roosevelt, who had been publicly urging an AFL-CIO merger since the outbreak of the war in Europe and had been conniving with Hillman and others toward this end, was enraged by Lewis's move. His hostility was further inflamed by A. H. Raskin's article in the January 19 *New York Times*. Raskin asserted that Lewis's unity move was based on a deal with AFL Teamsters President Daniel J. Tobin to retire Green from the presidency on a lifetime pension of $20,000 annually. George Meany, the AFL's secretary-treasurer, was to be boosted to president of a merged AFL-CIO and Philip Murray was to become its secretary-treasurer at $18,000 per annum, his salary as vice-president of the United Mine Workers. Murray's posts of CIO president and SWOC chairman were unsalaried.

Roosevelt called in both Murray and Green and bitterly denounced Lewis's proposition. Murray needed little prodding to express his disfavor with Lewis's plan and Lewis himself. It is reported that when Murray was apprised of the alleged Lewis-Tobin "plot" he exclaimed: "I will not be Pearl-Harbored!" He left his conference with Roosevelt breathing fire and brimstone at Lewis: "My manhood requires a little reciprocity and, by God, despite this feeble frame of mine, I will fight any living man to maintain my manhood."

Lewis had acted improperly in initiating a unity move without consultation with the president of his own organization, the CIO. But it was equally true that Murray did not come into court with "clean hands." Murray had been in collaboration with Lewis's mortal enemy, Roosevelt, and had been going to this union outsider for instructions, instead of consulting with the CIO membership.

No proof has ever been offered for Raskin's story. It might have been true that Lewis sought to take the initiative away from Roosevelt in the unity maneuvers. But Tobin was head of the National Labor Committee of the Democratic Party and newly indebted to Roosevelt for the federal trial and conviction of Tobin's internal union opposition in Minneapolis. He was not likely to plot against the President he worshiped. Moreover, other union leaders such as David Dubinsky and Emil Rieve had publicly applauded Lewis's proposition for "accouplement." Yet, they were all pro-Roosevelt to the core.

The merits of Lewis's unity proposal, apart from the manner in which he made it, must be judged in terms of the interests of the industrial workers and the effect such unity would have had on industrial unionism at that time. In November 1940, when the CIO membership was larger than the AFL's, Lewis had argued against unity, saying: "There is no peace because you are not strong enough to command peace upon honorable terms." In January 1942, he argued that "conditions are now changed."

However, nothing fundamental had changed save that the relative strengths of the two organizations had altered in favor of the AFL. There is no evidence that Tobin and the rest of the die-hard proponents of craft unionism in the AFL were ready in 1942 to accept the CIO industrial unions on the "honorable terms" of maintaining these unions intact without craft invasions.

The CIO's official and public repudiation of Lewis's unity proposal intensified the Lewis-Murray conflict. Moving to sharpen the attack on Lewis and the United Mine Workers, the Stalinist-controlled New York City CIO Council on March 14, 1942 expelled nine locals of the United Construction Workers Organizing Committee for "nonpayment of dues." The UCWOC was headed by A. D. Lewis, brother of the mine union president.

Michael Quill, head of the CIO Transport Workers Union, with a group of his henchmen invaded the UMW's District 50 offices in New York City looking for "dual unionists." Furniture was smashed and several UMW organizers threatened. Quill posed for press photographs with a smashed picture of John L. Lewis and charged Lewis with being "part and parcel of an isolationist plot." A UMW protest to Murray about Quill's assault was ignored.

On March 18, 1942, the CIO received a request from the UMW to deduct two months' per capita — $60,000 — owed the CIO from the $1,665,000 which Lewis claimed the miners had advanced over the years. In early April, UMW representatives withdrew from the Illinois CIO Council and Lewis men resigned from other CIO bodies. Late in April Lewis called a meeting of the UMW's Policy Board for May 25. Murray, a paid vice-president of the UMW, was explicitly instructed to attend.

Murray knew that the axe was poised over his head. This was the one and only side of Lewis that Murray himself had learned—the bureaucratic side. Murray tried to mount a counterattack. He assailed Lewis before a meeting of the Pennsylvania CIO Council, calling the UMW's claims for per capita credit nothing but "lousy low-life sabotage." Finally, Murray consolidated his own union base by calling a constitutional convention of the steelworkers, establishing the United Steelworkers of America with himself as president at $20,000 a year—$2,000 more than he was getting from the mine workers.

Three days later, on May 25, the UMW Policy Committee met. Murray made a commendatory talk in which he fervently pleaded his admiration and respect for Lewis. Murray claimed that "no one has taken greater pride in the leadership which you have than I have, and I speak with particular reference to the accomplishments of our distinguished President when I say so."

The next day's session began with a review by Lewis of his moves for "accouplement" of the CIO and AFL. He claimed he had the right to initiate these moves since he was chairman of the Standing Peace-Negotiating Committee of the CIO, not appointed, but elected by convention. Then he gave details of the UMW's financial and organizational aid to the rising CIO: In the first two years of the CIO, the UMW had provided more than 88 per cent of the total costs of the CIO. The other founding unions together had provided less than 12 per cent.

Suddenly, Lewis interjected the matter of Murray's attacks on Lewis's patriotism. Not only had Murray refused to credit $60,000 of per capita to the UMW from the sums contributed or loaned to the CIO, "but Vice-President Murray had already called me a Jap." (Lewis's resentment was not directed at Murray's use of the racial epithet, "Jap," but at his imputation that Lewis did not support the imperialist war.)

Murray loudly denied that he had ever called Lewis a "Jap." In fact, he was fulsome in his praise of Lewis, the patriot. "I don't know how often it should become necessary for me to repeat and repeat and repeat that as a man and as a citizen and as an American I have always regarded Mr. Lewis as without a peer in the realm of America. I dislike and I resent, no matter whose mouth it flows from, the implication that I made any filthy insinuating remark concerning President Lewis's Americanism."

Lewis then pulled the rug from under Murray's feet. He inquired whether Murray had accepted a paid post with the United Steelworkers in addition to his paid position with the UMW. Unable to deny that he was on the steelworkers' payroll as president at $20,000 per annum, Murray finally asked to be excused from the session and went weeping from the United Mine Workers headquarters, never to return.

Lewis did not bother to go through formal trial proceedings. On May 28, using his unrestricted constitutional powers to remove officials for "just and sufficient cause," Lewis declared Murray no longer a UMW vice-president, an action later approved by the Executive Board. Since Murray had incorporated precisely the same powers for himself into the steel union's new constitution, he could scarcely condemn Lewis's procedure. After the UMW Board had acted, Murray said resignedly: "I cannot question the authority of the international executive board in these matters."

Murray unleashed a two-hour attack on Lewis at the CIO Executive Board meeting on June 4 in the presence of the press. He said Lewis was "hell-bent on creating national confusion and national disunity." Murray no longer resented the "implication that I made any filthy insinuating remark concerning President Lewis's Americanism." In fact, he told the CIO tops that at the time of the October 1941 CIO convention Lewis had privately sought his support to "an act of treason" by urging him "to fight the foreign policies of the United States."

When the United Mine Workers met in convention on October 7, 1942, Lewis delivered one of his most biting speeches, scoring the leaders he himself had raised to power in the CIO, and calling for a split. The convention voted 2,867 to 5 for immediate withdrawal.

Some have viewed Lewis's break with the CIO as merely an act of personal pique, the expression of a grudge against Roosevelt and therefore against Roosevelt's handmaidens in the CIO. Undoubtedly, there was a good deal of individual animus in Lewis's action. No less impelling was the question of retaining the UMW's freedom to act amidst the increasing signs of pressure and restraints on the miners. Lewis feared government interference—and his fears were more than justified.

But the wisdom of his withdrawal from the CIO was questionable on other and more principled grounds. He weakened those who might have rallied around him to fight effectively within it for an independent militant policy during the war and to smash the Little Steel Formula wage freeze. Above all, he weakened the CIO in relation to the AFL and helped encourage those within the AFL who still hoped to destroy the CIO as an effective force for industrial unionism.

Lewis's pretexts for splitting certainly did him no credit. His claim that the funds advanced by the UMW to the CIO were a "loan" put the unselfish role of the miners in the building of the CIO in the light purely of a business transaction. In turn, the heroic battles of the workers in steel, auto, rubber and other industries had immeasurably aided and strengthened the miners and more than repaid the UMW for its monetary advances. Moreover, the chief reason Lewis gave to the UMW for splitting from the CIO was a personal one—he had been attacked and slandered by the other CIO leaders. This was true, but did it justify his abandoning millions of workers to these leaders, and withdrawing the miners from the organization they had helped so much to build?

18

How the Miners Won

There were many signs of the growing restiveness of the industrial workers as 1942 drew to a close and during the opening months of 1943. These indicate that if the miners had not been isolated, the coal mine strikes of 1943 would have aroused a far more active sympathy and even emulation from the CIO ranks.

There was a growing volume of protest from leading unions at the burial of wage demands and grievances within the War Labor Board — that "Graveyard of Grievances." The CIO United Auto Workers Executive Board, at its December 1942 meeting in Los Angeles, protested the WLB's stalling on its wage demands. Even the Stalinist-led CIO United Electrical Workers protested on December 22 because the "backlog of unsettled disputes is mounting each week." These protests reflected the pressure from the ranks. In January 1943, the anti-strike UAW leaders "were in a cold sweat," as one labor reporter put it, because of a spreading wave of flash departmental strikes in Michigan war plants, where the UAW leaders helped army officials suppress the strikes but clamored for a "revamped and streamlined" WLB.

The coal miners, for the most part isolated in small towns, were squeezed worst of all. When Pennsylvania anthracite miners started an unauthorized walkout on January 2, 1943, it was clear that they had reached a point of open revolt against economic conditions. A false rumor that the strikers were opposing a dues increase voted by the previous UMW convention was scotched by Senator Truman, who revealed in the Senate that a survey by the government found the miners demanding higher wages — $2 more a day.

The War Labor Board stepped in to "mediate" the strike on January 15 by ordering the men back to work. Lewis himself called the strikes unauthorized and ordered the workers to return to the pits. At the same time, he lashed at the WLB and announced he would present a demand for a "wholesome increase" in wages when the contract expired on April 30. The WLB back-to-work order only provoked the miners to extend their strike. Roosevelt himself, at the WLB's request, on January 16 ordered the miners back to work as "your Commander in Chief," raising the thinly veiled threat of military strikebreaking when he said that "your government will take the necessary steps to protect the security of the nation against the strike..." For the most part, the strikers ignored Roosevelt and his threats and returned to work on January 22 only at the pleading of their own leaders.

On January 30, OPA head Prentiss Brown approved a price boost of 23 cents a ton to Western Pennsylvania soft coal operators. He blandly told the press: "I don't believe and Congress never intended, that prices could be held at a flat level. We thought a slow, well-ordered rise of one-half of one per cent a month would occur under the most favorable circumstances." Secretary of Labor Perkins admitted in the same week that prices since Pearl Harbor rose nine per cent and were more than 22 per cent higher than in August 1939.

This was a conservative estimate. The UAW–CIO Executive Board, meeting in emergency session in Chicago the last week in January 1943, called on the national CIO to adopt a "realistic formula recognizing an advance of at least 30% in the cost of living since January 1941, so that the workers through their unions can commence to bargain now for comparable increases in wages." ILGWU-AFL President Dubinsky protested that the rise in living costs since adoption of the Little Steel Formula was 22 per cent "while the dressmakers in that period have had an increase of only 10%."

Lewis announced on January 28 that the UMW's Policy Committee would meet in Washington on February 2 to formulate wage demands on the soft coal operators for 450,000 mine workers. He minced no words about his attitude toward Roosevelt's WLB:

"Under the arbitrary and miserably stupid formula [Little Steel], it [WLB] chains labor to the wheels of industry without compensation for increased costs, while other agencies of government reward and fatten industry by charging its increased costs to the public purse. Assuredly, labor, despite its present weak and vacillating leadership, cannot long tolerate such economically paradoxical and socially unjust treatment."

WLB Chairman William H. Davis answered Lewis by recalling that the board's wage policy had been adopted by unanimous vote of labor, industry and "public" members, and was in line with "the specific instructions of the President in Executive Order 9250 of October 3, 1942," the decree freezing wages and naming Byrnes as economic czar.

Murray and Green on February 3 together visited Roosevelt in the White House to express dissatisfaction with the Little Steel Formula. They reported afterwards that while the President "showed deep interest, he made no specific commitments of any kind."(*New York Times,* February 4, 1943.)

On the day the CIO and AFL chiefs made their plaints to Roosevelt, Lewis announced the UMW Policy Committee would demand a $2-a-day raise for the bituminous miners. Lewis pointed out that if the soft coal miners were restricted to the Little Steel Formula they would have to "give back two per cent of their current wages."

A few days later the CIO Executive Board, meeting February 6 in Washington, said in a wage policy resolution that "allowance must be made for wage adjustments due to the increased cost of living which has resulted since May 1942," the date the Little Steel Formula was adopted.

In the whole labor movement, only the Stalinists and their followers supported the government's wage freeze. Harry Bridges, according to the February 7 *New York Times* report of the CIO Board meeting, "supported the current government wage policy and had urged that the CIO put its emphasis on demands for stricter price control enforcement and universal rationing of essential commodities. Mr. Bridges was answered sharply by Mr. Murray, who contended that some upward revision of the government wage policy was essential to maintain the support of workers whose living costs, especially for foods, have been going up sharply in recent months."

In a radio broadcast of February 9, Economic Stabilization Director Byrnes reaffirmed the administration's wage-freeze policy: "There must be no further increases in wages beyond the Little Steel Formula except in limited cases and special cases to correct gross inequities and to rectify plainly substandard wages."

To emphasize the point, the WLB on February 9 denied any wage increase to the badly exploited and underpaid CIO packinghouse workers of the "Big Four" meatpacking corporations: Armour, Swift, Wilson, and Cudahy. This ruling was accomplished by a proposal for a 48-hour week in the industry similar to the longer work week instituted in certain areas by presidential decree just the week before. War Manpower Commissioner McNutt threatened on February 15 that the work week might even be raised "beyond 48 hours a week, possibly to 52."

The statements and actions of the various government agencies and administration spokesmen were more and more focused on the coming assault on the miners. To Lewis's credit, he did not flinch from the battle or sweeten his tone toward the enemies. Speaking before the UMW's Tri-District convention on March 3 in Scranton, Pennsylvania, Lewis called the combination of the WLB, OPA and Economic Stabilizer Byrnes "a court packed against labor."

"I challenge anyone to deny," he said, "that industry and finance under our government's policy are guaranteed against the high cost of production, the high cost of living, and profit on top of that."

On March 10, the UMW opened negotiations with the Appalachian soft coal operators. Among the seven demands Lewis and the UMW committee presented to the mine owners were: (1) retention of the existing 35-hour, five-day week in the coal mining industry; (2) inclusion of all time traveled from the pit entrance to the point of work and back to the surface as part of the paid work time; (3) a $2-per-day raise in base pay.

In presenting these demands, Lewis unleashed a four-hour denunciation of the conspiracy of the Roosevelt administration and the coal operators "who smugly hope the government will chastise the mine worker for daring to make known the miserable facts of his existence." He pointed out that a UMW survey in 80 Pennsylvania mining towns showed that between 1939 and 1943 food costs for the miners had gone up 124.6 per cent, a fact later confirmed by government surveys.

Lewis spoke over the heads of the mine owners to the organized workers of America. The policies of the government and corporations "inflame the workers in industries who know that their rights are being withheld from them by this strange combination of government and industry. Let me warn you this afternoon that you can't do this to our people with impunity...

"Mine workers are hungry. They are asking for food, and if they don't get it, and if their contract runs out, it is a safe assumption that the mine workers, in the absence of a contract, will not trespass upon your property the first and second of April this year."

Lewis further solemnly warned the operators: "Your policy of do-nothing, and of waiting to see what the government will do for you will not buy you anything in 1943."

The UMW president cited the terrific accident rate in the mines due to lack of safety equipment: 64,000 men killed and injured in 1941; 75,000 in 1942; an estimated 100,000 in 1943, with the intensification of war production.

"That's a lot of meat," he said, "a lot of human meat to grind up in one year. There are too many funerals in this industry, gentlemen."

Demanding elimination of the third shift, thus permitting the mines to "bleed" and slow down the formation of explosive gasses, Lewis continued, "We care not if the elimination of this third shift takes a few shekels out of some operators' pockets."

From the Big Business lines came a drum-roll barrage against the miners. The press and radio wheeled up their heavy artillery. Lewis was subjected to a propaganda assault such as no man in American history had ever known. "Traitor," "treasonous," and "a Hitler" were repeated epithets flung at him. The March 13 *New York Herald Tribune* typified all of the press, both Republican and Democratic, when it blared:

"The government of the United States... has got to do something about John L. Lewis... It is not easy to exaggerate Lewis's challenge, not only to the nation's prosecution of the war but to the basic conception of American democracy."

The Executive Board of the CIO Amalgamated Clothing Workers, in the face of the CIO's own campaign for higher wages as well as mine negotiations, demonstratively announced that the ACW would not ask for a general wage increase for 125,000 workers whose contracts were up for renewal in May. This could have no other effect than to encourage Roosevelt and the mine owners in their resistance to the miners' demands.

The Stalinists openly sought to ingratiate themselves with the employers and government by an unrestrained slander campaign against Lewis. The *Daily Worker* editorialized: "The Lewis line is disruption of the war effort and provocation that could only result in irreparable harm to labor... He wants to throw the country into a home-front war against the President, not against Hitler."

Brushed aside in this wild swirl of words against Lewis was the simple fact that the operators were authorized to raise the price of coal while the miners were on the edge of hunger due to war inflation and war profiteering.

Truman's Senate War Investigating Committee, dropping its queries about war profiteering and the collusion of government agencies and big corporations, diverted its attention to the miners. Lewis was summoned before the committee on March 26.

The committee did not even attempt to conceal its hostility to the miners and its solicitude for the operators. Lewis easily deflected the barbs aimed at him and flayed the senators so mercilessly, exposing their stupid arguments with such withering scorn, that they publicly flinched before him at this open hearing. When they questioned the UMW's demand for "portal-to-portal" pay, Lewis pointed out that the Federal Circuit Court of Appeals in New Orleans the previous month had ruled that ore miners must be paid from the time they enter the mine to the time they leave it. The coal miners were asking nothing more.

When Senator Brewster of Maine interrupted Lewis's exposure of the cost-plus war contracts with the claim that under "proposed tax legislation. . . we will hope the rich will not get richer out of this war," Lewis snapped: "We all hope with you, but hope deferred maketh the heart sick." Brewster then asserted that Hitler would have been at America's shores "if we had waited to work out reasonable prices" for war goods. "Do you mean to imply," Lewis shot at Brewster, "that American industry wouldn't provide essential war goods to a nation that needed them unless guaranteed profits first?"

As the reeling senators were preparing to call it a day, Burton of Ohio told Lewis: "We want to help to make sure we don't start off inflation from this corner." Lewis answered: "Do you mind first inflating the stomachs of some of my members?" The flushed senator cried: "If we restrain industry and finance, are you willing to work on holding down the wages?" Rising to leave, Lewis glanced contemptuously at Burton and purred: "My dear Senator, whenever you have restrained industry and finance, just call me on the telephone and let me know."

The mine owners brushed aside the UMW's demands and the Roosevelt administration intensified pressure on the union to capitulate. On March 22, the industry and "public" members of the War Labor Board rejected the demand of the CIO and AFL representatives that the Little Steel Formula be junked and that the CIO packinghouse and West Coast aircraft cases be reopened. Wage raises had been denied in both cases to low paid workers.

The action of the CIO and AFL members of the WLB reflected both the pressure of their own ranks and their fear that Lewis, by appearing as the sole real opponent of the wage freeze, would gain the moral leadership of wide sections of organized labor. In fact, for the first time, the union members on the WLB characterized the Little Steel Formula as a "wage-freezing" device and not simply wage stabilization.

Roosevelt himself intervened as the April 1 mine strike deadline approached. He asked the operators on March 27 to agree to extend the existing contract beyond April 1 and make any subsequent wage adjustment retroactive to that date. At the same time he said that the dispute must be settled "under the national no-strike agreement of December 26, 1941" with "final determination, if necessary, by the National War Labor Board."

The moral position of the miners was becoming stronger every day. The CIO and AFL leaders backed the miners' demands and, for the time being, refrained from open attacks on the UMW's threat to strike. Local bodies of the United Auto Workers and other CIO unions passed resolutions of unconditional support for the miners. Only the Stalinist-controlled leadership of the CIO National Maritime Union, headed by Joseph Curran, chose the occasion to pass a resolution that openly smeared the UMW leaders.

The showdown was temporarily averted when a 30-day truce was accepted by the UMW leaders on the agreement of the mine owners to make any upward wage adjustment retroactive. This period of grace was used by the operators and the administration to build up the assault. The mine owners just sat tight and refused to discuss any settlement. Thomas Kennedy, UMW secretary-treasurer who had been originally appointed a CIO member of the WLB, resigned from that government board.

On April 8, Roosevelt issued what he called his "Hold-the-Line" executive decree, placing wages under the most sweeping and drastic controls in United States history. In his decree, which Roosevelt said was so "clear and specific" no one could misunderstand or misinterpret his meaning, he ordered all government agencies involved "to authorize no further increases in wages and salaries except such as are clearly necessary to correct substandards of living." This "substandard" had not been defined. The order made no mention of "inequities" this time. It did authorize War Manpower Commissioner McNutt to prevent workers from shifting to higher paid jobs.

Roosevelt's wage-freeze order was joyously hailed in an April 12 telegram to the White House from Edward R. Burke, head of the Southern Coal Producers Association. Burke said he interpreted the order as ruling out any wage increase for the miners and urged that the coal controversy be certified immediately to the WLB.

The top CIO and AFL leaders at first expressed shock and apprehension at the edict. They could scarcely do less — especially when Roosevelt, two days after his wage-freezing order, refused to veto the Public Debt Expansion Bill which carried a rider repealing any $25,000-a-year salary limitation. The *Daily Worker* alone of the entire working-class press hailed the "Hold-the-Line" order.

Lewis did not retreat before Roosevelt's new attack. He said on April 10:

"The farmer and miner in effect are being asked to maintain their living standards on a status quo, ante-bellum basis with no consideration of wear or tear or depreciation of human plant facilities while corporate industry is given ample allowance for maintenance of plant and equipment and $6,250,000,000 in nine months of monetary awards [net profits] for luxurious living...

"It is beside the point that other labor organizations such as the AFL and CIO, through their leaders, have adopted a policy of cringing toadyism to the administration coupled with a blind worship of the astoundingly unsound economic policies of the administration.

"The United Mine Workers and its membership will continue to make the fight."

Lewis's appraisal of the CIO and AFL leaders was confirmed a few days later when the union members on the WLB concurred in its decision to limit to two cents an hour a wage increase approved in the Atlas Cement case. This was the first case to come before the board after Roosevelt's "Hold-the-Line" order.

On April 17, McNutt issued a sweeping order freezing 27,000,000 workers to their jobs. CIO President Murray on April 19 approved the general principle of the order, with the reservation that certain features of the order be "clarified."

Roosevelt indicated that he would not permit even a token compromise but would attempt to force the UMW to total surrender, when he withdrew John Steelman, federal conciliator, and Secretary of Labor Perkins from their participation in the mine dispute. These officials had indicated a willingness to consider some compromise. But the operators insisted only that the case must be referred to the WLB.

On April 22, the WLB announced it was assuming jurisdiction of the case. The UMW refused to appear before this "court packed against labor." On April 24, WLB Chairman Davis announced that the board would consider the case only within the framework of the Little Steel Formula, which automatically ruled out any raises for the miners. The CIO and AFL members of the WLB concurred in the board's order to the miners for "the uninterrupted production of coal."

Instead, miners in Western Pennsylvania and Alabama left the pits that same day, a week in advance of the truce deadline. The UMW was demanding resumption of direct negotiations with the operators and genuine collective bargaining. On April 28, Steelman himself reported to the White House that the operators had deliberately blown up the negotiations by refusing any semblance of bargaining. The President showed no interest. The United Press reported that 41,000 bituminous miners were already out.

"As matters now stand," Lewis had said the night before, "there will be no bituminous contract by April 30. It is perfectly reasonable to assume at all times that the mine workers of the country will not trespass on the properties of the coal operators in the absence of a contract."

As for submitting the miners' case to the WLB, a UMW Policy Committee letter to Secretary of Labor Perkins said: "This board wields the headsman's axe against the workers of this country" and "has already rendered a decision in the mine workers' case."

The spreading coal strike forced Roosevelt to step forward personally to take public responsibility for leading the opposition to the miners. He telegraphed Lewis on April 29 that he would use "all the powers vested in me as President and Commander in Chief of the Army and Navy" if the strikes were not ended by the morning of May 1. Roosevelt's threat brought an immediate defiant reply from the mine workers. Nearly 10,000 Ohio miners left the pits. By the morning of Saturday, May 1, every union soft coal mine in the country was closed.

The national strike of the miners was not only the largest coal strike the country had seen up to this time. It was the largest single strike of any kind the land had ever known. It was carried out with a dispatch, discipline and single-minded determination that had never been surpassed in the American labor movement.

The press did surpass itself in the volume of vituperation, slanders and threats hurled at the miners and Lewis. Lewis was linked with Hitler in newsreels, on the radio, in countless newspaper cartoons. Union leaders joined the chorus of anti-labor forces who were screaming for nothing less than the destruction of the miners union under the guise of aiding the war for "democracy." UAW-CIO President R. J. Thomas said that the miners' walkout was "a political strike against the President."

On May 1 Roosevelt himself ordered government seizure of the struck coal mines and their operation under Solid Fuels Administrator Harold L. Ickes. Ickes "seized" the mines by promptly ordering the American flag to be flown over all mine properties and directing all mine owners and managers to run the mines as government agents in the name of the government—all profits to continue as usual. Ickes then declared the miners were working "for the Government" and ordered them back to work.

The miners didn't budge. They waited for the decision of the union. On Sunday night of May 2 Roosevelt was scheduled for a nation-wide radio address to the miners. Just before the President's broadcast, Lewis called a press conference and announced that starting Tuesday morning, May 4, another 15-day truce would be observed to give the government time to show whether it would make a just settlement with the miners. Right after the radio networks had flashed this news, Roosevelt, speaking in a savage tone, attacked Lewis and the miners, claiming that the strike involved "a gamble with the lives of American soldiers and sailors..." This was a baseless accusation. At no time during that strike and the three subsequent ones was there less than a full month's supply of coal above the ground, as the U. S. Bureau of Mines records show.

This writer was an eyewitness to the response of the miners after Roosevelt's diatribe. I toured the Western Pennsylvania mining area near Pittsburgh and wrote on May 3 for the May 8 *Militant:*

"The hope of the mine operators and every other boss in the country that President Roosevelt's speech last night would send the coal miners scurrying back to the pits this morning in a demoralized rout has been completely smashed.

"Sticking by their guns in a magnificent display of union discipline and solidarity, and in the face of an unparalleled barrage of government threat and intimidation, the miners throughout this key soft coal area today held hundreds of local meetings and in an organized, deliberate fashion voted to return to work tomorrow pending the outcome of the 15-day mine truce announced by United Mine Workers President John L. Lewis."

The *Militant* was the only significant press voice, in or out of the labor movement, that spoke unconditionally in defense of the mine strike.

The wartime miners strikes became the touchstone by which to judge the true loyalty of every union leader and working-class group toward the American workers. It revealed great masses of CIO workers in strong sympathy with the coal miners. But the whole top layer of the CIO bureaucracy opposed the miners in fear lest a UMW victory might force them to take more vigorous action against the wage freeze and thereby come in conflict with Roosevelt.

In Detroit on May 2, the day of Roosevelt's radio call to the miners, a thousand delegates representing 350,000 members of the United Auto Workers in Michigan overrode their national officers and adopted by overwhelming vote a resolution to support not only the UMW's demands but the strike as well. The UAW national leaders, which included President Thomas and Vice-President Reuther, introduced and backed a minority resolution opposing the strike. Thomas, Reuther and the Stalinist delegates spoke against Lewis and the strike. But the delegates would not be swayed. Only a half dozen or so — recognized Stalinists — openly voted against the majority resolution to back the coal strike.

An East Coast UAW conference of some 1,000 delegates, meeting in New York City on May 6, adopted a resolution which declared that "the fight against John L. Lewis is not the issue in this case" and that "it is evident that the miners' fight, involving as it does the struggle against lowering the living standards, is actually the fight of every working man and woman in America..."

An outpouring of similar resolutions from hundreds of local CIO unions in auto, rubber, steel, etc., and of thousands of individual messages of encouragement from CIO members revealed the true sentiments of the industrial workers toward the miners' battle.

The government-employer "blitz" against the miners was designed to arouse a veritable lynch spirit. Here is a sample from the May 10 *Time* magazine:

"In Orlando, Fla., an Army flying ace with 13 Jap planes to his credit, Col. Robert L. Scott, former aide to Major General Claire L. Chennault in China, boiled over in anger: 'I know I could do one service—this service would be the destruction with six fifty-caliber machine guns on an American fighter plane of John L. Lewis...'" The press prominently featured such morsels as: "I'd just as soon shoot one of those strikers as Japs."

Buried under this landslide of violent threats and abuse was the fact that the miners, every year, in peacetime and war, suffered a higher rate of casualties in proportion to their numbers than the United States armed forces during World War II. Every day, every hour, every second down in the pits the miners faced the cruelest forms of death and injury as a matter of course, as part of the routine of their livelihood. If Roosevelt had been so anxious about the effect of the mine strike on the war, if the war had been his overriding consideration, then he would have granted the miners their meager and just demands.

This union-busting campaign, whose success could have opened the way for a savage offensive against the whole labor movement and particularly the industrial unions, received encouragement from those who should have been resisting the attack most fiercely—the top leaders of the CIO. During the week of May 15, the CIO Executive Board met in Cleveland and found no more important matters to take up than the denunciation of Lewis and the mine strike. Ex-miner Philip Murray, CIO president, claimed the strike was nothing but part of Lewis's "political vendetta" against "our Commander in Chief."

It was during the first of the series of wartime coal mine strikes that the Communist Party revealed to what depths of treachery it could really sink in order to demonstrate to the United States capitalists how useful the CP could be to them if American capitalism would make some kind of permanent deal with the Kremlin.

When the American Stalinists shifted from their brief Stalin-Hitler Pact period of isolationist and pacifist opposition to the war, they swung all the way over to the extreme right of the labor movement. They opposed even the most elementary and feeble defense of labor and Negro rights as "aid to Hitler." They became so flagrant in their betrayal of the workers that not even the most conservative, hidebound, pro-war union leaders dared to go along with them—at least, not openly. An Extraordinary Conference of the top CIO leaders in Washington in March 1942 featured a clash between Murray and the Stalinists. The left-liberal New York daily *P M* reported on March 25, 1942:

"Murray and CIO left-wingers [Stalinists] clashed briefly for the first time since the Nazi-Soviet war began. The dispute arose over a speech by Harry Bridges, West Coast longshore leader, who charged, it is understood, that the CIO has not fashioned an adequate war program.

"Bridges is said to have deprecated agitation over current anti-labor legislation and labor's economic status, demanding greater emphasis on production."

Bridges had spelled out precisely what he meant by "an adequate war program" for the CIO in a speech he gave, shortly before the Washington conference, to the San Francisco CIO Council and subsequently published in the *Labor Herald,* organ of the California CIO. Bridges said:

"If we place stress on hours and wages so that we interfere with the fighting we're slackers and selling out our unions and our country...

"The majority of the time of officers, of grievance committeemen, of the unions as a whole must go to winning the war. How? Production. I'd rather say speed-up, and I mean speed-up.

"To put it bluntly, I mean your unions today must become instruments of speed-up of the working people of America."

At the same time the Stalinist-controlled leadership of the CIO United Electrical, Radio and Machine Workers demanded that their members increase their individual production 15 per cent. They made clear that "this increase shall be by the direct additional expenditure of energy and effort, over and above such increases as will be effected through improved methods or techniques instituted by our war production councils."

The speed-up urged by the Communist Party and its followers in the unions was attractively packaged in what the CP in early 1943 called the "wage incentive plan" and adopted as an official plank of its program. This was simply the old-fashioned sweat shop piece-work system. The CIO Executive Board in February 1943 at a Washington meeting voted down a motion to advocate this incentive wage plan.

The Michigan State convention of the Communist Party in March 1943 voted to send a letter to the FBI, demanding that it "discover and expose" the sponsors of leaflets being distributed at war plants in the Detroit areas, which denounced the Stalinist incentive pay plan as a return to the notorious "Bedaux piece-work system." Before FBI Chief J. Edgar Hoover even got this letter, UAW Ford Local 600 President Paul Ste. Marie issued a statement saying that he took responsibility for the leaflet and he again denounced the Stalinists for trying "to bring back the stretchout and speedup which the UAW has eliminated from most organized plants."

Subsequently, in March 1943, the UAW International Executive Board unanimously rejected incentive pay and the UAW convention in October defeated it overwhelmingly.

The May 1-4 national coal strike brought the anti-labor, strike-breaking activities of the Communist Party to a peak of ferocity that the vilest capitalist enemies of the unions did not surpass. On April 29 the *Daily Worker* carried a front-page appeal by CP National Chairman William Z. Foster, urging the miners not to respond to their union's strike call. He claimed: "If Mr. Lewis... had given support to Roosevelt's seven-point program for economic stabilization, the miners and other workers would not be finding themselves in their present difficult economic situation." This referred to nothing but Roosevelt's wage-freezing program. After the miners returned to work under a truce, the *Worker* gloated that the "Lewis line" of militant mass action in defense of the miners had been checked, and demanded that it be "utterly defeated."

This strikebreaking agitation was not confined to the columns of the *Daily Worker*. The Communist Party sent organizers and speakers into the coal fields to try to mobilize such scab elements as might be found for a back-to-work movement. Among these Stalinist mine-field tourists was Louis Budenz, managing editor of the *Daily Worker*. His articles falsely attempted to portray widespread wavering among the miners.

On May 2, Foster himself invaded the chief coal state — Pennsylvania. He addressed a meeting at the Town Hall in Philadelphia where he urged the miners to return to the pits and submit to what Lewis had called the "headsman's axe" of the War Labor Board. Charles Spencer, CP secretary in the Wilkes-Barre anthracite area, spoke over a local station on May 2 to tell the miners "not to follow Lewis into a treasonable strike."

Roosevelt's threats, lynch cries of the press, Murray's stab-in-the-back attacks, the Stalinist strikebreaking attempts — all these made no dent on the miners. For the next six months they were to carry on a bitter, tenacious struggle, a succession of four national strikes conducted with such matchless solidarity and discipline that the massive assault upon them finally cracked up and broke to pieces.

No sooner had the miners returned to work after their first strike in early May than Ickes, the administration's agent in charge of the seizure, announced that the miners would not negotiate with the ostensible new operator of the mines, the government, but only with the regular owners.

On May 17, the UMW Policy Committee announced an extension of the strike truce until midnight, May 31. This was done at the special request of Ickes. The WLB that same day denounced Lewis for "defying the lawfully established procedures of the Government." The operators simultaneously announced that the WLB had "forbidden" them to resume negotiations with the UMW.

As the date for the new strike deadline approached, there were plenty of indications that the miners' sentiments were shared by wide sectors of American workers. In Detroit, some 30,000 Chrysler and Dodge auto workers struck for four days in protest against an 11-month accumulation of grievances and demands. In Akron, Ohio, some 50,000 rubber workers struck for five days when the WLB conceded only a three-cent increase after a year's delay. These strike actions were smothered by the combined efforts of the WLB, army and navy officials, FBI, the raging press and radio and, above all, the top union leaders of the CIO United Auto Workers and United Rubber Workers. Indeed, the UAW and URW leaders publicly upbraided their striking members.

The successful strikebreaking by the government and union officials in the auto, rubber and other strikes during the interim of the coal mines truce, further emboldened the operators to sit back and wait for the government to smash the miners and their union. On May 25, the WLB had denied the miners all their major demands, making only two minor concessions.

The operators began to get the point when the truce deadline, May 31, passed. On the morning of June 1, some 530,000 miners refrained from entering the pits "without any special strike call being issued and with casual matter-of-factness," as George Breitman, the *Militant's* correspondent, wrote from the mining area around Pittsburgh.

Roosevelt thundered at the striking miners that they "are employees of the Government and have no right to strike." Ickes telegraphed the union that Lewis "cannot escape responsibility for the cessation of work." But Ickes conceded that "there are a few powerful operators who from the beginning had deliberately opposed any compromise which might lead to a reasonable settlement."

What was decisive, however, was the attitude of the miners, their belief in their rights, their understanding of their organized power and their strategic position in the economy. George Breitman, in a May 26 dispatch from Uniontown, Pennsylvania, to *The Militant* summarized the results of his numerous interviews with miners in the important UMW District 4:

"The question I asked was: 'Do you think you will obtain a substantial portion of your demands?' And always the answer was an unhesitating yes. When I asked why, their answer generally went like this:

"'Because we're the only ones who can mine coal and they're not going to make us do it unless they give us enough wages to do it right and feed our families on at least the same standard we had before the war. You know you can lead a horse to water but you can't make him drink.'"

Roosevelt, on June 3, threatened to call out the troops unless the miners returned to work by June 7 — and, as Alinsky noted in his biography of Lewis, the President no longer referred to "my friends, the miners." The miners merely shrugged and repeated their classic phrase: "You can't dig coal with bayonets." Roosevelt added a further threat—miners of draft age who did not respond to his order would be reclassified for military service. This made no impact either.

For the first time some of the coal operators began to question the ability of the government to terrorize the miners into submission. They also were fearful of the principle of government seizure of their property, even though they were aware that in this instance it was strictly a strikebreaking device.

Lewis had proposed that the miners be paid $1.50 a day more as portal-to-portal travel pay and the operators began what appeared to be some serious consideration of this compromise proposal. At this point the WLB ordered the negotiations to end until the miners went back to work. The board's labor members voted for the order. Aware that the operators were beginning to weaken, the UMW again pulled a truce move. The union's Policy Committee voted a return to work on June 7—but only "up to and including June 20" unless a satisfactory agreement had been reached.

The closer the miners moved to wresting an acceptable settlement from the mine owners, the more desperately the government

tried to beat the miners down. Congress pushed through the first federal anti-strike bill in the country's history—the Smith-Connally War
Labor Disputes Bill — whose major provisions had been proposed
by Roosevelt as early as November 1941. This drastic anti-labor
measure evoked such protest inside labor's ranks that both William
Green and Philip Murray felt impelled to plead for Roosevelt's veto.

Prior to passage of the anti-strike bill, demonstratively pushed
through as a threat to the miners, Lewis and the operators had come
to a verbal agreement on $1.30 a day for travel pay in the mines.
At this point, Ickes announced he was levying a $5 fine on every
miner who had participated in the June 1 to 5 strike, which would
have represented a collective fine of more than $2,500,000. So im-
mediate and violent was the miners' reaction that Ickes speedily
backtracked. In the face of hundreds of meetings of mine locals that
voted immediate strike action, Ickes lamely explained he was leaving
the collection of fines up to the individual operators—who promptly
said they preferred to let bygones be bygones.

The Smith-Connally Bill, although not yet law, emboldened the
WLB members. This bill would give the WLB power to subpoena
union leaders and make it a felony for them even to advocate a strike
in any government-seized plant or industry. On June 18, two days
before the strike deadline, the WLB turned down the agreement on
$1.30 portal-to-portal pay reached between the UMW and the opera-
tors. The board's report claimed that the miners were getting 65
per cent more average weekly take-home pay in March 1943 than in
January 1941, due to the greater average number of hours per week
worked in 1943. The WLB majority announced that the portal-to-
portal issue must first be handled by the Wages and Hours Administrator and the courts. But even if these decided favorably for the
miners, the WLB reserved the final decision.

Despite the fact that the Illinois operators had agreed to $1.50
and the Pennsylvania operators to $1.30 portal-to-portal pay daily,
the CIO and AFL members on the WLB voted to grant only 80 cents
a day for mine travel time. AFL Teamsters President Daniel Tobin
actually hailed the WLB majority's denial of portal-to-portal pay.
The Stalinists, as usual, went all the way in aiding the administration's and WLB's campaign against the miners. National Secretary
Earl Browder told the National Committee of the Communist Party
that Lewis headed the CP's list of "the main enemies at home."

The WLB's labor members, including the CIO's Van Bittner and
John Brophy, ex-UMW officials now on Murray's payroll, issued a
statement that the no-strike pledge "must be carried out today as it
was the day we made it."

On June 19 the miners began the walkout; 58,000 of them beat the deadline. The next day all bituminous and anthracite miners in the country stayed away from the mines. This writer reported the strike for *The Militant:*

"PITTSBURGH, June 21 — Today has been like a peaceful Sunday in the scores of coal mining towns in this area. It has been hard to realize that in these quiet communities, set amidst sunny, rolling countryside marred only by the inevitable tipples and ugly slag heaps, one of the greatest and grimmest struggles in American labor history is in progress.

"There was no outward sign of conflict as the third nation-wide wartime coal strike paralyzed the hundreds of mines in this vital Western Pennsylvania region. The mine workers just remained at home—to a man. There were no pickets. None were needed... A big, burly miner with whom I was walking down the road in Library, Pa., site of one of the biggest mines of Mellon's Pittsburgh Coal Company, stopped once and cocked his ear over to one side. A smile both sly and wistful crossed his face. 'At last we can hear the birds sing.' All the tumult and shouting of this tremendous struggle are confined to the columns of the capitalist press, the halls of Congress, the corridors of federal buildings, and the hysterical strike-breaking Stalinist sheets and meetings..."

Two days after the strike officially started, Lewis once more announced a truce—this time until October 31—and instructed the miners to return to work. A UMW Policy Committee statement said: "This arrangement is predicated upon operation of the mines... by the United States government and will automatically terminate if government control is vacated prior to the above-mentioned date."

Roosevelt, in turn, issued an hysterical attack on the miners after they had already started to return to work following the latest UMW Policy Committee directions. He threatened to force them to work as military conscripts and stated he had initiated measures "to set up the machinery" to draft strikers into the armed forces and compel them to mine coal under military orders, subject to courts-martial for refusal.

Nothing could have been more calculated to infuriate the miners. It is estimated that 40 per cent of the miners continued their strike for from four to six days after Lewis had asked them to return to work because of their indignation.

Roosevelt's threat to force the miners to work under military regulations, as one UMW official in Pittsburgh told this writer, was like "throwing gasoline on a hot fire." At a meeting of UMW Local 73 in Library, one old mining veteran said:

"Going into a mine is no easy thing. Every time you go in, you never know if you're coming out. If they want to pass such a law on us men, let 'em pass it. We've worked in these mines and risked our lives and damned near at times had to eat grass and frozen apples to stay alive. But we're still living and we're still fighting."

The bulk of the Western Pennsylvania miners voted not to return to work until June 28, six days after Roosevelt's threat. It was a deliberate demonstration of defiance and contempt from men who had voted for Roosevelt in 1932 and 1936 and even in 1940, after Lewis himself had broken with him.

On June 25 Roosevelt vetoed the Smith-Connally Bill, but it was enacted over his veto within two hours by a Democratic Congress. Among other things, this bill made it a crime punishable by one year imprisonment and $5,000 fine to "coerce, instigate, induce, conspire with or encourage any person to interfere by lockout, strike, slowdown or other interruption with the operations of plants in possession of the government." The bill authorized the seizure of plants for strikebreaking purposes, required prior notice and a 30-day "cooling-off period" before all strikes, and a provision for government-supervised strike votes.

Both Philip Murray and William Green hastened to write messages of effusive thanks to Roosevelt for his veto and, as Murray put it, "to assure you that our organizations will maintain their no-strike pledge."

So eager were these union leaders to represent Roosevelt's action as a sign of his "pro-labor" attitude, that they overlooked the real point of his veto message—he had openly stated the bill wasn't tough enough to suit him. He thought it had loopholes which still opened the way for strikes. In his veto message to Congress, he said he approved of seven of the bill's nine points — including those that provided for government plant seizures to break strikes, a ban on strikes in seized industries, jail for strikers and strike "inducers," fines on unions and impounding of union treasuries. "If the bill were limited to these seven measures," said Roosevelt, "I would sign it."

He objected only to the provisions that would permit strikes after a declaration of intention, a special vote and "cooling off." He also objected to the fact that his own special proposal—to place all workers between the ages of 18 and 65 under the provisions of a labor draft law, a labor conscription act — was excluded from the Smith-Connally Act.

The reaction to the Smith-Connally Act in the CIO ranks could be gauged by the debate and decisions of the 1,800 delegates to the Michigan State CIO convention in Detroit a few days after the

anti-strike law was passed. These delegates, representing 700,000
industrial unionists, adopted by a two-to-one majority a resolution
"recommending to all of the affiliated unions and to the CIO that unless assurances that were made to labor are immediately and effectively put into operation, we consider our 'no-strike' pledge no
longer binding..."

This resolution was bitterly opposed by CIO National Organization
Director Allan S. Haywood, representing Murray; John Brophy,
head of the Industrial Union Councils Department of the CIO; UAW
President R. J. Thomas; Michigan State CIO President August
Scholle and all the Stalinist delegates. As individuals and groups
the Stalinists took the floor and repeated the phrase that they would
"follow Brother Philip Murray in the no-strike pledge which he gave
to our Commander in Chief."

An additional response of the convention to the anti-strike law
was the adoption of a resolution which, while still favoring support
of Roosevelt, said this "can best be served by an independent labor
party." The resolution proposed a referendum vote by affiliated
unions on whether or not they "favored setting up an independent
labor party." The vote for this resolution was 2,519 to 1,909, with
the Stalinists again offering the bitterest opposition.

The convention also passed a resolution which declared that the
Smith-Connally Act "made a mockery out of avowed claims that this
is a war for democracy." Stalinist floor leader Nat Ganley, business
agent of UAW Local 155, asserted: "Regardless of what reactionary
legislation is passed, this still remains a just, progressive war
against fascism." Even Victor Reuther, going along with the pre-
dominant sentiment, said: "It is not a war for democracy if we allow
fascists to destroy our democratic rights at home."

Most indicative of the sentiments of these delegates — representing
workers in auto, steel, glass and many other CIO unions — was their
overwhelming adoption of a resolution of unconditional support to
the miners. In doing so, they brushed aside the attempts of the
Stalinists to insert an attack on Lewis in the resolution. "You cannot pass on the miners' question and ignore Lewis. You cannot win
the war and strike as you damn please," complained John Anderson,
Stalinist president of Local 155. To which one delegate replied amid
applause: "If Lewis pulled the strike to protect the rank and file,
hats off to Lewis."

Following the Michigan CIO convention, the Murray-Hillman-
Stalinist forces drew even closer together in their opposition to the
militant ranks and in their enmity and fear of Lewis. A special
meeting of the CIO National Executive Board was held in Washington,

July 7 to 10. This meeting resolved to fight the Smith-Connally Act, which Murray had said set aside the Bill of Rights, by reaffirmation of the no-strike pledge. When Emil Rieve and George Baldanzi, president and vice-president respectively of the United Textile Workers Union, objected to the attack on Lewis and the miners, they were subjected to fierce denunciation by the other board members. Murray raged particularly against the actions of the Michigan CIO convention and mysteriously hinted at "outside influence" at work.

The miners drew their strength from their own just cause, the solidity of their union, and the support of millions of other union workers like those in the Michigan CIO. They could ignore with equal calm the rantings of a Murray and the ultimatums of a Roosevelt.

The War Labor Board called on Roosevelt either to force Lewis to sign the WLB-dictated contract, or to seize the UMW's treasury as a punitive measure and cancel the checkoff of union dues. The board, including its CIO and AFL members, also demanded that Lewis be prosecuted under the Smith-Connally Act. A federal grand jury was convened on July 14 at the behest of the Western Pennsylvania operators and federal agents were sent into the mine fields by Attorney General Biddle to investigate charges under the anti-strike law. Unauthorized strikes, which followed the WLB threats, continued in some instances until July 5.

When Roosevelt was asked on July 9 what he would do to force Lewis to sign the WLB's contract, he finally conceded he could not force Lewis to do so. A day later, Edward R. Burke and R. L. Ireland Jr., leading spokesmen for the operators, revealed they were at the point of capitulation when they said that Roosevelt's statement proved that "Mr. Lewis, through his defiance of the Government, had gained his point."

During the four-month period of uneasy truce, the Roosevelt administration and its WLB did all in their power to prevent and upset all agreements between the United Mine Workers and the operators that provided for pay increases in any form. In the middle of July, Lewis had announced that an agreement had been reached and a contract signed with the Illinois Operators Association for $1.25 daily portal-to-portal travel pay, 50 cents of it retroactive to October 24, 1938, when the Fair Labor Standards Act went into effect. With other provisions, including extra hours, this would have raised the Illinois miners' pay by $3 instead of the originally demanded $2 a day.

With this contract in writing and signed by the Illinois operators, Lewis discontinued his boycott of the WLB. On August 3, Lewis appeared personally before the WLB hearing and defended the Illinois contract. On August 25, this "court stacked against labor" flatly rejected the Illinois pact and called the portal-to-portal agreement a "hidden wage increase." The board members were emboldened by Roosevelt's August 16 executive order which provided drastic sanctions against striking unions and strikers—including the withholding of "any benefits, privileges and rights"—in industries seized by the government, like the coal mines.

Even the right-wing Social Democratic *New Leader,* strongly pro-war and pro-Roosevelt, complained in its August 21 issue that Roosevelt's sanction order was "the high wave of reaction." It lamented: "The President appeared to serve notice that he has come to an open break with the New Deal." (Later, on December 28, Roosevelt himself was to declare that the "New Deal" was over.)

Once more the UMW officials and the Illinois operators went into a huddle. They finally agreed on a contract providing $2 a day more for a five-day week with overtime allowances, omitting the portal-to-portal issue. Fuel Coordinator Ickes took this occasion to announce the end of the mine seizures on October 13. The fiction of government operation was removed. Promptly, the miners began striking without any instructions from Lewis and the policy committee. Twenty-two thousand Alabama and 3,500 Indiana miners were the first to defy the Smith-Connally Act and Roosevelt's executive sanctions.

Lewis wired the strikers and asked their locals to meet and vote to go back pending a WLB ruling on the revised Illinois contract. The WLB threatened the miners with sanctions and the penalties of the law. The Indiana miners reluctantly returned; the Alabama miners refused.

"According to reports from the striking areas," said the October 19 *New York Times,* "the miners were refusing to attend meetings lest they incur the penalties of the Connally-Smith Act and they had somehow set up some form of a silent understanding with each other whereby they did not even need to speak, but would act as individuals as long as their wage grievances were not redressed."

Lewis had hinted that the WLB might bring forth a favorable decision. But new groups of strikers—in Ohio, Pennsylvania, Indiana, West Virginia, Kentucky and Illinois—followed the lead of the Alabama workers. The WLB again "poured gasoline on the fire" when it rejected the second Illinois pact on October 26. By the time the official strike deadline, November 1, had arrived, all 530,000 coal miners were out, for their fourth official national wartime strike within one year.

Roosevelt was at the end of his rope. He could not arrest 530,000 miners. He could not force them to go down into the pits at bayonet point, and even if he could, they need not mine an ounce of coal. He could not jail Lewis and the UMW leaders, for the miners swore they would strike "until Hell freezes over" if Lewis were victimized in any way. The President again seized the struck mines and authorized Ickes to negotiate a contract.

The Ickes-approved contract gave the miners $1.50 a day more – $8.50 a day. The WLB on November 20 finally agreed to a contract acceptable to the union and contractors. This fixed the mine wage at $57.07 a week and provided $40 to each miner for retroactive payment for travel time.

The UMW Policy Committee ratified the new contract on November 3 and instructed the miners to return to work. They had cracked the wage freeze and broken through the barrier of the Little Steel Formula. Except for a reduction of 15 minutes in their lunch time, the contract was virtually the same as the second agreement reached with the Illinois operators. Of the total increase, $1 to $1.25 a day was an actual increase in terms of the previous work week. The rest of the increase was due to more hours of work.

As the final mine walkout was going into full swing on November 1, Philip Murray was calling the CIO convention to order in Philadelphia. Murray made an unrestrained attack on Lewis and intimated that the miners, the men who had first raised Murray to a position of influence in the labor movement, were nothing less than agents of Hitler and the Japanese Mikado. A round of tirades against the miners followed Murray's slanderous attack. Frederick Myers, vice-president of Curran's Stalinist-controlled National Maritime Union, on November 2 called the struggle of the miners "the greatest treason against America."

Murray had opened the CIO convention by his attack on the miners and by pushing through a resolution reaffirming the no-strike pledge "without qualification or condition." But when the word was received that the miners had won, that they had cracked the Little Steel Formula ceiling, Murray and his lieutenants were in a dither. They knew Lewis's prestige would rise high among the CIO workers. Quickly, Murray introduced a resolution to open a labor drive for higher wages, above the Little Steel Formula. He even had the impudence to call on the coal miners (whose magnificent struggle had already demolished the Little Steel Formula) and the railroad workers (who at that moment were taking a nation-wide strike poll) to join with him in the fight for higher wages.

Although the United Mine Workers was no longer in the CIO and the CIO leadership had bitterly attacked the mine strikes, the wartime struggle and victory of the coal miners was of incalculable importance for American unionism, particularly for the CIO. It may be said that the CIO had two "Gettysburgs" — the Flint General Motors sit-down of 1936-37 and the 1943 coal miners strikes, although in the latter the CIO leaders were sniping from the enemy lines.

Until the miners fought back in 1943, the war brought with it one measure of repression after another, and ever increasing assaults on the living standards and liberties of the workers. The ruling class looked on the war as their supreme opportunity to destroy union contractual conditions and even unionism itself.

We have only to ask ourselves, "What if the miners had not waged their fight?" or "What if they had lost?" to realize the enormous stake the whole American labor movement had in the outcome of the miners' battles. If the miners had not fought and won, if they had been defeated, it would have meant not only the crippling and possibly the crushing of one of the most powerful industrial unions — the UMW — but a demoralizing blow of shattering proportions for the auto, rubber, steel, electrical equipment, and other CIO workers. In the wake of a miners' defeat, the corporate interests and their government agents would have fallen like a ravenous wolf pack on the most vulnerable unions. The government would have introduced new "formulas" to slash wages, increase hours of work and intensify the exploitation of labor in the name of patriotism and the "needs of the war." The defeat of the miners would have become another and more convincing pretext for the union leaders, like Murray and Hillman, to give away the workers' rights and conditions and to restrain every impulse of the CIO workers to fight back.

Instead, the miners' victory opened a whole new wave of labor struggle, mounting steadily through 1943, 1944 and 1945, reaching a titanic climax in the winter of 1945-46. The employers' postwar plan to turn the war veterans against the workers and smash the unions was never able to get going.

The miners themselves were able to go on from victory to victory in the war and immediate postwar period, winning many new gains, such as health and welfare funds, retirement pensions and other conditions, which then became objectives of the CIO unions as well.

Above all, the miners demonstrated as never before the fact that nothing can produce coal — or any other form of wealth — but the labor of workers. When the miners said "you can't dig coal with bayonets," they were saying that organized labor, united and determined to defend itself and its rights, is invincible. That is why, in hailing the miners' victory, *The Militant* of November 13, 1943, said:

"The miners strikes of 1943, taking place in the midst of the Second World War, will forever remain a landmark in the history of the American class struggle."

19

"The Situation Is Intolerable"

Shortly after Pearl Harbor, in his radio address of March 6, 1942, CIO President Philip Murray had exhorted labor to "Work! Work! Work! Produce! Produce! Produce!" He boasted: "There has not been a single authorized strike in a war industry and all the efforts of the CIO and its unions have been directed to ending at once such minor incidents as have occurred."

Murray's stress on "authorized" strikes and "minor" incidents was a bit misleading but not too far from the truth. As the war unfolded, however, and the workers' conditions worsened, Murray's emphasis on "Work! Work! Work!" became weaker. Moreover, the four 1943 national coal strikes undercut all talk about "not a single authorized strike" and only "minor incidents."

While reaffirming the no-strike pledge and low-rating Lewis, Murray increasingly complained about the WLB decisions and the rapidly widening gap between frozen wages and soaring living costs. WLB Vice-Chairman George W. Taylor had claimed on August 26, 1943, that average hourly factory wages had increased only six-tenths of a cent since September 15, 1942, date of Roosevelt's wage-freeze order. But even the most conservative and super-patriotic union leaders had to attest to the phenomenal leap in prices.

Speaking in Los Angeles on April 24, 1943, Murray said that since the previous September 15 "living costs, particularly in foodstuffs, had increased approximately 38 per cent for the average worker in the United States." His figure, it must be understood, referred to the general cost of living. AFL President Green said in Detroit in July that food prices alone "have gone up from 50 to 400 per cent."

During this period millions of union workers had been denied their wage demands or granted only the skimpiest concessions by the WLB. General Motors and Chrysler workers were "awarded" only four cents an hour; Ford workers, nothing. The WLB turned away 230,000 aircraft workers empty handed. The board did approve a three-cent raise for rubber workers who were entitled, however, to at least eight cents under the board's own formula. The WLB also ruled out any gains for 1,100,000 shipyard workers, both CIO and AFL.

As the miners' struggle drew to a climax, Roosevelt's labor policies came under attack from other large sectors of the labor movement. A threatened revolt of a million and a half railroad workers against the run-around they had been receiving on their wage demands confronted Roosevelt with one of the most serious crises of his presidential career. This rail labor crisis coincided with an upsurge of the CIO steelworkers that almost got out of Murray's control.

The 15 railway non-operating unions, affiliated with the AFL, had been seeking a 20 per cent wage increase since September 1942. The five operating unions of the railroad brotherhoods, representing 350,000 members, had been negotiating for 30 per cent more since February 1943. On May 24 Roosevelt's special railway emergency board recommended an eight-cent raise. This was vetoed by Economic Stabilization Director Fred M. Vinson on June 30. Late in September Vinson saw fit to approve a mere four-cent raise for operating employees.

The railway unions labeled the proposed increase an "insult." Brotherhood officials on October 25 informed Roosevelt that they had authorized a strike vote among the 350,000 operating workers. The next day a similar announcement was made for the 15 non-operating railway unions. Only a few months before, the leaders of the brotherhoods had denounced the mine strikes.

The fighting temper of the railroad workers at this time was reflected in the utterances of some of the most hardened railway union bureaucrats. A. F. Whitney, president of the Brotherhood of Railway Trainmen, largest of the "Big Five" operating brotherhoods, told the October 25 meeting of his union's general chairmen in Chicago:

"The President is in a weakened condition. He is almost now a 'political prisoner' in the White House... Nearly all the positions in our government are now held by big business reactionaries or at best by ultra-conservatives, and the President has put them there... We are now, despite the President's noble speeches, making war millionaires at a rate which... will make the profiteering of World War I look like a WPA payroll."

Apart from portraying Roosevelt, a shrewd and tough capitalist politician, as something of a bumbling idiot who allowed himself to become the "prisoner" of men he himself had appointed, Whitney's words were a far cry from the idolatry that customarily characterized the speeches of the pro-Roosevelt union leaders when speaking of "our Commander in Chief." And this was just an echo of the fury felt by the railroad workers. The operating workers voted 97.7 per cent for a strike to begin December 30, 1943. The non-operating workers, lowest-paid sector of the railroad industry, likewise voted over-whelmingly to strike on the same date.

The triumph of the miners and the rail labor upsurge, plus an al-most continuous rash of unauthorized departmental and plant strikes in the CIO-organized industries, forced Murray and the other CIO leaders to make some gestures in the direction of a fight for the workers' interests. Late in November and in December, the CIO in steel, aluminum, auto, textiles and even in the electrical equip-ment industry where Stalinists dominated the union, advanced de-mands for wage increases of from 10 to 17 cents an hour.

American workers were seething with unrest. A subsequent re-port of the U. S. Bureau of Labor Statistics revealed that in the period from June 25, 1943, when the Smith-Connally Anti-Strike Act was adopted, to December 31, 1943, there were 1,919 strikes, of which only 34 were in compliance with the law. Despite the fulmin-ations of Murray and other CIO leaders, CIO locals in the war in-dustries contributed heavily to these statistics.

With a national railway strike due December 30, Roosevelt's hand was forced. With one hand he offered the railroad workers a carrot while the other held a club. He said he would personally arbitrate the issues. Two of the railroad brotherhood officials, Alvanley Johnson of the Brotherhood of Railroad Engineers and A. F. Whitney of the Trainmen, abandoned the other railway unions, accepted Roosevelt's offer and called off their scheduled strikes. The three other brotherhood unions refused Roosevelt's arbitration offer.

Roosevelt then granted the two compliant unions an additional "five cents per hour in lieu of claims for time and a half pay for time over forty hours and for expenses away from home." This, added to the four cents previously approved by Economic Stabilizer Vinson, made a total raise of nine cents an hour, or one cent more than the original recommendation of the railway emergency board.

But Roosevelt did not wait for the strike deadline. He ordered the army to seize the railroads. Secretary of War Stimson imme-diately assured the railroad corporations that the government had no intention of interfering with their management and profits. He set up seven regional headquarters for the railroads, each headed by a railroad corporation president who was given a colonel's commission in the United States Army.

In the midst of this strike-preventive railroad seizure, scores of thousands of steelworkers started to strike on Christmas Eve. Their unauthorized action was provoked by the refusal of the War Labor Board to approve retroactive payment of any wage increase back to the time of the expiration of the old contracts. When the contracts expired on Christmas Eve, the steelworkers began quitting the plants shouting the famous slogan of Lewis's coal miners, "No contract, no work!" By the day after Christmas, more than 200,000 CIO steelworkers were on strike.

It was no longer John L. Lewis who was under fire from the Roosevelt administration and the heavy artillery of capitalist reaction. The strike threat of the railroad workers and the actual walkout of the steelworkers could not be blamed on any "political vendetta" waged by the ultra-conservative railway union leaders or on Philip Murray, head of the steel union. General George Marshall, Army Chief of Staff, took time out from his military duties for a special news conference to assail the railroad workers' demands and strike vote as "the damnedest crime that was ever committed against America." It was made plain immediately afterward that this professional militarist, never known for the slightest sympathy for labor, was speaking the views of Roosevelt. White House Secretary Stephen Early told the press that Roosevelt "is thinking along the same line" as Marshall.

George M. Harrison, president of the Brotherhood of Railway Clerks, had said after the miners' victory, "Maybe it pays to get tough." But Harrison and all the brotherhood leaders buckled under Roosevelt's seizure order and stand-by call for troops. The railroad strike was never called. But, as a result of the strike threat, the railroad workers did end up with a nine to eleven-cent hourly increase, more than double the original grant.

Murray frantically appealed to the steelworkers to end their unauthorized walkout. Roosevelt made an apparent concession on the retroactive pay issue. He sent a telegram to Murray which proposed extension of the old agreements and that "if the new agreements include any wage adjustments, such adjustments shall be computed and applied retroactively to the date when the particular contract in question would have expired by virtue of the notice of termination of such contract." Roosevelt then slipped in the joker: "If any wage adjustments are made they must of course be made in accordance with the act of Congress of October 2, 1942 [the Economic Stabilization Act] and executive orders numbers 9250 and 9328 and the policy directive of May 12, 1943." In short, wages must remain within the Little Steel Formula and the wage-freeze policy.

With this tricky formulation, which promised the principle of retroactivity but forbade any wage increases, Murray was able to lure most of the steel strikers back to their jobs by New Year's Eve. Ten months later, in the October 9, 1944 *New York Times,* labor reporter Louis Stark revealed that Roosevelt's retroactive pay promise had a double hook. Stark wrote that "if, following November 7 [election day] the President should decide to make a change in the General Wage Stabilization policy," then "no retroactive pay would be forthcoming to the CIO workers, although the steelworkers, in many cases, according to reports, have 'spent their back pay already.'"

Thus, what Roosevelt actually promised the steelworkers was that they could not get a wage increase so long as the Little Steel Formula was in effect but if it were changed to permit higher pay throughout all industry then the principle of retroactivity would not apply. The formulation used to trick the steelworkers was also used in the cases of other CIO unions before the WLB. The steel wage case was protracted and delayed until after Roosevelt's re-election. During all that time it was being given the WLB "treatment." For it was solely within the confines of the WLB hearings that Murray chose to "fight" for the steel union's 17-cent demand.

A labor reporter for the *New York Herald Tribune,* writing on the steel strike, said: "The strike now ending is only a curtain-raiser to a head-on collision expected when the actual demands of the steelworkers come to the WLB. Right behind the steelworkers and equally pledged to break the wage formula are the United Auto Workers of America, who are heading for showdowns with General Motors and Ford; the Aluminum Workers of America, who are demanding increases of the Aluminum Company of America; the Oil Workers International Union, which is preparing to take on the entire petroleum industry; the textile workers, likewise tackling an entire industry; the United Electrical, Radio and Machine Workers of America, which is taking on the Westinghouse Electric and Manufacturing Company, and many other CIO unions in various industries."

This was the labor picture at the start of the third year of United States participation in World War II. The forecast of big struggles to come was based, in part, on the experiences of the year just past. The number of strikes in 1943 totaled 3,752 and the number of strikers, 1,981,000. There were more strikes in mid-war 1943 than in any year since 1919, except those peak years of CIO battles, 1937 and 1941. The number of man-days lost in strikes more than tripled in 1943 over 1942. It was obvious that the war had ended the class struggle nowhere but in the heads of the union bureaucrats.

Roosevelt's action in ordering army seizure of the railroads was part of a buildup for the most dictatorial legislation any president ever attempted to impose on the American people—a national labor conscription law. It was noted in December 1943 that Roosevelt's spectacular use of the army in the railroad case contrasted markedly with his use of a civilian agency, the Solid Fuels Administration, to take control in the coal mines strikes. General Marshall's threatening diatribe against the rail and steel workers was intended to prepare public opinion for Roosevelt's proposal for virtual military control of the civilian labor force.

In his message to Congress on January 11, 1944, Roosevelt called for enactment of a "national service act" to outlaw strikes. As the fifth point of his five-point program, Roosevelt urged:

"A national service law—which, for the duration of the war, will prevent strikes and, with appropriate exceptions, will make available for war production or any other essential services every able-bodied adult in this nation."

Just as his first seven-point program of April 27, 1942 was designed to present his wage freeze in a demagogic disguise, so Roosevelt called for universal forced labor as part of a series of measures which he claimed formed an "indivisible" and "just and equitable whole. I would not recommend a service law unless the other laws were passed to keep down the cost of living, to share equitably the burdens of taxation, to hold the stabilization line and to prevent undue profits."

Roosevelt virtually confessed in his congressional message that only the wage stabilization point of his seven-point program of 1942 had been carried out. He admitted:

"For two long years I have pleaded with the Congress to take undue profits out of war."

How Congress had responded to his "plea" on profits (he had frozen wages by presidential decree without waiting for Congress) was shown by the December 18, 1943 report of the Department of Commerce. In the third quarter of 1943, corporation profits were "the highest for any quarter in American economic history and 16 per cent above the same quarter in 1942." In the very week Roosevelt demanded that Congress adopt a labor conscription law, a Senate group issued a report revealing that the net profits of 200 leading and representative corporations in 1942 were five to ten times greater than their best peacetime years. These cases, the senators reported, "are not exceptional instances." As Roosevelt issued his

new "plea" to Congress, the steelworkers union, presenting its 17-
cent wage demand to the War Labor Board, submitted figures revealing that U. S. Steel Corporation had almost tripled its net profits
during the two war years.

Senator Langer of North Dakota, in a speech to the Senate on
January 17, 1944, showed how little the American people could depend
on Roosevelt's "equality of sacrifice." Langer charged:

"Both the Republican and the Democratic Party pledged themselves that if ever war came again no new group of war millionaires
should be created. Yet look at the record in this very body. Almost
every single measure which would have prevented the creation of
war millionaires has been defeated. The platforms of the Republican
Party and the Democratic Party have been sterile, because at each
convention the great monopolists, the millionaires, have had control,
and the poor people, the average common men, have had nothing
to say."

CIO President Murray denounced the national service act proposal as "quack medicine." On January 14 and 15, 1944, the recently-
formed CIO Political Action Committee (PAC) held a national conference in New York City. It was attended by all the top CIO leaders,
including Philip Murray, Sidney Hillman, R. J. Thomas and Walter
Reuther. Murray inveighed at length against the proposed labor conscription law without ever mentioning the name of its chief proponent,
Roosevelt. This may have been out of consideration for the sensi-
bilities of Vice-President Henry Wallace, honored guest of the conference, who explained that the President had to do "many things
which some of us have not been able to understand."

After Roosevelt had submitted his proposal for labor conscription
to Congress, he summoned Murray and Green to the White House.
He gave them an ultimatum either to accept his national service law
proposal or face even more drastic anti-strike legislation. According to the *New York Post* account,

"The labor chiefs asked for assurance that the rest of the President's program — calling for higher taxes, control of profits, food
price subsidies, and continuance of the stabilization program—would
be approved. Mr. Roosevelt replied that he was unable to give that
assurance."

On the very day Roosevelt had sent his message to Congress,
Senator Austin submitted to the Senate a revised version of his na-
tional service bill, the only such measure before the Upper House.
The heart of this measure was contained in the sections stating:
"Every person assigned to service under this act shall receive the
compensation and work the hours applicable to the kind of work

which he or she is required to perform in the place of employment to which he or she is assigned." Every worker so assigned "shall have the right to join any union or organization of employes, but no such person shall be obliged to join such union or organization."

This was clearly intended to nullify every closed shop, union shop or maintenance of membership union contract. Under its provisions workers could be compelled to work anywhere, shift to any designated industry or job, and accept working conditions, hours and wages dictated by the employers backed by the government. When Senator Austin was asked if the Austin-Wadsworth national service bill, if adopted, would institute forced labor, the February 17, 1944 *New York Herald Tribune* reported his reply as follows:

"The Senator maintained steadfastly that there was no compulsion involved in his bill. 'Nobody would be compelled to work,' he said. However, if anyone refused to, after losing the various appeals, he would go to jail."

At the hearings on the Austin-Wadsworth bill before the Senate Military Affairs Committee, the leading wartime officials of the Roosevelt administration appeared to testify in favor of the forced labor provisions of the measure and to reassert the President's demand for enactment of a national service law. Secretary of War Stimson claimed to speak in the name of the "men in the armed forces" who, he alleged, had "a feeling of resentment" at the "industrial unrest."

What many drafted soldiers really thought of the anti-labor drive back home was indicated by an editorial, "Soldiers Are Workingmen Too," in the January 15, 1944 issue of the mid-Pacific *Army Newspaper,* published in Hawaii. It said:

"Note must be taken of the way certain periodicals reaching soldiers have begun to campaign against labor. This is not new. As in the present case, the drives are based on half-truths, omissions and paternalistic 'This hurts me more than it does you' attitude.

"Soldiers generally are concerned about this unfair carping. Most of them are workingmen. It is estimated that nearly a million are trade union members...

"Any time a labor dispute is reported, the public version, with few exceptions, is colored in favor of the employer... In these days the working people need a few dollars more to cover the ever-rising cost of living."

So intense was the popular opposition to the Austin-Wadsworth bill, that the Roosevelt administration switched to a "modified" form of the original labor conscription proposal. This was the Brewster-Bailey "Work-or-Fight" bill, which provided that the Selective Service draft boards have the power to assign any worker, between the ages of 18 and 45, to any job, anywhere. Refusal to accept such assignment would make a worker subject to military draft and assignment in a military labor battalion at the low army pay and subject to courts-martial for any violations of orders.

Representatives of the CIO, AFL and railroad brotherhoods spoke vehemently against this measure at Senate hearings, where Secretary of the Navy James V. Forrestal gave it the Roosevelt administration's blessings. A joint CIO-AFL protest called such a bill or any other form of labor draft not "wise or necessary." Martin H. Miller, legislative representative of the railroad brotherhoods, told the Senate hearings:

"The great majority of the people when they understand, oppose and resent conscription of civilians who would be driven like cattle to the private profit-making industries of the nation."

At least one senator — Edwin C. Johnson of Colorado — punctured the claim that labor regimentation was being demanded by the "boys in the foxholes." He declared:

"Be not deceived. No boy in the slime and mud of the jungles wants his father, his mother or his sister kicked around like dogs by bungling Washington bureaucrats."

In addition to Roosevelt's cabinet appointees, the totalitarian-minded military brass, and the labor-hating elements in Congress, there were others who approved Roosevelt's labor conscription scheme. One was the Nazis. Radio Berlin, as recorded on January 11, 1944 in New York City by the Columbia Broadcasting System, trumpeted:

"Roosevelt is now going to announce details of the compulsory universal service act in his message to Congress and propose the introduction of universal service in the United States. Thus Roosevelt once more tries to imitate a National Socialist [Nazi] measure which has proven itself for more than ten years in the Reich."

Another was the Stalinists. In conformity with their policy of supporting even the most anti-labor measures for the sake of the Kremlin's foreign policy and its wartime alliance with the American capitalists, they were the only elements in the American labor movement to openly back the forced labor plan of Roosevelt.

CP National Secretary Earl Browder, in an official report to the National Committee of the Communist Party which was unanimously adopted on January 7 to 9, 1944, summarized the basic line of Stalinism as follows:

"We must be prepared to give the hand of cooperation and fellowship to everyone who fights for the realization of this coalition [the

Teheran Agreement and the Anglo-Soviet-American coalition]. If
J. P. Morgan supports this coalition and goes down the line for it, I
as a Communist am prepared to clasp his hand and join with him to
realize it. Class divisions or political groupings have no significance
now except as they reflect one side or the other of the issue."

The *Daily Worker* not only endorsed Roosevelt's demand for a labor
draft, but lied when it stated in the issue of January 22, 1944:

"One fact stands out beyond a shadow of a doubt when we talk of
labor's sentiment on the President's message to Congress, ALL
LABOR, including even the miners if we leave out the Lewis bureaucracy, is behind it." [Original emphasis.]

Harry Bridges, Joseph Curran, Julius Emspak and similar well-
known followers of Stalinist policy echoed the line of the *Daily Worker*.
But virtually every leading figure in the labor movement, including
Philip Murray and William Green, bitterly denounced the labor draft
proposal.

The Stalinists got so far out of line with official CIO policy at that
time that CIO National Secretary James B. Carey, at the January 31
meeting of the CIO National Executive Board, condemned the action
of the Stalinist-controlled Greater New York Industrial Union Council
for adopting a resolution endorsing a fourth term for Roosevelt.
The CIO tops felt that his recent anti-union actions in the coal, railroad and steel cases and his advocacy of labor conscription made it
unpropitious to call for a Roosevelt fourth term *at that time*. They
hoped, by appearing to withhold support from Roosevelt, to wangle
at least some token concessions from him.

It was revealed by the well-informed *New Leader* on February 5
that when Roosevelt had called Murray and Green to a White House
conference to win their support for a labor draft, Murray had vehemently repeated his opposition to such a measure. The *New Leader*
reported:

"Roosevelt's reply was to tell Murray scornfully that he could not
speak for the CIO on that view... and in proof showed Murray a telegram from Harry Bridges endorsing a labor conscription act."

Murray was so alarmed by this that he called the special CIO
Board meeting in Washington at which Carey assailed the fourth-
term political resolution of the Greater New York CIO Council. The
entire board unconditionally reaffirmed the previous stand of the
CIO convention opposing any form of labor conscription. Bridges,
Quill, Curran, Merrill and Emspak were forced to vote for the con-
demnatory resolution. They complained later to reporters that the
press had "misinterpreted" their endorsement of forced labor.

Roosevelt's pressure for labor conscription was timed to meet the workers' pressure for wage increases. It was intended to intimidate the workers from exercising their right to strike and to scare the union leaders into a more vigorous enforcement of the no-strike pledge. But during the summer and fall of 1944, Roosevelt cagily quieted his labor conscription campaign in order to press more effectively his fourth-term election campaign. He revived his labor conscription scheme only after the votes were counted.

Once Murray had successfully hurdled the crisis of the 1943 year-end steel strike, he and the other CIO leaders sought desperately to keep the struggle for the CIO's wage demand confined within the framework of government arbitration. Murray and the other CIO leaders alternated between appeals to the War Labor Board and complaints to Roosevelt against the delays and unfavorable rulings of his WLB puppets. At the same time, they battled inside their own organization to stifle the growing unrest of their members and head off or break the increasing number of strikes.

Hearings had opened on January 3, 1944, before a special WLB fact-finding panel in Detroit, on the UAW's demand for a ten-cent hourly raise for 250,000 General Motors workers. This and other CIO wage demands were quickly sidetracked by the WLB, while it centered its attention on the steel wage hearings. Walter Reuther, UAW vice-president and head of its GM Division, on March 10 sent a letter to all GM locals explaining that the undue delay in their case was really a clever move to "time" the hearings on the GM demands "so that they are acted upon by the NWLB at the same time that the Steel case is acted upon." Reuther conceded this "will involve a certain amount of delay" but claimed that "we must measure the results of our Labor Board case not by how quickly we are able to clear it through the machinery, but rather by the concrete results obtained."

Meanwhile, all CIO action was deferred pending the WLB's hearings and decisions on the steel union's 17-cent demand. In February 1944, at the hearings of the WLB, Murray complained that the steel companies were refusing to bargain with the union in good faith and were insisting that every issue raised by the union—numbering 22 in all, including wages — be tossed into the WLB's lap. This was precisely the complaint Lewis had made in 1943 prior to the coal miners strikes. Murray charged:

"The companies made it perfectly clear that their answer was 'no' from start to finish. There was no counter-proposal offered on any of the basic issues that involved a single penny of cost to the companies... At the outset they were determined that they were going to bring all these issues before the National War Labor Board and dump the entire problem before this board."

The first representative of the steel companies to appear before the steel panel hearings, John A. Stephens, a U. S. Steel Corporation vice-president, disputed the right of the panel even to consider the issue of a wage increase. He argued that this involved the "national stabilization policy" and that such a panel was not the place "in which to determine a change in the national stabilization policy." Murray proclaimed that he did not intend to "obstruct the work of the panel or encourage in any way a stoppage of work."

In March 1944, CIO and AFL representatives requested a conference with Roosevelt on the whole wage stabilization program. They were informed by WLB Vice-Chairman Taylor that the President had rejected any conference on the administration's wage policy. The CIO and AFL spokesmen then petitioned the WLB for its "approval" in "requesting" Roosevelt to "modify realistically" the Little Steel Formula. This petition too was promptly rejected. The labor leaders then proposed a public hearing on the petition previously turned down. The WLB tossed this into the waste basket. Finally, the union officials asked merely that the board hold "a hearing on wage stabilization for the purpose of providing Congress with information on the subject." The WLB refused even this.

The United Steelworkers filed an ironclad brief with the WLB supporting the union's demands for wage increases. The brief showed that the corporations had boosted their share of income by 62 per cent during the war, while the relative share of the workers had declined almost ten per cent. The brief also proved that the average steelworker was going $8.44 a week into the red and was forced to cash his war bonds or borrow from loan sharks to keep from drowning in debt. The brief summed up the union's conclusions on Roosevelt's wage stabilization:

"The economic events since April 1942, reveal the most shocking injustices perpetrated on American workers. Wage stabilization, as one point of the program, was immediately put into effect by the National War Labor Board. By executive order and the administrative policies of the board, wage stabilization was studiously transformed into a national wage freeze."

At the steel union's international convention in Cleveland, May 9-13, 1944, the "Officers' Report" made no reference to the specific demand for a 17-cent hourly wage increase and mentioned only in passing "our demands for a general wage increase." The big emphasis was on the union's demand for a guaranteed weekly and annual wage, a worthy demand which Murray was using to sidetrack the basic issue before the WLB. Murray's first programmatic point in the officers' report was support of Roosevelt's "national wage stabilization" program— that is, support of the very basis of the wage freeze.

In August, after the WLB had batted the steel union's demands around for seven months, Murray wailed in frustration:

"We have suffered the inequities of frozen wages for some three and one-half years. We have had wage regimentation since January 1941. The only portion of the national population which has suffered the effects of these atrocities are the wage earners, and particularly those in the steel industry."

So, month after month, the "shadowboxing" before the WLB, as the April 8 *Business Week* had called the steel proceedings, continued. Early in October Roosevelt's War Mobilization Director James F. Byrnes announced that the administration would continue to "hold the line" on wages "until the dangers of inflation are passed." Such dangers, he said, would continue not only until "total victory" over both Germany and Japan but long afterwards. He predicted that "wage controls would remain at home indefinitely."

A few days later, Roosevelt summoned Murray and Green to hear their views on the Little Steel Formula and wage stabilization. After they had talked for an hour, Roosevelt gave them no reply but "bade them adieu in his usual friendly manner," reported the *New York Times*.

In December 1944, almost a year to the day after the Steelworkers had initiated their 17-cent demand and a month after Roosevelt had won his fourth term with the all-out support of the CIO leadership, his WLB gave an answer to the steel union: Demand rejected.

At the time of the National CIO convention in Chicago, November 20-24, 1944, the CIO possessed full information on the WLB's steel decision, which the board had obligingly withheld from public announcement until convention adjournment. On the opening day, however, the Washington correspondent of the *New York Times* had reported the exact details of the pending order. The CIO leaders, who had two members on the WLB, pretended they knew nothing about the board's rebuff in the decisive steel case. They turned the convention into a gala celebration of labor's election "victory" just as the first fruit of that "victory," the WLB steel decision, dropped on the heads of the delegates.

Subsequently, Philip Murray hailed the WLB's rejection of the steel union's major demands as "one of the greatest victories in labor's history." He based his claim on the board's grant of several minor fringe concessions. But WLB Chairman Davis, on the day he officially released the steel ruling, boasted that the Little Steel Formula was "not even bent." This was a far cry from Davis's melodramatic expression of despair when the miners settlement had been announced a year earlier.

While the 1944 CIO convention was in session, the November 25 issue of *Business Week* revealed that the WLB had rejected the wage demands of 75,000 Chrysler workers on October 20, three weeks before the November 7 presidential election, and that the United Automobile Workers leadership, the Chrysler Corporation and the Roosevelt administration had contrived to keep the decision secret from the general public as well as from the auto workers. *Business Week* noted that customarily such WLB decisions were issued with great fanfare. It also pointed out that the Chrysler contract expired on November 29 and that negotiations on a new contract were about to begin. After a year and a half of negotiations through the WLB, the UAW leaders decided to "forget" the old Chrysler demands and to start negotiating for a new wage contract within the framework of WLB rulings.

At the September convention of the United Automobile Workers, where a bitter five-day struggle had taken place over the no-strike pledge, Murray had declared with an air of intimate knowledge: "I am just as sure as I am living that the Little Steel Formula is going to be revised." This proved no more accurate than most of his predictions.

Six months later — just after another presidential "impartial" committee had recommended continuation of the Little Steel Formula and after the WLB, on March 3, 1945, had officially said "No!" to the 19-month-old wage demands of 300,000 General Motors workers — Murray could not refrain from an anguished outcry:

"The situation in which labor now finds itself is intolerable."

That accurately summed up the results of the CIO leadership's three-year collaboration with and reliance on Roosevelt's War Labor Board.

20

The War Labor Board and the Montgomery Ward Strike

If the CIO had at any time withdrawn its members from the War Labor Board, the latter's ability to function would have abruptly halted. Only the presence of the union representatives enabled the WLB to maintain its masquerade of impartiality. Murray and the other CIO leaders well understood this. They remained on the board and accepted its dictates because they agreed with its anti-strike function. They were most concerned with preserving their political alliance with Roosevelt and the Democratic Party and did not wish to jeopardize that alliance by a showdown over the WLB.

It was a devious game. The board could be blamed for anti-labor policies that were really determined by Roosevelt and thus protect Roosevelt's brittle "pro-labor" reputation. In addition, they welcomed the farcical hearings and delaying actions of the WLB as a pretext for staving off strikes. In the final analysis, however, they were forced to use more direct methods within the unions to appease or quell the militant workers.

When the nerve-frazzled and fatigued industrial workers became less and less responsive to flag-waving and patriotic exhortations, the CIO leaders tried to distract them from their demands for real wage increases with all sorts of tricky gimmicks and "pie-in-the-sky" promises for the postwar period.

The Stalinist-influenced union leaders, as previously noted, proposed to tie wage increases to increased individual output. This restoration of a form of the hated piecework system was labeled "incentive pay." Wherever the CIO had penetrated into mass industry during the Thirties, one of the first evils it attacked was the speed-up, particularly any and all forms of the piecework system. Now the Stalinists sought to lure the American workers back to this system bred in the dark ages of open-shop industrialism.

The CIO nationally and most of its affiliates flatly rejected and opposed incentive pay. Not surprisingly, many companies readily agreed to these schemes. In October 1943, the WLB approved an incentive pay plan of the Gruman Aircraft Corporation which provided for a five per cent increase in wages for every ten per cent increase in output by the individual worker. By September 1944 the WLB had approved some form of incentive pay for more than 3,000 plants. A survey of 1,000 of these plants showed that for wage increases of 15 to 20 per cent, the workers were turning out an average of 40 per cent more production, simply through intensified labor.

In the few CIO unions tightly controlled by them, the Stalinists put over a number of incentive pay contracts. These were usually negotiated in locked-room deals between union officials and company lawyers. The July 10, 1943 issue of *UE News,* organ of the CIO United Electrical Workers, reported the establishment of an incentive pay plan for 78,000 Westinghouse Electric workers, thus restoring a piecework system that the workers had fought militantly to destroy during the UE's founding struggles of the Thirties.

In December 1943, less than six months later, the UE leaders were forced by the miners' victory and by the wage policy hastily adopted by the 1943 CIO national convention to call a Westinghouse union wage conference. The delegates voted to demand a wage increase of 17 cents an hour. Of course, the UE leaders buried this demand in the "graveyard of grievances" — the WLB. The board got around to rejecting it in 1945. Fifteen years later, workers in certain plants and industries were still trying to throw off incentive pay speed-up schemes imposed during World War II.

Throughout 1942 and most of 1943, the CIO leadership tried to sidetrack efforts for pay increases by a campaign for a "rollback of prices." Murray's proposition was simple. Instead of labor fighting for higher wages to catch up with rising prices, the government was to be persuaded to force the capitalists to roll back prices to their level at the time the Little Steel Formula was introduced.

This notion, pressed by the whole CIO leadership, would require the capitalist government to finance some of the astronomical costs of the war out of profits instead of wages. After a year and a half of pleading for a price rollback, Murray finally started to "talk tough" to Congress. During the first week of July 1943, Murray issued an "ultimatum." He said that if Congress did not pass price rollback legislation by July 15, 1943, the CIO would be compelled to demand higher wages.

Roosevelt replied several days later. In connection with his veto of the Commodity Credit Corporation Bill, Roosevelt said: "I do not think that a reduction of all living costs...to the September 1942 level is practicable. We all must be prepared in total war to accept a substantial cut in our accustomed standards."

Roosevelt's "we all" did not include the corporation owners. By the end of 1943 their net profits had doubled over 1940. The capitalists' living standards could have been cut substantially and still have represented luxurious living; the workers' standards had been cut to the bone long since.

When Murray's July 15 price rollback deadline had come and gone, he still kept quiet about wage increases. On July 22, 1943, he and AFL President Green, accompanied by a retinue of high CIO and AFL officials, trekked to the White House. Green told the President: "Either prices must be brought down or the board must ask for revision of the Little Steel Formula."

After the fruitless conference Murray was reminded by reporters of his July 15 deadline. He claimed that "we want to give the President an opportunity to apply the rollback permitted by Congress." (The ultimatum had been addressed originally to Congress for legislation never enacted.) Asked if this was his last notice, Murray said: "I am not in the habit of issuing ultimatums to the President of the United States."

At Roosevelt's press conference that same day, the President genially dismissed the issue of price rollbacks. "Rollback," said Roosevelt, is an "awful" word and he wished someone would invent a new one.

CIO spokesmen continued to issue statements — especially just before the 1944 presidential elections — which gave the false impression that Roosevelt was seriously contemplating a price rollback measure.

On January 25, 1944, Murray presented before a subcommittee hearing of the Senate Education and Labor Committee the startling findings of a CIO cost of living survey made among 1,500 steelworkers. From January 1, 1941, base date of the Little Steel Formula, to January 1, 1944, the cost of living had soared more than double the 23.5 per cent rise claimed by the U. S. Bureau of Labor Statistics. Murray called the official statistics "worthless."

The AFL and CIO members of the Presidential Committee on the Cost of Living on January 30 made public a joint report showing that living costs had risen 43.5 per cent since January 1, 1941. UAW-CIO President R. J. Thomas and AFL Secretary-Treasurer George Meany, who had submitted the report, charged that there was a "discrepancy of 28.5 per cent between the rise in living costs and the wage adjustments [15 per cent above January 1, 1941] allowed under the Little Steel Formula."

By March 1944, Meany put into plain words what the whole labor bureaucracy dared no longer deny. He wrote in the *American Federationist:* "Is there anyone in America who really believes that the cost of living has been controlled by the government in the last two years? Is there anyone so simple-minded as to believe that price control as it now functions can be relied on by the American workers... ?"

When all the schemes like incentive pay and price rollback failed to halt the increasing strikes for higher wages, the CIO leaders tried to dissuade the workers from immediate defense of their interests by promises of glowing reforms for the postwar future. These reforms, incidentally, were aimed mainly at preventing the great scourge all workers feared would follow the end of the war — mass unemployment.

CIO President Murray, in a speech at Columbus, Ohio, in January 1944, put forth the proposal for a guaranteed annual wage to ensure security against postwar plans of Big Business to bring "the old apple man back on the street corners." Murray asked: "Can't we do better than the old-fashioned system of spreading the work, spreading the starvation, spreading discontent, spreading death?" There was nothing in his remarks about a return to any "good old days" of the New Deal.

In his keynote address to the steelworkers convention on May 9, 1944, Murray laid stress on the guaranteed weekly and annual wage. The steelworkers union actually raised the demand, but the WLB rejected it in December 1944. The idea was turned over to a "study" commission set up by Roosevelt. This commission went into such a deep study that the guaranteed weekly and annual wage proposal did not reappear in the CIO until 1954, almost two years after Murray's death.

In the United Automobile Workers, where the heaviest pressure was put on the leaders to end the no-strike pledge, the International Executive Board endorsed and issued a most far-reaching postwar plan. A meeting of the UAW Board on July 3, 1943, adopted a postwar program with government ownership and operation of the basic industries as its key plank. The program also called for the establishment of the 30-hour week.

The radical terms in which the UAW leaders spoke in their attempts to pacify the militant ranks are indicated by the text of the UAW Board's program published in the July 15, 1943 *United Automobile Worker*. It reads in part:

"Our industries can no longer be operated to serve private interests where these interests conflict with the public need... [The UAW-CIO calls for]:

"Government or municipal ownership and operation of monopolistic industries and of industries strategically essential to national safety...

"Government control and regulation of other industries to prevent the abuses of monopoly and to assure production in the public interest...

"Reduction of working week to thirty hours without reduction of pay, as a result of a full production program."

At the UAW Board meeting in December 1943, following the miners victory, the auto union leaders proposed to demand in the next contract an escalator clause which would provide for automatic increases in wages corresponding to the rises in the cost of living.

Every one of these proposals put forward by the UAW leaders—government ownership and operation of basic industries, the 30-hour week at 40 hours' pay, the escalator clause to combat inflation—had been taken over intact from the program of the UAW left-wing (anti-Stalinist) militants and had been projected originally in *The Militant*.

The real militants in the UAW were vocal and adamant opponents of the no-strike pledge. By appearing to adopt the radical program, Thomas, Addes, Reuther and Frankensteen hoped to appeal to the ranks and to quiet their rising clamor for revocation of the no-strike pledge.

This clamor was more than vocal. There was a steady and swelling stream of strikes, especially in the CIO-organized basic industries. The U. S. Bureau of Labor Statistics reported that the number of strikes had increased from 571 in the first quarter of 1942 to 643 in the same period of 1943, then to 1,040 for the first three months of 1944. *Business Week* of August 5, 1944, noted with concern an uninterrupted rise in strikes from a total of 270 in September 1943 to 610 in May 1944. This businessman's magazine observed that the D-Day invasion of France by the Allies had been expected to put a halt to the strike wave, but there were still 500 strikes in June 1944.

The July 30, 1944 *New York Times* described a spreading strike wave in Detroit as "a symbol of intense agitation within the plants and of discontent among the rank and file of workers. They are discontented with policies of management and government alike. They blame management for refusing to negotiate grievances and they blame the Government for freezing wages."

In April 1944 there occurred the most significant and dramatic wartime strike next to the miners' battles of 1943. This was the Montgomery Ward and Co. strike in Chicago. This strike further revealed the class character of Roosevelt's labor machinery, the strikebreaking role of the Stalinists, the submissiveness of the top CIO leaders and the deep sense of labor solidarity that permeated the organized ranks of industrial workers.

The Montgomery Ward management, headed by Sewell L. Avery, had announced in November 1943 that the $600,000,000 mail-order firm would not renew its one-year contract, signed the previous December with the CIO United Retail, Wholesale and Department Store Employees of America. The company said it would seek a federal court injunction to restrain the WLB from "forcing" it to sign a union contract. Montgomery Ward also instituted suit for $1,000,000 against the union and 14 of its officers for alleged libel in the union's paper, *The Spotlight,* and in the *CIO News.*

When the old agreement expired on December 8, 1943, the company informed the union that it would not renew the contract, using the pretext that the union did not represent a majority of the employees. Then, according to the paper of the local union directly involved — United Mail Order, Warehouse and Retail Employees Local 20 — "the Company instituted a wave of wage cuts, demotions, layoffs and firings...furthermore stepped up its campaign of persecution of union members..."

On January 15, 1944, the WLB ordered a 30-day extension of the old contract while the union filed for a new NLRB election. The company announced it would defy the extension order. On March 29, the WLB issued a second order. The company ignored it.

The WLB took no further action until after April 12, 1944, when some 5,000 Ward workers went on strike in Chicago, throwing mass picket lines around three buildings, including the main warehouse. Within a few days virtually the entire Chicago labor movement, with the exception of the Stalinist-controlled locals, declared its support of the strikers.

AFL Teamsters members and the railroad brotherhoods refused to handle "hot" cargo; the AFL Building Service Employees publicly backed the strike and contributed financial aid. The independent Illinois Union of Telephone Workers informed Local 20 that its members would not service Montgomery Ward until the strike was settled. The Chicago Printing Trades Union, which had previously refused to print the Ward catalogue, offered moral and material support to the strike.

URWDSE-CIO President Samuel Wolchok, despite the opposition of the Stalinist elements in his union, promptly sanctioned the strike and threw the international union's support behind the strikers. Subsequently, the union's General Executive Board endorsed Wolchok's action.

The April 15 issue of Local 20's *Spotlight* reported that "in a call from Washington today, Allan Haywood, National CIO Director of Organization, informed Leonard Levy [Local 20 president] that the CIO is prepared to aid and assist us immediately." This included the news that "the CIO WILL NOT PERMIT CHICAGO ORDERS TO BE SHIPPED FROM ST. PAUL." (Original emphasis.)

Philip Murray could no longer boast that no CIO union had ever gone on an "authorized" wartime strike.

Montgomery Ward's defiance of the WLB's directives to renew the old contract was an attempt to abrogate union security in the form of the WLB-approved maintenance of membership clause and to restore the complete open shop. Sewell Avery had undertaken this move as the beginning of a national drive by the large employers to nullify all forms of the union shop.

A day after the strike began, the WLB certified the case to Roosevelt. On April 26 Roosevelt ordered seizure of the strike-bound Chicago Montgomery Ward buildings. He issued a statement condemning both the strikers and the company. The CIO leaders hailed this seizure as a union "victory," although the strikers went back to work without any contract.

The "victory" myth was reinforced by the fact that Avery himself had refused to vacate his office and had been removed bodily, still seated calmly with arms folded, by two soldiers. This scene was photographed and published on the front pages of almost every newspaper in the country.

On Roosevelt's orders, the union leaders called off the Chicago strike and prevented its spread to other establishments of the far-flung Ward empire. While the government was in possession of the Chicago Ward building, the NLRB held an election which the union won overwhelmingly.

Roosevelt had told a press conference: "If the election shows that the union does not have a majority of the employees, that will end the case. On the other hand, if the election shows that the union has a majority, then the management has declared that it is willing to continue its contract and that will end the case." But it did not end the case. Sewell Avery promptly repudiated Roosevelt, saying: "We have never made such a statement and we never intend to. The only thing the election will settle is whether the union represents a majority of Ward workers."

After the NLRB election Avery said its results were of "no consequence." Ward "would sign no contract demanding maintenance of membership or a closed shop clause, nor would Montgomery Ward renew the former contract, containing a maintenance of membership provision."

Avery's removal from the Chicago plant did not have its calculated effect of intimidating him or forcing Montgomery Ward to accept the WLB ruling. But if Ward could defy the WLB, why couldn't the workers? Indeed, the WLB had referred the case to Roosevelt precisely because Avery's defiance had jeopardized the board's authority over labor.

The eviction of Avery, while giving the impression that Roosevelt was acting against the company, actually was a smokescreen for government strikebreaking. "The seizure of the plant has been a farce," the union's attorney subsequently complained.

Secretary of Commerce Jesse Jones, in his order returning the plant to the company, carefully noted that "at no time during the period of Government possession have the normal routine business procedures of Montgomery Ward and Co. been disturbed." The May 1 *CIO News* had already complained that "certain executives and supervisors of the company are continuing Avery's fight against the government. Workers are being shifted from job to job, discrimination is rife and seniority and the grievance procedure are being totally ignored."

Once the government's token seizure had ended on May 9, the union had no recourse except to appeal once more to the WLB or to renew the strike. Avery proceeded to victimize the active unionists and to reject a maintenance of membership contract. In June, Local 20's *Spotlight* reported that the Ward management had refused to consider 17 of the union's 20 demands, including such standard matters as seniority and time and a half for overtime. A month after the end of the seizure, the WLB for the fourth time ordered Montgomery Ward to extend the old contract, with no gains for the union. Avery bluntly refused. The WLB made no outcry and the press barely noted this continued defiance.

A month before the national elections, the October 7, 1944 *Militant* published an embarrassing reminder to the CIO leaders:

"Although the pro-Roosevelt 'labor statesmen' have been keeping quiet recently on the still-unsettled Montgomery Ward case... Sewell Avery has still refused to comply with the numerous WLB orders to sign a contract..."

On December 9 some 2,000 members of Local 332, CIO United Retail, Wholesale and Department Store Employees, struck the Ward stores in Detroit. All local CIO unions except those under complete

Stalinist domination pledged full support to the strike. Mass picketing aided by hundreds of CIO auto workers helped close the Ward stores. The strike spread to six other cities.

President Roosevelt again intervened, ordering all the struck establishments seized on December 28, 1944. Although he said that the company had defied the WLB "for more than a year," Roosevelt's statement made clear he was acting now only because Avery's recalcitrance "threatened" the "confidence" of the workers in the government's "structure for the impartial adjudication of disputes" and had led to the "distinct threat" of sympathy walkouts in support of the Ward strikers. The seizure order conceded a seven-cent wage raise, boosting the prevailing hourly rate of 39 cents to the grand sum of 46 cents — a concession Avery already had agreed to at the start of the strike and before Roosevelt intervened.

A federal court ruled on January 27, 1945, that Roosevelt's seizure was illegal. The army officers in charge of the seizure that same day announced they were withholding application of all WLB directives in the Ward case. By the last week in February 1945 the army officials had relinquished all control over the 13 Ward units that had been seized. On June 8, 1945, a Federal Circuit Court ruled that the earlier seizure had been legal after all. The army officials then said they would enforce the WLB rulings. At the court hearing WLB officials had revealed there were at least 102 other cases of employer non-compliance with board rulings, some going back more than two years. Since there were no strikes in these cases, the WLB took no further action to enforce its rulings.

Even after the Federal Circuit Court's decision Avery reiterated his determination not to accept the WLB's orders. The army officials, again in control of the previously struck plants, said they would put some of the WLB rulings into effect, but would not pay the more than $2,000,000 in retroactive wages due the Ward workers. At the war's close in August 1945, the properties were speedily restored to Montgomery Ward, which refused to the very end to sign a maintenance of membership union contract. Thus, Avery successfully defied the WLB, Roosevelt, and the federal courts. The various seizures had served only to break the Ward strikes. The union was left in a shambles until a postwar strike, without government interference, forced concessions.

Although the wartime Ward strikers had had the sympathy and even active support of most sectors of organized labor, they had faced one antagonist even more hostile than Avery — the Stalinist movement and its spokesmen in the unions. By 1944 the American Communist Party had launched its full-scale campaign to win the

American rulers to a postwar alliance with the Kremlin. This alliance would have the objective of dividing the world into fixed spheres of influence between the Kremlin bureaucracy and the capitalist powers, principally the United States. The deal would provide for the mutual suppression of working-class and colonial revolts.

In a radio broadcast on January 9, 1944, CP Chairman William Z. Foster had declared: "Communists do not believe it would be of benefit to national unity to make proposals of a specific communistic or socialistic nature at this time or in the immediate postwar future." This was one of the first clear declarations that the Stalinists intended to extend their opposition to socialist struggle into the postwar period. Earl Browder, the CP national secretary, had spelled out the Stalinist policy even more fully at the CP National Committee meeting which had concluded on the day of Foster's broadcast. Browder had stated that "we frankly declare that we are ready to cooperate in making [American] capitalism work effectively in the postwar period... We Communists are opposed to permitting an explosion of class conflict in our country when the war ends... we are now extending the perspective of national unity for many years into the future." The CP National Committee, including Foster, voted unanimously to adopt Browder's declaration of policy. These were the political considerations that underlay the policy of the Stalinist-influenced union officials during the Montgomery Ward strikes.

When the big Chicago strike was called in late April 1944, the URWDSEA-CIO had appealed immediately to the officials of the CIO International Longshoremen's and Warehousemen's Union, headed by Harry Bridges, to refrain from handling orders diverted from the Chicago Ward plant to its St. Paul branch. The ILWU officials replied that "we will handle Chicago orders eight hours a day, call it scabbing if you want to."

The April 21, 1944 *Dispatcher,* official organ of Bridges' union, publicly endorsed the declaration of scabbery by the ILWU's St. Paul local. It boasted: "ILWU Local 215, which is the bargaining agent for employes of Montgomery Ward in St. Paul, immediately reaffirmed its no-strike pledge, although it received requests from the Chicago strike leaders not to handle goods."

Bridges himself wrote in the May 5, 1944 *Dispatcher* that "under no circumstances will our union be a party to the game that was played in Chicago or anything like it. If anything we'll be more affirmative than ever in our adherence to the no-strike pledge."

The April 17, 1944 *Daily Worker* even proclaimed: "Mr. Avery owes his success in provoking the strike in large measure to a group of Trotskyites who are in the leadership of the striking local...

irresponsible elements who, like Avery, also want to embarrass
the Roosevelt administration and hamper the war effort and national
unity."

The only reason Avery did not succeed "in fomenting disorder
and disunity," according to this same *Daily Worker* article, was the
"restraining hand of responsible labor leaders and the city administration under Mayor Kelly..." This Mayor Kelly is the same New
Dealer whose cops slaughtered ten Republic Steel strikers in the
Memorial Day Massacre of 1937.

The Montgomery Ward strike in Chicago signaled a declaration
of unconditional surrender by the Stalinist-influenced union leaders
to the American capitalists. Harry Bridges not only ordered members of the CIO International Longshoremen's and Warehousemen's
Union to handle hot cargo of the Ward strike, he urged all labor
to give a *permanent* no-strike pledge to the corporations. On May 25,
1944, Bridges spoke before a meeting of ILWU Local 6 in San Francisco to push through a resolution stating that strikes were "treason"; that the unions should back the capitalist government "in any
actions necessary to prevent strikes"; that the government should
"refuse to give consideration to the demands of any section of labor"
that went on strike; and that the no-strike policy should be maintained not only for the period of the war but "indefinitely thereafter."

The June 9, 1944 *Pilot,* organ of Joseph Curran's CIO National
Maritime Union, featured an extensive article signed by Bridges
urging the permanent no-strike policy. Curran himself, in a radio
broadcast on July 12, declared that the NMU officialdom "wants none
[strikes] now—or in the postwar period." He urged a no-strike
policy after the war if the ship operators continued the "same attitude and thinking" they had allegedly displayed during the war.

The June 19, 1944 *Daily Worker* set the tone for the whole campaign
against union militants with an editorial that screamed: "Those who
violate the no-strike pledge are scabs and should be so treated.
Scabs were never handled with kid gloves."

Although the enormous spread of unauthorized strikes in the very
midst of war showed the real temper of the workers, the Stalinists
persisted in their attempts to tie American labor's hands, even into
the postwar period. At the Massachusetts CIO Council convention
in Boston on July 8 and 9, 1944, leaders of the United Electrical
Workers delegation attempted to amend the no-strike resolution to
extend the pledge after the war. This evoked a chorus of boos and
angry shouts from the outraged delegates. The amendment was defeated by a huge majority.

In September 1944, Bridges signed an ILWU contract with the

Pacific Coast waterfront employers containing a "security preamble" pledging no strikes for the duration of the war "and beyond."

Non-Stalinist leaders like Murray, Thomas, Reuther, Hillman, Rieve and others could parade as virtual leftists compared to the "communists." "See," they said in effect to the workers, "we ask you to forego strikes only until the war is over, while the radical communists tell you to give up strikes even after the war."

In essence, however, Stalinists and non-Stalinists in the CIO leadership had a common strikebreaking policy. The employers, the government and the union leaders worked as a bloc to crush the resistance of the workers. In the end, the gimmicks and postwar promises and elaborate maneuvers through the War Labor Board could not quiet the workers whose living standards and conditions of work had become intolerable.

21

The Fight against
the No-Strike Pledge

The case of the coal miners in 1943 had demonstrated that where the union leaders stood solidly with the workers, the War Labor Board and the whole administration could not crush the workers' resistance. It took the union bureaucracies with their powerful machines of paid functionaries to beat down the union militants, disorient the ranks and systematically smother every strike. They did it with threats, expulsions, receiverships over recalcitrant locals, suspensions of local officers, "community" fines against entire locals, even mobilization of strikebreakers and scabs to cross picket lines and operate struck plants.

Intimidation, punitive measures and victimization were the principal weapons employed to keep recalcitrant workers "in line." In a 1943 Chrysler case, for instance, the WLB denied a maintenance of membership clause because the workers had gone on strike. It fined Cramp Shipyard workers. It approved the pay deduction of a $10,000 fine from U. S. Rubber Company workers ordered by United Rubber Workers President Dalrymple.

As usual, the Stalinists were a step ahead of the run-of-the-mill union officials in anti-democratic assaults on the ranks. The August 28, 1943 *Daily Worker* proudly recounted how UE Local 1102 of St. Louis had "suspended 10 members for six-month and three-month periods for their part in unauthorized stoppage of work at the Emerson Electric Manufacturing Co. turret plant. The union asked the management to lay off the 10 for the period of suspension." The company graciously granted this "concession."

The conservative old-line CIO leaders did not take long to emulate the Stalinists. The National Executive Board of the Industrial Union of Marine and Shipbuilding Workers, at its meeting during the first week in September 1943, empowered its president, John Green, to set up a three-man committee, including himself, to police the union locals and deal "severe punishment" to individual members who violated the no-strike pledge.

At the IUMSW national convention in New York City, September 21-24, 1943, the "Officers' Report" disclosed that charters of four locals had been revoked and five other locals had been placed in receivership in the preceding 12 months, while 25 per cent of all locals had been "disciplined."

In the United Rubber Workers, a smaller but strategically situated CIO union, a number of the militants from key Akron locals at Goodrich, Goodyear and Firestone had caucused together to organize resistance to the no-strike policy and the anti-democratic actions of the top leaders. President Sherman Dalrymple had great difficulty in suppressing a general rubber strike in Akron in June 1943.

Early in January 1944, Dalrymple ordered the summary expulsion of 72 members of General Tire and Rubber Company Local 9 in Akron for participation in a strike. The company promptly fired the accused men. This set off a battle for reinstatement of the expelled members. The big Firestone and Goodrich locals took formal action in support of the victimized workers.

In retaliation, a general membership meeting of Goodrich Local 5, Dalrymple's home local, early in April 1944 voted his expulsion after a local trial board convicted him of violating the URW constitution on six counts. Both Firestone Local 7 and the Akron CIO Council backed the action of Local 5 against Dalrymple. The URW's General Executive Board held a closed hearing on the case of the 72 expelled by Dalrymple, found them "guilty" but reinstated all except seven singled out as "ringleaders." The board, composed of Dalrymple's own faction supporters, then ordered Local 5 to reinstate Dalrymple. To avoid a showdown fight and a possible split in the union, Local 5 complied.

The URW convention struggle in September 1944 revolved about the issue of union democracy. At the opening of the convention in New York City, a Firestone Local 7 delegate introduced a motion to wire the army commanding officers of Ray Sullivan and Howard Haas, requesting they be given special leave to attend the convention. Sullivan and Haas were past presidents of General Tire Local 9, among the 72 workers expelled, blacklisted in the industry, and drafted into the army. The Dalrymple machine did not oppose the motion. An attempt by the militants to modify the union constitution to reduce the bureaucratic power of the top officials was defeated by 774 votes to 384. They were able to obtain a compromise concession providing for reinstatement of all expelled members, and the re-funding of 50 per cent of the fines levied on members who had gone on strike. Debate on the no-strike pledge was relegated to the last day. One-third of the delegates voted against the official resolution to reaffirm the pledge "without qualification or reservation."

President Philip Murray's own steel industry recorded more strikes and strikers in wartime 1944 than in any previous year. In the case of an unauthorized strike of Local 1519 against American Steel and Wire Company's Cleveland works in March 1944, the Steel-workers International Executive Board suspended all five officers and the entire grievance committee of the local. Its records and funds were taken over and a receivership established. According to the workers, the company had been particularly provocative in re-fusing to adjust grievances and in violation of the contract. Raymond Jablonowski, who had been president of Local 1519, was inducted into the navy right after his suspension.

Despite Murray's powerful bureaucratic machine, he failed in his attempts to stifle all opposition to the no-strike policy at the United Steelworkers second constitutional convention in Cleveland, May 9-13, 1944. More than 500 machine men sat as delegates among the 2,300 in attendance. During the five-day convention not more than 40 delegates succeeded in getting the floor. Murray, his paid lieu-tenants and a host of guest speakers took the time of the convention.

In describing Murray's conduct of the convention, I wrote in the May 20, 1944 *Militant:* "For almost two days the delegates had been subjected to a relentless pounding by Murray, his top lieutenants and sundry guest speakers on the need to reaffirm the no-strike pledge... Whatever opposition might have existed appeared to be thoroughly stifled and cowed. Murray rode high, completely dom-inating the convention... intervening at the first intimation of dis-cussion from the floor. His speeches alone took well over half the convention's time... Every time a delegate spoke, even on the most minor question, Murray would begin pacing up and down the long stage, nervously apprehensive lest any discussion lead to an ex-pression of opposition sentiment."

By the afternoon of the second day, Murray felt the delegates were sufficiently browbeaten to risk introduction of resolutions. Since copies of the resolutions were received only a few minutes before they were introduced, one delegate suggested that the reso-lutions be held over until the next morning to give the delegates a chance to study them. Murray slurringly replied: "We'd all like a day off. But this is a working convention and there's a war on."

Several resolutions were promptly rushed through. Murray's

hand-picked Resolutions Committee brought forward a resolution to reaffirm the no-strike pledge. One delegate spoke for it to only mild applause. Then, Mark L. Brown, president of Reading, Pennsylvania Local 2715, a member of the Resolutions Committee, stepped up to the "mike." He told the surprised delegates that he had not learned of his appointment to the committee until his name had been announced at the convention itself. He further declared that if he had had the opportunity to help in drafting the resolution he would have opposed the reaffirmation of the no-strike pledge. Although some yelled "Sit down!" and "Throw him out!" the youthful Brown stuck to his guns. Soon the entire convention was listening intently and when he concluded his sharp attack on the no-strike policy there was a thunder of applause. My report continued:

"Murray, visibly disturbed and red-faced, quickly strode to the 'mike,'... used every trick of oratory, every threat and demagogic appeal he could muster to beat the delegates back into line... Above all, he placed at stake his own leadership, using his personal prestige to beguile the convention..." As soon as he concluded, "he hurriedly put to vote a motion to end debate... Loud, angry shouts arose from every section of the hall... Delegates started moving down the aisles to get to the 'mike.' Scores were on their feet frantically waving their arms and demanding the floor. To appease the rank and file, Murray... was compelled to back down and permit further debate."

This was an historic occasion in the steel union. Never before, in his eight years as head of the Steelworkers, had Murray ever had to yield on any point to the rank and file.

Timothy Smith, president of Buffalo, New York Local 2603, a Negro delegate, indignantly scored Murray's insulting insinuations about the patriotism of the militant delegates. He pointed out: "I have a son and two nephews in this war, who started out in perfect health, and two of them have already been shot up." He challenged Murray: "I have four or five grievances which I'll give the Executive Board. If they can settle them, I'll support the no-strike pledge. But I know they can't." He aroused applause when he charged: "Grievances are piled high in the War Labor Board. Yes, we can take our grievances to arbitration. But what happens? The lawyer gets $12,000 —we get two cents." He then directly accused the top union officials of aiding the companies against good union men:

"There is a tendency among executives of this union to pick out and discipline stewards and local leaders for strikes in local plants. Those who have given blood, sweat and tears to build this union are being pinned up against the wall by the executives."

In a voice vote taken on the no-strike resolution, the Murray machine secured a majority. But an estimated one-fourth of the delegates voted against the no-strike pledge. This was a considerable vote in light of the power of the machine, the reprisals that threatened opposition delegates and their lack of organization. The opposition was a temporary, loosely-knit formation which reflected the sentiments of the workers in the mills but had no real program to counter to Murray's. They had no outstanding leaders and spokesmen. Above all, most of them were still committed, however reluctantly, to political support of Roosevelt and his war program.

The struggle against the no-strike policy was strongest and most protracted inside the United Automobile Workers. Throughout 1944 the union officers ran around frantically from strike to strike like a rural fire company rushing to put out brush and grass fires in a hot, dry summer.

The 224 strikes involving 388,763 strikers in the auto industry during 1944 set an annual record. A couple of typical strikes were the walkouts in February of 6,500 members of Chevrolet Gear & Axle Division UAW Local 235, and of 5,600 members of Local 400 at Ford's Highland Park plant in Detroit. Both of these strikes were provoked by "disciplinary" firings of union members. R. J. Thomas and Walter Reuther ordered the Chevrolet strikers back to work with the threat that UAW officials "will not protect any workers who are penalized as a result of the continuance of the unauthorized action." Ford Local 400 President Ben Garrison, who was to play a leading role at the September UAW convention in the fight against the no-strike pledge, charged management with "severest discipline for the pettiest of infractions."

The UAW Executive Board adopted a resolution declaring that "an increasing number of corporations... have deliberately pursued a course intended to deny them [the workers] their rights under their contracts and to provoke them into engaging in work stoppages." No action was proposed against such companies. Instead, the Executive Board threatened drastic penalties, including withholding of "any intervention in their behalf in the event of disciplinary actions against them by management" for workers who "resort to work stoppages in response to the provocative acts of management."

President Thomas, acting on behalf of his entire Executive Board, called on Ford Local 600 to take "drastic and effective action" against members involved in a stoppage. Whereupon Ford Motor Company fired ten men and suspended ten more. Within a few weeks Ford had fired or otherwise "disciplined" 121 members of Local 600 at the River Rouge plants.

A mass meeting of Local 600 Aircraft Unit members on March 19 in Detroit proposed a city-wide UAW conference to initiate a movement to rescind the no-strike pledge. The large and influential Briggs Local 212 on March 26 voted to urge the Executive Board to call a special convention to revoke the no-strike policy. Scores of locals sent in similar resolutions.

The UAW leadership, uniting solidly against the ranks, intensified its acts of intimidation and repression. By unanimous action, the Executive Board removed all the elected officers of Chrysler Local 490 and appointed a receivership over the local. Shortly afterwards—at the end of May—Thomas issued another anti-strike statement: "Within recent weeks, there have been too many wildcat strikes. Public opinion has become inflamed against our union ... Our union cannot survive if the nation and our soldiers believe that we are obstructing the war effort."

The Searchlight, organ of Flint's Chevrolet Local 659 which urged the end of the no-strike pledge, issued some tart comments: "For a man that is drawing a salary from the union for doing union work, Thomas is performing some acts that look mighty queer to some of us. In fact every time he draws his salary there are those who think that he is coming dangerously close to obtaining money under false pretenses. Thomas draws a nice fat salary from the union and it is about time that he stopped worrying about the companies' problems and started to devote himself to union problems. If he wants to keep his belly pressed up to the union pie counter he had better get down to business."

In July, the Chrysler Highland Park Local 490 membership repudiated the dictatorial receivership imposed on it. The local reelected the entire group of officers who had been removed in April by the Thomas-Addes-Reuther-Frankensteen anti-strike coalition.

A series of walkouts by 7,000 members of Local 235 at the Chevrolet Gear and Axle plants in August, when the workers defied a WLB command to end their strike "forthwith," brought the heavy hand of the bureaucracy down on the local. Its leaders were expelled from office and a receivership placed over it. The ousted officers were charged with failure "to exert themselves sufficiently" to halt the strike. The company fired the seven expelled Local 235 leaders and the workers struck again. Walter Reuther, UAW vice-president and General Motors Division director, complained to the WLB that GM had used "subterfuge, trickery and duplicity" in firing the local union officers, after the WLB ordered the company to take back without discrimination all strikers who engaged in the first walkout. The WLB ignored Reuther and demanded the end of the second strike before it would even consider the case of the fired men. Under Reuther's pressure, the local ended the strike after four days. His plea to the WLB could not cover up the fact that he had supported the expulsion of the Local 235 officers which had given GM the tip to fire them from their jobs.

Late in August there was another strike of Ford Local 400 at the Detroit Highland Park plant. Richard T. Leonard, the UAW's Ford Division director, was jeered at a strike meeting when he tried to mobilize a back-to-work movement. He was chased from the scene when he ordered picketing workers into the plant.

Strikers on the picket line wore jackets with the slogan on the back, "Scrap the No Strike Pledge — Local 400." This was the slogan of a new broad movement which was mobilizing its forces for the coming UAW convention. The central and dominant point of the Rank and File Caucus program was the revocation of the no-strike pledge. It also urged withdrawal of the labor members from the WLB and establishment of a labor party.

At the Michigan CIO convention in July 1943, the delegates had voted to urge the CIO to withdraw the no-strike pledge. The UAW delegates spearheaded this action and even Victor Reuther, Walter's brother, had gone along with the anti-no-strike sentiment.

But the action of the convention, while revealing the true sentiment of the workers, was not binding on the international unions. At the October 1943 UAW convention, the Reuther-Leonard and the Addes-Frankensteen-Stalinist caucuses had joined forces to push over a resolution to "reaffirm without any qualification" the no-strike pledge. Reuther tried to establish a "principled difference" between his no-strike resolution and that of the Stalinists. His contained a few complaints about the WLB in the "whereases" and proposed government seizure of plants where managements refused "fair collective bargaining." The Stalinists promptly embraced these "differences," which were incorporated into a single "unconditional no-strike pledge" resolution behind which the whole leadership united to browbeat the ranks into line. No delegate from the floor defended this no-strike resolution. Reuther did take a position against the Stalinists by leading the opposition to their incentive pay proposals.

By the time of the 1944 Michigan State CIO convention, held July 12–15 in Grand Rapids, the national and state leaders, combined with the UAW top officials, were concentrating their forces to beat back the powerful rank-and-file campaign against the no-strike policy. They were mindful of the 1943 state CIO convention's revolt.

A massive array of CIO and UAW top officers poured it on the Michigan delegates hour after hour in denunciation of any attempt to abrogate the no-strike pledge. They were joined by army and navy brass hats, clergymen and specially selected Purple Heart war veterans.

Only six delegates were able to get the floor to speak in opposition to the no-strike pledge after the resolutions were finally introduced. The Reuther and the Addes-Stalinist caucuses were lined up together from the start. Nevertheless, more than a third of the delegates braved the tirades and jingoism to vote against the no-strike pledge. This opposition was concentrated largely in the UAW delegation.

The stormiest convention in the whole stormy history of the CIO United Automobile, Aircraft and Agricultural Implement Workers, at that time the largest union in America, opened September 11, 1944, in Grand Rapids. The entire convention machinery, including all committees, had been organized to enable the two top leadership caucuses to keep a tight grip on the workings of the convention.

Everything did not go according to plan, however. When the hand-picked Rules Committee brought forward its proposed convention rules, a mighty roar of disapproval greeted the motions to hold the election of officers on the fourth day of the convention and to limit reports of committees to a minority and a majority.

In the debate on the question of elections, the angry delegates stated they wanted them on the last day of the convention, "so that we know what every officer's opinion is before we vote," as one delegate put it. The Rules Committee backed down and then returned with a compromise—elections on the fifth day. The delegates howled: "Last thing! Last thing!" Delegate DeLorenzo, from Brewster Local 365, a member of the Rules Committee, then offered a minority report to postpone elections to "the last order of business." It was adopted by a close-to-unanimous vote. Thus the delegates frustrated the scheme of the leaders to divert convention discussion on issues into a discussion of personalities.

The determination of the delegates to have a full and free discussion was further expressed on the question of limiting committee reports to a single minority and majority. This proposal was aimed at preventing any resolution coming out of the Resolutions Committee calling for revocation of the no-strike pledge, since the Reuther and Addes-Stalinist factions each had its own no-strike resolution. Ben Garrison of Highland Park Ford Local 400, the one member of the Resolutions Committee who opposed the no-strike pledge, revealed to the convention that the proposed rule was "some sort of subterfuge" since "both majority and minority of the resolutions committee are for reaffirmation." He demanded amendment of the rule to permit "all shades of opinion." The convention finally voted to permit all points of view on the no-strike pledge to be reported out of committee and voted on by the convention.

The delegates had still not heard or received copies of the proposed no-strike resolution by 3 P.M. of the second day of the convention when all convention business was recessed to hear CIO President Philip Murray orate for an hour and a half. His opening was a campaign speech for Roosevelt in which he claimed the "CIO is being fought today because it is supporting President Roosevelt" and not, presumably, because it had destroyed the open shop in America's basic mass production industries. On the no-strike pledge, Murray asked for the "tolerant indulgence" of the delegates to speak on this boiling issue. He was received with some boos.

Murray said he wanted to speak on the issue in "the most moderate way" and then proceeded to an outburst of impassioned oratory and demagogy. He claimed they would hurt Roosevelt's chances for re-election if they ended the no-strike pledge; that the union itself would be "jeopardized." "War, war—war occasioned the No-Strike Pledge."

With Murray's dire warnings and emotional appeal still ringing in the delegates' ears, the UAW leaders tried another grand maneuver. Thomas suddenly announced that the Resolutions Committee would immediately report out a "supplementary resolution"—on the no-strike pledge. This was obviously a move to catch the delegates unprepared. The jeers, groans and boos of the delegates showed they were not napping or hypnotized. They demanded and endorsed a motion to postpone debate on the no-strike issue until the next morning.

Early the next day, the delegates came to grips with this crucial issue. The Resolutions Committee reported out three resolutions on the no-strike pledge. The majority resolution, presented by five members of the committee, called for reaffirmation of the no-strike pledge "for the duration of the war." Reuther's so-called minority resolution proved to be identical in principle to that of the majority, but used more confusing and misleading phrases. It resolved that "this Convention reaffirms its no-strike pledge for the duration of the war." It contained, however, a tricky and meaningless section that "between the period after the defeat of Germany and the end of the war with Japan" the International Executive Board be empowered to "authorize strike actions" in plants "reconverted to the exclusive and sole manufacture of civilian production."

The "super-minority" report—which turned out to have ten times the support of Reuther's "minority" resolution—clearly and unequivocally resolved that "this great convention rescind our no-strike pledge." It further proposed to prove that this position represented the will of the members by submitting the decision to a membership referendum.

Almost a full day's debate ensued. The leadership, which started off its attack by belittling the "super-minority" report and its backers found itself confronting an opposition that at several points appeared to verge on a majority. When Thomas, in the chair, referred to the anti-no-strike resolution as the "super-duper" report, fifty delegates hit the floor calling him to order. Thereafter, as the leadership found itself fighting with its back to the wall, its feeble attempts at derision turned to fearful pleas.

The delegates, true to the democratic traditions of the UAW, would not permit a vote on the resolutions until the discussion was exhausted and every point of view thoroughly explained.

The Stalinists, who had hoped to make capital for themselves by appearing as the loudest patriots, revealed little independent strength. They could appear as a significant factor only when they clung to the coat tails of one of the powerful leadership factions—in this instance, the Addes-Thomas-Frankensteen group. Their known spokesmen were repeatedly jeered and booed by the delegates. When W. G. Grant of Ford Local 600 started to speak about "showing our wholehearted support to the election of President Roosevelt" by reaffirming the pledge, the entire sizeable Briggs Local 212 delegation began waving tiny American flags in demonstration against the flag-waving tactics of the leadership.

Secretary-Treasurer Addes began by pleading with the delegates to "refrain from expressing their enthusiasm until I have concluded." He promised that if the delegates would "go out and do the job on November 7th" by re-electing Roosevelt "we will be able to secure from this Congress all of those things that the workers are entitled to."

Walter Reuther, a highly articulate and almost inexhaustible speaker, kept strangely in the background during most of the debate. He spoke only briefly and then his main emphasis was on maintaining the no-strike pledge, while trying to convey the impression that his resolution left some sort of opening for the defense of the workers on "civilian production." Victor Reuther, a member of the Resolutions Committee, argued that his was a "middle of the road position" satisfying both "the needs of our nation and the needs of our union." "Keep the no-strike pledge. Keep it—keep it on war work," he urged.

The few delegates who spoke from the floor in favor of Reuther's position quickly revealed themselves to be either in favor of the no-strike pledge or against it. They simply tried to read into Reuther's deliberately ambiguous resolution what they wanted to find. Their conflicting arguments confirmed the contention of delegate Paul Silver of Detroit Local 351, who called Reuther's position "more vicious" than the openly reactionary one, because the Addes-Thomas-Frankensteen-Stalinist resolution was "a report of defeatism" while Reuther's was "a report of confusion."

Ben Garrison, the only spokesman on the nine-man Resolutions Committee for the almost 40 per cent of the delegates who opposed the no-strike pledge, pointed out the fraud of "equality of sacrifice" on which the no-strike pledge was supposed to have been based. "Management has taken advantage of the war to break down collective bargaining and render our grievance procedure inactive and void. The gains labor has made have been steadily taken away from us." As for the argument that revoking the pledge would "hurt our boys in uniform," Garrison replied, "I want to make damn certain that a just share of victory means that a union will be here when they do come home."

The delegates demanded roll-call votes on both the majority and super-minority reports. When the roll call on the super-minority report to rescind the no-strike pledge was completed, this resolution had received 36 per cent of the total vote, or a vote of 3,750 to 6,617. Reuther's position was voted down by a simple hand vote. Scarcely a hundred delegates of the more than 2,300 present favored Reuther's straddling resolution.

Finally, a roll call was taken on the majority resolution. To the astonishment and chagrin of the leadership, the unconditional reaffirmation of the no-strike pledge was defeated by 5,232 votes to 4,988. As the matter then stood, the UAW no longer had a no-strike pledge.

At this point the Reutherites pulled what one delegate called the "dirtiest trick" of any UAW convention. The delegates, unable to come to a decisive position, were prepared to put the issue directly into the hands of the membership through a referendum. The Reuther group joined forces with the Addes-Stalinist faction on the Resolutions Committee to bring out a two-part resolution: (1) to reaffirm the no-strike pledge "for the duration of the war"; and (2) to authorize a membership referendum, "to be conducted within 90 days," on concurrence or non-concurrence.

Garrison offered his own minority resolution in four parts: (1) "that the No Strike Pledge remain in effect until a referendum vote" was taken; (2) that the convention authorize a referendum "commencing ninety (90) days after adjournment"; (3) that a nine-man referendum committee be selected to conduct the referendum, with all three views equally represented on the committee; (4) that "none of these officers and International representatives shall use union funds or the International Union newspaper or the International Union magazine or Educational Department nor any other agency of the union in propagandizing this issue."

Garrison did not belong to the new Rank and File Caucus which had mobilized the opposition forces and led them in the floor fight. He was one of those who tried to maneuver between the contending power caucuses and make deals with them where possible.

The delegates were confronted with two resolutions which called for retention of the no-strike pledge at least until a referendum. These seemed to differ only in minor details. Victor Reuther, in the ensuing discussion, gave the impression that if the majority proposal on the no-strike pledge were adopted, they were all in agreement on holding a referendum. Thus a majority of delegates, in a hand vote, voted about three to two for the majority no-strike position.

After the no-strike part of the report was adopted, the committee majority blandly announced they opposed a vote on the question of the referendum. Pandemonium ensued.

Walter Reuther, who had maintained an "eloquent silence" throughout most of the convention, continued it. Victor Reuther stepped forward to try to retrieve the Reutherite position. He spoke in favor of a referendum "within 90 days." Garrison reread the minority resolution which said "commencing 90 days after the adjournment." Thomas, Reuther and Garrison all reinforced the impression that the resolution called for a referendum "within ninety days" when its actual wording was "commencing 90 days after adjournment." The delegates, in a roll-call vote, adopted the referendum resolution by 6,622 votes to 3,354.

The convention's only other significant action was to record a decline in Reuther's popularity as a result of his shifty behavior. He was defeated for re-election as first vice-president by Richard Frankensteen, who was detested for his role in the 1941 North American Aviation Corporation strike. This was a low point in ambitious Reuther's career. He salvaged the second vice-presidency, however, defeating his old caucus ally Richard T. Leonard. The new Rank and File Caucus did not campaign for leadership. It contested only one post, that of the presidency, running a last-minute token candidate against R. J. Thomas. The candidate, Robert Carter of Flint, withdrew in the midst of the roll call when he had taken an eighth of the votes from Thomas but obviously could not win. This was the first time Thomas had been challenged since his election in 1939.

The UAW's no-strike referendum was dragged out for nearly six months after the convention. A protracted wrangle occurred in the Referendum Committee over whether the resolution said "within ninety days" or "commencing ninety days" after adjournment. Murray's speech and other material promoting the no-strike pledge was published in the union paper, thus circumventing the convention decision.

In the middle of March 1945, Ben Garrison made public the "unofficial returns" of the referendum. Out of 1,200,000 ballots distributed, according to Garrison, less than 300,000 had been returned. About 105,000 were for rescinding the no-strike pledge, 185,000 were against rescinding it and 6,000 ballots were voided.

But the question of the UAW referendum had become largely academic. *Business Week* noted that the votes were being counted when there were more workers on strike in Detroit than at any time since the start of the war. The majority of the UAW Executive Board had voted to call on the CIO to demand an end to the old War Labor Board — to be replaced, of course, by some new tripartite arbitration machinery.

A volcanic pressure was developing among the workers in all the CIO industries. Strikes were steadily increasing. If a complete blowup did not come before the official Japanese surrender, it was largely because many workers saw the end of the war was near and had decided they could now afford to wait it out and then force the union officials to call "authorized," united, industry-wide strikes.

When the war came to a close on August 14, 1945, the American workers had chalked up more strikes and strikers during the period from December 7, 1941, to the day of Japanese surrender three years and eight months later, than in any similar period of time in American labor history. During the war period there had been a total of 14,471 strikes and 6,774,000 strikers. These were far more strikes and strikers than during the whole first four years of the CIO —1936 through 1939. These strikes were largely isolated and quelled with little gains, but the belief that the war achieved "national unity" of capital and labor, or negated the class struggle, was proved false. The immediate postwar upsurge of labor resulted in the most powerful strike wave ever known; the class struggle in America rose to a new peak.

22

Labor Political Action

The greatest concern of the labor "statesmen" was how to disguise the anti-labor character of the war and how to conceal the anti-labor function of the government in the war. Above all, the union officials were constantly calculating how to persuade the workers that Roosevelt, the war leader, was in no way responsible for its anti-labor consequences.

During this period there was increasing political ferment among the organized workers, particularly in the CIO. Sentiment for independent labor political action through a third or labor party gained ground. This development in 1943 and 1944, which followed a drastic decline in the Democratic vote in 1942, inspired the CIO leaders to intensified activity and new organizational moves in the political field.

In a statement reflecting the growing concern of the CIO ranks for effective labor political action, the CIO Executive Board on February 4, 1944, observed: "Our national economic problems are problems which go far beyond any question of mere negotiations with employers and the statement of grievances with employers."

The CIO statement pointed out that government agencies determined the questions of wages and prices and that Congress, through tax legislation, was able to slice deeply into the workers' incomes. "All of this," said the Executive Board, "has placed on the shoulders of the CIO and its members an increased responsibility which goes far beyond wage negotiations and grievance adjustments...the real questions relating to their everyday working life are being decided in legislative and political fields."

In part, these views were intended to discourage union action on the economic plane, such as strikes. But this statement also endorsed a progressive principle of labor political action that had been generally opposed by the top union bureaucracy.

The idea that unions should engage in organized political activity and that the union ranks should participate in political action through special union-directed and union-built organizations, had been abhorrent to the majority of union officials attending the 1935 AFL convention that led to the formation of the Committee for Industrial Organization. Up to the fourth year of Roosevelt's first term there had been no official coalition between the labor leaders and the Democratic administration and political machine. Union officials made personal endorsements of political candidates on the basis of "reward your friends and punish your enemies." But union members were not expected or encouraged to engage in political work.

The workers were not indifferent to politics. The very forces that had driven them to industrial unionism in the early Thirties had also stirred them up politically. Their tendency, however, was in the direction of independent class politics through a working-class party. In 1932, when Roosevelt ran for his first term, the Socialist and Communist parties had won a combined total of a million votes for their presidential candidates. At the 1935 AFL convention, discussion of political action revolved around the issue of formation of a labor party. Even Francis J. Gorman, head of the United Textile Workers, speaking in favor of a resolution to set up a labor party, had been moved to say:

"We looked with what now seems to us naive faith to the proponents of a 'New Deal'—believing, I guess, that it meant a New Deal for labor as well as a New Deal for industry. We have been sorely disappointed. We do not impugn the honesty of the President of the United States, because whether or not Franklin Delano Roosevelt is sincere is of little consequence here. He cannot, out of the very nature of our economic and political machinery, do other than what he has done. We know, for instance, that his electoral success depends on the 'Solid South' and the Southland is composed of the most bitter anti-labor, most viciously unmerciful employer groups in the United States. The Administration has done nothing effective about protecting the Southern worker against the cruel persecution of the Southern boss—not because the New Dealers revel in the blood spilled on the economic battle front, but because Franklin Delano Roosevelt must have the Southern employer in order to be re-elected President of the United States. So, what difference does it make if he be the most ardent of the so-called friends of the working man. There is nothing he can do and at the same time stay within the limits of our present order."

In the spring of 1936 AFL Teamsters President Daniel J. Tobin, a leading opponent of the Lewis-led CIO, had been reappointed by Roosevelt's campaign manager James Farley to head the Democratic Party's National Labor Committee. Fearful that this might place the CIO at a disadvantage, John L. Lewis, Sidney Hillman, David Dubinsky, and other leaders of the CIO set up Labor's Non-Partisan League to mobilize the working-class vote for Roosevelt, thereby expecting to win his grateful reciprocity.

George L. Berry, head of the AFL Printing Pressmen's Union, agreed to serve as LNPL chairman; Lewis, as director in charge of organization; Hillman, as treasurer. The phrase "Non-Partisan" emphasized not merely that the new organization claimed no permanent ties with either of the two major parties, but that it was open to membership of all unions of whatever faction. Fifty-nine international unions did, in fact, join the LNPL in 1936, most of them not adherents of the CIO tendency. The LNPL raised the then enormous sum of more than $1,500,000 for Roosevelt's 1936 campaign. Lewis's United Mine Workers alone contributed $500,000.

The New York State section of the LNPL was set up in the form of a separate labor party with its own line on the ballot. Among its founders were not only CIO leaders like Hillman, Dubinsky and Alex Rose, but Joseph P. Ryan, head of the AFL International Longshoremen's Association and president of the New York City Central Trades and Labor Council, and George Meany, president of the New York State Federation of Labor. They knew that in New York hundreds of thousands of workers would refuse to mark the ballot or pull the lever for any capitalist party. The American Labor Party of New York State was organized on July 16, 1936, to get these workers to vote for Roosevelt on an independent party line.

Hillman, in particular, sought to convey the impression that this was the beginning of a new national labor party. On September 15, 1936, he made a speech in New York City in which he maintained that the LNPL was "not supporting the Democratic Party" but was mainly interested in re-electing President Roosevelt as an individual.

"After November 3," he said, "Labor's Non-Partisan League will remain a permanent political organization. In this state it is organizing under a separate emblem as a separate party, known as the American Labor Party. The interest of the country as well as labor demands a realignment of all progressives into one party, and the basis for that kind of realignment ought to be the reorganization of labor on the political field."

Not supporting the Democratic Party; a new permanent political organization; an "American" labor party; a realignment of all progressives into one party. Who could blame many for assuming that Hillman and others were laying the basis for a real labor party and that this would be the last time they would be called on to vote for a "lesser evil" capitalist candidate?

Factions and cliques which were at each other's throats competing for positions of power within the unions — AFL and CIO officials, right-wing socialists and Stalinists — combined within the LNPL, and especially in the American Labor Party, to put over a deliberate political swindle on workers who were seeking genuine independent labor political organization and action.

By 1938 a feud began between the Dubinsky and the Hillman forces within the ALP. Dubinsky was preparing to withdraw his International Ladies Garment Workers Union from the CIO. He attacked Hillman in the public press when the Amalgamated Clothing Workers' president appeared to be encouraging a movement to boom himself for the United States Senate. Hillman withdrew from the race at Roosevelt's request.

In August 1939, following the Stalin-Hitler Pact, the ALP was split into a right and left wing. Dubinsky's faction controlled the State Committee of the ALP. Congressman Vito Marcantonio and Stalinist-inspired union leaders like Curran and Quill dominated the New York County Committee of the ALP.

In the 1940 presidential elections, despite the objections of the Stalinists and the supporters of Lewis, the state ALP supported Roosevelt. He was also endorsed by the New York State CIO, in which the Hillman forces held sway.

After the election Labor's Non-Partisan League went into decline. The Lewis forces continued to control the LNPL apparatus but the main body of the CIO leadership, the Murray-Hillman-Stalinist bloc, was unconditionally committed to the Democrats.

In 1942 the New York State ALP under Dubinsky's command ran its own candidate, Dean Alfange, for governor against Democrat John J. Bennett, a Tammany Hall hack, and Republican Thomas Dewey. A week prior to the elections, at the personal insistence of Roosevelt, Hillman and his union endorsed Bennett. In spite of the defection of the Hillmanites and Stalinists, Alfange won 409,000 votes — ten per cent of the total state vote and almost 20 per cent of the vote in New York City, the highest percentage scored by the ALP in its history.

The total of the national vote cast in the 1942 state and congressional elections was almost 50 per cent below the 1940 figure. This was far greater than the normal mid-term voting decline and resulted in severe losses for the Democrats.

It was obvious to the most militant and thoughtful elements in the labor movement that the Democratic Party, dominated by conservative and ultra-reactionary elements, particularly the anti-union Southern racists, could not advance labor's interests. There was widespread discussion of the need for a labor party and moves were made toward the establishment of labor parties in such key states as Michigan and New Jersey.

At a meeting in Philadelphia on March 14, 1943, sponsored by the Social Democratic *New Leader* magazine, with representatives of more than 40 labor organizations in attendance, Dean Alfange urged the heads of the Pennsylvania AFL and CIO, who were present as speakers, to "launch in this strategic Keystone state a labor party comparable in beneficent influence to the American Labor Party in New York. We must build similar political units in every state..."

James McDevitt, president of the Pennsylvania State Federation of Labor, admitted that many workers in his key industrial state waited for the day of the organization of a labor party but, he added, in his opinion "the day was not yet." This reflection of the political mood at that time is an example of the way in which union officials maneuvered with the question of a labor party. It was not until a decade or more later that the labor officialdom attacked the very concept of a labor party.

So great was the antipathy of the union ranks to the Democratic Party and so openly reactionary did that party's representatives in government appear, that even AFL Teamsters President Daniel J. Tobin made a public attack in the March 1943 issue of the *Teamsters Journal*. Under the title, "Democratic Party Forgets How Hungry It Used To Be," Tobin, who in three presidential election campaigns had headed the Democratic National Labor Committee and was a frequent guest of the White House, asserted that many labor leaders now felt they were "being sold down the river" by the party they had helped put in power. He warned: "If we are going to be crucified, let us be crucified by those who don't claim to our friends."

In Michigan, center of the auto workers who represented about 20 per cent of the entire CIO membership, the workers did not intend to be crucified. On March 14, 1943, the Greater Detroit and Wayne County CIO Industrial Union Council held a political action conference attended by 900 union delegates. They adopted a plan to set up political action committees in every local union, to coordinate these committees by congressional districts and to select delegates to work in conjunction with state and national CIO bodies and in cooperation with non-CIO unions to abolish or prevent anti-labor legislation.

The pressure for independent labor political action was evidenced in New Jersey at the seventh annual convention of the American Labor League, held in Trenton during the latter part of May 1943. The American Labor League had been formed by both CIO and AFL representatives to deal with general problems confronting all labor in New Jersey. The convention of 300 delegates, representing about 40 local unions and 300,000 AFL and CIO members, voted measures to intensify independent labor political action. They refused to go on record, as several Stalinist delegates had proposed, to back Roosevelt for a fourth term in 1944. Samuel Colton, state executive secretary of the League, said:

"By 1944, it may be dangerous to go to labor and say, 'Support President Roosevelt.' The Chrysler strikes and the rubber strikes in Akron are anti-administration strikes. We want an independent labor party so that we can tell the President that he won't have labor's support in 1944 under any and all circumstances."

Labor party sentiment had been strong among the auto workers since the UAW's founding in 1935. At the 1936 UAW convention, a labor party resolution had been adopted and only intervention by John L. Lewis and Sidney Hillman secured an amending motion to support Roosevelt for a second term.

Some indication of this desire for a labor party was given at the June 1943 convention of the Wayne County (Detroit) Labor's Non-Partisan League. The LNPL was no longer fully representative of the CIO unions in that area but it still had a formal status as a political arm of the CIO. The 262 delegates represented some 200,000 members of affiliated CIO unions. Leading CIO officials, including Michigan President August Scholle, participated in the convention. After a heated debate, with Scholle and the other officials speaking against labor party action at that time, the convention adopted, with but ten dissenting votes, a resolution favoring formation of a labor party in Michigan. This resolution said in part:

"Whereas: Labor is sick and tired of depending on so-called 'friends' in public office who are, in fact, in almost all instances, better friends of employers and reactionaries than they are of labor, and...

"Whereas: The Republican and Democratic parties have demonstrated their growing inability and unwillingness to solve the basic social problems of the workers of the nation, and

"Whereas: Labor must have its own political party to successfully cope with problems of unemployment and the social disorder that will exist in America in the postwar period; therefore be it

"Resolved: That this Convention...go on record in favor of the immediate establishment of an independent party of labor and working farmers, and be it further

"Resolved: That this Convention recommend to the Michigan State CIO Convention the formation of a Labor Party... within ninety (90) days after adjournment of the Convention..."

Less than a month later the Michigan State CIO convention, meeting on June 30 in Detroit, witnessed a bitter debate over the labor party question. Here again the top CIO and UAW officials, with the Stalinists giving them vociferous backing from the floor, opposed any suggestion of a labor party. The debate was abruptly cut short and, amid general confusion, a voice vote was called on the labor party resolution. It was declared lost.

Nevertheless, the convention's Political Action Committee felt impelled the next morning to introduce a resolution giving lip service to the idea of a labor party. This resolution stated that "support of Roosevelt can best be served by an independent labor party" and instructed the Michigan CIO officers to initiate a referendum of its affiliated unions on whether or not they "favored setting up an independent labor party." Opposition to this resolution by the top leaders and the Stalinists was just as strong as it was to the original resolution, but it was adopted by a ballot vote of 2,519 to 1,909.

The 17-man committee set up by the convention "to explore and build sentiment for independent political action" and to conduct the referendum did everything possible to discourage the idea. It was reported in the August 20 *Michigan CIO News* that the members of the committee all "concede the desirability of having a third party *eventually,* while differing as to the desirability of launching it immediately." (My emphasis. A. P.) Finally, the convention's order was disobeyed and the referendum was never held.

Less than two weeks after the Michigan CIO convention had revealed the feeling of the ranks, Philip Murray convened the CIO National Executive Board in Washington, D. C., July 7-10, 1943, for the purpose of setting up political action machinery to head off the developing labor party movement in key industrial areas. Only Samuel Wolchok, head of the United Retail, Wholesale and Department Store Employees, suggested consideration of the Michigan position. He was immediately pounced on by the rest of the board members. Murray himself declared that "now is not the time" for a labor party. He launched a direct attack on the Michigan CIO convention and darkly hinted it had been under the control of "outside influences" which he did not name.

At Murray's suggestion, the board established a CIO Political Action Committee to mobilize labor votes for Roosevelt in next year's elections. Sidney Hillman, who had been summarily dropped from his war agency post by Roosevelt, was appointed to head this CIO-PAC.

The PAC was formally established on July 11 at a meeting in Philadelphia of 127 selected union officials. A top committee was formed which included Van Bittner, R. J. Thomas, Sherman Dalrymple and David J. McDonald, Steelworkers secretary-treasurer. Hillman told the PAC founding meeting:

"We are opposed to the organization of a third party at this time because it would divide the forces of the progressives throughout the nation. We are here to mobilize our power for political action now — not to wait until a few months before the election of 1944."

In an August 20 Federated Press interview Hillman noted that "third party movements in Michigan and New Jersey have died out." In this he echoed the August 15 *Daily Worker* which had announced that "the CIO program has headed off a dangerous third party movement..."

*   *   *

During this period of the growth of the labor party movement and the formation of the CIO-PAC, an unprincipled factional brawl raged inside New York's American Labor Party. The Dubinsky-Rose clique in control of the State Committee and the Hillman-Stalinist faction vied for absolute power. Hillman and the Stalinists especially wanted no conflict with the Democratic Party. This meant no support for any independent candidate, such as Dean Alfange in 1942, no matter how obnoxious and anti-labor the Democratic candidates might be.

Both sides in the ALP fracas insisted they were the best, most loyal and unconditional supporters of Roosevelt. They opposed each other in the August 1943 New York City primary elections and the Hillman-Stalinist group won. By the March 1944 state primaries, the warfare had reached a peak. The Hillman-Stalinist bloc won the primaries by a three-to-two margin. Hillman and his supporters secured control of the ALP State Committee and he was elected state chairman. Dubinsky and his cohorts split from the ALP and in June set up their own American Liberal Party, later called just the Liberal Party. The latter is still in existence but is confined organizationally to New York State.

*   *   *

Hillman's contention that "third party movements... have died out" was not strictly accurate. After the 1943 UAW and CIO national conventions, a Committee for the Promotion of a Farmer-Labor Party was initiated. This action was taken at a conference in Detroit on December 12, headed by Emil Mazey and Paul Silvers and attended by 70 local union leaders from AFL and CIO unions totaling 200,000 members.

The call to this political conference evoked a threatening response from UAW Vice-President Frankensteen. He issued a public statement charging that the conference was "in open defiance of the policies of Murray, R. J. Thomas, Hillman, August Scholle, and all other responsible leaders of labor." The fact was that Scholle and the others had deliberately violated the instructions of the Michigan CIO convention to hold a referendum on the labor party question.

It will be recalled that the United Mine Workers had just victoriously ended four national coal strikes against the Little Steel Formula wage freeze; the railroad workers had voted for a nation-wide strike; more than 200,000 steelworkers had walked out the week after Christmas. Labor's ranks were infuriated by enactment of the Smith-Connally Anti-Strike Act, initiated by the Democrats and passed by a Democratic-controlled Congress, and in January 1944 Roosevelt had demanded a labor conscription law so brutal that the Nazis could liken it to their own.

At this point the top CIO leaders, with the exception of Hillman and the Stalinist elements, assumed the attitude that they were not committed to the Democratic ticket in the forthcoming November presidential elections. Philip Murray wrote an article on the "CIO Political Action Committee," published in the February 1944 *American Magazine,* in which he stated:

"We shall, before the national conventions of the two major parties, hold a national meeting or conference of our own. We shall draw up and present to the American people a specific set of principles for the general welfare. Then, after the political conventions, we can decide what action to take regarding the two parties and the individual candidates, whether for state or national office, or for the presidency."

Murray was also careful to make clear that the CIO-PAC "is not a 'Labor Party' or a 'Third Party.' There is no *present* intention to form such a party." (My emphasis. A. P.) CIO National Secretary James B. Carey had previously emphasized this position at the January 31, 1944 National Executive Board meeting, when he condemned the Stalinist-controlled New York City CIO Council for adopting a resolution endorsing a fourth term for Roosevelt. CIO-PAC Chairman Hillman, however, had stated publicly as early as September 14, 1943, in an interview with the *Detroit Free Press,* that the CIO would support Roosevelt if he ran for a fourth term.

In Detroit on March 4 and 5, 1944, some 415 delegates from 85 CIO and AFL unions in Michigan with a total of 225,000 members, participated in a conference called by the Michigan Committee for a Farmer-Labor Party. The conference voted to form a farmer-labor type party under the name of the Michigan Commonwealth Federation. This choice of name was based on the influence of the Canadian Commonwealth Federation, whose national secretary participated in the conference. The CCF was designed as the Canadian counterpart of the British Labor Party, but with less official union backing and more emphasis on trying to win the middle-class voters. It had had great initial successes.

Some of the leaders of the MCF continued to be supporters of Roosevelt, or did not want to oppose his re-election. An influential section of the leadership were members or sympathizers of Norman Thomas's Socialist Party. They were not really interested in building a labor party, but desired rather a new liberal party soliciting support from the middle class. They discouraged and opposed efforts to win the unions as an official base of the new party and pushed instead for an organization based on community clubs. In any event, the March conference sought to avoid conflict with the stand of the CIO leaders and decided against running a presidential candidate.

The UAW National Executive Board attacked the launching of the Michigan party and claimed that the auto workers could engage in political action only through PAC. Reuther, whose caucus was supported by most of the leaders of the new party who believed he would give them at least sub rosa backing, voted for the UAW Board's motion attacking the MCF.

The MCF ran a slate of only six candidates in the November 1944 elections. It refrained from nominating candidates in opposition to any major candidates of the Democratic Party who were backed by UAW leaders. The six received the support of the most class-conscious elements in the Michigan labor movement but failed to win strong backing from the wider ranks of labor. By failing to direct its appeal to the organized workers and to seek broad union backing, the MCF condemned itself to decline and disappearance.

Meanwhile Murray's pretense of "impartiality" and "non-partisanship" toward the parties and candidates was quickly abandoned. At the steelworkers convention in May, Murray, Hillman (a guest speaker), Van Bittner and other CIO leaders pushed through a resolution of support for Roosevelt. They claimed that Roosevelt stood above parties — "vote for him not as a Democrat, nor a Republican, but as the only candidate labor can trust," as one of the union leaders put it. The CIO leaders asked no commitment from Roosevelt to any "specific set of principles for the general welfare" drawn up by the CIO-PAC, contrary to what Murray had promised in his *American Magazine* article.

At the first national conference of the CIO Political Action Committee held in Washington during June, there was no question of waiting until "after the political conventions." The conference endorsed Roosevelt and Vice-President Wallace.

The CIO leaders at this PAC conference conveniently shaped their program to fit Roosevelt's. "The program," commented the *New York Times* in its report of the conference, "contained no serious note of dissent from Administration policies." It repeated Roosevelt's slogans about "the four freedoms, the good neighbor policy, the Atlantic Charter, etc.," and endorsed his "New Bill of Rights" for home. This "New Bill of Rights" had been included in Roosevelt's January message to Congress which had also advocated a labor conscription law, the wage freeze, job freeze and anti-strike measures.

At the Michigan State CIO convention in July 1944, the national and state union officials squeezed through a resolution to endorse the national CIO political policy, thus excluding genuine independent labor political action. Leaders of the Michigan Commonwealth Federation acquiesced in the policy of supporting Roosevelt and offered no counter-resolution. In spite of this, almost 50 per cent of the delegates voted against the official resolution.

There was quite a contingent of CIO leaders at the Democratic National Convention in Chicago during the week of July 16. Roosevelt, acting at the behest of the Southern racists and the Northern city bosses behind the scenes, had already turned thumbs down on the renomination of Wallace. Matthew Josephson, in his *Sidney Hillman: Statesman of American Labor,* has given a revealing account of how Hillman was called into Roosevelt's presence a week before the convention and instructed not to try to block the drive for Truman. Hillman formulated it afterwards for the press: "We were for Wallace always, but not against Truman."

Roosevelt did not want to be accused of cutting down either Wallace or Byrnes who was the choice of the party bosses. He made it appear that Hillman was to have a final choice. Roosevelt is reported to have told this to Democratic National Chairman Robert Hannegan, saying, "Clear it with Sidney." Sidney, however, had been "wised up" in advance not to "veto" Truman.

The CIO contingent went through the motions of continuing the fight for Wallace, even mobilizing a 20-minute pro-Wallace demonstration in the spectators gallery. Hillman had already told Truman (who was backing Byrnes) that he could count on the CIO's backing at the right moment. Wallace was shortly thrown to the wolves and Senator Truman was nominated in his stead for vice-president. Later, according to Josephson's account, it was claimed either that the CIO group had been out-maneuvered by the party bosses or that Hillman had played the dominant role. The fact was that Roosevelt made the decision. Hillman had merely carried the ball.

Roosevelt had offered nothing for the CIO's support. He had made not a single commitment to labor—not only on the issues growing out of the war, such as the Little Steel Formula wage freeze, but on the grave problems that would arise with the war's end, particularly the mass unemployment that was expected to come with the decline of war production.

The problem of war production cutbacks and resultant layoffs of workers had loomed even while the war was on. In early June 1944, for instance, American labor was aroused by a two-day sit-in of 3,500 members of UAW Local 365 who refused to vacate the Brewster Aeronautical Corporation plant in Long Island City, New York, after the navy had canceled contracts and the plant was being closed down. This action dramatized the postwar prospects for labor.

Civilian employment in July 1944 was one million less than in January. The AFL's research department in its July report estimated that as many as four million workers would be unemployed by the year's end. The only measure Roosevelt signed that year to meet the needs of the postwar period was the George Demobilization Bill. This Act had been drafted at the behest of the big war corporations to ensure that the government-built war plants, machinery and equipment would be turned over to them for a song at the end of the war. There were no provisions for labor and especially the unemployed, who faced the prospect of unemployment insurance ranging, according to the state, from $2 to $20 a week. The George Bill had been bitterly opposed by organized labor. Roosevelt professed that he signed it with "considerable reluctance" because it "does not deal adequately with the human side of reconversion." But his own colleagues had authored and pushed the measure through.

Eight years later the pro-Democratic labor leaders were to speak scornfully of Republican President Eisenhower's "Cadillac Cabinet" of millionaires. Roosevelt's cabinet at the time of the 1944 election would have made Eisenhower's look like a bunch of poor relations. Roosevelt's was a "Rolls-Royce Cabinet," including representatives of the most powerful financial interests in America. To name a few: Secretary of War Henry L. Stimson, of the Wall Street law firm of Stimson & Winthrop, legal agents for the Morgan interests;

Undersecretary of War Robert Patterson, of another big Wall Street law firm with top financial connections; Henry S. Morgan, son of J. P. Morgan, in the War Department's top council; Secretary of State Cordell Hull, of Southern railroad interests; Undersecretary of State Edward R. Stettinius, former head of U. S. Steel Corporation; Secretary of the Navy James V. Forrestal, of Dillon, Read and Co., leading investment bankers; Secretary of Commerce Jesse Jones, multi-millionaire Texas banker; Attorney General Francis Biddle, scion of Philadelphia's wealthiest family, the Chestnut Street Biddles. Nelson Rockefeller, of the Standard Oil dynasty, headed the important Committee of Latin American Relations.

Shortly before the elections some leading Republican newspapers, columnists and politicians publicly announced their support of Roosevelt, thus emphasizing the fact that they considered him a reliable defender of capitalist interests. The October 16 *New York Times,* one of the most authoritative mouthpieces of capitalism, announced its switch to Roosevelt in a three-column editorial. Walter Lippmann, political sage of the *New York Herald Tribune,* a beacon of Republican conservatism, declared his choice fell on Roosevelt this time. Finally, Republican Senator Ball of Minnesota, who had made a seconding speech for Thomas Dewey at the Republican National Convention, also proclaimed his preference for Dewey's opponent.

Immediately following its formation, the CIO Political Action Committee was subjected to public attack and harassment. Agents of the Department of Justice swooped down on PAC's national offices to go through its books and records. The House Un-American Activities Committee headed by Democratic Congressman Dies of Texas, twice denounced PAC in witch-hunt fashion. Hillman himself defended PAC on June 13, 1944, before a hearing of the Senate Committee on Privileges and Elections. On August 28 before the House Special Committee on Campaign Expenditures Hillman explained:

"We are not interested in establishing a third party... We are not an appendage of either major political party. Nor, as has sometimes been charged, have we any desire or ambition to 'capture' either party... we seek to influence the thinking, the program, the choice of candidates of both parties..." He added at a later point: "The objectives of this committee [PAC] are the election of Roosevelt and Truman and a progressive Congress."

PAC was attacked as part of the drive against the very right of labor to organize on the political field. Inherent in the mobilization of the workers was a threat to the two-party political monopoly by the ruling capitalist interests. It represented a departure from Samuel Gompers' old traditional AFL policy of keeping the workers politically atomized. PAC sought to mobilize the workers into a political unit capable of intervening as an organized class force in elections. At another stage, it might become a springboard for the launching of an independent labor political party.

In spite of this harassment by Congress and the FBI, PAC played a decisive part in the re-election of Roosevelt. It mobilized scores of thousands of active campaigners for him in key states where the Democratic Party was moribund and incapable of appealing to the workers. It distributed over 83 million pieces of its own campaign literature. C. Thomas described the effect of PAC propaganda in the November 18, 1944 *Militant:*

"...Fear was crowned king in the 1944 presidential election campaign. Fear of unemployment, insecurity and want, drove the workers to the polls to cast their votes AGAINST a return to the catastrophic crisis which followed shortly after the last war...Dewey was equated with Hoover and the economic crisis. Roosevelt was portrayed as the 'savior' who rescued the workers from the 1929 crash...The labor bureaucrats carefully refrained from mentioning the labor record of the past Roosevelt administration. The wage and job freeze, the rising cost of living, the fraud of Roosevelt's 'equality of sacrifice' program, labor conscription, anti-strike laws and anti-labor repressions, the fact that Roosevelt himself had declared the New Deal dead, found no place in the campaign literature of the CIO-PAC..."

PAC's effectiveness in getting out the labor and liberal vote amazed the old party professionals. Even more amazing was the vote secured by the two independent parties in New York State, the American Labor Party and the Liberal Party. These two parties, based on unions, amassed a total of almost 800,000 votes—double the ALP vote in 1940. The ALP won 485,000 votes; the Liberal Party, more than 300,000. Roosevelt's majority was a mere 300,000 votes in the state. This indicated that he might have lost the state had he relied on the Democratic machine alone. This huge independent vote also indicated the sentiment that existed for an independent labor party.

In their post-election statement, the CIO-PAC leaders boasted that labor had won a "great victory" with the election of Roosevelt and a "progressive Congress." Of the 219 congressmen who voted for the Smith-Connally Anti-Strike Act (which the union leaders had denounced as a "fascistic" law and a "nullification of the Bill of Rights"), 191 representatives were re-elected. The PAC leaders boasted of the fact that 17 senators, with their endorsement, were elected. Five of these senators were Southern Bourbon Democrats, anti-labor defenders of "White Supremacy." Two of these PAC-backed "progressive" senators were Republicans who openly championed the interests of the corporations in their campaigns.

A by-product of this "great victory" was the enactment of the first state "right to work" law aimed at making any form of the union shop or closed shop illegal. The pro-Roosevelt states of Arkansas and Florida voted in favor of precedent-making state constitutional amendments prohibiting the requirement of union membership for the retention or securing of jobs. Within 15 years similar laws were to be placed on the statute books of 19 states, most of them under Democratic Party control.

The CIO national convention was held November 20 through 24 — after the elections. It was staged as a "victory" convention. The CIO-PAC was established as a permanent organization. The delegates were told this was necessary to ensure the election of a "progressive" Congress in 1946. As was noted in a previous chapter, the shadow of the WLB's rejection of steel and auto wage demands hung over this CIO convention, although mentioned by no one.

However, both Philip Murray and R. J. Thomas felt constrained, by the pressure of their memberships, to "speak bitterness" a little. Murray made so bold as to say in his keynote address that the Little Steel Formula had "riveted... shackles of bondage" on labor. Thomas blurted out: "We cannot go out much longer and sell the workers on the idea that the President is the greatest man in the world unless the President moves to equalize conditions of all classes of society."

Within the first month of his fourth-term victory, Roosevelt had moved to "equalize conditions" — by reaffirming the wage freeze; rejecting the steel union's demands after an 11-month stall; renewing his demand for a national labor conscription law; calling for a permanent national compulsory military training act to establish a Prussian-type military system in America; and naming Stettinius, a direct representative of the House of Morgan, as Secretary of State, and Nelson Rockefeller, of the Standard Oil family, as Assistant Secretary of State.

On December 19, 1944, Roosevelt blithely told his press conference that a "formal Atlantic Charter" did not exist. Up to then even the newspaper editors believed that the statement of noble war aims — the "Four Freedoms," no territorial aggrandizement, self-determination of peoples, freely-elected governments, etc., — issued by Roosevelt and Churchill on August 14, 1941, and called the "Atlantic Charter," had real status, like an international treaty. Roosevelt himself had likened it to the Magna Charta and the Ten

Commandments. No, said Roosevelt, more than three years and
millions of casualties later, it was just a press release stating certain desirable aims but "like the Ten Commandments, may never
be achieved."

Roosevelt's message to Congress in early January 1945 called
for the enactment of a general labor conscription law "at the earliest possible moment" and the immediate passage of legislation to
draft all men of military age classified 4-F (unfit for military duty)
for conscript labor. He also asked Congress to establish universal
peacetime compulsory military training for American youth.

Why did Roosevelt seek to maintain a system of permanent militarism?

In September 1944 General Electric President Charles E. Wilson
had told the army ordinance association that it was necessary "to
set the machinery in motion" for a peacetime militarization program because "the revulsion against war not too long hence will
be an almost insuperable obstacle to overcome." Citing this sentiment, the January 13, 1945 *Militant* charged: "Roosevelt's demand
for peacetime conscription proves that Big Business is already preparing for a Third World War."

As for his labor conscription demand, the pro-Roosevelt railroad brotherhoods organ, *Labor,* pointed out editorially: "Strangely
enough, the President did not have anything to say about this scheme
to draft labor for private profit when he was facing the voters in the
last campaign. He opened his battle for the presidency at a dinner
arranged by the Teamsters' union. On that occasion he might have
said something like this:

" 'My friends, I assure you that if you will re-elect me for a
fourth term the first thing I will do will be to demand that Congress
pass a law to draft American workers.' We all know he didn't say
anything like that. So far as we recall he never mentioned the labor
draft during the campaign."

Roosevelt's death in office on April 12, 1945, stunned the CIO leaders. But it might well be asked if he did not prove more politically
valuable to them dead than had he stayed alive to bear responsibility
for the development of the cold war, the witch hunt, the anti-labor
laws and government strikebreaking that flourished under his successor, Truman. Had Roosevelt lived to complete his term, the
pro-Democratic labor leaders, the liberals, Social Democrats and
Stalinists might have found it far more difficult to keep alive the
myth of Roosevelt, labor's savior.

Truman was not easy to depict as a savior of the working class.
He had voted for the Smith-Connally anti-strike law and for the tax

bill that Roosevelt had signed but described as "relief for the greedy" because it offered so many loopholes to the big corporations. Truman was known as strictly a "party man," loyal to the party machine and to his cronies of the Pendergast gang in Missouri who had given him his big start in politics. His most notable role had been as chairman of the Senate war investigations committee which had lifted the lid a bit from a few of the more noisome war-profits scandals. But his committee had done little to halt the more than fifty billion dollars in excess war profits that Comptroller General Lindsay Warren said the corporations had looted in the first three years of the war.

Within a few months of his inheritance of the presidency, Truman printed his name indelibly on the pages of history by ordering the dropping of the first two atomic bombs on the Japanese cities of Hiroshima and Nagasaki.

Before the war had come to its radioactive mushroom-cloud climax, the seeds of World War III were already being sown. With the defeat of Nazi Germany, the May 26, 1945 *Militant* said: "A new relation of forces has been established on the international arena and is finding its first expression in growing friction between the Allied imperialists and the Soviet Union. The gushing 'friendliness' which marked the period of the Allied-Soviet alliance against Germany has all but disappeared..."

American labor entered the postwar period with none of its old problems resolved, while the catastrophe of war had left in its wake immense new problems and issues. As the roar of the shells and bombs subsided, the thunder of the class struggle was heard throughout the land.

PART IV

THE POSTWAR STRIKE WAVE

1945-1946

23

American Labor's Greatest Upsurge

"It's Industrial Peace for the Postwar Period!" This was the front-page headline of the *CIO News,* April 2, 1945, just six months before the greatest strike wave in history.

CIO President Philip Murray and AFL President William Green had just signed with Eric Johnston, United States Chamber of Commerce president, a "peace pact for postwar prosperity." This "Peace Charter" proposed to eliminate strikes by the peaceful disposition of "differences between management and labor." Thus did the "labor statesmen" command the advancing wave of labor battles to stand still.

However, none of the problems of the depression decade had been solved by the war. The war itself had created a host of new problems and conflicts, both national and international. Through the steady rise of unauthorized strikes in 1944 and 1945, the American workers had been serving notice that the end of the war would bring a day of reckoning. The CIO and AFL leaders did nothing to prepare and inspire the workers for the gigantic battle ahead. They did all in their power to head it off. To be sure, Murray and Green did not dare go as far as the Stalinists who demanded a permanent no-strike pledge. But they based their whole program on class collaboration and class harmony in the postwar era.

Spokesmen of the National Association of Manufacturers and the Automotive Council for War Production said they didn't know anything about a "peace pact." In the same week the "Peace Charter" was proclaimed, B. E. Hutchison, Chrysler Corporation vice-president and a director of the NAM, announced that the NAM and the Chamber of Commerce were campaigning for a five-point legislative program to outlaw strikes, guarantee government protection to scabs and strikebreakers, and prohibit the closed shop. On April 23 NAM President Ira Mosher said in Boston that the NAM opposed any truce which would "uphold the legislative status quo" on labor. It sought to "modify" the National Labor Relations Act along the lines of the five-point union-busting program.

The workers themselves had little faith in the peaceful intentions of the employers. Although they had raised their output per man-hour by 26 per cent during the war years, their average hourly wage rates had risen only six-tenths of one per cent. From 1943 through 1944, productivity had increased 11 per cent while employment declined 16 per cent. Workers faced the specter of mass unemployment while the war was still on. Between the surrender of Germany on May 2, 1945 and the surrender of Japan on August 14, more than a million workers were swept out of the plants like so much scrap.

Between January 1 and May 30, 1945, 558,570 workers had voted for strikes in NLRB polls, compared to 42,922 in the same period of 1944. In early May forty presidents of UAW-CIO locals in Detroit held a conference and agreed to begin a campaign for the 40-hour week at 48 hours' pay to compensate for a cutback in hours with resultant loss in take-home pay.

If the union leaders had expected the Democratic administration in Washington to play the dove of industrial peace, Truman quickly disenchanted them by ordering four strikebreaking plant-and-industry seizures within a month of his taking office. When the CIO and AFL simultaneously called upon him to revise the Little Steel Formula upward, a June 7 Washington dispatch in the *New York Times* said Truman "declared emphatically today that the 'Little Steel' formula still stood and the inference drawn by the press conference was that for the present no change in the wage stabilization yardstick was contemplated." Truman also said he would not veto a measure, passed by the House, voting each representative a $2,500 "annual expense account," tax-free.

On June 14, 1945, a conference took place in Detroit that was to set the program and direction of the CIO in the crucial months following the end of the war. More than 400 local officers representing over 400,000 members of the UAW-CIO in Regions 1 and 1A, Detroit, adopted a resolution calling on the UAW International Executive Board to initiate a strike vote in all UAW plants "under the terms of the Smith-Connally Act." The conference also resolved "that we go on record in favor of the 30-hour week at no reduction in take-home pay"; that the Executive Board "take the first practical steps in this direction" by immediately initiating negotiations for "the 40-hour week at 48 hours' pay, that is, with a 30% hourly rate pay increase."

The conference referred to the success of the United Mine Workers during April and May in wresting new wage gains of $1.37-1/2 a day from the operators for both the soft coal and hard coal miners. The operators had agreed to full portal-to-portal pay instead of the two-thirds won in the previous contract, and a reduction of the work week to 35 hours with overtime rates to start at 35 hours instead of 40. (Truman had seized the hard coal mines for four weeks but the miners had defied the seizure.)

The Detroit UAW conference revolved around a struggle over a "majority" and "minority" resolution, identical but for one clause—the "majority," backed by the union heads, omitted any reference to strike action. The Resolutions Committee had been hand-picked by the conference chairman, Richard T. Leonard, who ruled the "minority" resolution, submitted from the floor, "out of order." He was overruled by a vote of the delegates and the "minority" resolution calling for a strike vote was finally adopted with only ten dissenting votes.

This Detroit UAW conference recorded an especially significant political incident. It gave a standing ovation to UAW First Vice-President Richard T. Frankensteen who had announced he was running for mayor of Detroit in the "nonpartisan" primaries in August against Republican Mayor Edward J. Jeffries Jr. and six other candidates, including the choice of the Democratic machine. Frankensteen's campaign, officially backed by PAC and the UAW, was considered by most of the labor militants as a highly progressive development in the direction of independent labor political action. CIO officialdom frowned upon unionists running for office and insisted on backing the professional capitalist politicians, especially the Democratic ones.

In the August 7 primaries, Frankensteen led the entire list, out-distancing his nearest rival, Mayor Jeffries, by 14,182 votes. Part of the impetus for Frankensteen's success was the great victory of the British Labor Party which had been voted into power over Churchill and the Tories in July. But the major propulsion for the Frankensteen campaign was the sweeping tide of American labor revolt and growing revulsion with the policies of the Democratic administration.

Industrial and business interests viewed the Frankensteen campaign with the greatest concern. Although Frankensteen himself claimed he was not a "labor" candidate but a candidate of "all the people," mouthpieces of the employers like the Detroit Citizens League, thundered: "The issue is whether the City government should be turned over to the organized unions."

*　　*　　*

"The threat of sudden peace is almost as terrifying as the sudden coming of war," the May 18, 1945 *Toledo Union Journal,* a CIO paper, had written, "for many realize that at no time has peace provided an adequate number of jobs for the workers." In a matter of four weeks two million more workers were dumped out of jobs. Their prospects were unemployment compensation as low as $2 a week for 13 weeks to a maximum of $20 for 20 weeks.

Within a week of V-J Day, mass demonstrations of jobless CIO members under official CIO leadership began to surge through the streets of major industrial centers. On August 21 some 7,000 CIO workers demonstrated through Chicago's Loop. Among other banners were "Negro and White Unite for Jobs" and "It Happened in England, It Can Happen Here!" Richard T. Frankensteen, fresh from his triumph in the Detroit primaries, was the chief speaker. He urged the workers to wire Truman demanding that $30 billion of unexpended war appropriations be used for severance pay for the jobless. This and his threat of a "march on Washington" won clamorous approval.

New York City's Madison Square saw a rally of 50,000 on August 29; about 25,000 shipyard workers marched on August 28 in Camden, New Jersey; some 30,000 paraded in San Francisco on September 3. In Detroit on September 4 more than 20,000 marched two miles down Woodward Avenue to Cadillac Square where scores of thousands joined them for a demonstration against the layoff of more than 300,000 from the war plants. Among the banners conspicuously displayed were: "Is War the Only Answer to Unemployment?"; "We Did It in '37—We Can Do It in '45;" and "Elect Labor's Candidates."

Adapting himself to these sentiments, UAW President Thomas told the Detroit demonstrators: "If we are turned down on the question of unemployment, it will become increasingly clear that the two old parties used their programs only for window dressing... Politicians in this country may find themselves in the same situation as Churchill in England... I cannot see why the mayor of Detroit should not be a member of our union."

CIO President Philip Murray on August 22 had fearfully warned the Senate committee hearing on a "full employment" bill that "if private enterprise fails to give workers jobs at good wages, turning out things we all need, the people will recognize the failure of private capitalism and vigorously call for government operation..."

Four days later at a mass rally of steelworkers at Westfield, Pa., Murray declared: "If business fails to keep in operation war plants, built at government expense, then it is the responsibility of the Government to keep them in operation... If private enterprise is unwilling to operate these plants or lease or purchase these plants, then it is the responsibility of the American Government to see to it that these plants are operated."

This was not the only problem on Murray's mind. Pressure for strike action in the CIO unions, with the 30 per cent wage increase demand sweeping every industry, was reaching the explosion point. At the news of Japan's surrender Murray rushed to assert that "no rash of strikes" would be permitted and "that no change will be made in the CIO's no-strike policy until the entire matter has been explored and... submitted to the executive board." Murray's counterpart in the AFL, William Green, pledged that "V-J Day will not mean an automatic ending of restraint on strikes."

Four days after V-J Day Truman hastened to make plain the administration's labor policy. His executive order reaffirmed the authority of the War Labor Board. He directed "officials charged with the settlement of labor disputes" to treat those disputes which "interfere with effective transition to a peacetime economy" as "disputes which interrupt work contributing to the effective prosecution of the war." The war curbs on labor were supposed to continue, although the war was over.

However, Truman appeared to loosen up the wage policy by authorizing the War Labor Board "to release voluntary wage increases from the necessity of approval"— but only "upon condition that they will not be used in whole or in part as the basis for seeking an increase in the price ceilings." This left little possibility for workers to get raises that the WLB would approve. For the future, Truman proposed to hold a labor-management-government "peace" conference.

If Truman considered the war still on so far as labor restrictions were concerned, he displayed a considerably different attitude toward the employers. On August 25 Truman returned the plants, mines and other facilities of 24 companies that had been seized during the war. These seizures had been designed to halt strikes, most of them called in protest at the refusal of employers to accept WLB decisions. Among the properties restored were those of Montgomery Ward, which never had complied with WLB rulings.

The national CIO leaders met in Washington on August 16 in a special meeting where they "unanimously" adopted resolutions stating that the "National War Labor Board must be temporarily continued" and that "it is the unshakable policy of the CIO and its affiliated organizations to adhere to their contractual obligations in letter and in spirit."

This "unshakable policy," however, immediately ran into an irresistible force—the determination of the workers. This pressure was felt most strongly in the CIO auto union. A week after V-J Day the UAW International Executive Board sent telegrams to the union's more than 1,000 locals advising them that "our no-strike pledge came to an end at the moment President Truman announced the surrender of Japan..."

Early in September, under continuous prodding from the ranks, the Executive Board announced plans for strike votes at General Motors, Chrysler and Ford. It declared that the UAW would demand a general industry-wide wage increase of 30 per cent. As the board made its announcement, some 90 auto and auto-parts plants were on strike in the Detroit area alone.

On September 14, in response to a report that the UAW leaders planned to strike the Big Three companies one at a time, Ford Motor Company locked out 50,000 workers, claiming that a strike of the Kelsey-Hayes Wheel workers had created a parts shortage. The Ford lockout was in reality intended to serve notice that the Big Three would not be divided by any one-at-a-time strategy.

The national General Motors delegated conference on September 14 and 15 spiritedly endorsed a resolution for a corporation-wide strike "to take place within two months" for a 30 per cent increase. In addition, the delegates, representing 225,000 GM auto workers, urged all unions to join in "one gigantic Congress of American Labor in Washington, D. C., at the shortest possible time" to take unified action in defense of the working people. This resolution expressly stated that "we cannot expect any relief from the forthcoming labor-government-management conference called by President Truman..."

In the next few months unions representing more than five million members launched the greatest wage offensive in U. S. labor history. The first shot was fired by the CIO Oil Workers Industrial Union on September 17 when 43,000 members in 20 states were called out on strike by their International President, O. A. Knight. Their slogan was "52-40 or Fight"—a 40-hour week at 52 hours' pay or a 30 per cent increase in wages.

Some 200,000 coal miners left the pits on September 21 to back the rights of supervisory employees to collective bargaining through the independent United Mine Workers. In the Northwest, 44,000 AFL lumber workers struck on September 24. A strike of the east coast members of the AFL International Longshoremen's Association tied up the New York and other key waterfronts for 19 days and marked a rank and file revolt against the sellout policies of Joseph Ryan, then holding a "lifetime" ILA presidency. The CIO Glass Workers struck the flat glass industry and held the line for 102 days. About 40,000 AFL and CIO machinists of the San Francisco-Oakland

Bay area, in a notable display of labor solidarity, joined forces on October 29 in a strike that was to last 140 days. CIO textile workers in New England on November 1 launched a 133-day struggle. On November 12 the strike ranks were joined by 70,000 AFL truck drivers in the Midwest who were not to touch hand to wheel for 81 days.

All these, however, were the preliminary skirmishes. The decisive battles were yet to come — in the two key industrial citadels of American capitalism, auto and steel.

Following the GM Conference, the local unions in GM, Ford and Chrysler began to take their own strike votes. The UAW leaders held back, spreading the illusion voiced by President R. J. Thomas that the 30 per cent demand could be settled "without a work stoppage." He appealed to the auto industry's Big Three to make a "good faith offer" similar to Studebaker's offer of a mere 12 per cent. The UAW officials insisted on going through every delaying action of the Smith-Connally Anti-Strike Law.

Only after key GM locals in Flint took their own strike votes and proceeded to file their own strike petitions under the law, did Reuther finally file the petition on September 22 for a corporation-wide strike. The strike was delayed, however, for another two months. On October 24, voting under the terms of the wartime Smith-Connally Act, the GM workers were polled on the question: "Do you wish to permit an interruption of war production in wartime as a result of this dispute?" The "war production" of 350,000 Detroit workers already had been "interrupted" by layoffs right after V-J Day.

Meanwhile, the CIO Oil Workers, who were spearheading the wage fight, were being pounded by the Truman administration to return to work and put their demands to government arbitration. The union officers threatened to call out 225,000 more workers in addition to those on strike, but never followed through. Truman did not wait. He ordered the navy to seize the struck refineries, demanding that the oil workers halt their strike "against the government" and submit their demands to his Fact-Finding Board. The OWIU-CIO officials ended the strike. Truman's seizure order provided that the companies bargain on the difference between the 15 per cent raise they had said they were willing to grant during the strike and the 30 per cent sought by the union.

On October 30 in a radio speech Truman told labor: "We must understand that we cannot hope with a reduced work week, to maintain now the same take-home pay for labor generally that it has had during the war. There will have to be a drop." He made no reference to the report submitted to him earlier by the Reconversion

Advisory Board. This Truman-appointed board revealed that the corporations were in a position to raise wages 24 per cent without boosting prices, and still get more than double their 1936-39 profits after taxes.

But his Secretary of Commerce, Henry Wallace, wartime darling of the union leaders, issued a report that same week stating that the corporations generally could pay only a ten per cent wage increase; the auto industry, 15 per cent.

The strategy of the government acting as a front for the corporations was, first break the strikes; then whittle down the wage settlements by pressure on labor. Truman promised: "Industry will not be asked to take an unreasonable chance in absorbing such wage increases."

The attitude of the corporations was exemplified by General Motors. GM President Charles E. Wilson, four days before the scheduled General Motors and Chrysler strike votes, made an arrogant and provocative offer to the UAW to increase the work week from 40 to 48 hours at straight-time pay, coupled with a rise in wage rates of from five to eight per cent. Wilson also claimed that General Motors, which had piled up unprecedented war profits, could not "afford" higher wages. He refused to permit the NLRB strike poll on GM property.

Both the GM and Chrysler workers voted by huge majorities that they did "wish to permit an interruption of war production in wartime as a result of this dispute." At the same time the CIO United Steelworkers announced that it was filing for an industry-wide strike vote. A week later the Ford workers balloted 11 to 1 for strike. Some 200,000 meatpacking workers and 275,000 CIO workers in Westinghouse Electric, General Electric and other UE-organized companies prepared for strike polls as even the Stalinist-controlled unions were swept along in the militant tide.

During this period the Detroit election campaign was reaching a sizzling heat. The auto companies and other business interests had mounted a campaign of unbridled ferocity and mendacity to defeat Frankensteen in his bid for mayor.

A chain of 16 neighborhood newspapers carried every type of anti-Frankensteen smear the Detroit bosses could think of. One paper circulated in white neighborhoods ran the scarehead, "White Neighborhoods Again in Peril." At the same time the Negro community was flooded with leaflets screaming "So Why Should Colored Folks Vote for Frankensteen? Frankensteen Has Not Proved Himself a True Friend of Negro Race." In Jewish neighborhoods, Frankensteen was described as an "anti-Semite." In other neighborhoods, the word was spread that he was a Jew. He was linked in Polish neighborhoods with the "Communist Gang Who Praise the Russian Conquest of Poland." Elsewhere they shrilled: "New Violent Group in Frankensteen's Camp. Trotskyites on Rampage Here. Want Power... The Socialist Workers Party known as Trotskyites is openly campaigning for Frankensteen..."

Even while the backers of Mayor Jeffries were crying that the "CIO is going to take over City Hall," they spread confusion in the workers' ranks with a leaflet distributed at factory gates: "Is Frankensteen Ashamed to be a Labor Candidate?" This was the real weak spot of his campaign. The AFL and independent unions were not drawn into the campaign. Frankensteen tried to put on a front of "respectability" rather than offer a program that would arouse and inspire the workers. The lack of a genuine labor party to organize and unify the workers politically proved costly. Frankensteen received the impressive total of 216,917 votes. Jeffries, however, received the unprecedented vote of 274,455 to win.

Another expression of the developing class struggle was the slogan raised by the General Motors workers in answer to the corporation's claim of "inability" to pay higher wages: "Open the Books and Records of the Corporation!"

This demand threw the GM officials and the capitalist press into a frenzy. For corporations to open their books to outside inspection, to reveal their "business secrets," to expose their real profits, their possible tax frauds and shady dealings — this would be nothing less than "abdicating the responsibility of management." GM Vice-President Harry W. Anderson told the UAW negotiators that under no circumstances would the corporation reveal its profits records. He exclaimed: "We don't even open our books to our stockholders."

The slogan, "Open the Books of the Corporations," originated in the program of the Socialist Workers Party. Its supporters had projected this concept in the unions, particularly in the UAW. This program had a profoundly revolutionary side, as the corporations well understood, and it put them on the spot as no other demand could do. In huge newspaper advertisements GM sought to counter this slogan with their own: "A 'Peek at the Books' — Or a Finger in the Pie?" This was a first step, the corporations claimed, to union control of the company.

Reuther used the slogan as effective propaganda to show the public that GM was trying to conceal its profits. But he never pressed the point as a serious demand to force GM and the other big corporations to reveal their real inside workings and methods.

Truman's Labor-Management conference the week of November 5

left the CIO leaders with no reasonable pretext for further delay of strike action. The employer spokesmen at Truman's conference indicated from the first that they had no other thought than to exact commitments from labor for the setting up of new government machinery to take over the function of the discredited War Labor Board, and to establish "procedures" to prevent strikes. To this, UAW President R. J. Thomas, fresh from the fury of the struggle in the auto towns, bitterly replied:

"If all this procedure is adopted I can't see how it will put one more slice of bread in many workers' mouths...I can't see how procedure will furnish clothes. I can't see how procedure will do away with unemployment. Procedure will not as a rule foment strikes, and procedure will not stop strikes."

The breakup of Truman's "peace" conference and the contemptuous attitude of the auto companies, in particular GM, would not permit the UAW leaders to withhold a strike call. At the same time they did nothing to inspire the members and prepare them for a long, hard battle. In the last week before the GM shutdown local union leaders, largely on their own initiative and backed by their ranks, started practical preparations for a prolonged strike. Strike funds were assessed locally; food stocks were piled up in union commissaries.

A City-Wide Strike Committee was set up by all GM locals in Detroit. A speakers bureau and publicity committee were set to work to unify the strike, boost morale, explain the issues, win support and counter the company propaganda. Support by AFL construction workers, thousands of whom were working on GM plant constructions, was assured in advance.

As 200 GM union delegates were assembling in Detroit for a national conference three days before the strike, the Ford Motor Company demonstratively lined itself up with General Motors. "We do not believe," said the Ford statement, "that this is the time to settle on general wage increases." Instead, the Ford company made 31 demands of its own for what it called "company security." The demands included the company's unrestricted right to hire and fire, promote and demote, fix production schedules and standards and, above all, discipline strikers and others charged with violating company rules.

On November 19 the GM delegates sent a final proposal to the company for arbitration procedure by a three-man panel—one from the union, one from the company, and a third to be jointly agreed upon—provided the arbitrators had full access to the company books. The next day, one hour before the deadline set by the conference, the company sent a curt reply demanding a three-day extension of the deadline. The conference refused.

On November 21, 1945, the greatest and one of the toughest strikes in labor history began. Some 225,000 General Motors workers poured out of 92 plants in 50 cities. For the first time the largest industrial corporation in America was shut down completely. During the previous two months there had never been less than 400,000 workers on strike; now the total rose to more than 600,000 — with 2,000,000 others on strike notice.

In Flint, Detroit, Cleveland, Toledo — in all the far-flung empire of General Motors — the workers set up their singing, shouting, mass picket lines. The union locals' "Flying Squadrons" in their uniform caps and blouses were on the alert to preserve order and protect the pickets from molestation. The coffee urns were steaming, the hot soups were being ladled into bowls, the fresh sandwiches were piled high. An army marches on its belly, said Napoleon — and so does a picket line, especially in a Michigan winter.

Throughout the initial weeks of the strike, General Motors and its local police and court agents were to poke and prod and pry, looking for local weak spots. Here and there they tried injunctions to limit picketing or made a show of running supervisory and office help through the picket lines with a show of police force. But they couldn't find a crack anywhere.

The very day the GM strike began Truman found the pretext to bare his teeth against labor. He issued a fiery blast at local municipal transportation strikers in Washington, D. C. He called this little local District of Columbia strike a "blow at the sanctity of labor agreements. It strikes at the very roots of orderly government."

Truman made his position more explicit on December 3. He called directly on the General Motors workers to return to work in the "public interest." He ordered them to submit their demands to a fact-finding board to be appointed by him. The House Committee on Labor promptly went to work on a bill, the "Labor Fact-Findings Board Act." This provided for compulsory fact-finding procedure in any plant or industry, during which it "shall be unlawful for any person to coerce, instigate, induce, conspire with, or encourage any person to interfere with or prevent such work or operations by lockout, strike or otherwise."

CIO President Philip Murray, himself confronted with the adamant stand of the steel companies, had no alternative but to answer Truman's threat of anti-labor legislation. Murray spoke the next night over a nation-wide radio hookup. He compared the fantastic corporate profits to wage cuts of 23 to 50 per cent suffered by workers since V-J Day. He cited government reports disclosing that the big corporations could raise wages 24 per cent and still make double their pre-war net profits. He complained that Congress had done nothing for the workers while passing tax laws favoring the rich and large corporations. Finally he assailed Truman, but not directly. "To all this arrogance," said Murray, "the Federal Administration yields in abject cowardice. Its rancor is confined to labor." The purpose of the Truman-inspired bill could be only "to weaken and ultimately to destroy labor union organizations. It can be but the first step for even more savage legislative repression."

Murray's first open challenge to the Democratic administration in 13 years was not altogether motivated by high principle. Reuther's conduct of the GM negotiations, and his adoption of such far-reaching slogans as "Open the Books of the Corporation" and "Wage Increases without Price Increases" had helped to focus the national spotlight on the GM struggle and on Reuther as its leader. The GM workers were setting the pace and Murray and the other top CIO leaders were being forced to follow.

Reuther's own factional opponents in the UAW were in the position of holding back the struggle. Thomas, Addes, Frankensteen and the Stalinists did not wish to be forced into any showdown battles with Ford, Chrysler and the other big corporations. They were for a policy of "flexibility" — that is, readiness to accept inferior and unsatisfactory terms rather than lead militant mass actions that might win concessions closer to the workers' demands and needs. Reuther, on the other hand, realized that his future as a UAW and CIO leader was at stake. He had lost much influence and status among the auto workers in the 1944 "no-strike" convention. He could regain his prestige—and more—through his leadership of the key GM strike.

After Murray's radio speech, the CIO leader summoned a conference in Pittsburgh of the UAW leaders, the heads of the Stalinist-controlled United Electrical, Radio and Machine Workers, and Murray's own chief lieutenants. This conference had been called at the insistence of the UE leaders. Pressure was put on Reuther to take the negotiations out of the hands of the elected nine-man top negotiating committee set up by the GM delegates and to shift the negotiations out of Detroit. In this way, Murray and the UE leaders hoped to cook up some sort of "reasonable compromise" formula for General Motors, thus setting a pattern for settlements in steel, electrical equipment and other major industries without strikes.

Reuther, however, insisted that the GM negotiations were in the hands of the elected GM committee. He had never before hesitated to negotiate with GM behind locked doors with only a few of his trusted paid departmental organizers present. This time, harassed by factional opponents, he was forced to fall back upon the power of the ranks.

A national delegates conference of the striking GM workers on December 8, 1945 in Detroit defiantly rejected Truman's back-to-work demand and the corporation's counter offer of 13-1/2 cents. This body adopted the proposal of the Flint City-Wide Strike Committee to appeal to the National CIO to convoke a national labor conference in Washington, D. C., to launch a united fight against threatened anti-labor laws and build a united labor front against government strikebreaking.

The GM conference resolution directly charged that "President Truman and his administration have lined up with General Motors and the other major corporate interests to break the General Motors strike" and that "President Truman's ultimatum to the auto and steel workers and his advocacy of anti-labor legislation, coupled with the furious campaign in Congress . . . have confronted the CIO with a deadly threat to its existence, and immediately menaces the General Motors strike. . ."

*   *   *

A unique action of the GM conference was the adoption of a resolution urging the CIO United Electrical, Radio and Machine Workers Union to call out 30,000 UE members working in the electrical appliances division of General Motors. Such UE action was essential to apply maximum pressure on the corporation. Normally, such a public appeal should not have been required. Elementary labor solidarity should have brought a UE stoppage in General Motors the instant the auto workers struck. But the UE leadership was Stalinist-dominated and still following its wartime policies. The Communist Party was in much disrepute with workers because of its wartime strikebreaking policy, its advocacy of the incentive pay plan, and its campaign for a permanent no-strike pledge. It felt impelled to make a shift in line. This shift was made possible following an attack on the American CP policy by Jacques Duclos, French Communist Party leader, on May 24, 1945.

The growing rift between the Stalin regime and its capitalist allies of the West impelled the Kremlin to dictate a pseudo class-struggle policy to its satellite political agencies as pressure for extension of the wartime American-Anglo-Soviet alliance into the postwar era. Earl Browder, CP national secretary since 1929, was made the scapegoat for its wartime betrayals and driven from the party. However, their shift in line was largely verbal.

Not only did the Stalinist union leaders hang back and drag their feet during the titanic postwar labor struggle; in some instances they continued to play the role of strikebreakers. Their withholding of aid in the GM strike received considerable publicity. But less has been told of their actions during the strike of some 60,000 AFL Lumber and Sawmill Workers in California, Oregon, Washington, Idaho and Montana from September 24 to November 25, 1945.

The Stalinist-influenced leadership of the CIO International Woodworkers of America, whose members had voted for strike action in support of the same demands as those of the AFL union, refused to call out the IWA members. When LSW-AFL strikers picketed IWA-CIO operations, the leaders of the IWA teamed up with employers to obtain anti-picketing injunctions. At the U. S. Plywood plant in Seattle the IWA members had actually welcomed the LSW pickets and had immediately shut down the plant. Subsequently, the IWA leadership, failing to win an injunction against picketing, rounded up forces to crash the LSW picket line. The secretary of the Stalinist-controlled Seattle CIO Council helped lead the picket-line smashers. An LSW picket sadly noted: "Here goes 90 cents an hour going through a $1.10 an hour picket line."

*   *   *

The leadership of the steel, electrical equipment, packinghouse and other CIO unions protracted their negotiations and did not schedule strike action until well into January 1946, at least two months after the GM strike began. Although the steelworkers had voted by a tremendous majority on November 28, 1945 for strike, the United Steelworkers leaders met on December 11 and fixed a strike date for January 14. The UE leaders, backed by a similar pro-strike vote of the ranks, fixed January 15, 1946 as the date for strikes in the major concerns under UE jurisdiction.

There was no coordinated CIO planning, strategy or action. Instead, rumors were spread by both the Stalinists and those close to Murray's office that Reuther "had jumped the gun," etc. In this fashion the failure to take prompt action to back the GM strikers was covered up with a whispering campaign.

Inside the UAW itself, the Ford and Chrysler workers were held back by the one-at-a-time strategy from shutting down the whole industry at one blow, putting the maximum squeeze on the auto barons. The UAW leaders in the Ford and Chrysler negotiations were undercutting the GM workers' bargaining power by accepting various Ford proposals for "company security," fines for strikers and increased "disciplinary" powers for the company. In addition, Thomas and Reuther agreed to cooperate with the fact-finding board appointed by Truman to "investigate" the General Motors strike. This was in violation of the explicit decision of the GM delegated conference.

As for General Motors, it went along with the fact-finding procedure only as long as Truman's board did not solicit any of the pertinent facts on its profits. On December 28, 1945, GM's representatives walked out of the fact-finding commission's hearings. They categorically refused to make their books and records subject to examination even by friendly government officials.

The very next day UAW President R. J. Thomas charged: "There is definite collusion between General Motors and Chrysler. Ford is sitting on the sidelines waiting to see what happens in the GM case. All of them...are in sympathy with each other. All the others are waiting on GM."

Thus, the GM workers found themselves for a period holding the fort alone in what was to be a terrible, drawn-out battle of attrition. But the strikers were buoyed by the prospect of being joined eventually by the steel, electrical, packinghouse and other CIO workers. Added to this were expressions of solidarity in money, food and picket-line support the GM workers received from local unions of every affiliation and from many international bodies.

A tremendous feeling of labor unity pervaded the organized workers during this period that tended to break down in action the divisions set up by bureaucratic, factional, and craft interests. There were several city-wide general strikes and joint mass demonstrations in defense of strikers. On January 3, 1946, in Stamford, Conn., some 30 local unions of the CIO and AFL combined in a 24-hour general strike to aid 3,000 striking AFL Machinists in the Yale & Towne Manufacturing Company against the brutality of city and state police. The Lancaster, Pa. workers engaged in a two-day city-wide strike and demonstration in February to halt police attacks on AFL transit strikers and win a contract for them. An estimated 20,000 AFL and CIO workers struck and demonstrated in Houston, Texas on February 26 to force City Hall to deal with 700 striking members of the AFL City-County Employees Union.

All the schemes of the employers to divide the workers and smash their strikes failed. During the postwar strike wave in 1919, the employers had brought thousands of unwary Negro workers from the South to use as scab labor. The end of World War II, however, found 1,600,000 Negro workers in unions, primarily in steel, coal,

automobiles and meat packing. A third of the delegates to the CIO
United Packinghouse Workers convention were Negroes, and hundreds of thousands of Negro militants bolstered the picket lines.

The use of women, particularly the wives of strikers, to start
back-to-work movements and break the morale of the strikers proved
a fiasco after World War II. Millions of women had been brought
into industry during the war. A high percentage of them were married
women forced to work to make ends meet. In the first eight months
after V-J Day, according to the report of the Women's Bureau of the
U. S. Department of Labor, some four million women were dropped
from the labor force. They had no love for the employers. Not only
did women strikers and strikers' wives help man the picket lines
and run the soup kitchens in all the major strikes, but in a series
of strikes the miserably exploited telephone operators were to force
the powerful American Telephone and Telegraph Company trust to
deal with their unions.

Two misguided wives in Flint called a meeting of over 300 women
to start a back-to-work movement in GM. But after a discussion of
the issues, the meeting sent a telegram to Truman demanding he
make GM bargain in good faith with the union. Part of the meeting
collection was turned over to the strike fund and the two who had
called the meeting volunteered for strike kitchen duty.

Above all, the employers had hoped to use returning war veterans
as strikebreakers. The veterans, however, proved to be staunchly
pro-union. There was scarcely a city or town that did not witness
veterans in uniform in the vanguard of picket lines. Numerous parades and marches of union war veterans descended on city halls
and even state capitals—Indiana, Pennsylvania, New York, Illinois—
to back demands of strikers to halt police intimidation or to secure
unemployment compensation.

*   *   *

At the close of the war the American soldiers in Europe and Asia
engaged in the most remarkable series of struggles for their rights
that has ever been waged in a victorious imperialist army. This
was the "Bring Us Home" demonstrations that swept the armed forces
overseas at the end of 1945 and the beginning of 1946. These demonstrations coincided with the peak of the strike wave at home and the
GIs' methods clearly reflected those employed in labor struggles.

Right after V-J Day Congress was bombarded with petitions and
letters from combat troops who had been in Europe protesting their
transfer to the Pacific area for occupation duty. The White House

itself on August 21 announced the receipt of a protest telegram signed by 580 members of the Ninety-fifth Division, a combat-hardened group then stationed in Camp Shelby, Mississippi.

Troop trains carrying members of the Ninety-seventh Infantry Division were reported from St. Paul to have displayed signs saying, "Shanghaied for the Pacific" and "We're Being Sold Down the River While Congress Vacations."

Parents and wives held mass meetings demanding that the GIs be sent home. When General Harry Lewis Twaddle, commander of the Ninety-fifth Division, assembled his troops to explain about occupation duty in Japan, reported Washington columnist Drew Pearson on September 15, 1945, "the boos from the soldiers were so prolonged and frequent, it took him 40 minutes to deliver a 15-minute speech."

Protests extended even to the elite troops, the marines. A December 22, 1945 dispatch from China to the *New York Times,* printed after a week's censorship delay, revealed that U. S. marines guarding a railroad were bitter about their assignment and this bitterness "extends to complaints that high point men are not being sent home fast enough and to protests that they did not enlist to guard British property." This same *Times* dispatch reports on an article in the Shanghai edition of *Stars and Stripes.* The paper's correspondent, Dick Wilson, said that morale of marines in North China was "lousy" and "more and more of the Leathernecks are cracking up daily... [These men] who have had too much fighting want desperately to go home and nothing else matters."

This resentment was felt even more deeply as U. S. ships were used to carry French forces to re-invade Indo-China and Dutch troops to Indonesia, to re-enslave colonial peoples just released from Japanese imperialist rule.

On Christmas Day, 1945, 4,000 U. S. troops in Manila marched on the Twenty-first Replacement Depot Headquarters carrying banners demanding: "We want ships." The depot commander, Col. J. C. Campbell, ordered the men back to their barracks, saying: "You men forget you're not working for General Motors. You're still in the Army."

As thousands of American troops demonstrated twice more in Manila, their example inspired GIs in all parts of the globe. In Guam, troop mass meetings protested the point score system for releasing soldiers to civilian life and 3,500 staged a reported "hunger strike" against demobilization slowdowns. Mass meetings, parades, petitions, letters to Congress expressed their protests.

U. S. troops in Seoul, Korea, on January 10, 1946 adopted a resolution: "We cannot understand the War Department's insistence on keeping an oversized peacetime army overseas under present conditions."

In Paris on January 8, thousands of GIs marched down the Champs Elysees to gather in front of the American Embassy, shouting: "Get us home!" Speakers at a GI demonstration on January 9 in Frankfort on the Main in Germany declared that the commanding general was "too scared to face us here" and the troops cabled Congress: "Are the brass hats to be permitted to build empires?"

A Nuremberg dispatch in the New York daily *P M,* January 13, described the GI demonstrations in terms of a labor struggle. "The fact is the GIs have strike fever. Almost every soldier you talk to is full of resentment, humiliation and anger. He acts exactly as workers have acted and by so doing drew the GIs' criticism in the past...But now the shoe is on the other foot. The GIs now feel they have a legitimate gripe against their employers."

One of the leaders of the Manila demonstrations was Emil Mazey, former president of UAW Briggs Local 212, who had led the opposition to the no-strike pledge at the 1943 UAW convention. He was named to the soldiers committee elected at a delegated convention representing 139,000 GIs in the Philippines. His own group had cabled the UAW asking it to transmit their demands to Congress. UAW President Thomas made the cable public and stated support for the GIs' demands. Both the CIO and AFL also made official declarations of support for the speedy return of the troops.

The Stalinists alone withheld or tempered their support of the GIs. Unlike *The Militant* which had campaigned for withdrawal of all U. S. troops from foreign soil, the December 23, 1945 *Worker,* Sunday paper of the Communist Party, stated editorially: "Americans wanted their boys home now, *except those essential to occupation.*" (My emphasis.) On January 8, 1946, the *Daily Worker* told soldiers and their families: "We have duties to fulfill in the armies of occupation." This was precisely the argument of the War Department.

Senator Elbert D. Thomas, head of the Military Affairs Committee, describing the "Bring Us Home" pressure on members of Congress, said: "Constituents are on their necks day and night. The pressure is unbelievable. Mail from wives, mothers and sweethearts demanding that their men be brought home is running to almost 100,000 letters daily."

The story of these "Bring Us Home" demonstrations awaits its historian. Their tremendous scope and effect have not been recounted in the official histories — for understandable reasons. The truth is that the victorious United States Army almost disintegrated as an effective fighting force at the end of the war. These world-wide troop demonstrations and protests were akin to mutiny in the eyes of the professional officer caste and proclaimed the armed forces as unreliable.

The American workers' strikes and the GI demonstrations played a profound role in encouraging the refusal of colonial peoples to submit to the return of their old imperialist masters from Western Europe. Less fearful of direct armed intervention by the United States, the peoples of India, Indonesia, Indo-China, China and Burma pressed their struggles for national freedom and social emancipation. These struggles in turn were to spark the uprisings against foreign rule and imperialism that have since spread to the Middle East, Africa and Latin America.

*   *   *

The struggles of the American workers and soldiers became interlinked and confronted the American capitalist ruling class with an invincible power. This played an important part in giving the GM workers the will to hold on until the legions of mass industry swelled the nation's picket lines into the mightiest strike army in this country's history.

As the GM workers waited for the steel, electrical and packinghouse workers to launch their strikes, Truman intervened with his Fact-Finding Board's proposals. On January 10, the board recommended an increase of 19-1/2 cents an hour — a raise of 17-1/2 per cent instead of the 30 per cent demanded and needed just to keep the workers even with their take-home pay at the end of the war.

CIO Steelworkers President Philip Murray offered to accept the recommendation; the steel corporations declined. Nevertheless, at Truman's insistence, Murray wilted and postponed for one week the national steel strike originally set for January 14. This gave the steel corporations, which had already been offered a $4 a ton price increase by Truman's OPA, time to press for even higher price rises.

Murray's postponement of the steel strike and his acceptance of the 19-1/2-cent settlement proposal came as the GM strike delegates were meeting in Detroit. The delegates were confronted with a proposal of the entire UAW Executive Board for acceptance of the Fact-Finding Board's recommendation. Reuther urged acceptance, although he claimed that Truman's fact-finding body would have favored a 24 per cent raise for GM workers if the issue of wages and price rises in steel were not also under consideration. He complained about the steel union leadership's failure to oppose price increases and the Stalinist-led UE's refusal to pull out the General Motors electrical division workers. The conference finally voted to accept the 19-1/2-cent proposal, with about one-third voting in opposition. General Motors, however, refused to add even a penny to its original offer.

On January 15 the GM workers finally received the long-awaited reinforcements. Some 200,000 members of the CIO United Electrical, Radio and Machine Workers set up mass picket lines around 78 plants of General Electric, Westinghouse—and the General Motors Electrical Division. The UE leaders had offered in advance to call off the strike if the companies would meet the 15-cent offer made by U. S. Steel to the steelworkers and then negotiate the difference between that offer and the 25 cents the UE originally demanded. GE, GM and Westinghouse refused even to consider the UE proposal.

The next day 125,000 members of the CIO United Packinghouse Workers and 90,000 of the AFL Amalgamated Meat Cutters and Butcher Workmen jointly struck the national meatpacking corporations — Armour, Swift, Wilson, Cudahy, and Morrell. This strike was especially notable because the rival CIO and AFL unions agreed not to return to work until both had settled. The CIO union demanded 25 cents more an hour: 17-1/2 cents immediately and the balance to be negotiated.

The one-week delay gained nothing for the steelworkers. On January 21 some 800,000, encompassing the entire basic steel and steel-fabricating industry, joined the more than one million workers already on strike. For the first time in modern American labor history the entire U. S. Steel Corporation was closed down. With one blow of their mighty fist, the steelworkers brought American monopoly capitalism's most important basic industry to a halt.

The 1946 national steel strike was the largest single strike this country has ever known. When the steelworkers hit the picket lines on that fateful January 21, a total of almost 2,000,000 American workers in the basic industries were on strike at one time.

In the twelve months following V-J Day more than 5,000,000 workers engaged in strikes. For the number of strikers, their weight in industry and the duration of the struggle, the 1945-46 strike wave in the U. S. surpassed anything of its kind in any capitalist country, including the British General Strike of 1926. Before its ebb it was to include the whole coal, railroad, maritime and communications industries, although not simultaneously.

It is clear, in retrospect, that the American monopolies stood helpless before this awesome display of labor power. The corporations used their usual devices of trying to break picket lines with force and violence, police terror and injunctions. In Philadelphia, Chicago, Los Angeles, even Detroit, the cops beat up strikers, and workers were sentenced to jail terms for "contempt" of injunctions. But the forces of corporate power and political reaction were met by stiff mass resistance. The American industrial workers had learned a thing or two since their first great awakening in the Thirties. In 1946 there were few would-be scabs, — and very few of them got through the picket lines.

The 1946 national steel strike was the climax of more than a half century of terrible bloody struggles against the brutal steel monopolists. In 1892 and again in 1919, the steelworkers had gone on strike only to be crushed with such violence that each time it took years for the workers to recover and fight anew. I observed the steelworkers in action on the very spot where the old defeats had left their awful scars and it was a never-to-be-forgotten experience.

In my report to *The Militant* datelined Pittsburgh, January 23, I described how "immense tentacles of steel plants reach out from this city of smoke and steel and stretch for scores of miles along the river banks.

"For the past three days, these plants have sprawled lifeless. No smoke or flame belches forth from the squatting steel monsters with their huge spines of stacks rising from the open hearths and furnaces...

"Other and smaller fires are burning now, visible only as glowing red dots from a short distance. They are far different from the ore-eating, man-eating conflagrations that a few days ago roared and blazed inside the mills. These are friendly fires, meant to warm and comfort pickets in the long, freezing vigil of the near-zero night.

"These glowing coals in coke-fueled steel barrels called salamanders form a mighty chain up and down the valley and the river banks. They have become symbols of union strength and hope opposed to the tyrannical power of the steel bosses.

"Hundreds and hundreds of these metal-barrel heaters burn night and day at the innumerable gates, entrances and possible entrances to the steel kingdoms. And always near and around them are the slow-circling clusters of men and women of steel, keeping their day and night-long guards in American labor's greatest strike siege."

I also visited Homestead, Pa., where I saw the simple white stone marker put up in 1941 by the local steel union to commemorate the pioneer unionists who fought and died in 1892. There I got my most gratifying experience:

"... Looking down the hill toward the main gate of the plant, we saw a mass picket line circling before the entrance. Strung before the gate was another, small straight line of individuals, from which every few seconds one would detach himself and hurry into the plant gates.

"We hurried over and learned it was time for the administrative and supervisory people, as well as the CIO maintenance crews, to go into the plant [Carnegie-Illinois, U. S. Steel Corp.] under the rigid inspection of the union pickets...

"The pickets threw their circle close, so that only one man could pass at a time. Meanwhile the picket captain and assistant picket captains closely inspected the passes and jerked back the coat collars to inspect each white badge to insure that only legitimate 'pushers' and supervisors went in, according to the agreement with the union...

'They can only come in through this one gate, and some of them have to go two miles inside the plant to their departments. There's nothing to do in there. All they do is play cards. But the management thinks it's playing psychology.'

"We watched the most aggressive of the picket captains, a little, wiry young fellow who had recently returned from 33 months' army service in Europe. As each 'white badge' came up to the line, the veteran's elbow would jut out and catch the supervisor in the crook of the arm. 'Pass?' he would snap. 'Badge?' he would bark, pulling open a coat collar to get a better view. 'OK.' We watched that elbow jab out methodically and halt the meek 'white badge' men. In one pause, the little tough veteran turned to us and grinned slyly: 'That's psychology, too!'"

Similar scenes were being played throughout the length and breadth of America in a half-dozen major industries. This was a token of a new power in the land. In 1937 the industrial workers had risen from atomization to organization. In 1946, the industrial workers demonstrated that their organized power could command the nation, if they but willed to do so.

Unfortunately, the firmness and determination of the striking workers were not matched by their leadership. The CIO leaders, so united in suppressing the workers during the war and in political support of the Democratic administration, had no unified, coordinated policy for wresting the greatest possible gains in the postwar strikes. In almost every international union the leaders proceeded to make settlements without consideration of other unions still on strike.

The first break in the CIO strike lines came on January 26, five days after the steelworkers came out. A conference of the CIO United Packinghouse Workers in Chicago voted to end the picket lines that day after defying Truman's seizure of the packinghouse industry for 24 hours. The day before, the conference had voted to disregard the seizure under which the workers were to go back pending fact-finding procedure. UPWA President Lewis Clark charged that Truman "has engaged in a strikebreaking action the sole effect of which can be but to play into the hands of the packers."

On February 7 Truman's fact-finding panel proposed a 16-cent hourly raise instead of the demanded 25 cents. The recommendation opened the way for a big hike in meat prices by proposing that only five cents of the wage increase be "absorbed" by the companies from their 800 per cent increase in profits since 1940. The other 11 cents were to be paid from price increases and government subsidies.

The hope that the Chrysler and Ford workers might come out in support of the prolonged GM strike ended on January 26 when the UAW came to terms with Chrysler and Ford for 18 and 18-1/2-cent hourly raises respectively. These contracts were later to be supplemented by onerous "company security" clauses. Formally the GM workers were still demanding a 30 per cent increase, but they were actually holding out for not less than the 19-1/2 cents proposed by the "fact-finders."

As the GM strike dragged through its third month, the Stalinist-dominated United Electrical, Radio and Machine Workers suddenly announced a settlement for its 30,000 striking members in GM's Electrical Division. The UE leaders revealed on February 9 that they had accepted a wage agreement of 18-1/2 cents. UAW President Thomas expressed "terrible shock" when informed of the UE leaders' secret deal and said it "puts us in an awful spot since GM now will come to us insisting that we settle on the same terms." (The UAW leaders had already settled "on the same terms"— and less—with Chrysler and Ford.) The February 11 meeting of the UAW General Motors City-Wide Strike Committee in Detroit adopted a resolution that "emphatically condemns this inferred 'double-crossing' of the UAW-GM workers by the UE leadership."

The national shutdown by 800,000 CIO steelworkers came to a victorious end on its 26th day when the giant U.S. Steel Corporation capitulated on February 15. It agreed to the union's final demand for an 18-1/2-cent across-the-board wage increase. This was the first time U.S. Steel had ever yielded to a strike and this was the largest single wage concession ever won in the industry. But the greatest gain of the strike was the industry-wide unity forged among the steelworkers. Four more times within the next decade the industry was to challenge the steelworkers and four times bow before national strike actions.

Before the U.S. Steel wage settlement, Truman had agreed to a

$5 a ton steel price increase — a 10-1/2 per cent rise. Every penny of it was pure gravy for the steel companies.

The NAM initiated a campaign through full-page advertisements in 600 newspapers to end all price controls at the expiration of the Price Control Act on June 30, 1946. The OPA was already handing out thousands of authorizations for price increases. The scarcity of civilian goods, from safety pins and canned foods to clothing and housing, provided a field day for black market and under-the-counter illegal price gouging.

On the 95th day of the GM auto workers strike, the UAW International Executive Board issued an appeal to all UAW locals to support the GM strikers "to the utmost of your resources." Negotiations were almost dead as General Motors put the final squeeze on the grim strikers whose resources were nearing total exhaustion.

On March 2, the GM delegates conference voted to ask General Motors to accept arbitration of the remaining issues, which included wages, maintenance of membership, transfers and promotions, vacation pay and local union grievances. GM promptly said "No."

During this conference Reuther called the separate settlement made earlier by the UE leaders "an act of treachery unparalleled in the history of the labor movement." This was something of an exaggeration, although it expressed the feelings of the GM workers. The no-strike pledge had been a considerably greater act of treachery.

As the GM workers continued their dogged battle on the picket lines, the CIO United Rubber Workers announced on March 2 a clean-cut victory over the Big Four rubber corporations: Goodyear, Firestone, Goodrich, and U. S. Rubber. Two days before a national strike deadline these companies signed the first contracts achieved by industry-wide bargaining in the rubber industry. The contracts called for an 18-1/2-cent wage increase plus retroactive pay equivalent to four cents an hour for an entire year, double time for Sundays, and six designated holidays with pay. All told, the wage gains amounted to 24 cents an hour. This was the best contract signed in this period by any major industry. Representatives of all local unions were on the URW's negotiating committee. They rejected all attempts at government intervention and firmly refused to discuss corporation propositions for "company security" and similar devices. In short, the rubber workers meant business; and the companies knew it.

The CIO auto union board on March 7 filed charges with the National Labor Relations Board that General Motors was engaged in a lockout because of its refusal to accept the Fact-Finding Board's wage recommendations and to arbitrate the issues. The UAW leaders issued "an appeal to all organized labor and all American citizens who believe in justice to come quickly and generously to the aid of the GM workers."

The negotiating committee on March 6 attacked the corporation "because the...corporation is trying to interfere in the internal affairs of the UAW-CIO...General Motors doesn't want the strike to be settled until the UAW-CIO convention, March 23-31."

There were strong indications that General Motors was putting off the settlement in hopes of hurting Reuther's position in the UAW, for he had become the symbol of the GM strike.

A labor reporter for the *Detroit Free Press,* after interviewing numerous GM workers, wrote on March 9: "Whether you like it or not, it appears that the GM executives who hoped that a long strike would destroy Walter Reuther have outsmarted themselves in this fight." At the same time, a group of local union presidents announced a meeting for March 17 to form a "Reuther for President Committee" to campaign to replace R. J. Thomas and elect Reuther as President of the UAW.

General Motors' resistance to the paralyzing power of the union collapsed on March 13. On March 15 the GM delegates conference approved a new contract. After 113 days on the picket lines, the 225,000 GM auto workers had forced the corporation to agree to an 18-1/2-cent across-the-board wage raise, 13-1/2 cents of it retroactive to November 7, 1945; correction of local plant inequities; no "company security" clauses; and paid vacations. If this was considerably less than what was demanded and needed, it was none the less a proud victory. The GM workers had been made to bear the brunt of corporate resistance; their stand had sparked the whole labor struggle which won the largest and most extensive wage increases that had ever been secured in a single period.

The eight-day convention of the CIO United Automobile Workers, March 23-30, 1946, was treated as top-ranking national news by press and radio. Enraged by the GM strike victory, the capitalist press openly campaigned against the "socialistic" Reuther. CIO President Philip Murray appeared in person at the UAW convention to throw his prestige and influence behind the Thomas-Addes-Stalinist faction and against Reuther.

The factional struggle for office overshadowed and distorted the real issue before the convention—the methods of the GM struggle as against the methods of the Chrysler and Ford settlements. Reuther himself did not seriously attempt any clarification or put himself on record for the future. Discussion of issues took place in caucus meetings outside the convention hall. Such caucus meetings, held almost nightly, were accepted as part of the normal processes of union democracy in action. But there was no direct confrontation of program and ideas in the convention hall. It was noteworthy that Reuther did not speak once on the central issue of GM policy even in his caucus rallies.

The Thomas-Addes caucus, with close prompting from the Stalinists, evaded the GM strike issues and struck at Reuther through a slander campaign. In the course of one caucus speech Thomas shouted: "Don't forget that Mussolini was once a socialist too!"— a snide reference to Reuther's long-abandoned socialism.

When the election for UAW president took place, the great majority of the most militant wing of the delegates supported Reuther. In a roll-call vote, Reuther won by a narrow margin of 124 votes out of some 8,800 cast. The next day, however, Thomas was elected first vice-president over Reuther's candidate, Melvin Bishop, who was considered a bureaucratic reactionary by the militants. The Thomas-Addes group also captured the two other top posts. An interesting sidelight was the election of Emil Mazey in his absence to the UAW Executive Board.

When he was pushing his way to the top of the union, Reuther was more aggressive in action and bolder in his social program than the other UAW leaders. The 1945-46 strike wave gave him his chance and he grasped it. He was never again to display the same type of leadership. Even at the 1946 convention he tried to appear as a "responsible," conservative "labor statesman."

But the election of Reuther to the UAW presidency did not reflect any willingness of the UAW members to abdicate to bureaucratic procedures. They did not trust any of the officials. They voted down motions proposed by the top leaders to extend officers' terms to two years instead of one and to double the monthly dues. They rejected a proposal to increase by $1,000 to $1,500 the UAW officers' annual salaries, then ranging from $5,000 for board members to $9,000 for the UAW president. Reuther now commands a salary of $22,000 a year as UAW head, plus ample expense allowances. He is, however, one of the more "poorly" paid union leaders today.

The GM strike settlement ended the great 1945-46 CIO strike wave, which was the historic high point of the CIO in action. There were still some mighty class battles to be fought in 1946, such as the miners and the rail workers strikes, which raised issues of the most vital concern to all labor. These will be treated in the following chapter.

The tremendous advance of the class struggle during the postwar period can be seen by a comparison of the strike statistics for 1937 and 1945-46. In 1937, the epic year of the CIO's rise, there were 4,740 strikes involving 1,861,000 strikers, for a total loss of 28,425,000 man-days of work. In 1945 the number of strikes was 4,750 with 3,470,000 on strike, almost double the 1937 figure, and a loss of 38,000,000 man-days. In 1946 the number of strikes reached 4,985 with 4,600,000 strikers and 116,000,000 man-days lost.

Although the strike figures have not been so high in any year since, it may be noted at this point that the strike figures for every year without exception since 1946 have been higher than the 1935-39 average, and in most years higher than the pre-war peak in 1937. After 1946, labor never quite went back to the "old quiet days" of the Thirties—an illuminating fact which the union bureaucracy would prefer to see buried deeper than the gold at Fort Knox.

PART V

THE NEW OFFENSIVE
AGAINST LABOR

1946-1950

24

Truman's
Anti-Labor Drive

A highly publicized international event of 1946 was the visit to the United States of ex-Prime Minister Winston Churchill. On March 5 the recently-deposed British war lord made an address at Westminster College in Fulton, Missouri, Truman's home state. The President himself introduced Churchill. He later said he had read Churchill's speech in advance.

Churchill's address was the first public call to arms against the Soviet Union by a major Western capitalist leader. He urged that national armaments be maintained at continuous full wartime strength; that Washington and London monopolize the atomic bomb; and that an Anglo-U. S. "fraternal alliance" be formed to halt the alleged "expansive and proselytizing tendencies" of the Soviet Union.

Opposition to this war-like speech was so widespread that Churchill himself claimed on March 15 that he did not mean to propose an Anglo-American "military" alliance. Truman subsequently denied endorsement of Churchill's views. The British government, led by the Laborites, promptly dissociated itself from Churchill's bellicose talk.

Churchill and his Tory party had just suffered a stunning electoral defeat at the hands of the British Labor Party. His appearance in the United States with his anti-Soviet war alarms came in the midst of the great labor upsurge.

The American ruling class, headed by the President of the United States, gave a repudiated Churchill an American platform from which to address the world. By bolstering his prestige, America's rulers were assuring all the shaky capitalist regimes of Europe and Asia that they would not be deserted by U. S. imperialism should they find themselves confronted by opposition from their own people. At the same time, American labor was being warned against any aspirations toward political power. From this standpoint, Churchill's speech was also a call to arms of world capitalism against insurgent labor, and first of all in Britain and America.

Shortly after Churchill's Missouri speech, the Truman administration opened a new assault on the labor movement. The occasion was the national coal and railroad strikes in April and May.

Two weeks after the General Motors settlement, 400,000 soft coal miners quit the pits at the April 1 termination of their contract. The strike was called when the operators rejected the United Mine Workers' demand for a health and welfare fund, to be financed by a small levy on each ton of coal mined.

Prior to the strike UMW President Lewis had indicted the coal profiteers for "gross mismanagement, cupidity, stupidity and wanton neglect" resulting in 28,000 deaths and more than a million injuries in the mines over the previous 14 years. Lewis charged that every ton of coal mined was "smeared with the blood" of mine workers.

The mine owners called the UMW's demands "time-killing trivia with the obvious intent of stalling negotiations and creating a national crisis." The UMW negotiators broke off the futile proceedings on April 10. As Lewis stalked out he flung back at the operators: "We trust that time, as it shrinks your purse, may modify your niggardly and anti-social propensities."

While the mine negotiations stood stalemated, two railroad brotherhoods — the locomotive engineers and the trainmen — on April 15 announced a May 18 strike date for 295,000 operating rail workers. Truman's Fact-Finding Board had recommended an hourly raise of 16 cents, a cut below the 18 to 18-1/2-cent pattern set in most of the CIO strike settlements. The two operating unions rejected the recommendation. Truman promptly threatened to seize the railroads and break the strike, as Roosevelt had done in 1943.

On May 4 Truman lashed out at the coal strike as a "national disaster." He called the miners' bid for health and welfare royalties an "illegal" demand. He threatened "militant action" to break what he said was "gradually" assuming the proportions of "a strike against the government."

Scores of anti-union bills were poured into the congressional hoppers. The Senate shoved aside its consideration of the new military program and voted 66 to 9 for immediate consideration of the Case Labor Disputes Bill, a forerunner of the Taft-Hartley Act adopted a year later. Both houses of Congress began consideration of a bill to make it illegal for employers to grant union health and welfare funds financed by royalties based on production, such as coal tonnage.

The newspapers printed horror stories of imminent strike-induced famine, of water supplies and utilities cut off, of millions unemployed and the country in ruins. One week after General Motors had calmly announced it had accumulated a huge reserve of coal as a result of the 113-day GM strike, the company suddenly discovered it would be down to its last lump within ten days.

The UMW had rejoined the AFL on January 25, 1946, and AFL President William Green felt obliged to give public endorsement to the miners strike. On May 8 Green urged the Pennsylvania Federation of Labor to give unqualified support to the miners' struggle. He told the cheering delegates that "the UMW is in a life and death struggle and the organization is making a fine fight of it. Our duty is to rally around the mine workers until they win their battle."

On May 9, at the very height of the savage campaign against the miners, CIO President Murray venomously attacked Lewis before the Amalgamated Clothing Workers convention. Murray boasted that "no one in the CIO has turned against the Government." The CIO president's attack on Lewis was unaccompanied by any statement of support for the miners strike or their demands.

"From another quarter," reported the May 18, 1946 *Militant,* "the Communist Party and its *Daily Worker* were conducting a continuous sniping attack on Lewis ... the *Daily Worker* called on the capitalist government 'to act' in the mine strike ... 'in the interests of the miners.'"

On May 10 government spokesmen led the miners to believe that the operators were agreed "in principle" on the health, safety and welfare royalty. The UMW called a two-week truce. The following day, the UMW announced its further demands for a wage increase of 27 cents an hour.

On May 15 Truman commandeered the railroads in advance of a strike. Minutes before the May 18 rail strike deadline, Whitney and Johnston, heads respectively of the Brotherhood of Railroad Trainmen and the Brotherhood of Locomotive Engineers, postponed the strike for another five days. Nevertheless, the railroad workers engaged in a spontaneous national strike of several hours which for the first time tied up the railroads from coast to coast.

During the five days ending May 18, the CIO United Steelworkers were meeting in convention at Atlantic City, New Jersey. Headed by Philip Murray, the convention took no action in behalf of the embattled mine and rail workers. Murray himself maintained a demonstrative silence. (This same convention marked the public beginnings of the anti-communist cold war inside the CIO that was to rack the organization for almost five years and lead to a major split.)

The locomotive engineers and railway trainmen struck officially on May 23, halting the entire railway system. They were ordered back by Whitney and Johnston two days later. The night before, over the radio, Truman had given the union leaders a 24-hour ultimatum to end the strike or he would use troops to run the railroads. Although among the most conservative unionists, the railroad operating workers for more than 48 hours had defied Truman's seizure under the wartime Smith-Connally Act. Truman had to slip in a concession: an 18-1/2-cent raise instead of the 16 cents recommended by his "fact-finders."

Truman did not wait for his ultimatum to expire before seeking powers for further drastic strike-breaking measures. The day after his radio blast he called a special joint session of Congress and demanded that it enact the most repressive legislation against organized labor ever advocated by a president. He urged Congress "immediately to authorize the President to draft into the armed forces" all workers "who are on strike against the government." And this was in peacetime!

Truman's bill further provided that those who continued to strike at seized facilities would be subject to a $5,000 fine and a year's imprisonment, plus loss of job or seniority rights. Even "officials of labor organizations representing the employes" could be "inducted into the Army... at such time, in such manner... and on such terms as may be prescribed by the President." The bill, however, proposed to take good care of the railroad corporations. It provided for "fixing of just compensation to the owners...to the value the use of such properties would have had to their owners" had the lines continued to operate under private control.

Within two hours of Truman's demand, the Democrats and Republicans in the House of Representatives had approved his proposed "emergency" measure by a majority of 306 to 13. The measure was delayed in the Senate only because ultra-reactionary elements wanted to make it "foolproof" and to tack it on to the Case Anti-Strike Bill, which previously had been given precedence on the Senate floor.

The Republican *New York Herald Tribune* of May 26 wrote with smug satisfaction: "Now all that remains to be done is the issuance of an executive order turning the seized railroads back to their owners. The formality probably will be put off until Monday." The roads were actually returned that same day, a Sunday. The railroad workers returned to the 10-hour day, the 60 to 80-hour week, no paid holidays, no sick leave, and wages which had fallen from second highest, by industry, in 1933 to 27th in 1946.

During the period of the mine truce, many of the undaunted miners had refused to abandon their traditional position of "no contract, no work." More than 200,000 were already on strike, despite Truman's seizure, when the official truce ended on May 27. As the entire force of 400,000 soft coal miners stayed out of the pits, Truman made an ominous gesture. An armored detachment of 150 soldiers from Camp Campbell moved into the Madisonville, Kentucky mine fields to escort a few scabs who had been rounded up.

Two days later, however, the miners chalked up another triumph. Not they, but the administration capitulated. The government, as operator of the mines, signed a contract granting wage increases of $1.85 a day, including an 18-1/2-cent an hour raise for a 35-hour week instead of the previous forty, plus two hours a day guaranteed overtime at time and a half rates.

Above all, the government had to concede the principle of health and welfare royalties. The miners were to secure a five-cent levy on each ton of coal. This would provide a health-and-welfare fund of about $25,000,000 a year, administered jointly by the government and the United Mine Workers. The UMW was also to get complete control over the millions of dollars which the companies had been deducting from miners' pay over many years for company-controlled "welfare" funds that rarely returned any benefits to needy miners. The government also promised to enforce the federal mine-safety code, which had been non-compulsory.

Truman's demand for a "draft strikers" bill and the anti-union campaign in Congress posed with renewed sharpness the question of labor's independent political action. It was impossible, at least for the moment, for the union leaders to pretend that Truman was a "friend of labor."

Murray had complained in his concluding speech at the Steelworkers convention on May 18 that Congress "has not adopted a single piece of constructive legislation since the year 1937" and that for nine years "labor has been fighting with its back to the wall." This illuminating admission was wrung from Murray by the Senate's rejection of a bill to raise the federal minimum wage from 40 cents an hour to 65 cents.

But it was not a question merely of congressional failure to enact new and improved welfare measures. Under the incitation of a Democratic President, a Democratic Congress was driving to pass laws designed to restrict, damage, undermine and ultimately destroy labor unions and the right to strike. Fifty of the 90 PAC-endorsed congressmen, whose election in 1944 Murray had hailed as a "great victory," had voted for the Truman-proposed bill to draft strikers; 33 prudently abstained from voting; only seven voted against.

The Democratic-controlled Senate put aside Truman's bill only because it wished to hasten action on the Case Labor Disputes Bill. This provided for semi-compulsory government mediation, enforceable 60-day "cooling off" periods to prevent strikes, damage suits against unions and other measures to curb strikes and subject unions to employer reprisals. It also forbade boycotts and jurisdictional strikes. The Senate approved the Case Bill by a vote of 61 to 20. Of 46 Democrats voting, 33 backed this anti-labor measure. The House had already passed the Case Bill on February 9, also with a majority of the Democrats — 97 — voting for it, and 91 against.

The labor leaders rose to peaks of verbal violence in denunciation of both the Truman and Case Bills. CIO President Murray charged that the "draft strikers" bill was a "beachhead for those sinister forces which seek to use the military power as a means of crushing labor." AFL President Green likened the labor draft to "slave labor under fascism" and pledged that the AFL "will resist such punitive, restrictive and un-American legislation as the Case Bill and Government Seizure [Truman] Bill to its last breath."

Sidney Hillman, who had helped engineer the nomination of Truman at the 1944 Democratic national convention, now found the Truman and Case bills embodied "the most extreme and autocratic controls over the liberties and democratic rights of American workers ever seriously proposed in the history of our nation."

The *Daily Worker* claimed that Truman had "betrayed Roosevelt's program." But it was Roosevelt himself, in his message to Congress on June 25, 1943, who had said: "I recommend that the Selective Service Act be amended so that persons may be inducted into non-combat military service up to the age of 65 years. This will enable us to induct into military service all persons who engage in strikes or stoppages or other interruptions of work in plants in the possession of the United States."

The anti-labor offensive brought no concerted action or even a proposal for action from the top CIO and AFL officers. They complained, blustered and issued dire warnings—but did nothing. Nevertheless, the general desire of the ranks for some effective resistance did find expression.

On May 27, two days after Truman had called for a military labor draft bill, United Auto Workers President Reuther announced that the UAW leaders proposed to the national CIO, AFL and railroad brotherhoods that they convene a united labor conference to jointly fight against the legislative union-busting campaign. This proposal, which had been suggested since the end of the war by the Socialist Workers Party and *The Militant,* had been widely discussed and publicized in

CIO circles. Resolutions proposing such action had been adopted by leading militant locals of the UAW in Detroit and Flint. In his statement of May 27, Reuther said:

"The top officers of the UAW-CIO today decided to ask President Philip Murray of the CIO to take immediate steps to bring about joint action by all organized labor to prevent passage in the Senate of restrictive labor legislation proposed Saturday to Congress by President Harry S. Truman.

"Vice-Presidents Richard T. Leonard and R. J. Thomas agreed with me to ask President Murray to confer immediately with officers of the American Federation of Labor and the railroad brotherhoods to plan the calling at the earliest possible date of a national united labor conference for the specific purpose of combating President Truman's proposals and all other restrictive legislation aimed at labor now pending in Congress."

Some 35,000 workers, summoned on 24-hours' notice, rallied on May 29 in New York City's Madison Square Park to hear leaders of the CIO, AFL and railroad brotherhoods, including A. F. Whitney, head of the Trainmen whose strike Truman had broken. There was no question of the sentiments of the workers, for every denunciation of Truman brought thunderous applause. But the meeting ended in silence when the speakers offered no program of action.

Local CIO councils and mass rallies in a number of large cities adopted resolutions supporting the UAW proposal. Local AFL groups, including a one-day stop-work meeting of 5,000 AFL seamen in New York City on June 6, passed motions to support the national labor conference proposal.

Sentiment for a labor party was swiftly revived by Truman's open anti-labor stand. In Flint, Michigan, within 38 hours of Truman's congressional message, signs were posted throughout Chevrolet plants reading, "BUILD A LABOR PARTY!" This and similar local pressure from other parts of the state forced the adoption of a pro-labor party resolution by the Michigan State CIO convention, held in Detroit from June 10 to 13. The resolution called for "full support of the formation of a new political party comprising all sections of the labor movement, the AFL, CIO and Railroad Brotherhoods, and independent unions, working farmers, professional workers, consumers, members of minority racial and religious groups, and all people advocating a progressive and liberal program." However, the effect of the resolution was weakened when the leadership, including both factions in the UAW, secured the inclusion of a qualifying clause calling for "endorsement and support of liberal and progressive candidates of the existing parties during this election year."

In the discussion on the labor party resolution, UAW Detroit East Side Regional Director Emil Mazey told the delegates: "This is a timely resolution although I wish it were a firmer one. It is time we built a party of our own. If we had started building a labor party years back we would today not find ourselves in the present mess. We must not only pass this resolution, but we must go out after this convention and do something about it."

Even David Dubinsky made so bold as to endorse the creation of an independent labor party. In Dubinsky's address to the United Hatters, Cap and Millinery Workers convention early in June, he declared that the unions "cannot satisfy themselves with a party that includes the Southern reactionaries or the industrialists in the Republican party."

Truman's strikebreaking actions were not confined to the coal and rail strikes. A May 6 CIO maritime "unity" conference in San Francisco, held by six CIO seafaring and waterfront unions, had announced a nation-wide maritime strike for June 15. These unions, including Curran's National Maritime Union and Bridges' International Longshoremen's and Warehousemen's Union, were strongly dominated by the Stalinists. They had adopted a "statement of policy" exempting not less than 75 per cent of all vessels in operation from strike action on the grounds that they were "troop ships" or "relief ships." Nevertheless, on June 2 Truman announced he intended to use the government's maritime agencies, including the U. S. Navy, Coast Guard, and War Shipping Administration, to load cargo and man struck ships in the event of a maritime strike.

The CIO maritime situation was of special interest. The Stalinist leadership of the NMU had stalled off union action for eight months, throughout the whole strike wave. This leadership had finally received a nine per cent wage increase offer from the shipowners in contrast with the 30 per cent the NMU had demanded originally. They tried to shove through this proposal for a $12.50 per month increase, which amounted to little more than five cents an hour. This touched off a revolt at a large NMU membership meeting in New York City on May 27. As a result, the NMU leaders beat a retreat. By the end of the meeting they had switched to opposition to the miserable settlement they had at first proposed to accept.

The militant stand of the CIO seamen, plus the declaration of the AFL seamen's unions that they would strike all ships under their contracts if Truman tried to man CIO-struck ships, forced a further limited concession from the government. The NMU leaders agreed to accept a $17.50 monthly increase.

The passage of the Case Bill by Congress took the focus of attention away from Truman's even more Draconic proposal for military strikebreaking. Truman kept silent about the Case Bill and gave no indication of whether or not he would sign it. However, the union leaders, particularly Murray and Dubinsky, had indicated that they were prepared once more to overlook Truman's strikebreaking and anti-labor proposals if he were to veto the Case Bill.

Truman was too shrewd a politician to risk a break with his labor supporters. Labor represented the decisive block of votes for the Democrats, although labor had very little real voice in the Democratic Party and none in the government. Moreover, since the Case Bill had been initiated by the Republicans, Truman could evade political responsibility for it even if it were passed over his veto. On June 11 Truman vetoed the Case Bill while repeating his demand for a "draft strikers" law. The Case Bill died in the House when the vote was just four short of the necessary two-thirds majority to override the Presidential veto.

Three weeks later, on July 3, Truman did sign the notorious Hobbs Bill. This was ostensibly aimed at labor "racketeers," particularly in the AFL teamsters union. The Act provided for fines up to $10,000 and 20 years' imprisonment for strikers and pickets who might be convicted of "racketeering" which in any way "obstructs, delays or affects" interstate commerce. The CIO called the "anti-racketeering" label on the Hobbs Bill a "gross deception."

There was already an Anti-Racketeering Act in the federal statutes, but its language specified that its provisions were not to apply to "the payment of wages to a bona fide employee" and it was not to be construed "in such manner as to impart, diminish, or in any manner affect the rights of bona fide labor organizations in lawfully carrying out the legitimate objects thereof." The Hobbs Act excluded these safeguards.

Despite the intensified campaign to curb the unions, the momentum of the 1946 strike wave continued into the latter half of the year. In September, every coastal port in the country was paralyzed by the greatest maritime strike in our history. In November, another national coal strike broke out.

The maritime strike was spearheaded not by the CIO but by the AFL seamen's unions—the Seafarers International Union and the Sailors Union of the Pacific. These unions had won an agreement from the ship operators under AFL contract for wage raises of $22.50 to $27.50 a month, compared to the $17.50 accepted by the CIO maritime unions in June. The AFL seamen's unions struck on September 5 after the Wage Stabilization Board turned down their raise as "inflationary." The board insisted that the lower rate accepted by the CIO maritime unions was the "ceiling" and the "prevailing rate."

The SIU-SUP strike, which was promptly backed by the CIO seamen, completely immobilized U.S. shipping. It was the greatest demonstration of maritime labor solidarity since the beginning of American unionism. The AFL Teamsters refused to make deliveries or pickups to and from the piers. There was only one small break in the strike front. Joseph Ryan had ordered his AFL longshoremen to go through the picket lines of the CIO National Maritime Union. The longshoremen refused to obey.

Within eight days the Truman administration capitulated. Under a formula designed to save face Economic Stabilization Director Steelman announced his approval of the SIU-SUP demands. As the AFL seamen withdrew their picket lines, the CIO unions extended their picketing to all ships in the ports, thus keeping the full stoppage in effect. On September 21 the 17-day national maritime strike came to a victorious end. This time the U.S. Maritime Commission was forced to concede that equal wages were to be paid to all American seamen and that the CIO seamen were entitled to the same wages as the AFL seafarers. The joint action between the previously feuding AFL and CIO unions was such a demonstration of maritime labor power that Truman did not dare to repeat his threats of armed force.

Less than two months after the maritime crisis, the government was confronted by the demand of the United Mine Workers for a reopening of the contract signed after the spring strike and government seizure which was still in effect. Under the threat of a national coal strike to begin November 1, just before elections, Truman intervened personally. He instructed officials in charge of the government-operated mines to open discussion on all disputed issues, including wages, hours and working conditions. The UMW committee indicated that it expected improvements in the contract by November 20.

The UMW move coincided with an important political shift in Congress. In the November 5 elections, the Republicans captured both houses of Congress and a majority of the state governments from the Democrats. There had been no enthusiastic turnout of the workers for the Democrats. A big shift had taken place in the middle class, particularly that section of it which had supported the Democrats since 1932. This group included farmers, the urban middle class of shopkeepers, professionals, and small businessmen. A tide of reaction had set in with the war, the inflation, the labor-baiting, the mounting anti-Soviet propaganda campaign, and the

growing witch hunt against communists, which the Democrats themselves had fostered. The Republicans got the benefit of it.

Once the elections were over, Truman felt free to drop any pretense of friendliness to the miners. He had nothing to lose politically
by getting "tough." He announced on November 15 there would be
no reopening of the UMW contract.

Actually, government operation of the mines was a fiction, as
the November 24 *New York Times* indicated: "American flags were
hoisted over the tipples; officials of the mining companies were
designated as Government officers in charge of the mines and mining
areas. These were the only signs of Government rule."

Since the operators themselves were acting as the government's
agents in control of the mines, the terms of the government's contract with the union were systematically violated.

The miners had no choice but to announce that the contract would
expire on November 20. After that date their principle of "no contract, no work!" would become automatically operative and a nation-
wide coal-mine strike would again be in force.

Truman had repeatedly scurried in retreat before the demands
of the price-gouging profiteers. When the meat trust cut off 90% of
the country's meat supply in October to enforce a demand for removal
of all price controls, Truman bowed abjectly before the meat packers.
On November 9 he had followed the NAM's dictates and ordered the
removal of government price controls from all commodities except
sugar, rice and rental housing.

These acts were fresh in the minds of the workers when Truman
announced from a warm vacation retreat in Florida on November 17
that "we will fight Lewis on all fronts." He commanded the miners
to stay in the pits.

The very next day, Lewis was haled before Federal Judge T. Alan
Goldsborough in Washington, D. C. Truman's Attorney General Tom
C. Clark, armed with affidavits from the heads of the War, Navy and
six other government departments, asked for a restraining order—
an injunction—against the impending mine strike. Goldsborough
promptly granted it.

Miners nevertheless began to leave the pits. A day before the
official contract termination, about 127,000 miners were out in defiance of the injunction. By November 20, some 400,000 miners were
on strike. Truman rushed back from Florida and called a White
House conference of all government officials involved. Judge Goldsborough ordered Lewis to stand trial on November 27 for "contempt."

Acting as plaintiff, prosecutor, judge and jury, Goldsborough
found the United Mine Workers and Lewis "guilty" of "contempt" of

one of the most fantastic injunctions ever issued by a court of law. It literally commanded Lewis not merely to withdraw his announcement of the termination of the UMW contract with the Truman administration but not even to mention that the contract might be terminated at any time in the future.

The whole labor movement was stunned by this overriding of the Norris-La Guardia Anti-Injunction Act of 1932. The CIO national convention, in session at the time Goldsborough issued his injunction, adopted a strong resolution attacking the government's use of "a sweeping injunction against the United Mine Workers of America... No labor injunctions can dispose of the problems now confronting workers who see their earnings shrink before the fast-rising cost of living. American democracy cannot tolerate any attempt to impose economic slavery through vicious anti-labor injunctions."

There had been a report on December 3 that the mine owners were at last ready to come to terms. Word went out from the White House that Truman wanted no settlement until the miners and Lewis had been "slapped down" by the federal court. On December 4 Judge Goldsborough imposed a $3,500,000 fine on the United Mine Workers and $10,000 on Lewis personally for "contempt." The UMW said it would appeal the sentence and the Attorney General asked the Supreme Court to review the case immediately. The Supreme Court withheld decision until March 1947.

Throughout the whole period of this struggle the miners and Lewis had been under ferocious assault from the daily press and public officials. A government drive to incite mass hysteria against them was launched. The Office of Defense Transportation announced a 25 per cent curtailment in train service. A "brown-out" to conserve coal for power was ordered in major cities. A bloodcurdling howl arose in Congress for anti-labor laws. The press spread scareheads about "25,000,000 Workers to Face Unemployment in Coal Crisis."

Using the Department of Justice and federal judiciary, Truman put Lewis in the position where continuation of the strike might mean not only bankruptcy for the union but imprisonment for its leaders. Even a Lewis could not withstand such pressure. On December 7 he called off the strike until March 31, 1947, in order, he said, to permit the United States Supreme Court to consider the miners' case "free from public pressure superinduced by the hysteria and frenzy of an economic crisis."

*   *   *

It is necessary to recall an aspect of Truman's policy during this phase of the battle that has been lost sight of. On December 3, the day he had let it be known that he opposed a coal settlement before the courts had "slapped down" the miners, Truman also held a press conference during which he discussed his legislative program for labor. He declared that he would demand revision of the Wagner Labor Relations Act—an objective eagerly sought by the corporations and publicly proclaimed by the Republican Party. He indicated that he hoped to achieve the end of the closed shop. Truman boasted that he hoped to "steal the march" and "beat the Republicans to the punch."

Three days after Truman's press conference, CIO President Murray issued an appeal to the AFL and railroad brotherhoods for "unified action" to fight anti-labor legislation. He said "it has become self-evident that there is a deliberate and monstrous movement under way to cripple, if not destroy the labor movement of this country..."

Who was in the forefront of this assault? Murray spoke only of "the dictatorship of a reactionary coalition in Congress" and the "predatory interests." He did not mention Truman. Other CIO leaders went further than Murray in their proposals for action against the anti-labor drive. New York State CIO President Louis Hollander had warned Truman that if he did not "return to Roosevelt's policies" there would be increased pressure for a third party which, Hollander said, would become the "first party," as the Labor Party had in England. The United Automobile Workers Executive Board renewed its appeal for a national united labor conference.

But none of the CIO leaders fixed direct responsibility on Truman and the Democrats for their role in the anti-union offensive, which Truman personally led. There was, in fact, a direct line leading from his labor policies in 1946 and early 1947 to the passage of the notorious Taft-Hartley Act in June 1947.

Truman even refused to call World War II formally to an end. "President Truman today said the recent soft coal strike had made it impossible to declare the war formally at an end now," said a December 12 United Press dispatch from Washington. "He said he thought if it had not been for recent strikes, he might have been able by now to have declared the war at an end."

Truman won praise from the capitalist press and the Republican leaders in Congress for his proposals on labor legislation in his January 6, 1947 State of the Union speech to the new Congress. Except for slight differences in detail, the proposals were similar to those contained in the Case bill which he had vetoed six months earlier. Truman told Congress he wanted a law to bar "jurisdictional" strikes and "secondary boycotts" and to forbid "the use of economic force by labor." His proposals were almost identical to those that were to be made twelve years later, in 1959, by Republican President Eisenhower and to be denounced unconditionally by organized labor.

After Truman's State of the Union speech, Senator Robert Taft, Ohio Republican who was heading the GOP anti-labor drive in Congress, said he could see in Truman's labor program "no substantial difference with our point of view." Representative Case noted: "We offered him some of those objectives last spring in the Case bill... I'm glad to see he is moving in that direction." Republican Senator Bricker of Ohio found that Truman "anticipated the Republican position."

Truman's repeated incitations against labor; his seizures of the mines and railroads for purposes of strikebreaking; his threat of armed force against the maritime workers; his demand for a "draft strikers" bill; his signing of the Hobbs Act; his invoking of an injunction and a "vengeful" fine against the coal miners; his call for revision of the Wagner Act; his boast that he would "beat the Republicans to the punch" in pushing anti-labor legislation; his speech to Congress calling for a federal ban on many traditional union activities —all these were vital elements in the birth-process of the Taft-Hartley Act.

Truman was to disown the Taft-Hartley Act. But anyone who studies objectively the origin of the postwar anti-labor legislation must be struck by the startling resemblance between certain features of the Taft-Hartley foundling and some of the brain-children of the Democratic politician and "friend of labor" from Independence, Missouri who occupied the White House after Roosevelt.

25

Economic and Legislative War on Labor

The postwar anti-labor drive was powered by economic forces inherent within the American capitalist system. This system had been revived from a prolonged depression only by government war spending. The abnormal war economy had added new contradictions to those revealed by the depression decade. The American capitalists sought to overcome these contradictions at the expense of the working people and lower middle class.

U. S. Comptroller General Lindsay C. Warren in April 1944 had testified to the House Naval Affairs Committee that the government agencies "are dishing and shoveling out Government money with reckless abandon." The war corporations, he charged, had looted "untold billions." He subsequently estimated "excess profits" on government war contracts at not less than 50 billion dollars. Most of this money, plus some 20 billion dollars worth of government-built war plants, went to a tiny group of giant corporations. Thus, the American economy emerged from the war more completely concentrated in the hands of a few great privately owned monopolies. These monopolies were in turn controlled by a tiny oligarchy of immensely rich families and shareowners.

The pertinent facts and statistical data are contained in a 358-page report issued in 1946 by the United States Senate Small Business Committee under the title, *Economic Concentration in World War II*. This Senate study found that the 250 largest manufacturing companies at the end of the war controlled "66.5 per cent of total usable facilities and almost as much as the entire 39.6 billion dollars held before the war by all the more than 75,000 manufacturing corporations in existence."

The instability of the postwar economy was most strongly embodied in the national debt. Karl Marx had written in his late 19th

Century work, *Capital:* " The only part of the so-called national wealth that actually enters into the collective possession of modern peoples is their national debt." At the end of World War II the American people "owned" more national debt than any people of any age. By 1946 the federal debt had shot to 229.7 billion dollars—almost 5-1/2 times the 1939 figure and almost 14 times that of 1929.

This cancerous expansion of the federal debt was due to war spending. In 1946 federal spending was nearly 64 billion dollars, of which 43-1/2 billion dollars were for direct military purposes. The latter item had been a mere billion dollars in 1939. Debt-building government spending sparked a terrific price inflation. A rapid and sharp rise in prices has been under way almost continuously since the start of World War II. By September 1948 the food-cost index was to rise to 215.2 or over 115 per cent; clothing, to 201.0.

By supporting the war program, the union leaders automatically supported inflation; by concealing the major relationship between government war spending and inflation, they disarmed labor in the fight to maintain and improve its standard of living.

Keeping these facts in mind, we can more clearly understand the CIO's policies and actions after the great strike wave and during the drive to saddle the unions with restrictive laws.

The wage increases won by the strikes in 1945 and 1946 did not compensate even for the wartime price rises. While the strikes were in progress the OPA was shooting out new price ceiling orders. All meat ceilings, for instance, were raised on February 26, 1946. Ten days later, price boosts up to 15 per cent were handed the textile and clothing manufacturers. Spokesmen of the manufacturing and business organizations appeared before hearings of the House Banking and Currency Committee in March 1946 and threatened continuation and worsening of the consumer goods shortage—that is, withholding of goods from the market — unless the flimsy price controls were eliminated altogether. They opposed renewal of the Price Control Act, which was to lapse June 30.

Thousands of workers in the nation's largest meatpacking plants were laid off in the latter half of March 1946 and production was greatly curtailed to force an additional increase in prices. On March 29 the OPA granted further increases on both pork and beef products. In April, price ceilings were completely removed from several thousand items, representing about 15 per cent of consumer goods in dollar value.

A joint committee of the CIO, AFL and railroad brotherhoods appealed directly to OPA Administrator Paul Porter and Economic Stabilizer Chester Bowles to rescind their order to abolish price ceilings on a wide variety of consumer goods. The unionists failed to move Truman's two appointees.

While the meat industry continued to withhold meat and curtail production despite several OPA price rises, Truman sought to blame food shortages on famine conditions in Europe. He could have seized the meat industry, which was deliberately sabotaging production to impose high prices. Instead, in his radio broadcast of April 19 Truman opined that "we would all be better off, physically and spiritually, if we ate less." He even proposed that "on two days a week let us reduce our food consumption to that of the average person in the hungry lands."

In a period of nine months after the war, the OPA had removed price ceilings entirely from 3,000 items, granted the full price demands of 6,000 companies claiming "individual hardship" and given partial increases to 2,000 others. Scarcely a month after the GM strike was settled, UAW President Walter Reuther, on April 27, 1946, asserted that if the inflation continued, "we will be forced to reopen wage issues." CIO Secretary-Treasurer James B. Carey told the Senate Banking and Currency Committee on April 25 that if there was no "effective price control" then "a whole new hand will have to be dealt" on wages.

In June the grain speculators, big flour mill operators and baking corporations imposed a bread famine on the country. Overnight, bread disappeared from the grocery shelves and wheat and flour piled up in huge elevators. The June 5 *New York Times* said that the national bread shortage was marked in the country's largest city "by an increase in black marketeering and an apparent abundance of cake" — the latter not covered by price ceilings. In Philadelphia, breadlines formed before dawn and on June 16 police were called out to subdue crowds angrily demanding bread. Two ten per cent price increases and the reduction in the size of the legal loaf failed to satisfy the grain and baking interests.

Congress enacted a bill to extend OPA beyond June 30. However, this bill was so obviously inflationary that Truman did not dare take political responsibility for it. Although the Democrats in Congress urged him to sign the bill, he vetoed it as "worse than no OPA at all." The OPA was allowed to expire on June 30.

A timely piece of advice was offered by *The Militant,* May 4, 1946, which foresaw inflation of "a more and more unbridled character." It said:

"It [labor] must fight for a program that anticipates inevitable price rises and continuously combats the consequences of inflation... by raising the demand now for the inclusion in all union contracts of the sliding scale of wages which will rise automatically with every increase of general living costs."

This proposal was given practical expression in demands for a cost-of-living bonus and the escalator clause in wage contracts. Leading United Automobile Workers locals initiated the demand for a sliding wage scale to meet rising prices. These included Ford Local 600, Briggs Local 212 and Budd Local 306. Although Reuther warned at the Michigan State CIO convention in June 1946 that labor might have to strike again for higher wages, he remained demonstratively silent on the issue of the escalator clause.

The CIO United Packinghouse Workers on June 28 demanded a "cost of living bonus," in addition to regular wages, to be paid weekly or monthly in proportion to the rise in living costs. UPWA President Ralph Helstein said the far-reaching plan contemplated the use of a reliable cost-of-living index rather than the U. S. Bureau of Labor Statistics index which grossly understated the actual increase in living expenses.

With the ending of the OPA and the last pretense of price control, "economic stabilization" collapsed. Some 40,000 wage contracts approved by the Wage Stabilization Board were, in effect, tossed out the window, since wages were fixed on the basis of price control.

A meeting of 1,200 officers, committeemen and stewards of the UAW and other CIO unions in Detroit vigorously applauded Walter Reuther's proposal to "reopen all wage contracts if a new and better OPA is not passed by Congress." The officers of the Packinghouse Workers in Chicago, in the same week, said the union "will press during negotiations for the inclusion of a clause in the contract providing for a cost of living bonus." They pointed out that Truman had not hesitated to seize the packing plants in February when the workers had struck against low wages. But, they said, when the meat trust withheld meat for months, the administration viewed the matter "with complete calm."

The CIO Executive Board, meeting in Washington on July 18, urged the President to call a labor-industry conference with the aim of giving "full and official recognition" to the need for higher wages and to meet "the crisis created by the drive to cripple and destroy price control..." President Philip Murray refused to answer questions of the press about what action the CIO would take in the event such a conference were not called or if it did not accept the CIO's wage proposals.

Meanwhile, on July 16, some 100,000 workers had packed into Cadillac Square in Detroit to protest the skyrocketing prices. To their disappointment, Reuther and the other speakers called for a "buyers' strike." Most of the workers were already on an involuntary "buyers' strike." Meat, bread and other essentials were so hard to obtain and so expensive that many could scarcely buy less.

On July 25, Truman signed a new OPA bill which permanently ended price controls for such necessities as milk, eggs and tobacco, and left prices uncontrolled on 60 per cent of all foods until August 21. Prices were allowed to zoom on clothing and thousands of household items. Final authority to decontrol any commodity was vested in a three-man decontrol board, to which Truman appointed two bankers and an industrialist. Truman admitted, as he signed the bill, that it "by no means guarantees that inflation can be avoided." The new OPA began ordering price increases so fast that the newspapers could not keep up with them.

Congress itself gave a tip-off to labor on the course the unions should follow. The members of Congress voted themselves a 50 per cent pay increase—half of it a tax-exempt "expense" account—right after passing the new OPA bill.

Reuther and the other CIO leaders turned once more to the discredited program of the "price rollback." Murray on August 2 wrote to all CIO officials "to urge President Truman to call a conference of labor and management." Reuther backed down on his earlier threat of "reopening the wage contract." Instead, he adopted the false argument that the only way to stop inflation was to get "more production."

The fallacious theory that wage increases cause price increases, which the employers and government officials were chanting in every key, was echoed by both the CIO and AFL leaders. The *CIO Economic Outlook* in August argued against demanding higher wages "at this time" because "if won, they are likely to be promptly reflected in further price increases." The CIO publication concluded that "at the present stage of events we can accomplish more by price action than by wage action." No real action was taken on either front.

The August AFL *Labor's Monthly Survey* went so far as to blame the inflation on the CIO strikes in the spring and claimed that "practically the entire living cost rise" was due to the CIO steel strike which had "forced" a "price ceiling break."

A Flint–Lansing regional conference of UAW locals representing 65,000 General Motors workers recommended that the UAW "reopen wage contracts to regain the losses suffered during the war and postwar period" and that "a clause for an upward sliding scale of wages be inserted in each union contract." Chrysler locals with 85,000 members and the giant Ford Local 600 representing 80,000 members called for reopening of wage contracts to provide for "cost-of-living" bonuses. Leading locals of the United Rubber Workers in Akron and other areas, under the initiative of Goodrich Local 5 in Akron, adopted resolutions advocating an escalator wage clause. Even in the Stalinist-dominated United Electrical Workers, the membership of the large Philadelphia Westinghouse Electric Local 107 adopted a resolution calling for the inclusion of an escalator clause in all UE contracts. In the CIO United Steelworkers, the New England District convention in September voted 300 to 50 to overturn the official Resolutions Committee's report opposing the sliding scale of wages.

The national CIO leaders, with a couple of notable exceptions, were opposed to the escalator clause. The Stalinists provided the "ideological" arguments against the sliding scale of wages. They opened the public attack in the August 23, 1946 issue of *Minnesota Labor,* Stalinist-controlled organ of the Minnesota State CIO.

The Stalinist-authored editorial, titled "Escalator Trap," misrepresented the cost-of-living bonus advocated by the CIO United Packinghouse Workers and the escalator clause proposed by CIO local unions. The editorial claimed that the proponents of the sliding scale of wages committed "the fundamental error of tying the wage rates to a disputed cost of living index" and that this "is a tacit admission that the present basic wages are adequate and need never be advanced."

Both the Packinghouse Workers and the auto and rubber locals had explicitly pointed out the inadequacy of the government's cost-of-living index. Moreover, the Stalinists were deliberately confusing two different aspects of the wage question. The fight for higher basic wage scales is intended primarily to improve the workers' living standards. The fight for the escalator clause is to maintain the buying power of basic wages during the life of the contract. Thus, the UPWA was demanding 12 to 22 cents an hour more in basic wage rates and the additional protection of an automatic cost-of-living bonus during the life of the contract. Between 1948 and 1952 most of the CIO leaders, including the Stalinists in the UE, were to approve escalator clauses. In every instance, however, they were to sacrifice increases in the basic wage rates and to tie the sliding wage clause to the BLS index. Nevertheless, those unions which adopted even inadequate escalator clauses by and large made the best wage gains between 1948 and 1959.

The CIO leaders continued for several months after the new Price Decontrol Board was set up in July 1946 to emphasize the "rollback of prices." On August 21, CIO President Philip Murray charged that the Decontrol Board's decisions had already removed 50 per cent of all foods from price regulations. Once more the meat industry withheld meat supplies, laid off thousands of packinghouse workers and demanded unlimited price ceilings. Truman's OPA tried to coax a bit more meat on the market by granting new price increases to the packers on September 6.

Leaders of 25 United Packinghouse Workers locals in Chicago and Milwaukee on September 8 demanded that the government take over and nationalize the entire meat industry. The New York State CIO also called for nationalization.

In Toledo, Ohio, the Housewives Emergency Committee organized by CIO unionists' wives demonstrated several times at City Hall. Backed by both CIO and AFL unions, the Toledo housewives forced the City Council to call on Washington to nationalize the meat industry under the control of union workers. The resolution adopted was introduced by Thomas Burke, a local CIO leader and a City Councilman. Vice-Mayor Michael V. DiSalle (later Democratic governor of Ohio) claimed the resolution was foisted on the City Council by "Trotskyites."

The September 1946 *CIO Economic Outlook* in an article, "Exploding the 'High Wage-High Price' Myth," revealed that the average industrial worker's weekly take-home pay was $4.05 less in dollars — not to speak of purchasing power — in July 1946 than in April 1945. "In fact, if you add the sharp price rise to the $4.05 cut in money wages," said the *Economic Outlook,* "poor Joe finds that his weekly pay check is now worth 19 per cent less than it was in 1945."

On October 14, "Horsemeat" Harry, as Truman had become known because of the widely-advertised sale of horse flesh, announced that he was removing all meat price controls. Within another month all but three commodity price controls were liquidated amid an orgy of price-gouging. Beef suddenly reappeared — at $1 a pound for hamburger that had sold before the war at less than 20 cents. The stock market, which since May had suffered the third longest and deepest decline in the history of the New York Stock Exchange, registered a sudden rebound the day after Truman removed all meat price controls.

The CIO United Automobile Workers International Executive Board, meeting in Cleveland October 20, announced a campaign for "substantial wage adjustments." At the same time, the CIO textile, electrical, shipbuilding, packinghouse, and oil workers unions also opened new wage campaigns. Philip Murray stated on October 26 that the United Steelworkers would ask for "healthy wage increases" after the old contracts expired in January 1947. The CIO United Rubber Workers called for a straight 26-cent hourly raise and the Oil Workers International Union on November 1 demanded $2 more per day.

At the CIO's Eighth Constitutional Convention in Atlantic City, November 18 through 22, 1946, Murray's keynote address contained no reference to communists and stressed that "without doubt the most important considerations to be presented to the convention will be the economic or wage aspects."

This was altogether different, at least as far as words went, from the program offered by William Green at the AFL convention in October. Green's entire address was centered on the fight against "totalitarian communism" and his proposal on how to protect workers against the rising cost of living was "not so much price control as the centering upon full production by the workers."

The CIO convention adopted a strongly-worded resolution on the need for "substantial wage increases" but gave no hint of a program of action to attain it. Murray concluded the wage policy discussion with one of his appeals to the rapacious industrial barons to "Come on, be decent, be gentlemen, sit around the bargaining table ... in the spirit of good faith." That was like asking wolves to say grace before meals.

O. A. Knight, President of the Oil Workers International Union, described to the CIO convention the new escalator clause contract won from the Sinclair Oil Company. "Under this plan all employes of the company receive an upward adjustment of 18 cents an hour retroactive to October 1, 1946," said Knight. "If the cost of living increases, additional upward adjustments will be made, based upon the amount of increase in the cost-of-living index and with no ceiling on upward adjustments." At the end of each quarter of the year, if the index rose three per cent, the wages would rise a corresponding percentage. Knight made it plain that in the event of a fall in living costs the downward adjustment could not go below the basic wage which included the 18-cent increase.

President Joseph Curran of the National Maritime Union made a veiled attack on the sliding scale principle. Curran, although he had developed differences with the Stalinists in the NMU, was still running interference for Stalinist ideology. He declared that "if we tie ourselves too closely to that kind of theory we will find that our standard of living will remain static." This was a distortion of the clear meaning of Knight's remarks.

On December 11, 1946, CIO President Murray made public an economic survey showing that without raising prices "total corporate business can support a 25 per cent increase in wages." By November 1946, the report showed, real weekly wages in industry were 23 per cent below the January 1945 average, "paralleled by the lushest profits in history."

The *Eighteenth Quarterly Report of OPA,* filed on November 5, gave a devastating refutation to the claim that wage increases cause price increases. It revealed that in 11 major industries the price increases granted between January 1945 and June 1946 were anywhere between 30 and 900 per cent higher than added wage costs. Of particular interest is the government agency's findings on the steel industry. Added costs due to wage increases in the iron and steel industry were only 1.6 per cent; price rises granted by OPA amounted to 11.1 per cent—almost seven times the added wage costs.

On December 16, 1946, the top leaders of the CIO steel, auto and electrical unions met in Pittsburgh for what was called a "general strategy conference" to lay plans for coordinating their wage campaigns. Murray had agreed to an extension of the U. S. Steel contract pending further negotiations. The CIO United Packinghouse Workers leaders had accepted a meager 7-1/2-cent hourly increase and dropped the demands for both the cost-of-living bonus and the guaranteed annual wage.

At this point, the CIO Oil Workers announced that its members employed by the Sinclair Oil Company had received an automatic seven-cent raise, retroactive to January 1, based on the 7.4 rise in the BLS living-cost index for the last three months of 1946. This seven-cent boost was added to the basic raise of 18 cents an hour secured in the November 15, 1946 contract.

At the UAW's National General Motors Delegates Conference on March 8, 1947 in Detroit, a resolution advocating that the GM workers demand an escalator clause similar to that won by the Sinclair Oil workers was presented by John W. Anderson, president of Detroit Fleetwood Local 15. Reuther blocked discussion on the resolution and it was referred without recommendations to the UAW's International Policy Committee, where it was buried.

In the end, each CIO union took what it could get without a struggle. The United Rubber Workers settled for 11-1/2 cents; the United Steelworkers in April accepted 12-1/2 cents plus 2-1/2 cents to adjust differentials; the United Electrical Workers took 11-1/2 cents plus 3-1/2 cents for "fringe" items. The United Automobile Workers also accepted the 15-cent pattern.

Within the first year of the Sinclair Oil escalator contract, the wage increase totalled 28 cents an hour; the other CIO workers received total gains of from 7-1/2 to 15 cents.

The CIO leaders' appeasement policy on the wage front during the spring of 1947 only emboldened the reactionary drive of the administration and Congress. This drive combined (1) the new Truman Doctrine of world-wide military intervention against anti-colonial and anti-capitalist struggles; (2) a witch hunt against communists that virtually scuttled the Bill of Rights and led to the menace of McCarthyism; (3) the enactment of an omnibus anti-labor law that wiped out the Wagner Act.

It was in this atmosphere of war-incitement, witch hunting and labor-baiting that the coal miners' struggle, suspended since December 7, 1946, was to be resumed. By a five-to-four decision on March 6, 1947, the Supreme Court upheld the federal district court injunction prohibiting the miners strike of the previous November. In addition to approving Judge Goldsborough's injunction, the Supreme Court also upheld his "contempt" citation against the United Mine Workers and John L. Lewis. But the court reduced the $3,500,000 fine on the union to $700,000 provided the UMW withdrew its cancellation of the contract with the government. Otherwise the original fine of $3,500,000 would stand.

On March 19, Lewis rescinded his previous cancellation of the contract, in compliance with the Supreme Court's order.

Justice Frank Murphy, one of the two dissenting Justices, warned that "government could easily utilize seizure as a subterfuge for breaking any and all strikes in private industry." The mine strike, he pointed out, grew out of a dispute between "the private coal operators and the private miners... The miners remained private employes despite the temporary gloss of government possession and operation of the mines."

Congressmen and senators almost to a man jubilantly hailed the Supreme Court's judicial blow against labor. Republican Representative Fred A. Hartley Jr., head of the House Labor Committee, announced that the court's decision in the miners case would be incorporated into permanent legislation binding on all unions. In this way Truman's initiation of injunction procedure against the miners led to one of the most vicious features of the impending Taft-Hartley Act.

The Centralia, Illinois mine disaster on March 25, the worst such catastrophe since 1928, gave new impetus to the miners' struggle. One hundred and eleven miners died in an explosion and fire resulting from the failure to enforce state and federal mine safety codes. A year before, the Centralia miners had warned Illinois Governor Green about the dangerous conditions that prevailed and had pleaded "please save our lives!" Of the four UMW local officers who had signed that appeal, three died in the mine and one worked on the rescue squad that sought in vain to reach them.

On April 1, 1947, at the call of Lewis, the nation's 400,000 coal miners left the pits for a six-day mourning period for the 111 dead in Centralia.

At the end of the mourning period, however, some 350,000 miners refused to re-enter pits deemed in violation of the Federal Mine Safety Code. Previously, on April 3, Secretary of the Interior Krug had ordered the closing of 518 mines violating the safety code. This was a virtual admission of the failure of the Truman administration, while operating the mines, to maintain the government's own minimum standards. The Federal Bureau of Mines, in an independent report, found that only two mines, both in Wyoming, lived up to the federal safety code.

Lewis wired the union districts to announce "the policy of immediate resumption of production at each mine as fast as it is certified by federal mine inspectors as being in conformity with the federal mine safety code." Gradually, the miners straggled back to work.

In this same month some 340,000 telephone workers waged their first national strike against the mighty American Telephone & Telegraph monopoly. Organized in the independent National Federation of Telephone Workers, the telephone strikers, the great majority of them women, fought valiantly against local injunctions, anti-picketing laws and the high-powered propaganda of the press. After five weeks the strike was gradually liquidated by local settlements, mostly for small wage gains. But it revealed the readiness for militant union action of sectors of the American working class previously considered indifferent and even hostile to unionism.

From the start of the anti-union legislative drive, it was clear that the entire labor movement was menaced. The idea of a National Congress of Labor, uniting all sections of organized labor in joint action, had won wide currency among local unions, especially in the CIO. President Philip Murray had echoed this sentiment when he appealed on December 5, 1946 to the AFL and railroad brotherhood leaders to organize joint action together with the CIO to oppose the impending anti-labor bills.

The AFL Executive Council at the end of January 1947 responded to Murray's appeal for joint action with a counter-proposal for "organic unity." The AFL leaders rejected joint defense of the labor movement short of the CIO's rejoining the AFL under its terms and conditions. At that very moment, AFL unions were stepping up their raids to chop the CIO mass industrial unions into small, weak, divided craft bodies.

Among the top AFL bureaucrats were some who were suggesting that labor itself help draft laws regulating unions. Charles J. MacGowen, president of the AFL Boilermakers, had proposed in the December 1946 issue of his *Boilermakers Journal* that the unions themselves should "see if it is not possible to pass legislation which will make strikes unnecessary except in very rare instances."

As public hearings began February 5, 1947, before the House Labor and Education Committee on a measure aimed at labor, union spokesmen issued statements that such a bill was "unjustified" and "unnecessary." A meeting of AFL lobbyists tipped off the press that they were ready to make "concessions" and "are ready to accept some milder restrictions."

Leaders of the AFL Building Trades department, keystone of the AFL craft union structure, imposed an indefinite no-strike arbitration policy on 2,000,000 building trades workers. This action was publicly announced not by the union leaders but by Truman, who early in February hailed it as a pattern of "voluntary" surrender for the entire labor movement.

Some CIO leaders, echoing Congress, sought to convey the impression that the drive for anti-labor legislation was inspired by the mine strikes which in turn were the result of Lewis's "megalomania" and "dictatorship complex." What emboldened Congress, however, was the obvious reluctance of both CIO and AFL top leaders to organize any real mass struggle against anti-union laws.

On the local level, the union ranks and leaders were eager and even pressing for united militant action to oppose the threatened union-curbing laws. During February 1947, local joint action committees of CIO, AFL and railroad brotherhoods sprang up in various cities. A state Co-operative Legislative Council was set up in West Virginia by all labor bodies. The mood of the workers, as contrasted to that of the leaders, was exemplified by a united labor demonstration on February 13 in Nashville, Tennessee.

On the streets of that Southern state capital were heard the marching feet of 2,500 white and Negro unionists united behind one banner that read: "Opposed to the Open Shop!" They entered the capitol building in a body, filed past the Governor's first-floor office and up the stairs into the gallery of the General Assembly chambers where the State Senate and House were in joint session considering a bill to ban all closed shop contracts in Tennessee. The unionists denounced the bill in a two-hour hearing. The State Senate Labor Committee subsequently reported the bill out without recommendations and the State House Labor Committee tabled it.

This dramatic demonstration of united labor action received little attention in the official labor press and no mention from top union leaders.

Both CIO President Murray and AFL President Green testified before the United States Senate Labor and Welfare Committee on

February 18-19 against the more than 250 anti-labor bills then pending in both houses of Congress. These representatives of a combined force of 15,000,000 organized workers were completely powerless, politically. There was not a single CIO or AFL voice in the whole of Congress.

Green was taunted by Republican Congressman Clare Hoffman of Michigan for offering no "constructive" proposals to "improve" the Wagner Act. The AFL chief pleaded:

"Now wait! I'm willing that the Wagner Act be changed so that the employer can engage in free speech [to attack unionism before his captive audience of employees]. On financial reports of unions, we're willing. If it's a matter of union registration, licensed on a voluntary basis, we have no objection."

The CIO National Executive Board on March 15 had designated April as "Defend Labor Month." Here and there isolated mass actions were undertaken to protest the anti-labor measures pending in both national and state legislatures. On April 16 some 20,000 Chicago packinghouse workers, many of them still wearing bloodstained work clothes, staged a one-hour work stoppage and mass demonstration to protest the anti-labor drive. In Iowa, on April 22, an estimated 100,000 CIO and AFL members went on a one-day strike to oppose a pending state bill to outlaw the closed shop.

Under the initiating pressures of local bodies the United Automobile Workers International Executive Board on April 15 called a cease-work mass demonstration in Cadillac Square, Detroit, for the afternoon of April 24. An estimated half million workers quit the plants at the appointed time and 275,000 jammed the Square and all the streets for blocks around. It was the greatest outpouring of labor in the auto center's history.

The Greater Flint CIO Council adopted a proposal for a national 24-hour protest strike to be initiated and organized by a united National Labor Conference of representatives of all locals of the CIO, AFL and railroad brotherhoods. The CIO United Packinghouse Workers convention, the National Foundry Council of the UAW, the CIO United Office and Professional Workers, and leaders of the five national CIO maritime and waterfront unions at a San Francisco conference endorsed the proposal for a 24-hour national "labor holiday." So did scores of local unions and CIO councils throughout the country.

There was definite hostility to such action in the higher labor circles. Within the CIO, the growing conflict between the Murray-Reuther and Stalinist factions and the intensified witch hunt against "communists" were fortifying the most reactionary and anti-militant

elements. An example was the Pennsylvania CIO convention in May
which banned members of the Communist Party from holding office
and then voted two-to-one against a one-day stoppage of 600,000
state CIO workers to protest the anti-labor bills.

In the House of Representatives the Hartley Bill was passed by
a vote of 308 to 107 on April 17. The House Democrats backed this
bill 93 to 84. The Taft Bill passed the Senate on May 13 by a vote
of 68 to 24, with the Democrats evenly split 21 to 21. Senate-House
conferees worked to merge the bills into one measure. The labor
leaders concentrated on an appeal to Truman to veto the impending
Taft-Hartley Bill and to persuade six Senators who had voted for
the Taft Bill to reverse their votes and thus prevent the two-thirds
majority needed to override a presidential veto.

In a nation-wide radio broadcast on May 16, CIO President Murray called for the "immediate rallying of support from millions of
Americans inside and outside the ranks of labor to enable [Truman]
to veto the bill and secure a favorable vote upholding his veto."

How were the workers to rally? What specific action were they
to take? Murray, like AFL President Green who had made a similar
broadcast on May 11, could recommend only petitions, postcards
and prayers. They feared to summon 15,000,000 workers, with their
hands on the basic means of production and distribution, to assert
their potential power.

On May 29, the joint conference committee of Congress approved
a combined measure called the Taft-Hartley Bill. This was a com-
pendium of many of the most onerous anti-labor proposals. It out-
lawed the closed shop and prohibited union shop contracts except
under very restricted conditions. It expanded the National Labor
Relations Board from three to five members and added a General
Counsel, appointed by the President, with power to determine which
cases of alleged violations were to be prosecuted in the courts. It
required a 60-day prior notice, the so-called cooling off period,
before termination or modification of a contract. It empowered the
President to set up a fact-finding board, without powers of recommendation, to inquire into any strike which he deemed to affect the
national health and safety. Upon receiving this board's report, the
President could then seek a federal court injunction to make a strike
illegal for a "cooling off" period of 80 days. It also authorized the
NLRB to seek injunctions or restraining orders to halt a whole series
of so-called unfair labor practices by unions as well as employers.
The bill made illegal secondary boycotts and jurisdictional strikes
and barred the collection of "excessive" initiation fees or dues. It
directed the NLRB to take "forthwith" legal restraining action against

any union involved in alleged secondary boycotts or "jurisdictional" strikes. It permitted employers to file damage suits against unions for breach of contract.

It also required unions to file with the Secretary of Labor annual financial statements, copies of their constitutions and by-laws, full details of how all officers were elected and their initiation fees and dues. It forbade unions and employers from contributing in cash or by indirect means, such as publicity, to the campaign funds of any candidates for federal office. It prohibited strikes by federal government employees or workers in government-owned corporations. It permitted the checkoff of dues only if the employee gave written permission to the employer. It required officers of local, national and international unions to file an affidavit swearing they were not members of the Communist Party and did not support any organization advocating overthrow of the government by force or any "unconstitutional" means.

The penalty for each violation was fixed at a year in prison or $1,000 fine or both.

The Taft-Hartley Bill thus sought to impose direct continuous government regulation over the unions in the selection of their officers, in their economic and organizational struggles and in their political activity. It established government by injunction not only in order to break strikes in private industry but to prevent unions from engaging in a host of traditional labor activities. It opened the unions to destructive damage suits by employers. It undermined union security. It made labor union officials take a special discriminatory and insulting "loyalty" oath on pain of being denied union recognition by the NLRB and of being excluded from NLRB collective bargaining polls.

The House on June 4 passed the Taft-Hartley Bill by a vote of 320 to 79. The great majority of Republicans backed the measure, as expected. But 103 Democrats also voted for it, while only 66 voted against. On June 6, the Senate endorsed the bill by a 54 to 17 vote with Senate Democrats voting 17 to 15 in favor.

Appeals for a national protest strike poured into the national CIO office from more than 100 different areas. Similar resolutions were adopted by AFL and independent locals. Some 17,000 Pennsylvania coal miners struck for several days in protest. In Los Angeles a special emergency meeting of the local AFL Central Labor Council voted to launch a Labor Caravan to Washington and invited all other labor organizations to participate.

The union motorcade left Los Angeles on June 12 and was joined en route by several hundred cars loaded with unionists of all affiliations from Detroit, Akron, Pittsburgh, Buffalo, Rochester, New York, Newark, Baltimore and other cities. The motorcade arrived in Washington on June 17 with about 1,000 union militants.

The AFL contingents were promptly summoned to national head-quarters and told to cease their joint action with the "communist"-led CIO delegations and to return home forthwith. Defying this in-junction, the AFL militants rejoined their CIO brothers and marched together down Pennsylvania Avenue to the Capitol.

The CIO top leaders also opposed the caravan. Allen Haywood, CIO national organizational director, telegraphed every CIO regional director that the caravan "has not received approval of CIO nor has national CIO authorized anyone to speak for it in behalf of caravan project. Neither has there been any consultation between national CIO and AFL officers. You are advised that CIO and national offi-cers are doing everything possible to prevent Taft-Hartley Bill from becoming law. Under these circumstances the caravan in our judg-ment is unnecessary."

CIO President Murray sent the White House a 10,000-word letter scoring the bill. Truman kept complete silence on what action he would take. On June 20 Truman announced his veto and sent a con-demnatory message to Congress. His principal argument was that the bill would not lessen strikes and would "weaken the national unity and economy at a critical time in world affairs."

Truman could count on Congress to override his veto and he could still retain the pose of "labor's friend." Indeed, Murray, Green, Reuther, Whitney and other labor leaders promptly hailed Truman, forgetting his virulent anti-labor record. Truman's veto action was to prove a vital factor in rallying labor support for his re-election in 1948, although he was to use the Taft-Hartley Act against labor more zealously than a Republican might have dared.

Within a couple of hours of Truman's veto, the House overrode it by a vote of 331 to 83, with the Democrats voting 106 to 71 to uphold what the unions called a "slave labor bill." On June 23 the Senate defeated the veto by a vote of 68 to 25. Twenty Senate Demo-crats, three more than those who voted originally for Taft-Hartley, voted to override Truman's veto; 22 voted to uphold it. Several of the latter were so-called liberals who had abstained from voting on the original passage of the Act.

AFL President Green announced that the AFL would launch "an immediate campaign for the prompt repeal" of the new Act. He asserted that "labor would never become reconciled to this law" and would fight to have it abolished if it took "fifty or 100 years." Within four months he was to propose capitulation to the Act.

Following a meeting of the CIO National Executive Board at the end of June, President Murray announced that the CIO will "work unceasingly in the political field to ensure the political repudiation of those reactionaries who are responsible for the Taft-Hartley Bill." He added: "I am not thinking in terms of a third party."

Despite the threat of the Taft-Hartley Act, hundreds of thousands of workers immediately defied it in the shipyards and coal fields. The CIO Industrial Union of Marine and Shipbuilding Workers on July 1 called out some 132,000 East Coast workers in a wage strike that lasted 84 days, when most of the struck shipyards settled for a 12-cent hourly raise. The shipbuilding division of Bethlehem Steel held out for five weeks more.

The final passage of the Act on June 23 aroused the miners to fury. About 212,000 quit the pits in Pennsylvania, Alabama, Ohio, Virginia and West Virginia. On June 30, 1947, the Smith-Connally Anti-Strike Act, under which Truman had seized the mines in May 1946, expired. Simultaneously the UMW's contract with the government also ended. But all the soft coal mines were shut down before the beginning of the ten-day scheduled vacation period ending July 8. Throughout the mining regions the embittered war cry sounded: "Let the Senators dig the coal!"

The miners scored their greatest wage victory. The leading coal operators gave in before the vacation period ended. On July 8 the miners re-entered the pits under a new contract granting a 44-1/2-cent hourly wage increase, a ten-cent per ton royalty for a union health and welfare fund and the first private contract ever to incorporate the Federal Mine Safety Code.

Especially significant were new contract clauses to protect the miners and the UMW from possible damage suits and other reprisals under the Taft-Hartley Act. The contract could be terminated on 30-day notice. Previous clauses providing penalties for "wildcat" strikes were made "null and void." To limit the possibility of civil suits under Taft-Hartley, the contract was made operative only "during such time as such persons [employees] are able and willing to work."

Both the CIO and AFL immediately announced their opposition to inclusion of no-strike clauses in union contracts and advised against use of the new NLRB machinery in negotiations or disputes. The legal department of the AFL in its official *Bulletin No. 1* on the Taft-Hartley Act advised against signing no-strike contracts as a means of avoiding breach-of-contract suits. Previously, most union leaders had encouraged no-strike clauses and urged dependence on such government agencies as the NLRB.

The CIO United Steelworkers Executive Board barred no-strike contracts because the union "will not commit itself to no-strike obligations enforceable by harassing law suits." The board also announced that it "has determined not to use the facilities of the new labor board" because it would be "deluding" its own members "if it holds any hope that use of the facilities of the new labor board would provide any protection for workers seeking to organize unions and exercising their rights to engage in collective bargaining."

The CIO United Electrical Workers urged a boycott of the NLRB because "nothing but injury can result to the interests of the membership of any union that takes a seat in this crooked game, where the rules are rigged and the dice are loaded against them..." On July 16, the United Automobile Workers announced from Detroit that it would have nothing to do with the Taft-Hartley NLRB. President John Green of the CIO Shipbuilding Workers, then on strike, advised his local unions that "it would be extremely dangerous to include no-strike clauses in your agreement."

Within two years every international union but the United Mine Workers and the International Typographical Union was to capitulate, take the Taft-Hartley "yellow dog" oath and submit to the NLRB.

The Ford Motor Company on August 6, just nine hours before a strike deadline for 108,000 workers, signed an interim agreement to waive all rights under the Taft-Hartley Act to sue the UAW-CIO or any of its officers and members for alleged damages due to strikes. The UAW negotiators were headed by Vice-President Richard T. Leonard, one of the leaders of the Thomas-Addes faction in a showdown struggle against Reuther's drive for one-man rule. Reuther had made communism the central issue and was pressing for compliance with the non-communist oath clause of the Taft-Hartley Act.

On the very day the Ford workers had made their breach in the Taft-Hartley Act, President David Dubinsky of the AFL International Ladies Garment Workers Union sent a memorandum to 450 locals and joint boards of the ILGWU advising them to sign no-strike contracts and to be prepared to file affidavits with the NLRB that their officers were not communists.

Other CIO leaders, including President L. S. Buckmaster of the United Rubber Workers, President John Green of the Shipbuilding Workers and President Emil Rieve of the Textile Workers, quickly announced their agreement with the policy of "living with" the Taft-Hartley Act. On the other hand, President Murray had made known that he opposed a compulsory "loyalty" oath "in principle" and would not comply with the Taft-Hartley law in this respect.

In the AFL, Mine Workers President John L. Lewis single-handedly blocked the AFL Executive Council from accepting NLRB General Counsel Robert N. Denham's first ruling that all AFL and CIO top officers had to sign Taft-Hartley oaths to qualify affiliated internationals for NLRB recognition. Many of the AFL craft moguls were even eager to sign the Taft-Hartley affidavit because they saw a possible advantage in this over the CIO.

At the October 1947 AFL convention in San Francisco, Lewis pleaded with the AFL leaders not to "debase" themselves by "groveling" before Congress and amending the constitution to permit them to sign the non-communist Taft-Hartley oath. He publicly lashed the AFL leaders "who run like cravens before the Taft-Hartley law."

"At least once in your lives," he thundered at the squirming Executive Council members on the convention platform, "you should do your duty by your membership." Those AFL leaders who refused to fight the "first ugly, savage thrust of fascism in America," he said, reminded him of the Biblical passage, "Lions led by asses." For the mighty host of eight million AFL workers are "marching across the plains of America and having their thinking done for them by fat and stately asses."

Tobin, Meany and Dubinsky spoke in favor of an AFL constitutional amendment eliminating all officers excepting president and secretary-treasurer so that AFL Vice-President Lewis could no longer block NLRB recognition of AFL affiliates by his refusal to sign the Taft-Hartley oath. Tobin even proclaimed that "I'm happy to have the chance to say by affidavit, 'I'm not a Communist.'" The convention voted to eliminate vice-presidencies.

Lewis pulled the miners out of the AFL without trying to organize a serious battle. He did not think in terms of mobilizing the ranks to fight against the leadership. His answer to the bureaucracy's act of twisting the organization's constitution was to send a contemptuous note on a crumpled slip of paper to the AFL president: "Green. We disaffiliate. Lewis."

The CIO Executive Board on October 10 adopted a policy of "neutrality" toward the question of signing or not signing the Taft-Hartley affidavit. The board proposed to leave the determination up to each affiliated union. No opposition in principle was raised to submission to the Taft-Hartley law.

Three days later, the 600 delegates to the Ninth Constitutional Convention of the CIO, held in Boston, adopted a resolution presented by the Resolutions Committee headed by Lee Pressman, stating that each affiliated international union "will determine for itself the policy to be pursued in relation to the new Labor Board."

Murray told the CIO convention that he had "personal convictions" against filing a Taft-Hartley affidavit. But he urged the convention to adopt a resolution permitting any other CIO officer to sign. The Textile Workers, Shipbuilding Workers, and Brewery Workers leaders promptly announced their decision to take the Taft-Hartley oath.

On October 31, President Walter Reuther informed the NLRB that the UAW Executive Board had voted to comply with the Taft-Hartley provisions. This was heralded in the daily press as a "capitulation" that would "break the log jam" in the CIO against submission to the oath. Vice-President R. J. Thomas, however, informed the NLRB the next day: "I have no intentions of and will not sign such affidavit..." A resolution to conform with the Taft-Hartley Act was finally pushed through the auto union's convention by a two-to-one vote on November 10.

The CIO was in wild retreat before the forces of reaction. Instead of uniting in struggle against the profiteering employers, the CIO leaders were engaged in a "cold war" against each other and the membership.

PART VI

COLD WAR
IN THE CIO

1946-1947

26

The Cold-War
Witch Hunt Begins

The CIO's policies and activities in the years following the 1946 strike wave were increasingly influenced by the international conflict between the capitalist and non-capitalist world called the "cold war." This was tied up with the savage faction fight between the Murray-Reuther and the Stalinist factions from 1946 to 1950 that ended in a damaging split. How did it happen and who was responsible?

Just as imperial Rome stamped its "Pax Romana" — its "Roman Peace" — on the ancient world, so American capitalism dreamed of imposing a "Pax Americana" on the modern postwar world. The United States felt assured of global domination not merely because of industrial and technological superiority. America's monopoly of the atomic bomb meant it could bully, blackmail or blow into submission any other part of the world—the Soviet Union, first of all.

However, the hopes of America's ruling class that its World War II victory would assure it world dominance and super-profits were rudely shattered. The Soviet Union had survived the Nazi onslaught and revealed an astonishing military strength. China, the great prize of the Pacific War, was snatched away by the vast revolutionary upheaval of the Chinese people. American troops were reluctant to be used as suppressors of colonial peoples. Moreover, the colossal strike wave of 1945-46 had shown that the very home base of U. S. imperialism was none too secure.

A quick, easy settlement of world issues was ruled out. American capitalism faced an unexpectedly drawn-out period of costly attempts to restabilize its world system and prepare a new world war. There were to be no short cuts. Popular opposition at home, actual or potential, had to be suppressed; civil liberties had to be crushed; labor's rights had to be strangled. A protracted, nerve-wracking course of maneuvers to line up international allies had to be pursued. "Communism" had to be "contained."

The internal warfare that dominated the CIO from 1947 to 1950 was initiated by the top CIO leadership against the Stalinists in conformity with the "cold war" foreign policy pursued by the U. S. State Department and in line with directions from the White House. The policy of class collaboration on domestic issues had its counter-part in collaboration with American imperialism in the international sphere. In matters of foreign policy, the union officialdom main-tained an attitude of unconcealed servility and conformity.

During the period of the U. S.-Soviet wartime alliance, the pro-Roosevelt CIO leaders had maintained an actual, if informal, alli-ance with the Stalinists. At the November 1944 CIO convention, for example, the alliance of the Murray machine and the Stalinists was so close that Lee Pressman wrote the resolutions presented to the convention.

The "togetherness" of the CIO bureaucracy and the Stalinists reached a high point on the international arena when the CIO and the pro-Empire British union leaders engineered the formation in Feb-ruary 1945 of the World Federation of Trade Unions together with the Soviet Union's representatives. The WFTU eventually suffered the fate of the U. S.-Soviet alliance itself and the CIO leaders, along with their British trade union allies, found the occasion in 1949 for splitting the WFTU when the State Department required it.

The struggle against the Stalinist wing of the CIO bureaucracy was initially a fight of the real militants against the bureaucratic misrule and class collaboration policy pursued by the Stalinists. It was an extension of the resistance to the similar policies of the whole trade union bureaucracy. This was a necessary and progres-sive fight.

Although the Stalinists played only a secondary role in the UAW, during the war and in early 1946 they supported the wing of the UAW leadership which opposed the militant General Motors strike policies. In the struggle over the issues and conduct of the strike, the militants had supported the Reuther wing of the UAW leadership as against the Thomas-Addes faction and elected Reuther to his first term as UAW president. Many of these same militants then voted to make Thomas the first vice-president, indicating that they by no means desired to entrust unchallenged rule to Reuther.

In an article on the UAW convention in the May 1946 *Fourth Inter-national* magazine, I noted that Reuther in his bid for the UAW presi-dency had "played conservative," that his supporters had included not only progressive elements but "many questionable and reactionary elements" and that "in evaluating the role of the various top leaders and tendencies in the coming period, the militants will have to keep in mind the possibilities of shifts and changes." I recalled that "Reuther himself, the most progressive of the UAW leaders in 1946, was a chief spokesman in 1941 for the right-wing tendency which sought to bar 'communists' and which advanced a pro-war policy."

Paradoxically, the first open and direct battle against the Stalinists following the war began within a union under their complete control and within their own faction. That was the National Maritime Union.

The NMU had been organized in 1937 in struggle against the reactionary leadership of the old AFL Seafarers International Union. Joseph Curran had first won prominence in the great West Coast maritime and waterfront strike of 1936. He then worked to mobilize the East Coast seamen to join this battle. The bitter opposition of the SIU-AFL leaders and of Ryan's machine in the International Longshoremen's Association inspired the East Coast seamen to form the National Maritime Union under Curran's leadership and to affiliate with the CIO.

When the war began, the Stalinist machine had a complete stranglehold on the NMU. The seamen pressed in vain to break through the bureaucratic crust that had formed around the union. Since the Stalinists were the most zealous supporters of United States participation in the war, they dealt mercilessly with the rank and file. The NMU leaders collaborated with the National Maritime Commission and the Coast Guard in victimizing militants who tried to defend the interests of the merchant seamen. Curran himself before the end of the war was calling for a permanent postwar no-strike policy.

The postwar shift in the world Stalinist line, which resulted in the removal of Earl Browder as national secretary of the Communist Party in 1945 and his expulsion in February 1946, had repercussions within the unions. The shake-up within the CP apparatus and the pressure of the NMU membership as the CIO strike wave began to roll set off a conflict in the top NMU leadership. This conflict, which had been bottled up for many months in the top circles finally broke out into the open.

The November 23, 1945 *Pilot,* official NMU paper, reported the resignation of several leaders, including Ralph Rogers, a national director, whose statement of charges against a section of the Stalinist leaders was published, as well as counter-charges against him. He revealed the pressure and harassment put on him after his opposition to a campaign by the NMU National Council to sell as a "great victory" a 1944 WLB decision which gave the seamen nothing. Other NMU officials, including old-time Communist Party adherents, were also forced to resign. Curran and Treasurer Hedley Stone charged that their telephones had been tapped at the direction of Joseph Stack, NMU New York Port Agent.

An NMU "investigating committee," heavily weighted with loyal supporters of the Foster faction in the Communist Party, was set up to "study" the various charges and counter-charges. When the results of the "investigation" were reported, Curran, the committee's sole dissenter, called the findings a "whitewash" of the Stalinist machine's policies and of those then adhering to it.

At an NMU membership meeting in New York City on February 18, 1946, Curran partially revealed for the first time the scandalous conduct of the Stalinist machine of which he had been a part. He said that "the union is in the hands of a machine...that is going to tell you how you are going to work or else...The machine tells you who is a phony in the union, the machine tells you who to elect, who to fire. The machine tells you who to bring on charges."

Curran revealed how Stalinist policy cost the NMU the key collective bargaining election in the Standard Oil tanker fleet. He reported that New York Port Agent Stack, who was also a member of the New York State Committee of the Communist Party, "keeps a regular FBI set of cards in the Port Registration Office" on the working seamen. Curran demanded the resignation of the four top Stalinist NMU officials, Vice-Presidents Frederick "Blackie" Meyers and Howard McKenzie, National Secretary Ferdinand Smith, and Stack.

However, at a meeting of the National Committee of the Communist Party on February 5, National Chairman William Z. Foster stated: "We have a very dangerous situation in the NMU. We have done our best to try to adjust the situation and have been unable to accomplish it...There has been a little surgery in the NMU but apparently not enough. If these comrades continue in defying the party line we will have to do some more surgery."

In the initial stages of the NMU internal fight Curran was forced to take his case to the membership, to appeal to the militants and carry on a progressive battle against the entrenched bureaucracy he himself had helped to create. The Stalinist machine was attacked for its real crimes against the workers and there was no resort to redbaiting or patriotic flag-waving.

One of the first manifestations of the redbaiting drive occurred in another union, the United Steelworkers. As the Truman administration, Congress, and the press whipped up anti-Soviet hatred, a campaign was launched in the United Steelworkers against "communists" and "reds."

In preparation for the convention on May 14-18, 1946, Murray's appointees toured the steel locals to line up nearly 300 local resolutions, calling for constitutional amendments to deny the right of "communists and socialists" to hold office and even to deny union membership to "reds." At the convention itself it became increasingly clear that most of the rank-and-file delegates, fresh from their recent triumph in the first national steel strike, were in no mood for a redbaiting campaign. Just before the convention, Murray, sensing the mood, summoned a meeting of the Steelworkers Executive Board and instructed them to call off the whole campaign. Instead, he introduced a "Statement of Policy" which included no proposals for constitutional restrictions on radicals. The "Statement" did, however, say that "this union will not tolerate efforts by outsiders—individuals, organizations or groups—whether they be Communists, Socialists or any other group, to infiltrate, dictate or meddle in our affairs." The chief outside meddlers in the steel union, as in the whole labor movement, were the Democratic administration and the Democratic Party, of which Murray and his faction were members and agents. In addition, the Association of Catholic Trade Unionists, an organization directed by the clergy, was freely roiling the waters inside the CIO and inciting the anti-communist campaign. But no one was under the misapprehension that Murray intended the resolution to be directed against either the Democratic Party or the ACTU.

At the same time, the "Statement of Policy" insisted that "we will not permit any limitation on the free and democratic right of full discussion of trade union problems in our own ranks. We must not and do not seek interference with the free and democratic right of each member to harbor such views as he chooses. Our union has not been and will not be an instrument of repression... As a democratic institution, we engage in no purges, no witch hunts. We do not dictate a man's thoughts or beliefs."

The inclusion of a promise of "no purges, no witch hunts" was designed to allay the fears of many steelworkers that a purge of the militants was being contemplated at that time. The steel convention did, in fact, revolt against attempts by the Murray machine to increase its powers and control through constitutional amendments. The delegates voted down proposals to increase the term of office for national executives from two to four years, or to change the basis of representation in order to greatly reduce the number of delegates to conventions.

With each new move of the Truman administration's "get tough with Russia" campaign, the Democratic Party forces in the CIO introduced new bureaucratic measures against the Stalinist faction. The latter had entrenched themselves in a number of key local CIO councils, including the New York, Cleveland, Detroit and Los Angeles bodies, as well as a number of international unions. While Murray himself maintained a formal attitude of seeking to preserve unity in the CIO, his right-wing machine and allies were intensifying their attack on communists in the local councils.

In August 1946, the Philadelphia CIO Council took action to bar communists from holding office in that body. The leader of the redbaiting right-wing faction was Harry Block, a vice-president of the CIO United Electrical Workers and ally of James B. Carey, former UE president and the CIO national secretary. The Stalinists surrendered without a fight on the basis of a deal to accept the resolution barring communists in return for the withdrawal by their opponents of more drastic measures. (From first to last in the four-year struggle within the CIO, the Stalinists followed a similar supine policy except when they had mechanical majorities. Then they met their opposition with the same sort of anti-democratic, repressive organizational measures.)

At the UE's national convention in September 1946, the Carey-Block faction opened an attack on the communists and ran a slate against the incumbent officers. The right-wingers had no program for the workers except unrestrained redbaiting. The Stalinist leadership, for its part, put forward a seemingly more militant program. They backtracked on their wartime incentive-pay program by calling for safeguards in existing incentive-pay plans and no further introduction of such plans. They also endorsed the 30-hour week and guaranteed annual wage. The Carey-Block slate was defeated by a nearly six-to-one margin.

One of the ironies of this UE convention was the address of CIO President Murray in which he felt impelled to praise the UE leadership for the "splendid support" they had given "all national policies" of the CIO and to Murray personally. At that very moment Murray's emissaries were moving to clip the power of the Stalinists in local councils where the latter had succeeded in imposing their rule.

In Cleveland, the CIO Council had been split when the Amalgamated Clothing Workers delegates walked out in May, followed by the Steel, Utility and Oil Workers in July. The Stalinists who dominated the council provoked the split when they tried to fire the editor of the local CIO paper on flimsy charges and without a fair hearing. In order to counter a motion that they draw up charges and hold a fair trial, the Stalinist faction pushed through a motion asking CIO President Murray to intervene. He did so by sending the national organizational director, Allan S. Haywood, who placed the Cleveland Council in the hands of a receiver.

On this occasion Haywood laid down the terms of a "peace program" which embodied conditions for the conduct of the Cleveland Council that were to be formally adopted by the national CIO several months later for all local councils. In addition to stipulating that George De Nucci, the administrator, was to preside at all Cleveland Council meetings, that five resigned right-wingers be restored to the local Executive Board and that new council elections be held at a time De Nucci should decide, the council was to refrain from acting on resolutions dealing with international matters, except those endorsed by the national CIO. It must also cease to send delegates to gatherings of other organizations, specifically the National Negro Congress and Civil Rights Federation, unless endorsed by the national CIO. This was part of the technique that was subsequently used to break the control of the Stalinists in all local and state councils, even where they had a clear majority, and to proscribe all views different from or contrary to those held by the right wing. Pressed between the two powerful bureaucratic blocs, the rank and file and the real militants were increasingly silenced. The Stalinist leaders in the Cleveland CIO agreed not only to the imposition of an outside dictator-receiver but to far-reaching anti-democratic restrictions on expressions of views and on fraternal association. These latter restrictions violated the traditional policies of the CIO since its founding.

On the eve of the CIO national convention, the CIO Executive Board on November 15, 1946 adopted a ruling directing local and state CIO councils to limit their activities and statements "to issues of local and state concern and to matters of general policy that have been passed upon by the national CIO. Councils shall take no action or issue statements in conflict with CIO policy. They shall not send delegates or make any contributions to national organizations not recognized by the CIO." This ruling also asserted the power of the national office of the CIO "to assign duly accredited CIO Representatives" to "work closely" with local and state councils to see that they "comport themselves" in line with the directive.

This ruling, which strengthened the hand of the top bureaucracy against the ranks, was adopted with the assenting votes of the Stalinist members of the CIO National Executive Board. Although the Stalinists pretended otherwise, this decision was aimed immediately against their rule in numerous local and state bodies. But it had the broader effect of restricting these CIO organizations in assisting civil liberties and civil rights groups, or in freely expressing views on current national and international problems.

27

Conflict over
the Marshall Plan

The CIO national convention, held in Atlantic City, November 18-22, 1946, took the organization's first formal action directed specifically at the Stalinists. Prior to the convention, the capitalist press had conducted a propaganda campaign to incite a rabid drive against communists at the CIO gathering. Professional anticommunists like the social democrats and the Association of Catholic Trade Unionists had tried to whip up an all-out offensive against the so-called left wing. Stalinist "leftism" consisted, not in more militant trade union policies, but in the single point of advocating a peace pact between Washington and Moscow.

Murray was fearful of any open strife inside the CIO. He was still looking back over his shoulder at John L. Lewis, then leading a great struggle against the attempt to break the AFL United Mine Workers strike with a government seizure and injunction. The CIO president secured Stalinist agreement in advance of the convention to a "Declaration of Policy" that was not as strong as the extreme right-wingers were demanding but still directly condemned the Stalinists and opened the way for attack on them throughout the CIO.

The CIO convention gave a surface impression of harmony. Indeed, the emphasis appeared to be on the opening of the "second round" wage campaign to offset the bounding inflation. Resolutions were strongly anti-militarist. The convention voted for discontinuation of the stockpiling of atom bombs; denounced compulsory military conscription; demanded withdrawal of American troops from China. However, the most decisive and lasting action of the convention occurred in the half hour of the first afternoon's session devoted to the communist issue.

Murray introduced his "Declaration of Policy" that said "we resent and reject efforts of the Communist Party or other political parties and their adherents to interfere in the affairs of the CIO." Three well-known Stalinist union leaders were part of the six-man committee which drafted the declaration and made the vital concession to the redbaiters. A number of Stalinist heads of unions were on the 51-man CIO Executive Board that unanimously endorsed the declaration.

In presenting the declaration to the convention, Murray claimed that "it should not be misconstrued to be a repressive measure...It does not convey the impression to a single, solitary member of this Union that this organization is going to engage itself in diabolical pursuits. That must not be resorted to."

Murray demanded a vote on the "resent and reject" statement without "needless debate." The "Declaration of Policy" was adopted by an overwhelming majority. When Murray called for the opposition vote, the convention was surprised to see two well-known Communist Party followers in the National Maritime Union, Howard McKenzie and Joseph Stack, break party discipline and vote against the declaration. At adjournment of the session, a group of Stalinists surrounded McKenzie and Stack to harangue them publicly. Under this pressure, the two rushed to the platform and buttonholed Murray. He called the convention to order and reported that the two dissenting votes were withdrawn and he was happy to announce that the declaration against the interference of the Communist Party in the CIO was adopted "unanimously."

The day before the convention, George Morris had written in the November 17 issue of the *Sunday Worker* that any "knuckling down [to the redbaiters] by the CIO would only whet the reactionary appetite..." Two days later, in the November 19 *Daily Worker,* Morris wrote that the CIO's declaration that "we resent and reject efforts of the Communist Party...to interfere in the affairs of the CIO" was "the long sought-for answer of the CIO" to the demands for a reactionary red-purge. The Communist Party "especially," Morris wrote, had "always favored a statement telling the world the CIO isn't Communist." He concluded that the declaration "leaves the basis for continued unity, freedom of thought and political affiliation."

This Stalinist "statesmanship" tried to conceal the fact that the CIO "Declaration of Policy" actually provided the formula for continuing and extending the witch hunt. The December, 1946 issue of *Steel Labor,* official paper of Murray's own United Steelworkers, reported the CIO's declaration and revised local council rules under the headline, "Red Activity in Local Councils Barred by CIO." The Connecticut CIO's *Connecticut Vanguard* blazoned on its masthead, "We Resent and Reject Communism."

Within two weeks of the adoption of the "resent and reject" dec-claration, the Massachusetts CIO convention in early December passed a resolution barring "members of the Communist Party and other Communist organizations" from holding office. The right-wing leadership also pushed through constitutional amendments cut-ting the size of the state executive committee from 34 to 10, thus eliminating representation from several unions then under Stalinist influence.

The New Jersey CIO convention, a few days later, was the scene of a prolonged debate and redbaiting outburst over a resolution to endorse the national "Declaration of Policy" and to "resist and fight, in democratic fashion, any and all attempts of the Communist Party and its adherents in or out of the CIO to foist their policies on our organization."

At the California State CIO convention, December 12-15, 1946, a militant minority opposed a resolution, introduced by the state Executive Board, to endorse the CIO's "resent and reject" decla-ration. The Stalinists themselves supported the resolution. One, Henry Gliksohn of Harry Bridges' Longshoremen's and Warehouse-men's Union, pledged himself and his party to "loyally carry out the decision."

Administrative measures against the Stalinist faction came thick and fast. One of the first moves was a letter from the national CIO to all local and state councils to "discontinue forthwith all fund-raising, membership solicitation and other work in support of" the National Negro Congress and to work only with the National Association for the Advancement of Colored People. The November *Textile Labor,* organ of the CIO Textile Workers, advised "sincere rightists" who did not think the CIO convention had gone "far enough" that it "is on the administrative level that the Declaration of Policy... and the new industrial union council rules will be implemented."

Some of the Stalinist union leaders took the Communist Party's line of "statesmanlike" support of the "resent and reject" resolu-tion so seriously that they put out their own "resent and reject" statements in unions under their control. On December 15, Lewis Merrill, president of the CIO United Office and Professional Workers union and long identified with Stalinist policies, issued a UOPWA statement directing members and officers not to "become identified with this or that wing" of the labor movement, including the Com-munist Party. In fact, the Merrill statement threatened that "any effort to impose the viewpoint of outside organizations" on the union "will be met by the firmest exercise of union discipline." He set the example by publicly resigning as a contributing editor to the

New Masses magazine and from the Board of Trustees of the Communist Party's Jefferson School of Social Science in New York City.

The *Daily Worker* then had to take notice of such an obsequious concession to the redbaiters by one of the CP's more prominent followers. The CP organ dissociated itself from Merrill's move in an editorial headed: "Appeasement of Redbaiting Never Paid." But Merrill was carrying to its logical conclusion the "statesmanship" of the CP itself.

By January 1947, the internal struggle within the CIO was given new impetus by external political developments. This was the formation of two organizations—the Progressive Citizens of America (PCA) representing the Wallace tendency, and the Americans for Democratic Action (ADA) representing the liberals adhering to the official foreign policy of the Truman administration.

At the PCA's founding conference in New York City on December 29, 1946, a statement was adopted strongly criticizing the Democratic Party but leaving open the possibility of remaining within its framework. "It is not clear now whether this party will recover its progressive tradition or surrender to its own brand of ignorance and bigotry," said the PCA preamble. It added, "We cannot...rule out the possibility of a new political party, whose fidelity to our goals can be relied upon." From the start, the Stalinists were active in the Wallace movement, although Wallace and his colleagues in the Democratic Party left wing dictated the program, officers and political moves of the PCA.

Henry A. Wallace served more than three terms under Roosevelt either as a member of Roosevelt's cabinet or as vice-president. He had been editor and publisher of *Wallace's Farmer,* a leading farm journal established by his father, whose hybrid corn business Henry inherited. He had hailed the atomic bomb as a major triumph of the Roosevelt "New Deal." When Roosevelt had demanded Saudi Arabian oil during the war, Wallace had boasted that "this was not ruthless imperialism" but "good old-fashioned American imperialism" and "the United States is proud of it." He stated during a tour abroad in Stockholm on April 18, 1947:

"I am not a Communist, I am not a Socialist, I am only an American capitalist—or as I told the House of Parliament in London—I am a progressive Tory who believes it is absolutely essential to have peace and understanding with Russia."

Wallace summed up his program in that period with his words: "We must talk with Stalin." This was scarcely a radical program, but Wallace was denounced as a "traitor" for prematurely advocating discussions with Moscow. On the other hand, the Stalinists

began to depict Wallace as a great "savior" and "man of the people."
George Morris, labor editor of the *Daily Worker,* wrote approvingly
of the Wallace-type "progressive capitalist": "Liberals who favor
further advances along the Roosevelt path to 'make capitalism work'
won't get us sore. On the contrary, they have and will continue, to
find us among the most vigorous supporters of every step."

Within a couple of weeks of the formation of Wallace's Progressive Citizens of America, another section of "New Deal" liberals
who had been associated with Roosevelt, together with some of the
most actively anti-communist union leaders, formed the Americans for Democratic Action. It included such notables as Eleanor
Roosevelt, former OPA Director Leon Henderson, former Housing
Expediter Wilson Wyatt and former Governor and later Senator
Herbert Lehman of New York. Sponsoring and attending the conference was a group of CIO leaders which included Walter Reuther.
James Carey and Allan Haywood were there as personal representatives of CIO President Murray.

The ADA represented itself as the liberal defender of "democracy" against "communism"—meaning supporters of the "get tough
with Russia" policy of the Truman administration. Murray adopted
a neutral attitude since he did not wish as yet to precipitate an open
fight between the PCA and ADA forces inside the CIO. At his bidding, the CIO Executive Board issued a statement that the CIO was
not supporting either organization. However, individual CIO leaders
continued to give support to the two opponent political groupings.

The establishment of the Progressive Citizens of America posed
the threat of split in the Democratic Party and the building of an
opponent party along neo-New Deal lines. One response to this
threat was not only the founding of ADA; another was stepped-up
organizational measures against all those in the CIO who did not
toe the political mark laid down by the right wing. The Stalinists,
who continued until 1948 to avow their desire to function within the
Democratic Party machine, were subjected to increasing attack and
harsh redbaiting.

The Carey faction in the United Electrical Workers, using the
CIO convention's "resent and reject" declaration as a springboard,
launched a drive against the UE leadership. Running on a strictly
anti-communist program with no policy for defending the ranks
against the employer attacks, the right-wingers in January 1947
ousted the Stalinist leadership in two key UE units —Westinghouse
Local 601 in Pittsburgh and General Electric Local 203 at Bridge-
port, Connecticut. No-holds-barred factional struggle followed.

One of the groups campaigning most aggressively against the

"outside interference" of the Communist Party in the CIO was the Association of Catholic Trade Unionists. This group was under the direct leadership of Catholic priests. It was able to put a great deal of pressure on some Catholic unionists like Philip Murray.

The ACTU is a unique formation, representing a specifically religious labor policy based on the dogmas of the Roman Catholic Church. These dogmas are not an outgrowth of the development and experience of the labor movement. They are not the expression of a working-class tendency. They are the product of an organized, world-wide religious institution, centuries old, and now closely linked by property interests with the capitalist system. The ACTU is a power bloc advancing in the labor movement the divisive doctrine of special religious groupings fighting for their various religious programs.

This agency, directed by the Catholic hierarchy, incited the most reactionary tendencies inside the CIO to wage the witch hunt against communists. The January 17, 1947 issue of the ACTU's *Labor Leader* tells how the ACTU "rescued" UE Local 453 in Yonkers, New York, from the "outside interference" of the Communist Party by helping the right wing take control of the local. The paper boasted: "The ACTU was invited by both the executive board and the membership to set up a Labor School right in the union hall to train the local's membership."

Such moves to destroy the Stalinist control of unions like the UE and Mine, Mill and Smelter Workers even to the extent of fostering splits, were paralleled by direct measures of the national CIO against individual Stalinists. One of the most significant was Murray's removal of Harry Bridges, head of the CIO Longshoremen's and Warehousemen's Union, from the post of director of the California CIO in early 1947. This was done under the guise of separating the state CIO into two divisions, northern and southern, leaving Bridges in charge only of the northern wing.

Murray struck a further blow at the democratic rights of state and local CIO councils when he issued a national ruling early in January 1947, prohibiting the lower bodies from making contributions or sending delegates to any national organization except a hand-picked list of 36 approved by the top CIO leaders. The bias of the list was very clear. Among the 36 approved bodies were a number of foreign relief agencies — but not those of Yugoslavia and Poland, two of the most terribly stricken countries in the war.

Agitation for a more active purge of communists in the CIO was intensified with the initiation of the Truman Doctrine. On March 12, 1947, Truman announced the new doctrine of American imperialist intervention in the eastern hemisphere, specifically Europe and Asia, when he asked Congress for authority to send military supplies and missions to Greece and Turkey. The President sought to buttress the Greek monarchy and the Turkish military dictatorship against civil uprisings as the first open moves in the military encirclement of the Soviet Union. This Greek-Turkish "aid" program was pushed through Congress and enacted within two months.

ILGWU-AFL President David Dubinsky was the first of the top union leaders to endorse Truman's new foreign policy. Murray at first steered clear of any explicit endorsement of the Truman Doctrine. It was too obviously a form of militarist intervention in the affairs of other countries. In the meantime, the right-wing offensive against the Stalinists and their allies in the CIO was intensified. Murray himself gave the signal at a meeting of the CIO National Executive Board in May 1947.

Members of the CIO Board had complained that their unions were under attack for "harboring Communists." Murray replied: "It is high time the CIO leaders stopped apologizing for Communism. If Communism is an issue in any of your unions, throw it to hell out, and throw its advocates out along with it. When a man accepts office...to render service to workers, and then delivers that service to other outside interests, that man is nothing but a damned traitor." He did not apply that term to union leaders like himself who served the "outside interests" of the party of Southern Bourbons and big city bosses.

Murray's CIO Executive Board statement was adopted as the masthead statement of *The Real UE,* organ of the Carey-Block right-wing faction, which called itself the UE Members for Democratic Action and carried on an unmitigated redbaiting campaign inside the United Electrical, Radio and Machine Workers.

The Communist Party and its publications had pretended all along that Murray was no party to the campaign against them. Not until a month after his statement to throw "to hell out" the "advocates" of "Communism," did the Stalinist press venture a faint bleat of protest. The June 10, 1947 *Daily Worker* conceded that the "generally progressive CIO at its last convention took the first false step" when it adopted the resolution to "resent and reject" the "interference of the Communist Party."

At this juncture, the Marshall Plan, first proclaimed by Secretary of State George C. Marshall in a speech at Harvard University on June 5, 1947, provided the camouflage the CIO leaders needed to put over the Truman Doctrine. United States foreign policy looked to the remilitarization of the Western European capitalist nations

and their combination into an anti-Soviet alliance. Before this could
be accomplished, the private profit economies of these war-bereft
and bankrupt countries, whose workers had moved in mass to the
left, had to be stabilized.

Murray responded to these foreign policy developments with further moves to drive suspected Communists from appointive CIO
posts. In July he forced the resignation of four Stalinists on his staff
who had served him faithfully for years. They were *CIO News* Editor
Len De Caux, Associate Editor Fred Avila, Circulation Manager
Harry Gantt and Robert Lamb, Washington legislative representative
of the United Steelworkers.

A struggle inside the International Union of Mine, Mill and Smelter Workers, which had long been Stalinist-dominated, led to direct
intervention of the national CIO in the affairs of an international
union. The anti-"red" faction had come close to putting over a resolution at the IUMMSW convention in 1946 to bar communists from
union posts. It was defeated by a vote of 439 to 401. In the subsequent election for national officers by referendum vote, the election
committee split. A majority declared Reid Robinson, incumbent
president, re-elected. Maurice Travis, Robinson's appointed assistant, was declared elected to the vice-presidency. The minority
of the election committee charged that the opposition had really
won. This provided a pretext for a right-wing split of a claimed
one-fourth of the Mine-Mill locals. Most of them joined the CIO
International Union of Marine and Shipbuilding Workers, run by
right-winger John Green.

The national CIO stepped in after Robinson resigned from the
Mine-Mill presidency and Travis assumed Robinson's post. At the
direction of the CIO National Executive Board, Philip Murray set up
a three-man committee of Amalgamated Clothing Workers President Jacob Potofsky, United Steelworkers Vice-President Van A.
Bittner, and United Rubber Workers President L. S. Buckmaster,
all dependable right-wingers, to lend their "good offices" toward
the settlement of the Mine-Mill dispute. This committee reported
back in July. It proposed the removal of Travis as IUMMSW president and the appointment by Murray of an administrator over the
union. While the committee chided the splitters and the shipbuilding
union for taking them in, it dealt its main blows at the IUMMSW
officers who "have allowed the influence of the Communist Party to
interfere with the internal affairs of the international union."

The Stalinists, for their part, were doing their share to exacer-
bate the situation. In August, the Wallace forces and the Stalinists in
California launched a state third party—the Independent Progressive

Party. Most of the members of the 34-man committee heading the drive to put the IPP on the state ballot were union officials. The chairman was Hugh Bryson, head of the CIO Marine Cooks and Stewards. Bryson was quoted in the August 26, 1947 *Daily Worker* as saying the new party was designed to "strengthen the position of progressives in the Democratic Party" and to "help send a Wallace delegation to the Democratic National Convention in 1948."

The Murray machine seized an important sector of the CIO from the Stalinists at the Illinois State convention in August. Joseph Germano, District 31 Steelworkers director, was elected Illinois State CIO president in a rough-and-tumble convention which saw right-wingers using physical tactics as well as violent redbaiting against the Stalinists. The latter, no novices themselves in the use of such methods, sent up a wail of protest which Murray did not deign to notice.

When the rights of unionists who supported them were under attack, the Stalinists raised a hue and cry about "democracy." But where they were in control, as in the United Electrical Workers, they used the club on all opposition. In March 1947, the Stalinist-controlled General Executive Board of the UE-CIO adopted a resolution terming the Carey-Block caucus — the UE Committee for Democratic Action—a "dual movement" and calling on it "to dissolve." This was followed by a campaign in the locals which poured forth a flood of resolutions urging the coming UE convention to take drastic action against the "outside interference in the affairs of the union" by the Carey-Block CDA.

At the UE convention in Boston the last week of September 1947, the Stalinist caucus rammed through a resolution aimed to illegalize all factions but its own. The resolution ordered the dissolution of the UE Committee for Democratic Action, the leading opposition caucus. This group was a bloc of social democratic elements, the Association of Catholic Trade Unionists, and others united on the sole program of anti-communism and support of the Truman Doctrine. The resolution further stated that if opposition members "persist in their disruption" the UE leaders would "drive them out of the union." A constitutional amendment was passed that empowered the UE General Executive Board to suspend any local "in circumstances which might lead to revocation of charter."

The ninth convention of the CIO opened October 13, 1947 in Boston. The pro-U. S. State Department wing was eager for the "kill." Philip Murray, as he had done at the 1946 convention, still kept a restraining hand on those who wanted to drive out the communists forthwith. He tried to preserve a surface unity while imposing his

line with ambiguously worded resolutions which he would be free
to interpret as he saw fit after the convention.

All resolutions submitted to the convention by the CIO Executive
Board had been adopted unanimously by the board, including its
Stalinist members. All recommendations from the resolutions committee were submitted unanimously and the convention adopted them
unanimously. The foreign policy resolution did not directly support
the Marshall Plan; it approved the shipment of food and other aid
to needy countries, provided it was not used "to coerce free peoples."
Walter Reuther, UAW president, and George Baldanzi, executive
vice-president of the Textile Workers, proclaimed their full support of the Marshall Plan. Murray then added that he personally
favored the "Marshall idea."

Murray attained his ends by converting the convention into a
demonstration for Secretary of State George C. Marshall, the chief
guest speaker. The former Army Chief of Staff was escorted to the
platform with the blare of a navy band and a host of dignitaries. Murray introduced him with effusive and grandiloquent homage. Marshall
addressed the convention, warning against "enemies of democracy"
and those who would "undermine the confidence of the labor element in the stability of our institutions and the soundness of our
tradition."

This convention, held only four months after passage of the Taft-
Hartley Act, virtually abandoned any real struggle either to defy
or repeal the "Slave Labor" Law. The demonstration for Marshall
and the retreat on Taft-Hartley were two sides of the same coin.
The total effect of the convention was to intensify the onslaught
against all opponents of the Murray-Reuther-Carey faction.

One of the most immediate beneficiaries of the 1947 CIO convention was Walter Reuther in the United Automobile Workers. His
caucus more and more attracted the most reactionary elements,
including the ACTU followers and the supporters of anti-Negro policies, although a section of the militants, swayed by antipathy to the
Stalinists, also continued to support Reuther.

In the course of the power struggle during 1946 and 1947, the
Thomas-Addes-Leonard caucus indicated a better stand on union
democracy and on other major issues, such as the Taft-Hartley
oath, than Reuther. Reuther's caucus hammered on one point—
the "commies," and brushed aside all discussion of program. The
ACTU's Detroit paper, *The Wage Earner,* acted as an unofficial factional voice of the Reuther machine.

The Reutherite charge that Thomas, Addes, Leonard and other
leading figures of their caucus were either Communists or under

their direction was an outright falsification. In this period the Stalinists had no voice in the top counsels of the opposition caucus and no significant influence in its lower ranks. The Thomas-Addes-Leonard group, in order to protect its own position in the UAW, had to defend union democracy, including the principle of no discrimination for political views, from both the Stalinists and the Reutherites.

Riding the tide of anti-communist reaction that flowed from the State Department, the Reuther machine seized full control of the top union apparatus at the UAW convention, November 9-14, 1947. With the cry, "Get the Commies!" the Reuther forces ousted Thomas, Addes, Leonard and most of their supporters from top office. Addes was replaced by Emil Mazey as secretary-treasurer. Mazey, who had a reputation as a militant, linked up with Reuther and led the main convention debate to approve the policy of complying with the Taft-Hartley anti-communist oath provision. R. J. Thomas, who led the fight against the oath, was defeated for vice-president by Richard Gosser of Toledo.

CIO President Philip Murray addressed the UAW convention before its election of officers and plainly indicated his support of Reuther's machine. Murray made a condescending reference to Thomas as one who "makes his mistakes" and is "sometimes mischievous, but nevertheless not a bad guy." He praised Reuther "for the splendid support that little red-head has given Phil Murray since his incumbency [as UAW president]."

Reuther emerged from the convention not only as one-man ruler of the UAW—his machine had captured all top officerships and 18 out of 22 members of the National Executive Board—but as chief spokesman for the Truman Doctrine inside the labor movement. He was to use his new power to attempt to silence and drive out all opposition. He was never to succeed fully. To this day there remain strong pockets of non-Stalinist opposition to Reuther in the UAW despite his many bureaucratic measures, including imposition of receiverships on recalcitrant locals, removal of local officers, etc.

The outcome of the UAW convention chiefly affected the non-Stalinist militants. The Stalinist forces in the UAW had suffered a severe decline between 1944 and 1947 due to their ultra-reactionary trade union line during the war, while the real militants had been on the ascendency during that period. Reuther was able to swing to his side a portion of the militants, of whom Emil Mazey was representative. These militants—or former militants—lacking any firm class political program, continued to act as a left cover for him. Reuther emerged as the dominant figure of the CIO next to Murray, and was in position to succeed him as president of the CIO in the event of his retirement or death.

The Wallace developments intensified the factional war inside the CIO. The national leaders moved more vigorously to recapture state and local councils from the Stalinists. At the Minnesota CIO convention, October 31-November 2, 1947, their ten-year rule came to an end.

Murray sent a large group of top CIO officials to the convention to organize the faction fight. The anti-Stalinist opposition, which in this instance also included delegates who favored a labor party and opposed redbaiting, emerged from the convention with a 14-6 majority on the new state executive board. Then the right wing of the new majority and the Stalinists voted together to put over an endorsement of Minneapolis Mayor Hubert Humphrey, a Democrat, for senator in 1948.

Following the Minnesota convention, a number of key Stalinists were ousted from the CIO's paper, *Minnesota Labor,* and from various departments of the state organization. On August 11, 1948, the Hennepin County (Minneapolis) CIO Council, largest body in the Minnesota CIO, adopted a resolution calling for the restoration of the civil rights of the 18 Socialist Workers Party and Minneapolis Drivers Local 544-CIO leaders who had been sent to prison in 1944 under the Smith Act. This reversed the stand taken when the council had been under Stalinist control during the war. The same resolution, it might be added, also opposed the pending prosecution of the 12 Communist Party leaders under the Smith Act.

At the New Jersey CIO convention the first week in December 1947, the right-wingers "ran wild," as *The Militant* reported. They pushed through a resolution specifically supporting the Marshall Plan by name, which the national convention had not done. They also tried but failed to win adoption of a resolution to bar communists from state CIO office. They were successful in putting over a resolution calling on local CIO unions to "fight and defeat for office all members of the Communist Party and their fascist adherents."

The New Jersey CIO right-wingers provoked a split at the convention when they used their mechanical majority to overrule the nominations offered by delegations from unions under Stalinist leadership, contrary to the traditional procedure. The UE delegation's nomination of James McLeish for vice-president by a 79 to 9 vote was ignored. Ernest Pollock, the right-winger who got the nine votes, was nominated and elected. Most of the UE delegates as well as many others walked out of the convention at this point—an action which did not displease the redbaiters who were eager to get undisputed control.

In the internal CIO struggle, the Stalinist union officials revealed how much they had been corrupted by more than a decade of adaptation to the general union bureaucracy. When the Communist Party ordered a "left" shift that involved conflict with the pro-Democratic Party union leaders, many of the CP's trade union cadre buckled and broke. Shortly after the UAW convention, John Williamson complained in a *Daily Worker* series that "the disease of factionalism and jobs had penetrated even the fabric of more than a few in the Communist ranks."

One of those for whom the lure of his job proved greater than his loyalty to Stalinism was Michael Quill, head of the CIO Transport Workers Union, whose chief success had been the organization of the New York City transit workers. Quill was a member of the City Council of New York City. He had made deals with the ruling powers in City Hall regularly and had supported both the La Guardia and O'Dwyer city administrations from election to election. In all of Quill's moves, the Communist Party and its press had supported him or applied to him the necessary whitewash.

On December 22, 1947, the *Daily Worker* startled its readers with a blistering attack on "certain leaders" of the Transport Workers Union for "opportunism...fundamentally unsound strategy...departing from elementary principles of sound trade unionism...sacrifice of the workers' interests and demands." Quill had come to a break with the Communist Party. Within a few months he would "spill his guts" about the Communist Party's trade union policy, and make common cause with the pro-State Department CIO leaders.

His defection was an even more telling revelation of the inner rot of the Stalinist tendency than Curran's, for Quill had been more closely identified with the Communist Party's political activity as a city councilman elected on the American Labor Party ticket. It was, in fact, when Quill became aware that the Communist Party was serious about pressing a third-party campaign for Wallace and expressed qualms about provoking a split in the CIO over this issue that the *Daily Worker* discovered his crimes.

The "third party," as the Communist Party viewed it, rested on a single individual, Wallace, and on his sole decision to run as a presidential candidate in opposition to the two old parties. As late as December 10, 1947, Wallace told an audience in Syracuse that he would be a candidate of a third party only "if it is apparent that the Democratic Party is a war party." That had been made apparent, of course, in both World War I and World War II. On December

29, 1947, Wallace finally announced in Chicago that he would run for the presidency on a third-party ticket with the support of the Progressive Citizens of America and other "liberal" groups. He would offer "a positive program of abundance and security, not scarcity and war."

The *Daily Worker* was elated. In an editorial, "A Historic Candidacy," Wallace's announcement was hailed as "the call for a national fight for peace." That paper now admitted the very opposite of what the Stalinist delegates in the unions had previously affirmed. "Every honest American must know," the *Daily Worker* said, "that the Truman Democratic and the Taft-Dewey GOP are at bottom a single party, united on the same platform of reaction, profiteering and war..."

The idea that Wallace could prove any kind of bulwark against imperialist war was promptly exposed in *The Militant*. James P. Cannon, writing on "Henry Wallace and the Next War" on May 10, 1948, prophesied: "By seizing hold of the mass sentiment against war, and by diverting it from the basic cause of war, the Wallace party sterilizes the anti-war movement and prepares it for collapse when the first shot is fired or the first bomb is dropped." Within 26 months Wallace was to quit the Progressive Party and hail Truman's "police action" in Korea. This was foreshadowed in an interview with Wallace, published in the April 25 *New York Times,* which quoted him as saying: "If the United States should go to war I, of course, would withdraw [from the election campaign]."

The Stalinist campaign for Wallace was thus sheer adventurism. The Wallace party lacked the elementary ingredient for any successful progressive mass third party in modern-day America. It was not based on the main body of the trade unions; it was outside either the influence or the control of the organized workers. It was, as *The Militant* of January 5, 1948 said, "a caricature of a new party — Wallace plus the Stalinists plus their fellow travelers." Programmatically and in its Wallace leadership it was a third capitalist party.

The Wallace campaign sidetracked the movement for a genuine labor party and heightened the factional atmosphere inside the CIO. The first consequence of Wallace's announcement of his candidacy was a split in New York State's American Labor Party—the only third party formation with a genuine trade-union base in the country. The New York State CIO Council had voted on January 5, 1948 against endorsement of Wallace. A number of key CIO unions on January 8 walked out of the ALP in protest against the proposal to endorse Wallace. These unions included the Amalgamated Clothing

Workers, United Automobile Workers and United Steelworkers. Quill and his Transport Workers Union were soon to follow.

There was nothing progressive in the CIO leadership's opposition to the Wallace candidacy. They, like the Stalinists, opposed the formation of an independent party based on the unions and controlled by labor. The Murray-Reuther-Carey wing of the CIO leadership was motivated strictly by a desire to maintain its ties with the old-line capitalist political machines.

A parade of union leaders was already on the march back to the Democratic Party. A. F. Whitney, president of the Brotherhood of Railroad Trainmen, emerged from the White House on January 20, 1948, to tell newsmen he'd had a "wonderful chat" with Truman and was going to raise union funds to help re-elect him. In May 1946, when Truman broke the railroad strike, Whitney charged that the President had "double-crossed" the railway workers. At that time Whitney publicly vowed to use the millions in the trainmen's treasury to help defeat the "political accident" who urged Congress to enact a law to draft railroad strikers into the army.

A meeting of the CIO Executive Board in Washington, D. C., January 22-23, 1948, made more explicit the top leadership's stand. The board voted 33 to 11 for a resolution which came out flatly "for the adoption and implementation of the Marshall Plan." On the question of Wallace's candidacy, the board by the same 33-to-11 vote declared that a third party in 1948 was "politically unwise," although "at this time the CIO is in no way committed to any presidential candidate."

Emil Mazey, newly elected UAW secretary-treasurer, wrote a statement in the January 1948 *United Automobile Worker* turning thumbs down on Wallace that did not give the same motivation as the CIO Executive Board. "We must build an independent party of our own composed of workers and working farmers if we hope to get results on the political arena," said Mazey. "Workers must not be misled by the third-party rantings of Wallace. His movement does not represent a genuine party of the workers, but is, in fact, a third capitalist party. . ." But Mazey, who was a member of the Executive Board, failed to show up at its January 22 meeting to defend this point of view.

UE President Albert Fitzgerald had asked at the CIO Executive Board meeting for postponement of action on the political resolution so he could "consult" with the UE membership first. "Bunk!" retorted Murray and reminded the Stalinists and Fitzgerald that they voted for the anti-third-party resolution in the 1944 CIO convention—without consulting their members.

The political and economic needs of the workers were subordinated first to the CIO leadership's drive against the "commies" and then to the re-election of a president who in 1948 was to wield more strikebreaking injunctions against labor than any previous president.

28

Taft-Hartley Injunctions and Faction Strife

While the CIO leaders were preoccupied with the pursuit of communists, the CIO workers were feeling increasing economic pressure. Job insecurity and mounting prices continued to hound the workers despite what Truman in his 1947 "Midyear Economic Report" called "unprecedented prosperity." Indeed it was—for the corporations. Their net profits after taxes had risen from a record $10 billion wartime peak in 1943 to $12 billion in 1946 and was on the way to an estimated $17 billion in 1947.

The September 1947 *Fortune* magazine published the results of a poll showing that 35 per cent of the American people were finding it harder to make a living than before the war. *Fortune's* editors expressed surprise at so many reports of discontent.

While average unemployment for any week in 1947 was about 2,500,000, during the entire year 14 million workers suffered some period of layoff. Of those laid off, only 4,100,000 collected unemployment compensation—an average of $18.05 a week, with an individual maximum of $22.80. Some 2,270,000 needy aged received an average of $36.04 a month in federal old age assistance.

A U. S. Bureau of Labor Statistics report on November 19, 1947, revealed that while physical output of industrial production was 85 per cent higher in August 1947 than in 1939, real wages of all manufacturing workers averaged only $32.45 a week—$9 a week more during "unprecedented prosperity" than during a prewar depression year. Only the soft coal miners had average real wages over $40 a week. They had lifted their weekly dollar wages in those eight years from $23.88 to $71.19, equal to $42.81 in 1939 dollars. But there were 12 per cent fewer miners producing 51 per cent more coal than in 1939.

Less than five months after the springtime "second round" of wage increases, the *CIO News* in September observed that "if the trend continues at the present rate much longer, American workers will find themselves in about the same economic position they were back in 1939...unless they receive another round of pay increases."

The Boston convention of the CIO in October took further note of the economic situation with adoption of a resolution advocating a "vigorous collective bargaining program" to increase real wages, secure a guaranteed annual wage and a shorter work week with no reduction in take-home pay. On December 3, after a meeting in Washington of Philip Murray and the nine vice-presidents, the CIO president announced his organization would seek a "third round" of "substantial wage increases" to offset prices soaring at the rate of two to three per cent a month. The CIO leaders indicated they intended to take no wage action until the spring of 1948.

Engrossed in the UAW's internal power fight, the Reuther caucus at the United Automobile Workers convention in November 1947 choked off debate and action on economic issues. They placed their main emphasis on the discredited program of a "rollback of prices." Reuther himself, in his keynote and closing speeches, even fixed the amount of the proposed "rollback" at 12 per cent.

The majority report of the Resolutions Committee, which represented the views of the Thomas-Addes-Leonard group, recommended that the UAW "immediately embark on a new drive for wage increases," including "cost-of-living bonuses during the life of the wage clauses with the negotiated rates as the base minimum." In addition, it called for the resignation of union leaders, including Reuther, from the National Planning Association, which was pushing speed-up propaganda.

In Flint on December 21, the presidents of five General Motors locals put forth a three-point program with specific wage proposals: (1) a 25-cent hourly wage increase and a sliding scale cost-of-living bonus clause; (2) revision of the GM contract; (3) a single termination date for all contracts in the auto industry. The December 22 *Detroit News* reported that as a result of the "wage clamor" Reuther had called a UAW Executive Board meeting for January 15, 1948, to discuss the wage issue. "It was obvious," commented that newspaper, "that the locals had upset the national CIO's strategy by making public the account of their demands and launching the drive prematurely..." A December 21 meeting of Briggs Local 212 in Detroit, home local of UAW Secretary-Treasurer Emil Mazey, adopted the Flint program against Mazey's opposition. He had asked the local to wait for the top UAW leadership's decision.

By the beginning of 1948, UAW locals representing more than 200,000 auto workers had gone on record favoring the Flint three-point program. In addition to the Flint GM locals, Ford Local 600, largest local union in the world, Briggs Local 212, Budd Local 306, Plymouth Local 51, Fleetwood Local 15 and other local unions had endorsed the 25-cent wage boost plus the sliding-scale cost-of-living clause. The Detroit GM Regional Sub-Council on December 22 had likewise approved the escalator wage program.

When the UAW Wage Policy Committee met on January 6, however, it took no action on the proposals of the local unions. The International Executive Board announced on January 16, two days before a GM delegates conference in Detroit, that the UAW's "economic objectives for 1948" would be a 25-cent hourly wage increase plus five cents for health and welfare. At the GM conference Reuther pushed through a proposition that the union cut the wage demand to 15 cents if GM should grant an "acceptable" retirement pension plan. Reuther himself had voiced opposition to a similar pension scheme proposed for the previous Ford contract. A third of the GM delegates voted against the pension gimmick which they considered a doubtful future benefit in place of immediate wage gains needed to meet the ever rising cost of living. Reuther's proposition was also considered a virtual invitation to the corporation to whittle down wage demands. A motion to include an adequate escalator clause in the forthcoming contracts was ruled out of order.

Reuther's program to substitute indefinite future benefits for present needs was attacked by Chevrolet Local 659 President Jack Palmer in a radio talk over Flint station WFDF on January 20. After stating that "we want an adequate pension plan" and that this must not be confused with the problem of inflation, Palmer said:

"Brother Reuther's complaint [at the GM conference] against the sliding scale of wages — and he had only one — was that this clause made no provisions for improving our wage scale over and above prices. This sounds like a mighty poor argument when he can only propose a 15-cent wage increase while he states we need 25 cents to close the gap with prices. On the contrary, the sliding-scale-of-wages clause in no way prevents us from improving our contract. All it does is keep wages from lagging constantly *behind* prices." (Original emphasis.)

The corporate propaganda for more output through a longer work week found an echo in Reuther's speech on February 5 before the Senate Foreign Relations Committee. The auto workers, Reuther claimed, "are ready to work longer work weeks whenever management . . . can supply the materials and the work." He explained that even with overtime pay after 40 hours, the auto corporations could sweat out of the auto workers in a 44-hour week ten per cent more production with an additional wage cost of only 4.4 per cent.

All the CIO unions but the Packinghouse Workers marked time throughout the spring of 1948. Some 100,000 packinghouse workers began a strike on March 16 for a 29-cent wage increase and a cost-of-living bonus clause. There was little supporting action from the other CIO unions. Murray announced in advance that the steelworkers would not strike under any condition.

Once again it was the coal miners who set the example. On March 15 a swiftly spreading strike began in protest against an eight-month tie-up of $30,000,000 in welfare funds by the coal operators. On March 22 John L. Lewis announced that the mine owners had "dishonored" and "defaulted" on the 1947 contract. Within 24 hours all 400,000 bituminous miners had declared themselves "not willing and not able" to work so long as the operators prevented release of the welfare funds.

Although it was an election year, Truman threw off his "friend of labor" mask. He swung the Taft-Hartley club at the miners, packinghouse workers, AFL atomic workers and the AFL International Typographical Union. The ITU, like the UMW, had refused to submit to the Taft-Hartley non-communist oath requirement.

Truman first invoked a Taft-Hartley anti-strike injunction on March 19 against 800 members of the AFL Atomic Trades and Labor Council at the Oak Ridge (Tenn.) National Laboratory, which was being operated for private profit by the Carbide and Carbon Chemicals Company. The workers had voted to strike when the company threatened to cut the contractual wage scales and to reduce sick leave. Under the old contract the workers had been granted 90 days sick leave a year because of the extreme radiation hazard.

On March 27 Federal Judge Luther M. Swygert granted an injunction against the ITU and its officers to halt strikes against the five Chicago dailies. In this case, the injunction was so far-reaching that it prohibited any deed or word in furtherance of a strike or any other form of action to enforce demands which might be held at some future date to be in violation of the Taft-Hartley Act.

The packinghouse workers had a Taft-Hartley fact-finding board imposed on them by Truman, while local judges in a dozen Midwest towns and cities bombarded them with anti-picketing injunctions. Truman's board approved the companies' offer of a nine-cent raise instead of the union's 29-cent demand, even though the meatpacking industry's 1948 profits were running double those of 1947. Kansas

City police, under orders to "crack skulls," invaded a CIO packing-house workers union hall on April 23 and injured 110 workers, ten of whom had to be hospitalized. The "Kansas City Outrage" drew nothing more than a brief bleat of protest from Murray and other CIO leaders. On May 22 the CIO packinghouse union, after a ten-week strike, was forced to settle on the "Big Four" terms as backed by the fact-finding board.

The heaviest blows were aimed at the coal miners. At Truman's behest, Justice Matthew F. McGuire of the United States District Court in Washington issued a temporary injunction on April 3. He banned a mine strike until April 13 when a hearing on a permanent injunction was to be held. The temporary injunction ordered Lewis personally to "instruct forthwith" the miners to re-enter the pits.

Lewis contended he had not called the strike. He sent a letter to the mine locals on the day the injunction was issued, stating that "any action or decision that you may now care to take continues to be entirely of your own determination." The Taft-Hartley Act said that "nothing in this act shall be construed to require an individual employe to render labor or service without his consent...nor shall any court issue any process to compel performance by an individ-ual employe of such labor or service without his consent."

Four days after the injunction had been issued and in the face of the continued refusal of each of the 400,000 coal miners "to render labor or service," a revamped Board of Trustees of the miners' welfare fund agreed to a $100 a month pension for all miners over 62 years of age with 20 years' service. Other industries subse-quently won provisions of $100 *including* federal social security. The UMW pensions provided $100 a month *above* any government old-age payment.

Some two-thirds of the miners continued to strike after the pen-sion grant because Truman was pressing for "contempt" action against the UMW and Lewis. The President had again procured the services of Federal Judge T. Allan Goldsborough who in 1946 had fined the UMW $3,500,000. The miners were afraid that if they ceased resistance the judge would "throw the book" at their union and even jail Lewis. The UMW leader, meanwhile, had already wired the local unions to notify them "pensions granted, agreement now honored" and had advised that "your voluntary cessation of work should now be terminated." On April 20 Judge Goldsborough levied a punitive $1,400,000 fine against the union and $20,000 against Lewis personally. During the whole Taft-Hartley proceedings against the miners, CIO President Murray and AFL President Green kept silent.

The UMW and Lewis were not convicted of breaking any law. They were charged with violating an arbitrary, judge-made ruling— an injunction. To convict them, the judge had to establish first that the UMW officials had called the strike. He therefore claimed that the mere statement by Lewis that the mine owners had "dishonored" their pact was, in effect, "like a nod or a wink or a code." In short, the judge held that for Lewis to inform the union membership of the status of the union contract was in itself an order to strike.

This argument was so novel that Judge Goldsborough had to admit he had invented a new point of law, "a principle of law which, as far as I know, no court has ever been called upon to announce." This principle was: "As long as a union is functioning as a union it must be held responsible for the mass action of its members."

Under this deadly legal formula a corporation could deliberately provoke a strike in hopes of breaking a union. If the strikers did not respond to a back-to-work order by a court, the union leaders could be sent to jail and the union's treasury looted by the same court under the "responsibility" principle enunciated by Judge Goldsborough.

In the case in question, Lewis had done nothing more than refrain for a period from urging the miners, who had struck on their own initiative, to return to work. Even after he did so urge them, two-thirds of the miners continued their walkout for several weeks. The fact is that more than once both before and after this strike Lewis was forced to go along with revolts of the miners. He was by no means able to turn strikes off and on like a water tap.

At the end of June the miners emerged from another long hard battle, vindicated and triumphant. The "break" came when Judge Goldsborough ruled on June 22 that the miners' pension demand was legal. Thereafter, the mine owners signed a contract doubling the royalty payments into the health and welfare fund and raising regular wages by $1 a day, or about 12-1/2 cents an hour. The Truman administration's intervention had served only to delay a settlement and to victimize the union with a Taft-Hartley assault and extortionate fine.

In this same period, the railroad workers also felt the heavy hand of the Truman regime. In advance of a scheduled strike of three railway operating unions, Truman on May 10 secured an anti-strike injunction against the Brotherhood of Locomotive Engineers, the Brotherhood of Locomotive Firemen and Enginemen, and the Switchmen's Union. He seized the railroads under a 1916 law which provided for such action "in time of war." This was a particularly flagrant act of injustice because the rail workers had not received even a "second round" wage increase since the truncated gains they were forced to take in 1946, when Truman had seized the lines, made army colonels of the railroad presidents, and called for a draft-strikers law. In 1948, a presidential "fact-finding" board imposed a 15-1/2 cent an hour settlement, which could scarcely begin to compensate for the bounding price rises between 1946 and 1948. In the course of this conflict the Railway Labor Executives Association, an organization of top leaders of railroad unions representing the majority of the 1,400,000 railroad workers, adopted a resolution calling for government nationalization and ownership of the nation's railroads.

When it came to strikebreaking by injunction, Truman was as much at home on sea as on land. The President obtained a temporary injunction on June 14, pending a hearing on an 80-day Taft-Hartley restraining order, to forbid seven CIO maritime and waterfront unions from calling a scheduled strike on June 24. The Stalinists, who were steadily losing ground in the National Maritime Union, attacked President Curran for not defying the injunction. Their bold talk evaporated when it was revealed that Howard McKenzie and Ferdinand Smith, who were associated with the Stalinists, had signed a joint statement with Curran postponing the strike. The Stalinists kept silent about the stand of Harry Bridges, head of the West Coast CIO longshoremen, and the leaders of the Marine Cooks and Stewards, who also had agreed to abide by the injunctions. A federal court in New York City issued an 80-day Taft-Hartley injunction on June 23. All the CIO maritime and waterfront unions bowed to this order. On September 1 the West Coast longshoremen and marine cooks went on strike. Truman promptly ordered federal troops to load struck ships when the employers rejected a union offer to load army cargo as a "communist trick."

By June 23, 1948, the first anniversary of the Taft-Hartley Act, the Truman administration had secured no less than 12 anti-strike injunctions under either the "national health and safety" clause of the Act or its "unfair labor practices" provisions. On a straight statistical basis, Truman was the most anti-labor president ever to hold that office and he carried out some of his worst depredations against labor in the election year of 1948.

While the coal and railroad struggles were in progress, the CIO wage campaign shuffled along through the spring of 1948. Attention increasingly focused on the automobile industry. Some 75,000 Chrysler workers went on strike May 12 and the General Motors and Ford workers voted to follow. A GM delegates conference had scheduled a strike poll for May 23. Then Reuther made a coup — he secured a General Motors agreement, the main feature of which was an escalator clause proposed by General Motors itself. As *New York Times* labor reporter A. H. Raskin recalled on January 3, 1960, the escalator clause was "part of the inducement held out to Walter P. Reuther's United Automobile Workers for accepting a long-term contract."

Seventy-two hours before the GM strike deadline, Reuther and his negotiating committee on May 25 reached an agreement for an 11-cent hourly wage increase: three cents an "improvement factor" based on increased output, and eight cents allowed as a cost-of-living bonus under an escalator clause. The contract was to run for two years, the longest in GM history up to that time, and contained the onerous "penalty" clauses designed to penalize resistance to speed-up.

Specifically, the GM escalator clause provided that for each two-thirds of one per cent rise in the BLS cost-of-living index, which then stood at 169.3 points based on the 1939 figure of 100, there would be a one-cent raise in hourly wages, automatically adjusted every three months. Wages could be cut in the event of a fall in prices, but not more than a total of five cents. This would leave six cents of the initial 11-cent increase intact, no matter how much prices might fall.

UAW Secretary-Treasurer Emil Mazey, in a letter published in the May 28, 1948 *New York Times*, admitted that "the present agreement, though headed in the right direction, starts with a depressed base period and allows too small an annual increase in wage rates." In spite of such deficiencies, the GM escalator clause in the long run proved to be an important protection to GM wages, although Reuther had sacrificed a good bit of the "improvement" to obtain it.

An ironic footnote to the Reuther escalator contract was the almost simultaneous attack on it by the Stalinist press and Lewis's *United Mine Workers Journal*. The *Daily Worker* promptly dubbed the GM sliding-scale pact the "wage-cutting escalator clause" and concentrated its fire on the provision that allowed a total of up to five cents to be cut from the wage rate in the event of a drop in prices. But the Communist Party itself had adopted a resolution warning of the "direct inflationary effect" of the Marshall Plan and the "swollen war economy." (*Sunday Worker*, May 30, 1948.) The Stalinist attack on the contract failed to mention that the Stalinist-dominated United Electrical Workers had just signed an identical "wage-cutting escalator clause" pact for the 40,000 workers in GM's Electrical Division.

The UMW *Journal* attacked the government index base of the UAW escalator clause, a sound criticism in itself. But it went on to liken the clause to the Little Steel Formula that had frozen all wages during the war. This wartime formula was, of course, not a negotiated union contract but a government-imposed wage freeze over all wage rates for a long period and regardless of price rises.

The escalator clause, inadequate as it was, worked to the advantage of the GM workers, as was soon evidenced. Three days after the GM settlement, the 17-day Chrysler strike was ended with a fixed 13-cent boost in the hourly rate. Ford, which had originally demanded that the union accept a pay cut, also settled for a 13-cent increase. Then, on July 15 the GM escalator clause automatically added three cents to the eleven cents received in May, bringing the total increase to one cent more than the Ford and Chrysler gains. During the 12-year inflationary period from 1948 to 1960, the GM escalator clause brought regular automatic wage increases. Only once, during the 1949 recession, did the cost-of-living index decline sufficiently to permit a one-cent cut in the wage rates.

Most of the other CIO unions settled for a wage pattern of from nine to eleven cents. The rubber workers took eleven cents and dropped the escalator demand. The UE leadership accepted a nine to eleven-cent boost in General Electric, but minus the sliding-scale cost-of-living protection. Unable to get the major sections of the oil industry to match the gains of the Sinclair Oil workers under their escalator clause, the union leaders scrapped the Sinclair escalator clause in order to get a flat 17-cent uniform increase throughout the organized sector of the industry. Murray signed a two-year contract on July 15, providing an average increase of 13 cents but less than 11 cents for the majority of steelworkers.

By the beginning of 1948 the U. S. State Department was attempting actively to intervene in trade union affairs of the Western European and Latin American countries. It had already inspired an anticommunist split from the French Confederation of Labor and was engineering a similar development within the General Confederation of Italian Workers.

CIO leaders were traveling abroad and working within the World Federation of Trade Unions, in order to line up international labor in the service of the cold war machine's anti-Soviet policy. A week after Philip Murray had heatedly denied that the Marshall Plan was anything other than a "civilian economic rehabilitation job," CIO Secretary-Treasurer Carey threatened the Italian workers that if they did not vote against the Communist-Socialist ticket in the April 18 elections, "they could hardly expect to share in the benefits of the ERP [European Recovery Plan]."

During the "third round" wage campaign, both sides in the CIO factional war had aggressively pushed their political policies. When the CIO National Executive Board on January 22, 1948 abjured Wallace and any third party move, the Communist Party followers in the unions insisted on pressing the Wallace campaign even if it meant provoking expulsions and splits. As for the Murray leadership, support of Wallace was treated as a violation of CIO policy, although Murray himself had stated, following the CIO Board meeting, that the anti-Wallace resolution was not binding on the members and that they had only a "moral obligation" to abide by it.

This "moral obligation" was enforced by more than moral persuasion, however. Murray announced on February 6 that Lee Pressman, the CIO's General Counsel for more than ten years and legal adviser of the Steelworkers union, had "resigned" his CIO posts. Pressman stated that he was entering private practice and would actively campaign for Wallace.

Two years later, in August 1950, Pressman broke publicly with the Stalinists in an appearance before the House Un-American Activities Committee and repudiated the American Labor Party, which had become the New York section of Wallace's Progressive Party. Pressman's recantation came after Wallace had announced his support of Truman's Korean "police action." In his August 8, 1950 letter of resignation from the ALP, Pressman stated:

"It is crucial for any progressive political parties to have the full and energetic support of organized labor. This, the American Labor Party does not enjoy. The basic reason is the outstanding conviction that the policies, activity and political direction of the American Labor Party do not represent or reflect the democratic or progressive interests or aspirations of the American people but rather the Communist Party."

Pressman was only one of many talented men and women who had initially lent their services to the CIO in the belief that they were advancing the cause of labor and socialism, but who became so disoriented and disillusioned by Stalinism that they eventually were lost to the labor movement. Pressman was replaced by Arthur J. Goldberg, a career lawyer.

Murray opened his first public attack on Wallace supporters in a vitriolic speech on February 10 to the Cleveland convention of the Industrial Union of Marine and Shipbuilding Workers of America, which was controlled completely by right-wing elements. The union was down to a shadow as the result of postwar layoffs. Its leaders were seeking to build up the union again by serving as a catch-all for split-off groups from Stalinist-controlled unions and such new unions as Murray wanted under his own thumb. This very convention had received into IUMSWA membership some 25,000 members of the Progressive Metal Workers Council, a right-wing split from the Mine, Mill and Smelter Workers.

Murray's choice of the IUMSWA convention in Cleveland for his open declaration of war on the Wallace forces was influenced in part by the fact that a bitter fight was reaching a climax in the Cleveland Industrial Union Council, where the Murray-Reuther forces were driving to take control after a long Stalinist reign. At a turbulent council meeting on March 10 the right-wingers succeeded in passing a motion calling for full support of the Marshall Plan and opposition to a third party.

CIUC Administrator James C. Quinn as chairman instructed the delegates that local councils could not oppose the CIO National Executive Board's political position and that "you have to vote yes on CIO policy." Adoption of the right-wing motion was the first major defeat suffered by the Stalinist faction in the Cleveland Council in ten years.

Where the Murray-Reuther-Carey forces could not win the support of the majority of local council delegates, they engineered splits and set up competing bodies. In the Greater Newark CIO Council, a minority composed of auto, steel, textile and other union delegates walked out in February and set up another council headed by William Mackey, a field representative of Murray's steel union. In the Los Angeles Council, on February 20, 114 delegates walked out after the majority refused to rescind a previous motion to "take no action pro or con" on such controversial questions as the Marshall Plan, the third party or Wallace's candidacy. The Stalinists had tried to evade a public stand and thus avoid a fight and split.

But the right-wing minority in Los Angeles had been forearmed. John Brophy, National Director of CIO Councils, had sent a letter to the Los Angeles Council demanding that it make an affirmative declaration for the Marshall Plan and against a third party. Brophy wrote that even a "compromise position" violated the national CIO rules governing local councils.

No compromise, evasion or abstention was to be tolerated. Brophy's letter to all state and city councils on March 8 spelled out the position each had to take, which was "one to express opposition to any third party in 1948 and one of positive support for the Marshall Plan."

"Rejecting, tabling, ignoring communications and statements from or by CIO officers, CIO-PAC or the CIO Executive Board on these matters, or the adoption of compromise or conflicting reso-

lutions constitutes a rejection of the CIO communications and statements and is action in conflict with CIO policy."

In short, the Stalinists were given but one choice—they had to
openly affirm opposition to the Kremlin's foreign policy and to declare positive support for the foreign policy of U. S. capitalism as
expressed in the Marshall Plan. But that was precisely where the
American Stalinists could not yield. Foreign policy was the one
point where neither bureaucratic faction could be flexible in 1948.

Murray early in March backed his threat to purge non-supporters
of his policy by ousting Harry Bridges from his appointive post as
CIO regional director for northern California. CIO Director of Organization Allan S. Haywood, in his statement announcing Bridges'
ouster, reaffirmed the Murray machine's position that nothing less
than a positive declaration for the Marshall Plan and against a third
party would be acceptable. Haywood stated further that the action
against Bridges was only the start of similar coast-to-coast reprisals
against the Stalinists and Wallace supporters. Haywood cited, as
specific targets for national CIO intervention and "reorganization,"
the councils of New York City, Newark, Los Angeles, San Francisco
and California. This meant that majorities of local elective bodies
would be overridden by national CIO executive fiat, even if it meant
the establishment of new dual councils.

The March 22 *CIO News* reported all state CIO Councils but California and Iowa had endorsed the Marshall Plan. Murray asked all
state and local CIO bodies to act with "utmost speed" to pressure
Congress to pass the Marshall Plan bill (European Recovery Act).
His letter said that all CIO groups must make this the "No. 1 pri-
ority task."

The national CIO leaders now carried their factional offensive
directly to international unions under Stalinist influence or control.
Kid-glove methods were abandoned. Raids to split members from
the UE, Farm Equipment Workers, and other Stalinist-led unions
were made. The UAW attempted to snatch the UE local in Cleveland,
and gave haven to dissident UE members in New York. Reuther moved
to squeeze the FE from the Caterpillar Tractor plant in Illinois.
The right-wingers did not hesitate to take advantage of the Taft-
Hartley Act. Since some of the Stalinist-led unions had refused to
take the Taft-Hartley oath, the raiding unions could win unopposed
in the NLRB elections.

A jurisdictional dispute had been in progress several years between the Farm Equipment Workers and the UAW. In 1945 the CIO
Jurisdictional Committee had proposed a merger which was approved
by the CIO National Executive Board, but rejected by the FE lead-

ership. They did accept the merger terms offered in 1947 by the UAW National Executive Board majority. Reuther, who feared the FE forces might strengthen the Thomas-Addes faction, had opposed the plan. A UAW membership referendum then rejected it.

When the FE in early 1948 called a strike at the large Caterpillar Tractor plant in Peoria, Illinois, four other unions moved in to claim jurisdiction. They knew the FE would be ruled ineligible in an NLRB poll because of refusal to take the Taft-Hartley oath. In addition to the UAW, the invading unions were the AFL Boilermakers, the International Association of Machinists, and the AFL United Automobile Workers, the remnant of the group which Homer Martin had led back into the AFL in 1939.

The FE suffered a shattering defeat at the Caterpillar plant, where the UAW won an NLRB election in June. Thereafter, the FE leaders voted to take the Taft-Hartley oath and four well-known Stalinists had to resign from the Executive Board.

Raids on Stalinist-led unions by the UAW, as well as similar activities by the Steelworkers, Shipbuilding and other unions, served notice on the Stalinist union leaders that any hope they might have of re-establishing peaceful coexistence with the top CIO bureaucracy was illusory.

In March 1948, the National Maritime Union's Rank and File Caucus headed by Curran announced a complete slate to contest all the posts held by the Stalinists in the regular elections to start April 1. Representing a genuine revolt against the rule-and-ruin policies of the Stalinists, the Rank and File Caucus was composed of various elements united on a general program aimed at establishing the basis for union democracy. Although Curran personally had voted for the Marshall Plan resolution at the January 22 CIO Executive Board meeting, the caucus refrained from adopting a position on the disputed international and political questions.

The results of the NMU's three-month election referendum, announced in July, revealed a crushing defeat for the Stalinist machine. They had lost every post by margins of two and even three to one. Some 41,000 NMU members had voted, the largest such turnout in the union's history. The Stalinists had had virtually unrestricted opportunity for a decade to demonstrate what their leadership could do for the seamen. Discredited, they were swept away by the hostility of the ranks. The NMU and the CIO Newspaper Guild then announced their withdrawal from the Greater New York CIO Council.

Another stiff jolt was handed the Stalinists in April when Michael Quill announced in a telegram to Philip Murray that he was resigning as President of the Greater New York CIO Council. In his statement

Quill heaped opprobrium on the comrades and party he had served so loyally for many years. He now found that "disagreements" in the TWU were being "seized upon by a group of strange people" he called "communist crackpots" who were engaged in a "cheap and underhanded way of splitting the unity of the CIO."

On April 20 Quill followed his defection from the Stalinists and his resignation from the council by quitting the American Labor Party, of which he was vice-chairman. He was still a city councilman elected on the ALP ticket. In the TWU's key Local 100 in New York City, Quill secured a vote of 24 to 10 at its Executive Board meeting to condemn the ALP, the Communist Party and the Greater New York CIO Council. At the same time, Quill began a "now it can be told" series in the TWU paper.

He described Stalinist sabotage of TWU organizing campaigns during World War II in the name of "national unity." He told how the Stalinists in 1941 worked to prevent a bus drivers strike to safeguard their "progressive coalition" with Mayor La Guardia. He claimed that Stalinist TWU officials Austin Hogan and John Santo met in Quill's absence with Mayor O'Dwyer and agreed to support a New York transit fare increase in order to secure a wage deal. Since Quill himself had been a party to Stalinist acts and policies he now denounced, he could explain his own role only as that of an honest yokel to whom the Stalinists had sold the Brooklyn Bridge.

At the May 1948 Fourth Constitutional Convention of the United Steelworkers of America, the delegates, in the words of Farrell Dobbs' eyewitness report in the May 24 *Militant,* "witnessed a wild orgy of redbaiting, used by Philip Murray to smother criticism of his policies which deprived workers in basic steel of a wage increase, and to ram through the convention" decisions to empower the officers to take the Taft-Hartley oath; denunciation of the Wallace party; authorization for the leaders to endorse one of the major party candidates; endorsement of the Marshall Plan and support of peacetime conscription "in case of a possible further worsening of international relations." Members of the Communist Party were barred from holding office in the union. Murray and his staff were voted salary increases ranging from $5,000 a year for Murray down to $2,000 for district representatives.

Here we see exemplified the process through which the whole CIO was moving: the intensification of political reaction; the hardening of the bureaucratic crust; the greater centralization of power in the hands of the top leaders; the elimination of democratic rights; and, of course, increased privileges and emoluments that went with greater bureaucratic power.

In the course of the Steelworkers convention, Director Germano of District 31 denounced as a "Communist" Delegate Nick Migas of Local 1010, East Chicago, Indiana. Migas had signed a leaflet to the delegates which opposed Murray's "no-strike" policy in the "third round" wage campaign, and his opposition to Wallace. While Migas was on the convention floor facing 3,200 delegates and attempting to reply, Murray took the microphone and whipped the convention into a frenzy against the helpless Migas who could not be heard. Murray charged Migas with "treasonous conduct." Threats of physical violence were hurled at him from various parts of the hall.

Migas tried to slip quietly from the convention hall. Almost a third of the delegates trailed out after him into Boston's Huntington Avenue where he was caught and savagely beaten. After the police, who were on the scene and had been in the hall, thought Migas had received "enough," they hauled him to the police station under "protective custody." The next day the constitutional amendment barring communists and "other subversives" from steel union office was easily pushed through. Murray no longer acted as a moderating influence on the extreme right-wingers. He incited the pack.

This drive in the CIO against "subversives" derived its impulse from the virulent anti-communist campaign of the capitalist press and government that was designed to silence all opposition to the cold-war strategy. The basis of this witch hunt against political dissenters was Truman's executive order of March 24, 1947, providing for a "loyalty" investigation of more than two million federal employees. They were to be fired for mere suspicion of disloyalty— a term never defined—and for association or connection with any so-called subversive organizations.

The methods of the purge were disclosed on December 27, 1947, in a statement by Seth Richardson, Chairman of the Loyalty Review Board of the United States Civil Service Commission. These methods paralleled in a number of respects those made notorious by Hitler's infamous Gestapo. "Evidence" against federal workers would be supplied by the Federal Bureau of Investigation (FBI) which would function as a secret political police, ferreting out intimate details of the private lives, activities and opinions of federal employees. All "loyalty" proceedings were to "be kept entirely secret," said Richardson. Accused persons would be denied the elementary right to confront and cross-examine their accusers and detractors and "will not be permitted to examine or inspect" FBI reports alleged to contain damaging information against those charged with "disloyalty."

One of the first victims of Truman's "loyalty" purge was James

Kutcher, a veteran who lost both legs in Italy in the Battle of San Pietro. Employed as a clerk in the Veterans Administration office in Newark, New Jersey, he was fired as a "security risk" and "subversive" because of his acknowledged membership in the Socialist Workers Party. Kutcher was reinstated in his job in 1956 only after an eight-year civil liberties fight that won the backing of unions representing several million members.

Thousands of careers were ruined, reputations dishonored and lives destroyed, without the accused having the chance to defend themselves against their unknown, unseen defamers. In the wake of this gigantic purge, scores of bills to eliminate basic constitutional rights of free opinion and expression were introduced into Congress. Several such bills fostered or backed by Democrats, including prominent liberals, were eventually passed.

Organizations branded "subversive" by a single attorney general, with but one or two exceptions in over a decade, were denied any opportunity for a public hearing and defense against the label of "subversive" and the political blacklist. "Guilt by association" became the standard formula for public degradation and intimidation.

From the very first, union members were made the target of this drive to smother independent or critical thought and opinion. A few days after Richardson's disclosure of the "loyalty" review procedure, army brass began to move into private plants and to secure summary dismissals of workers they designated "bad security risks." In many instances, those fingered as risks were active union shop stewards and grievance committeemen whom the corporations had previously spotted as "troublemakers."

It was in this fertile soil that "McCarthyism" — that incipient American fascist movement personified in the late Senator Joseph McCarthy of Wisconsin — flourished with such vigor in the first half of the Fifties.

29

The Wallace Campaign and Truman's Victory

The most vital question facing labor in 1948 was that of political action.

From the standpoint of program, it would appear that the CIO leadership could have had no hesitancy. It had already been demonstrated that they were prepared to tear the CIO apart, if need be, in support of Truman's foreign policy. The Truman Doctrine was their doctrine. They had rejected Wallace, Truman's leading opponent from within the liberal capitalist political camp. They even required that all CIO leaders and bodies declare positive and open opposition to Wallace. They did make a few formal protests against some of the more atrocious aspects of Truman's "loyalty" purge but they emulated the spirit of this purge in their own factional war against "subversives." Yet the CIO leaders showed the greatest reluctance to endorse Truman's candidacy for President.

The fact was simply that they had grave doubts that he could win. He was a poor bet. In a keen analysis of the Democratic Party's dilemma at that stage, George Breitman had summed up the situation in the March 15 *Militant:* "To tell the plain truth, if it weren't for the hope that the Murrays, Greens and Whitneys can pull it through, the Democratic Party might well disintegrate by the end of the year."

The Democratic Party was, as it still is, a coalition of disparate and even conflicting elements. It was ruled from the top by a clique of big city bosses and Southern white supremacists, but its mass base was primarily the wage earners. In the spring of 1948, this coalition appeared to be coming apart at the seams. Under the pressure of a growing and increasingly aggressive Negro civil rights movement, Truman was being forced to take verbal positions on

civil rights that antagonized many elements of the powerful Southern bloc in the Democratic Party. At the same time, the initial
response to the Wallace movement, which held out a promise to
settle the United States-Soviet conflict by diplomatic means, had
been extremely promising. Wallace's sponsors were confidently
predicting he would capture as many as four million votes in November; early in the campaign this did not appear to be outside the
realm of possibility.

Since the political philosophy of the opportunist labor bureaucrats holds that it is better to back a winning candidate who may
give only a few crumbs than to back a losing candidate who will have
no crumbs to give, the CIO leaders were scanning the political horizon for a sure Democratic Party winner in place of Truman. The
immediate concern of the union leaders was how to salvage the
Democratic Party and how to reinforce the Democratic-labor coalition to the advantage of the labor bureaucracy. The first thing the
union officialdom had to do was to sell the workers on the proposition
that it was imperative to secure a Democratic Party administration
in Washington just this one more time. After that, there would be
a new political realignment of all the "progressive" forces versus
all the reactionary forces from which would emerge a fresh party
in which labor would assume its rightful place as a leading, even a
commanding, sector.

This concept was embodied in a resolution adopted March 3, 1948,
by the CIO United Automobile Workers International Executive Board.
The board voted to reject Wallace's third party not only "as a political maneuver contrary to the best interests of labor and the
nation" but also "as an obstacle in the way of establishing a successful and genuine progressive political party in the U. S. A."

Less than a week after the adoption of the resolution, Max Zaritsky
of the AFL Hatters, Cap and Millinery Workers further disclosed
the trepidations of union officials about Truman's candidacy. Truman's nomination by the Democratic Party, said Zaritsky, would
be a "misfortune" because the President had "completely lost" the
confidence of the workers and could not be elected in November.
The *New York Times* commented that Zaritsky was not alone in his
views: "It is an open secret that his opinion that Mr. Truman cannot
command any important section of the labor vote is almost universally shared by ranking officials of both the American Federation
of Labor and the Congress of Industrial Organizations."

Louis Hollander, head of the New York State CIO, also held
out the prospect of a new party after 1948. "Some day we will have
a real independent Labor Party," he said in an interview in the

March 29 *Labor Leader,* organ of the Association of Catholic Trade Unionists, "built from the bottom up," that "won't have to call itself 'the third party.' It will be the second or even the first party."

In the meantime, the argument went, it was crucial that the Democratic Party again be put in the driver's seat. But Truman was unfit for the presidency and, besides, he couldn't win. Whom did Hollander, Reuther, Carey, Murray have in mind? Their man—General Dwight D. Eisenhower.

The "labor statesmen" set afoot a "Draft Eisenhower" campaign. They didn't know if he would run and, especially, if he would run as a Democrat. But they were sure he could win a lot of votes.

On April 4 the *Detroit Free Press* carried an interview with Walter Reuther. The head of the CIO's largest affiliate complained that "Truman is hopelessly inadequate" and hoped that "some competent man like Eisenhower will be nominated by the Democrats." CIO Secretary-Treasurer James Carey appeared at a gathering of Americans for Democratic Action to make a veritable stump speech for Eisenhower. At the same time, "spontaneous" Eisenhower-for-President resolutions began sprouting in CIO Steelworkers locals in preparation for the steel union convention. Nothing came of these attempts. Eisenhower declared on July 5 that he would not accept any nomination for public office "or participate in a partisan political contest."

The Republican national convention on June 24 nominated Governor Thomas E. Dewey for President and Governor Earl Warren for Vice-President. Heady with high hopes of victory after 16 years of exile from the White House, the Republicans included in their platform praise for the Taft-Hartley Act and a pledge of its strict enforcement. They also promised to reduce the national debt, cut taxes and maintain the "bipartisan" foreign policy initiated by the Democrats.

The day before the Democratic Party national convention opened in Philadelphia, a closed caucus of 75 leaders of the CIO Political Action Committee met in the City of Brotherly Love. PAC Chairman Jack Kroll glumly forecast that the CIO members may "just sit on their hands and wait" in November and "this may well result in a Republican victory."

On July 15 the Democrats nominated Truman for President and Senate Minority Leader Alben W. Barkley of Kentucky for Vice-President. In winning the nomination, Truman made strong gestures designed to hold or win labor and Negro support. The labor plank of the Democratic platform promised unconditional repeal of the Taft-Hartley Act—organized labor's main demand. Truman also advanced a civil rights program including abolition of poll taxes in federal elections, a federal anti-lynch law and a fair employment practices act. This was adopted against Southern opposition by a vote of 651 to 582. As a result, some Southern Democrats bolted the regular ticket and set up a States Rights Party which ran Governor J. Strom Thurmond of South Carolina for President. The main group of Southern Democrats backed the Truman ticket, knowing full well that the civil rights plank was intended solely as a vote-catching device for Negroes in Northern states where they represented a possible balance of power.

The Wallace movement held its national convention July 23-26 in Philadelphia and formally established the Progressive Party. Of the 3,240 convention delegates, only 529 were trade-union members. The largest convention delegations came from Stalinist-ruled organizations such as the New York ALP, the California IPP and the Illinois Progressive Party, as well as fraternal and foreign-language societies. The convention nominated Wallace for President and United States Senator Glen H. Taylor, Idaho Democrat, for Vice-President.

The Progressive Party convention adopted a platform somewhat to the left of the Democrats, including a plank calling for nationalization of some large banks, railroads, utilities and industries based on government subsidies. But Wallace's acceptance speech still stressed his claim to being the best defender of the capitalist system. His "anti-war" program boiled down to some improvements in the United Nations setup and man-to-man talks with Stalin.

Although the Stalinists supplied much of the working forces and apparatus of the Wallace movement, they ran it on behalf of Wallace and his political cronies. Wallace and Taylor, who provided the Progressive Party's reason for existence, were subject to no membership control; they did or said anything they pleased. On the opening day of his nominating convention, Wallace conceded in a press interview that he had a lot of "Communist party support" but that he regarded this as a "liability."

Early in August Kroll indicated that the CIO leadership had managed to overcome its strong distaste for Truman and would most likely back his candidacy. On August 31 the CIO Executive Board meeting in Chicago voted 35 to 12 — with only the pro-Wallaceites dissenting — to endorse the Democratic slate.

Two days later the CIO Political Action Committee issued a statement of support to the Democratic ticket, which completely reversed almost everything the CIO leaders had been saying about Truman for two years. It ignored the President's strikebreaking use of the Taft-Hartley Act, his demands for anti-labor legislation such as a "draft strikers" law. Now the CIO-PAC leaders discovered that "the platform of the Democratic Party and the record of Harry S. Truman and Senator Alben W. Barkley are deserving of enthusiastic support."

The CIO leaders threw every resource into the Democratic campaign. So did the AFL leadership, who had abandoned their previous opposition to any form of labor political organization and had set up Labor's League for Political Education (LLPE) at the 1947 AFL convention. The CIO-PAC reportedly spent $1,500,000 to aid the Democratic campaign, and the LLPE a like amount. Even more decisive were the human resources — the hundreds of thousands of union organizers and members mobilized by the CIO and AFL as doorbell ringers, leaflet distributors, and chauffeurs to drive voters to the polls.

Not all the union leaders were supporting Truman. At the United Mine Workers convention which opened on October 5, John L. Lewis denounced those who ran to the White House "at the whim of the President" and there "sell out the labor movement and sell out their own union for a lunch...They seem to fawn too much in the presence of the rich and powerful, and they are untrue to the men who work and pay their salaries and sustain them in the comforts they enjoy. I have a contempt for such men."

But when he had finished uttering these powerful truths, Lewis proposed only to lead labor into the political camp of another deadly enemy of labor — the Republican Dewey. The next day Dewey demonstratively declared his support for the Taft-Hartley Act. But if Lewis had to eat his own words about Dewey, he at least added an extra pinch of salt to give them savor. The UMW convention raised his annual salary from $25,000 to $50,000 to sustain him in the comforts he enjoyed. Lewis became the highest paid union official in the world. Capitalism was good to Lewis and, in the final analysis, he remained loyal to it.

Truman cleverly pitched his election campaign to the sentiments of the workers. In his Labor Day message he called for repeal of the Taft-Hartley Act which, he said, "unfairly restricts labor unions and their members." He opened his campaign in the Michigan auto centers of Flint and Detroit. On September 6 he claimed that if the Republicans were elected there would be a depression within a year or two. This prediction of economic crisis turned out to be true — in 1949 and early 1950 after the workers returned Truman to the White House. As the campaign proceeded, Truman "poured it on" in a series of speeches full of radical-sounding demagogy. The

Republican Party, he said on September 18, was in the hands of "Wall Street gluttons," and on October 8 he said the major issue was "hard times or prosperity."

In August and September, Truman's Republican opponents, using Truman's own "loyalty" purge as a springboard, conducted red-scare hearings before the House Un-American Activities Committee and before a Senate Investigating Committee subcommittee at which former Communist Party members, including Elizabeth T. Bentley and Louis F. Budenz, claimed that a fantastic number of "Communists" and "Soviet spies" infested the Truman administration, especially the State Department. On September 22 in San Francisco, Truman even appeared as defender of civil liberties against the witch-hunters when he denounced the House Un-American Activities Committee as "more un-American than the activities it is investigating."

As the international crisis grew with the conflict over Berlin, Truman in October yanked Wallace's chief plank from under him by announcing a plan to send Chief Justice Frederick M. Vinson of the United States Supreme Court to Moscow to negotiate personally with Stalin.

When all the votes were counted by the morning of November 3, Truman had scored an upset. He won with 304 electoral votes in 28 states to Dewey's 189 electoral votes in 16 states. The popular vote for Truman was 23,667,727; for Dewey, 21,542,581. The States Rights Party carried four Southern states with 38 electoral votes and 1,005,945 popular votes. Wallace did not win a single electoral vote; his popular vote, however, was 1,116,379. In several states the Progressive Party had been ruled off the ballot which deprived Wallace of thousands of votes more.

"Labor did it!" were the first words of Truman when he heard the news of his unexpected victory on the morning of November 3. This was the truth. Later Truman was to shrug off the decisive role of organized labor in his re-election, but that was the ungrateful act of an unprincipled politician trying to minimize the debt he owed those he was preparing to stab in the back. Senator J. Howard McGrath, Democratic Party National Chairman, in the very first words of his victory statement paid full tribute to organized labor for his party's victory.

The chief positive result of the election was to indicate strongly that organized labor, if mobilized on a correct program and in its own party, could sweep the nation and take political power outright in the name of the working class. Said the November 8 *Militant:* "Such is the weight of organized labor in the American population that it could pick out a discredited medocrity like Truman, conceded by the union leaders themselves not to have a chance if they could not arouse the labor vote, and put him back in the White House."

Within 24 hours of his election, Truman began to hedge on his pledge to fight for unconditional repeal of the Taft-Hartley Act, the major plank of the Democratic platform. On November 4 Secretary of Labor Maurice J. Tobin revealed that the President was preparing a new labor law to offer as a substitute. At the same time he would ask Congress to repeal the Taft-Hartley Act. The Democratic Party's promise turned out to be the tricky gambit of seeking to replace one anti-labor law with another. Truman had already spelled out his substitute: a "draft strikers" law; "fact-finding" government intervention and a 60-day "cooling off" period before strikes; binding arbitration in all labor disputes involving interpretations of contracts; outlawing of "jurisdictional" strikes and secondary boycotts; government seizure of plants and the use of injunctions against strikes affecting the "public welfare."

At the AFL convention three weeks after the election, George Meany and other leaders indicated they were prepared to leave the door open for a "substitute" labor law. Their resolution called for legislation to ensure that "the public welfare is paramount...and must not again be placed in jeopardy by the irresponsible action of anyone," the standard formula for legislation to illegalize industry-wide strikes. Meany explained that the AFL would look "favorably" on the type of legislation, for instance, that Truman had asked for in his January 1947 message to Congress.

The CIO national convention in Portland, Oregon, November 22-26, was converted into a post-election "victory" jubilee. To be sure, the convention reiterated the CIO's call for repeal of the Taft-Hartley Act, but sounded no warning about the obvious intent of Truman and the Democrats to weasel out of their campaign promises. With rapidly increasing unemployment, with the cost of living registering new highs, the CIO leaders turned instead to the matter of gravest concern to them—the factional war in the CIO. Riding the crest of their "great labor victory" in having won Truman a new four-year rent-free lease on the White House, the CIO right wing concentrated on internal dissenters.

Wallace's unexpectedly small vote dealt a devastating blow to the pretensions of the new Progressive Party and its chief supporters, the Stalinists. Even the November 4 *Daily Worker* had to confess: "The vote for Wallace, it must be admitted, fell below not only the unrealistic quotas assigned to him by certain forces, but even below what his most sober supporters, including this paper, had suspected."

Nothing was said by the *Worker* on the chief and fatal flaw in the Wallace movement—its attempt to circumvent the labor unions. It complained in its post-mortem on "The Meaning of Truman's Election" that "Truman won the election by a hypocritical copying of the speeches of Franklin D. Roosevelt and by imitating as much as he dared the charges of the Progressive Party and Henry Wallace." He even "stole" Wallace's "peace" program, lamented the *Worker,* for "Truman won support when he announced—even though he did not carry out—the Vinson peace mission to Moscow."

Discouraged, disoriented and depressed by the debacle of their Wallace adventure, the Stalinists came into the 1948 CIO convention a sickly crew. The only question was how far Murray was prepared to go in dealing with them, since the Stalinists were still formidably entrenched in about a fourth of the CIO unions with a claimed composite membership of up to one million.

30

Raids and Purges

In the months immediately preceding the November 1948 CIO convention, the one CIO activity that had not slackened, except for electioneering, was the factional war. The CIO majority leaders had not organized many unorganized workers, but they had "reorganized" quite a few dues-paying members in raids on the Stalinist-led unions. Reuther, for one, took advantage of the Taft-Hartley Act to grab the large Royal Typewriter UE-CIO local at Hartford, Connecticut, in an NLRB election from which the UE was barred. The UE decision not to take the Taft-Hartley oath had been in strict conformity with the 1947 CIO convention resolution.

John Green's CIO Shipbuilding Workers took over sections of the CIO United Public Workers; the Mine, Mill and Smelter Workers; and other unions even more remote from the shipyards. The CIO United Paperworkers of America, headed by Harry Sayre, invaded the CIO United Office and Professional Workers Union. In August, the CIO United Auto Workers Executive Board accepted the affiliation of 20,000 members of the National Association of Die Casting Workers, which had split in June from the Mine, Mill and Smelter Workers.

CIO raids on established CIO locals and international unions under Stalinist influence were occurring in the midst of a drive by the AFL Teamsters leadership to swallow up various unions, both CIO and AFL. This aroused justified CIO protest against "cannibal unionism."

As the 1948 CIO convention approached, the factional divisions had almost hardened into the form they were to take at the 1949 split convention. The Stalinists, in a bloc with independents like UE-CIO President Albert J. Fitzgerald who had headed the Labor Committee for Wallace, had succeeded in nailing down their control of the UE at its September 1948 convention. The Stalinists led about 75 per cent of its delegates, although a sizable minority of the union had seceded before the convention and affiliated with raiding CIO unions.

After the defeat of the Stalinists in the NMU elections, Curran consolidated his position by expelling leading Stalinists. On August 30 a general membership meeting in the New York City port heard charges of misconduct and mishandling of funds against Ferdinand Smith, Howard McKenzie and Paul Palazzi, all former officers of the union. The meeting upheld the charges by a vote of 1,462 to 523. Although Curran denied any intention of a political purge, C. Thomas reported in the September 6 *Militant* that "the most conscious members are apprehensive of any move, even though directed against the hated CP hacks, that smacks of minority persecution." This apprehension was to prove entirely justified within the next year.

At the same time, the Quill forces in the TWU had captured one stronghold after another and had left the Stalinists with only mechanical control of the International Executive Board. The Stalinists sought to safeguard their board positions by decreeing a change in the union's election procedure. This decree would deprive the forthcoming TWU convention of its constitutional power to elect the international officers, substituting a 40-day membership referendum. But Quill, who now based himself on Murray's program, gave the Stalinist faction a stunning defeat at the convention in December shortly after the CIO convention. The Stalinists were driven out of office after a 14-year reign.

Prior to the national CIO convention in Portland, the Murray-Reuther-Carey forces moved to take over two important CIO councils. On September 3, after a turbulent two and a half days, national CIO representative Adolph Germer assumed authority over the Wayne County (Detroit) CIO convention as an administrator. He then called a new convention, with committees designated by him. A majority of delegates, despite strong opposition to the dictatorial methods employed, remained with the new convention rather than risk a split in the largest industrial center of the CIO movement.

On November 20 — two days before the convention — a meeting of the National Executive Board by a 38 to 5 vote revoked the charter of the New York City CIO Council, the greatest national stronghold of the Stalinists, placing it under a Murray-appointed administrator. The board instructed Louis Hollander to take over the offices, funds, records and properties of the council. The CIO National Board declared the New York City body guilty of "slavish adherence" to the "line and dictates of the Communist Party." Four of the ten CIO Board members who had been associated with Stalinist policy abstained on the vote; five voted against; Bridges was absent. However, the dissenting Stalinists later meekly announced they would not contest the decision at the convention "in the interests of unity."

In his opening speech on November 22 to the convention, Murray demanded to know if the Stalinists were going to "continue expressing their criticism and condemnation of the national CIO in its support of the Marshall Plan." He also assailed them for wanting "to drive Truman out of the White House"—a sentiment Murray, Reuther and Carey had themselves voiced when they sought Eisenhower as a candidate.

Murray solemnly denied that he was engaged in a politically-motivated purge: "It is not a question of communism with me. If a communist is leading a labor organization in the CIO and, after years of existence he is unable to demonstrate his fitness to organize the unorganized, then, in justice to the people employed in that industry, he should resign. That is a practical, realistic, factual description of certain situations which confront the Congress of Industrial Organizations today."

In this fashion Murray tried to foist upon the Stalinists sole responsibility for the failures and organizational shortcomings of the CIO. He also sought to gain exceptional centralized powers to take organizational measures not only against recalcitrant state and local CIO councils but also against affiliated international industrial unions. A resolution granting the Executive Board such dictatorial reorganizational powers over international unions was adopted on November 25 by a ten-to-one majority.

On the second day, Murray announced there would be no more minority reports. Selly, head of the American Communications Association, tried to raise the issue of internal raiding while speaking in support of Murray's resolution for "Organizing the Unorganized." Convention Chairman Emil Rieve ruled out of order all discussion of "so-called raids" as being within the purview only of the convention's Jurisdictional Committee.

Discussion on the political action resolution came on the third day. This was the supreme moment for the right-wing leaders. Murray and his lieutenants flogged the Stalinists with the "great labor victory" of Truman's election. Murray described his decision to support Truman as of almost divine revelation:

"I thought of you [CIO leaders and delegates]. I thought of the millions whom you are privileged and honored to represent. I thought of your children and their homes, and the millions of children of your constituents. I thought of my country. I thought of my God. And I made my decision."

The political action resolution, adopted by a vote of 537 to 49, stated categorically: "We reaffirm our decision and reject any and all proposals for a third party, at this time." Walter Reuther and Emil Mazey remained silent throughout the debate and voted for the resolution, although the UAW Executive Board a few months before had adopted Reuther's resolution calling for a "new political realignment" after the 1948 elections.

CIO-PAC Chairman Jack Kroll falsely castigated the Stalinists as supporters of Thomas E. Dewey, the Republican. He claimed that through the Wallace campaign "we saw the extremists of the left make their brazen bid to put Tom Dewey in the White House." The real Stalinist crime, of course, consisted in disorienting the movement for a genuine labor party by creating a political vehicle for a single capitalist politician, Wallace, who was totally undependable as a defender of labor's rights or as a fighter against imperialist war.

One important motivation for the intensity of the attack on the Stalinists was the desire of official CIO leaders to cover up for their own failure to lead an effective defense of the membership's living standards. This failure was indicated by Murray himself in his report to the CIO. Demonstrating the need for "fourth round" wage increases, Murray cited government figures showing that the share of employees in the national income had declined from 67.6% in 1945 to 61.2% in 1948 while all forms of ownership had raised their share in the same four years. Corporate net profits had increased from 4.8% to 9.1% of the national income. In the same period all net profits had risen 134.5%; prices, 35.2%; money wages, 23.1%.

There was another big problem the CIO leaders had to confront: Why was the CIO unable to grow? Why was it no longer sweeping in new hundreds of thousands and even millions of members as it had in the prewar days?

The CIO leadership did not relate this stagnation to their own policies — their dependence on political favors rather than independent labor action; their retreat before political reaction, as in the case of the Taft-Hartley Law; their class collaboration, which vitiated any effective struggle on the economic and political battlefronts. The big drawback, as they saw it, was — the "Communists." If only the CIO wasn't "tainted" with the "Communists," it would be able to attract new layers of workers, gain greater favor in the eyes of the politicians and government officials, attain more "respectability," even soften the flinty hearts of the employers.

This view was expressed most blatantly at the 1948 convention by George Baldanzi, executive vice-president of the Textile Workers Union. In response to veiled threats of split by James Matles of the United Electrical Workers, Baldanzi replied: "It is high time that we shed ourselves of our own internal enemies to make the job [of organizing] a little easier." He claimed that the whole organization work of the CIO, particularly in the South, "will be wasted until we can...face the workers of America as a one hundred per cent American organization."

Years after most of the Stalinists and all the Stalinist-led unions were expelled or split from the CIO, even the merged AFL-CIO made no significant inroads in those very fields where the CIO leaders in 1948 charged the "Communists" with responsibility for failure. At the 1955 merger convention, the organization of the white-collar workers — from office workers and government employees to store clerks and scientific technicians — was to be made a top-priority task of the new fifteen-million-member unified labor organization. Yet, as late as January 1960, the top brass of the AFL-CIO were to complain once more about the abysmal results in the campaign to organize the white-collar workers.

Even more appalling has been the record of the official labor bureaucracy on the organization of the South, the most formidable citadel of both the anti-Negro and anti-union elements in the country. The open-shop South, with its low living standards and cheap labor supply, has been for decades the chief haven for runaway plants from the North, particularly in the textile industry. During the late 1920's the old AFL had launched a special campaign to organize the South. Twenty years later Baldanzi blamed the failure of the CIO in this area on the Communist Party which, during its early period, had made the greatest sacrifices and most heroic efforts to help organize the Southern textile and agricultural workers.

The question of the organization of the South, which looms with especial magnitude because of the great Negro upsurge of the past decade, touches on some of the gravest weaknesses in the policies and methods of the American labor bureaucracy.

The CIO in its rise represented a great step forward in many spheres, including that of racial integration. It was founded on the principle of no discrimination. All forms of the color line were constitutionally banned from all CIO affiliates and from the national CIO. This was a far cry from the traditional situation in the AFL and railroad brotherhoods. As late as the AFL-CIO merger in 1955, there were still some thirty AFL international unions with constitutional color bars and restrictions.

At its peak membership of six million, the CIO included a half million Negro workers. They were a significant force in such major unions as steel, automobile and packinghouse. At the 1947 convention of the CIO packinghouse workers, one-third of all the delegates were Negroes. This does not mean that Negro workers achieved equality with all other workers in the CIO-organized industries or even were accorded their proper representation in the unions. The CIO did a little to change the discriminating corporation pattern in the hiring and upgrading of the Negro, but he remained the last hired and the first fired, and was restricted to the hardest, dirtiest and lowest-paid work. The CIO did give him, where he was able to enter basic industries, union status and a measure of union protection. In return, the Negro worker gave the CIO unbounded loyalty and fighting support.

Just before Pearl Harbor, at the 1941 CIO convention, a campaign was initiated to organize the South. This campaign was to be, in Philip Murray's words, the CIO's "Task Number One." The CIO leadership, which included the Stalinists, abandoned this number one task during the whole of World War II, just as they sacrificed the general interests of labor to the demands of the capitalist war machine.

During the war, the insistent demand of the Negro workers for jobs in the better-paying war industries and for an end to segregation in housing and education led to the establishment in 1944 of the CIO Committee to Abolish Racial Discrimination. Between March 15 and August 15, state and local committees had increased from 50 to 85, with organizations even in Georgia, North Carolina, West Virginia, Kentucky, Texas, Kansas and Alabama. They succeeded in winning a number of cases involving such issues as job upgrading and integrated government housing. But this CIO activity did not touch at the core of the problem. The vast Southland remained generally unorganized and constantly fed the springs of anti-Negro and anti-labor poison throughout the country. In the South, the issues of civil rights and labor rights fused.

In May 1946, the CIO opened what was announced as its greatest organizing campaign since the 1936-37 founding drive — a campaign called "Operation Dixie." This phrase indicated a grand offensive to be run with the power, precision and organization of a military drive. Murray called it a "crusade" to mobilize not less than one million Southern workers into the CIO within a year. To this end the national CIO sent 400 organizers to key selected points in the South and placed a million-dollar fund at their disposal.

On the occasion of the opening of "Operation Dixie," I wrote in the May 4, 1946 *Militant* an estimation of the scope of the task and what was required to carry it out successfully: "United organization of the cruelly exploited Southern Negro and white workers would constitute the first great advance in what inevitably must develop into a social, economic and political struggle aimed at a profound transformation of the entire South... Anyone acquainted with the Southern scene recognizes that a real drive to bring the white and Negro workers together will be resisted with all the ferocity and violence that the Southern ruling class can muster... Any policy that... seeks to confine itself to the most narrow trade-union aims or tries to adapt itself... to the prejudices of the Southern system can only hamper and weaken 'Operation Dixie'..."

For a while Van A. Bittner, the CIO's Southern campaign director and a vice-president of the CIO Steelworkers, kept announcing "real progress." By February 1947, the CIO Southern Organizing Committee was able to report establishment of 324 new local unions in the South. But as time passed, the campaign lagged more and more. By 1948 it had become half buried and almost forgotten.

The reason for the failure of "Operation Dixie" was not the Stalinists. Their contribution to its failure had been the same as that of the official CIO bureaucracy. It was impossible to support the Democratic Party and not reinforce its Southern wing, the chief political prop of the Jim Crow system and one-party dictatorship in the South. The CIO leaders refused to wage political war against the Southern ruling class because that would undermine the whole Democratic Party and put an end to the Democratic Party-labor coalition. The Stalinists had supported that policy and had reinforced the leadership in its bankrupt political course. To this day, the organization of the South remains unachieved because the union leadership is in an alliance with a political machine that is built in large part on the rule of the white supremacists and labor-haters of the South.

31

The "Fourth Round" Wage Campaign

Between the CIO's 1948 convention and its final cold war split in early 1950, the country suffered serious economic difficulties.

Democratic Party propaganda has represented the five-year period between the end of the second world war and the beginning of the Korean intervention as a time of healthy economic growth. This falsification is accomplished by lumping the years of the Korean war boom with the preceding years of stagnation and decline. It hides the real conditions that prevailed during the peacetime years of Truman's administration. It tends to cover up the most vital fact of modern American economic history: At no time since 1929 has American capitalism maintained even a semblance of economic stability and growth without huge military spending and war debt.

There has been only one brief period, from June 1947 to June 1950, when the American capitalist economy did not operate under conditions in which vast government deficit spending, particularly for military purposes, has not been clearly decisive in sustaining the economy, although even in 1947-50 the annual direct military budget remained from eleven to fourteen times higher than in 1939. But Truman's "unprecedented prosperity" of 1947 had already evaporated before he sent his message to the new Congress on the fifth of January, 1949.

In the "Economic Report" that accompanied his "State of the Union" message to Congress, Truman acknowledged that the "prosperity of the postwar years...has rested considerably on somewhat temporary factors which were the aftermath of war..." Now, he admitted, "the momentum of war-created demand and war-created purchasing power has waned."

He conceded other flaws in the prosperity: "Five million families are still living in slums and firetraps. Three million families share their homes with others." He expressed some dissatisfaction with the social security system which after fourteen years left more than a third of all wage earners uncovered and paid a starvation pittance averaging only $25 a month to the pauperized aged. But even if the benefits in 1949 had been doubled, they would merely have been restored to their meager purchasing power of 1939, since they had never been increased during the entire wartime and postwar inflation decade.

The one precise point of Truman's message was his proposal of a $15 billion direct military budget for fiscal 1950, a sum which the *New York Times* called the "most audacious for any non-war period in American history."

Truman hardly had time to get comfortably resettled in the White House when a January 14, 1949 United Press dispatch from Washington reported that both government and labor economists were predicting a postwar peak in unemployment by spring.

By July, the Truman administration's official figures on unemployment rose above the four million mark. The *CIO News Service* on August 15 pointed out that in addition to the four million totally jobless, there were "nine million or more persons working only part time — many of them not more than 20 hours a week."

For some years the AFL had maintained a Shorter Work Week Committee, headed by Daniel W. Tracy, president of the International Brotherhood of Electrical Workers. This committee had been lifeless until, one day in January 1949, Tracy issued a press statement saying that "we don't know how long present employment will continue, but we must be prepared to move toward a shorter work week."

UAW President Walter Reuther announced on January 16, 1949 that the union's Executive Board had adopted a program of "fourth round" demands, as follows:

"An adequate pension and retirement program. 2) A comprehensive social security program including health, hospitalization, surgical and life insurance provisions. 3) A wage increase to restore the buying power of wages to the level of June 1946, when OPA was destroyed."

Conspicuously absent from this program was any reference to the long-established UAW and CIO program for the 30-hour week and six-hour day with no reduction in take-home pay. Large layoffs were already beginning in the automobile industry. Reuther's failure to raise the demand was not an oversight.

In his remarks to the UAW economic conference of national and

regional auto union leaders on February 20 in Detroit, Reuther referred to the demand for the 30-hour week at 40 hours' pay as the
program of the Communist Party and *Daily Worker*. He inferred that
this demand was a plot to cut American production to the advantage
of the Soviet Union. He said that people advocating this program
were not to be considered loyal union members.

How the 30-hour week, which would provide for the employment
of more workers, would curtail production, Reuther failed to explain. Such a program might force the industry to shift some of its
monumental profits into workers' pay checks by requiring the payment of overtime rates after 30 instead of 40 hours. This had been
the official program of the UAW before the war and had been re-
adopted at both the 1944 and 1946 conventions in anticipation of the
very unemployment situation facing the auto workers in 1949. The
auto corporations were already instituting the 32, 24 and 16-hour
week for scores of thousands of workers, in addition to those laid
off. These part-time workers, however, were getting equivalent
cuts in take-home pay.

The Committee for a Militant and Democratic UAW, a progressive grouping of UAW members formed after the 1947 convention,
charged that Reuther was seeking "peace at any price" with the corporations. This committee's paper, the *Auto Union Builder,* reported
in February, after Reuther's attack on the shorter work-week program, that there was a "deep sense of dissatisfaction" among many
UAW members and local officers with the Reuther administration's
policies.

"We refer particularly," said the *Auto Union Builder,* "to the [UAW]
administration's soft policy toward the corporations on speed-up
and its collusion and collaboration with management against militant members of the UAW; we refer particularly to the signing of
the two-year outrageously inadequate contract in General Motors,
which moreover takes one-quarter of our union membership out of
wage and pension negotiations in 1949; we refer particularly to the
throttling of the democratic processes inside our union and the attempt to fasten on the membership the dictatorial rule of a self-
perpetuating machine."

The paper then called attention to the fact that "in the past year
over 5,000 GM workers have been disciplined by layoffs of from
three to 90 days and dozens more have been fired for attempting to
resist the raising of production standards." It stated that Reuther
had not fought the speed-up and had "refused to permit the ranks to
defend themselves against this evil."

The general tendency of the CIO leaders in the face of advancing unemployment was to put up no fight, reduce wage demands to a minimum and settle for so-called fringe benefits which added little or nothing to take-home pay. Some CIO unions, such as the oil, shipbuilding, rubber and packinghouse workers, did raise the formal demand for the shorter work week and no cut in pay. In June, the CIO Brewery Workers in New York City won a 37-1/2-hour week at 40 hours' pay. But the leaders of the big key unions used the very fear of unemployment to discourage wage demands and to put a damper on the fight for an effective program which would tend to spread existing work more widely without loss of weekly income. At the first sign of unemployment, the leaders of the 350,000-member Amalgamated Clothing Workers had hastened to announce in February that they would "postpone" their efforts to get wage increases in 1949. The CIO Textile Workers leaders, representing 400,000 workers, similarly announced they were dropping wage demands. The Stalinist-influenced leadership of the CIO United Electrical Workers, after much blarney earlier in the year about militancy, in July indefinitely postponed wage negotiations with the General Electric Corporation.

Harry Bridges proposed to solve the problem of unemployment among the CIO West Coast longshoremen by an ingenious plan to eliminate 1,000 union members from the industry. A meeting in February of 4,000 ILWU-CIO members in San Francisco, enraged by the proposal, booed him down when he attempted to defend his slick plan. It was denounced from the floor as a "union-busting" proposition and voted down by a three-to-one majority.

The growing unemployment in 1949 did not mean that the previous two years of "unprecedented prosperity" had been a golden age for labor. "One-third of a nation," in the words of Roosevelt 12 years before, was still "ill-housed, ill-clad, ill-nourished." This had been affirmed in a report released on November 12, 1949, by the Subcommittee on Low-Income Families of the Joint Congressional Committee on the Economic Report, headed by Senator Sparkman of Alabama.

This committee's conservative findings on living conditions in 1948, when production and employment had reached the then highest peacetime peak in history, revealed that some 16 million American family units had received an annual cash income of less than $2,000. Eight million of these family units subsisted on less than $1,000 annually. Another nine million families had scraped by on less than $3,000. The minimum decency and health income, as established by the U.S. Bureau of Labor Statistics in 1948, was between $3,200 and $3,500 a year for the average family.

When the official government figures on unemployment neared five million in early 1950, Truman was quoted in an interview with Arthur Krock in the *New York Times* of February 15: "A certain amount of unemployment, say from three to five million, is supportable. It is a good thing that job-seeking should go on at all times; this is healthy for the economic body."

Economic developments in 1949-50 again demonstrated that the Democrats like the Republicans were unable to solve the anarchy and instability of American monopoly capitalism, as reflected in mass unemployment. Not even government spending, almost five times greater than in 1939, could keep the economy stable.

Before November 1948 was over, Democratic Senator James E. Murray, scheduled to head the Joint Congressional Committee on Labor-Management Relations in the new Congress, had announced that a "single bill" was being prepared which would enact a new union-restricting law while repealing the Taft-Hartley Act. Thus the Truman administration indicated opposition to repeal of the Act.

Some union leaders responded with blustering threats of possible third-party action to Truman's obvious moves to wriggle out of his Taft-Hartley repeal promise. Jacob Potofsky, Hillman's heir to the presidency of the CIO Amalgamated Clothing Workers, at the December 1948 convention of the New York State CIO warned Truman that the CIO is "not a tail to anyone's political kite" and that "we of labor... will not permit any going back on promises that have been made during the campaign." AFL Teamsters President Tobin rumbled about the American workers taking the political road of British labor if Truman continued to give labor a "runaround." *CIO News* Editor Allan L. Swim advised the Democrats not to fail on their pledges if "the nation is to avoid the creation of a real third party." These third-party threats were simply pressure on the Democratic machine by its loyal supporters.

AFL International Ladies Garment Workers President David Dubinsky, who frequently ran interference for the Democratic Party in these matters, tried to put a union label on Truman's revision of his Taft-Hartley repeal pledge. On December 26 he announced that his Executive Board had approved a proposed substitute. Dubinsky's "substitute" contained such features as compulsory "cooling-off" periods before strikes, government "fact-finding" boards, and other forms of government intervention in union affairs and delaying powers in strikes. Dubinsky also advocated government settlement of jurisdictional disputes and a ban on "unjustifiable" boycotts, matters ultimately embodied in the 1959 Kennedy-Landrum-Griffin law known to labor as the "killer" act.

The Big Business press hailed Dubinsky's "statesmanship." Among other dailies, the ultra-conservative *New York Sun* recalled Dubinsky's "fine reputation for responsibility and foresight" and noted that the ILGWU leadership "recommends retention, and in some instances even extension, of policies incorporated in the present legislation... Clearly it is the name rather than the character of the law which is under attack here."

The new Democratic Congress, elected as a result of the "great labor victory" in the 1948 election, was as anti-labor as the previous Republican Congress which had enacted Taft-Hartley. There were 58 members in the new Senate and 227 in the House who had voted for the Act in 1947.

In February 1949, the Senate Labor Committee began consideration of a bill sponsored by the Truman administration. This bill made several formal concessions to labor. It provided for repeal of Taft-Hartley and restoration of the Wagner Act—but with new broad amendments embodying some key features of the Taft-Hartley Act. These included curbs on so-called unfair labor practices by unions: "unjustifiable" secondary boycotts and jurisdictional strikes; strikes to compel an employer to bargain when he claims he is under obligation to bargain with another union; and failure to give at least 30 days' notice before termination or modification of contracts. It also provided for final and binding compulsory arbitration in certain types of labor conflicts.

Although the proposed bill did not specifically authorize the use of strikebreaking injunctions, on February 4 Truman approved a memorandum on this point submitted by Attorney General Tom Clark to the Senate Labor Committee. Clark had asserted in his memorandum that no special law was needed to permit the President to smash strikes which affect "health, safety and welfare." The Chief Executive, according to Clark, had "inherent power" to invoke government machinery and court injunctions to break strikes.

Both the CIO and AFL leaders went along with Truman's Taft-Hartley substitute. AFL President Green evaded any denunciation of the dangerous doctrine of "inherent power" by saying it was "a matter for the courts yet to determine." CIO General Counsel Arthur Goldberg, prior to Truman's testimony, had stated that "repeal of Taft-Hartley is necessary before there can be consideration of points raised by the President." After Truman had testified for his "one package" bill, Goldberg told the hearing that "we do not oppose in principle" Truman's amendments, adding that he did not "think that this statute was intended to provide for injunctions." Senator Taft pressed Goldberg on the matter of presidential "inherent powers," but the CIO representative evaded a straight answer by saying it was simply Clark's opinion and not Truman's.

"It's Time to Slug Back!" was the headline over a feature editorial in the April 1949 issue of the *United Automobile Worker*. This headline was not an exhortation to the workers to fight the anti-labor legislation pushed by Truman; it was an appeal to Truman and the Democrats in Congress to halt their retreat on all their promised "Fair Deal" reforms. The response in Congress was to agree to further union-curbing amendments of the Truman-sponsored Thomas-Lesinski bill which contained the administration's original labor proposals. This Sims amendment specifically provided for the enjoinment of strikes, already included in the Taft-Hartley Act. It also contained other concessions demanded by the most openly reactionary wing of Congress.

The union leaders and liberals were lamenting bitterly the failure of the Democratic Party to deliver on its "Fair Deal" promises. In Washington at the end of May, a conference of Americans for Democratic Action, among whose chief leaders were Senator Hubert Humphrey and Walter Reuther, angrily protested against the Truman administration's moves to abandon most of its reform promises and to hastily adjourn Congress by July 31. The ADA termed this "more than a flag of surrender, a flat betrayal of the Democratic Party platform." The real betrayal was their own action in telling the voters that Truman and his party ever intended to live up to their vote-catching promises. AFL Secretary-Treasurer Meany even told the fifth annual dinner of the Liberal Party in New York that he did not consider the two-party system vital any longer to this country; that it would be "no catastrophe" if the two-party system were "weakened" by a "third party"; and that the situation in Congress "to my mind is an indictment against the two-party system."

The May 15 *Advance* used its entire front page for an editorial bewailing the fate of the Democratic Party's campaign pledges. Its views were summed up in the plaintive question: "Who Won the Elections?" Just a few months before, the ACW leaders had jubilantly claimed it as a "great labor victory."

Daniel Tobin of the AFL Teamsters thundered in the May issue of *International Teamster:* "Quit soft-soaping our enemies, Democratic leaders, and get down to business or else you will destroy the party that has so continuously broken its campaign pledges and promises..." Tobin knew whereof he spoke because he had headed the National Labor Committee of the Democratic Party in four presidential elections.

The Democratic leaders did get down to business. Truman announced on June 2 that he would make no fight to prevent amendment of the Thomas -Lesinski bill along the lines of the Sims bill, which contained five "compromise" amendments denounced by labor. The only difference between the Truman "compromise" and the labor-opposed Sims bill was a provision for breaking strikes by plant seizures instead of injunctions.

Senator Taft took Truman at his word when he said he had no objection to Congress spelling out his "inherent" injunction powers. Taft offered to give Truman double-barreled power to blast strikes by an amendment authorizing the President to use both seizures and injunctions. In the House, it was the Democrats who had previously pushed through the Sims bill which also contained enjoinment powers. On June 29 William Green and Philip Murray issued simultaneous statements calling for defeat of the Taft-amended Thomas-Lesinski bill, thus leaving the Taft-Hartley Law intact. The Senate ended the sorry farce by rejecting Truman's whole "compromise" bill and adopting Taft's 28 "improvements" on his Taft-Hartley Act. The "Fair Deal" fizzled out before it even got off the launching pad.

A revealing light was thrown on the labor bureaucracy's role in the Thomas -Lesinski and Sims bills episode as reported in the May 16, 1949 *New Republic*. The weekly magazine charged that during the House debate on the Sims bill which had been publicly denounced by the CIO and AFL, lobbyists for the national CIO and a majority of its affiliates including steel, textile and auto, had buttonholed every congressman they could approach and urged them to vote for the Sims bill as the "least evil" they could get to replace Taft-Hartley. The AFL's chief legislative representative had simply stayed away during the crucial period—a case of silence bidding consent. These grave charges, similar to those published by the *United Mine Workers Journal*, were never answered by either the CIO or AFL leaders.

Instead of bringing workers the fruits of the "greatest labor victory," the year 1949 brought a new upsurge in bitter, drawn-out strikes. That year was not only one of recession and mass unemployment; it was also the second greatest strike year in American labor history in the number of man-days lost due to strikes. Only the explosive year of 1946 with its 116 million strike man-days was greater; the 1949 figure scaled 50,500,000.

If ever a union leader had a right to expect some reward for political service rendered, Murray was that man. Truman and the Democrats unquestionably owed it to him. His theory of dependence on capitalist "friends of labor" should have paid off in the year of 1949. The fact of the steel strike was to prove once more how fallacious

Murray's political concept was. Moreover, the strike came as a
swift and devastating rejoinder to Murray's stated views on the alleged new class harmony and understanding prevailing in the country
generally and in the steel industry in particular. Writing in the July
1948 issue of *American Magazine,* Murray had said:

"Today, progressive businessmen regard their workers, not as
antagonists, but as welcome partners ... They accept trade unionism...In the steel industry, especially, we have found that the free
and frank exchange of ideas by management and labor at all levels
has generated a better spirit and better understanding of our mutual
problems."

When the CIO Steelworkers, prior to the contract terminations
in 1949, raised the issue of "fourth round" wage increases, the steel
bosses' "better spirit and better understanding of our mutual problems" evaporated like a drop of water on a hot iron stove. In June
the U. S. Steel Corporation contemptuously rejected the union's bid
for a 20-cent hourly wage increase, health and insurance benefits,
and a "non-contributory" $150-a-month retirement pension. The
Ford Motor Company and General Electric rejected similar demands
by the United Auto Workers and the United Electrical Workers. The
union leaderships just sat back, waiting for the steel union to set
the "pattern."

Murray frantically sought the intervention of Truman, who proposed to set up a special fact-finding board in return for a 60-day
cooling-off period. Murray promptly accepted the proposal. The
steel companies turned it down. They wanted Truman to set up the
board and enforce the cooling-off period under the terms of the
Taft-Hartley Law. Murray was thus forced to set a strike date.

Truman issued a second appeal to the steel companies to accept
his Taft-Hartley procedure without invoking the Taft-Hartley Act.
He sweetened the offer by publicly assuring the steel corporations
that his fact-finding board would have power only to make recommendations which would not be binding on either party. Thus, the
companies would still be able to refuse any concessions, however
slight, the board might propose. Moreover, a further two-month
delay would give the corporations time to pile up a large inventory
if they decided to force a strike. Murray, however, had virtually
committed the steelworkers in the eyes of the public to accept any
recommendation the board might make. The steel companies, having jockeyed the union into this unfavorable strategic position with
the aid of Truman and Murray, finally agreed to Truman's procedure. Murray called off the July 16 strike deadline.

The steel firms used the 60-day delay of the strike not only to build up stockpiles but to propagandize against the "danger" of steel wage increases to the economy. Their literature and advertisements warned that higher wages and pensions for steelworkers would lead to "depression." Ten years later they opposed similar demands as "inflationary." At neither time did they see reason to object to all-time-high steel profits.

Truman's steel fact-finding board issued its report September 10. It recommended total rejection of the union's immediate wage demands, with not one cent in wage increases.

The board stepped beyond the steel wage issue and leveled a general attack on the whole "fourth round" wage campaign. Repeating the steel companies' arguments, the board claimed that steel wage increases would set a "pattern to be followed in other industries" and would have "an adverse effect on the whole economy." It called in effect for a peacetime national wage freeze: "In general it seems desirable at this time to stabilize the level of wage rates."

A sop was thrown to the union in the form of the board's endorsement of the principle of insurance and pensions financed wholly by the companies. However, it cut down the union's demand for a $125 monthly pension at age 64 to a maximum of $65 which, it said, the companies should pay into such funds, but fixed no clear obligation on the companies to make any specific concession. The board proposed a maximum of six cents per hour per worker for pensions and four cents for insurance. "Our rough estimate," said the board, "is that the net result would be eight cents an hour." The recommendation also provided that each company could negotiate separately and seek any terms below the maximum.

Murray agreed to this insignificant recommendation. He did not even insist on it as a bedrock demand. All he asked was that it be accepted as the "basis" for further negotiations.

Unlike union advocates of "class harmony," the steel companies never gave concessions in advance and always fought for the last penny. U. S. Steel, Republic Steel, and other leading firms denounced the very principle of company financed pensions as a "revolutionary doctrine" and "socialistic," although these same corporations were paying 20 cents a ton royalty on coal from their captive mines to the United Mine Workers for retirement pensions of $100 a month.

After months of delay while piling up steel backlogs for the companies, the steelworkers had to strike anyway. But they were striking for a "remnant of the remnant" of their original demands. That was the end result of Murray's policy. The 1949 steel events once again revealed Murray as a "labor statesman of the giveaway school"—

the apt description James P. Cannon once applied to another prominent graduate of that school, Sidney Hillman.

Once again a decision was thrust on Murray by the pressure of outside events. On September 19 some 480,000 coal miners, shouting their slogan, "No contract, no work!" closed down almost all mining operations. They demanded an improved contract and payment of all pension, health and welfare royalties due the miners' fund from defaulting Southern operators. About the same time there was an outbreak of wildcat steel strikes in the Pittsburgh area, indicating rank-and-file resistance to further stalling.

At this point, the Ford Motor Company announced it was prepared to concede the UAW no more than the maximum proposed by Truman's steel board—ten cents for insurance and pensions minus the one and three-quarter cents Ford claimed it was already paying into a fund. Wage increases were out. Thus, government intervention in steel had immediate adverse consequences in other key industries.

With only three days until the second strike deadline, set for October 1, Benjamin F. Fairless of U. S. Steel flung a provocation at the union by offering pension and insurance payments "up to" the ten-cent maximum—provided the workers agreed to a wage reduction as a contribution to the fund. Murray then threatened that if the companies did not accept the government board's recommendations, the union would be "free to strike for its original demand" of 30 cents an hour in wage and fringe benefits. But Murray had already compromised the original demands. The steel union leaders had publicly indicated by their hasty acceptance of the board's report that their only remaining point of resistance was the question of company-financing for the proposed pension fund.

As the national steel strike deadline approached, Truman on September 23 made his momentous announcement that the United States no longer had a monopoly on the atomic bomb. He reported that "an atomic explosion occurred in the U. S. S. R." Pointing to the Soviet A-bomb, Arthur Krock of the *New York Times* promptly asked: "Has not the baleful potential of great strikes been made even clearer?" His colleague on the same influential paper, business columnist C. F. Hughes, asserted: "Public opinion is not likely to condone industrial bickering in the face of this new threat."

Goaded by the arrogant steel monopolists who were demanding nothing less than unconditional surrender, the steelworkers on October 1 closed down most of the industry. They had to face the hardships and uncertainties of a prolonged national steel strike just to win a couple of fringe demands promising only some meager benefits in the future.

The 500,000 steel strikers joined the 480,000 coal miners who had been on the picket lines for three weeks. Only in February 1946, during the massive postwar strike wave, had there been more American workers on strike at one time.

* * *

Any intention Murray might have had of fighting for more than the mite offered by Truman's steel board must certainly have been washed away by Reuther's settlement with the Ford Motor Company on September 29, two days before the steel walkout. In return for a miserable pension plan to cost Ford only eight and three-quarter cents an hour per worker, Reuther agreed to a 17-1/2-month wage freeze from July 16, 1949 to January 1, 1951, with no pension payments until April 1, 1950. The contract was to run for two and a half years — from October 1, 1949 until April 1, 1952 — with one wage reopener on January 1, 1951. Pension demands, however, could not be reopened before March 1955.

Publicized as a $100-a-month benefit to Ford workers retired at age 65 after 30 years of service, the plan actually provided that Ford pay only the difference between what a retired worker might get monthly from federal social security and $100. As government benefits increased, Ford was to pay a correspondingly smaller portion of the $100 maximum. This contrasted with the coal miners' pension of $100 a month from a company financed fund, regardless of government payments, at the age of 62 and after only 20 years' service. A large portion of the Ford pension was nothing but government social security to which the workers themselves were contributing a special tax, deducted from their pay.

For the pension-insurance plan, Reuther had agreed not only to a long-term contract and wage freeze; he had accepted in slightly modified form the notorious "company-security" clause which permitted Ford to discipline workers provoked into unauthorized strikes by speed-up or abuses. The renewal of that clause was in violation of a resolution adopted by the UAW's July convention in Milwaukee. This resolution instructed all negotiators not to sign any agreement with a company-security clause.

By allowing the corporations to wring more output per hour from every worker, especially by speed-up, the UAW leaders were able to wheedle a few secondary concessions from the employers. That was the purpose of the company-security clause. The term itself, but not the provisions, was dropped from the Ford contract. Through this clause, aggressive resisters to speed-up were eliminated from the plants. Many of those victimized just happened to be opponents of Reuther's policies.

Eight months earlier, Reuther, Mazey, and UAW Vice-Presidents Gosser and Livingston had published a statement in the January 1949 *United Automobile Worker,* claiming that the anti-Reuther caucus members "have exaggerated the extent of the speed-up as the reports of unions to the International will show." Events quickly showed, however, that the speed-up charges had not been emphatic enough. In May the Ford workers had to strike for 24 days against the unbearable speed-up. Reuther did not dare to refuse authorization of this strike. He succeeded, however, in ending the stoppages with no improvements but with an arbitration agreement almost identical to one offered by Ford before the strike. John W. Love, business columnist of the *Cleveland Press,* jibed at Reuther's *tour de force* in jumping to the head of the Ford strikers and bringing them "back through a gate which turned out to be the side door of the Ford works."

At the subsequent UAW convention in Milwaukee, Reuther sought in his opening address to fend off anticipated attacks against his feeble policy on speed-up. "We take the position we will mobilize our union to fight against speed-up wherever it raises its ugly head," he stated. But during August some 18,000 Chrysler workers were forced to engage in a five-day unauthorized strike against speed-up, firings and disciplinary layoffs. Again Reuther was able to maneuver the workers back to work without a correction of the unsatisfactory conditions. Similarly, a whole series of wildcat strikes against speed-up hit General Motors plants in August, which were stifled by the Reuther leadership.

Reuther's Ford settlement was the worst ever made in a major section of the automobile industry up to that time. He had serious difficulty in securing ratification of the pact at the October 9 and 10 meeting of the UAW's National Ford Council, representing 49 Ford locals. After pounding the delegates for two days of stormy sessions, Reuther wrested a 659 to 381 vote for the agreement. He had told the press previously that the contract was opposed only by "Communist" and other "minor" elements. However, at the National Ford Council meeting, the pact was attacked by such staunch supporters of Reuther as Al Musilli, president of Highland Park Local 400; Art Valenti, president of Lincoln Local 900; Archie Acacia, president of the pressed steel unit of Ford Local 600. Thomas Thompson, then president of Local 600, swung the majority in favor of the contract. He admitted that the contract was bad but argued that the workers had no choice at that time.

There was sharp criticism of the Ford contract in other divisions of the union. A rebellious meeting of 250 officers and committeemen of the five GM locals in Flint on October 22 reaffirmed their previous motion of opposition to the Ford settlement, despite a personal appeal made by Emil Mazey. Chevrolet Local 659, Buick Local 599, and the Fisher Plant 2 local in Flint adopted their own resolutions hitting the Ford pact as did the Greater Flint CIO Council.

In addition to the Ford settlement, another CIO agreement had an important bearing on the outcome of the steel strike. After a 35-day corporation-wide strike, the CIO United Rubber Workers secured a new contract from the Goodrich Company on October 1. The action and the settlement had been complicated by the internal struggle in the URW. George Bass, head of the Policy Committee and president of the large Akron Goodrich Local 5, was also the leader of a militant opposition to the conservative machine of President L. S. Buckmaster. Buckmaster had been suspended from his post in June by the Executive Board majority on charges of violating the rights of a union local. In the atmosphere of the cold war and witch hunt, Buckmaster at the September URW convention succeeded in winning re-election in a fairly close race. With Buckmaster once more in control, the 17,000 Goodrich strikers could no longer count on strong and active support from the international union. The final settlement did not include the "fourth round" wage increase for which the strike had been called.

Nevertheless, the Goodrich contract was superior to the Ford pact in several important respects. The Goodrich pension plan provided for a maximum of $140, instead of $100, in monthly benefits. Like the Ford plan, this was to include social security payments to which the workers themselves contributed. The Goodrich contract, however, contained no company-security clause. It extended for only one year and provided for a wage reopener within seven and a half months instead of the fifteen months of the Ford agreement.

*   *   *

The steel strike, begun October 1, settled down to a defensive, holding operation with the aim chiefly of preserving the union and forcing the steel firms to grant the pittance proposed by the fact-finding board. The steel corporations "could have easily ducked" a strike, according to the October 8 *Business Week,* but "raised their sights beyond their immediate economic interest and have taken on a battle for a principle important to every business in the land." This principle was "to stop appeasing labor leaders." The steel industry viewed the strike as an opportunity to give the union such a smashing defeat or to make the strike so costly to the workers that the demoralization and disgust engendered would turn the workers against the union itself. But the steelworkers held firm.

Lewis on October 14 proposed to William Green that the nine largest AFL affiliates join with the United Mine Workers to raise a weekly fund of $2,500,000 to aid "one of the greatest segments of organized labor" to meet the "vast and barbaric attack" by the "entrenched" steel industry and its "formidable allies." But Green answered that the proposed action was "impossible and impracticable" and that the immediate urgent needs of the labor struggle must wait until there would be a "united labor movement" through organic merger with the AFL on the terms of its craft-minded leaders.

The first big break in the steel strike came on its thirty-second day. Bethlehem Steel agreed to a pension plan for its 75,000 workers along the lines of the Ford pension but with slightly better terms. Pensions were to begin at $100 a month, including federal social security, but no ceiling on benefits. The plan covered workers at the age of 65 with 25 years of service. A contributory health and welfare fund, including hospital benefits and life insurance of a most modest amount, was to be financed by equal 2-1/2-cent hourly contributions from the company and the worker. The previous plan had been paid entirely by the workers.

U. S. Steel settled on November 11, the forty-second day of the strike. The terms were similar to those in Little Steel.

To the extent of beating off the industry's union-busting attack, the steelworkers won. But in all other respects, except for the compromise pension plan, the settlement represented a victory for the corporations. The workers were not only forced to sacrifice their "fourth round" wage increase, but also to accept an average of $1 a week less take-home pay in U. S. Steel for extremely meager fringe benefits. They were bound to a 2-1/2-year contract with a wage reopener on December 31, 1950, or 18 months after the termination of the previous contract. Using the miserly pension settlement as an excuse, the steel companies on December 15, 1949 hiked their prices $4 a ton, although the pension plan did not become operative until March 1950.

The weak steel settlement made the miners' stand more difficult. On November 9 the striking coal miners who had been out 52 days went back into the pits under a three-week truce. Just two days before the truce announcement, the United States Supreme Court upheld the $1,400,000 fine levied against the union the year before for "contempt" of a Taft-Hartley injunction.

Truman issued a press statement on November 17 saying he would "not hesitate" to use the Taft-Hartley Act against the miners "if it becomes necessary" with renewal of their strike. The Truman administration had already battered labor with 58 Taft-Hartley injunctions, under various sections of the Act, within 29 months of its enactment.

Eleven hours after 400,000 soft coal miners began their fourth strike of the year on December 1, the UMW Policy Committee, acting on Lewis's advice, instructed the miners to return to work on December 5—on a three-day-week basis. The Southern Coal Producers Association, the most obdurate holdout against the miners, demanded a federal injunction against the tactic under the "unfair labor practices" section of the Taft-Hartley Act—the procedure used in 1948 against the AFL International Typographical Union.

Starting on January 3, 1950, the miners began a series of "rolling strikes," involving at various stages between 10,000 and 100,-000 men. Despite Lewis's "suggestion" that the miners stop these actions, they continued until February 1. Truman's NLRB General Counsel Robert N. Denham on January 18 sought an injunction against the UMW to halt these unauthorized walkouts as an "unfair labor practice." Even Senator Taft charged that Denham's demand went far beyond the intent of Taft's own vicious class legislation, which the senator said was not designed to coerce workers back to work without a contract.

Senator Hubert Humphrey and other Democratic liberals asserted that Denham was acting on his own. However, Denham told the press that Truman had been continuously informed of all his moves and that the "White House had raised no objections to our proceedings." CIO President Murray authorized General Counsel Goldberg to offer legal aid to the miners but took no steps to mobilize any CIO membership action on the UMW's behalf, nor did he breathe a word about Truman's role in the NLRB's proceedings.

As the miners were being called before a federal court on January 26, 1950, a corporation-wide strike of 90,000 Chrysler workers began. On the eve of this strike Reuther had reduced the United Automobile Workers demands to ten cents an hour, leaving it up to the company to decide whether this increase should be applied to wages or a pension-insurance program. The Chrysler Corporation precipitated the strike when it insisted on a fringe benefit plan that would have meant only three cents an hour more in labor costs. Chrysler decided to "stick tough" on the fact-finding formula applied in Ford and the steel industry as a maximum concession.

Truman on January 31 issued an ultimatum to the miners to end their "wildcat" actions and to resume work on a "normal production" basis of a five-day week. He tried to wangle the miners into accepting a "fact-finding" procedure with a 70-day "cooling-off" period similar to the provisions of the Taft-Hartley Act. Government intervention stiffened the mine owners' resistance and they walked out of the renewed negotiations they themselves had requested with the UMW. Lewis announced that "the miners will continue their struggle to achieve justice." Truman again struck at the UMW and at his political foe, John L. Lewis. On February 6, 1950, the President invoked a Taft-Hartley "national emergency" injunction. Thereupon, another 270,000 soft coal miners joined the 100,000 already on strike.

Meanwhile, the AFL officials, according to Louis Stark in the February 3 *New York Times,* had refused to offer the UMW any legal support on the grounds that its "able and willing" clause, under which the miners were striking without union authorization, set an example for nullification of "disciplinary authority" by international unions over their local affiliates. This appeared to the AFL moguls as a greater danger than the Taft-Hartley Act which the miners were challenging. In fact, the miners were defying two Taft-Hartley injunctions at one time, which brought the total of such injunctions under Truman to sixty-one.

A wave of sympathy and solidarity with the miners swept through the CIO ranks, particularly in the auto plants. A number of UAW locals adopted resolutions for a 24-hour national strike to back the miners. The major GM locals in Flint and others throughout the country voted financial aid to the miners and organized food and clothing collections for them. A city-wide Detroit labor caravan carried aid to the hard-pressed miners.

Once again the miners proved the superiority of fighting independent mass action over dependence on treacherous "friends of labor" in Washington. On March 5 the striking miners scored another historic victory. The operators collapsed and agreed to a new contract containing a 70-cent daily wage increase — despite Truman's fact-finding recommendation of a national wage freeze — plus another ten cents per ton royalty for the health and welfare fund, bringing the total royalties to 30 cents. Moreover, the UMW retained almost all the contract terms in dispute, including the union shop. The "willing and able" clause suffered a language change — now the miners would remain at work so long as there was "good faith" and "mutual understanding" in the carrying out of the new contract.

The Chrysler strike dragged on, with Reuther proposing to settle for mere arbitration. This was precisely what the miners had just successfully rejected when Lewis said he would not permit "three strangers" to determine conditions of work for miners. On May 6, 1950, the hundred-day strike was settled with a pension plan similar to Ford's but payable after 25 instead of 30 years' service. The union estimated the total cost to the company would be a maximum of seven cents an hour per worker. Wages and conditions of work remained unchanged.

The debacle of the CIO's "fourth round" wage campaign and the pitiful settlements secured in steel, auto, rubber, and other CIO industries cannot be attributed solely to government intervention— which the CIO leaders had invited in the steel conflict—or to the "unfavorable economic conjuncture" of the Truman recession. In the very midst of the steel and auto battles the CIO officialdom had been pursuing the irresponsible fratricidal war, begun in 1946, to its culmination. By the spring of 1950 the contending power blocs had torn a gaping hole in the CIO from which it was never to fully recover.

32

Splits and Expulsions

The Stalinist union leaders, during the cold war in the CIO, were taunted and held up to public ridicule on the basis of their miserable record in the labor struggle by bureaucrats whose own records certainly cannot bear close scrutiny by the American workers.

This is worth emphasizing because the ranks of the Communist Party played a far from disreputable role in the awakening struggles of the American workers in the early Thirties and in the rise of the CIO. It was the Communist Party, still imbued with class instinct and revolutionary zeal although already badly disoriented by Stalinism, which gave the first great impulse and leadership to working-class mass action in the early years of the great depression. From 1931 to 1933 the Communist Party built the first mass organizations of the unemployed and led the earliest demonstrations and marches to demand relief and jobs for starving millions. The activities of the CP-led Unemployed Councils, followed by the battles of the Unemployed Leagues built by the American Workers Party and the Workers (Trotskyist) Party, and the united front of all these tendencies in the Socialist Party-led Workers Alliance, trained hundreds of thousands of workers in labor organization and class-struggle tactics. Many of these became the rank-and-file organizers, along with thousands of radicalized workers in the mass production industries, who did the basic grass-roots job of building the CIO. Indeed, even a number of the paid organizers sent out by the United Mine Workers, Amalgamated Clothing Workers and International Ladies Garment Workers had been originally inspired and educated by the radical tendencies.

The Communist Party provided by far the largest number of zealous and courageous local organizers in the early days. In finally demoralizing this generation of militants with its opportunist, class-collaboration line, the Stalinist movement dissipated the greatest capital of the American working class, its most conscious vanguard.

This must be said because the elements who seized exclusive power in the CIO in 1949-50 have tried to erase this vital and decisive role of the radicalized workers, including the Communists, in the successful rise of the CIO. The Stalinist leaders, of whom much sport was made and who skulked out of the 1949 CIO convention, were only shadows of the men who had helped advance the banner of the CIO in a score of industries in the Thirties. They had been corroded by opportunism and adaptation to the official labor bureaucracy long before that bureaucracy tossed them away like squeezed lemons.

A three-day session of the CIO National Executive Board in May 1949 set the Murray machine's final course toward driving out the Stalinist-influenced opposition — and any other opposition — to right-wing policies. The board's majority demanded the resignation of all members who did not actively support the Marshall Plan and the political line laid down by Murray. It also ordered affiliated unions to remove from the board those representatives who failed to carry out Murray's political edicts and to nominate replacements who would support his policies. This decision implied reprisals against any affiliated union which failed to comply.

No part of Murray's political and foreign policy program had been submitted to the CIO membership for discussion and decision. A handful of top executives under Murray's command was enforcing this program by means of bureaucratic compulsion, redbaiting and purges.

At this same CIO Board meeting in Washington a resolution was adopted ordering the Farm Equipment Workers to "merge with the Auto Workers or face possible revocation of their charter." The Mine, Mill and Smelter Workers Union was denounced for "vilifying" Murray by protesting the beating of its secretary, Maurice Travis, by goons linked to the Murray forces.

The period prior to the November 1949 CIO convention was used by both factions to consolidate their forces and make preparations for the swiftly approaching separation. Neither side tried seriously to avert the split, although the right wing was deliberately intent on carrying it through, whatever the damage to CIO unity and strength.

If the Stalinists could not have avoided serious blows under the circumstances, they might have held their own forces and followers intact and even gained sympathy in the wider ranks. But they came into labor's court with unclean hands on such elementary issues as wages and working conditions, racial equality, civil liberties and union democracy. The developments in the United Electrical Workers, third largest union of the CIO, illustrate how the Stalinists rated on these issues during the very period when their own rights were under heaviest fire.

The Stalinists succeeded in retaining their grip on the central apparatus of the UE. But, in addition to numerous groups and locals which split from the UE and joined other CIO affiliates, there were an increasing number of key UE locals which the right wing took over in union local elections after the 1948 CIO convention. These included the 16,500-member Pittsburgh Westinghouse Local 601 and the General Electric local in Schenectady. The January 17, 1949 *Labor Leader,* voice of the Association of Catholic Trade Unionists which was actively intervening in the UE struggle, described the right-wing inroads: "The recent victories mean that the anti-red camp has practically doubled its strength and now represents about 140,000 members while the Stalinists retain the support of 280,000, a 2 to 1 margin."

As the largest Stalinist base in the CIO, the UE might have been expected to set the pattern for economic gains and militant tactics. But the UE trailed behind the steel, auto and other major CIO unions. It was generally the last of the CIO "Big Three" to make settlements and then on the basis of gains made by the others. During the war the UE leadership had set up labor-management speed-up committees and imposed incentive pay plans. Plants under UE contract were plagued with piecework systems that led to wages and working conditions inferior to the far-from-ideal standards in auto and steel.

Labor Department figures disclosed that average hourly earnings in UE-organized industries in 1948 ran a poor fifth to coal, with $1.96 per hour; rubber tires, $1.73; auto, $1.68-1/2; and iron and steel, $1.52-1/2. The UE industries averaged $1.50 in electrical equipment; $1.45 in electrical machinery; and only $1.28 in radio and phonographs. Basic hourly wage rates, as compared to earnings, were much lower, since earnings were swollen by piecework, bonus plans and other speed-up schemes.

When challenged by militant members who fought to remain in the CIO as the mainstream of industrial unionism, the UE top leaders adopted a verbal militancy. President Fitzgerald, speaking in September before the dissident Philadelphia UE Local 107 on the "1949 Wage Fight," devoted most of his time to elaborating arguments to justify a possible split. He claimed: "They are good trade union arguments and cannot be answered...If we have to toe the line as they see it, then the time will come when we must build a new or-

ganization just as the people who left the AFL to form the CIO did."
But he was considerably less forceful in reply to a question about
how he proposed to win the 30-hour week which the Fitzgerald-
Matles-Emspak leadership said it supported. Fitzgerald answered:
"We are going to start a real honest-to-God petition campaign."

Another major issue which the Stalinists tried to exploit dema-
gogically was discrimination against Negroes inside unions led by
the right wing. A special propaganda campaign by the Stalinists was
directed at the Negro members. Following the November 1949 split
convention of the CIO, the November 20 *Sunday Worker* ran a long
article by Abner Berry which tried to convince Negro unionists to
go along with the Stalinists and break with the CIO. Berry stressed
the fact, correct in itself, that the word "Negro" had appeared only
a few times in the official convention proceedings.

The right wing, led by Murray-Reuther-Carey forces, was indeed weak and vacillating on such issues as upgrading of Negroes,
removing barriers to skilled and better-paid jobs for Negroes, and
ensuring Negro representation on all union committees, including
the highest. But the UE leaders were as guilty as the right-wingers
on all these counts. Berry had to concede: "Not all of the progressive [Stalinist-controlled] unions have adhered fully to the fight for
the rights of Negro workers."

Berry listed a series of demands on the race issue which the
Stalinists were then emphasizing, including "recognition of Negro
leadership in the trade unions by securing representation on the
policy-making boards of the steel and auto workers and of the CIO
itself." The Stalinists had raised this demand several times at UAW
conventions as a factional weapon against the Reuther wing which
was highly vulnerable on this point. Neither of the UAW factions
nominated Negroes on their convention election slates. The Reutherites defended this policy on the specious grounds that to run Negroes who were "not qualified" just to provide Negro representation
was "Jim Crow in reverse." This argument was not only false but
ridiculous, considering the caliber of most of the white UAW office-
holders.

But Berry's accusations of racial exclusion from the leadership
of the CIO international unions failed to cite a particularly flagrant
example: the Stalinist-controlled United Electrical Workers. Not
only did the UE have no Negroes on its General Executive Board,
but very few were in the leaderships of its districts or large locals.
The UE was a prime sample of the lack of conformity between Stalinist words and their deeds on Negro rights, as on labor's rights
in general.

The Stalinists in the CIO unions were caught in the cross-fire of a redbaiting purge in the CIO and the Truman administration's fierce witch hunt. In 1948, the 12 top leaders of the Communist Party had been indicted under the Smith "Gag" Act of 1940 for allegedly "teaching and advocating" the "overthrow of the government by force and violence" and for "conspiring" to advocate the same. This was the same law and charge under which 18 leaders of Minneapolis Drivers Local 544-CIO and the Socialist Workers Party had been tried and sentenced in 1941. Even though the Stalinists had approved this prosecution which paved the way for their own, in 1948 and 1949 the only group outside of the Stalinist-influenced organizations that consistently denounced the move to frame up the CP leaders under the Smith Act was the Socialist Workers Party. Its 1948 presidential candidate, Farrell Dobbs, had publicly offered a united front to defend the Stalinists in the interests of civil liberties.

George Morris complained in the April 28, 1949 *Daily Worker:* "Why is the CIO silent on the trial of the 12?" In a May 16 letter to that paper, Irving Abramson, eastern regional representative of the national CIO and chairman of the National CIO Community Services Committee, cited the CP's own stand on the Smith Act in the Minneapolis case as an argument for refusing to defend civil liberties in the CP case.

Abramson pointed out that he had opposed the Smith Act in 1941 and still did in 1949. "That doesn't mean the Smith Act is unconstitutional against the Communist Party but is a model piece of sound legislation when used to jail its enemies," wrote Abramson. "Incredible as it may sound, this is, nevertheless, the recorded position of the Communist Party."

Abramson wrote further: "You were 'vindictive.' You hated the Trotskyites more than you loved civil liberties. Yes, you were not even decent enough to be 'silent.' You saw the opportunity to get rid of hated political enemies...to help the hangman do his work on the '18' even if your scaffold was the Smith Act."

Yet, with their own leaders in the dock, the CP and its union fractions still paid no heed to admonitions like Abramson's. The Conference for Civil and Human Rights in New York City, June 25, 1949, rejected the proposal to include in a resolution protesting attacks on civil liberties references to the Minneapolis case and the firing of legless veteran James Kutcher from his government job for being an SWP member. At a June 29 meeting of San Francisco Local 10 of the International Longshoremen's and Warehousemen's Union, Kutcher in person was slandered from the floor by Stalinists after he had presented his own case and declared his unconditional support to the defense of the CP leaders on trial. More than 2,500 workers, infuriated by the attack on Kutcher, shouted "shame" and "sit down, you phony" at the Stalinist spokesman. In a standing vote, with only 12 dissenting, the meeting voted to back Kutcher and contribute financially to his defense.

Only after 11 CP leaders had been convicted and sentenced to prison in October did the Stalinists discontinue open and aggressive opposition to support of Kutcher's defense.

Due to the violations of union democracy in unions under their control and their unscrupulous stand on civil liberties for other victims of the witch hunt, the majority of CIO workers were indifferent to the expulsion of the Stalinists. The UE again offers the most vivid example.

At the 1949 convention in Cleveland, September 19-23, the Stalinist machine retained its control by only a three-to-two margin. Because of their monopoly of the convention machinery, the Stalinists were able to exclude some right-wing delegates. They were also able to persuade delegates from eight locals, who had been instructed to vote for the right-wing slate, to disregard instructions and vote for the incumbent leadership. But the Stalinists were able to retain their majority primarily because they out-promised the right-wingers on such bread-and-butter issues as the "fourth round" wage demands. Of course, the UE leaders only talked a good fight at the convention. Matles was careful to state, when he told the delegates that negotiations were being resumed with GE and Westinghouse, that "we are not talking about a strike, we are talking about collective bargaining."

Once the convention had voted the old leadership back into office, with 40 per cent voting in opposition, the leaders rammed through a series of purge measures. An amendment was adopted to allow suspension of the constitutional clause which permitted charges and trials of members only in their own locals. In the cases of members accused by the General Executive Board of "raiding and secession" activities, the board was empowered to "assume original jurisdiction." This meant that the GEB could reach into the locals and expel any member through its own drumhead hearings. At the same time, the GEB secured a convention majority for its statement calling on the members to "drive the traitors out of their locals and the union."

Finally, the UE convention adopted a series of ultimatums to the forthcoming CIO convention. These demands concluded by stating that in the event the UE was not given the assurances sought from the CIO, "this convention authorizes the board to withhold per capita tax to the CIO for such time as it deems necessary for the protection of the interests of the UE." It gave Murray the constitutional pretext he needed to suspend the UE.

In unions like the UE the Stalinists set a direct example for bureaucratic repressions used against them in other unions. NMU President Curran's practices after the November 1948 CIO convention deserve special review on this account. His purge of the Stalinists was the ripe fruit of the CP's own methods.

In the last week of December 1948, Curran had secured the expulsion of three prominent Stalinists and the one-year suspensions of four others. The Stalinist defendants, who were charged with participating in "illegal" meetings and "disruption," were lumped with individuals accused of genuine offenses such as shipping off the docks instead of through the union hiring hall; use of deadly weapons; falsifying union shipping cards; etc. All were put in the same pot, stewed in a mass trial and thrown out together.

Even as the NMU *Pilot* complained that the union's National Council was being forced to meet "in the shadow of the Taft-Hartley Act," the NMU Council in April 1949 submitted to a 30-day referendum several Taft-Hartley-type amendments to the NMU constitution.

The chief proposal required that all NMU members affirm in writing that they were not members of the Communist Party or any other "subversive" organization. The resolution also stated that NMU membership might not be retained by any seamen who "subscribe to, support, sponsor or otherwise follow a course of action consistent with and demonstrating membership in or adherence to the policy and program of the Communist Party or any other subversive or totalitarian doctrine." Also designated for the purge list were any members "who join together and are members of anti-union groups or factions within the NMU." An "anti-union group" was any that criticized the Curran administration.

In June 1949, the Judges of Election and the Honest Ballot Association, which had conducted the poll on the constitutional amendments, invalidated the referendum for violations of voting procedure and glaring irregularities.

At the opening of the NMU convention in New York City on September 12, 1949, pledge cards, binding them to support Curran in expelling all communists, were circulated among the delegates. Curran threatened that all delegates would be required to "stand up and be counted" on their "loyalty." The convention, under Curran's control, adopted a resolution to purge all "communists and other subversive groups" by a vote of 405 to 189. Two other amendments —to expel all alleged members of "Nazi, Fascist or Communist organizations" and to expel members "issuing, distributing or mailing literature" that "vilifies" the NMU leaders — were narrowly defeated for lack of a two-thirds majority. Curran, as convention chairman, had ruled out of order all proposals and amendments from the floor.

After the November 1949 CIO convention which set in motion the mass expulsion of Stalinist-led unions, the Curran machine in the NMU mounted a blitzkrieg against all opposition. The battlecry became: "Dump the aliens and kick out the reds!"

Only two years before, in his "President's Report" to the Sixth National Convention of the NMU, Curran himself had made an especially strong appeal for the defense and protection of the alien seamen. The "Report," dated September 22, 1947, had been written long after his break with the Stalinists and his policy on alien seamen had the support of the national CIO. Curran then said in part:

"Our Union fought to have these war-service aliens receive citizenship as small payment for their valiant services in wartime. Instead, the reactionary Congress passed laws reducing the alien quotas on our ships, and eliminating the waivers that existed during the war. This meant that thousands of war-service alien seamen, members of our Union, were thrown on the beach to starve and daily face the prospect of deportation, with the consequent breakup of their families here in the United States."

Despite the hordes of city police and detectives who did their best to intimidate the members, Curran at first sustained several defeats at New York membership meetings. However, on November 25 Curran initiated a putsch. Members who arrived that day at the NMU hiring hall found all but one entrance sealed and a large concentration of police surrounding the entire block. They were lined up and permitted to enter only one at a time and forced to surrender their union books. Those who were identified with any opposition to Curran were pointed out to the police, their books taken away and they were forcibly ejected from the hall.

On December 1, at a New York membership meeting which was packed with an estimated thousand supporters from other ports, Curran secured a vote approving removal of 15 local NMU port officials and union patrolmen who opposed him. Some 400 police and detectives swarmed over the auditorium. They stood shoulder to shoulder, forming a cordon across the front of the hall and along every aisle. Several hundred Curran men had also been deputized as "masters-at-arms." Curran jammed through a vote to sustain his action against the 15, with 1,714 voting for the trial committee's recommendation; 566 opposed; and 1,700 abstaining. He had learned from Stalinism that international labor solidarity was a phrase to be exploited only when it served some bureaucratic interest. He had also learned to accommodate his policies to the demands of such government agencies as the War Shipping Administration, the navy and the Coast Guard, which from the start of the war had increasingly intervened in the hiring of merchant seamen. Curran had not changed when he joined the right wing; he had merely continued his opportunism, in part Stalinist-taught, jumping over to the strongest side while the jumping was good.

Michael Quill also proved to be an apt pupil of Stalinist methods even when he used them against his mentors. A. H. Raskin, in the March 5, 1950 *New York Times Magazine,* delightedly described how Quill tricked his membership as well as his former political associates. On one occasion, as related by Raskin, Austin Hogan, the president of New York's biggest TWU local and leader of the Stalinist caucus, had called a meeting of 18 section chairmen to line up the anti-Quill forces. Asked whether he would attend the meeting, Quill said no, because "the fact is there won't be any meeting. I've just sent out 18 telegrams signed by Austin Hogan calling the meeting off."

When Quill prepared to visit the TWU's Omaha local where he faced a strong opposition, Raskin wrote, he first issued a leaflet denouncing himself as a "redbaiter" and urging the Omaha local to repudiate him and go over to the AFL. The hoodwinked members accepted the leaflets as genuine and were naturally outraged that the opposition planned to split the CIO in favor of the AFL. Before the opposition could disprove the fraud, the Omaha delegates to the TWU convention had been elected. They were, of course, pro-Quill.

Raskin recited several such forgeries and misrepresentations used by Quill. But the *Times* labor reporter passed them off as the product of clever calculation in the good cause of "responsible" unionism.

The CIO's internal cold war reached its climax at the Eleventh Constitutional Convention, held in Cleveland, October 31-November 4, 1949. The Stalinists boasted that their faction represented 20 per cent of the CIO membership, or more than a million workers. However, apart from the United Electrical Workers, in which the Stalinists had mustered support from locals representing about 250,-000 members at the UE's convention in September, the other ten unions had very small memberships, several of them numbering only a few thousand each. The official "Officers Report" to the CIO convention spoke of the eleven unions facing expulsion "whose membership is less than ten per cent of our total." Murray himself, on the second day of the gathering, described "those eleven industrial unions, representing approximately six and one-half per cent of the dues-paying membership of the National CIO."

If the Stalinist faction, even at its reduced strength, had been composed of genuine militants and real socialists, Murray might have faced the roughest time of his career at this CIO convention. His position was very shaky because of his timid, feeble leadership in the steel struggle. More than 80 per cent of the steelworkers were in the fifth week of their strike. Murray had given away their major demands and had committed them to Truman's fact-finding recommendation of a miserable fringe benefit.

Fearful of an attack on this weak flank, Murray in his "Officers Report" accused the Stalinists of "psuedo-militancy" and of "carping, unjustified criticism" that was "diabolical, prejudiced and illfounded" and the "most flagrant approach to union strikebreaking" in CIO history. His keynote speech further complained that "Wall Street not only attacked us, the steel industry not only attacked us ...but the Communist party attacked us as well." He thought that Wall Street and the Communist Party "ought to get together and sleep in the same bed."

It is most revealing that Murray never once spoke out during the war about the "most flagrant approach to union strikebreaking" of the Stalinists when they stood at his right hand and helped to enforce the no-strike policy. That was when the CP really did "sleep in the same bed" with Wall Street.

The Stalinists at the CIO convention did not let out the tiniest peep about Murray's steel policy, not even when it was certain they were going to have their heads chopped off, organizationally speaking, and had nothing to lose. On October 31, after the Committee on the Officers Report had moved to concur "with respect to the entire report," delegate Irving Pickman of the Stalinist-ruled Fur and Leather Workers Union indignantly demurred: "We never accused President Murray of subservience to corporate interests, of selling out the interests of American workers, of red baiting, of company unionism, as stated in the report. On the contrary, we have always spoken of the President of the CIO with respect and recognized his great contributions to the CIO..."

Neither Ben Gold, Fur Workers' president, nor any other delegate directly attacked Murray's trade-union or political policies or openly defended the Stalinist line on the Marshall Plan and Wallace. Gold, Bridges and the few other Stalinist-line delegates who spoke, stuck to the themes of "unity," "trade-union democracy" and "no crossing of picket lines." These were scarcely subjects on which the Stalinists in the CIO could convince by example — as the debate amply demonstrated. Indeed, the right wing had a field day in answering the Stalinists.

The main debate of the convention occurred on the first of three related constitutional amendments designed to facilitate the expulsion of the Stalinists and Stalinist-run unions and councils. George Baldanzi as head of the Committee on Constitution placed before the delegates the first proposed amendment which read: "No individual shall be eligible to serve either as an officer or as a member of the Executive Board who is a member of the Communist Party, any fascist organization, or other totalitarian movement, or who consistently pursues policies and activities directed toward the achievement of the program or the purposes of the Communist Party, any fascist organization, or other totalitarian movement, rather than the objectives and policies set forth in the constitution of the CIO."

This amendment, which Murray's mechanical majority adopted by voice vote that same afternoon, was the first in the CIO's history to fix discriminatory political qualifications and limitations on CIO members and unions. Although it spoke of "any fascist organization," it was intended specifically for the Stalinists. But it could be used against any other radical tendency within the working class which might oppose the official labor bureaucracy from the left, or anti-capitalist, position.

The UE delegation quietly withdrew from the convention without a fight and without a declaration of any kind to the delegates. This fact was not generally known until the second afternoon of the convention when TWU President Quill, while discussing the anti-Communist amendment, shouted that "the UE have left the CIO, they have walked out, they have deserted the fight. They didn't come in here with Bridges and the others and stand up and be counted. They deserted about four hours ago..."

Delegate John J. Stanley of the United Office and Professional Workers opened the discussion on the amendment to bar Communists from CIO office. He laid down the main line of argument followed by the Stalinists. "This legislation," he said, "runs directly contrary to the traditional CIO policy, and its evils were recognized by no less a leader...than Philip Murray himself. In 1946 at the Atlantic City convention of the CIO, when some people in CIO were already advising that the CIO engage itself in an atmosphere of witch hunts, I remember Philip Murray...castigating those who would turn the efforts of this organization into such fruitless paths..."

The 1946 convention, of course, had opened the witch hunt by passing Murray's Statement of Policy declaring "we resent and reject the interference of the Communist Party"—a statement endorsed by every Stalinist delegate. Immediately afterwards various state CIO conventions had adopted resolutions barring communists from office.

Another spokesman for the Stalinist caucus, Joseph P. Selly of the American Communications Association, charged that the CIO was "enacting a little Taft-Hartley law into the CIO constitution" and that "the adoption of this resolution so completely reverses the fundamental policies of the CIO on which it was founded as to make the organization unrecognizable, as to give it a character not only different but the opposite of the character it formerly enjoyed."

Actually, most CIO affiliates had never enjoyed much union democracy. Original CIO unions like the United Mine Workers and the Amalgamated Clothing Workers, both of which had barred communists from the start, had little union democracy. The Stalinist-led unions were held in a bureaucratic vise. The steelworkers were not permitted to vote for their national officers for six years—until 1942. Reuther had succeeded by 1941 in putting over an anti-communist amendment to the auto union's constitution.

It was not their democratic character so much as their industrial structure that distinguished the CIO unions from the AFL. It was this great advance of industrial unionism that both factions were weakening and endangering by their split tactics.

With the exception of Murray, ex-radicals from both the social-democratic and communist circles waged the attack on the Stalinists. Reuther, Quill, Curran, Rieve, Potofsky and Baldanzi used the crimes of the Stalinists as a pretext for imposing anti-democratic, bureaucratic restrictions on all CIO members.

Textile Workers President Emil Rieve led off the debate for the Murray wing. He evaded discussion of his own abandonment of wage demands by denouncing Stalinist totalitarianism abroad. National Maritime Union President Curran, sliding over his own pro-Stalinist role for ten years including the entire war period, sarcastically recalled how the Communist Party in 1944 "decided that it need no longer carry on the policy of all-out struggle against the employers; that it need not continue the all-out struggle for a revolution of the proletariat...the time had come for a program of collaboration with the boss..."

Using his rapid-fire auctioneer-style delivery and hurling bits of liberal and even radical phraseology, UAW President Reuther assailed both the international and domestic policies of the Stalinists from the left. He declared: "They [the Stalinist faction] are not free men, they are not free agents...They are colonial agents using the trade union movement as a base of operations in order to carry out the needs of the Soviet foreign office...Every time there is a shift in basic policy they have betrayed us in our most critical hour in the past...We fought more strikes when we started to build our union to abolish piecework and the speed-up, and yet when the party line dictated, these comrades were willing to lay our union on the altar of sacrifice, and they tried to initiate piecework and the speed-up in every plant...We remember, when the Party Line dictated, they were talking about the five-year no-strike pledge..."

Reuther did not fail to nail Bridges' claim that the ILWU "has never failed to respond in support of a strike." The UAW president dramatically stated: "Ask the boys from Montgomery-Ward what happened during the war. Ask them to ask Harry Bridges what his position was during the war when the Montgomery-Ward workers were fighting against Sewell Avery and American Fascism...They are the phony Left, they are the corrupted Left...because every basic concept that is associated with the Left they have either corrupted or destroyed..."

Reuther was not urging a return to the real Left as against the "phony Left." He was no fiery apostle of class struggle; he was engaged in defending American capitalism, its aggressive foreign policy and the proponents of that policy in the labor movement.

As final speaker on the anti-communist amendment, CIO President Philip Murray—who so often plaintively begged the steel barons to "be gentlemen, be decent"—berated Bridges for his wartime betrayal of labor and his fanciful claim of "democracy" in the ILWU. Turning on all the organ stops of his sonorous voice, Murray told the convention:

"I have no dislike for Harry Bridges, none whatsoever, but I remember in the year 1945 Harry Bridges attending a meeting of the CIO Executive Board and proposing...that the National CIO and all its affiliated organizations agree not to have any strikes in any of our unions for five years following the war. I wonder if Mr. Bridges had submitted that proposition to his rank and file before he made it to the CIO Executive Board. Had we accepted that kind of a proposal offered by Mr. Bridges, the ranks of our movement would have been decimated, the steelworkers would not have been striking for pensions, the great labor gains made in 1946, 1947, and 1948 would not have been attained, the organization would have been decrepit and completely destroyed..."

It is true that the CIO Board had rejected Bridges' proposal. But it adopted Murray's "Peace Pact" with the United States Chamber of Commerce and National Association of Manufacturers only a few months before the outbreak of the greatest industrial strike wave in American history. Murray might have gone on smoking the peace pipe with labor's worst exploiters until the day he died if a few million CIO workers hadn't decided to try their luck with those class struggle methods both Murray and Bridges had deplored.

But Murray did stress with more candor than his colleagues the real basis for the internal struggle, which had nothing to do either with Stalinist collaboration with the employers or with strikebreaking. Murray reviewed his own relations with the Stalinists and conceded that throughout the entire course of the war "I received the united support of all the Left Wing elements of this organization." But "on the day that Japan capitulated," Murray had found, "the policy of the Communist Party in the United States and elsewhere changed." That, according to Murray, was the real source of the split.

His dating was right but his explanation stood the truth on its head. The shift in line inside the CIO took place on the part of the official leadership in response to the anti-Soviet foreign policy aggressively pursued by the Truman administration under the banner of United States A-bomb monopoly.

Once the resolution to ban communists from CIO office was accepted, the rest of the convention was simply a mopping-up operation. The very next morning, November 2, Baldanzi presented two more constitutional amendments. The first empowered the CIO National Executive Board "to refuse to seat or to remove" any board member who was deemed ineligible by virtue of the anti-communist amendment passed the day before. The second gave the Executive Board "further power, upon a two-thirds vote," to revoke the charter or expel any affiliated national or international union whose "policies and activities . . . are consistently directed toward the achievement of the program or the purposes" of the previously proscribed political organizations.

Following enactment of these amendments with scarcely any debate, the next major action of the convention was to adopt a special resolution declaring that the UE, which had bolted the convention and withheld its per capita owed to the national CIO, had become "the Communist Party masquerading as a labor union" and was expelled by voice vote.

A similar resolution was then speedily adopted to expel the Farm Equipment Workers which had merged with the UE prior to the CIO convention in defiance of a CIO Board decision. In a formal ceremony at the convention, Murray then presented James Carey with a charter for a new union, the International Union of Electrical, Radio and Machine Workers.

Finally, a resolution was adopted formally instructing the incoming Executive Board "immediately to exercise its powers" to "take appropriate action" against CIO affiliates held in violation of "CIO policy" and the new anti-communist amendments.

After the convention, charges were brought against ten unions: American Communications Association; Food, Tobacco, Agricultural and Allied Workers; Fishermen and Allied Workers; International Fur and Leather Workers; International Longshoremen's and Warehousemen's Union; International Union of Mine, Mill and Smelter Workers; National Union of Marine Cooks and Stewards; United Furniture Workers; United Office and Professional Workers; and United Public Workers.

Witnesses were heard and elaborate testimony was recorded at a series of formal hearings. The testimony was almost exclusively designed to show "Communist" and "Communist Front" connections of officials of the accused unions. Most of the witnesses were former Stalinists who tried to outdo each other in supplying lurid "evidence" against their former comrades and thus buy themselves into the good graces of the Murray machine. These hearings, however, were a mere formality. The split was already completed and the factional war was being fought out at the plant and job level.

In the spring of 1950 the CIO Executive Board expelled all the accused unions but one. Shortly after the CIO convention Morris Pizer, president of the Furniture Workers, declared his support for Murray's policies. The charges against the UFW were then withdrawn. At the Furniture Workers convention in June 1950, the Pizer forces took full control by a more than three-to-one majority.

By June 1950, the new IUE-CIO had won collective bargaining rights through NLRB elections in a majority of the plants of General Electric, Westinghouse, and other large corporations in the electrical equipment industry. But many plants of these corporations remained with the UE. Thus, in a poll held on May 25, the IUE-CIO with 47,486 votes captured 49 out of 89 GE units; the UE with 36,683 votes retained 40 plants. It is interesting to note that the UE officers not only complied with the Taft-Hartley non-communist-oath regulation but that the NLRB was compelled in numerous instances to recognize the UE as a bona fide union and not as "the Communist Party masquerading as a labor union."

The UE was whittled down by 1959 to 80,000 members, while the IUE, affiliated with the AFL-CIO, claims a membership of 280,000. But the industry remains in a three-way split because the International Brotherhood of Electrical Workers, also AFL-CIO, had competed with some success in the field. As a result, the corporations have been able to play one union against another. The workers in the electrical industry are still paying the price in marginal wages, bad conditions and inferior bargaining position for the 1949 split and expulsions from the CIO.

The only other independent unions of consequence that have survived the 1949 expulsions from the CIO are Bridges' West Coast longshoremen's union, with a claimed 65,000 members in 1959, and the Mine, Mill and Smelter Workers, now claiming 100,000 members. But the influence of the Stalinists in all these unions is greatly reduced. The unions remain as small, isolated groups clinging to a few contracts, trying to survive away from the mainstream of organized workers.

It was revealed at the November 1950 CIO convention that at the time of the 1949 convention the CIO membership had been reduced to 3,700,000. There was to be some growth after that but the membership was never again to reach the peak of the CIO's halcyon days. The relative stagnation in the CIO's growth was not, however, the only or most important development following the split.

The 1949 convention was almost immediately followed by a further great shift in the direction of closer collaboration between the CIO leaders and the corporations. Freed from the restraints that would have been imposed by the mere existence of any large organized opposition, the CIO officialdom could proceed to contractual concessions they would not have dared to accept before the split. These were epitomized by the five-year no-strike contract Walter Reuther signed with General Motors.

Unlike the coal and steel unions, the United Automobile Workers under Reuther adopted the "one-at-a-time" strategy of bargaining with each great corporation in the industry. The General Motors, Ford and Chrysler contracts were carefully designed to terminate not only in different months but in different years. This reduced the possibility of industry-wide strikes and industry-wide contracts. Thus it was easier in the automobile industry to cut corners on contractual conditions from corporation to corporation and even from plant to plant.

The two-year escalator contract secured with General Motors in 1948 ended on May 29, 1950. A few days before this termination date Reuther announced that he had agreed to an unprecedentedly long-term contract with GM. GM had proposed and Reuther had accepted a contract binding the UAW not to make any further demands until May 29, 1955. In return, the GM workers would get a continuation of the escalator wage clause, a $100-a-month pension plan on the Ford and steel industry models, an improved welfare and insurance program and an actual hourly wage increase of four cents an hour each year for five years. The wage increase was based on a "productivity improvement factor." This four-cent annual wage increase, based on the previous average basic wage of $1.65 an hour, amounted to less than two and a half per cent and would decline percentage-wise each year in relation to the previous year's basic wage rate.

Since General Motors had already intensified the speed-up in its plants, this alone would have insured a rate of productivity increase annually greater than the rate of wage increases. Reuther was able to secure ratification of the five-year no-strike contract at a GM delegates' conference on May 25-26 by playing on the fear of a prolonged strike. The contract he had signed with Chrysler after the hundred-day strike did not make the GM workers eager to engage in such a struggle.

Why was General Motors, which had to be driven by the sitdowns in 1937 to sign even a six-month contract, now demanding a five-year contract? The *U.S. News and World Report* of June 2 pointed out that in seeking labor peace for five years, GM expected that the "rewards to be gained from stability will outweigh" the meager increases in wages and benefits because GM retained the right to put in new machinery, use new methods and "reduce the labor force, if necessary." The May 27 *Business Week* hailed the long-term GM pact as a means of softening up the union ranks so that in five years they "will almost forget they are union men."

In September, Reuther put over a five-year contract in Ford's, after a series of wildcat strikes which had forced wage concessions from Chrysler and had spread to Ford plants. A Chrysler five-year pact was consummated in December.

This policy of long-term contracts which the Amalgamated Clothing Workers had adopted earlier was to become widespread among CIO unions in the Fifties. However, some unions like the Steelworkers limited their pacts to three years. By March 1953, the strangling five-year contracts in auto had become so insufferable that the auto workers forced their leaders to retreat. Future contracts were limited to no longer than three years.

Long-term contracts combined with built-in—if severely limited—periodic wage increases were to considerably modify the number and intensity of CIO strikes during the Fifties. Disparity between contract termination dates in the various industries restricted simultaneous industry-wide strikes like those of 1946. But in no sense was there to be a return to the quiescence of the Twenties and early Thirties. Every year between 1950 and 1960 was to witness some important industry-wide or big corporation-wide strikes. These struggles were mainly defensive, unlike the aggressive temper of the 1934, 1937, 1941 and 1946 strikes. Conservatism in the CIO, consolidated by the expulsions of 1949 and 1950, was to clamp a heavy lid on the militancy of the CIO unionists during the last five years of the organization's independent existence.

PART VII

THE
KOREAN WAR
YEARS

1950-1953

33

Labor's Near-Break with Truman

For its duration and area, the Korean War, termed by President Truman as "merely" a police action, was the most murderous and destructive war in history. The majority of American people opposed the invasion of Korea, suspected its motives, and felt disgust and shame at its consequences.

Within a few hours of radio reports on June 25, 1950 that North Korean troops had crossed the South Korean border, Truman announced he had dispatched planes, warships and troops to "defend" South Korea. The State Department, after midnight, rounded up sleepy-eyed members of the United Nations Security Council and stampeded them into an immediate statement branding North Korea an "aggressor." Before the week was out and without a congressional declaration of war, United States troops were killing and dying in Korea.

According to Secretary of State Dean Acheson, the U.S. aim was to "establish a free, independent and democratic Korea." This was to require more than five million members of the United States armed forces alone during the entire war and cost America more than 150,000 battle casualties. Total war deaths surpassed five million—about four million of them Korean civilians.

All of Korea was being "reduced to grave mounds, tree stumps and ruined homes," reported the *Voice of Korea,* organ of the Korean Affairs Institute in Washington, D. C., on March 31, 1951. J. Donald Kingsley, agent general of the United Nations Reconstruction Agency, said: "I doubt that ever in the history of the world, since perhaps the sacking of Carthage, has there been such complete destruction as has occurred in Korea."

On January 23, 1951, Dr. George Gallup of the American Institute of Public Opinion made public the findings of a national poll which indicated that 66 per cent of the American people wanted to "pull our troops out of Korea as fast as possible." In another Gallup poll in March 1952, 51 per cent answered "yes" to a question whether it had been a "mistake" to intervene in the first place; only 39 per cent said "no." It was the most unpopular war in America's history.

One force alone could have halted that atrocity which still lies so heavily on the American conscience. The American labor movement, had it not been crippled by a leadership overwhelmingly committed to U. S. imperialism and capitalist politics, could have compelled Washington to stop its armed invasion of Korea. But without pausing even to question Truman's "police action" in Korea, the trade union leaders promptly fell into line like orderlies snapping to attention. AFL President William Green called for the "mobilization of labor" and "all-out preparedness." CIO President Philip Murray wired Truman his "wholehearted and unstinting support."

Nevertheless, when Truman began his Korean "police action" he also launched an undeclared war against labor at home.

On the same day the Korean War began, the Switchmen's Union struck five railroads. The union was demanding reduction of the work week from 48 to 40 hours with no cut in take-home pay. On July 6, 1950, Truman threatened "drastic action" unless the strike was halted at once. The union called off the strike on four lines but continued the Rock Island walkout. Truman's seizure order followed on July 8. At the same time, he secured an injunction directing the union to cease the Rock Island strike.

The day before, both Murray and Green had declared their support of the switchmen's strike. After Truman took over the Rock Island line, they said not another word on the subject.

On August 28, in advance of a threatened strike, Truman seized the country's entire railroad system. He put a million railroad workers under military control. Seven railroad magnates were vested with military authority as regional directors of operations for the nation's railroads. Six of them didn't even have to be sworn in; they were called into "active duty" as reserve officers who had been named colonels during the May 1948 rail strike and army seizure.

Truman's order fully protected the railway owners' profits, their ownership and control, but forbade any changes in wages, hours and working conditions except by consent of the corporations. The latter felt under no compulsion to make concessions. The switchmen were coerced eventually into accepting continuation of the 48-hour week.

Domestic economic developments at the start of the Korean War paralleled in many respects those following Pearl Harbor. Prices shot up immediately. The tempo of production quickened with the stimulus of new war orders. Unemployment declined, although this was as much the result of the military draft as of increased civilian employment. Profits, particularly in the war-related industries, bounded upward at an accelerated pace.

As the war boom developed, some of the staunchest supporters of capitalism felt impelled to comment on the magical effect on the American economy. Senator George D. Aiken, Vermont Republican, told a meeting of Missouri farm owners that "only 14 months ago, the economy of our country seemed headed for a slump or at least a descent to lower levels...Then came the Korean outbreak and the situation changed virtually overnight. The trend toward depression was definitely off. Unemployment began to ease off. Demand and prices stiffened." (*Congressional Record,* August 10, 1951.) Then Senator Aiken admitted: "What a tragedy it is that as a nation we must rely upon war or the threat of war to maintain full employment and economic prosperity...Should the time come when war clouds no longer threaten...we will be confronted with a problem of major degree."

AFL Secretary-Treasurer George Meany, addressing the New York State Federation of Labor convention on July 31, 1950, asserted: "I haven't any doubt at all that labor will give a no-strike pledge when the time comes." He complained, however, that food prices had risen nine per cent since the war began and asked for a pledge from the Republican senators "to lay off their war against labor while the country is in danger." He said nothing about Truman who was leading this attack upon labor and breaking strikes with Taft-Hartley injunctions and plant seizures.

The top CIO leaders were more cautious about a no-strike pledge and kept silent about it.

John L. Lewis told Green in a letter dated August 29, 1950 that he was "distressed" at having "to disturb the calm placidity of your ordered existence" but that "the rights of American workers in industry should not be bartered to appease your innate craving for orthodox respectability." Lewis wrote further: "The press chronicles you as plodding about the country seeking someone to whom you can give a 'no-strike pledge.' I am sure you will pardon me when I suggest that the mine workers are not yet ready for you to sell them down the river. Restrict your pledges to your own outfit. We do our own no-striking."

Unlike World War II, the Korean War failed to put an official damper on the class struggle in America. The period of the Korean

War witnessed more strikes and strikers than any other comparable period of time in American history. Here is the table of the average strike figures per year during the key periods from 1935 to 1953.

Annual Average of Strikes

	No. of Strikes	No. of Strikers	Strike Man-days
1935-1939	2 867	1 130 000	16 900 000
World War II —			
Dec. 8, 1941-Aug. 14, 1945	3 919	1 839 272	9 900 000
1947-1949	3 573	2 380 000	39 700 000
Korean War 1950-1953	4 847	2 642 500	37 275 000

The strike figures cited above take on added significance when the Korean War period is compared with that of World War II. Although the Korean War put heavy economic pressure on the workers, this increased stress was not as intense as that suffered during the second world war. Yet the workers struck much more often and in greater numbers during the Korean War. There is a startling difference in the man-hours of strike for the two war periods. The annual average was four times greater during the Korean War.

With the exception of the 1943 coal strikes, almost all war-industry strikes during World War II were unauthorized and were quickly broken by the Roosevelt government with the indispensable aid of the union leaders. During the Korean War the union bureaucracy did not dare play such an open strikebreaking role. Indeed, the year 1952 saw all strike records broken save for those set in the year of mightiest upsurge —1946.

We can fully perceive the extraordinary sweep of the class struggle in the very midst of the Korean War only by comparison with the peak strike years since the beginning of the CIO in 1935.

Year	No. of Strikes	No. of Strikers	Strike Man-days
1937	4 740	1 860 000	28 400 000
1941	4 288	2 360 000	23 000 000
1946	4 985	4 600 000	116 000 000
1949	3 606	3 030 000	50 500 000
1950	4 843	2 410 000	38 800 000
1951	4 737	2 220 000	22 900 000
1952	5 117	3 540 000	59 100 000
1953	5 091	2 400 000	28 300 000

These figures reveal a large quantitative difference between the pre-Pearl Harbor period and the years following World War II. Although the number of strikes in 1949 was less than in either 1937 or 1941, the number of strikers and man-days lost were far higher. The year 1949 was the second full year of the Taft-Hartley Act, which Truman had been enforcing with zeal and vigor. Small, isolated strikes were undoubtedly discouraged by the Act, but it did not prevent great industry-wide or corporation-wide stoppages in such giants as coal, steel, auto and rubber.

The war and the Taft-Hartley Act combined could not prevent the greatest annual number of strikes in American history. For the first time, the number surpassed 5,000 in a single calendar year. The number of strikers and strike man-days were second only to the all-time peak year of 1946.

Moreover, the post-World War II strikes, including those of the Korean War years, were qualitatively different from those of the Thirties. During the Roosevelt "New Deal" years, the great majority of strikes were for union recognition. Many of those were spontaneous local uprisings of workers who frequently shut down the plants first and then called on some national union to come in to "organize us." Then, a nickle or three-cent wage increase was considered "gravy" on top of a six-month agreement or stipulation by the company simply to negotiate with a union committee. Many strikes were completely smashed and numerous local unions wiped out in the struggles of the Thirties. We need only recall the tragic fate of the national textile strike in 1934 and the Little Steel strike in 1937. As late as 1941, the historic Ford and Bethlehem Steel strikes were fought for union recognition.

The strikes of the late Forties and early Fifties, including those of the Korean War period, were largely authorized actions. More and more often these strikes were on a national scale, for tangible gains in wages, shorter hours, improved working conditions, health and welfare funds, paid vacations, pensions, and other benefits. Rarely was a strike broken or a union smashed by direct violence. Instead, legal nets were woven and spread to entangle the unions in the delaying procedures of courts and governmental agencies.

However, the relationship of class forces in America had become such that mere legal devices did not suffice to strangle organized labor. Determined mass action by union workers could tear great gaping holes in the legal net, as the coal miners had proved more than once. The government had the Taft-Hartley Act, but it was used with great caution and only when it could expect the union leaders involved to capitulate without a struggle or when the law could be brought to bear on an isolated union. Thus, in every single year which encompassed the Korean War—1950 through 1953—the number of strikes and strikers was at a high level. This can be seen when the figures of the Korean War period are compared with the two peak strike years before World War II.

In August and September 1950, Detroit and other auto centers witnessed a strike wave involving the major corporations which led to wage concessions—and to the five-year no-strike contracts negotiated by Reuther. Millions of workers began clamoring for wage increases in the wake of war price rises. In November, a million workers, covered by escalator wage clauses, got automatic wage raises. Last in line again, Murray's steelworkers did not obtain wage boosts until December.

In the November 7, 1950 elections, the Republicans made sweeping gains in both Senate and House. The Democrats barely kept their majorities in both houses of Congress. This was exactly two years after the "great labor victory" in the 1948 national elections.

On December 15, 1950, Truman declared a state of "national emergency" for the "full mobilization" of the country. He announced his assumption of wartime powers. In the course of his speech he threatened "mandatory controls" on wages. He warned there would be "a lot of changes in our ordinary way of doing things." The first big change, he made clear, would be in the workers' living standards: "We shall have to cut back on many lines of civilian production. Workers will be called upon to work more hours ... A defense effort of the size we must now undertake will inevitably push up prices ... We've increased taxes ... Still further taxes will be needed..."

Most disturbing were two actions proclaimed in Truman's address. At the last minute he had inserted a direct attack on 10,000 striking railroad yardmen, ordering them to end their strike and accept the 48-hour week against which they had been fighting for two years. And he demonstratively turned the direction of the war economy over to the direct guidance of the big corporations by naming Charles E. Wilson, president of the General Electric Corporation and a notorious union hater, as Director of the Office of Defense Mobilization. Wilson was vested with supreme power over production, manpower and "economic stabilization," including wage and price controls.

Truman's "national emergency" proclamation so alarmed the unions that for the first time since the 1935 split in the AFL, a united front of the CIO, AFL, railroad brotherhoods and International Association of Machinists was established through the formation of the United Labor Policy Committee. The ULPC was composed of all the top labor leaders with the exception of Lewis.

No one expected Truman to control prices. His new measures to regulate the cost of living proposed an honor system for voluntary maintenance of government-fixed "fair standards" of prices. The cost of living had shot up more than 15 per cent in the first five months of Truman's "police action." But this pretense of price control, the unions feared, would provide the pretext for a wage freeze.

On December 20, 1950, the newly formed United Labor Policy Committee issued a declaration in the name of all participating unions which criticized virtually every phase of Truman's economic "stabilization" program. It was feared that escalator cost-of-living wage clauses and other built-in wage protection factors in existing union contracts would be nullified by administration decree. "Any wage stabilization policy," the ULPC statement insisted, "must recognize existing collective bargaining agreements which themselves assure stability" such as those in "automobile and other industries where existing contracts provide for the orderly adjustment of wage rates."

The union leaders were soon completely frozen out of the war machinery appointments. They were denied even their customary role of "labor advisers." Charles E. Wilson as director of the Office of Defense Mobilization had "unparalleled controls over the country's economy... subject only to Presidential veto," observed the *New York Times.* Truman named a slew of big-name agents of the monopolies — Republicans, notorious anti-New Dealers, Chamber of Commerce officials — almost every one, it seemed, but the union leaders who were most responsible for Truman's election in November 1948. "We regret," said a United Labor Policy Committee statement late in December 1950, "that to date labor has not enjoyed opportunity for full participation in the mobilization effort..."

On December 28 the *New York Times* stated that an independent sampling of congressional mail showed tremendous sentiment for bringing the troops back from Korea. In Detroit, America's greatest industrial city, the *Detroit Free Press* published the results of its local poll that showed 75 per cent of those questioned were in favor of bringing the troops home as fast as possible. In UAW-CIO Ford Local 600, largest union local in the world, a candidate campaigning for the first time for the presidency came within a hair's-breadth of winning from Reuther-backed candidate Carl Stellato. Joe Hogan received 16,188 votes to the incumbent Stellato's 16,664. Hogan's surprising strength was based on his two-point program in the campaign: (1) End the Korean War; (2) Build a Labor Party.

As the other union leaders fretted because Truman ignored their suggestions on the war economy and froze them out of government appointments, the United Mine Workers drove through to a resounding victory in negotiations with the soft coal industry. By pursuing an independent and militant policy, on January 18, 1951 they secured a 20-cent-an-hour wage increase. Through Lewis they made it absolutely plain they would not tolerate a wage freeze and would not consider a no-strike policy. For the first time in over a decade the operators decided not to force the miners into a strike. If the other union leaders were considering submission to the government's new "stabilization" machinery, the miners' victory for the time being undermined their plans. It was not the season for willing surrender by labor leaders.

On January 19 Truman appointed Eric Johnston, former motion picture industry "czar" and four-time head of the Chamber of Commerce, as Economic Stabilization Administrator under the overall economic command of Wilson. On January 26 the administration agencies announced that most wages were frozen as of January 25 and that most prices were fixed as of their highest point between December 19, 1950 and January 25, 1951. But the Wage Stabilization Board on which the union leaders were participating hastened to rule that wage increases agreed upon before January 25 — specifically the miners' raise—were not to be affected by the wage freeze.

In addition to General Electric's Wilson and the motion picture industry's Johnston, Truman appointed W. H. Harrison, president of the International Telephone and Telegraph Corporation, to complete a Big Business triumvirate empowered to run the war economy. Harrison was named Administrator of Defense Production. Columnist Murray Kempton of the *New York Post* noted that "a single corporation—the telephone industry—has more personnel in important government posts today than the entire labor movement."

The trio of mobilization chiefs quickly revealed the nature of the program they intended to impose on the American people. William Green complained from Miami, following issuance of the price control order, that "prices have been steadily rising while wages have been pretty much standing still." Michael Quill called the order for "voluntary" enforcement of price ceilings a "cowardly retreat on the part of the administration reeling under the blows of profit-mad Wall Street lobbyists." This open and direct attack on the Truman administration was a new note. But, as it turned out, Quill's was not a lone voice.

On February 16 the Wage Stabilization Board by a vote of six to three adopted a new wage-freeze formula. This fixed a ten per cent ceiling above basic wage levels of January 15, 1950, six months before the war began. The coal miners' raise had been previously exempted. The three labor members of the WSB — Emil Rieve of the CIO Textile Workers, Harry C. Bates of the AFL Bricklayers, and Elmer E. Walker of the independent International Association of Machinists — who had asked a 12 per cent wage ceiling, cast the three dissenting votes. They then walked off the board.

"Our decision here cannot and must not be interpreted merely as a protest against an unfair and unworkable [wage] formula," the three dissenters said in their statement of resignation. "That formula culminated a whole series of shocking developments which we find unsupportable."

John L. Lewis promptly gave public praise to the three labor dissidents who had quit the WSB. The sweet dram he poured for them was not without a drop of acid: "In equity and good conscience all American workers are entitled to receive at least the same comparative wage improvement from the base of January 1950 that has been negotiated and made effective in the ... coal industry."

The WSB's wage-freeze formula served notice that labor was to carry the whole economic burden of the Korean War and the new rearmament program. At that very moment the government reported corporate profits before taxes in 1950 had risen to almost 50 billion dollars compared to 27.6 billion dollars in 1949, the last full nonwar year.

The pressure of the ranks on the union leaders at this stage was revealed in officially-sanctioned strikes and strike threats. As the WSB wage formula was being announced, the CIO Textile Workers of America was waging a major strike against the woolen manufacturers. TWA President Rieve wired Truman to remind him that he had been elected on a "Fair Deal" program and urged the President "to take the mobilization program out of the hands of the big business men." Ralph Helstein, president of the CIO United Packinghouse Workers, labeled the wage freeze "monstrously unfair." The freeze had been ordered just after the packinghouse workers, following a strike vote, had secured a wage-increase agreement from Swift, Armour and Cudahy which was subject to WSB approval and didn't fit the formula.

Although the CIO auto workers were tied down with five-year pacts, their cost-of-living escalator clauses and annual productivity-improvement wage increases were threatened by the WSB's policy. The day after the WSB wage ruling the auto union's International Executive Board announced: "We are prepared to fight just as hard to maintain our contracts as we had to fight to win them.

That means in plain language, full use of the strike weapon if such a course is forced upon us. We shall recommend such a course of action at our convention in Cleveland, April 1-5."

This was said as the Chinese forces were battering the American troops out of North Korea. Such an expression of militancy by the UAW officials testified to the anger of the UAW members against Truman's policies. The leaders did not dare to go along with his policies and face the UAW convention.

Once more the Democratic-labor coalition appeared strained to the breaking point. This marriage of convenience had barely survived the post-World War II strike wave and the anti-labor legislative drive. Now the ULPC directly confronted the Democratic administration. On February 28, 1951, it announced that it was following up the resignation of the three labor members from the Wage Stabilization Board by withdrawing all 24 labor representatives from war mobilization agencies. This action was taken, the ULPC said, to "impress upon the American people the great wrongs being perpetrated against them." Among those who quit were Murray, Green, Meany, Reuther, James B. Carey and George Harrison. Never had these conservative union leaders adopted such a sharp tone in denunciation of government policies. They stated:

"On February 16 we announced that we had become thoroughly disillusioned with the conduct of the defense mobilization program. We made the deliberate charge that big business was dominating the program ... Since then we have spelled out our indictment in detail to the President of the United States and to the heads of agencies under him. We have talked and we have listened. After full and complete exchanges of information, our original convictions have been more than confirmed...

"1. We are today confronted with a price order which amounts to a legalized robbery of every American consumer, together with a wage order which denies justice and fair play to every American who works for wages ... Wages and salaries of all Americans are now bound under the most rigid controls in the history of our country.

"2. The door has been slammed in our faces on the vital problem of manpower, which directly affects the workers we represent ... So long as the control of manpower rests in the Office of Defense Mobilization no wage or salary earner may feel safe that the big business clique in control of that agency may not seek to achieve a compulsory draft of the nation's workers.

"3. There has been no affirmative action to meet our basic position that equality of sacrifices must be the guiding and indispensable principle in the defense program.

"4. We have also arrived at the inescapable conclusion that such representation which already has been accorded to labor... and such further representation as is now offered are merely for the purpose of window dressing...Mr. [Charles E.] Wilson...would now accept window dressing, supplied by labor, to cover the back-room activities of the leaders of industry who staff the ODM. He will get no such window dressing from the men and women of American labor.

"5. We have, however, publicly stated, and we now reiterate, that we are prepared to participate in a reconstituted tripartite Wage Stabilization and Disputes Board which would administer a fair and equitable policy."

Despite the bitter tone and specific accusations there is nothing in this bill of particulars that could not have fitted even more closely the war labor program of the late President Roosevelt. Indeed, Roosevelt had been the chief exponent of a compulsory labor draft during World War II.

The real gripe of the union officialdom was that the Truman administration gave them not even a tattered cloak to cover the nakedness of their readiness to comply with the fundamentally anti-labor war program. Truman gave them no demagogic peg on which to hang an "equality of sacrifice" program. Hence their demand for a "Disputes" board to which all union conflicts with the corporations might be siphoned. They wanted an extension of the Wage Stabilization Board principle — although they had just quit the existing WSB.

Even as they defied and denounced Truman's policies, the union leaders sought to build a bridge back to a firm political alliance and full collaboration in enforcing the war program. Nevertheless, the break was real. For the time being they felt more intensely the hot breath of the disgruntled workers than the cold contempt of the political bosses they served. They were forced to a rupture with the Democratic administration in the midst of war by the pressure of the ranks.

In addition to the official indictment handed down by the United Labor Policy Committee, prominent individual union leaders, particularly in the CIO, made even sharper attacks on the whole two-party political domination and ventured feelers in the direction of a third party or labor party.

Louis Hollander, a leader of the Amalgamated Clothing Workers and president of the New York State CIO, declared that the Democratic and Republican parties were united in "a reactionary coalition to gang up on the wage earner" and "it is possible that we may have to develop an independent political party — not a third party, but a first party of the American people."

CIO Secretary-Treasurer James B. Carey, who had been one of the President's ardent supporters, openly denounced Truman. In the heat of a protest meeting in Boston, Carey read a letter criticizing Truman personally for handing the war machine over to Big Business — but the letter was never sent. Robert S. Allen, *New York Post* columnist, quoted Carey as saying at a closed meeting of the ULPC:

"Truman doesn't even bother to pay lip service any more on social legislation. What remnants of the Fair Deal were left have been completely junked. Not only is labor's advice being disregarded, it's not even being sought any more. With a few exceptions, everyone in inner Administration circles is now practically openly hostile to labor. There is no use kidding ourselves about that. It's a fact and we might as well realize it and deal with it."

The ULPC sought to "deal with it" at a delegated conference in Washington, D.C. on March 21. Some 700 delegates participated from the ULPC's component unions, mainly CIO and AFL. The day before, these two major bodies had held separate meetings to hear reports of their ULPC representatives. At the CIO meeting, Reuther sought to implicate Truman in the government program which gave Big Business control of war mobilization. Murray, however, pointedly refrained from any reference to Truman and placed the entire blame on Truman's appointee, C. E. Wilson, and on Congress. At the AFL gathering, President Green refused to accept a motion to call on Truman to remove Wilson as Defense Mobilization Administrator. When both organizations met together on March 21, Reuther said nothing about Truman.

The conference was very significant as a reflection of the desires of the union ranks and many union leaders to reunite the forces of labor. But it was almost wholly dominated by the top leaders who consumed most of the time in windy speeches. Reuther's speech was the most applauded because of its militant tone, although he did not step out of line. Only two delegates not on the official speakers' list managed to get the floor. They were CIO United Automobile Workers Secretary-Treasurer Emil Mazey, and Ed Wells of the Knoxville, Tennessee Central Labor Union. Mazey did direct his fire at Truman:

"One phase of the problem has not been adequately covered here today. Truman was elected on a fair deal program. I respectfully submit that the President has made but feeble attempts to put that program into effect. And we are getting a raw deal today. Truman has the responsibility of removing C. E. Wilson. The President can't escape his share of responsibility for the mess today."

However, Mazey's lips were glued shut on political action. It remained for Wells, the only local delegate to get the floor, to speak out: "The speeches yesterday and today have been fine. But the big question that arises here today is what can we do to be effective about the information we are getting. I am not at all satisfied despite what has gone on here today that we have steered the labor movement to what it wants to accomplish...

"If United Labor is going to walk out of the Truman administration and out of the Democratic Party then we are going to get somewhere. The least we can do is get the Central Labor Unions and the State Federation of Labor to pass resolutions for a democratic Labor Party or a Farmer-Labor Party."

This opened the question the labor leadership has had to confront continuously in the quarter century of the great flowering of the union movement: If the Democratic Party betrays the interests of labor, what alternative does labor have besides a switch to the Republicans?

The ULPC conference, called to deal with an open break with the Truman administration, offered no answer to this key question. The delegates were offered and adopted without debate a Declaration of Principles that was limited substantially to a repetition of the complaints and grievances that had led to the dramatic withdrawal of the union representatives from the war mobilization agencies. "We are shocked by the cruel disregard being shown for the interests of every-day American families. We are shocked by the privilege and favoritism bestowed upon a single group," the conference declared. But the labor bureaucracy was not "shocked" enough to propose any effective action by labor's 16,000,000 organized workers.

The CIO United Automobile Workers held its convention on the heels of the ULPC conference. This convention, meeting in Cleveland April 1-6, proved notable in several respects, none of them connected with Reuther's own major objective of a substantial dues increase. It was the first time since 1936, when the UAW advocated a labor party, that a UAW convention was permitted to debate and vote on a labor party resolution. It was the first time a top officer of the UAW ever attacked a President of the United States from the platform of a UAW convention. And, perhaps most unusual, it was the first time a UAW convention — or any CIO convention — ever heard a principled declaration of opposition to a capitalist war in progress.

In his keynote address at the opening session, Walter Reuther did not say anything that could be quoted as an explicit attack on Truman. The farthest he dared to go was, "Mr. Wilson is responsible

for a lot of things in Washington, and people in administrative position who were elected to office may be able to delegate authority,
but they cannot abdicate responsibility."

UAW Secretary-Treasurer Mazey, just as he had done at the
ULPC conference a month earlier, assailed Truman by name. He
charged that "the President in this administration has given the nation a raw deal" and "President Truman cannot escape his full share
of responsibility for the confusion and for the mess that the mobilization program finds itself in..." Later in the convention Mazey
supported the official resolution on political action which deliberately avoided even mention of a labor party.

Delegates from the floor quickly picked up Mazey's attack on
Truman and proposed that it be attached to the resolution in support
of the United Labor Policy Committee program, on which Mazey
had been speaking. Reuther sidetracked the issue by stating that
the "newspapers are all here" and would report Mazey's remarks;
that Mazey had made the same general remarks at the ULPC conference of all the top labor leaders, "so they heard it." However,
he added that "I am sure we will be glad to get copies to all members of Congress so they will know also." This was accepted by the
delegates as giving a more formal status to Mazey's attack on Truman. But Reuther had actually prevented any formal action by the
convention that would have put the UAW on record in criticism of
Truman.

Before the convention could get down to a discussion of the urgent political question, the Reuther machine occupied two days in
hammering through the decisions and policies that were its prime
objectives at this convention. First, Reuther sought to place the
convention on record for unconditional and uncritical support of Truman's armed intervention in the Korean civil war. Then, he pressed
for his chief immediate organizational goal — a two-thirds increase
in membership dues: from $1.50 a month to a $2.50 minimum.

A dramatic debate on the Korean War unexpectedly climaxed the
second morning's session. The Resolutions Committee presented a
resolution proposing complete support to Truman's Korean policies.
A half-dozen delegates took the floor to offer sharp criticism. The
debate was opened by John Anderson, president of Detroit Fleetwood Local 15. He was well known for his left socialist views, as
an anti-Stalinist and a World War II veteran. He charged that the
resolution did not reflect the sentiments of the majority of American
people. "Numerous polls" taken throughout the country had shown,
he said, that "the people have criticized and have been in overwhelming opposition to our intervention... They have been for the

withdrawal of the troops in Korea. I am for the withdrawal of our troops from Korea."

Anderson recalled that a national CIO representative in South Korea before the outbreak of the war "gave a lot of factual information as to what the Syngman Rhee regime represented in Korea and it was no different than Chiang Kai-Shek and Bao Dai [Emperor of French Indo-China] and other puppets of the wealthy class in the Far East."

The Korean War, he pointed out, "is not just inspired by Soviet agents, as the public press would have us believe, but it is to a large extent a civil war, a revolutionary war such as the American people fought back in 1776 and our American Civil War... The workers in South Korea are as hostile to the American troops and their policies as they have been to the Russian policies."

During World War II no delegate at any CIO union convention had ever felt free and safe enough to voice opposition to U. S. participation in the war. During the Korean War, the most conservative union leaders felt obliged to openly refuse collaboration with the government war agencies and to endorse strikes. But it was unique for a major union convention to hear a debate on the question of supporting the war itself.

Delegate Ernest Dillard, also of Fleetwood Local 15, drew strong applause when he directed attention to the investigation of the treatment of Negro GI's in Korea made by Thurgood Marshall, representative of the National Association for the Advancement of Colored People. Marshall's report, said Dillard, himself a Negro, had disclosed "how Negroes were snatched from the foxholes, taken to a kangaroo court in Korea in the battlefield and given years and years for the slightest infraction of war rules similar to what they do to us in GM for the slightest infraction of the book of rules." Dillard noted that the American press had played down Marshall's report because "the rulers of this country certainly cannot afford to be hollering about fighting for freedom in Korea and let it be shown to this nation the conditions under which black American GI's must suffer in Korea and on the battlefield."

Reuther "appeared visibly disturbed during Anderson's powerful indictment of U. S. policy in Korea," my eyewitness dispatch in the April 9, 1951 *Militant* reported. He broke into the middle of the debate to announce that "we are also opposed to the corrupt reactionary regime of Syngman Rhee" and that the Resolutions Committee was agreeable to "clarifying" the original resolution by adding a line expressing opposition to Rhee. But the Truman administration had repeatedly insisted that the war was being fought to keep the

Rhee regime in power as the true expression of "democracy" in Korea.

Reuther likewise intervened immediately after Dillard spoke. He replied from the chair that the question of racial discrimination had no bearing on the question of "who is basically responsible for aggression in Korea." Of course, Dillard had made plain that his references to the treatment of Negro Americans in Korea were intended to reveal whether or not U.S. imperialism was indeed engaged in a war for "democracy."

On a vote by show of hands, only a score of delegates dared to vote openly against the committee's "clarified" resolution. In the war and witch-hunt atmosphere of that period, the delegates were reluctant to expose themselves to possible reprisal, but a large number abstained from voting. Significantly, there was little violent jingoism voiced and no open hostility expressed toward those who opposed the war. Bert Foster of Cleveland Local 45, a delegate who spoke for Reuther's resolution, admitted that those opposed to the resolution were "good, honest trade union people."

After a heated four-hour debate in the afternoon session of the second day, the convention adopted by a three-to-one hand vote the monthly dues increase Reuther and his fellow-officers had been seeking.

Reuther did not depend only on his machine and sheer bulldozing to put over his dues increase. He also appealed to the delegates on the basis of program. The higher dues, he assured them, were required to finance a fight for such new far-reaching demands as a guaranteed annual wage, a $200-a-month retirement pension, and similar worthy objectives. He said nothing about the fact that this fight would be deferred at least four years—until expiration of the five-year contracts.

The vital question of political action did not come up for discussion until the night session on April 5, the fifth day of the convention. The delegates were worn out by then and many had already left.

It was at that late hour in the convention when most of the delegates first learned that the Resolutions Committee was divided on political action. Three members of the committee submitted a minority resolution calling for a "Congress of Labor and...an Independent Labor Party." The three were Bert Foster of the Cleveland Fisher Body Local 45; James Schuetz, Bell Aircraft Local 501, Buffalo; and Robert J. Winters, GM New Departure Local 626 in Bristol, Conn. Foster had recently been elected president of his local on a Reutherite slate.

The majority resolution, representing Reuther's position, made no reference to a new party. It did, however, refer guardedly to Truman's responsibility for appointment of the key war mobilization figures. It urged the "United Labor Policy Committee to call a representative Conference of Labor in the spring of 1952, prior to the convening of both old party conventions" to "determine the political course that should be taken in the 1952 campaign."

Reuther's resolution continued to put primary blame for labor's plight on an "unholy alliance of reactionary Northern Republicans and Southern Democrats." The minority resolution hit Truman and the whole Democratic Party, including its presumably liberal wing. It said: "These so-called Fair Dealers have turned out to be fake dealers. Their fair deal has become a raw deal. Truman has ceased giving even lip service to social legislation. The fight for a real Fair Deal now depends upon labor and the party it must and will create."

The majority position coincided with the official line of the ULPC. It was a "wait-and-see" policy designed to leave the door open for a reconciliation with the Democratic administration and for an election deal with the Democratic Party. The proposal to hold a "Conference of Labor" in the spring of 1952, even if seriously intended, almost automatically excluded a labor party from consideration in the 1952 elections.

No one during the debate, including Reuther, spoke against a labor party. Speakers for the majority resolution even expressed sympathy for the "sentiments" of the labor party advocates. Their difference, so they said, was with the "strategy and tactics" of the minority—the "timing" of the labor party resolution, as Reuther put it.

Before a single delegate had a chance to speak from the floor, Reuther supporters called the question to force an immediate vote. This move to cut off debate brought a howl of disapproval and was rejected by an immense majority. Due to the lateness of the hour the delegates agreed to limit debate to three speakers for each side with five minutes per speaker.

The majority speakers evoked little response from the delegates. They repeated the theme that for the UAW to advocate a labor party would "wreck" labor unity. One majority speaker even pleaded that "we are going to step into something that one little organization like the UAW is not going to be able to handle."

Reuther tried to blunt an effective presentation by the pro-labor party forces by recognizing those he called "unknowns" to speak from the floor.

When it came time to recognize the last minority speaker, Reuther pointed in the direction of John Anderson, president of Fleetwood Local 15. As Anderson approached the microphone, Reuther waved him aside and said: "Not you, Brother Anderson, but that other delegate next to you whose name I don't know." A tall lanky fellow came up to the "mike" and waited for silence. Then he said in a drawl, "Charles Carmack, Local 15. I yield the floor to Brother Anderson." The convention roared with laughter. Reuther, seldom "outfoxed," turned red. Grinning to cover his chagrin, he said, "I admit it. I've been tricked. But I'll never fall for that again. Go ahead, Brother Anderson."

Anderson recalled that he had been speaking for a labor party "on every possible occasion" since 1939. But "every time it comes up at a UAW convention it is put as a point on the agenda when we can get little time." Whenever the labor party question was raised, "we are told now is not the time...I say now is the right time to form a labor party. We've been boasting all week here that we're a million and a quarter strong and now we've suddenly become so small and weak when the labor party is being discussed." On the contrary, if the American workers form a labor party, "we will win national elections, we will win state elections, we will win city elections."

When Anderson finished, the applause was deafening. At this point Reuther brushed aside the convention decision and took the floor himself. He claimed that "all agree on the sentiments of both resolutions. Both criticize both political parties and that criticism is justified." But, he said, the difference was "not a matter of political principles" but a "division in strategy and tactics." He shouted, "If you want to make it impossible to further exploit the possibilities of the United Labor Policy Committee, then support the minority resolution." He pleaded with the delegates, "Don't isolate this movement of ours." The minority's "sentiment is fine," he conceded, "but their judgment is bad, their timing is bad." (Reuther still thinks the "timing is bad" for a labor party, and continues to espouse the Democratic Party.)

Immediately after this wind-up appeal he took the vote. A quarter of the convention resisted Reuther's influence and voted for the labor party resolution. The majority resolution was shoved through due to Reuther's prestige and his misleading "labor unity" argument.

*   *   *

The 1951 UAW convention was not one of those tempestuous factional brawls which had marked the auto conventions of the Thirties and Forties. No really bitter-end struggle on fundamental issues was waged, such as the historic five-day battle over the no-strike pledge during the 1944 convention. Indeed, the only unusual and positive action of the convention was to vote a dues increase. The entire discussion of program and issues, such as that on the Korean War and labor party, was compressed into about three hours of a five-day convention. The convention really did nothing—nothing at all. Reuther had unobstructed leadership. The old major factions had been liquidated. Nothing stood in the way of his putting forth a real, effective program to meet the great crisis in which labor was at that very moment engulfed. He had nothing to offer.

The 1951 UAW convention deserves closer study because it brought into exceptionally clear focus the true nature, program and methods of operation of the new strata of union bureaucrats which came into being with the rise of the CIO and of whom Reuther is the outstanding representative. The old school of union bureaucrats —the Tobins, Freys, Wolls, Greens, Hutchesons and their like—could never have survived in power in unions like the UAW. Direct and open suppression of opinion and opposition, while not rejected by the new bureaucrats, is used more cautiously and sparingly, and usually against very unpopular or isolated minorities. Reuther employed more refined and subtle methods, even appearing to agree with a principle or program he actually opposed in order to side-step an honest confrontation of views. He prevented the formal adoption of what he opposed on specious organizational and "tactical" grounds.

The Reuthers combine social demagogy and militant phraseology with great adroitness in organizational maneuvering. Inside the UAW itself, Reuther has always been regarded as sharp, crafty, slick, clever — a shrewd, calculating maneuverer. Above all, he readily sacrifices principles and program to "practical politics." This was clearly brought out in the 1951 debate on the labor party.

Reuther's use of social demagogy and his ability to conceal antidemocratic acts under a cloak of pseudo-democracy makes him popular with many intellectuals and professional liberals outside the labor movement. He is regarded as a man of "ideas" and "social vision" because of his ability to block or confuse the discussion of class struggle concepts and surround his basically bureaucratic conservative machine with an aura of social and political progressivism.

But of what positive accomplishment could Reuther boast at this auto convention, held amidst a labor crisis so profound that it had led to united labor's first open break with the Democratic administration in eighteen years? He had put over the first UAW dues increase in many years! When the logic of the situation led inexorably to a program of independent class political action, Reuther counterposed to it a "labor unity" based on such a flimsy program that it evaporated within four months of the UAW convention.

On the very day on which Reuther claimed a UAW pro-labor party resolution would "wreck" the "unity" of the United Labor Policy Committee, the union leaders were already in headlong retreat following their one brief bold act of withdrawal from the war mobilization agencies. In response to Truman's request, the top echelon of organized labor on April 5 accepted posts on Truman's National Advisory Board on Mobilization Policy. Green, Meany, Murray, and Reuther himself had joined the board. General Electric's Wilson was the chairman. The board had no authority to make policy; it could only "advise." The union leaders had agreed to serve in the very menial and deceptive capacity they had publicly vowed on February 28 they would never accept.

The union leaders' retreat became a wild rout when they agreed to serve on a reconstituted Wage Stabilization Board composed of 18 members instead of the original 12, but with the same proportion of representation for labor, industry, and "public" members. In essence, the new board remained a body rigged in favor of the employers and designed to freeze wages.

Not one of labor's grievances was solved by the coalition war agencies. All major complaints enumerated in the ULPC declaration of February 28 remained. Yet, on April 30, the United Labor Policy Committee agreed to resume all posts from which the labor leaders had withdrawn in February. The reason given for crawling back into these posts was "a significant change of attitude in Washington."

Reuther had reason to be pleased by the new arrangement. The Truman administration, threatened by an explosion of the auto workers, graciously permitted the WSB on June 6 to approve GM's compliance with its five-year contract by granting a five-cent-an-hour cost-of-living escalator increase and a four-cent annual productivity wage raise. The steelworkers, however, found no acceptable response from the steel industry and government.

Truman, on July 31, had signed a new Defense Production Act against which the whole labor movement protested. CIO Textile Workers President Rieve, speaking for the CIO, told a congressional hearing on the bill that labor would again withdraw from government posts if the old law was not improved. The new law was worse. Price and profit controls were reduced to a complete sham. The term "cost of production" was so broadened as to invite manufacturers to boost prices based on padded costs. The act prohibited future rollbacks on beef prices, a special concession to the packing-house interests who had created an artificial meat famine similar to that after World War II. At the same time, the new law contin-ued tight wage controls and enabled the complex WSB machinery to stall union demands. The ULPC met in Washington, sent messages of protest to individual congressmen about the law already enacted and signed, nervously quieted the ranks and discouraged all mani-festations of mass action.

The AFL Executive Council meeting in August expressed acute dissatisfaction with its Democratic political allies and went so far as to threaten to withhold AFL political support "if the Democrats don't come up with decent candidates." They dissolved the United Labor Policy Committee at its August 28 meeting by withdrawing on the grounds that the ULPC had already "accomplished its pur-pose." Green pointed to the "temporary basis" of the ULPC and in-sisted that what was required was "organic unity"; that is, a mer-ger of the two organizations, CIO and AFL. In Green's mind this meant the absorption of the CIO into the AFL and its division among the numerous craft bodies. Murray berated the AFL action in quit-ting the ULPC and charged that it had "scuttled a method of inter-union cooperation" hailed by the members of all organized labor. The AFL convention in September formally approved its dissocia-tion from the ULPC.

Reuther's argument that UAW advocacy of a labor party would "wreck" the ULPC was proved fraudulent by events. The ULPC was doomed from the moment it capitulated to the Truman administra-tion and ended its boycott of the war agencies. The CIO leaders, Reuther included, had gone along with the policy of surrender to Truman and by doing so were just as responsible as the AFL chiefs for "scuttling" labor unity in the form of the ULPC.

Unity was possible only on the basis of a program of struggle against the government's policies. Murray and Reuther, no less than Green and Meany, drew back from such a program. Without it, the foundation of the ULPC was washed away.

The conditions that had originally brought about formation of the ULPC remained. But the struggle against these conditions, in a partial sense at least, took another form. It was to be climaxed by the great 1952 national steel strike.

34

The Third
National Steel Strike

The Korean War, with its new outpouring of government expenditures, had solved the problem of recession for the owning class almost overnight. Profits and production scaled new heights. But surprisingly little of this blood-bought "prosperity" trickled down to the workers. The cost-of-living index, based on the 1935–39 average of 100, rose from 170.2 in 1949 to 185.6 in 1951, and to 190.4 by January 1953 when General Eisenhower took over the White House.

In April 1951 the Truman administration adopted a new base for the cost-of-living index and revised the method of computing the index to give greater weight to such items as automobiles, refrigerators and furniture, and less to food, housing and clothing. The new index started from a 1947–49 base of 100, thus tending to conceal the 100 per cent rise in living costs, including new taxes, in the decade from 1940 to 1950. The CIO attacked the revised index which worked to the advantage of the employers in computing wage increases under the escalator clauses. But even the new index showed an 11 per cent rise in the cost of living in just a year and a half, up to 111.0 in 1951, and 113.9 by January 1953. Of the total rise of 25.4 per cent in the index from 1949 to 1960, more than half occurred in the last two and a half years of Truman's administration.

Because of the united, if brief, stand of the CIO with the AFL and the official strikes in the railroad, packinghouse and textile industries, the administration decided on a slightly more flexible wage policy. In June 1951, the ten per cent wage-ceiling formula was scrapped and the CIO and AFL meatpacking workers were granted wage raises of 14 per cent over the January 1950 wage scale.

Back in January, in a letter to Senator Harry Byrd of Virginia, Truman had confided that he was for taxing the people "until it hurts."

General Motors President Charles E. Wilson (not to be confused with General Electric's Wilson who headed the economic mobilization program) had observed on January 4 that it would be "naive to think" that labor would not force wage increases "to make up for the increase in the cost of living." He proposed to hold down the workers' real income and purchasing power through taxation. "They will [accept lower living standards] more willingly," he said, "if their nation's necessities in the form of taxation force them to do so than they would if they were forced to the same conditions by employers holding down their wages."

Before Congress adjourned in 1951, Truman signed a new tax bill which was simon-pure class legislation. It raised taxes on workers' income 12 per cent while millionaires' taxes were notched up only one per cent.

But a new economic phenomenon appeared in the very midst of the war. In June 1951, mass layoffs began to plague the industrial workers. The auto layoffs were especially severe. This became a sharp issue in the UAW. The auto workers complained of intensified speed-up as layoffs mounted to more than 200,000 in the industry by late fall.

Reuther might have stifled all open attempts to fight the speed-up and layoffs but for new inner-union forces that had begun to line up against his policies after the April 1951 UAW convention. Among the most influential elements who broke with Reuther and began to voice more strongly a program to meet the needs of the workers were top leaders of UAW Ford Local 600 with its 65,000 members.

Scarcely a week after Reuther had shoved through his dues increase, Local 600 President Carl Stellato hurled a full-page attack at the UAW president in the April 14 *Ford Facts,* the local's paper. An eight-column head in giant type stated Stellato's views toward Reuther's policy in one word: "BETRAYAL!" Stellato had been stung by the epithet "anti-union" flung at him by Reuther and Emil Mazey after Stellato had opposed the dues increase during the convention debate.

"I have been confronted with every threat," Stellato wrote. "The fact that the membership of my Local Union demanded by a vote of 23,000 to 9,000 that delegates from Local 600...oppose any form of dues increase, made no difference whatsoever to those sending out these threats. I was supposed to be a 'good boy,' 'a smart politician,' 'fall in line' and otherwise violate the trust placed in me by the membership which elected me."

Having taken the bull by the horns, Stellato had to wrestle not only with the question of Reuther's conduct on the dues issue, but with his whole manner of ruling the union. He had to raise the basic question of union democracy. Stellato wrote that "the cardinal sin is to disagree with the top leadership. For this you can be exterminated politically, you can be fired if you are a Union representative, you can be brought to trial by the Executive Board and thrown out of the Union, you can be denied the right to criticize Union policy or Union officers in Local Union papers. Every such action is a denial of the great democratic traditions of our union." Stellato also described the "various 'smart' techniques" employed to stifle opposition expression at the conventions.

Thrust into opposition to Reuther over the elementary issue of union democracy, Ford Local 600 began to advance proposals designed to arouse the UAW membership on the great economic problems confronting them, particularly the mass unemployment amidst the war boom, the so-called conversion layoffs. In June, the local Executive Board proposed a campaign to secure from the federal government $60 weekly unemployment compensation instead of the $20 to $30 received by the jobless auto workers. The Local 600 leaders also urged an emergency conference of the UAW to map a fight against speed-up.

Strikes against speed-up broke out in key plants of the Chrysler Corporation, among them the Detroit Dodge and DeSoto plants. A conference of Chrysler-local union representatives called for corporation-wide strike action and backed Local 600's call for a national UAW conference to launch a general attack on speed-up. The Reuther machine did nothing effective about the spreading layoffs and the speed-up. But it acted with vigor against those who tried to defend themselves against these conditions.

The UAW International Executive Board on July 23 placed an administrator over DeSoto Local 227 because the plant had been closed 80 working days since the first of the year due to "unauthorized stoppages" and the local union had refused to "discipline" workers alleged to have led these strikes against speed-up. The Dodge strikers were driven back to work by the threats of UAW International Vice-President Richard Gosser of Toledo and Norman Matthews, UAW Detroit East Side Regional Director. They said that the International Union would not support the strike and would withhold any aid for workers, however numerous, who might be fired or disciplined by the company.

Reuther responded to the pressure of local demands for action against layoffs and speed-up by arranging a series of UAW regional conferences. These conferences, however, were permitted no real opportunity to discuss proposals like the $60 a week unemployment compensation and the 30-hour week at 40-hours' pay. At the Region 1 conference held in Detroit during late September, Reuther violently attacked the opposition Committee for a Democratic UAW-CIO, headed by Stellato, for advocating "30 for 40." Reuther called the shorter work-week proposal "unrealistic" and "poorly timed." The answer to mass unemployment, Reuther claimed, was "the guaranteed annual wage." He assured the assembled workers that the "facts were being assembled so that a fight can be made on this" —in 1955. In the meantime, he urged, "sharpen up your statistics, boys, we'll carry them to Washington."

The intensely ambitious Reuther could brook no other aspirants to his post or rule. His Executive Board summoned Stellato and Local 600 Vice-President Pat Rice to a hearing on charges of publishing certain material in *Ford Facts* that was "detrimental to the interests of the International Union." There is no doubt that it was detrimental to Walter Reuther and his lieutenants.

When the accused Local 600 leaders, accompanied by the entire Executive Board, appeared before the International Executive Board, they found themselves confronted with general and unsupported accusations. Stellato turned the hearing into a denunciation of Reuther's failure to act on the auto workers' critical problems and his unprincipled maneuvers to stifle opposition opinion. Moreover, Reuther had not even submitted a bill of particulars and written charges, as the UAW constitution required. Prior to this attempted drumhead court, Local 600's delegated General Council of more than 200 elected members had voted almost unanimously to condemn Reuther's action and support their local leadership. Reuther had to retreat for the time being and agree to submit his charges in writing.

At a large mass meeting in November, Stellato publicly urged Reuther to cease his attacks on Local 600 and use his leadership talents to lead a fight against layoffs and speed-up. Stellato specifically stressed the "30 for 40" program. This struggle within the UAW, a reflection of the dissatisfaction and discontent of the auto workers, was protracted over a number of years.

In the meantime, the attention of American labor was turning increasingly toward the steel industry. The Thirteenth Constitutional Convention of the CIO early in November served as a springboard for the Steelworkers' campaign to win concessions in the approaching contract negotiation. The entire contract was up for renegotiation for the first time in five years.

The CIO convention delegates heard a long series of complaints and tirades against the government's wage policies prefaced or intermixed by loud affirmations of support for Truman's war program.

A convention resolution declared that "we shall never submit to discriminatory wage freezes." Textile Union President Rieve mournfully confessed that he and the other labor members on the new Wage Stabilization Board "often times must vote —when we don't want to —to cut down wage increases won by other unions in negotiations..." Joseph Beirne, president of the CIO Communications Workers of America, the chief union of the telephone workers, referred to the WSB as the "graveyard of grievances." He revealed: "We have today over 10,000 cases tied up, 10,000 cases where we know and we feel... the keen desires of the workers whose wages are held up, and wanting those wages, wanting some relief..."

These outcries about Washington's wage policies were the opening barrage in the steelworkers' announced campaign for "substantial wage increases." Immediately following the CIO convention, the United Steelworkers Wage Policy Committee met in Atlantic City and formulated a 22-point program of demands on the steel corporations. These demands covered every issue from wages to seniority, from the upgrading of Negro workers without discrimination to the guaranteed annual wage. There would have been little uncertainty about the favorable outcome of the negotiations but for the role of the government. In his report to the CIO convention, Murray had voiced fear of government interference, since Defense Mobilization Director Wilson had already proclaimed that a steel strike would not be tolerated and that any dispute would have to be resolved by the WSB. Therefore Murray had warned the CIO delegates: "The heavy hand of government lurks forever around the corner. It may have a bludgeon in its hand ready to bash our brains in with..."

Contract negotiations with the U. S. Steel Corporation began on November 27, 1951. The union asked for an "across-the-board" wage increase of 15 cents an hour, in addition to 21 other demands. The corporation conceded nothing. Its resistance was stiffened by Wilson who said in a speech on December 13 that the whole stabilization program hung on the outcome of the steel fight and that "we must and we will maintain wage control." The steel union charged that the government had kept secret two reports which showed that the steel industry could raise wages 34 to 40 cents an hour without raising prices and still maintain the pre-Korean War average of profits.

Murray had accurately predicted the attitude of the steel companies when he had told the CIO convention: "What do you do when you meet an employer and he says to you at the beginning of a conference: 'Here it is, take it or leave it. If you don't like it, go on over to the Wage Stabilization Board. If they give you a couple of pennies, we will seek a price increase. Go on, get out of here.'"

Now, in the midst of the Korean War, Murray faced the same choice that had confronted John L. Lewis and the United Mine Workers in 1943, but without the opposition from within the labor camp. The 170-man International Policy Committee of the steel union, with Murray's concurrence, announced that 650,000 steelworkers starting midnight December 31, would not work "in the absence of mutually satisfactory contracts." In an unprecedented move, the Policy Committee also called the union's first special convention, to begin on January 3, 1952 in Atlantic City.

Truman promptly demanded that the dispute be placed in the hands of the Wage Stabilization Board and threatened to "use whatever laws there are on the books to prevent a strike." On Christmas Eve Truman phoned Murray. The December 29 *Business Week* reported Truman as telling Murray: "...We can't have a steel strike now...I can't think of what's going on over in Korea and stand by and let a steel strike happen." This, evidently, was all Murray needed. He announced on December 28 that the Policy Committee had called off the strike and that it would be up to the special convention to "answer the President's request."

On January 4, 1952, the CIO Steelworkers' special convention adopted the proposal of Murray and his Executive Board to postpone any strike until February 20. This, the resolution said, was intended to give the Wage Stabilization Board 45 days to "consider the case."

The two-day special convention was notable as the only convention in the steel union's history in which most of the time was taken up by the delegates. Great volleys of applause and cheers repeatedly ripped through the convention hall at the "shut 'em down" declarations. The *Wall Street Journal* in its convention report said: "Seldom has anger and sharp attack against industry flashed so frequently at a steel workers' meeting."

Why was this unusual convention called and militant sentiment permitted such free rein? It was a risky precedent to set, from Murray's point of view.

Murray found himself confronted with completely adamant steel corporations which were encouraged in their resistance by every agency of government up to and including the White House. He then used the convention as a medium for putting pressure on the companies and WSB. By unleashing some of the pent-up anger of the ranks at the convention, Murray hoped to impress industry and government with the fighting mood of the workers.

However, the convention was "much more than a 'clever' bureaucratic strategem," M. Stein reported in the January 4, 1952 *Militant*.

"Such a gigantic spectacle could never be staged even by professional actors with expert direction. It is the genuineness of the steelworkers' anger that made such a deep impression. The steelworkers are in mortal fear that the companies are out to smash their union. One convention speaker after another kept repeating: 'The company is out to smash us.'"

At the WSB hearings in February, the steel industry spokesmen said no to every one of the union's 22 demands. They even opposed productivity wage increases—raises based on higher man-hour output—as "inflationary." Anything that interfered with the companies' unrestricted right to determine job allocations, incentive plans, number and type of jobs to be filled, speed of operations, etc., was dismissed as "socialistic." The climax of the steel industry's performance came when Bradford B. Smith, economist for U. S. Steel, claimed the union's demand for a guaranteed annual wage was "a disguised form of unemployment insurance that would destroy the incentive to work." It would be preferable, said Smith, "for steelworkers to save $15 a week from their own paychecks to tide themselves over periods of unemployment." That, he said, was the "one non-socialistic thoroughly American way" for steelworkers to "minimize the unemployment hardships." He called the steelworkers the "economic royalists" of American labor.

Even Murray could not stomach this rank insult. "This piece of paper that your industry has presented here," Murray raged, "is the most reprehensible, filthy, lying, deceiving presentation that has ever been presented to a government agency in my lifetime." This time he did not plead with the steel moguls to "be decent, be gentlemen." Nevertheless, Murray pushed through two more strike postponements to give the stalling WSB "more time" to consider the case. Finally, the WSB announced it would make its decision known on March 20. A new strike deadline was set for Sunday midnight, March 23. The local steel unions were pushing their strike preparations zealously. Philip Murray was pictured by columnist Murray Kempton in his March 14 *New York Post* as "sitting and waiting in his office, fingering the letters from the wives of his members that call him a coward because he has waited so long..."

It was not simply cowardice. Twice before—in 1946 and 1949—Murray had called national steel strikes. He suffered from a false political philosophy and allegiance. The year 1952 was a presidential election year. Murray was committed "body and soul" to the Democratic Party and its national administration. A national steel strike might push Truman into use of the Taft-Hartley Act or other anti-labor measures which might help to destroy the pro-labor image of the Democratic President which the union leaders had been trying so desperately to preserve.

As for Truman, he had the problem of preventing or breaking a steel strike without formal use of the Taft-Hartley Act in an election year. He had to reassure the capitalist interests, who really dominate the Democratic Party, by limiting concessions to the union as much as possible. He had to appear to be resisting the anti-labor demands while putting the screws on the workers. "After all, he didn't use the Taft-Hartley Act," the pro-Democrat labor apologists would be able to say during the election campaign. Of course, Truman and his administration had used the notorious Act 66 times before the steel conflict.

The steel industry required the collaboration of the government in holding concessions to the union to an absolute minimum and then in using such concessions finally granted to justify a big price increase. The steel owners planned to play the game in which they had displayed such mastery in 1946 and 1949: force the union to strike for negligible gains; make a deal with the government to authorize large price increases; blame the price rises on the "inflationary" demands of the union.

The Wage Stabilization Board on March 20 announced a recommendation for a whittled-down, compromise settlement of the union's demands. The union had asked for an 18-1/2-cent hourly wage boost; the WSB agreed to 12-1/2 cents. The union sought eight paid holidays; the board said six. The union called for complete abolition of the Southern wage differential; the board cut the differential in half but did not eliminate it. With a show of disapproval, Murray nevertheless agreed to the WSB's terms.

But the higher administration economic agencies threw the WSB recommendations out the window. After a conference with Truman at Key West, Defense Mobilization Director C. E. Wilson announced: "If the wage increases contemplated under the WSB recommendation are put into effect it would be a serious threat in our year-old effort to stabilize the economy." The steelworkers were told in effect to start renegotiating with the steel industry for terms that would fit Wilson's — and Truman's — concept of "economic stabilization."

A fifth strike deadline was set for midnight, April 8. By squeezing four strike postponements out of the union leadership, Truman had staved off an industry shutdown for at least 99 days — 11 more than the maximum 80-day "cooling-off" period he could have imposed under the Taft-Hartley Act. In fact, had the union gone through the Taft-Hartley procedure formally, it would have been free to strike after the 80 days. Now, after a longer period, Truman could still use his claimed "inherent powers," or even the Taft-Hartley Act. Murray was using every pretext for delaying strike action in the hope of saving Truman from a politically embarrassing situation.

It may seem that the WSB recommendation, which had been turned down by Wilson, was a considerable concession to the union. Actually, it was only 3-1/2 cents more than what the companies had finally indicated they were prepared to give. The latter had offered a 14.1-cent wage package. The WSB "public" members favored 17.6 cents. The union was holding out for a 30-cent package. Bureau of Labor Statistics figures showed average hourly wages in all major industries had risen eight cents in 1951—but in steel not one cent.

The WSB's recommendation, as has been noted, was set aside. But before the scheduled strike could begin Murray once more called it off, after Truman seized the strike-threatened plants in advance of a shutdown.

Murray had said that in event of a seizure he "presumed" the government would put the WSB recommendations into effect. Instead, when Secretary of Commerce Charles Sawyer, who was in charge of the seizure, was asked by reporters what he intended to do about the recommendations, he replied, "Nothing. The present arrangements will continue until a settlement." Thus, the workers would lose the benefits to which even the WSB had to concede they were entitled. The operation of the steel mills would continue as usual, Sawyer said further. He had appointed the incumbent owners and managers as "operating managers" with full control.

While the Truman administration was holding off any wage concessions, on April 23 it authorized a $3-a-ton increase in steel prices. The steel companies, which had demanded $12, expressed dissatisfaction with the gratuity handed them by the government and instituted a series of court suits to end the government seizure. Although the seizure was intended to smash a strike, the companies refused to recognize the right of the government to interfere even in principle with their unrestricted "property rights."

On April 29, Federal Judge David A. Pine of the District of Columbia Court ruled that Truman's seizure of the steel plants was illegal. Within eight hours of the court's ruling, the nation's steelworkers had emptied the plants on notice from the international union headquarters that work was to cease "in the absence of a contract."

A day after the steel walkout, close to 100,000 oil workers of some 20 CIO and AFL unions also struck. They had received an eight-month runaround from the oil firms and the WSB on their demand for a 25-cent wage increase. After a three-week strike, the

WSB was persuaded to approve 15 cents of the demanded 18-cent-an-hour general wage increase plus other benefits. One contract that had already been signed for 18 cents was disallowed. Labor members of the WSB voted for the 15-cent limit.

Murray, at Truman's insistence, called off the steel strike on its fourth day, May 3, in spite of his own earlier revelation of the union's disastrous experiences with government agencies, made to the Senate Labor and Welfare Committee hearing on April 23. He had then said: "We did not want to go to Washington in December 1951... The process of going to a board has, in the experience of this union, been a method of forcing the union to accept a compromise of its position before a strike has begun. We did not want to go through that process again."

Yet, he did. The result, as Murray complained to the Senate hearing, was that "at this moment, despite the seizure, the Steelworkers of America are still receiving 1950 wages and paying 1952 prices." Workers in almost every major industry, he said, had already received increases in excess of what the WSB had approved for the steelworkers but "they and their families, almost alone in America, still today have received nothing, absolutely nothing."

Judge Pine not only ended the steel seizure but he forebade the government to put wage increases into effect. The four-day strike that had followed the removal of Truman's strikebreaking weapon had quickly reversed the relationship of forces. A federal appeals court then hastily overruled Judge Pine's injunction against government enforcement of wage increases. Murray had again sent the workers back on the job after Truman's appeal and his vague hint that he might put some pay award into effect. The United States Supreme Court, largely handpicked by Roosevelt and Truman, then intervened to declare that wage increases could not be given until the seizure issue had been finally settled, since Truman had appealed Judge Pine's rulings to the highest juridical authority. Murray acceded to Truman's insistence that the steel union await the outcome of the Supreme Court hearing—whenever that might be.

At the Sixth Constitutional Convention of the United Steelworkers of America on May 14 in Atlantic City, some 3,000 embittered delegates voted unanimously to authorize strike action. But the leaders were able to keep from the resolution any specific strike deadline. If they were forced to strike, as Murray told the steel delegates, it would not be for their own demands. He had to admit: "The Wage Board has already compromised your situation; it has given you much less than you hoped to get through collective bargaining." Once more, as in 1949, the steelworkers were faced with a full-scale struggle for only the remnants of their demands.

Then, on June 2, the Supreme Court upheld the lower court's ruling that the seizure of the steel industry was illegal. Now if Truman wanted to break the strike he could no longer hide behind subterfuges; he would have to use the Taft-Hartley Act. But, with Murray's collaboration, Truman had already delayed a strike almost twice as long as a Taft-Hartley 80-day "cooling-off" injunction, and he did not dare evoke the Act because of the generally shaky position of the Democratic machine. It was not widely known then that Adlai Stevenson, who was to be 1952 Democratic presidential candidate, had proposed the use of the Taft-Hartley Act against the steelworkers. But Truman was too shrewd to place the Democrats under that handicap. Now it was up to the steel industry itself to drag out a settlement as long as possible.

The showdown steel strike, delayed more than six months and postponed six times, began on June 3 immediately following the action of the Supreme Court. At last the steelworkers were able to use their fighting powers in an open test of strength against the corporations.

On June 10 Truman addressed Congress with an appeal to enact special legislation empowering him to break the steel strike by plant seizures. He boasted: "I had managed to keep production going from the end of December to the second of June—a period of more than 150 days—even though the companies and the union had no collective-bargaining contract."

Truman was not opposed in principle to using a Taft-Hartley injunction. What he wanted, he now asserted, was speed in its application. "If however," he told the legislators, "the judgment of the Congress, contrary to mine, is that an injunction of the Taft-Hartley type should be used, there is a quicker way to do so than by appointing a board of inquiry under the Taft-Hartley Act. That would be for the Congress to enact legislation authorizing and directing the President to seek an injunction...In any event, I hope the Congress will act quickly."

This quotation refutes the propaganda subsequently circulated in the election campaign that Truman's intervention in the steel crisis was in the interests of the steelworkers.

As the grim strike—showing all signs of becoming a long struggle of attrition—went into its third week, John L. Lewis informed Murray in a June 18 telegram: "Our union is in this fight with you. Indicative of this fact and as a preliminary step, United Mine Workers of America has today established financial credit for the United Steelworkers of America in the National Bank of Washington, D. C., in the amount of $10,000,000 subject to your draft and order, as your need warrants and circumstances require. The men in the mining industry and those of our membership in associated industries salute the men in the steel industry and commend their brave hearts..."

The United Mine Workers was facing contract negotiations and did not want to go through all the delaying actions the Steelworkers had suffered. Undoubtedly, Lewis was anxious to strengthen the resistance of the steelworkers and thereby aid the stand of the miners. Whatever Lewis's motives, there was no question of the genuineness of the offer. Murray never took advantage of it. Even at that late date Murray feared a renewal of Lewis's influence among the CIO workers.

On the other side of the battle line, the Truman administration dangled an offer of a bigger price increase before the steel companies. The President hoped to induce the steel firms to come to terms with the union and end the politically embarrassing strike. Economic Stabilizer Roger L. Putnam, who had succeeded Eric Johnston, indicated on June 18 that his agency was prepared to give "friendly and sympathetic" consideration to a $4.50-a-ton steel price hike instead of the $3 previously approved.

In their public propaganda the steel corporations made it appear that wages and the union shop were the only real issues in the strike. However, there were other issues most crucial to the steelworkers. Among these were job classifications, so-called management rights and the company manipulation of incentive plans to cut down the pay of workers.

As recently as 1947 the union had succeeded in securing an agreement on the precise description, wage rate and production speed of the thousands of different types of jobs in the industry. For the first time the duties of all categories of workers had been clearly defined and graded according to skill and responsibility. The companies could no longer shift the workers around at will, redefine a job to reduce the wage scale, compel the workers to "fill in" their "spare minutes" with other work like floor sweeping, etc. Certain rights and conditions for which the workers had fought for years and decades were spelled out in the contract.

These conditions and rules had no sooner been wrested from the companies and formalized by agreement in 1947 than the steel bosses began to hedge and chisel. A bitter guerrilla war, involving hundreds of work stoppages as well as numerous firings and other reprisals against the workers, had grown in intensity for two or three years before the 1952 strike. The prime aim of the steel employers was to restore "management prerogatives"—that is, the right to hire and fire at will, to speed up output per man-hour, to reduce "labor costs" at whatever expense to the workers. In short, the steel bosses sought restoration of the pre-union, open-shop era.

Throughout the Fifties and coming to a head in the great steel strike of 1959, the struggle in the steel industry would revolve around the crucial issue of the intensity of labor exploitation as expressed in job conditions, working rules, speed-up, rest periods, etc. In 1952, however, the government and corporations succeeded to a large extent in disguising these underlying issues and focusing attention almost entirely on the union shop and "inflationary wage demands." It must be added that Murray himself directed little public attention to the issue of working rules.

The steelworkers understood very well the objectives of the corporations. That is what gave the union ranks the tenacity to hold on for 54 days in the longest major steel strike up to that time—a strike, moreover, in the midst of a war. As in the previous steel strikes, the local unions received no advice, no instructions, no help in the actual conduct of the struggle. Each union local was left to its own devices to organize picket lines, aid the needy, keep up the morale. The actual mobilization, organization and conduct of the strike were done from below. The strong arms of the steelworkers retrieved, in part, what the flabby hands of their leaders were letting slip away.

Rather than concede anything, the steel industry preferred a long wartime strike in which it was hoped the steelworkers union would suffer a shattering defeat. Truman put no real pressure on the steel companies to yield. Certainly the President waged no such vigorous campaign to compel industry compliance in the steel conflict as he had waged to compel union compliance.

The attitude of the steel companies was summed up in an admission by Roland Sawyer, Pittsburgh correspondent, in the July 14 *Christian Science Monitor:* "However, in a struggle of the intensity of the present one, in which the issue has become one of who is running the mills, the management or the union, *national defense comes second.* The steel companies fought the President's seizure order on the issue that he had seized private property without warrant and won." (My emphasis.)

As the steel strike dragged on week after week, Murray made little effort to appeal to the labor movement on the steelworkers' behalf. He made no serious effort even to mobilize the aid of the CIO unions and membership. There were a number of practical measures possible to bolster the resistance of the strikers and alleviate their hardship. But Murray did not think in terms of streng-thening the strike, but rather of ending it as quickly as possible on any terms he could represent to the workers as a "great victory."

Finally on July 24, the fifty-second day of the strike, Murray agreed to a new government proposal for settlement. The original recommendation of the WSB was sliced down. Its pre-strike for-mula had called for an across-the-board wage increase of 12-1/2 cents an hour, retroactive to January 1, the contract termination date. An additional 2-1/2 cents was to be added on July 1, and an-other 2-1/2 cents on January 1, 1953, for a total rise of 17-1/2 cents. With 8.9 cents in proposed fringe benefits, the total of the original "package" would have come to 26.4 cents. The new recommendation came to 21.4 cents, a drop of 5 cents. Even so, only the steelwor-kers' own stubborn strike finally secured this whittled-down offer. But the retroactive clause finally granted went back only to April 1 with most of the original WSB fringe concessions omitted. The steel companies agreed to these reduced contract terms only after the Truman administration approved a price increase of $5.20 per ton.

The steelworkers ended their strike in its fifty-fourth day — Ju-ly 26. But it was not until three weeks later that U. S. Steel agreed to retention of the original Section 2B from the previous contract covering "management rights." The corporation also withdrew the "incentive wage" plan it had unilaterally imposed before the old con-tract had terminated. These were major victories for the workers.

It was subsequently revealed that the companies had agreed to a pay rise before the strike and after Murray had conceded a further slash in the WSB's original wage recommendations. The steel own-ers had also been assured of the larger price increase. However, under the guise of opposing the union-shop demand the companies had unloosed an attack on all union conditions up and down the line. But for the intransigence of the steelworkers, many if not all of these conditions might have been bartered away. Only the threat of a renewed strike forced the companies to yield on the issue of work rules and conditions.

Murray died only a few months later—having been forced to head the three largest industrial strikes in American history and all in his last seven years — without renouncing or modifying by one iota his contention that America had no classes and that here "we are all workers."

35

End of an Era

By and large, American politics of the past hundred years has been channeled into the electoral struggles between the Democratic and Republican parties. Both parties are alike in their devotion to the private profit system and in their defense of monopoly capitalism; each party serves special-interest groupings among the capitalists themselves.

The two major parties are the property of wealthy business interests who select in advance judges and mayors and city councilmen, governors and state legislators, congressmen and senators and presidents of the United States. Bribery, payoffs and shakedowns are the "fringe benefits" picked up in modern American politics. The journalist Lincoln Steffens in his book, *The Shame of the Cities,* brilliantly exposed the source of this corruption. Steffens wrote:

"He is a self-righteous fraud, this big business man. He is the chief source of corruption...The commercial spirit is the spirit of profit, not patriotism; of credit, not honor; of individual gain, not national prosperity; of trade and dickering, not principle. 'My business is sacred,' says the business man in his heart. Whatever hinders it, is wrong, it must be. A bribe is bad; that is, it is a bad thing to take; but it is not so bad to give one, not if it is necessary to my business."

As a young reporter, Steffens had brashly asked a wealthy political boss how his group was able to "bribe even Supreme Court justices." The boss replied, "My boy, we don't bribe them. We select them." That is the real essence of the matter.

The Truman administration had its full share of the traditional and standard corruption of which Steffens wrote. Its last year was

permeated with the stench of scandals which reached inside the very
White House and involved expensive "gifts" from businessmen to
some of Truman's close personal aides. "The White House re-
sembles nothing so much as a supermarket for the sale of influence,
patronage and juicy government war contracts," I wrote in the April
14, 1952 *Militant*. "Truman, the once unsuccessful haberdasher, has
finally made good as the manager-in-chief of this supermarket."

The fact that both major parties are controlled by direct agents
of specific capitalist groups and interests has been obscured by the
union leaders who, especially since 1932, have lent their support
chiefly to the Democratic faction. The unions have had no real say
inside the Democratic Party at any time. Despite the absolute reliance on the labor vote, no union leaders hold any commanding
posts within the Democratic Party nor are there any labor leaders
in important posts in the executive, judicial or legislative branches
of the federal government. During national election campaigns a
few mild reform planks are written into the Democratic platform
as a propaganda inducement to workers. But it has always been a
party of propertied interests.

The modern Democratic Party is based first of all on the racist
Southern landowners, cotton factors, tobacco growers and manufacturers, textile mill owners, and oil speculators. Capitalist groups
from the rest of the country, including consumer goods and mer-
cantile interests, share control of the party machine with the South-
erners. The Republican Party, on the other hand, gets its support
from and is dominated by the heavy goods industries and large north-
eastern financial interests.

The March 1950 issue of *The Machinist,* publication of the IAM,
carried a list of 78 "big-money boys" who in 1949 contributed from
$2,000 to $5,000 each to the Democratic National Committee. They
included some of the wealthiest labor-haters in the country. The
Republican Party that year could find only 20 donors willing to part
with as much as $2,000 each. No labor leaders could be found in
the list of big personal donors to either party.

By the end of the Fifties it had become even more apparent that
big money dominates both parties. Scions of immense wealth play
an increasingly open and direct role within the dominant circles of
the Democratic Party. They are the visible and active symbols of
the rule of that party by the beneficiaries of the great American
fortunes.

The 1960 Democratic presidential candidate, John F. Kennedy,
who reputedly spent a fabulous sum to gain the nomination, on August 18, 1960 announced the formation of a National Committee of

Business and Professional Men and Women for Kennedy and [Senator Lyndon B.] Johnson. The five co-chairmen and 31 national committee members were executives of corporations whose combined assets, as listed in *Fortune* magazine and *Moody's Directory,* total more than $5.8 billion. The Kennedy family fortune itself was reported in *Fortune* to be between $250 million and $400 million—give or take a hundred million dollars.

Within this framework of capitalist dominance and direction of the Democratic Party, the pro-capitalist labor leaders are permitted the "privilege" of offering suggestions on a narrowly limited range of issues deemed of proper labor concern. These include, primarily, social welfare and labor legislation, provided the union officials do not press anything "too radical" or in conflict with the various capitalist special interest groups whose alliance forms the operating core of the Democratic Party.

The labor leaders who profess to speak for the largest and most necessary sector of American society—the wage workers—shun any independent political program and embrace the politics of labor's enemies. In his article, "Labor and Foreign Policy," in the July 7, 1952 *Militant,* James P. Cannon summed up the role of the labor leaders in international affairs:

"An increasing number of the organized workers are interested in foreign policy and recognize, to one degree or another, that it is the number one political question, but they have yet to work out a logical foreign policy of their own. The foreign policy recommended by such global thinkers as Green and Reuther is not the product of their independent thought. It is nothing but a mimeographed handout from the State Department, which in turn gets it from the New York bankers who are also the directing powers behind the antiunion drive. This policy doesn't make much sense for a steelworker on a picket line. The imposition of this foreign policy on the trade union movement is one of the main reasons why the instinctive strivings of the organized workers to participate effectively in American politics is bedeviled and frustrated at the outset."

The labor leaders have side-stepped their responsibility to defend American labor's interests in all the domestic conflicts of the postwar era. The two most vital of these conflicts have been the battle for Negro civil rights and the defense of civil liberties against the increasing encroachments of militarism and police-statism.

The issue of Negro rights to which both the Roosevelt and Truman administrations paid lip service had come sharply to the fore in the early days of World War II. Sixteen million Negro people—native-born Americans—saw in the manpower shortages of the war their opportunity to press for jobs and equal treatment in industry. After repeated unavailing pleas to Roosevelt, hundreds of thousands in the spring of 1942 had quickly rallied to the March on Washington Movement. This had been initiated and led by A. Philip Randolph, president of the AFL Brotherhood of Sleeping Car Porters. Faced with the threat of Negro mass action in the capital itself, Roosevelt set up a temporary Fair Employment Practices Commission to hear complaints of discriminatory practices in industry and to seek employer cooperation in utilizing Negro manpower in the war plants. Randolph and his associates then had called off the projected march on Washington.

During the immediate postwar years, the Negro people faced a new wave of racist terrorism in both North and South. Lynchings and murders of Negroes by whites flared up. Efforts to secure housing in white neighborhoods led to white mob actions in many parts of the country. Almost without exception, the police and public authorities openly or covertly aided the racist mobsters. After 20 years of the New Deal and the Fair Deal, the Negro remained a "second-class citizen" in almost every sphere. A report of the National Association for the Advancement of Colored People referred to 34 Negroes killed in 1949 while in "custody of the police"; to 41 cases of Negroes injured by mobs; and scores of attacks on Negroes seeking better housing in cases from Chicago and Chattanooga to Washington, D. C.

The upsurge of the non-white peoples in Asia and Africa in the late Forties and early Fifties inspired a new wave of Negro militancy in the United States, extending even into the deep South. But the labor movement, including the CIO which had made "Operation Dixie" its "Task Number One," lent to this developing Negro struggle only occasional and mild expressions of sympathy. The top union leaders made no response to the appeal of the NAACP Board of Directors in January 1952 for a national stop-work protest in the case of the bomb-murders of Mr. and Mrs. Harry T. Moore. Moore, head of the Florida NAACP, had incurred the special hatred of the racists.

In twenty years of Democratic rule, not a single piece of federal legislation nor a single presidential executive order, with the exception of Roosevelt's ineffectual wartime FEPC, had been put into effect. Racists ruled supreme in Congress. A most revealing event was the defeat in the Senate in 1950 of a permanent FEPC bill, although both parties in their 1948 election platforms had promised such a law. A motion to end a Southern Democratic filibuster against taking a vote on the FEPC bill was defeated. It required 64 votes to invoke cloture and permit the bill to be taken up. The vote was 52 for cloture, 32 against. Only 19 Democrats voted for cloture while 26 voted against it. Twelve senators, half of them professed supporters of an FEPC, had not bothered to show up for the voting. Nine of the twelve absentees were Democrats. Both Republicans and Democrats then dropped the issue. This was to be the pattern until late in the Eisenhower administration when Congress finally enacted a token and toothless civil rights voting bill.

In Washington, D. C., the seat of government, Jim Crow flourished in all federal agencies and in public transport, schools, hospitals, employment, housing. To one degree or another this reflected the position of the Negro people throughout the country. Even in the North they were set apart in black ghettos, crammed into dilapidated firetraps and charged exorbitant rents. Their economic status was indicated by a joint congressional committee's report on low-income families. While 11 per cent of America's families headed by white males had family incomes under $2,000 a year in 1948, some 39 per cent of families headed by non-white males were in the "under $2,000" — the poverty — classification.

By 1951, the above-cited NAACP report noted, "after the fighting broke out in Korea, the civil rights issue rapidly lost ground..." The police themselves often took over the function of the lynch mob. The NAACP reported 131 clear-cut cases of police violence towards Negroes and 33 killed "while in the custody of police." The racists resorted less to lynch mobs — the police did the lynchings by "due process of law."

Negro civil rights were closely tied with the problem of organizing Southern labor. This issue was partly reflected in the factional struggle within the CIO Textile Workers. A bitter fight at the union's five-day convention ending May 2, 1952, led to an eventual split. The forces led by President Emil Rieve defeated the caucus of George Baldanzi, executive vice-president, who sought to replace Rieve. This was primarily a power struggle on organizational issues. It was aggravated by what a convention resolution called "the depression in the industry" resulting in "more than 150,000 unemployed and hundreds of thousands more working on curtailed schedules."

The Baldanzi group blamed the Rieve leadership for failure to organize the two-thirds of the textile industry located in the South. More and more "runaway" textile plants from the North were re-opening in non-union Southern towns. Baldanzi and his supporters were defeated for office at the convention and were purged from international posts. Subsequently Baldanzi led a small split back into the AFL.

"Organize the South" still remains a high-sounding slogan without content in both the Textile Workers Union and the entire merged AFL-CIO.

No small part was played in the 1952 defeat of the Democratic-labor coalition by the raging anti-communist witch hunt. This had been given new impetus in 1949 and early 1950 both by the revolutionary events in China and the new atomic weapons developments leading to an intensification of United States militarism and the cold war. Truman had announced on September 23, 1949 that there was "evidence within recent weeks an atomic explosion has occurred in the U. S. S. R.," ending American monopoly of the atomic bomb. On January 31, 1950, Truman revealed that he had ordered production of a hydrogen bomb—promptly nicknamed the "Hell Bomb." Such a bomb would be 20,000 times as powerful as the "primitive" A-bomb that had liquidated Hiroshima. "This is not a weapon," said the February 4, 1950 *Business Week*. "It is a means of blackmail by suicide pact." It was also a pretext to intensify the attack on civil liberties, to jam through more "anti-subversion" legislation, to step up the search for "spies" and "traitors."

During the 1952 election campaign, the Democrats were scorched by the witch-hunt fires they had helped to light. The union leaders bemoaned the "smears" and "excesses" of McCarthyism. But their complaints and denunciations were almost exclusively in terms of defense of the Democratic regime from the Wisconsin Republican Senator's ridiculous charges that the Democrats were "coddling Communists."

McCarthyism was indeed a sinister movement—but precisely because the Democratic administration had created the atmosphere and preconditions in which such an incipient fascist tendency could thrive. By whipping up cold war hysteria, by constant fear propaganda about the "Russian menace" and by its ruthless "loyalty" purge, the Truman administration had led wide sectors of the American people to believe that this nation was in danger of imminent attack by the Soviet Union, that the government agencies were permeated with disloyal employees, that Russian spies and their American agents were harvesting vast fields of military secrets. McCarthy simply added that such inroads were possible only because of derelictions and even "treason in high places," not excluding the White House. The answer to why the United States fell "to a position of declared weakness," McCarthy told the Senate on June 15, 1951, could not be obtained "without uncovering a conspiracy so immense and an infamy so black as to dwarf any previous such venture in the history of man."

Long before McCarthy had emerged, the CIO leaders had been embroiled in a four-year cold war against a substantial minority of the CIO. McCarthy's first outbursts came just as the CIO bureaucracy itself was expelling in drumhead trials 11 international unions with all their members. The favorable atmosphere for McCarthyism also encouraged the CIO purges.

The CIO leaders were aware that the various "anti-subversive" laws were all devised with legal hooks on which to snag union officials. Such laws are aimed ultimately at the rights of all labor. Most conventions of CIO affiliates during the period just prior to the 1952 election campaign passed resolutions condemning the Smith "Gag" Act of 1940, under which a number of Communist Party leaders were being railroaded to prison, and the McCarran-Kilgore Internal Security Act of 1950. Conventions of the Steelworkers, Amalgamated Clothing Workers, Textile Workers and Packinghouse Workers in May 1952 voted for similar resolutions deploring the numerous federal, state and local laws undermining civil liberties on the pretext of fighting communism. The steel union's resolution stated: "We are confident that the American way of life is not endangered by free speech, even when this free speech is exercised by Communists, Fascists or reactionary enemies to our democracy. But we are fearful that legislative denials of civil liberties do endanger our democracy..."

The Amalgamated's resolution went so far as to assert: "The Smith Act and the McCarran Act have created, in effect, a legal system superseding the Bill of Rights, the Constitution and our traditional body of law." The ACW resolution also demanded the abolition of the House Un-American Activities Committee.

The Packinghouse Workers Union condemned the McCarran Act for providing "detention" camps which are "now being built for political prisoners." The Textile Workers convention, at which the bitter faction fight took place, adopted a resolution denouncing a Supreme Court decision upholding the conviction of 11 Communist Party leaders in the 1949 Smith Act trial. This resolution said: "These Communist Party leaders were convicted under the Smith Act, not for conspiring or attempting to overthrow the government by force and violence, but for conspiring to teach and advocate the propriety of such an overthrow...We insist that the prosecution of those who merely advocate ideas, however repulsive, is injurious to the cause of freedom."

All these resolutions were silent, however, about the need and duty of organized labor to actively defend and aid the victims of the repressive laws they deplored. Even worse, union leaders like Walter Reuther did not hesitate to use the activity of the witch-hunt agencies for factional advantage.

The House Un-American Activities Committee had been reactivated after the Democratic congressional sweep in 1948. Its activities had then become the source of repeated bitter complaints by the CIO leadership. In January 1952 this committee announced with great fanfare that it was going to investigate "un-American" activities in the Detroit area. Its special target was Ford Local 600 which had been pressing for the 30-hour week at 40 hours' pay and an end to the five-year contract. More than a hundred members had been questioned in preliminary hearings.

President Stellato wrote that "the politicians are building up a scare hysteria second to none...Why? So that the unemployed, standing in the soup lines in Hamtramck, talking about the unemployment, the graft, the corruption in America, can have their attention diverted by the Un-American Activities Committee."

The House committee conducted a "red" orgy for a week to the accompaniment of frenzied press scareheads about the "communist menace" in the unions. But Local 600 and its leaders remained unscathed. The local's organized defense and solid front prevented any victimizations by the committee or the Ford Company.

After a few days' recess, the committee renewed its attack on Local 600. The most important witness was saved for a grandstand play on March 11. He was Elesio Romano, a paid UAW international representative. Romano claimed that "the Communists and their supporters were in full control of Local 600's General Council, its executive board and its weekly newspaper, *Ford Facts*. "He cautiously stated, however, that the local's four top officers — Stellato, Rice, Hood and Financial Secretary William G. Grant — "are not, to my knowledge" members of the Communist Party.

Within four hours of the committee's adjournment the next day, Reuther ordered Local 600's officers to appear before the UAW International Executive Board to "show cause why an administrator should not be appointed to take charge of the local union."

Local 600's General Council voted to fight against an administrator. Its officers charged that Reuther and his board had "joined forces" with the House witch-hunt committee "in its efforts to destroy the unity and effectiveness of Local 600."

During the factional struggle with former UAW President Homer Martin from 1937 through 1939, Reuther had defended himself against a "Communist" smear with some eloquent words on redbaiting. The February 16, 1952 *Ford Facts* had republished Reuther's 1937 statement in the hope that it would cool his factional frenzy and persuade him to tone down his own redbaiting against Ford Local 600. Reuther had written:

"So now the bosses are trying a new stunt. They are raising a new scare: the red scare. They pay stools to go whispering around that so-and-so — usually a militant union leader — is a red. They think they will turn other workers against him.

"What the bosses really mean, however, is not that a leader is a red. They mean they don't like him because he is a loyal, dependable union man, a fighter who helps his brothers and sisters and is not afraid of the boss.

"So let's all be careful that we don't play the bosses' game by falling for their red scare...No union man worthy of the name will play the bosses' game. Some may do so through ignorance. But those who peddle the red scare and know what they are doing are dangerous enemies of the union."

Within three days of the ending of the House committee hearings in Detroit, Reuther and his International Executive Board had put Local 600 under an "Administrative Board." His formal reason for this action was alleged failure of the local leaders to enforce the UAW constitutional provision barring a member from holding "elective or appointive" office "if he is a member of or subservient to" the Communist Party.

At the board's hearing, Reuther personally assumed the role of prosecutor. Stellato's request for a postponement and a bill of particulars was denied. At the end of the "hearing," the board rendered a quick decision: to name a six-man administrative board to run Local 600. The next day, this "Administrative Board" removed five elected unit chairmen. The administrators also announced the suspension of all functions of the local, including its executive board, general council and membership meetings. Each of the top four officers of the local had an administrator assigned to his office.

The March 22 *Business Week* hailed Reuther's action and commented that "this week Reuther and the [House Un-American Activities] committee were working together on the UAW like a well-rehearsed vaudeville team."

Reuther's Administrative Board next removed a number of the Ford local's staff officials, including three committeemen of the Motor Building Unit. Now the reason given was not "communism"; it was "reorganization on a more efficient basis" and giving "the workers in the motor plant better representation."

Stellato demanded that the UAW officers comply with the union's constitution and hold an election within 60 days of the start of the administratorship. The administrators refused to hold such an election. In the meantime they took over *Ford Facts*. Stellato's group then issued a caucus paper, *Local 600 Union Facts*.

In the UAW local elections in July and early August, the Local 600 members voted down the Administrative Board's candidates, returned candidates of the anti-Reuther caucus in 15 out of 19 units, and swept the Stellato slate to victory. The UAW Executive Board was forced to remove the Administrative Board and restore the affairs of the country's largest union local to its elected officers.

Reuther's red-scare attack on Ford Local 600 coincided with the approach of new national elections. Truman could not hope to repeat his upset victory of 1948. His broken promises on Taft-Hartley repeal, civil rights, civil liberties and full employment could not be lightly dismissed. The unpopularity of the Korean "police action" and the growing threat of a world-annihilating atomic war had aroused strong resentment toward the Democratic administration. Truman correctly read the political barometer. On March 29, 1952 he formally announced he would not run for re-election.

After 20 years, the Democrats had to come up with an entirely new candidate. Illinois Governor Adlai Stevenson was the choice of many middle-class and well-to-do liberals.

To the union leaders Stevenson was an embarrassment. His program was to the right of Truman's. Edwin A. Lahey of the Washington Bureau of the Knight newspapers, in a pro-Stevenson article, "Labor, Adlai and Ike," published by the August 25, 1952 *New Republic,* reported:

"But the labor leaders know that Stevenson, despite his build-up by a lot of liberals... has been most unsympathetic with some of President Truman's actions, particularly in the steel strike... In a little-noticed speech in Portland, Ore., after Truman's seizure of the steel industry, Stevenson criticized the President for not using the Taft-Hartley Act."

Prior to the Democratic national convention, both AFL and CIO leaders indicated their support for W. Averell Harriman, chairman and principal stockholder in the Union Pacific Railroad as well as a leading investment banker. On May 14, President George M. Harrison of the AFL Brotherhood of Railroad Clerks held a luncheon for him. Harrison publicly proclaimed his support for Harriman, while William Green, George Meany and other AFL bigwigs vigorously applauded Harriman's speech. Washington columnist Robert Allen wrote in the May 13 *New York Post* that Philip Murray and Emil Rieve were among those union leaders "who have personally promised to support actively the candidacy of the wealthy New Yorker." Subsequently, Reuther also indicated his preference for Harriman.

Stevenson was the choice of the Democratic national convention in July. His nomination was dictated by the fact, as the *New York Times* put it, that he "has managed to retain the admiration of the Northern liberals without alienating the Southern conservatives." The true nature of the deal they struck at the convention was underscored by the nomination of Senator John J. Sparkman of Alabama as Stevenson's running mate for vice-president. Congressman Adam Clayton Powell Jr., Harlem Democrat, told the press on August 3 that Sparkman "has voted every single time against every single civil rights issue in the House of Representatives and in the Senate" and had also voted against the minimum wage law and for the Smith-Connally anti-strike law. Later Powell swallowed his scruples and backed Stevenson and Sparkman.

The Republican convention scored a big coup when it nominated General Eisenhower, the man whom the Democrats had tried to persuade to run for them. This professional militarist was backed by many of America's richest financial groups. His army brass background had been given a civilian veneer by a brief career as president of Columbia University. He could thus be represented to the American voters as a man of culture, intellect and "peace."

As soon as possible after the Democratic convention, Philip Murray convened the CIO National Executive Board. It promptly endorsed the Stevenson-Sparkman slate. The CIO membership had had no opportunity to discuss the election issues and endorsements. The top leaders simply handed down their decision. On August 14 the CIO Board stated: "Under a Stevenson administration...we can look forward to an unfaltering continuity of the best traditions and ideals of the New Deal and Fair Deal."

UMW President John L. Lewis followed the CIO and AFL lead. Lewis lined up the UMW convention in October behind a pro-Stevenson resolution that falsely called him a humanitarian pledged to repeal of the Taft-Hartley Act. The July 1 *United Mine Workers Journal* had reported more accurately that "neither Republicans nor Democrats made any serious effort to rewrite the law or repeal it, or to live up to the pledges in their 1948 platforms. The labor sections of these platforms were dishonored and the Taft-Hartley law... still remains on the statute books. Indeed, members of both parties in Congress have been clamoring for its use in the steel situation..." As did Stevenson.

Within a week of Lewis's endorsement of Stevenson, the four employer and four "public" members of Truman's Wage Stabilization Board outvoted the four labor members and cut 40 cents from the $1.90-a-day raise Lewis had negotiated for 350,000 soft coal miners.

The miners were forced to strike on October 20. After a week's stoppage, at Truman's personal request following a 24-minute conference Lewis urged the miners to suspend their strike—at least until after the elections. At a special hearing in Washington Lewis argued for the full $1.90 increase. Knowing the miners would strike again if denied their whole increase, Truman on December 4 reversed the WSB ruling and approved the full raise.

The decisive issue of the election was the Korean War. At the start of the election campaigns, both parties had tacitly agreed to keep the Korean situation out of the public debate. But the electorate insistently demanded of the candidates: "What are you going to do to bring our boys back from Korea?"

Eisenhower's implied promise to end the war quickly was sufficient to arouse the hopes of millions. The greatest outpouring of voters in American history on November 4, 1952 ended the twenty-year reign of the Democratic Party. Eisenhower got 442 electoral votes to Stevenson's 89. The General's victory appeared less massive, however, in the popular vote. He received 33,936,252 popular votes to Stevenson's 27,314,992.

The New Deal–Fair Deal era, whose last social reform measures had been enacted in 1938, ended amidst the bomb bursts and fiery napalm of Korea. After 20 years, American capitalism of the liberal reform epoch had brought neither the "welfare state" nor the prospect of peace. All the material and technical means were at hand to usher in a society of full freedom and abundance for all. But these means had been converted, for private profit, into the arsenals of war. One of Truman's last official acts was his warning to the Soviet Union on January 7, 1953 that the United States had developed a successful hydrogen bomb. Eight months later Moscow in turn announced the explosion of a "hydrogen device."

Militarism and war had become an indispensable way of life for American capitalism. Eisenhower himself attributed the relative stabilization of American capitalism to government war spending. Speaking in Peoria, Illinois, early in October 1952, he said:

"If we look closely at the last twenty... years we find a startling thing. Nineteen twenty-nine was the last year in which we enjoyed prosperity in a time of peace. From then until 1939, when World War II began, our economy showed no growth whatever in real output per person.

"The New Deal never actually solved the unemployment problem. In 1939, after seven years of New Deal doctoring, 9-1/2 million Americans were still out of work... Then came World War II... World War II did what the New Deal was unable to do..."

After the war, Eisenhower added, there was "no economic growth and no rise in living standards...Just as...the economy was beginning to weaken, along came Korea. Defense production again propped up the economy."

Eisenhower didn't know it, but he was indicting the capitalist system. His own program for the "jitters" of the United States in the Fifties was to be the tripling and quadrupling of Truman's peacetime military expenditures of the 1946-50 period. But Eisenhower's facts about the primacy of war spending in the resuscitation of American capitalism are indisputable.

The changes in the Gross National Product (GNP) — the total national production of goods and services — reveal the relationship between the economy and war most clearly. The GNP is the chief measure of economic growth used by the capitalist economists. Here are the GNP figures, expressed in constant 1954 dollars, for the key years from 1929 through 1952:

Gross National Product
(in billions of 1954 dollars)

1929	181.8	1947	282.3
1939	189.3	1948	293.1
1944	317.9	1949	292.7
1945	314.0	1950	318.1
1946	282.5	1952	353.5

In 1939 the GNP just slightly surpassed the 1929 figure, although technology had improved greatly and the population had grown by some 10 million. Most of the decade's slight increase represented greater government spending. Within five years (1944), however, war spending had boosted the GNP by more than $128 billion (in constant dollars). There followed a gradual sag over the next five years, although by 1949 the population had grown another nine million. In the Korean War years, 1950-52, the GNP leaped another $61 billion. Eisenhower was to raise the GNP in the 1953-60 "peace" period— but only by an unprecedented outpouring of military expenditures.

In his 1950 federal budget message six months before the Korean War, Truman himself had summed up the results of Democratic rule. He had asked $42.4 billion for 1951. "As in all recent years," he said, this budget was "dominated by financial requirements" of war, past or in preparation. "Estimated expenditures for these purposes are...about 71 per cent of the total budget." On the other hand, "The budget proposes total funds of 2.1 billion dollars for social welfare, health and security, and 434 million dollars for education and general research, about one-sixteenth of total federal expenditures." About 6-1/4 per cent for welfare; 71 per cent for war.

By the end of Truman's rule, price inflation and taxes were eating ever more deeply into living standards. Food prices in June 1952 were 133.7 per cent higher than in 1939 and 37 per cent steeper than at the start of the Korean War. Taxes, which had soared to 28 per cent of national income in World War II, rose to a new high of 32 per cent in 1952.

A worker had to earn between $2,250 and $2,500 a year, before taxes, to have a buying power equivalent to $1,000 in 1939. The official data shows that exactly 40% of the American population in 1949 got less than $2,289 per year. The share of the national income obtained by this lowest 40% had drastically declined over the 40 years from 1910 to 1950. The following figures show the percentage of national income received by the poorest 40% of the people:

1910	19.8%	1929	15.5%	1947	14.0%
1918	19.4	1934	17.4	1948	15.0
1921	15.7	1937	14.0	1950	12.0

All the great wage struggles, particularly from 1933 to 1953, plus the social reforms wrested from the "New Deal," did not suffice to halt the historical trend toward an ever widening gap between the proportional rewards for productive labor and for parasitic capital.

What of the much vaunted social measures of the "New Deal"? After five continuous presidential terms under the Democrats, what did these benefits amount to?

The Wages and Hours Act, passed in 1938 after the massive upsurge of the CIO, established an original minimum of 25 cents an hour. It covered workers in industries engaged in interstate commerce, but excluded large categories including farm labor and retail store employees. The 25-cent minimum was just half the hourly relief wage of 50 cents paid in 1935 to Northern unskilled laborers on WPA. The law provided for a 40-cent minimum in 1944. Few workers covered by the minimum wage law benefited by it. Unionized workers had raised their own minimums far above the government floor. By 1944 almost all workers coming under the Act were receiving more than the starvation legal minimum wage of $16 for a 40-hour week. The 40-cent minimum was maintained, despite inflation, until 1950. Then a 75-cent minimum wage adopted in 1949 went into effect. The new minimum merely restored the approximate purchasing power of the 40-cent rate in 1939. About 200,000 workers were estimated to have benefited by the new minimum wage. A $1 minimum — a hunger wage at current prices and taxes — was adopted in 1955, during Eisenhower's first term.

By the time Truman departed from the White House, the social security fund begun in 1935 had collected by direct wage deductions and taxes on payrolls a total of slightly under $26 billion. By the end of June 1953—some 18 years later—the government had returned to elderly retired workers and their dependents a little less than $9-1/2 billion. These payments were in no sense a government handout. They were deferred wage payments withheld from the workers as a whole by social security taxes. In 1952 this richest country in the world ranked only twentieth in the percentage of national income spent on social security. On a per capita basis, America ranked only sixth. Even after improvements in social security payments were voted in August 1950, the 2,977,476 recipients of federal old age retirement pensions in the fiscal year ending June 30, 1953, received average benefits of $50.42 — per month.

The "states' rights" unemployment insurance system set up in 1935 is a hodgepodge of 51 different state and territorial systems with varying rates and durations of payments. In the fiscal year 1952-53, the average payment received by 3,980,000 eligible unemployed applicants was $23.32 a week for an average of 10.2 weeks. A third of all wage earners were not even covered by the unemployment compensation laws. Unemployment insurance still is a form of subsistence relief for limited periods for workers laid off through no fault of their own.

The social security system, which went into effect in 1938, appears as a considerable advance. But viewed in terms of the enormous productivity of American labor and vast tax outlays by the workers, the benefits are piddling. As a means of stabilizing the economy or solving the ever pressing tendency toward mass unemployment, these measures serve merely as a slightly soothing ointment for some of the worst ulcers of capitalist society. Over the years, social security taxes have removed a greater sum from mass purchasing power than the total benefits paid out have restored to it.

The most lasting legacy of those two decades has been permanent militarism and a public debt swollen from $30.6 billion in 1930 to $61.3 billion in 1940 and then to $248.7 billion by the time Truman was retired.

The end of the Roosevelt-Truman era appeared to the pro–Democratic union leaders as a staggering setback to their program for effectuating class peace through the intercession of a "pro–labor" capitalist government. The sudden deaths of Philip Murray on November 9, 1952, and William Green on November 21, followed closely on what to them was a political defeat. Under Murray's stewardship, the CIO he had inherited from John L. Lewis had declined to less than four million actual dues-paying members from a peak of more than six million. His yearning pleas to the steel barons to "be gentlemen" and maintain class harmony by generous, gracious, across-the-table accord, had been rudely rejected. He had been dragged, vainly offering compromises, into the three largest industrial strikes the country had ever experienced up to that time—the 1946, 1949, and 1952 national steel strikes.

Murray's "great and good friends" in the White House had repaid his servile devotion with small coin or none at all. He may have died still believing that in America "we're all workers here." But there was nothing in the steelworkers' experience, and particularly in 1952, to give weight to this gossamer theory.

PART VIII

AFTER THE
NEW DEAL — FAIR DEAL
ERA

1953-1955

36

New Moves
toward AFL-CIO Merger

The dominant labor development of the three years following the Democratic defeat was the moves toward reunification of the CIO and AFL. One school of thought attributes this stronger unity trend largely to personal factors, particularly that of the passing from the scene of Murray and Green. Some commentators hold that the chief obstacle to unity had been the "ingrained suspicion and distrust" between Murray and Green. This was not, however, the most serious factor in the unity developments. Previous unity moves had collapsed because the top circles of both organizations had felt no overriding, self-preserving necessity to fuse into one organization. Now the electoral defeat of the Democratic-labor coalition provided the irresistible motive.

Most of the CIO and AFL leaders believed that their union positions and control rested on the foundation of their political alliance with the Democratic machine. The ruling bureaucracies in the rival unions had repeatedly sidetracked or derailed labor party moves and thereby salvaged the Democratic Party. They had received a certain quid pro quo for their services. The Democratic administrations had thrown scraps of concessions to the labor officials with which to impress the workers. The top union officials had been permitted to confer with the President and a few had even been treated to free lunches at the White House. They were called "Bill" or "Phil" or "Walter" by high government dignitaries who appeared as guest speakers at union conventions; they were photographed in the company of prominent candidates for high office; they were invited to express their views before congressional hearings and to expound their class-collaboration philosophy on TV and radio.

In short, they were provided the opportunity to impress the union members with their political contacts, their standing with powerful governmental figures, their prestige in the highest ruling circles. They were often hailed in governmental chambers and in the daily press as "labor statesmen," especially when they displayed a conciliatory attitude toward the employers and a readiness to give away the workers' demands. To all this was added a number of appointments with commensurate salaries to non-policy making posts in government bureaus and agencies. A flock of union agents had been put on the State Department expense accounts for travel to foreign lands to line up the labor movements of other countries in support of Washington's cold war policies.

The friendly smile and condescending pat on the back by presidents, cabinet members and federal legislators was no small asset to the union bureaucrats in selling themselves to many workers. That is what the union leaders feared to lose with the defeat of the Democrats in 1952.

Whatever wistful hopes they may have cherished about an "understanding" with the Republicans were quickly frustrated. Political events more and more forced the thoughts of the great majority of CIO and AFL leaders toward serious merger efforts. Such a merger, they believed, would consolidate the union movement as a more powerful political influence and thereby strengthen the political prestige of the union officialdom.

William Green's death created no problem of leadership for the AFL. Secretary-Treasurer George Meany had already assumed many of the functions of the ailing Green. Meany had come up from the apparatus of the AFL Plumbers Union and risen by orderly progression through successively higher layers of the AFL hierarchy. For many years he had been president of the New York State Federation of Labor and had then been promoted to the second-highest post in the AFL. After Green's death the Executive Council quickly named Meany president of the AFL. In his general union outlook, Meany was regarded as a solid conservative, class-collaborationist to the bone and completely devoted to the interests of the bureaucracy. But he also represented the more politically aggressive and strongly pro-Democratic sector of the AFL leadership. This leadership in 1948 had pushed through the establishment of the first AFL political organization — Labor's League for Political Education. In 1952 the AFL convention had formally endorsed a presidential candidate for the first time. Meany had been a consistent, fervent Democrat and New Dealer — one of the founders, in fact, of New York State's American Labor Party in 1936.

In contrast, Murray's death had confronted the CIO with a potential crisis of leadership. There had been a longstanding but subdued conflict within the top stratum of CIO leaders. There was no real difference in principles or program between the two cliques. But there was a certain difference of background and association. The chief representatives of the two factions were David J. McDonald, who succeeded Murray in the Steelworkers presidency, and Walter Reuther, president of the CIO's largest union.

The top leaders of the steel union had come originally from the old officialdom of the United Mine Workers. They had been grafted onto the steelworkers' organization. They were steeped in the methods of the Lewis machine in the miners' union. Murray's closest associates in both the Steelworkers and the CIO apparatus had been figures like Allan S. Haywood, the CIO's executive vice-president and national director of organization, and McDonald, Murray's own hand-picked secretary-treasurer of the steel union. Haywood, who had served the Lewis machine in the Illinois mine region, had been assigned by Lewis to aid Murray in the early days of the Steel Workers Organizing Committee drive in 1937. Many of Murray's organizational moves in his cold war with the Stalinists from 1946 to 1950 had been carried through by Haywood.

McDonald, who succeeded Murray as head of the second largest union in America, is one of the most incongruous figures ever to appear in the labor movement. All sorts of elements from professional gangsters to career lawyers and preachers have wangled or strong-armed their way from the outside into leadership of American labor unions. McDonald's entry was wholly accidental.

He was an office clerk with dreams of a career in the theater or motion pictures. His introduction to the labor movement came when he secured a job as a stenographer for Philip Murray, then a UMW vice-president. Just prior to the formation of the Committee for Industrial Organization and the subsequent setting up of SWOC, McDonald had taken a course in motion picture technique and had seriously contemplated a movie career. His theatrical mannerisms and poses, his speech, studied dress and grooming still reveal his earlier ambition. When Murray died, McDonald had the apparatus of the steelworkers union in his hands and by that fact alone was able to take over its presidency.

McDonald was regarded as a lightweight by most of the CIO top leaders. While he had been named acting president of the Steelworkers by its Executive Board, he had little status in the wider circles of the CIO. It was not even certain that he would retain the presidency of his union at its convention in March 1953, and if he did, whether he could maintain his position very long. As it turned out, he was elected president by the convention and has been able to keep his grip on that union's leadership. But he could not hope to step into Murray's shoes as head of the CIO. Instead, he pressed the candidacy of Allan S. Haywood.

The first CIO convention without Murray was convened on December 1, 1952. Aside from adopting routine resolutions that contained no fresh interpretation of events or new programmatic ideas, the 700 convention delegates were embroiled in a power struggle for Murray's mantle. For several years Reuther had been regarded as the likely successor to Murray. He was certainly the most politically aggressive leader in the UAW. In the internal struggles of the UAW he had outmaneuvered all other factions, tendencies and leaders, and had succeeded in fixing one-man rule on the dynamic auto union. Fearing that they faced parlous times ahead, the great majority of the CIO leaders preferred to entrust their organizational fortunes to the dextrous and wily Reuther. He differed in no basic principle from McDonald and Haywood, but he was expected to make a more effective public image of CIO leadership and a more efficient administrator. Reuther won the CIO presidency easily.

The convention made no effort to seriously analyze labor's political experiences or to account for the Republican break-through despite the touted advances under the 20-year "New Deal—Fair Deal" rule. The 75,000-word report of the late Philip Murray threw only a few candle gleams on this shadowed subject. The report complained that no new social legislation had been enacted since the end of the war and, indeed, not since 1938.

In their pre-election propaganda the union leaders had depicted a Republican victory as a ghastly disaster which would plunge the country into a depression and initiate a government pogrom against organized labor. Immediately after the election, however, a number of union leaders, particularly in the AFL, made overtures of peace and cooperation toward the new Republican administration. Some sought a political *modus vivendi* if not an outright alliance of the type they had enjoyed under the Democratic administrations. There was no lack of readiness within both the CIO and AFL leaderships to "play ball" with the new regime.

Advance, newspaper of the Amalgamated Clothing Workers, on November 15, 1952 expressed the view that it was unnecessary to discuss what had brought about the Democratic defeat—"post-mortems have no place in our affairs." The Amalgamated paper went on: "So long as the forthcoming Republican Administration does not tamper with the gains at home and the program abroad, it will have our support." Speaking for the AFL leaders, the November 7 *AFL*

News-Reporter actually summoned labor to "unite now behind Gen. Eisenhower for survival against Communism."

Both the union leaders and the Democratic Party leaders dreaded other possible political consequences of the elections far more than they did Republican rule in Washington. They feared, above all, a movement of labor away from the apparently ineffectual Democratic Party and toward active resistance to the Republican regime through the formation of an independent, union-based labor party. There was considerable revival of labor party sentiment in the union ranks with the Republican advance to power. Ford Local 600 and other UAW locals, for instance, adopted strong labor party resolutions and submitted them to the pending CIO convention.

The union leaders were relieved by President-elect Eisenhower's announcement early in December 1952 that he intended to appoint AFL Plumbers President Martin Durkin as Secretary of Labor. The December 5 *AFL Newsletter* called the Durkin appointment a "master stroke" and evidence that "Eisenhower has recognized the fact that his administration must represent all the people; not merely those who supported him in the election campaign." The CIO leaders sent Durkin "warm" congratulations and a pledge of "wholehearted support."

Durkin's selection for the purely decorative post of Secretary of Labor was intended as window dressing for Eisenhower's "Cadillac Cabinet." It indicated how cheaply Eisenhower thought the labor leaders could be bought—with one powerless cabinet post.

Durkin plugged along with Eisenhower, assuring the AFL Executive Council that the President was preparing a series of amendments to the Taft-Hartley Act that would be "favorable to labor." The former plumbers union president even reproved his successor, Peter J. Schoemann, for stating in the union's journal that the administration was trying "to steal from the American people what is rightfully theirs" through bills to relinquish federal claims to offshore oil reserves, to raise interest rates, and to turn over government-owned atomic installations to private profit interests.

On September 11, 1953, after only eight months in office, Durkin resigned. Eisenhower had not been willing to press for the few token alterations in the Taft-Hartley Act (which even Taft was willing to grant) that would in no wise have altered the basic anti-labor character or effect of that law.

Even before the Durkin episode had concluded, the CIO and AFL leaders took their first big preliminary step toward reunification. On June 2, 1953 their conferees adopted a two-year no-raiding agreement effective January 1, 1954, whereby each organization agreed to refrain from seeking members where the other already held a collective bargaining contract. This pact, later approved by the national conventions of both bodies, also provided for machinery to discuss and ameliorate jurisdictional disputes between CIO and AFL unions.

This step was dictated by the continued fierce invasion of CIO unions by AFL affiliates, including such large and powerful unions as the Teamsters, International Brotherhood of Electrical Workers, and the Carpenters. Although the political climate was favorable to unity efforts, there remained numerous organizational obstacles to a merger. These were based primarily on the narrow interests of the bureaucracies controlling various affiliated unions. The AFL had a large group still determined to war on the CIO and to grow at the expense of the established industrial unions. At the same time the CIO was developing centrifugal tendencies. Its internal ties were being loosened. Several CIO affiliates were engaging independently in merger talks with AFL unions. McDonald of the Steelworkers was rumored to be meeting with John L. Lewis and discussing the possibility of a new union realignment in which they would play the leading roles.

By 1953, the issue of industrial versus craft unionism was settled in life. The AFL bowed to the inevitable and accepted industrial and semi-industrial forms of organization among several of its own key affiliates. There was no longer a deep principled difference over this issue between the two organizations. Certainly it was not an insuperable barrier to unification. For both Reuther and Meany, the big issue was organizational unity in order to strengthen their political influence and their power to exert pressure on capitalist political parties and government agencies. They also wished to be in a stronger position to resist anticipated new attacks on their union bases by the Republican regime.

Especially stubborn resistance to the no-raiding pact came from the AFL Teamsters and Carpenters. William "Big Bill" Hutcheson, the president emeritus of the 750,000-member United Brotherhood of Carpenters and Joiners, second largest AFL affiliate, had not altered his attitude in the slightest since the memorable session of the October 1935 AFL convention when Lewis had felled him with one punch for calling the miners' leader a name too rude to be incorporated in the official minutes. As one of the few avowed Republicans in the AFL leadership, Hutcheson felt no political impulsion toward unity. After the CIO-AFL no-raiding agreement was drawn up, Hutcheson on August 12 pulled the Carpenters out. But on September 8 he restored the union to the AFL. The following October

20 "Big Bill" died, leaving his son and heir Maurice not only his "business," the carpenters union, but a personal estate valued, according to an October 26 Associated Press report, at "several hundred thousand dollars."

Another bitter opponent of the no-raiding agreement was AFL Teamsters President Daniel J. Tobin. A venerable pillar of the AFL Executive Council and long a member of the Democratic National Committee, Tobin had dragged his feet in the 1952 presidential elections. In the August 1952 issue of *International Teamster* he had expressed his dissatisfaction with the treatment the teamsters union was getting from the government by confessing: "I have lost confidence in the leaders of both parties, so far as carrying out the pledges to labor contained in their platform." In October 1953, the 85-year-old Tobin turned over his union presidency to David Beck, whose "cannibal unionism" and strikebreaking on the West Coast had made his name anathema to decent unionists. Tobin's declining years — he died in 1955 — were cushioned by a $50,000 annual salary as president emeritus of the Teamsters. Tobin's heir, Beck, commenting on his own newly increased salary of $50,000 per annum as head of the union, confided to the press: "I don't need the money. I've been very successful in business and investments."

Unmoved by the political considerations motivating Meany and Reuther, Beck announced he would not sign the no-raiding pact for the Teamsters. As a preliminary to his rejection of the peace pact, Beck had issued a declaration of jurisdictional war against not only the CIO but a dozen AFL unions as well. In a general letter to the membership, published in the October 1953 *International Teamster,* Beck declared: "We desire the affiliation of workers belonging to us held in membership by various international unions. We respectfully ask them to recognize our jurisdiction and transfer them to us. We do not want misunderstandings and conflict...Neither do we intend to sit idly by and watch...pirating of our members." This "pirating" of "our" members was a defensive formulation to mask aggression.

In spite of opposition by Beck, Maurice Hutcheson and several other AFL officials, the AFL and CIO Peace committees, which had not met since drafting the no-raiding pact in June, resumed their joint discussions on December 16.

The CIO convention, November 15-20, had complained of Beck's stand in its resolution approving the no-raiding agreement. But it was not direct raiding that the Reuther leadership feared most. From the moment the pact was drafted, there appeared a tendency for individual CIO affiliates to seek their own accords directly with rival

AFL Unions. At least three CIO international unions were reported to be discussing merger with AFL unions. The 65,000-member CIO International Brewery Workers, with 329 locals, was said to be conferring with the huge AFL Teamsters which had been attempting to rip the beer drivers from the industrial organization of the brewery workers. Similarly, executive officers of the CIO's 78,500-member Utility Workers were conferring with their opposite numbers in the AFL International Brotherhood of Electrical Workers. Ralph Helstein, head of the CIO United Packinghouse Workers, was holding fusion talks with Patrick Gorman, secretary-treasurer of the AFL Amalgamated Meat Cutters and Butcher Workmen. These negotiations — none of which came to fruition — were motivated on the part of the CIO participants by fears that the Reuther leadership might come to general merger terms less advantageous than those that might be secured by direct dealings of the affiliates themselves.

Secession of ten locals of the CIO Brewery Workers drivers to Beck's Teamsters in July had brought angry protests from Reuther that such actions might damage merger negotiations between the CIO and AFL. These loosening and decentralizing tendencies threatened to gravely impair the CIO's negotiating position in any merger move.

Reuther's conduct as head of the CIO helped to deepen its internal crisis. Thus, he threatened to place a receivership over the Packinghouse Workers whose leaders Reuther had falsely accused of holding communist views. It had become almost a reflex for Reuther to raise the communist bogey whenever anyone disagreed with him or acted without his sanction.

Reuther's redbaiting method of attack could not be effectively used against McDonald. The latter had been repeatedly linked with Lewis in allegedly secret moves to set up some sort of "third force" in the American union movement. As early as the United Automobile Workers convention in March 1953 where he was a guest speaker, McDonald felt obliged to dispel the rumors of his separatist aims. This was intended in large measure to scotch speculation about an impending split in the CIO, as well as to prepare the way for introducing a resolution on Reuther's newest proposal, the Guaranteed Annual Wage, which had been the brain child of the late Philip Murray. In June, after the no-raiding pact had been drafted, McDonald was repeatedly reported to be in touch with Lewis. When he could no longer continue to deny the fact, McDonald claimed that a much publicized visit with Lewis had involved only a friendly personal chat about "old times" in the miners union. However, this fiction could not be maintained when McDonald, Lewis and David Beck in May 1954, after having met privately in Washington, made a joint public announcement that they had reached an accord to act together on unemployment, a major problem plaguing the American workers once more.

No one knowledgeable in the ways of the American labor bureaucracy put much stock in their talk about joint action in behalf of the unemployed. This skeptical view was to become more fixed on June 9, 1954, when leaders of 94 unions, 65 in the AFL and 29 in the CIO, affixed their signatures to a new no-raiding agreement extending to December 31, 1955. The heads of the Steelworkers, Shipyard Workers, American Newspaper Guild, and Amalgamated Lithographers, all of the CIO, and the AFL Teamsters refused to sign. However, the strong pro-CIO sentiment of the rank-and-file steelworkers, as reflected at their 1954 convention, ultimately proved a strong deterrent to any aspiration McDonald might have had to take an independent course in company with Lewis and Beck. At the convention he declared himself for an AFL-CIO merger in advance of any public statement of policy by the CIO itself. His motivation in part may have been the belief that in such a merger he, rather than Reuther, would best thrive in the company of the old AFL leadership.

One of the most serious obstacles to a merger was the gangsterism and racketeering in a few prominent AFL affiliates. It was sometimes difficult to differentiate between the common run of union officials who fattened off the union treasuries, and the professional criminals who sought to use the unions as a means to extort personal payoffs from the employers or as a cover for other criminal operations. The latter type of racketeer was a problem which the CIO industrial unions had scarcely confronted, for they dealt in the main with the larger corporations and concentrated groups of workers. Racketeering was an evil that could thrive more easily in those trades and industries that were relatively small-scale and local and with many competing units. In such cases, many employers themselves gladly bought the favors of corrupt and gangster-ridden union leaderships to gain their aid in enforcing some competitive advantage and in keeping down the workers' demands. The existence of these conditions in some AFL bodies made CIO leaders and members alike wary of formal merger with their old parent organization.

Meany had an opportunity late in 1952 and in 1953 to make a move that would reassure the CIO leaders on the score of gangsterism. It aimed at the same time to strengthen the central AFL leadership in its power to deal with internal elements who lowered the status and prestige of the AFL bureaucracy as a whole and interfered with the process of unification in which both the Meany and Reuther groups saw advantages. The occasion was the New York State Crime Commission's hearings in December 1952 into criminal activities on the New York City waterfront. Testimony at the hearings confirmed the long-known fact of the ties between the waterfront employers, racketeers associated with Murder Inc., and the leadership of the AFL International Longshoremen's Association headed by Joseph "King" Ryan, who had had himself elected ILA president for a "lifetime" term.

Why the employers went along willingly with gangster rule on the docks and payoffs to the Ryan machine was explained by Harry Ring in *The Militant* of December 15, 1952:

"The unholy alliance between the shipowners, stevedore companies and union officials is revealed by their unanimous defense of the vicious 'shape-up' system by which the dockworkers are hired daily. The shape-up, where the men are arbitrarily selected for each day's work by the hiring boss, is the weapon (along with brute force) by which such things as [gangsterism] maintain their vise-like grip on the union. In addition to being a source of rampant favoritism for supporters of the machine, it is a highly lucrative means of shaking down men in need of a day's work."

The Ryan machine and its gangster allies finally elicited the disfavor of the waterfront employers because the dockworkers between 1945 and 1952 had repeatedly revolted. In 1951 they had refused to accept Ryan's sellout agreement and had forced better wages and conditions by a powerful wildcat strike. From the employers' point of view, Ryan was failing to "deliver the goods." Moreover, the gangster elements were beginning to "get out of hand" and were making independent exactions that the employers considered prohibitive for such "protection." The "anti-Communist" fund, to which the stevedoring companies made liberal "contributions," was one of the weapons the employers used to get rid of Ryan.

Ryan somehow got his personal funds mixed with the "anti-Communist" fund. He spent part of the latter to acquire such weapons of anti-red struggle as $35 silk shirts, a Cadillac, and insurance premiums. In five years he had lightened the fund by $17,000 and withdrawn $31,650.81 from the assets of the union's *I.L.A. Journal.*

Having outlived his usefulness to the waterfront employers, city officials, big-time racketeers and the Tammany Hall politicians, Ryan was cast to the wolves in response to the clamor for a "clean-up" on the waterfront. He was indicted on grand larceny charges in connection with his depredations on the union funds.

The State Crime Commission's disclosures and the public scandal put pressure on the AFL leaders to clear themselves of any implication in the unsavory affairs of the Ryan machine.

Meany was encouraged to intervene in the ILA situation by the political circumstances of 1953, the need to provide the atmosphere for reunification of the CIO and AFL, the discreditment of Ryan, and the attack on him by the government agencies. He wanted to demonstrate that the AFL leadership could and would deal firmly with any elements in its own ranks who might threaten the hegemony of the CIO leaders in their own unions in any future alliance or merger.

The AFL Executive Council in May 1953, under Meany's inspiration, ordered the ILA leaders to abolish the shape-up; oust all union officials who had taken gifts or bribes from the employers or had appointed ex-convicts to union posts; oust all union representatives with criminal records; and establish democratic practices in the ILA so that "true and capable" leaders could be elected. In short, the AFL chiefs ordered the ILA leaders to abolish themselves. On August 11, 1953, the AFL Executive Council voted to propose to the AFL convention in September that it suspend the ILA for failure to carry out the four measures demanded three months before.

Although the investigation had proved that the employers had been the chief beneficiaries of the racketeer-domination of the ILA, the only government action taken was directed at the dock workers. At the time of the AFL's suspension move, a bill had been signed by Eisenhower to sanction a New York–New Jersey port commission with dictatorial powers to regulate longshore hiring. The bill provided for state-controlled hiring halls and permanent registration of all dock workers. This was to become the basis for a blacklist of union militants and any so-called communists.

The AFL convention on September 22 expelled the entire ILA. The Executive Council then voted to set up a new AFL longshoremen's union. It was chartered on September 25 and placed under the supervision of five appointed trustees. In the meantime Ryan had been indicted for "misusing" union funds. The ILA leadership called a special convention at which Ryan, on November 18, resigned his $20,000-a-year ILA presidency. However, his henchmen made sure to absolve him of the thievery charges and cushioned his fall by voting him an annual pension of $10,000. The convention named Captain William V. Bradley, head of the union's tugboat division, as Ryan's successor. A committee was set up to seek readmission into the AFL or merger with the CIO. Both bodies refused the ILA's application.

Confronted with the AFL's rival union, the ILA leaders were compelled on September 30 to call out 50,000 longshoremen at the expiration of their contracts. Ryan had originally asked 50 cents

more in hourly rates and ten cents for a welfare fund. Within 24
hours of the ILA's expulsion from the AFL and the establishment of
a rival setup, the demands were scaled down to an additional ten
cents in hourly wage rates and three cents for welfare. But the employers turned down every ILA compromise offer.

Appointed to head the AFL drive against the now-independent ILA
were Paul Hall, leader of the AFL Seafarers International Union,
and AFL Teamsters President Dave Beck. Hall and Beck openly
collaborated with federal, state, and local government officials, including New York's Republican Governor Thomas Dewey, who were
engaged in attempts to break the longshoremen's strike. A Taft-
Hartley injunction, issued at Eisenhower's request, was honored by
Ryan who ordered the strike ended on October 7.

The National Labor Relations Board voided the results of a representation election, held December 23, 1953, which the ILA won
against the Hall-Beck machine. On March 5, 1954, some 24,000 New
York area ILA members struck in protest against the hiring of AFL
members on some docks. This action was fought for the right of the
dock workers to a union of their own choice, free from coercion and
intimidation by government agencies in collusion with the AFL leaders, including Hall and Beck. This major dock strike followed the
action of the NLRB in obtaining a federal court injunction, under
the secondary boycott provisions of the Taft-Hartley Act, ordering
the ILA and eight of its locals to end work stoppages allegedly interfering with truck freight on the piers. Following a 29-day strike,
the longest in the port's history, the dock workers returned to work
after the NLRB threatened to rule the independent ILA off the ballot
in a new collective bargaining election scheduled for May 26.

On May 11 the Federal District Court found the union guilty of
"contempt" and fined the ILA $50,000. On May 25, the ILA was or-
dered into federal receivership which ended July 7 when the union
posted a $50,000 bond pending a ruling on its appeal. The next day
the independent ILA again won an NLRB poll over the ILA-AFL. The
NLRB finally certified the original ILA on August 27, 1954. The AFL
union's name was changed in July to the International Brotherhood
of Longshoremen. But discredited in advance by the reputations of
those assigned to organize it, the AFL union gradually faded from
the picture.

The ILA developments in 1952 and thereafter revealed the true
nature of the AFL leadership as a whole. These events pointed the
way to the policies that were to be pursued in connection with the
ousting of the Teamsters and other unions under government pressure in the late Fifties. Like the Murray-Reuther-Carey leadership

which ruthlessly split the CIO in response to the Truman administration's cold war requirements, the Meany leadership showed in the ILA struggle its willingness to sacrifice labor unity and organizational strength at the behest of the government. In all the later AFL-CIO actions designed to end racketeering in the unions, the AFL and CIO leaderships together were to show that they could split organized labor but they could or would not provide democratic solutions to the evils they so belatedly but loudly deplored.

37

"30 for 40" and "GAW"

Another impelling factor in the CIO and AFL unification moves was the worsening economic situation in 1953 and 1954. With the slowing and halting of the Korean War, new economic pressures were exerted on labor and new discontents arose in the union ranks. Unemployment and reduced work weeks with no compensating wage increases began to restore the pattern of the economy just before the outbreak of the Korean War.

Employment declined by nearly 1,500,000 between January and December 1953. By March 1954, unemployment reached a post-Korean War peak of 4,052,000. Between January 1953 and May 1955, except for one month the official number of jobless never fell below three million.

The death on March 5, 1953 of Premier Joseph V. Stalin, dictator of the Soviet Union, brought a renewed and vigorous bid by his political heirs for a truce in Korea. This had combined with popular pressure on the new President to make good his election promise to end the Korean War. The resultant "peace scare" in American financial circles was registered upon the ticker tapes of the stock exchanges of world capitalism. Michael L. Hoffman, chief European economic correspondent for the *New York Times*, described the shock waves that spread over the capitalist sector of the globe:

"Evidence pours in from nearly every European capital, from Tokyo, Washington and Southeast Asia, that the economic framework of the non-Communist world has an alarming tendency to melt in any atmosphere less frigid than the 'cold war.' In the face of this evidence, economists can only repeat earlier warnings that real relaxation of international tensions would find the West in a serious and perhaps fatal economic condition."

Eisenhower himself went right to the material heart of the matter when he warned American capitalists against any relaxation of their military posture, whatever the outcome of the Korean truce talks. Addressing the Junior Chamber of Commerce in Minneapolis on June 10, 1953, he said:

"Again and again we must remind ourselves that this is a matter not only of political principle but of economic necessity. It involves our need for markets for our agricultural and industrial products, our need to receive in turn from the rest of the world such essentials as manganese and cobalt, tin and tungsten, without which our economy cannot function."

The tactical shifts which called for a cessation of war in Korea caused economic tremors that were among the principal matters of concern at the important United Automobile Workers convention held in March 1953. It was at this convention that Reuther laid out the main lines of his policy for the whole period of "peace" that was to follow the Korean War.

The approach of the convention, scheduled to begin March 22 in Atlantic City, inspired numerous local resolutions calling for a ban on the notorious five-year contracts Reuther had put over in 1950. The swift inflation of the Korean War period meant that even with the escalator clause the UAW members could not keep pace with rising living costs. Moreover, problems of layoffs and speed-up could not be met by effective organizational action for another two years and more because of contract restrictions in force until June 1955. Anticipating moves at the pending UAW convention to ban long-term contracts in the future and to condemn the existing five-year pacts, Reuther himself sought to reopen negotiations with General Motors on wage factors despite the five-year clause.

The UAW demanded a revision of the escalator clause and other contractual provisions because long-term agreements must be regarded as "living documents" that "must not...foreclose the working out of such practical problems that may arise which the parties could not anticipate at the time such agreements were negotiated." Any view of the contract "as a legalistic, static document," said the Reuther statement, "makes long-term agreements unworkable, impractical, impossible and unacceptable."

Reuther did not repudiate the principle of the five-year or long-term contract. One of his chief concerns at the 1953 UAW convention was to prevent the delegates from voting time limits on contracts and from putting on the record a specific condemnation of the existing five-year agreements. He made an impassioned plea not to disavow the five-year pact with General Motors because, he claimed,

that would force the UAW negotiators to expose their hand "by laying all their cards on the table" in the negotiations for changes in
the existing long-term contract.

Fearful of taking any step that might injure the union's current
bargaining position, the delegates adopted without amendment Reuther's resolution on the GM negotiations. Reuther never again dared
to agree to a five-year contract, although the convention's failure
to put a time limit on agreements enabled the UAW leaders to stretch
future contracts from the earlier traditional one-year and two-year
limits to three years.

Following the UAW convention, Reuther and Vice-President Livingston, head of the GM negotiating committee, announced on May
22 that amendments to the old GM contract had been secured. These
would raise GM's wage bill a mere $15 million a year as against its
annual net profits of half a billion dollars — which rose to more than
a billion dollars in 1955. A new formula for figuring cost-of-living
wage increases, adapted to the new BLS index, was obtained. Nineteen cents of the previous escalator clause gains of 24 cents would
be incorporated into the basic wage scale on June 1, 1953. The
skilled workers were also given a special ten-cent hourly raise.
The annual improvement factor was increased from four cents an
hour to five cents. Wildcat strikes affecting an estimated 135,000
GM workers had been principally responsible for nudging GM into
these concessions.

The most significant debate at the UAW convention occurred on
the program to combat unemployment. Reuther's chief emphasis
was on the so-called Guaranteed Annual Wage. This was represented
to the delegates as the panacea for their economic ills — and, indeed, no one could be against a program to assure the workers of a
full year's income equivalent to 52 weeks of his full-time take-home
pay. This proposal was counterposed to the traditional program of
the shorter work week with no reduction in weekly earnings.

Immediately following adoption of the annual wage resolution,
another resolution was presented by Reuther's Resolutions Committee condemning those who advocated a campaign "now" for the 30-
hour week at 40 hours' pay. There was no contradiction between the
two demands, but the Reuther resolution stigmatized the proponents
of "30 for 40" as communists, fellow travelers, opportunists and
demagogues. Ford Local 600 President Stellato, against whom much
of the fire was directed, correctly pointed out that the demand for
the shorter workday and work week was long-established UAW policy
reaffirmed at almost every previous convention.

Reuther's resolution on the shorter work week set forth the burden of his argument against such a program "now." It claimed that "30 for 40" would "reduce America's production by one-fourth." A shorter work week was a good idea, the resolution admitted, and the auto workers should demand it "as soon as and whenever the productive capacity of our national economy make it possible to maintain high and satisfactory living standards with fewer hours of work." Meanwhile, a shorter work week, the resolution alleged, would have the effect of "impairing the national defense effort and undermining the economic and military strength of the free world in the face of totalitarian aggression."

This resolution inspired appalling expressions of reactionary sentiments from a few delegates. One boasted he was now working 55 hours and wouldn't mind working more. Another announced he was working 60 to 70 hours a week, which he didn't think was too much.

A number of delegates took the floor to protest strongly the insinuation that the advocates of the shorter work week were Communist-inspired and unpatriotic. Delegate Lou Ciccone of GM Local 216 in Los Angeles charged that Reuther's resolution "represents a dangerous and false course for our union. It contains within it false propositions which, in effect, challenge the legitimacy of the historic struggle of the American labor movement for the shorter workday and week without reduction in take-home pay."

Ciccone pointed out that the 30-hour week did not mean that a worker would be limited to 30 hours of work. "It means," he said, "that overtime penalty provisions will begin after 30 hours' work and the length of the workday can continue to be a flexible one subject to these overtime provisions." This was the nub of the issue and hit at the real motivation of Reuther's resolution—his unwillingness to fight for a bigger share of corporation profits.

The Reutherites, by distorting and misrepresenting the effect of the 30-hour week, were able to push over their resolution, although not without a sizeable minority opposition vote. This, however, did not settle the issue. In the next seven years, during which the auto workers were to be hard hit by three economic recessions and "automation" was to become a household word, the program of the shorter work week with no loss of take-home pay came to the fore again and again. At the same time, Reuther's guaranteed annual wage was to fade into a program of limited unemployment handouts which in no way met the fundamental problem of mass layoffs and unemployment.

On June 20, less than two months after the convention, Reuther offered a five-point program to "maintain full employment." He did not talk about the lack of labor power "impairing production." He said that two million more jobs had to be created each year to avoid a sag in the economy. An accompanying CIO study reported that "rising man-hour output tends to displace from 1,000,000 to 1,750,-000 working people each year." Meanwhile, the auto workers would have to wait two more years before pressing their guaranteed annual wage demand. Reuther and his fellow officers, however, had made sure they secured their own "GAW" immediately. Their salaries had been substantially raised by the convention.

During the two years following the 1953 UAW convention and while the auto workers impatiently awaited the termination of the five-year contracts, Reuther lost no opportunity to attack the shorter work week and workday program both in his home union and throughout the CIO. He never opposed it in "principle." He promised instead that his own guaranteed annual wage plan would do what the shorter work week was designed to accomplish.

On September 26, 1953, the 72nd convention of the American Federation of Labor adopted a resolution calling for a federal law to reduce the legal 40-hour work week to 35 hours "without loss of 'take-home' pay" in order to combat what the resolution called a "creeping depression." At its next convention a year later the AFL delegates voted to call on Congress to enact a 35-hour week by 1956. They also set as their ultimate goal the 30-hour week without loss of weekly pay—that is, "30 for 40."

Inside the CIO auto union, considered the pace-setter for the entire CIO, sentiment for the shorter work-week program continued to intensify. UAW-GM Sub-Council No. 7, which included GM locals in California, in October 1953 followed up the decisions of its constituent locals by adopting a "30 for 40" resolution. The giant Ford Local 600 in its October 31 *Ford Facts* opened a sustained campaign for the 30-hour week at 40 hours' pay. The California State CIO convention, representing one of the largest state sectors of the CIO, on November 8 adopted a "30 for 40" resolution. UAW Flint Chevrolet Local 659, defender of the key citadel in the historic 1937 GM sit-down strike, likewise adopted this program. Subsequently, the entire Flint CIO Council, with delegates representing the heart of the GM empire, took similar action. Within the next half year the CIO Textile, Packinghouse, Clothing Workers and Woodworkers unions adopted shorter work-week demands. The Pennsylvania CIO in 1954 called for a six-hour day in all contracts. Even CIO Steelworkers President McDonald ventured to warn in May 1954 that "failure to overcome the present crisis in unemployment will lead us to propose the development of a program based on the six-hour day with eight hours' pay."

At the CIO convention in Cleveland, November 16-20, 1953, Reuther did not mention the shorter work week even as a long-term perspective. As was expected, he concentrated almost completely on the guaranteed annual wage. His proposals for action were exceptionally weak. He urged only "exchanging information so that each union may develop its own policies most effectively." Millions of workers who faced layoffs and part-time employment were restrained by long-term contracts from negotiating for a guaranteed annual wage. In fact, at this early stage, the Reuther-McDonald resolution on "GAW" already included a clause emphasizing the need for "flexibility" in adapting the plan to specific industries.

On July 1, 1954, the major steel manufacturers led by U. S. Steel concluded a new two-year contract with the Steelworkers. The contract provided a five-cent raise in hourly pay, plus two cents for the existing 2-1/2-cent welfare fund, if the workers themselves contributed a like amount. The agreement, signed by McDonald at the peak of steel unemployment, said nothing about a guaranteed annual wage.

The CIO never did develop a sustained, coordinated campaign for the "GAW." It became a live issue only in the steel and auto unions. The GM and Ford workers, who had fought the decisive battles in '37 and '41, called for an immediate fight to meet the existing conditions of mass layoffs and part-time work. The February 2, 1954 issue of *The Searchlight,* official paper of the 14,000-member UAW Chevrolet Local 659 in Flint, proclaimed in its headline: "CAR PRODUCTION FLOPS—4 Day Work Week Jolts Chevy Workers." Local 659 President Robert Murphy emphasized the need for "stressing the thirty-hour week with forty hours' pay." To Reuther's argument that this would "impair production," Murphy replied, "We are now faced with a thirty-two hour work week with only thirty-two hours' pay..."

But Reuther had a better plan—the "Guaranteed Annual Wage." It was thoroughly explained in "Preparing a Guaranteed Employment Plan," a brochure "prepared for the delegates to the 6th International UAW-CIO Education Conference, Chicago, April 8-11, 1954."

This official UAW pamphlet emphasized that the "principal objective of the program—the guarantee of steady full-time employment—is fundamental to the whole structure of the plan." And to make the point unambiguously clear, the brochure said again: "The goal must be kept clearly in mind. The UAW's purpose is really to develop a *Guaranteed Employment* plan. We use the phrase 'guaranteed wage' because it is widely used and understood. But it is not a completely accurate description of what our union will propose in collective bargaining. *Our main objective is steady full-time employment, week by week, the year around."* (Emphasis in original.)

The kind of "Guaranteed Annual Wage" the CIO leaders had in mind had been made explicit a month before the CIO convention at a Steelworkers Wage Policy Committee meeting in New York City. An article by this writer in the November 23, 1953 *Militant* discussed the union's plan in answer to a letter from a Cleveland steelworker:

"A guaranteed annual wage which requires the corporation to provide *all* the workers with a *full* income equal to full-time regular take-home pay for an *entire* year would merit a 100% vote..." But McDonald's "GAW" plan "contains several of the major gimmicks that union members should look out for in any proposed guaranteed annual wage clause... First of all it does not cover a large part of the workers. It would cover workers only with a minimum of three years' seniority. In some plants this would exclude a majority of workers..." The article quoted Otis Brubaker, the steel union's research director, who had said the plan would provide an eligible worker "with 60 or 70 per cent of his normal earnings." However, the company would be liable only for the difference between that 60 or 70 per cent and what the worker might receive from state unemployment compensation.

McDonald, at least, did not keep up the pretense so long. On March 16, in his talk before the Pennsylvania CIO convention, he spoke of the "misnamed" guaranteed annual wage and acknowledged that it should properly be called "supplemental unemployment compensation."

Toward the end of 1954, the UAW-CIO called an extraordinary national "economic conference" in Detroit to draft a program for contract demands in the 1955 negotiations with the auto "Big Three" and other concerns in the industry. By this time the entire AFL, most of the CIO affiliates, and the major GM, Ford and Chrysler locals in the UAW itself had adopted resolutions calling for a shorter work week with no cut in weekly take-home pay. Some 1,100 local delegates at the conference on November 12 reaffirmed the guaranteed annual wage as the chief demand for 1955. But they also spelled it out as a guarantee of 52 weeks of full-time work or the equivalent in pay for auto workers with two or more years seniority. Reuther had to defer to the clamor for the "30 for 40" demand by promising that the shorter work week "will take its place at the top of our collective bargaining agenda" after the "annual wage is secured."

Reuther was also forced to retreat on the five-year contracts. The conference voted in favor of a two-year limitation on all future contracts, and one year if they failed to include cost-of-living and productivity-improvement-factor clauses. Although these decisions reflected the opinions of the membership, they did not have the binding power of a formal convention.

The question remains: Why has Reuther been so stubbornly opposed over the years to seriously advancing the program of the shorter work week with no loss of pay? In the March 29, 1954 *Militant* I wrote: "The real reason why Reuther is obstructing the struggle for the shorter work week...has to do with the program of action required to win the demand. *This demand cannot be won without a major fight and it is the fight that Reuther opposes*." (Emphasis in original.)

Reuther did not dare to say this openly, but the clue to his reluctance to fight for the shorter work week is given in the official "Report on Automation" presented to the UAW Economic Conference in November 1954. This stated: "Barring an increase in international tensions requiring greatly increased diversion of economic resources to defense production, the timing of the fight for the shorter work week depends basically on the rate of acceleration of productivity advances..."

It was precisely because of the "rate of acceleration of productivity advances"—the word "automation" was already on everyone's lips—that the problem of mass unemployment was so immediate and pressing.

During that same period, AFL President Meany not only expected a giant increase in military outlay to prop up the sagging economy; he demanded it. At the September 1954 AFL convention, Meany attacked Eisenhower for slightly reducing the war budget. The AFL leader called for a bigger "defense" program. He declared that the $42 billion a year earmarked by Eisenhower for direct war spending was "not enough." Actually, it was more than three times greater than such military spending in any previous full peacetime year, including the Truman recession and cold war year of 1949.

Throughout Eisenhower's administration, union leaders including Reuther and Meany echoed the Democratic Party's propaganda that Eisenhower "puts balancing the budget ahead of defense against Communism." Eisenhower did not have to be told by anyone how to bolster American capitalism through government spending, expanded federal debt, and higher taxes. During his election campaign, he had described how it had been done for twenty years before. The official budget reports show how well he had learned this lesson. Following are the annual figures for total federal spending and for direct military expenditures, labeled "National Security," during the last full peacetime fiscal years under Truman and the first four under Eisenhower.

	Total Federal Expenditures	Direct Military Expenditures	Percentage
1947	$39 033 000 000	$14 392 000 000	37
1948	33 068 000 000	11 675 000 000	35
1949	39 507 000 000	12 902 000 000	33
1950	39 606 000 000	13 009 000 000	33
1954	67 772 000 000	46 904 000 000	69
1955	64 570 000 000	40 626 000 000	63
1956	66 540 000 000	40 641 000 000	61
1957	69 433 000 000	43 270 000 000	62

The Eisenhower administration succeeded in balancing the federal budget in only three fiscal years: 1955, 1956, and 1960. By June 30, 1960, the federal debt jumped from $266.0 billion in fiscal 1953 to $286.3 billion, an increase of $22 billion in seven years. By the spring of 1955 the decline in employment had been halted. Unemployment fell somewhat. The economy experienced a new boom that was to last, however, only until 1957. Under the temporary conditions of boom, the unemployment problem did not have the urgency for many workers that it had in 1954. At the United Auto Workers convention in Cleveland, March 27–April 1, 1955, the question of "30 for 40" slipped further into the background.

The Ford Local 600 leaders, who formed the core of a loose anti-Reuther tendency, did not seriously press the shorter work-week issue and, in fact, offered no serious opposition to Reuther's program.

While the UAW convention did not approve "30 for 40" as an immediate contract demand in the forthcoming negotiations, its attitude was considerably different than in 1953. This time, proponents of an immediate campaign for the shorter work week were not accused of being agents of the Kremlin. Reuther felt obliged to include in his guaranteed annual wage resolution a clause promising "to place the winning of the shorter work week at the top of our union's collective bargaining agenda after the guaranteed wage has been achieved."

Shortly after this convention the May 25 *Labor's Daily* reported that Walter Reuther's brother Victor had told the world congress of the International Confederation of Free Trade Unions in Vienna: "The battle for shorter work weeks will soon be opened on a grand scale by the American labor movement." It has not been opened on any scale to this day.

General Motors negotiations began on April 7, 1955. The company at once demanded another five-year contract. Ford also sought a five-year pact and offered in addition a gold-plated "savings and stock participation" scheme in which the workers were asked to put up two-thirds of the outlay for a combination of Ford shares and government bonds. Both the GM and Ford workers voted to authorize strikes if the companies failed to meet the union's demands.

On June 6, after virtually all Ford plants in the country except River Rouge had been struck, an agreement was announced. It provided for a meager supplement to state unemployment compensation for a period of "up to" six months for laid-off workers with at least one year seniority. No payments at all were allowed for the first week of layoff. For the next four weeks payments would equal "up to" 65 per cent of weekly take-home pay when combined with state unemployment insurance and then would be scaled down to 60 per cent for the final maximum of 22 weeks. The actual payments by Ford might range from $2 to $25 per week per worker, but would average only $9. Ford's contribution for this fund would be only five cents per hour per employed worker. The company would be liable for a fund of not more than $55 million. If the total payments should reduce the trust fund below this sum, the individual layoff payments would be reduced accordingly.

Just two days before the settlement, Reuther had urged arbitration to prevent a strike called for June 6. He charged that the company's proposal provided "inadequate levels of benefits." "Under the Ford proposal," he said, "a worker in Michigan with a wife and two children whose straight-time earnings excluding bonuses are $90 a week would draw from the fund nothing for the first week of layoff, $7.72 for the first four weeks thereafter, and then $3.66 a week."

Nevertheless, two days later Reuther accepted this fraudulent "guaranteed employment plan" with trivial changes, hailing it as the "largest economic package ever offered." Stellato went along, stating that the contract represented "more progress" than any the UAW ever negotiated.

In effect, the plan was the equivalent of a five-cent-an-hour deferred-wage payment to be collected for a limited time in tiny packets after the worker was laid off. In addition, the new contract provided for one to two and a half cents an hour increases in the annual improvement factor, small hourly increases for some of the skilled workers and slight improvements in the escalator, pension, insurance and vacation plans. In actual cash in his paycheck, the Ford worker got only six cents an hour more—minus withholding taxes. That was during 1955, the best year in automotive production history to this very day.

When the terms of the new contract were announced to the River Rouge workers, the only satisfaction they could find in it was indicated by the widely-repeated remark: "Well, three is better than five." But even a three-year pact violated the recommendation of the UAW Economic Conference in November 1954 to limit all future contracts to two years or less.

The guaranteed annual wage was dropped by the Steelworkers leadership during the 1955 negotiations held under the wage-reopening clause of the two-year pact signed in 1954. Steel unemployment was relatively low because the industry was running at close to 100 per cent capacity—hitting 101.6 per cent in the Pittsburgh area the week before the June 30 wage-reopening date. Under the spur of rivalry with Reuther and anxious to strengthen his shaky position in the steel union as well as his standing in the forthcoming AFL-CIO merger, Steelworkers President McDonald concentrated on securing a wage package of 21 cents an hour—one cent more than the Ford settlement.

At midnight, June 30, 600,000 CIO steelworkers went on strike without waiting for formal notice from the union's top leadership. About 90 per cent of the industry was closed down. By 10:30 the next morning, U. S. Steel hastened to sign a wage agreement granting an average hourly wage increase of 15 cents, ranging from 11-1/2 cents for the lowest wage categories to 27 cents for some of the skilled classifications. McDonald's boosters were able to claim that the increases meant "double the money in the pay envelope" over that which the auto agreement had secured. McDonald promised the steelworkers that the union would go after "an honest-to-God" guaranteed annual wage in 1956.

The 1955 steel agreement was indeed superior to the auto settlement in terms of a genuine wage boost. But it was still low enough for the corporations to avoid a showdown battle. They were reaping their highest profits. They had cut their labor costs by eliminating more than 156,000 steelworkers right during the boom conditions. In addition, the basic steel corporations raised the price of steel $7.30 a ton. AFL staff economist Seymour Brandwein calculated that the steel wage increase would cost about $200 million a year while the steel price rise would bring the corporations an additional $600 to $700 million—a $3 profit for each $1 of increased wages.

In December 1952 and January 1953, just after McDonald had taken over the Steelworkers presidency, he had made a highly publicized arm-in-arm tour of the U. S. Steel Corporation's plants with Benjamin F. Fairless, U. S. Steel's chairman. That public demonstration of mutual regard and harmonious relations between corpo-

ration and union heads had a dual purpose: to persuade the steelworkers that the steel employers had the friendliest and most generous attitude toward their workers, and that McDonald represented
the type of "responsible" union leader with whom the corporations
were prepared to cooperate. Shortly after that tour, Fairless stated
on May 21, 1953 that he believed the American capitalist system was
well on the way to solving its "knottiest problem," the struggle between capital and labor. "I believe," he said, "that we can, that we
shall and that we must find the way to industrial peace."

Despite this sentiment, shared in common by capitalists and labor leaders, the class struggle was far from completely muffled
during Eisenhower's first term. There was still a considerable
amount of strike activity and every once in a while bitter picket line
clashes served to remind American labor that the employing class
never ceases to probe for weaknesses in labor's front. Below are
comparative annual strike averages.

	Number of Strikes	Number of Strikers	Strike Man-days
1935-39	2 867	1 130 000	16 900 000
1950-53	4 847	2 642 500	37 275 000
1953-56	4 176	2 120 000	28 050 000

These figures merit careful study. They dispel the myth of the
quiescence of the class struggle and the near-harmony of capital
and labor in the Fifties. In general, the strikes of the Fifties did
not have the intensity, ferocity and physical conflict of the struggles
of the Thirties. And there was little resort to government strikebreaking compared to Truman's use of plant seizures and Taft-
Hartley injunctions.

The number of strikes and strikers during the Eisenhower administration did decline compared to the post-World War II and the
Korean War peaks. But this was not accompanied by any widespread
setbacks for the workers in the matter of wages and fringe benefits.
Long-term contracts staved off many battles, it is true. But there
were some built-in wage increases such as escalator clauses and
annual productivity boosts which tended to make the long-term pacts
a bit more acceptable. Moreover, the rapid acceleration of the cost
of living during Truman's two terms had slowed considerably. This
somewhat reduced economic pressure on the workers. In addition,
a number of corporations, enjoying phenomenal profits in the period
after the Korean War, made some modest wage concessions. Brief
strikes at Firestone Tire and Rubber Company and the U.S. Rubber
Company in August 1953 won small wage gains and additional fringe

benefits which Goodrich and Goodyear then accepted. Westinghouse Electric Corporation and General Electric likewise granted small wage increases. Some 43,000 seamen of the CIO National Maritime Union that same year secured raises of two to six per cent after a four-day general walkout. Even the telephone monopoly, the American Telephone and Telegraph Company and its subsidiaries, granted small but unprecedented wage increases after an effective 11-day strike in six states of 53,000 Southwestern Bell Telephone workers.

The gains were extended to 50,000 CWA-CIO members in the Southern Bell System in nine states. No exceptional generosity was involved in any of these settlements. The corporations simply weighed the cost of tolerable concessions against the cost of prolonged strikes that they no longer had the confidence they could break.

38

The Witch Hunt
and Labor Struggles

The assault on the organized workers during the first Eisenhower administration was primarily one which came under the heading of "McCarthyism." All wings and tendencies of capitalist politics, the Democratic liberals in Congress included, vied in a campaign of political terrorism disguised as anti-communism. The stifling atmosphere of intimidation created by threat of the communist smear, which was McCarthy's specialty, was thickened by new repressive legislation and direct victimization.

Behind the general smoke screen of anti-communism, one of the most sinister anti-union bills was introduced into the Senate in April 1953 by Senator John Marshall Butler, Maryland Republican. He had been elected with Senator Joseph McCarthy's direct aid. Butler's bill required the National Labor Relations Board to deny collective bargaining recognition or elections to any union under "investigation" by the Subversive Activities Control Board set up under the McCarran-Kilgore Act of 1950. Such investigation and denial of NLRB certification were to be based on any employer's mere complaint that a union seeking collective bargaining rights was "communist dominated." If the Subversive Board should "find" against the union, the latter would be permanently banned by the NLRB unless and until such a ruling was reversed by a regular federal court.

On November 1, 1953, the special Senate Internal Security subcommittee, headed by McCarthy's protege, Senator Butler, opened hearings on "Communist penetration of our trade unions." The targets of this inquisition, it was announced, were several of the independent unions which had split from the CIO in 1950, including the United Electrical Workers and the Mine, Mill and Smelter Workers, engaged at the time in conflicts with large corporations. McCarthy carried out one of his highly publicized and televised inquisitions of alleged Communists in General Electric plants in Massachusetts. Among those who received the stigma of his wild charges and innuendo-loaded questions were local officers of the CIO International Union of Electrical Workers.

McCarthy also conducted a smear hearing, February 19 and 20, 1954, in Albany, New York, on alleged subversive activity by the independent United Electrical Workers in General Electric's Schenectady plant. Hundreds of union workers traveled to Albany at their own expense and the loss of a day's pay to voice their opposition. "The workers jammed the hearing room and hundreds more milled through the corridors and outside the building," reported Harry Ring in *The Militant.* "They booed and jeered McCarthy's tirades and shouted approval of seven subpoenaed GE workers who defied the witch-hunters. Workers in the corridors held aloft for photographers an outsized valentine inscribed: 'GE Loves McCarthy.'"

A Negro worker, amid vigorous applause, turned the attack on McCarthy and denounced him. When McCarthy tried to intimidate this witness, he shouted back: "Go down South and subpoena Governor Byrnes and Talmadge. Yes, subpoena those enemies of my people, of America. Why don't you investigate subversion by GE, of the Jim Crow system, of the profits taken from the sweat of my people? You fascist bum, why don't you investigate that?"

Ring further reported: "When the seventh witness leaned forward in the stand to tell him, 'I don't want to be framed. I will rest upon the Fifth Amendment which guarantees that innocent people be protected,' McCarthy suddenly announced that he had received an 'urgent' phone call from New York City and abruptly ended the hearings. He left the courthouse with the boos of the audience ringing in his ears." He never went back.

A companion offensive against unions was unloosed by the House Un-American Activities Committee. The latter group, headed by Congressman Harold H. Velde, a Republican, ran into an unforeseen obstacle when it barged into San Francisco to open a "subversive" hearing in City Hall. Some 6,000 members of Local 10, ILWU (independent), "hit the bricks" on December 3, 1953, to protest Velde's investigation. The waterfront was paralyzed. The CIO Council in the East Bay area denounced the Velde committee as an enemy of democratic rights. The hearings were flooded with "unfriendly witnesses" and "unfriendly" spectators. Scheduled to last 11 days, the hearings were hastily terminated after five days. Velde retreated ignominiously. At the first real resistance by organized labor, the government witch-hunters had to cut and run.

Unfortunately, the top labor leaders did little more than whine that McCarthy, Velde and the like were not "really interested in suppressing communism." That objective, it appeared, was "sincerely" desired by the Democratic liberals in Congress, the traditional "defenders" of civil liberties and labor's rights.

During the Senate debate on the Butler bill in August, 1954, Senators Humphrey, Lehman and Douglas took the lead in opposing the measure, denouncing it as anti-union. Their proposal to defer it to the study of a 12-man board was defeated. The liberals then made an abrupt about-face. They became the most aggressive "anti-Communists," accusing the McCarthyites of unwillingness to take "real action" against "communism." Humphrey introduced a bill to outlaw the Communist Party. "I am tired of reading headlines about being 'soft' toward communism," thundered the embattled Humphrey. "...I want to come to grips with the Communist issue. I want the Senators to stand up and to answer whether they are for the Communist Party, or against it..." Liberal Wayne Morse cried: "We put it up to the Senators to 'fish or cut bait.'" Lehman hailed this bill to ban a political party for the first time in American history because it "avoids all pussyfooting."

Butler interposed a cautionary note by saying that the Humphrey bill "involves very serious constitutional questions." The liberals howled him down, shouting "let's quit horsing around" with "legal technicalities and details." That was all right with Butler and McCarthy. They added the Butler bill on "Communist-infiltrated" unions as an amendment to the Humphrey bill to outlaw the Communist Party. Democratic liberals and McCarthyites alike unanimously embraced the combined measure. After some revisions, two test votes and a final vote of 265 to 2 in the House and 79 to 0 in the Senate, Eisenhower on August 24 signed the bill into law.

Most of the liberal publications and commentators voiced dismay and shock. Historian Arthur Schlesinger Jr. wrote in the August 24 *New York Post* that "the Democrats succeeded triumphantly in placing their party to the right of Joe McCarthy, of Pat McCarran, of Judge Harold Medina [judge in the 1949 Smith Act trial of the CP leaders]..." The September 1 *Advance* called the whole debate and action "one of the most amazing acts of demagogy any Congress has put on display" and declared especially "heinous" the actions of the "champions of civil liberties." Only the official *CIO News* in its August 23 issue saw in the moves and countermoves over the Humphrey-Butler Bill a slick trick by which the Eisenhower administration "got the anti-labor provisions they asked for, but they had to swallow with them a bill they didn't want — a bill which outlaws the Communist Party..."

After the Department of Justice had announced that labor unions would be the first target of the new law, the August 30 *CIO News* editorial offered an apology for the liberals who had converted the Butler Bill into a full-scale attack on political liberties. Still, the CIO paper did find the law, which received the unanimous vote of the liberal Democrats in the Senate and most of them in the House, "dangerous to a free union labor movement since it would give the government power of life and death over unions."

It is an irrefutable fact that the New Deal—Fair Deal liberals were the chief authors and sponsors of the first federal laws to (1) make mere opinion a crime (the Smith Act of 1940, rushed through by a Democratic Congress and signed by President Roosevelt); (2) establish concentration (detention) camps in America where political dissenters can be imprisoned without trial during a "national emergency" (McCarran-Kilgore Internal Security Act of 1950); and (3) outlaw a political party (Communist Control Act of 1954).

The Communist Control Act immediately became a pretext for government intervention against a union economic struggle. Some 5,000 members of the independent International Union of Mine, Mill and Smelter Workers in 11 plants of the Kennecott Copper Corporation went on strike August 16 and another 15,000 from the Anaconda Copper Mining Company joined the walkout on August 23. These strikes were, in part, demonstrations of international labor solidarity with striking Chilean copper miners in one of Kennecott's subsidiaries. The day before a tentative unratified Kennecott agreement was reached for an eight-cent hourly wage increase and fringe benefits, "word came from Washington that the Justice Department was embarking on an inquiry into the mine-mill union under the Communist Control Act of 1954..." (*New York Times,* August 29.)

In spite of their isolation, the copper workers displayed unbreakable unity and withstood all blows. They waged a six-week, industry-wide strike during the summer of 1955 and won a new agreement with a 15-cent wage package. Neither the CIO nor AFL leaders protested the Justice Department's attempt to deprive the IUMMSW of legal standing because some communists were alleged to be members. The CIO and AFL leaders held the official view that this was no business of theirs since, they claimed, the Communist Control Act did not apply to their organizations. It applied, of course, to any union which the Subversive Activities Control Board might declare to be "Communist-infiltrated." A Communist-infiltrated union was interpreted to be a union with so much as one Communist Party member.

In the atmosphere of anti-subversive terrorism generated by the

various probes and anti-communist legislative activity, some corporations in 1954 were able to put over actual wage cuts. While the
Communist Control Bills were under debate, the Studebaker Corporation on August 7, 1954 sent personal letters to its 23,000 employees —12,000 of them already laid off—threatening to end its
UAW-CIO contract, close down its plants and throw all the workers
out of jobs, unless the union agreed to wage cuts of from 15 to 20
per cent.

A precedent for acceptance of such a proposal had been set in
April when UAW Vice-President Richard Gosser had pressured Local 12 in Toledo to accept a ten per cent wage cut for its members
at Willys Motors, a subsidiary of Kaiser Motors. (Local 12 was
originally the Toledo Auto-Lite union of the historic 1934 strike, but
Gosser had not appeared on the union scene until several years later. He subsequently became one of Reuther's right-hand men and
the false impression was permitted to circulate that Gosser was one
of the "heroes of the Auto-Lite strike.") Gosser's plan regarding
Willys in 1954 involved the elimination of an incentive-pay system
without higher wage rates to cover the loss in take-home pay. This
had been projected as a means to keep Willys Motors on a "competitive basis" with the "Big Three." Gosser also offered to shave
the company's production costs 20 per cent in three to six months
by increased "efficiency"— a term the workers had learned from
experience to associate with speed-up and reduction of the working
force. Then, if enough Willys cars were sold, the workers might
get an ultimate bonus. Reuther and his UAW Executive Board had
approved this wage-slashing proposition.

When Studebaker threatened in August to close down unless the
union accepted a pay cut, Reuther threw his weight behind the Studebaker Local 5 leaders who recommended surrender to the company's
demands. The workers were then on part time and averaging only
$35 a week. The proposed pay cut of $5 to $7 would reduce their
earnings to little more than what they might obtain in unemployment
compensation. The Reutherites argued that since Studebaker wages
averaged $2.37 an hour while the rates at GM, Ford and Chrysler
averaged only $2.07, the Studebaker rates must be brought down to
the level of the "Big Three" in order "to improve the competitive
position of Studebaker..." Under an incentive-pay system, the Studebaker workers had pushed their output up to the highest possible
level, enabling the company to lay off more than half the Local 5
members in the process. Now the remaining workers were expected
to keep up their grueling productivity pace without the "incentive."

The Local 5 members, in a meeting of about 5,000 workers, at first voted down the wage-cut proposition by a three to two margin. For a week they were subjected to a scare campaign by both the company and UAW leaders who chorused: "If you don't take the wage cut, it's goodbye to your jobs." At a second meeting, with more than 10,000 in attendance, the vote was 5,371 to accept the new contract, 627 against, and 4,000 who voted by walking out in disgust. The wage-cutting program came to be known as the "Studebaker Plan."

At this very time, Reuther and other union leaders were arguing in a general way that higher wages meant more mass purchasing power and was one of the major weapons to fight the current economic recession. Yet Reuther agreed to reduction of the wages of the highest-paid group of auto workers instead of demanding that GM, Ford and Chrysler wages be raised to the Studebaker level.

What aroused the greatest fears of CIO members, especially the auto workers, was an attempt to smash a small strike in Detroit by police violence. On September 2, 1954, one week after the Communist Control Act had been signed, about one hundred police, heavily armed with tear gas, riot guns and gas masks, descended on the picket line at the Square D Company's plant where 1,200 members of Local 957, United Electrical Workers, had been on strike for 12 weeks. The union's leaders had already pared its demands down to within one cent of the company's offer. The strikers were informed that the presence of the police armed for riot duty was to herd scabs into the struck plant. The cops, outnumbering the pickets two to one, escorted ten strikebreakers into the plant. Aghast workers on their way to jobs at nearby UAW plants witnessed this scab-herding sight —one that had not been seen in the city since 1940. The press had been hammering on the angle that this was a "communist" strike because the UE was one of the unions expelled from the CIO in 1950.

The Square D picket lines quickly began to grow, augmented by sympathetic UAW members. Police dispersed the pickets and workers who gathered to demonstrate their support. Police and company men took repeated photographs of those on the line and in the immediate vicinity. News stories were published that evening with exaggerated accounts of the "back-to-work" movement by "willing workers"—actually strikebreakers who had never worked at Square D before. Some of these scabs were quoted as saying they had crossed the picket line just to "fight communism." Square D inserted large ads in the papers inviting scabs to apply for jobs. Every local radio news broadcast gave instructions on how strikebreakers were to enter the plant.

Clearly, it had been decided to make a demonstration of union-busting in the very center of the automobile industry and the heart of militant industrial unionism under the guise of fighting a "Communist-infiltrated" union. For several days Square D strikers were yanked into police vans for alleged violence and an injunction was issued banning mass picketing.

On the morning of September 9, in addition to the UAW rank-and-filers who had been aiding the strikers, thirteen prominent officials of UAW locals joined the beleaguered pickets. They represented locals totaling more than 150,000 auto workers. The local Reutherite UAW leadership in Detroit took no official supporting action other than to deplore the police violence and to invite the Square D strikers to quit their union and join the CIO International Union of Electrical Workers. However, the 13 UAW local officers who gave direct aid to the strike issued a statement urging "all union members, whether they be CIO, AFL or members of independent unions, to give all-out support to this strike.

"The issue is clear: SQUARE D WORKERS TODAY; CIO AND AFL WORKERS TOMORROW!"

Ford Local 600 Flying Squad members distributed *Ford Facts,* headlining support of the strike and declaring: "Square D is a test tube. This strike is being used as a dry run experiment in how to smash a union which is striking for legitimate and basic contract objectives." The appearance of the UAW local officials and the first UAW Flying Squad formations changed the atmosphere immediately. The massed police suddenly lost their belligerency and assumed an "Aw gee whiz, fellas" attitude.

Thousands of UAW members from 41 Detroit UAW locals swarmed to the picket line. The eyes of labor and capital throughout the nation were now focused on this "test tube" struggle. Displaying more hope than accuracy, the September 11 *Business Week* prematurely gloated: "The first effort by a major employer in the Detroit area to break a strike since before the auto union seemed assured of success this week."

The tremendous and militant response of the CIO auto workers finally defeated the union-busting assault. On September 30, after 108 days of picket line battles, the Square D workers returned to their jobs with a signed contract, although they had been forced to yield some big concessions.

This battle had confirmed once again the lesson taught by the first great strike victories preceding the formation of the CIO—the epic struggles of 1934 in Minneapolis, Toledo and San Francisco. Any strike, however small, can be won if organized labor recognizes the principle of class solidarity and does not shrink from mobilizing the great mass of the working populace to active, militant defense of the picket lines.

One bitter UAW strike in 1954 was lost because Reuther did not carry out this principle. The strike, which began April 5, involved 3,600 workers of the Kohler Company, plumbingware manufacturers at Kohler, Wisconsin. Wages, pensions and similar demands were at stake. But the decisive issue was union security through sole collective bargaining rights for UAW Local 833. The Kohler Company had successfully resisted genuine unionism for 20 years. Company-armed special deputies and guards had violently smashed an AFL strike on July 27, 1934, when they murdered two workers and wounded 47 others. This had been followed by mass evictions from Kohler-owned houses. During the 1954 strike the company's president, Herbert Kohler, a relative of Governor Walter Kohler who was a political ally of Senator Joseph McCarthy, admitted before a Wisconsin Employment Relations Board hearing that guns, tear gas and clubs were stored in the plant with "my approval." The Kohler workers were at a disadvantage because they were isolated in a small company town where Kohler ruled like a medieval baron.

The early stages of the strike were militantly fought with the backing of almost all the Kohler production workers. Robert Burkart, the UAW international representative in charge of the strike, conscientiously tried to put into effect a strategy of mass support by the Wisconsin CIO workers and the hundreds of thousands of UAW members within a 400-mile radius of Kohler. On April 25 a five-mile motorcade of 1,250 cars loaded with sympathetic unionists entered Sheboygan County and surrounded the struck Kohler plant. But occasional demonstrations of this type were insufficient to meet the company's challenge, which was backed by armed force and court injunctions.

The UAW international union gave $100,000 a week to the strikers. A fund set up by Wisconsin unionists generously contributed $25 a week to each striker. But money alone could not keep the scabs from going through the plant gates each morning. By September a thousand strikebreakers a day were pouring into the works. The Wisconsin CIO leadership, undoubtedly under Reuther's orders, yielded to every demand of the Kohler officials made through the courts—no mass picketing, no "loitering," no "unlawful" assembly. A policy of consistent mass action by the massive UAW with its one and a quarter-million members could have shut the Kohler plant completely, cut off Kohler's profits and forced a just settlement. Instead, the strike was allowed to dribble away over long months of inaction, delay and attrition. The struggle was sidetracked from the picket line to the courts and the National Labor Relations Board. For more than six years the UAW continued the strike formally and maintained token pickets. Not until August 26, 1960 did the NLRB get around to ruling Kohler guilty of unfair labor practices and order reinstatement of 1,600 fired strikers. Many of those who still wanted their jobs back — a large percentage had taken employment elsewhere — were given inferior ratings. At this writing, according to UAW complaints, some have been reinstated as janitors, floor sweepers and washroom attendants.

Another small but ferociously fought UAW strike was linked to the pattern of strikebreaking set in the Square D and Kohler battles. This was the strike that began July 25, 1955 at four plants of the Perfect Circle Corporation, piston ring manufacturer in Indiana. Perfect Circle's main plant at Hagerstown employed 1,370 workers. Two smaller plants at Richmond employed 420, and 340 worked at the company's foundry in New Castle. The crucial events occurred at New Castle.

The company hired scabs and maintained partial production aided by an injunction, issued August 1, limiting the number of pickets to five. Perfect Circle then moved to secure an NLRB decertification election at the Richmond and Hagerstown plants and announced it would sign no contract until after such a poll. Under the Taft-Hartley Act only those actually on the job — the strikebreakers — would have the right to vote. The regular employees — the strikers — had been "fired." The union officials offered arbitration of the strike issues but the company refused.

Repeated acts of police violence at the forge plant culminated on September 27 in the smashing of a peaceful picket line by armed cops led by New Castle's Mayor Paul F. McCormack. Fifty union men and women were clubbed and arrested. On October 4 the company announced the dismissal of 35 members of UAW Local 370 for mass picketing. That night CIO workers from the Chrysler and Ingersoll Steel plants in New Castle helped to form a picket line of 300 cars which circled the forge plant. Few Chrysler and Ingersoll Steel workers reported to their own jobs the next morning. More than a thousand sympathetic workers augmented the Perfect Circle picket line.

Suddenly, from the fortress-like foundry, the strikebreakers and supervisory employees poured a fusillade of rifle, shotgun and pistol fire. Nine picketing workers were wounded. The marchers fell back to cover. A number of picketers rushed home, secured their own firearms and quickly returned to defend the picket line arms in hand. The police force hastily evacuated the plant after the shooting and "confiscated enough scab guns to cover four table tops — in addition to clubs and pipe lengths," wrote *Militant* reporter Henry Gitano from the scene. He also disclosed that "Company attorney Clyde Hoffman admitted firearms had been brought into the plant (some by helicopter) with the consent of the police and that the firing started from inside the plant."

For the moment, the strikers held sway and the plant was closed down. The next day Indiana's Governor George N. Craig, a former national commander of the American Legion, imposed "limited" martial law and sent a detachment of 300 National Guards, as he said, to "prevent any attempt to reopen the strikebound plant, and to disperse all picketing." His executive secretary, Horace Coats, insisted that the troops — equipped with full war paraphernalia, including bayoneted M-1 rifles, machine guns and four Sherman tanks —were "assigned only to protect lives and maintain law and order." He added that "certainly" the troops "are not going to escort workers into the plant." But on October 7, Guard officers informed Mayor McCormack they would withdraw their forces if Perfect Circle went through with its announced plan to reopen its plant on Monday, October 10.

On that date, however, Governor Craig declared full martial law in New Castle, Hagerstown and Richmond with the statement: "There is no law against an employer operating his plant if he can, and that right will be preserved by the military." The October 24 *Militant* published Henry Gitano's eyewitness account:

"With the guns of four Sherman tanks trained at the entrance to the Perfect Circle foundry and with the area bristling with sandbagged machine gun emplacements, the plant opened Monday to receive its contingent of [90] scabs. They were escorted by troops armed to the teeth. So warlike was this display of military force deployed against a handful of unarmed union pickets that the town looked on in bewildered amazement."

Reuther charged in a telegram to Secretary of Labor James P. Mitchell that "the full responsibility for the merciless shootings... [rests] squarely upon the shoulders of the Perfect Circle Company, whose president 'on leave' is Lothair Teetor, U.S. Assistant Secretary of Commerce." The UAW and CIO President added: "One of the principal difficulties in the relations between the Perfect Circle Company and its employes is its acceptance by the management of the company of the theory of the class struggle."

But the October 12, 1955 *New York Times* indicated that the Perfect Circle bosses were not scared by Reuther's jibe. The *Times* reported: "Company officials appeared to be elated at the turn of events that permitted them to reopen the foundry." As for Governor Craig, when he was charged with "placing property rights above human rights," he replied: "The right to property is the most basic of human rights and unless it is safeguarded, all other human rights stand in jeopardy." The Perfect Circle workers did not face this class view as a theory but as ruthless fact staring at them from the deadly barrels of machine guns.

Why were so many weapons and agencies of the American employing class—armed strikebreakers, court injunctions, city and state police, National Guards, the Taft-Hartley Act and its decertification procedure, the NLRB—brought to bear on a tiny segment of small town American workers in Indiana? The October 18 *Wall Street Journal* itself explained: "The strike's significance spreads far beyond the boundaries of these three small Indiana towns." Many businessmen, the *Journal* observed, regarded the Perfect Circle Corporation "as the leader of a crusade, fighting for the worker's right to hold a job without belonging to a union." For employers everywhere, the prospect of a smashed Perfect Circle strike was looked on as the hoped-for event that might trigger a successful open-shop offensive against all organized labor.

The NLRB's decertification election went through as planned on November 10 at the Hagerstown and Richmond plants. With the strikers barred, the scabs voted two to one against the UAW-CIO as their bargaining agent. At New Castle the Local 370 members, under the personal pressure of UAW Secretary-Treasurer Emil Mazey, reluctantly voted 86 to 72 on November 29 to accept a compromise agreement. This compromise recognized the UAW as bargaining agent and granted a 17-cent-an-hour wage increase plus another seven cents to go into effect in 1956. The demand for a supplemental unemployment benefit program, similar to that of the "Big Three," was denied. The local's president, Carl Batchfield, and six other militants who were among the 35 fired during the strike, were not reinstated.

That the employers never fail to press an advantage and to use any means they can to fight unionism was demonstrated by the experiences of other large CIO unions in this same period. The Textile Workers Union of America and the International Union of Electrical Radio and Machine Workers provided unfortunate examples.

TWUA President Emil Rieve announced in Boston on February 5, 1955 to a delegated conference of 500 locals that the international union would by-pass badly needed wage increases in 1955 because of the "serious depression" in the industry. The textile workers had received no general contractual raises since 1951. Two months after

Rieve's announcement, some 25,000 workers in 23 New England textile mills were forced to strike on April 16 rather than accept a further wage cut of ten cents an hour. The companies had succeeded in getting the TWUA leaders to agree to a 6-1/2 per cent wage cut in 1952. Now, when the union asked for renewal of the old contract which already included one wage cut, the employers figured they might as well try for a second. Rieve expressed surprise: "In our opinion, the action of our Boston conference was labor statesmanship of the highest order; indeed it was so heralded in the public press." After the New England strike began, the union then demanded elimination of the 1952 wage cut. However, it settled finally for the old contract with the original wage cut but without the additional ten-cent slash. Thus, "labor statesmanship" proved itself once more— with a little timely aid from a strike.

At that time a survey of 16 leading New England textile mills showed a range in wages of $1.25 to $1.37 an hour compared to $1.29 to $1.34 in 16 similar Southern mills. The average of $1.30 an hour in textile plants of both areas was 14 to 55 cents below the average wages in other local New England industries. This was one of the most telling arguments for organizing the South—the "Operation Dixie" which the CIO had voted its "Task Number One" at conventions since 1941.

Shortly after the automobile workers in 1955 threw off the yoke of Reuther's five-year contracts, President James Carey of the IUE on August 15 saddled 100,000 workers of the General Electric Corporation with a five-year pact. This agreement contained no supplemental unemployment benefits, although the union's main demand had been a "guaranteed annual wage." Instead, the contract contained a five-year plan of small gradual wage increases of three per cent each year for the first three years, and three per cent plus one cent per hour in the final two years. The actual increase during the first year ranged from a 4-1/2-cent minimum to ten cents for the highest-paid workers. The independent UE, chief rival of the IUE-CIO, charged that the settlement fell short of the concessions won by the UE from other electrical equipment firms and that the total package was five to ten cents below what was gained in steel, auto and copper. UE officials called the five-year feature of the IUE contract "retrogressive."

Westinghouse Electric Corporation, the second largest in its field, decided not to meet the IUE's meager terms and forced a corporation-wide strike that began on October 17, 1955. This walkout eventually involved more than 70,000 Westinghouse employees in 30 plants throughout the country. The strike was significant because

Westinghouse tried to do on a large scale and in major industrial areas what Square D, Kohler and Perfect Circle had done against relatively small and isolated groups of workers. The strike was met by a violent strikebreaking offensive, the first such attempt by a major industrial corporation since World War II.

Westinghouse enlisted the aid of police and sympathetic judges in a score of towns and cities. Backed by police clubs and injunctions, the company tried to run scabs into its plants. This led to numerous clashes between the mass picket lines and the police and strikebreakers. The most savage assault on peacefully picketing workers took place in Columbus, Ohio. At dawn on January 4, 1956, a heavy contingent of police threw itself at the picket line and mercilessly clubbed every picket they could reach. One young worker was beaten to death and eight were badly injured, while 89 others were jailed.

The strike was weakened by the division between the IUE-CIO and the independent UE which had been purged from the CIO in 1949. Of the 55,000 production workers on strike, about 10,500 belonged to the UE which had called its Westinghouse members out in support of the IUE strike. The IUE leaders, however, rejected a UE proposal for joint negotiations. Attorney General Brownell intervened to try to weaken the strike further by a move on December 20, 1955 to decertify the UE as a "Communist front." Another 1,500 Westinghouse employees were affiliated with the AFL International Brotherhood of Electrical Workers and 13,500 office workers belonged to the Independent Salaried Unions.

The fundamental issue of the strike was the company's insistence on renegotiation of the 1954 contract in order to extend it from three years to five and bring it in line with the GE agreement concluded in August 1955. The most recent IUE convention had adopted a resolution for across-the-board wage increases, instead of percentage raises which give the higher-paid workers a bigger dollars-and-cents package than the lower-paid categories receive. Another basic issue was the company's demand for a completely free hand in setting production standards without consideration of the workers or consultation with the union.

After 156 days of strike, the IUE-CIO leaders accepted a five-year contract, a three per cent annual wage increase, and a clause providing for consultation with the union before changes were made in work standards and job classifications. The UE made a similar settlement. Only the militancy and endurance of the workers saved the Westinghouse strike and the union from utter disaster. The IUE officials had offered no strategic plan of struggle and each local union had to fend for itself. Although this strike began before the

AFL-CIO merger, it became the first major strike under the aegis of the newly joined organizations. The AFL-CIO contributed a fund to the strike in its later stages. But not even the weight of the largest union organization in history could make up for the weakness of the IUE-CIO strike leadership.

In 1935-37, the battle generally was over the simple principle of union recognition and a written contract, if only for a few months. In 1955-56, the big corporations were insisting on such contracts for long periods —five years. Only in exceptional circumstances did the employer hold out against wage increases or for wage cuts. Westinghouse had never denied a wage concession; it was a matter of how much and the kind of wage formula to be granted. Even in the matter of production standards, Westinghouse had to concede in principle the right of the workers, through their union, to review and oppose unfair and oppressive work conditions. But the company squeezed a far greater compromise from the union leaders than it was entitled to get, considering the actual relationship of forces involved in the struggle.

One of the significant developments of this period was the beginning of labor struggles in the South. The Southern states, for the most part, had been a desert so far as unionism is concerned. The spring of 1955 witnessed a series of exceptionally militant strikes of Southern railroad, telephone, steel, hotel and bus workers. These strikes were fought against great odds. The workers confronted a terrifying array of local police forces and armed strikebreakers. One of the longest railroad strikes on record, waged for 57 days by 30,000 unionists of the Louisville & Nashville Railroad, forced the company to an agreement on May 9, 1955.

This victory in turn strengthened morale in the two-month-old strike of 50,000 members of the CIO Communications Workers in the Southern Bell Telephone system. The mayor of Knoxville, Tennessee, issued a "shoot-to-kill" order to police sent to establish "law and order" among the women telephone operators picketing the local telephone exchange. In New Orleans, more than 10,000 CIO, AFL and independent unionists paraded in support of the telephone workers. Attempts of Southern Bell to pit Negro workers against white had very little success. In Atlanta, for instance, the company sent all striking Negro workers a special letter asking them not to picket. It was defied. After 68 days of furious strikebreaking attempts, the Southern subsidiary of the giant AT&T monopoly was forced to yield and to sign a one-year contract granting from $1 to $4 in weekly wage increases.

The aggressive labor struggles and victories in the South, although still sporadic, gave hope at the time that a "new era" was opening for Southern labor. More than half of America's Negro workers were in the South and Negroes were one-fourth of the entire Southern labor force. Unless the Southern white wage workers could link their struggle with the growing fight of the Negro people to smash the Jim Crow system, the American labor movement could make no decisive inroads into that open-shop stronghold in the South.

These Southern labor battles in 1955 were stirred in part by a quickening of the Negro struggle for civil rights and equality. On May 17, 1954, the United States Supreme Court had issued its verdict on school desegregation that was to signal a whole new stage of Negro upsurge, particularly in the South. The attitude and actions of organized labor toward the historic movement of the Negro masses for a "Second Emancipation" was and remains one of the keys to the fate of all Southern labor and ultimately of the entire American working class.

39

The World's Largest Union

The final stage of the AFL-CIO merger occurred with no great clamor from the ranks for organic unity, although a majority of unionists were pleased by the prospect of "one big organization" and hoped it would bring them added protection and benefits. The unity developments were set in motion by the labor leaders themselves. Their aim was better defense of their union power and prerogatives, and a unified front against both their Republican political opponents and the union ranks.

The 16th Constitutional Convention of the CIO held in Los Angeles December 6-10, 1954, formally approved a proposal of the CIO subcommittee on organic unity to proceed at once to meet with the AFL representatives to discuss merger terms. AFL President Meany had sent a message to the convention urging a meeting of the AFL-CIO unity committee "as soon as possible." Reporting for the CIO subcommittee, Steelworkers President McDonald indicated to the convention that substantial understanding had been reached with the AFL on the basis for fusion. McDonald made the "prophecy" that unity would be achieved soon. However, he alarmed officials of smaller CIO unions when he said that to "lay down preconditions as to the terms upon which organic unity can be achieved...would be a guarantee that labor unity cannot be achieved." This evoked fears that small CIO unions might be absorbed into larger AFL affiliates in a unity "deal."

CIO President Reuther and Secretary-Treasurer Carey, who were the other members of the organic unity subcommittee, hastily reassured the delegates that unity would be secured without loss of principle. Reuther promised to safeguard the "cardinal principle that the integrity of every affiliated union would be fully protected."

A short but sharp debate on the "Political Action" resolution indicated the underlying political motivation for the merger move. The
resolution called for "supporting the progressive forces within both
major political parties and basing its judgments on platforms and records of performance." Thus, the resolution proposed a continuation
of political action through the two-party system, support to capitalist
"friends of labor" and the perspective of the eventual "fundamental
realignment" of the liberal and conservative elements of both parties
so that all the liberals would be in one party and all the conservatives
in another. Until then, the resolution indicated, vote Democrat. It
attacked the Republican administration sharply and hailed the re-
election of Democratic Senators Douglas, Murray and Humphrey.

President Michael Quill of the Transport Workers Union, who
was most distrustful of the merger developments, startled the convention on December 8 when he spoke from the floor on the political
action resolution. He said: "Serious consideration should be given
to building in America a really and truly independent political party
of CIO, so that the workers will have the choice to stand up separately and apart from any of the existing parties."

Quill was careful to explain: "I am not talking about a political
party that would nominate its own candidate for President of the
United States, but I am talking about a party that would be strong
enough to have something to say about that nomination." He further
qualified his proposal by adding that "we should at least give serious consideration to forming labor parties in the states...where it
is impossible for us to walk with the existing Democratic Party."

The first attack on Quill's proposal came from an unexpected
quarter. United Automobile Workers Secretary-Treasurer Emil
Mazey, whose forceful declarations for a labor party at UAW and
Michigan CIO conventions were well remembered, chose the occasion to make a demonstrative break with his political past. Now he
wanted to show the AFL leaders that they need not fear the "left
wing" of the Reuther machine on political grounds.

Mazey conceded that "the best possible conditions for making
progress in the political arena would be for labor to have its own
party, in association with farmers." He reminded the delegates
that he had fought for such a program: "I think most of you know
that I have been an advocate of independent political action and that
I strongly believe in that kind of movement, and I have been critical
of my elders in labor, CIO and elsewhere, who for years have said
now is not the time to launch out in the building of a political movement of our own, and I find myself in the embarrassing position of
having to repeat what I used to condemn in others."

Reuther had moved even further to the right. He argued that a labor party is undesirable as such because it is a class party and America is not a class society, at least in the traditional sense. Reuther asserted:

"In Europe where you have society developed along very classical economic lines, where you have rigid class groupings, there labor parties are a natural political expression. But America is a society in which social groups are in flux, in which we do not have this rigid class structure...

"A labor party would commit the American political system to the same narrow class structure upon which the political parties of Europe are built...Basically what we are trying to do is work within the two-party system of America and bring about within that two-party system a fundamental realignment of basic political forces..."

With this statement, Reuther broke the last link with his past. Meany and the other AFL "elders" could count on him to adhere to the most rigid capitalist class line in politics. After the merger, Meany and other old AFL leaders occasionally held up the threat of a possible labor party alternative in order to put pressure on the Democratic machine for small favors. But they did not make the smallest move in that direction.

Merger steps were speeded up after the CIO convention. A meeting of the CIO and AFL unity committees on January 4, 1955 agreed to consider in February a draft of specific unity measures. Twenty top AFL and CIO officials on February 12 signed a merger agreement, subject to ratification by their separate conventions. Final fusion was set for the end of the year.

The merger agreement accepted the principle of industrial unionism. It stated: "The merged federation shall be based upon a constitutional recognition that both craft and industrial unions are appropriate, equal and necessary as methods of trade union organizations." The AFL's denial of this proposition two decades before had led to the split and the formation of the CIO. The agreement also contained the assurance that "the integrity of each affiliated union in the merged federation shall be maintained and preserved."

One part of the merger agreement which was definitely retrogressive dealt with the question of racial discrimination. The CIO policy had marked an advance on this issue compared to the AFL, in which some affiliates maintained an official policy either of exclusion or segregation of Negro workers. While the CIO fell far short of an ideal policy in practice, it had maintained a constitutional ban against restrictions on the rights of Negroes as union members. The unity agreement, to all but eyes trained to detect verbal deceptions, appeared to uphold the principle of nondiscrimination without qualification. It was represented in this light by Meany and Reuther. The actual wording of the relevant clause in the merger compact reads:

"The merged federation shall constitutionally recognize the right of all workers, without regard to race, creed, color, or national origin to share in the full benefits of trade union organization in the merged federation. The merged federation shall establish appropriate internal machinery to bring about at the earliest possible date the effective implementation of this principle of nondiscrimination."

The phrases "full rights" or "equal rights" do not appear in this clause. Instead, the pivotal words are "full benefits." This was not an innocent or accidental choice of expressions. It contains in concealed form the "separate but equal" doctrine which the United States Supreme Court struck down only a few months before in its historic school desegregation ruling. The merger agreement promised to give the Negro worker whatever benefits the union gained for the white workers. It did not explicitly rule out the exclusion of Negroes from certain unions or their relegation to restricted "Class B" locals whose members are denied full organizational rights. This would continue to automatically bar Negro workers from certain jobs and occupations. They obviously could not enjoy the "full benefits" provided by a union if they could not get certain jobs because they were denied a union card, or segregated into all-Negro union locals or units — a common practice in a number of AFL unions.

For the union movement as well as for the Negro workers, the issue of equal rights was crucial. A Department of Labor survey in 1955 showed that over 90 per cent of the Detroit manufacturing workers were unionized, and an average of 80 per cent for the 17 largest American cities as a whole. But in the South, where Negroes were a quarter of the total work force, less than 15 per cent of the wage workers were unionized. Even in highly organized Detroit, the median income of Negro families in 1954 was $3,800 a year compared to $5,700 for white families, according to a University of Michigan "Detroit Area Study" cited in the Detroit edition of the *Pittsburgh Courier*, July 30, 1955. "Median" means that half the respective families fell below these figures and half were above. The differential between the Negro and the white medians was $1,900 a year or $37 a week.

A. Philip Randolph, president of the AFL Brotherhood of Sleeping Car Porters, correctly hailed the merger move as generally progressive and urged his fellow Negroes to support it. Nevertheless, he was impelled to make strong demands with respect to banning discrimination in the merged AFL-CIO. Randolph urged that the united organization deny affiliation to unions that practiced racial or other discrimination. The August 13, 1955 *New York Herald Tribune* reported that an AFL spokesman had indicated "that Randolph's request. . . is not likely to be granted."

This was to become the most controversial issue at the merger convention in December. It is instructive to recall that the CIO leadership had not hesitated at the prodding of the Truman administration to expel eleven affiliates with a sizable chunk of the CIO's membership for alleged subservience to the Communist Party. After the merger, the AFL-CIO leadership expelled the country's largest union, the Teamsters, for "unethical practices" by its leaders— also at the prodding of the Democratic Party leaders in Congress. Yet they recoiled from such drastic action when it came to eradicating the heinous crime of racial discrimination and segregation within their affiliates. Moreover, this issue had been given fresh urgency by the series of militant strikes in the South that spring.

The CIO Executive Board on February 24, 1955 voted 42 to 2 to approve the merger agreement. Quill remained the most vehement opponent of the move. But most of the CIO leaders regarded the action as imperative. They were mindful of the decline in CIO membership from its 1949 peak, the menace of the Taft-Hartley Law, the threat of wage cuts like those imposed by Studebaker, the growing number of state "right to work"—that is, "right to scab"—laws, the danger of mass unemployment through automation and, above all, the political weakness of organized labor. For similar reasons, the great majority of the AFL Executive Council also approved the merger terms.

A mutually satisfactory draft of a new constitution for the merged organization was completed by the AFL-CIO Joint Unity Committee on May 2, 1955. It was quickly approved by both the CIO Executive Board and the AFL Executive Council. A key clause in the proposed constitution prohibited raiding and encouraged mergers and agreements to eliminate jurisdictional disputes and conflicting organizations in the same fields.

What was left out was also significant. The leaders of both organizations eagerly assented to eliminate from the new constitution the historic preamble to the old AFL constitution. This preamble had somehow survived long after the AFL leaders had discarded its aims and principles in practice. Formally in effect since 1886, this preamble read:

"A struggle is going on in all the nations of the civilized world between the oppressors and the oppressed of all countries, a struggle between the capitalist and the laborer, which grows in intensity from year to year, and will work disastrous results to the toiling millions if they are not combined for mutual protection and benefit."

The language of class struggle did not fit in with the unity program and aims of the soft, complacent labor "statesmen" whose highest ambition is to win the badge of respectability from the employers and their agents.

The new constitution summoned labor not to combat oppression by the employing class but "to protect the labor movement from any and all corrupt influences and from the undermining efforts of Communist agencies and any and all others who are opposed to the basic principles of our democracy and free and democratic unionism..."

The top leaders of both bodies, except for mavericks like Beck and Hutcheson, were firmly united politically. Consequently, they easily agreed to merge the AFL Labor's League for Political Education with the CIO Political Action Committee to form the new Committee on Political Education (COPE).

After four days of separate preliminary conventions to ratify the merger agreement, 1,487 CIO and AFL delegates on December 5 combined in a single convention to constitute the AFL-CIO. Twenty years of split and bitter rivalry were brought to a close.

But if the great historic nature of the occasion was felt by the delegates, they scarcely showed it. It was more like a decorous convocation of church deacons, both in appearance and tone, than an assembly of the leaders of unions which had gone through two decades of often fierce class battle involving millions of strikers almost every year. Meany told the delegates that the unions had the "right and duty" to intensify their political activity to defeat anti-labor legislation. But he sharply disclaimed any AFL-CIO intention to "control" the workers' votes, to build a labor party or even to take over any of the existing major parties.

Art Sharon's description of the composition of the convention in the December 12 *Militant* tells volumes about the nature of the union leadership assembled at New York's 71st Regiment Armory. Sharon wrote:

"These delegates, as I have observed them in the sessions, are several times removed from the workers who make up the 15 million membership of the new labor body...To any serious student of the labor movement or to any dedicated unionist, the composition of the convention—the types who set the pattern—is of prime importance. Almost to a man the delegates are paid functionaries many years away from the trade or industry they presumably represent today. Indeed those who worked even in some distant past can claim special distinction from many whose hands have never touched a tool or machine in production.

"The delegates were not exactly youthful. In fact only the CIO, with many delegates still in their forties, keeps the convention from being strictly an old man's gathering."

Very few delegates were women, although women constitute the great majority of membership in such unions as the International Ladies Garment Workers, the Millinery Workers, and the Hotel and Restaurant Employees. The ILGWU had only one woman delegate out of eleven; the Millinery Workers, none; the Hotel and Restaurant Employees, one out of eight.

The small number of Negro delegates reflected their restricted position in the labor unions. At the preceding separate AFL convention, the Negro Trade Unionists Committee had issued an appeal to the AFL delegates to "clear its house of remaining undemocratic, divisive, discriminatory policies and practices..." The NTUC called for a clear provision in the new constitution guaranteeing equal rights and non-segregation; Negro representation on the new executive council; a campaign to organize the South on a non-segregated basis; strong and adequately financed Fair Employment Practices Committees with authority to act effectively; and expulsion of any union failing to eliminate discrimination after a fixed time limit.

The only concession made to the Negro delegates' demands was the election of two Negroes among the 27 vice-presidents named by the convention. They were A. Philip Randolph of the Sleeping Car Porters for the AFL, and Willard S. Townsend, head of the United Transport Service Employees, for the CIO. They were the first Negroes in the 69 years of the AFL to be elected to the top ruling body of the labor hierarchy in an AFL-connected federation. But on the issue most directly affecting the employment and incomes of Negro workers — full and equal rights of membership in all AFL-CIO affiliates — the Meany-Reuther leadership offered instead the slippery formulation of "full union benefits." This policy has remained a focal infection inside the AFL-CIO to this day.

One issue which stirred the delegates, although it was not brought out openly, was the effort of Teamsters President David Beck to maneuver his 1.4 million-member organization into the newly established Industrial Union Department (IUD), headed by Reuther as chairman and James Carey as secretary-treasurer. This department had been set up to compensate, in part, for the fact that the AFL secured the two top posts in the merged organization. Meany was elevated to the presidency and the secretary-treasurership went to William F. Schnitzler, who had occupied the same post in the old

AFL. Beck's aim appeared to be domination of the Industrial Union Department through a possible alliance with McDonald of the Steelworkers.

Reuther and Carey gave an absolute "no" to admission of the entire Teamsters to the IUD. At one point Beck threatened to bolt the convention over this issue, but the delegates ruled that only that portion of Beck's membership organized in an industrial structure could affiliate with the AFL-CIO's IUD.

Another source of conflict with Beck was his mutual assistance pacts with the independent International Longshoremen's Union, Joseph Ryan's former domain, and the Mine, Mill and Smelter Workers, one of the unions expelled in the CIO's 1950 cold war purge. These conflicts represented differences that were to come to a head in the next period and lead to a new split with the expulsion of the Teamsters union.

*   *   *

Whatever the aims and motives of the leaders, the very existence of a single labor organization of the monumental size of the merged AFL-CIO represented a tremendous historic achievement of the American working class. Only twenty years before, the entire organized labor movement had fewer members than the CIO alone at the time of the merger. The organization of the main sectors of American industrial labor, combined with the forces of the ten-million-member AFL, represented the largest independent labor organization in world history— an organization planted squarely in the middle of the most advanced capitalist country on the globe. Within two decades, a wholly new relationship of class forces had been established in capitalism's mightiest and most highly developed bastion. This is the biggest fact of twentieth-century America.

Most of the workers who entered the combined organization had never known a serious, insuperable defeat. They had a vast store of experience in class struggle. The anti-labor laws and legal traps, the capitalist agencies of force and violence, the instruments of repression, the propaganda deceptions, the intervention of the capitalist government, the venality, incompetence, timidity and even treachery of the official union leadership—all these had failed to halt American labor's giant step forward from class atomization to a class organization never equaled in size or surpassed in picket-line and shop militancy.

Within this mighty body of organized labor lay an incalculable potential of power, economic and political. Meany and Reuther may have disclaimed any intention of using this power in an effective in-dependent manner. But this latent power is a fact of such towering dimensions that it must loom before the workers at each new stage of national and international crisis.

So long as this immense inherent power of organized labor exists, the American workers are bound to ask themselves sooner or later: Why must we submit to exploitation, insecurity, recurrent unem-ployment, political suppression and the threat of eventual atomic annihilation? Why should we not use this organized power that lies so ready to our hands to effect our own solution of the impasse of modern society, to direct our own destiny?

Why not?

A Note
on Sources
and Acknowledgments

This history of the CIO is based largely on eyewitness and contemporary accounts. I have relied chiefly on two sources: the commercial daily press, and the union and socialist periodicals. I have also made extensive use of the published official proceedings of union conventions and conferences described in the text.

Such authoritative capitalist newspapers as the New York Times, Wall Street Journal, and Christian Science Monitor have provided my principal source of information on the general historical events that form the broad background for labor developments since 1929.

In addition, I have made extensive use of daily newspapers in the industrial centers where much of the labor activities described in this book took place. Among these newspapers are the Akron Beacon-Journal, Buffalo News, Chicago Daily News, Cleveland Plain Dealer, Detroit Free Press, New York Herald Tribune, New York Post, New York World-Telegram, Pittsburgh Press, St. Louis Post-Dispatch, Toledo Blade, and the Youngstown Vindicator.

General reference sources found particularly useful are the Congressional Record, Encyclopedia Britannica (including its annual supplements), and the annual editions of the World Almanac.

Since 1935 there has grown up a truly immense labor press. Virtually all international unions publish their own news weeklies and monthly magazines. In addition, there are hundreds of regional, district, and local union newspapers. Over the years, the unions have published thousands of educational pamphlets.

However, the official union press offers surprisingly little information on the great battles of labor in the past three decades that is not available in more extensive and accurate accounts from other sources. The main functions of the union publications have been to glorify the leaderships in power and to defend their policies. Their historical value is chiefly as a source of the viewpoints, policies and official programs advanced by the union leaders.

Among the union publications I cite most frequently are the CIO News and the AFL News Reporter, Advance (Amalgamated Clothing Workers), the Dispatcher (International Longshoremen's and Warehousemen's Union), Justice (International Ladies Garment Workers Union), International Teamster, the Pilot (National Maritime Union), Steel Labor, Textile Labor, United Automobile Workers, and the U. E. News (United Electrical Workers-CIO).

The CIO was an arena of great and continuous ideological and political struggle. To re-create and explain that struggle it is necessary to turn to the radical press—the publications especially of the American Communist Party (Stalinist), Socialist Party, Social-Democratic Federation, and the Socialist Workers Party (Trotskyist). Their chief periodicals in the period covered by this book were, respectively, the Daily Worker and the Sunday Worker, the Socialist Call, New Leader, and The Militant.

In the preparation of this book, I made a rigorous re-study of the Daily Worker and Sunday Worker, as well as other Stalinist periodicals and pamphlets. These papers provide the printed record of the remarkable twists and turns in the labor policies of the Communists and their followers who played a considerable role in the CIO and who also, at a certain stage, supplied a great deal of the ideological arguments for the political and economic policies of the CIO leadership as a whole. However, I approached all news reports in the Stalinist press with utmost caution because of the numerous politically motivated distortions and misrepresentations I discovered.

My greatest single source of eyewitness and participant information on the entire labor movement since November 1928 has been the weekly Militant. It is a rich mine of vivid, detailed accounts by informed worker-correspondents covering the whole panorama of the American labor struggle in modern times. I have contributed articles on strikes and other labor events to The Militant since January 1935 and have been privileged to serve as a regular staff member since October 1940. I have cited and quoted freely from my own eyewitness reports. I have the advantage over many writers of history. I can say not only that I wrote hundreds of contemporary articles about the events described in this book; I can add, in the case of many historic labor events: "I was there."

I have included a running account of economic developments during the years covered by this history. Unless some other source is given directly in the text, economic statistics cited are from official government data published by the Bureau of Labor Statistics of the United States Department of Labor and the Bureau of the Census and other agencies of the United States Department of Commerce.

In the case of all quotations, the source is acknowledged directly in the text. This has helped me greatly in my desire to eliminate all footnotes, which I personally find annoying and diverting.

* * *

Over the years I have had the rare good fortune to meet and converse with leading participants of many of the great labor struggles while the events were still fresh in their minds. I want to acknowledge especially the oral accounts I heard from Vincent R. Dunne, the late Carl Skoglund, and Farrell Dobbs about the Minneapolis truck drivers strikes in 1934; and from Samuel Pollock and T. G. Selander about the great Toledo Auto-Lite strike of 1934. I wish to express deep appreciation to Samuel Pollock for providing me with very rare documentary material on the historic pre-CIO Toledo auto struggles.

I am indebted to many kind friends for invaluable technical aid in the preparation of my notes and manuscript. I particularly want to thank Sylvia Bleeker, Carol DeBerry, Marvel Dobbs, Barbara Doritty, Sharon Finer, Virginia Halstead, Karolyn Kerry, Paul Montauk, Nora Roberts, Auda Romine, and last, but not least, my wife Ethel.

The entire responsibility and work in connection with the publishing of this book was handled by Anne and Robert Chester, ably assisted by Mary Henderson. Kathleen Burch did the proofreading and prepared the index. George Novack spent long and laborious hours in the careful editing of my manuscript. To each of them I owe a debt of gratitude which I feel can never be fully repaid.

Index